Rating : principles--practice--procedure.

Philip Michael Faraday

The Making of Modern Law collection of legal archives constitutes a genuine revolution in historical legal research because it opens up a wealth of rare and previously inaccessible sources in legal, constitutional, administrative, political, cultural, intellectual, and social history. This unique collection consists of three extensive archives that provide insight into more than 300 years of American and British history. These collections include:

Legal Treatises, 1800-1926: over 20,000 legal treatises provide a comprehensive collection in legal history, business and economics, politics and government.

Trials, 1600-1926: nearly 10,000 titles reveal the drama of famous, infamous, and obscure courtroom cases in America and the British Empire across three centuries.

Primary Sources, 1620-1926: includes reports, statutes and regulations in American history, including early state codes, municipal ordinances, constitutional conventions and compilations, and law dictionaries.

These archives provide a unique research tool for tracking the development of our modern legal system and how it has affected our culture, government, business – nearly every aspect of our everyday life. For the first time, these high-quality digital scans of original works are available via print-on-demand, making them readily accessible to libraries, students, independent scholars, and readers of all ages.

old books. new life.

The BiblioLife Network

This project was made possible in part by the BiblioLife Network (BLN), a project aimed at addressing some of the huge challenges facing book preservationists around the world. The BLN includes libraries, library networks, archives, subject matter experts, online communities and library service providers. We believe every book ever published should be available as a high-quality print reproduction; printed on-demand anywhere in the world. This insures the ongoing accessibility of the content and helps generate sustainable revenue for the libraries and organizations that work to preserve these important materials.

The following book is in the "public domain" and represents an authentic reproduction of the text as printed by the original publisher. While we have attempted to accurately maintain the integrity of the original work, there are sometimes problems with the original work or the micro-film from which the books were digitized. This can result in minor errors in reproduction. Possible imperfections include missing and blurred pages, poor pictures, markings and other reproduction issues beyond our control. Because this work is culturally important, we have made it available as part of our commitment to protecting, preserving, and promoting the world's literature.

GUIDE TO FOLD-OUTS MAPS and OVERSIZED IMAGES

The book you are reading was digitized from microfilm captured over the past thirty to forty years. Years after the creation of the original microfilm, the book was converted to digital files and made available in an online database.

In an online database, page images do not need to conform to the size restrictions found in a printed book. When converting these images back into a printed bound book, the page sizes are standardized in ways that maintain the detail of the original. For large images, such as fold-out maps, the original page image is split into two or more pages

Guidelines used to determine how to split the page image follows:

• Some images are split vertically; large images require vertical and horizontal splits.
• For horizontal splits, the content is split left to right.
• For vertical splits, the content is split from top to bottom.
• For both vertical and horizontal splits, the image is processed from top left to bottom right.

RATING:

PRINCIPLES—PRACTICE—PROCEDURE.

RATING:

PRINCIPLES—PRACTICE—PROCEDURE

THIRD EDITION

PARTS I. AND II

BY

PHILIP MICHAEL FARADAY

RATING SURVEYOR

PART III

BY

W. J. JEEVES

OF LINCOLN'S INN, BARRISTER-AT-LAW, AUTHOR OF THE ARTICLE ON
"LOANS" IN THE ENCYCLOPÆDIA OF LOCAL GOVERNMENT LAW

LONDON
THE ESTATES GAZETTE, LTD,
34 & 35, KIRBY STREET, CHARLES STREET,
HATTON GARDEN, E C

SWEET & MAXWELL LTD,
3, CHANCERY LANE, W C

1910

ↀ

LONDON

PRINTED AT THE OFFICE OF

THE ESTATES GAZETTE, LTD , 34 AND 35, KIRBY STREET,

CHARLES STREET, HATTON GARDEN, E C.

PREFACE

THE second edition of this book having been exhausted for some time past, I have, at the request of the publishers, the pleasure of submitting a third edition

May I point out to those critics of the second edition who expressed disappointment in not finding a book dealing with Rating Reform that they entirely misunderstood the intention of the work? Its sole aim was to shew as clearly as might be the working, from a practical point of view, of the existing system, and thereby to assist Overseers and Assessment Committees in the very complicated and difficult task they have to discharge in making and dealing with valuations for rating purposes   That is still my aim for the present

That there is field for reform no one can deny, but it appears to me to be rather in the elucidation and unification of the principles on which the value of rated properties is to be based, in the systematising of the practice with respect to statutable deductions or the abolition of the gross estimated value for purposes of rating, and in the perfecting of existing machinery, rather than in the setting up, in the place of authorities who have great experience in the work to help them, entirely new authorities without any such experience, and who, apart from such reform as that indicated, would have to contend with all the same difficulties that now exist

That I am not alone in this view, and that the opinions expressed in my Preface to the second edition with respect to the recommendations of the Royal Commission on Taxation are very largely held, may be said to be shewn, it seems to me, by the general disapproval with which the Bill in which it was proposed in the year 1904 to partially deal with the matter was received and by the ultimate withdrawal of such Bill

In this third edition I have endeavoured to bring the matters dealt with up to date, and this has involved a considerable increase in the size of the volume

Among other matters of importance the Rating of Machinery has been the subject of a decision of the House of Lords in the case of *Kirby v Hunslet Union*   This case, it is submitted, fully establishes the views put forward in the second edition on this vexed question

In Part I.—*Principles*
In Part II—*Practice*
In Part II—*Procedure*

Part III —*Procedure*—has been entirely re-written by Mr W J. Jeeves, barrister-at-law, and will be found to contain a concise statement of this branch of the subject, both within and without the Metropolis, which, it is hoped, will materially add to the practical usefulness of the book

It affords me much pleasure to acknowledge my indebtedness to Mr. Jeeves for the assistance thus given, and for his valuable criticism and advice on many points of interest and doubt

In Appendix I. and Appendix II every pains have been taken to include all the provisions of Statutes and Statutory Orders to which reference is likely to be required, and in Appendix III. is a Table shewing the working out of rates at amounts varying from 1s to 12s in the £, which, I trust, will be found to be of practical use to Clerks of Assessment Committees, to Assistant Overseers, and to Collectors of Rates and others

P MICHAEL FARADAY.

77, Chancery Lane,
         London, W C
April, 1910.

PREFACE TO THE SECOND EDITION.

THE reception given to the first edition of this work on Rating has encouraged me to greatly enlarge the scope of the book as now published in its second edition

Several important decisions have been given since its original publication, affecting the law, upon the subject, and the recommendations of the Royal Commission on Local Taxation have been comparatively recently made public.

It is unlikely, however, that many, if any, of the recommendations will become law in the immediate future, indeed, if some of the suggestions were adopted greater inequalities would exist than at present, and, although it cannot be denied that the evidence given before the Commission would be invaluable to the rating reformer, it is greatly to be regretted that the Commission, the work of which lasted some years, were unable to recommend more practical reforms.

As an instance, Gas, Water, Electric Light and similar concerns are valued for rating purposes in their entirety by a similar process to that of Railways, Tramways, Canals, etc, the allocation of the values, however, among the various parishes differs in the two classes of property, and whilst on the one hand no alteration whatever is suggested in the present method adopted (see page 80), on the other a recommendation is made which cannot be considered satisfactory either to the Companies affected or the Rating Authorities (see page 71) Another instance is the recommendation that all places in England and Wales should be re-valued at least once in every five years ; although there is little doubt that this should be done in every Urban District, in the majority of Rural Districts it is quite unnecessary and would impose a hardship on the ratepayers owing to the expense of the valuation—the Commission might well have extended the five years to ten years in such cases

What might be called the hardy annual, namely, the Bill to exempt machinery from Rating, has again been before Parliament this year, and is once more consigned to the pigeon-hole. It is altogether unlikely that any Government, with rates increasing practically all over the country, will reduce the area of taxation, and the fact of the existence of the proposed measure must be conclusive evidence that machinery is liable to be rated in the manner set forth in the chapter devoted entirely to this difficult subject It is however, a striking injustice to manufacturers that in certain Unions machinery is assessed, and that the manufacturers in these Unions should have to compete with those who are more fortunately situated in Unions where machinery is not taken into consideration at all Moreover, in these latter Unions, it is clear that the general body of ratepayers are paying more than their fair share of rates as the law at present exists, and it is open to any individual ratepayer to have a rate quashed under these circumstances

The valuer has now far greater scope in his enquiry as to the proper assessment of an hotel or public house since the decision of the House of Lords in the case of *Cartwright* v. *Sculcoates Union* (page 226).

I take this opportunity of thanking Mr A. F Vulliamy (Messrs. Callard and Vulliamy, 25, Golden Square, Regent Street, W) for his valuable assistance in editing the purely legal matter in the work. Mr Vulliamy stepped into the breach occasioned by the death of Mr. Stanley A. Latham, who edited the first edition

P. MICHAEL FARADAY.

77, Chancery Lane,
     London, W.C
November, 1903.

PREFACE TO THE FIRST EDITION.

NOTWITHSTANDING the number of important standard works already extant on the subject of Parochial Rating I venture to think, on placing this book before the public, that it will fulfil a want, at least as regards the practice of making valuations from a surveyor's point of view.

In order to present the subject clearly and intelligibly I have endeavoured to divide the principles which underlie and govern rating assessments from the practice or form in which the assessments themselves have to come before the different rating authorities

Whenever the opportunity has offered, I have separated as far as possible the classes of property, and have endeavoured to accentuate this division by giving particular forms of valuation suitable for each class. At the same time it was found impossible, without tedious repetition, to gather under each title all the factors which combine to make a complete valuation under that title, so that general information relative to the rating of a particular hereditament must sometimes be looked for in chapters other than the one specially relating to that particular class

I have much pleasure in acknowledging the assistance I have received from Mr Stanley A Latham, 45, Palace Chambers, Westminster, and I also take this opportunity of thanking those gentlemen who so courteously permitted me to refer to and make abstracts from their works upon the subject of Rating

P MICHAEL FARADAY

Rolls Chambers,
    89, Chancery Lane. W.C
December, 1896.

ERRATA.

TABLE OF CONTENTS.

PART I

PRINCIPLES.

CHAPTER I.

CHAPTER II

CHAPTER III

                    PART II.

                    PRACTICE.

                    CHAPTER I

PART III.

PROCEDURE.

TABLE OF CASES

M

S

TABLE OF STATUTES.

RATING.

PART I.—PRINCIPLES.

CHAPTER I.

INTRODUCTION

Introduction—Rating Acts, Cause of—General Foundation of Present Law of Rating—Principal Spending Authorities and Purposes of Rates

THE comparatively new science of sociology has set itself Introduction the task of discovering and formulating the rules which lie at the root of, and govern, the apparently always conflicting factors which go to constitute what is known as the life of the people

The formula to resolve these factors might be found in the answer to the question—' What is to be done to prevent Poverty ? " but, unfortunately, that formula still remains to be discovered, and as a more complete solution has so far eluded us, we have been working and shall, at least for our immediate future, continue to work, with the rough-and-ready methods known to us, and with which we are already practically acquainted, viz . Legislation in the form of the Poor Laws.

The first Statute dealing with the matter was 43 Eliza- Rating Acts, cause of beth, c 2, and the sound policy of its provisions has been established beyond all controversy, vagrancy and mendicarcy were on the increase to an alarming degree, accompanied by highway robberies and like felonies, and this Act was passed, to a certain extent at least, as a safeguard for both property and the person. Those who were incapable were to be provided for, whilst to those, on the other hand, who were willing to earn an honest livelihood work was to be given, the payment to consist of food and lodging, so that no man need steal to live, or commit crime to procure the mere necessaries of life

By 4 & 5 William IV., c. 76, s. 62, power was given to the ratepayers in any parish to raise money on the security of the rates for the purpose of sending abroad able-bodied paupers dwelling in such parish

Opportunities for work were, by these means, found for all who were willing; and to all who were incapable food and lodging were given. No tenable argument can therefore be reasonably adduced why able-bodied men, women and children should have courted starvation in our large cities.

General foundation of present law of rating
The Act 43 Elizabeth, c. 2, gave power to the parishioners to elect a certain number of householders in a parish, and provided that "together with the church-wardens of that parish, they shall become the guardians of the poor." "And they, or the greater part of them, shall take order from time to time, by and with the consent of two or more such justices of peace as is aforesaid, for setting to work the children of all such whose parents shall not, by the said churchwardens and overseers, or the greater part of them, be thought able to keep and maintain their children, and also for setting to work all such persons, married or unmarried, having no means to maintain them, as use no ordinary and daily trade of life to get their living by, also to raise, weekly or otherwise . . . a convenient stock of flax, hemp, wool, thread, iron, and other necessary ware and stuff to set the poor on work. And also competent sums of money for and towards the necessary relief of the lame, impotent, old, blind, and such other among them being poor, and not able to work, and also for the putting out of such children to be apprentices."

And it further gave power to raise money from adjoining parishes, and to help cases when a particular parish could not maintain its own poor This Act, which still remains in force as far as regards its leading principles, and the Act 4 & 5 William IV., c. 76, s 62, quoted above, make ample provision for the relief of the poor and destitute , yet we read day after day of cases of death from starvation, through want of work and absolute penury. Before Parliament took up this question, the poor were entirely dependent upon promiscuous charities and voluntary charitable institutions for their subsistence, and in view of the presumed moral duty to support our neighbour, or of the rich to help the poor, it was, perhaps, the best possible circumstance that could have happened when the Legislature made a tax on each "substantial householder" to keep the poor—a law the foundation of which is that each one pays according to his means, and the receiver is not dependent upon the varying impulses, generous or otherwise, of the donor.

This tax (by the Act of Elizabeth as above) extended to "every inhabitant, parson, vicar and other," and to "every occupier of lands, houses, tithes impropriate, or propriations of tithes, coal mines, or saleable underwoods" in every parish.

The fact that coal mines and saleable underwoods were so expressly mentioned as liable to assessment resulted in the Courts holding that it was the intention of the Legislature to exempt all other kinds of mines and woods, and these continued to be exempted from 1601, when the Act of Elizabeth was passed, until the year 1875, when the Rating Act, 1874, came into force. This Act repealed the before-mentioned provision as to saleable underwoods, but added to rateable property. "Land used for a plantation or a wood or for the growth of saleable underwood and not subject to any right of common." "Rights of fowling, of shooting, of taking or killing game or rabbits, and of fishing when severed from the occupation of the land", and "Mines of every kind not mentioned in 43 Eliz., c. 2"

In the year 1889 the Advertising Stations (Rating) Act, 1889 (52 & 53 Vict., c 27), extended the liability to be rated to advertisement hoardings

Section 3 reads as follows :—

" Where any land is used temporarily or permanently for the exhibition of advertisements, or for the erection of any hoarding, frame, post, wall or structure, used for the exhibition of advertisements, but not otherwise occupied, the person who shall admit the same to be so used, or (if he cannot be ascertained) the owner thereof, shall be deemed to be in beneficial occupation of such land or part thereof, and shall be rateable in respect thereof to the relief of the poor and to all local rates, according to the value of such use as aforesaid "

Section 4 of the same Act provides that, " Where any land or hereditament occupied for *other* purposes, and rateable in respect thereof, is used temporarily or permanently for the exhibition of advertisements, the gross and rateable value of such land or hereditament shall be so estimated as to include the increased value from such use as aforesaid."

It will be thus observed that since the Act of Elizabeth very few additional classes of property have been expressly made assessable to local rates, but it must be borne in mind, however, that the terms "land" and "house" have a far wider application than they had in 1601, and extend to various kinds of property which were not known or even thought of at that period. Such properties as railways, gas works, water works, tramways, electric lighting works, telephones, etc, etc, which have come into existence since 1601, are clearly rateable under the Act of Elizabeth. The owners are "beneficial occupiers of land," and although there is no Act which includes such concerns, it may be taken that all such properties, whether owned or occupied by companies (public or otherwise) or by private individuals, are clearly liable to be rated unless exempted by Statute or Common Law, as set out in the next chapter.

It is also to be observed that while in terms the Act of Elizabeth made personal property the subject of rating, yet in practice it was generally ignored, but what had been the general practice was followed and legalized in the Poor Rate (Exemption) Act, 1840, by which personal property is expressly exempted

It may perhaps be well to note here, too, that as the burden of local taxation has increased in later years, large amounts of money spent on purposes which have no connection with poor relief are for convenience levied, as part of the Poor Rate, on precepts received by the Overseers from the various spending authorities.

The following table shows the principal spending authorities outside the Metropolis, the rates to which they have recourse, and the more important purposes upon which the rates are spent[1].—

Principal spending authorities and purposes of rates

AUTHORITY	RATE	PURPOSE.
Guardians and Overseers	Poor Rate	Relief of Poor and minor services
County Council	County Rate (part of Poor Rate)	Police, Main Roads, Asylums, etc
Town Councils	Borough Rate and, in some cases, Watch Rate (both sometimes part of Poor Rate)	Municipal Services, Police and Asylums in some cases, etc
	General District Rate or Improvement Rate	Roads, Sanitary Services, etc
Urban District Councils	General District Rate or Improvement Rate	
Rural District Councils	Poor Rate	Highways and General Expenses
	Special Expenses Rate	Sanitary Works
Parish Councils	Poor Rate	General Parochial Services
	Lighting Rate	Lighting

[1] See Final Report of the Royal Commission on Local Taxation, p 4

CHAPTER II.

EXEMPTIONS.

**Exemptions
by Statute
and Common
Law**

IN the first place all Crown property is exempt from
liability to assessment to the Poor Rate; this, not only
because the Crown is not mentioned in the Act of
Elizabeth, but because the privileges of the Crown
cannot be affected except by special Act of Parliament

The *Mersey Docks* case[1] is made particularly conspicuous by the decisive judgment as to what constituted
property in the occupation of the Crown, whether
actually by the Crown itself, or by Government officials
in its service. Lord Cranworth said, in giving judgment
in this case, "Lands or houses occupied by the Crown,
or by servants of the Crown, are *not* liable to be rated."

Jones v Mersey Docks, (1865) 11 H L C 443; 35 L J M C 1; 12 L T.
643

From this same principle arises the exemption from rating not only of royal palaces, but also of the offices of the Secretaries of State, the Horse Guards, the Post Office, and many similar buildings

It is also to be noted that the Crown need not necessarily be the owners, as well as the occupiers of property in order to be non-liable to the Poor Rate. In the case of *R* v *Smith*,[1] Lord Campbell, C J., said "As the law now stands, if property is in the possession of the Crown, it is exempted from rateability, and it is immaterial whether the property be part of the hereditary possessions of the Crown *or be rented by the Crown.*" *Crown property (owned or rented by)*

So palaces are not rateable, unless where occupied by private persons, who may have beneficial occupation in no way connected with the Crown[2] The Houses of Parliament are not rateable, being property occupied for Government purposes *Palaces*

Gaols are not rateable, for by 40 & 41 Vict., c 21, all prisons became the property of the Government *Gaols*

Post offices are not rateable,[3] though it must not be forgotten that, where the persons in occupation of such hereditaments have accommodation in excess of that necessary for postal purposes, they are liable to be rated for such excess accommodation.[4] The same principle would equally apply to all property under this heading *Post Offices*

Barracks are not rateable,[5] and by 17 & 18 Vict., c. 105, s 9, places for keeping militia stores or "any premises or buildings appurtenant thereto" are also exempt *Barracks, Militia storehouses*

Volunteer storehouses are exempt by Statute The Volunteer Act. 1863 (26 & 27 Vict , c. 65), s 26, provides *Volunteer storehouses and drill halls*

---

[1] (1857) 26 L J M C 105, 7 El & Bl 483

[2] *R* v *Ponsonby*, (1842) 3 Q B 14, 11 L J M C 65

[3] *R* v *Smith*, (1857) 26 L J M.C 105, 7 El & Bl. 483

[4] *R* v *Terrott*, (1803) 3 East 506, *R* v *Fuller*, (1855) 8 El. & Bl 365 (n).

[5] *Lord Amherst* v *Lord Somers*, (1788) 2 T R 372

that " the commanding officer of a volunteer corps or administrative regiment, receiving any arms, ammunition, or other stores, supplied at the public expense or by subscription, shall, subject to the approval of the Lieutenant of the County to which the corps belongs, or in which the headquarters of the administrative regiment are situate (as the case may be), appoint a proper storehouse for the depositing and safe keeping of such arms, ammunition or stores," and "every such storehouse shall be free from all county, parochial, or other local rates and assessments "

Volunteer drill halls where attached to storehouses were held to be non-rateable in the case of *Pearson v Holborn Union*,[1] where three non-commissioned officers resided on the premises for the purpose of safely guarding the guns and ammunition, to comply with the demands of the military authorities, and there were also an officers' mess room, officers' ante-room, a canteen, a sergeants' room, and a men's mess room ; but from the judgment it will be seen that the whole of the premises were used solely for the purposes of the corps, and that the appellant had no use or occupation of the premises other than as colonel commanding the said corps, and in discharge of his duties as such.

In the case of *Hornsey Urban Council v. Hennell*[2] it was held that under Section 150 of the Public Health Act, 1875 (38 & 39 Vict, c 55), there is no liability attaching to the commanding officer of a volunteer corps to pay the apportioned part of the cost of sewering and paving the street on which the premises abut, where such premises consist solely of headquarters, storehouses, magazine, etc , used only for the purpose of the corps.

But where the commanding officer in barracks had apartments for the residence of himself and family, with

[1] (1893) 1 Q.B D 389, 62 L J. M C. 77, 57 J P 169
[2] (1902) 2 K B. 73 , 86 L T. 423.

a coach-house, stable and yard attached, separate from one for transacting the business of the corps. *Held,* there was a beneficial occupation enjoyed by him over and above that necessary for an officer for the purpose of the public [1]

Stables rented for the use of a corps are not rateable. [2]

Regimental stables

Where a drill hall was used for concerts in addition to volunteer purposes, it was held to be liable to the extent to which it was used for other than volunteer purposes. [3]

In the case of *Lewis* v. *Durham Union Assessment Committee* [4] certain freehold premises were used as a Volunteers' Drill Hall, and in addition there were the residence of the sergeant-instructor, certain officers' quarters, etc. Portions of the premises, however, were from time to time let for lectures, dramatic performances, concerts and other purposes not of a military nature. There was a caretaker of the premises, although he did not reside upon them, and the licenses for music and plays were taken out in his name. It is also important to note that profits from lettings in this case were used for the purpose of repaying the interest and capital to a mortgage which had been raised on the premises

Held, that only the portions of the premises used exclusively for volunteer purposes were exempt under Section 26 of the Volunteer Act, 1863, [5] and that those parts of the premises which were occasionally let out were not exempt.

This case also raised the question of who was the proper person to be rated as the occupier of the

[1] *R* v. *Terrott,* (1803) 3 East 506
[2] *Lord Amherst* v. *Lord Somers,* (1788) 2 T R 372
[3] *Rayner* v. *Drewitt,* (1900) 82 L.T. 718 ; 64 J.P. 567
[4] (1904) 90 L T. 388 , 68 J.P 220, 20 T L R. 227.
26 & 27 Vict., c. 65.

premises, the name of the caretaker had been inserted in the Valuation List, but this was held to be wrong

Telegraph undertakings Telegraph undertakings are by the Telegraph Act, 1868,[1] not exempt—(curiously enough that Statute makes property of this class acquired under the Act liable to the same extent that it was so liable before becoming Crown property)—but in the case[2] in which a postmaster disputed the valuation of the Assessment Committee and objected to payment—offering a smaller amount—the Assessment Committee refused the offer, and applied for a *mandamus* to compel the postmaster to pay the amount of their assessment The writ was refused, however, Blackburn, J, saying. "I have no doubt whatever but that it was intended by the 22nd section that the parish should not be the losers by the transfer of the telegraphs —that they should have the same rates they had, or ought to have had, previously. But the Act provides no means of enforcing the payment, and in that respect it is defective"

It was further held that the postmaster acted under the authority of the Treasury, over which the Court had no control.

Bridge in occupation of Crown In the case of the Victoria Bridge[3] at Chelsea, built by the Commissioners of Works and Buildings, with money borrowed from the Treasury, the tolls were to be divided, part going towards the expenses of the bridge and the rest to the Treasury in payment of the debt contracted. *Held*, that there was no beneficial occupation by any individual or body of persons other than an occupation by on behalf of the Crown, and that therefore the Commissioners were not liable to be rated in respect of the tolls

---

[1] 31 & 32 Vict, c 110
[2] *R v Postmaster-General*, (1873) 28 L.T. 337 , 37 J P. 196
 R v McCann, (1868) L R 3 Q B 667 , 37 L J M C 123, 19 L T 115.

National institutions are exempt [1] These would National institutions comprise such buildings as the National Gallery, British Museum, etc

Under a private Act relating to certain premises Public property belonging to His Majesty's Custom House it was enacted that such premises should be to all intents and purposes free and exempt from the payment of rates and assessments, although the premises might ultimately become private property by sale or assignment

The premises were subsequently sold, and by a later private Act the provision as to the payment of rates was repealed, but it was provided that the collectors of rates should only be entitled to certain fixed sums and that no more could be demanded from the occupiers of the said premises than provided by the Act.

The House of Lords held in this case [2] affirming the decision of the Court of Appeal, that the payment of rates under the private Acts was intended to extend for all time, and that the occupiers were liable only for such fixed sums, and, therefore, were not liable to be assessed for further rates, which happened in this particular case to be a Consolidated Rate and Sewers Rate under the City of London Sewers Act, 1848.

The above case is to be distinguished from the decision of the Court of Appeal in *Sion College v. City of London Corporation*,[3] where it was held that reclaimed land from the Thames was not exempt from the Consolidated Rate under Section 169 of the City of London Sewers Act, 1848,[4] notwithstanding that by a local Act it was provided that these lands reclaimed from the Thames should be free from all rates and taxes and assessments whatsoever.

---

[1] *R v Shee*, 3 G & D. 80, (1843) 4 Q B. 2, 12 L J M.C. 53, also *De la Beche v. St. James', Westminster*, (1855) 24 L J. M.C 74, 4 El. & Bl 385, 1 Jur N S. 375.

[2] *Netherlands Steamboat Co. v City of London Corporation*, (1905) 3 L G R 1087

[3] (1901) 1 Q B 617

[4] 11 & 12 Vict, c 68.

In addition to Crown and Government property there are various public properties which are exempt. There is an immense amount of uncertainty as to what constitutes such public property; the apparently conflicting decisions of the Courts, and the lack of definite legislative enactment, may in some degree account for this; but it is not proposed to give an exhaustive digest of all such cases, and reference will be made only to some of the leading decisions and to the hereditaments they affect.

Assize Courts — Assize Courts were held to be non-liable because they were used for public purposes [1]

Judges' lodgings — The County Hall, Courts of Justice, and Judges' lodgings were exempted in the case of *R. v The Justices of Worcestershire* [2]

County Courts — So, in the case of a County Court being occupied by a treasurer who is in possession of a lease under 9 & 10 Vict., c 95, s 48, it was held that there was no occupation of the building such as to render it liable to the Poor Rate. [3]

Sessions House — The Middlesex Sessions House was held not liable to the Poor Rate, because it was a building used for public purposes. [4]

Police Stations — Police stations are not rateable,[5] neither are the officers who live in the stations, under 2 & 3 Vict., c 9. But the case of *Showers v. Assessment Committee of Chelmsford Union* [6] must not be overlooked. Here the chief constable and other police officers of the County of Essex resided in parts of a block of buildings belonging to the county. The premises occupied three sides of a square,

---

[1] *R. v St. Martin's, Leicester*, and *R. v Castle View, Leicester*, (1867) L R. 2 Q.B 493, 36 L J. M C 99; 16 L T 625, 15 W R 1036, 8 B & S 536

[2] (1839) 11 A. & E. 57, 9 L J M C 17.

[3] *R. v Manchester Overseers*, (1854) 3 El. & Bl 336, 23 L J. M C 48

[4] *Nicholson v. Holborn Union*, (1886) 18 Q.B D. 161, 56 L J M C 54.

[5] *R. v St. Martin's, Leicester*, (1867) L R 2 Q B. 493, 36 L J. M C 99

[6] (1891) 1 Q B 339, 60 L J M C 55, 64 L T 755.

and the front door of each residence opened into one centre court The whole was surrounded by a wall, and the buildings were under one roof. Besides the officers' residences, the buildings comprised certain stores for police clothing, etc , which were not rated . but there were no cells for prisoners. The whole of the premises were used solely for the purposes of the county, the chief constable being required to reside there. Each officer paid rent for the premises in which he resided, such rent being deducted from his pay *Held*, upon the facts, that the premises were not a police station, and did not constitute a single building used as a whole for public purposes so as to be exempt from rateability ; and that each of the officers had a separate beneficial occupation of his own residence in respect of which he was rateable

But, on the other hand, where a county police station had within the boundary walls houses where certain officers were, by the terms of their appointment, bound to reside, it was held that the houses were part of the station, and, therefore, were exempt from rating.[1]

In the case where two constables occupied a building, in which, although a cell was attached, no charges were taken, and the police station was elsewhere, the building was held to be rateable [2]

As to whether reformatories are or are not exempt there is a variance of judicial opinion In the case of *Shepherd* v. *Bradford*[3] (a decision before the *Mersey Docks* case), it was held that a reformatory was not rateable. But in the later case of *Tunnicliffe* v. *Birkdale Overseers*[4] of premises occupied as a school, the managers

Reformatories

---

[1] *Cross* v *West Derby Guardians*, (1889) 81 L.T. 645 , 64 J.P 182 , 16 T L R 120

[2] *Monmouth Overseers* v *Monmouth County Council*, (1902) 87 L.T 65, 66 J P 788.

[3] (1864) 33 L.J M.C. 182

[4] (1888) 20 Q.B D. 450 , 56 L J M C 109.

having a certificate under the Reformatories Schools Act, 1866 (29 & 30 Vict, c 117, s 4), it was held that such premises were liable to the Poor Rate.

Embassies   Ambassadors are exempt. By a local Act (35 Geo. III , c. 73, s 190), which enacts that "every rate or assessment which shall be made, laid, or assessed by virtue of this Act for or in respect of any land, ground, house, shop, warehouse. wharf, coach-house, stable, cellar, vault building, tenement, or hereditament whatsoever, which any ambassador, envoy, resident agent or other public minister, of any foreign prince or state, or the servant of any such ambassador, envoy, resident agent or other public minister, or any other person not liable by law to pay such rate or assessment, now doth or hereafter shall inhabit, shall be paid by and recoverable from the landlord, owner, lessor, or proprietor of every such land, ground, house, shop, warehouse, wharf, coach-house, stable, cellar, vault, building, tenement or hereditament respectively, who shall be liable and compellable to the payment thereof, and the same shall be recovered and applied as the other rates hereby made payable are to be recovered and applied"—this is made clear. This Act, however, only applied to a limited area, but other areas are covered by a number of similar Acts. The parish in these cases is not the sufferer, as it is to be observed that the proprietor is made liable for payment of such rates, so that, in point of fact, ambassadors dwellings and offices are assessable, although indirectly, to the Poor Rate. See also the Metropolitan Police Act (10 Geo. IV , c. 44), which relates to the collection of the Police Rate from the owners of ambassadors' dwellings.

Contribution by Government to rates   It is to be noted, however, that while the principle of exemption is maintained, a contribution equivalent to the rates that would otherwise be leviable is now given in respect of most Government property. So long as this system is continued it would seem that the practical question as to Government property is really no longer one as to rateability, but as to method of valuation—the only peculiarity in the treatment of such property being that it is valued by a Treasury officer instead of by the ordinary valuation authorities.[1]

The Treasury officer, however, does not, as a rule, object to meet a valuer on behalf of the local authorities; indeed, he is often glad to do so, as various points arise in discussion which otherwise might have passed un-noticed. It should be noticed also that the Treasury make no contribution in respect of court houses, police stations and the premises of volunteer corps, on the ground that these properties are not maintained out of the money voted by Parliament. Contribution in respect of metropolitan police courts and stations, however, is made from the Metropolitan Police Fund

Churches and chapels are exempt by Statute 3 & 4 *Churches and chapels* William IV , c 30, which enacts that "no person or persons shall be rated or shall be liable to be rated, or to pay to any church, or poor rates, or cesses, for or in respect of any churches, district churches, chapels, meeting houses, or premises, or such part thereof as shall be exclusively appropriated to public religious worship, and which (other than churches, district churches, and episcopal chapels of the Established Church) shall be duly certified for the performance of such religious worship according to the provision of any Act or Acts now in force Provided always, that no person or persons shall be hereby exempted from any such rates or cesses for or in respect of any parts of such churches, district churches, chapels, meeting houses or other premises, which are not so exclusively appro-priated, and from which parts not so exclusively appropriated such person or persons shall receive any rent or rents, or shall derive any profit or advantage."

[1] See Final Report of the Royal Commission on Local Taxation.

This Statute also enacts that " no person or persons shall be liable to any such rates or cesses, because the said churches, district churches, chapels, meeting houses, or other premises, or any vestry rooms belonging thereto, or any part thereof, may be used for Sunday or other schools, or for the charitable education of the poor "

It will be observed from the above that, before exemption can be claimed for a church or chapel not belonging to the Established Church, it must be duly registered and be exclusively appropriated for public religious worship. It therefore follows that private chapels in monasteries, convents, schools, asylums, etc, must be so registered or they are liable to be rated. With regard to similar chapels of the Church of England, they should be used exclusively for *public* religious worship, and if not so used would. it is submitted, be liable to be rated, although the point does not seem to have been the subject of judicial decision

Literary societies

Literary societies are exempt by Statute 6 & 7 Vict, c 36, Section 1 of which reads as follows. " No person or persons shall be assessed or rated, or liable to be assessed or rated or liable to pay, to any county, borough, parochial, or other local rates or cesses, in respect of any land, houses, or buildings, or parts of houses or buildings, belonging to any society instituted for purposes of science, literature, or the fine arts exclusively, either as tenant or as owner, and occupied by it for the transaction of its business, and for carrying into effect its purposes, provided that such society shall be supported wholly or in part by annual voluntary contributions, and shall not, and by its own laws may not, make any dividend, gift, division, or bonus in money unto or between any of its members, and provided also that such society shall obtain the certificate of the barrister-at-law," who in the next Section of the Act is defined to be the barrister appointed to certify the rules of Friendly Societies, and to whom three copies of the rules of management signed as in the said section directed have first to be submitted, on each of which copies he is to give a certificate that the society applying therefor is entitled to the benefit of the Act

Further, in the event of refusal of a certificate, a right of appeal to Quarter Sessions is given, and any person assessed to any rate from which a society shall be exempted can also appeal to Quarter Sessions against a decision of the said barrister granting a certificate. *Prima facie*, therefore, the barrister's certificate is proof of exemption, but there is the right of appeal above referred to, and it is to be remembered that if the certificate be granted, and notwithstanding a rate be levied on the premises, it is necessary to appeal against the rate[1] and support the grounds on which the certificate purports to be granted, the certificate while a condition precedent to claim of exemption not being conclusive proof of right thereto[2]

It must also be noticed that the society must be supported wholly or in part by annual voluntary contributions.

The word "voluntary" does not necessarily mean that a society must not have a fixed subscription. In the case of the *Art Union of London* v *Overseers of Savoy*[3] there was a fixed subscription of one guinea per annum to entitle any person to membership, by reason and during payment of which he was entitled to receive every year a copy of an engraving and in addition one chance in the annual distribution of prizes, such person, however, ceasing to be a member on the non-payment of his

---

[1] *Birmingham Churchwardens* v *Shaw*, (1849) 10 Q.B 868, 18 L J M C 89

[2] *R* v *Phillips*, (1848) 8 Q B. 745, 17 L.J. M.C 83

[3] (1894) 2 Q B 609, 63 L J M.C. 253, and (1896) A.C. 296, 65 L.J. M C. 161.

subscription. In the Court of Appeal it was held that the word " voluntary " used in the Act (6 & 7 Vict., c 36) meant " not compulsory ". and, should a member cease to subscribe, the society could not enforce such subscription, but, as has been already stated. he ·ould cease to be a member. This decision was, however, overruled on appeal to the House of Lords,[1] who decided " voluntary " not to mean " not compulsory " but " gratuitous,' without any money or other material consideration.

A society must by its laws be incapable of letting its premises, or it cannot claim exemption—see *Purvis* v *Traill*,[2]—even if let to a society with the same object.

It is also to be further noted that there must also be a law of the society prohibiting " any dividend, gift, division or bonus in money unto or between any of its members."

The United Service Institution [3] was, however, held not exempt   Lord Campbell, C J , in delivering judgment, asked, " Is the United Service Institution a society for the support of which the Legislature intended to throw a burden by additional taxation upon the county, borough, and parish in which it is established ? But in this case, by the laws of the institution, the buildings and the funds of the society could be applied to purposes other than those of science, literature, or the fine arts.

Institutions for the instruction of students or members are not exempt *vide* the cases of the *Institution of Civil Engineers*,[4] and of the *British and Foreign School Society*,[5] an institution for the training of teachers. See also *R.* v *Brandt*,[6] the case of an institution formed for the advancement of the science of music, by giving concerts in a hall belonging to the society *Held*, that

[1] (1896) A.C 296 , 65 L J M C 161
[2] (1849) 3 Ex 344 , 18 L J M C 57 , 3 New Sess Cas 459.
[3] *R* v *St Martin's-in the-Fields*, (1851) 21 L J M.C. 53.
[4] (1879) L R 5 Q B.D. 48
[5] *R* v *Pocock*, (1846) 8 Q B 729 , 15 L J M C. 132 , 10 Jur. 662.
[6] (1851) 16 Q B 462 , 20 L J M.C 119 , 15 Jur 223

the society, though constituted for the purpose of promoting the fine arts, was not exempt, as it appeared that the promotion of the fine arts was not the primary object of the society, but only incidental, the primary object being the gratification of the subscribers. It should be stated that in the case of the *Royal College of Music* v. *Westminster Vestry*,[1] Hawkins, J, said that the effect of the judgment in *Commissioners of Inland Revenue* v. *Forrest*,[2] was virtually to overrule the decision with respect to the Institution of Civil Engineers above referred to, but the case in question turned on the construction of the Customs and Inland Revenue Act, 1885, and reference to the judgment in the case would seem to show that it was not intended to have the effect so suggested.

In the case of the *Zoological Society*,[3] the society was held not to be exempt, because it was not a society for the purpose of science exclusively according to the Act (6 & 7 Vict, c 36) The *Religious Tract Society*[4] was also held not exempt

So in the case of the *Jenner Institute of Preventive Medicine*[5] it was held that the premises were not occupied by the society for the purposes of science exclusively, but also for the sale of various medicines, and was therefore not exempt.

And in the case of *Soane's Museum Trustees* v. *St Giles' and St George's*,[6] where the public, subject to certain restrictions, were admitted, it was held to be rateable, as there was a beneficial occupation to others than the public.

[1] (1898) 1 Q B 304 and 809
[2] (1890) 15 A.C 334, (1887) 19 Q B D 610, (1888) 20 Q B D. 621
[3] (1854) 3 El & Bl 807, 2 C L R 766; 26 L J M C 139, 18 Jur 786
[4] R. v. Jones, (1846) 8 Q B 719, 15 L J M.C 129
[5] Jenner Institute v St. George's, Hanover Square, (1900) 69 L J Q B 814, 63 L T 344.
[6] 16 T L R 440

In the case of the *Royal College of Music* v *Westminster Vestry*,[1] however, the college was held to be exempt, the payments made to members of the teaching staff not constituting "any dividend, gift, division or bonus in money."

Public libraries and news rooms

Libraries and news rooms may be exempt—see the cases of the *Birmingham New Library*[2] and the *London Library*,[3] the latter a society established for the lending of books to its members and being supported within the meaning of the Act by annual subscriptions and voluntary contributions, and prevented by its laws from "making any dividend, gift, division, or bonus in money unto or between any of its members"[4] In the case of a society at Manchester,[5] which had let part of its premises to tenants (who were rated individually for the same), and applied the rents received to the objects of the society, it was held that this fact did not affect the exemption from liability to be rated of the part occupied by the society. But it must be noticed that a society cannot let the actual premises sought to be exempted for meetings, etc., applying the rent obtained to the common fund, but must use the premises exclusively for its own objects[6]

The following societies have also been exempted from liability —The *Linnaean Society*,[7] the *Bradford Library and Literary Society*,[8] and the *Liverpool Library*[9]

[1] (1896) 1 Q B 809

[2] (1849) 10 Q B 868, 18 L J. M C 80

[3] *Clarendon (Earl)* v *St James' (Rector)*, (1852) 10 C B. 806, 20 L J M.C 213, 15 Jur 492.

[4] (1843) 6 & 7 Vict, c 36

[5] *R* v *Manchester Overseers*, (1851) 16 Q B 449, 20 L J M.C 119, 15 Jur 219

[6] *Purves* v *Traill*, (1849) 3 Ex 344, 3 New Sess Cas 459, 18 L J. M C 57

[7] (1854) 23 L J M C 148, 18 Jur 859

[8] (1858) 1 El & El 88, 28 L J M C 73

[9] (1860) 5 H & N 526, 29 L J M C. 221, 8 W R. 198

But, on the other hand, in the case of the *Birmingham News Rooms*,[1] a society which had a news room where many of the newspapers, periodicals, and various shipping and share lists, etc, were taken for the benefit of its members, although a library was attached, it was held not exempt, as it was not instituted for purposes of the fine arts, literature, or science exclusively.

So in the case of the *Russell Institution*,[2] a society which had a library with news rooms. Certain lectures were also delivered there on scientific subjects, yet it was held that it was not a society instituted for the purposes of science, literature, or the fine arts exclusively within 6 & 7 Vict., c. 36

So in the case of *Purchas* v. *Holy Sepulchre, Cambridge (Overseers)*,[3] a society formed under the title of the Cambridge Philosophical Society. Its meeting house contained reading rooms in which newspapers were taken, and to which every member contributed in his annual subscription. *Held*, that the society was not entitled to be exempted from rateability, as the premises were not occupied for the purposes of science, art, or literature exclusively, and also that the society must be rated in respect of the whole building, not the reading room only.

In recent years, what are known as "Free Public Libraries" have sprung up in large numbers, and it is not infrequently found that they have escaped assessment altogether, or, as an alternative, that they have been rated only at a nominal sum.

There is, however, no justification for this practice, and in the case of the *Liverpool Corporation* v. *West Derby Union Assessment Committee*,[4] where a free public

[1] *R* v. *Phillips*, (1848) 8 Q B 745, 3 New Sess. Cas 134, 17 L J M C. 83, 12 Jur 431

[2] (1854) 3 El & Bl. 416, 2 C L R. 755, 23 L J M C 65, 18 Jur 597

[3] (1854) 4 El & Bl 156, 3 C L R 6, 24 L J M C 9, 1 Jur N S 304

[4] (1905) 92 L T 467, 53 W R 633, 69 J P 277, 21 T L R 469.

library had been established under a private Act and a certificate of exemption granted under the Scientific and Literary Societies Act, 1843,[1] it was held that, although the premises were for the time being used by the public, this of itself did not relieve the liability to be rated in respect of the occupation of the corporation, and that the corporation were not a society and their contributions not voluntary contributions within the meaning of Section 1 of the said Act, and that the words " for purposes of literature only " did not cover acquisition of knowledge from newspapers

It would, therefore, appear that similar free public libraries are not entitled to exemption and that they should be rated in a similar method to that applied to hospitals, board schools and other like institutions and dealt with in the chapter on buildings

The antithesis of this case is to be found in the decision in the case of the *Hornsey School of Art v Edmonton Union Assessment Committee and Hornsey Overseers*,[2] where it was held that certain grants were voluntary contributions within the meaning of the Scientific and Literary Societies Act, 1843,[1] although such grants were from the Board of Education and the County Council, and were augmented by the fees of students, but in this case the institution was admittedly established for the purpose of advancing and encouraging fine arts exclusively

Lighthouses   With regard to lighthouses, by the Merchant Shipping Act, 1894 (57 & 58 Vict, c 60), s 731 it is provided that " All lighthouses, buoys, beacons, and all light dues, and other rates, fees, or payments accruing to, or forming part of, the Mercantile Marine Fund, and all premises or property belonging to, or occupied by, any of the general lighthouse authorities or by the Board of Trade, which

---

[1] 6 & 7 Vict, c 36
[2] (1905) 94 L T 203, 70 J P 121

ale used or applied for the purposes of any of the services for which these dues, rates, fees, and payments are received, and all instruments or writing used by, or under the directions of any of the general lighthouse authorities or the Board of Trade in carrying on these services, shall be exempted from all public, parochial, and local taxes, duties and rates, of every kind," and by Section 634 the Commissioners of Irish Lights are constituted "general lighthouse authorities" As to the rating of other lighthouses see Part II., *post*.

With regard to Sunday and Ragged Schools,[1] "every authority having power to impose or levy any rate upon the occupier of any building or part of a building used exclusively as a Sunday School or Ragged School may exempt such building or part of a building from any rate for any purpose whatever which such authority has power to impose or levy Provided that nothing in this Act contained shall prejudice or affect the right of exemption from rating of Sunday or Infant Schools, or for the charitable education of the poor in any churches, district churches, chapels, meeting houses, or other premises, or any vestry rooms belonging thereto, or any part thereof, by virtue of the 3 & 4 William IV., c. 30, entitled ' An Act to exempt from poor and church rates all churches, chapels, and other places of religious worship ' "

The words " may exempt" do not mean "must exempt," so the rating authorities are at liberty to use their discretion in the matter.[2] By the Act in question (32 & 33 Vict , c 41, s 2) "a 'Sunday School' shall mean any school used for giving religious education gratuitously to children and young persons on Sunday, and on week days for the holding of classes and meetings in furtherance of

(right margin note: Sunday and Ragged Schools)

---

[1] The Sunday and Ragged Schools (Exemption from Rating) Act, 1869 (32 & 33 Vict , c 40) s 1

[2] *Bell v Crane*, (1873) L.R 8 Q.B 481, 29 L T (N S) 207, 42 L J M.C 122

the same object, and without pecuniary profit being derived therefrom, and a 'Ragged School' shall mean any school used for the gratuitous education of children and young persons of the poorest classes, and meetings in furtherance of the same object, and without any pecuniary benefit being derived therefrom, except to the teacher or teachers employed "

Voluntary Schools

By the Voluntary Schools Act, 1897 (60 & 61 Vict., c 5, s 3), no person is to be assessed or rated to or for any local rate in respect of lands or buildings used exclusively or mainly for the purposes of the schoolrooms, offices or playgrounds of a voluntary school   Should any profit however be derived by the managers of the school from letting the premises, such managers should be rated to the extent thereof   The definition in the Act of a voluntary school is "a public elementary day school not provided by a School Board "

In the case of the *Royal Commissioners of the Patriotic Fund* v. *Wandsworth Borough Council*,[1] where a school was administered as a charitable institution for the education of children (board and lodging being provided) and a grant earned by the institution as a public elementary day school, it was held that nevertheless, such a building may be liable to be rated because it is not used exclusively or mainly for the purpose of a schoolroom, offices or playgrounds   such as is required by the Voluntary Schools Act before referred to

Tolls

Tolls *per se* are not rateable, though upon this point many cases have been contested. The only statutory exemption there has been of tolls is in the case of *turnpike* tolls[2], but tolls may be of the nature of personal or private incomes or profits, and by 3 & 4 Vict., 1840, c 89,[3] it is provided that " it shall not be lawful for

---

[1] (1903) 88 L T 865 , 67 J.P 311 , 19 T L R 517
[2] 3 Geo IV , c 126 s 51, and 4 Geo IV , c 95, s 31
   The Act is kept in force by the Expiring Laws Continuance Acts

the overseers of any parish, township, or village, to tax
any inhabitant thereof, as such inhabitant, in respect of
his ability derived from the profits of stock in trade or
any other property." Toll houses, however, are rateable.[1]
See also the case of *R* v. *North and South Shields Ferry
Co.,*[2] where the landing places were held to be rateable, but
not the tolls *per se*, so in the case of *R*. v. *Fowke.*[3] where
a lighthouse was held to be rateable only as a building—
not in respect of the value of the tolls paid by ships passing
such light

It has also been recently held[4] that where a bridge was
leased the benefits of occupation rested with the lessee,
who had the power to charge tolls, and that the lessee
was liable to be rated for this hereditament and not the
lessors, although they in effect had only given an easement and not demised the bridge to the lessee

The bridge belonged to the York Corporation, and they
retained the power to open it at certain times for the
passage of ships. All officers of the Corporation, and
soldiers and volunteers in uniform, were entitled to free
use of the bridge, and the Corporation or their servants
had power at all times to enter upon the bridge for the
purpose of doing repairs   In addition to these restrictions the lessee was not allowed at any time during his
tenancy to erect any obstruction across the bridge or its
approaches without the consent of the Corporation

The Overseers rated the lessee, and levied a distress
warrant in respect of unpaid rates, and it was held, as
stated, that the lessee was liable for the rates

Public parks are exempt, the leading case here being
that of Brockwell Park, the London County Council
being the legal owners. This case was decided in the
House of Lords in 1897[5]

Public parks

---

[1] *Williams* v *Bedminster Union*, (1876) 45 L J M C 117, 34 L T 795
[2] (1852) 7 Railway Cases 849, 1 El & Bl 110, 22 L.J. M C 9,
17 Jur 181
[3] (1826) 9 D & R 120, 5 B & C 814.
[4] *Percy* v *Hall*, (1903) 88 L T 830, 67 J P 293, 17 T L R 503
[5] *Lambeth Overseers* v. *London County Council*, (1897) A C , 625 76 L T.
795, 46 W R 79, 61 J P 580, 66 L J Q B 806

The park was acquired by the London County Council
under a special Act, which provided that they should
maintain it for the perpetual use of the public, and the
Lord Chancellor, in his judgment in the case, said "The
public is not a rateable occupier, . .   the fact that
the park is vested in the County Council does not make
them the occupiers.   It would be absurd to contend that
wherever the legal estate is there is occupation   The
road is vested in someone, but, if a public road, there is
no occupation of it any more than a milestone or a direction post. . . .   I think there is no occupation at all,
the County Council being merely custodians and trustees
for the public."   Lord Herschell also said· "It seems clear
that the park and the buildings thereon have no rateable
value   No tenant would give anything for them, seeing
that every part of them is dedicated to the public use and
that the small sums of money which might be received in
respect of them would .   be more than absorbed
by the expense of keeping them in order"   So in the case
of the *Mayor, etc., of Manchester* v *Chorlton Union*,[1] and
the case of the *Mayor, etc, of Liverpool* v *West Derby
Union (No 2)*,[2] it was held that, although the Corporation
in whom the park in each of such cases was vested for the
benefit of the public, had power on occasions to close it
for the purpose of a flower or agricultural show, and to
make a charge for admission, the park was not rateable.

Public roads   Public roads are not rateable, as they are vested in
local authorities for the benefit of the public, and sewers
underground have not for many years been rated, but
this cannot be regarded as altogether a sound principle
Underground   and was discussed in the case of *Ystradyfodwg and
sewers   Pontypridd Sewerage Board* v. *Newport Union*,[3] in which
a large sewer, which ran partly beneath the ground,

_____

[1] (1899) 15 T L R 327
[2] (1908) 2 K B 647.
[3] (1901) 1 Q B 406, 70 L J K B. 318, 84 L T 40

partly in an embankment and partly on concrete ashes, and for the use of which the Board received certain annual payments from other authorities, was held to be rateable in its whole length

Extraordinary tithe rent-charge is also exempt [1] There are also many cases of partial exemption under private and local Acts. It was a particularly common provision in old Canal Acts that canals should be rated at the same value as the original agricultural land through which the canal was constructed. This was done in order to encourage the construction of canals, and frequently Parliament in granting an Act made this concession.

Extraordinary tithe rent

Partial exemptions

There is also partial exemption in the case of certain light railways—see The Light Railways Act, 1896 (59 & 60 Vict., c 48)—in Section 5 (1c) of which it is enacted that where the Treasury exercise the power conferred on them under that section to make a special free grant-in-aid of a light railway, " the order authorizing the railway may make provision as regards any parish that during a period not exceeding ten years, to be fixed by the order, so much of the railway as is in that parish shall not be assessed to any local rate at a higher value than that at which the land occupied by the railway would have been assessed, if it had remained in the condition in which it was, immediately before it was acquired for the purpose of the railway."

Light railways

There is also partial exemption in the case of Burial Grounds under the Burial Act of 1855,[2] Section 15 of which enacts that land purchased or acquired under the Burial Acts for the purpose of a Burial Ground (with or without any building erected or to be erected thereon) shall not, while used for such purposes, be assessed to any local rates at a higher value or more improved rent than the value or rent at which such land was assessed at the time of such purchase or acquisition.

Burial grounds

[1] 49 & 50 Vict (1886), c 54, s. 5
[2] 18 & 19 Vict , c 128

In the case of the *North Manchester Overseers* v. *Winstanley*,[1] the churchyard of a parish church had been closed and a new one, three hundred yards from the church, acquired and consecrated. The rector received the usual fees for burial and for the purchase of graves. There were no buildings on the land for religious purposes. The rector claimed exemption under the Poor Rate Exemption Act, 1833,[2] but this contention was not accepted by the Court of Appeal, and it was held that there was a rateable occupation by the rector, and in the judgments of the Court it is suggested that churchyards (*i.e.*, burial grounds attached to the church), though generally not rated, may be rateable; this view in fact was decided to be right on appeal to the House of Lords.[3]

Unoccupied property

Where there is no occupation of property whatsoever (that is, property to let), it is not rateable, but the question of occupation is dealt with in the next chapter.

Unproductive property

Unproductive property is also not rateable,[4] so where the supplies of a coal mine became exhausted, the tenant was held not liable as the beneficial occupier, although under his lease he still had to pay rent for the same as a tenant.

Stock in trade

Although by the Act of Elizabeth stock-in-trade was rateable, this has been exempted by an Act entitled the Poor Rate Exemption Act, 1840,[5] which has since been kept in force by the Expiring Laws Continuance Acts.

Excusal of rates

The excusal of rates on the ground of the poverty of the ratepayer is provided for as regards the Poor Rate under an Act of 1814,[6] as regards the Highway Rate under the Highways Act of 1835,[7] and as regards Urban Rates under the Public Health Act, 1875.[8]

---

[1] (1908) 1 K B 835, 77 L J K B 661, 72 J P 171, 98 L. T. 781, 24 T L R 388
[2] 3 & 4 William IV, c 30. See page 23 *ante*
[3] (1909) 26 T L R 90
[4] *R* v *Bedworth*, (1807) 8 East 387
[5] 3 & 4 Vict, c 89
[6] 54 Geo III, c 170, s 11.
[7] 5 & 6 William IV, c 50, s 32
[8] 38 & 39 Vict, c 55, s 225

CHAPTER III.

OCCUPATION

Occupier Liable—What Constitutes Occupation—Easement not an Occupation—Railway Bookstall—Tenants at Railway Stations—Stalls in Markets—User of Gas Mains of another Authority—Tunnel for Drainage—Water Main—Use of Quay Space, Sheds, etc, in Dock —Shooting Grounds—Possession under Breach of Agreement — Grazing Rights — Lodgers — Control of Outer Door—Flats and Chambers—Westminster Tontine Case —Right of Landlord to enter Premises—Occupation of Hotels—Possession of Outer Door—House Divided, two tenements — Structural Severance — What is Occupation?—Staircase, Common Entrance—Occupation must be Beneficial—London Sewers Case—School Board Case—Empty Houses, definition of—Liability of Owners in respect of Caretakers or Servants—Rateable Occupation, a question of fact—Empty Furnished Houses — Part Occupation by Owner — Property in Course of Construction — Theatres — Advertisement Hoardings—Occupation by Liquidator—Where Owner Liable—Non compliance of Owners with Liability to Pay Rate—Occupation for Short Term

THE Act of Elizabeth still obtains (with the exception of the question of personal property), and therein it is enacted "that by taxation of *every occupier of* lands," etc   So that it is necessary that there should, in the first place, be some person or persons in occupation of a hereditament before it can be held to be rateable.[1] It matters little under what tenure the property is held,[2] so

Occupier liable

What constitutes occupation

---

[1] *Norwood Overseers v Salter*, (1892) 2 Q B 118, 56 J P 535, 61 L J M C 193, 67 L T 376

[2] *Bute v Grindall*, (1793) 1 T R. 343, also *R v Bell*, (1798) 7 T R 598.

that there is an occupation.[1] Possession does not necessarily mean occupation, however, and in the case of
R v *St Pancras*,[2] Lush, J , said: " Occupation includes
possession as its primary element; but it also includes
something more   Legal possession does not *of itself*
constitute an occupation   The owner of a vacant house
is in possession, and may maintain trespass against any
one who invades it , but as long as he leaves it vacant he
is not rateable for it as an occupier "

To constitute liability to rating there must be exclusive occupation[3], and so while there may be an
interest in and even a beneficial enjoyment of a hereditament, yet if it does not involve exclusive occupation or

*Easement
not an
occupation*

possession, such interest is not rateable.   An easement is
not rateable   Thus where a canal company made use of
a towing path on the banks of a natural river they were
held not rateable, as they only possessed an easement
over same.[4] The question, however, as to whether there
is or is not an easement is a question of fact.[5]

*Railway
bookstalls*

In the case of *Smith* v. *Lambeth Assessment Committee*,[6]
the parish authorities sought to make liable bookstalls
on the platforms of a railway station   The railway company let to a firm of newsagents a space on the platform
for the sale of books and periodicals, the railway company
reserving to themselves the right of control of the
servants of the firm of newsagents, through the station
master, and also stipulating that no books of an
' indecent, immoral or seditious character, or *which
should be forbidden by the company* " should be sold

---

[1] *Kittow* v *Liskeard Union*, (1874) L R 10 Q B 7 , 44 L J M C 23,
39 J P 325, 31 L T 601

[2] (1877) L R 2 Q B D 581, 46 L J M C 243, 37 L T 126

[3] See judgment of Cockburn, C J , Westminster Tontine case, *post*,
p 39

[4] *Manchester, Sheffield and Lincolnshire Railway Co* v *Doncaster
Union*, (1894) 71 L T 585 · 10 T L R 567, 6 R 280—H L., 57 J P 792

[5] *Percy* v *Hall*, (1903) 88 L T. 830 , 67 J P 293, 17 T.L.R. 503

[6] (1882) 10 Q B D 327 52 L J M C 1, 48 L T. 57, 47 J P 244—C.A.

The Court held that there was no exclusive occupation by the newsagent of any portion of the platforms, therefore they were not rateable.

Although it thus appears that the tenant of the bookstall is not liable to the local rates, yet this does not prevent an enhancement of value to the station itself, for which the railway company are liable, by reason of the fact that the bookstall is situated on the station, it being obvious that if a railway company would give so much rent for a railway station *per se*, the fact that, from its position in or near a town, they could let for the purpose of a bookstall or otherwise, a certain part of such station not necessary for the use thereof as a station, would induce them to give a higher rent than if they were unable to so let part of it

In the case of the *London and North Western Railway Company* v *Buckmaster*[1] it was held that the railway company was properly rateable for certain stables which were situated within the premises of the railway station and approachable only through the gates between the station and the public roads Certain persons were permitted by agreements to occupy and use these stables at a monthly rent, and on the terms of agreeing to be bound by the bye-laws rules and regulations prescribed by the railway company for the use of their station, and to deliver up possession of the stables on the expiration of one month's notice from the company Although the company did not in fact exercise any control over the stables, it was held that, on the true construction of the agreement, looking at the situation of the stables, it was the intention of the company to retain the control It is, however, the common practice to look upon the tenants of a railway company as the occupiers liable to be rated, and in many agreements it is specified that the tenants shall pay the usual tenant's rates and taxes, but the

Tenants at railway stations

---

[1] (1875) L.R 10 Q B 70, 33 L T. 329, 39 J P 692, 44 L J M C 180.

question whether the tenant or the railway company is liable for the rates as the occupier would appear to have to be determined in each individual case, according to the specific terms of each individual agreement

Stalls in market

So in the case of *Spear v Bodmin Union*[1] Here there were two stalls rented by the appellant in Bodmin Market Place There was no agreement that the stalls should remain in the same place, but they were liable to be removed at the will of the market authorities The Court held there was no exclusive occupation of land. See also *Mayor of London v St Sepulchre*,[2] and *R. v Morrish*.[3]

User of gas mains of another authority

So also in the case of the *Mayor, Aldermen and Burgesses of Southport v. Ormskirk Union*[4] The borough of Southport adjoined the township of Birkdale. The Corporation of Southport were the owners of gas works situated in the borough The Local Board of Birkdale were the owners of gas pipes and mains within the township of Birkdale, and by a local Act the Local Board were given the exclusive right of laying pipes, etc, within the township, and were bound for ever to keep the existing and future pipes, etc, in good repair and condition, and to afford the use thereof to the Corporation of Southport for the supply of gas within the township of Birkdale in consideration of certain payments. *Held*, by the Court of Appeal affirming the decision of the Divisional Court, that the Corporation had an easement only, and were not the occupiers of the said pipes, etc

But in the event of a specific portion of land being rented, then the occupier becomes liable[5]

Tunnel for drainage

In the case of the *Halkyn District Mines Drainage Co v Holywell Union*[6] there was a tunnel made for

---

[1] (1880) 49 L J M C 69, 43 L T 127, 44 J P 764

[2] (1871) L R 7 Q B 333, *n*, 41 L J M.C 109 *n*

[3] (1863) 32 L J M C 245, 10 Jur N S 71, 8 L T. 697, 11 W R 960, 27 J.P 470 c

[4] (1894) 1 Q B 196, 69 L T 852, 58 J P 212

Yarmouth (Mayor of) v Groom, (1862) 32 L T Ex 74

[5] (1895) A C. 117, 71 L T 818, 11 T L R 232—H L , 59 J P 566

drainage of certain mines the owners of which *by deed granted the appellants exclusive use of the tunnel* It was held by the House of Lords that on the true construction of the deed the appellants had such exclusive enjoyment of the tunnel that they were liable to be rated. This case was quoted in *Mayor, &c of Liverpool* v *Birkenhead Assessment Committee and Wallasey Urban District Council,*[1] to which reference may be usefully made, it being there decided that in the case of a water main by means of which the Corporation of Liverpool supplied water to the Council the Corporation were in the exclusive occupation of the main, so that they and not the Council were liable to be rated in respect thereof. See also *Stourbridge Main Drainage Board* v. *Seisdon Union,*[2] in which the Board, though reserving certain powers of control for works, were held not to be the occupiers of a sewage farm let by them subject to such reservation

Water main

In *Allan* v *Overseers of Liverpool*[3] the question of exclusive occupation in relation to certain quay spaces and sheds in the Liverpool Docks was raised on facts on which the Court held that the appellants to whom such accommodation had been granted had not exclusive possession, and that, therefore, the Dock Board and not the appellants were liable to be rated in respect thereof. Blackburn, J , in his judgment said that, "In order to ascertain whether an occupation exists or not, the intention of the parties must be looked to, to see whether an *exclusive possession of the premises has been parted with.* And this, in many cases, depends not altogether upon the words that may have been used in a case as upon all the circumstances taken together. For example, the word "let" may have been used without

Use of quay space, sheds, etc , in docks

---

[1] (1904-8) "Konstam's Rating Appeals," p 390.

[2] (1902) 66 J P 372, 86 L T 415

[3] (1874) L R 9 Q.B. 180, 43 L J M.C 69, 30 L T 93, 22 W.R 330, 38 J P 261

D

there being a letting; also the word "let" may have been carefully avoided, and yet it may appear in fact that the occupation has been parted with."

The same principle was also laid down most precisely in the case of *Rochdale Canal Co.* v *Brewster*[1] and in the case of *Sutton Harbour Improvement Co* v. *Plymouth Guardians*[2]

Shooting grounds

Where rifle associations were permitted to use certain land for the purpose of a shooting ground and a place for encampment for the annual rifle meeting, and the agreement specified that the occupation was not to be for more than seventy-seven consecutive days in each year, which days were not to commence earlier than the 1st May nor terminate later than the 31st August, although the association were empowered to put a fence round the part occupied by them, it was held there was no such exclusive occupation of the land as to render the association liable to the Poor Rate, but with respect to a store shed, which was occupied by them for their own purpose throughout the whole year, they were held liable as the occupiers[3]

Possession under breach of agreement

In the case of *R* v *Trent and Mersey Navigation Co.*[4] an agreement was entered into whereby a canal company were supplied by the owners of a limestone quarry with as much limestone as they required, subject to the payment of a certain sum per ton. In the event of the latter not carrying out their part of the agreement the canal company were to be at liberty to enter into possession of the quarries and obtain the limestone themselves, paying to the owners a reduced rate per ton The owners made default, and the canal company entered and worked

---

[1] (1894) 2 Q B 852, 64 L J Q B. 37, 71 L T 243, 10 T.L R 595; 59 J P 132.

[2] (1890) 63 L T 772; 55 J P. 232, 6 T.L.R 400.

[3] *Mildmay* v *Wimbledon (Churchwardens and Overseers)*, (1871) 41 L J. M.C 133, 27 L T 265, 20 W R 985, 37 J P 247.

[4] (1825) 6 D & R. 47, 4 B & C. 57, 3 L.J K.B 140.

the quarry, and for twenty years were the only persons to do so. *Held*, that the canal company were not the rateable occupiers of the land, because they had not a sole and exclusive occupation but a mere privilege

A Corporation who were seised in fee of pasture land Grazing rights appointed a ranger to keep the keys of the gates, preserve the fences, and impound cattle trespassing The freemen turned their cattle on to the land, making in respect thereof certain payments to the Corporation, the balance of which, after deducting expenses of management, was distributed among the poorer burgesses. The Corporation and not the persons depasturing cattle were held to be rateable as beneficial occupiers of the land in question, although there was no pecuniary profit made by the Corporation.[1]

So where pasture was let for grazing purposes for a limited period the vendor of such pasture was held to be the occupier, the person having the right to graze being held to be only a licensee.[2]

So in the case of *R v Abney Park Cemetery Co*[3] Here a company in possession of a cemetery ground sold portions of the land on trust to be used as graves for private persons, but it was nevertheless held that the company were in occupation of the plots of land which had been sold as aforesaid and therefore rateable in respect of the same. It has also been decided by the House of Lords[4] that although churchyards may have escaped assessment ever since the Act of Elizabeth, yet under the Act they are clearly rateable.

A lodger cannot be considered an occupier, his occupa- Lodgers tion is more in the nature of a guest at an hotel; his rooms are entered by the landlord for the purpose of

---

[1] *R. v Sudbury (Mayor of)*, (1823) 1 B & C 389, 2 D & R 641
[2] *Mogg v Yatton Overseers*, (1880) L R 6 Q B.D. 10, 50 L J M C 17, 45 J P 324
[3] (1873) L.R. 8 Q B 515; 42 L J M C 124, 29 L T 174; 37 J P. 822.
[4] (1909) 26 T L R 90

keeping them clean and in order, he probably uses the
same common staircase to his set of rooms as the other
occupiers of the house, and his apartments are always
under the control of the landlord. This cannot, therefore,
be called exclusive occupation, such as would make him
personally liable to be rated for that portion of the house
used by him for dwelling purposes

But the case is not the same where the several parts
of one house are let in flats and chambers, or where a
house is divided into two parts, each being let separately
In these instances it has been held that there is separate
occupation by each tenant, and that accordingly each part
ought to be separately rated   The two leading cases of
R v. *St. George's Union*[1] and *Allchurch* v *Hendon
Assessment Committee*,[2] in which these questions were
raised and dealt with, are referred to in detail later.   In
considering these two cases, however, it is desirable that
the recent decision of the Court of Appeal in *White and
Hales* v *Islington Corporation*[3] should be borne in mind.
The effect of this last-mentioned decision would seem to
be that in a Parliamentary Borough, although there may
be what in other cases, on a practically similar state of
facts, has been held to be separate occupation such as to
entitle each of the several parts of one dwelling house or
other tenement let out in apartments or lodgings to be
separately rated, yet that by reason of the provision of
the concluding paragraph of Section 7 of the Representation of the People Act, 1867,[4] if such parts or
occupations were not separately rated at the passing of
the said Act, the owner of the dwelling house or tenements so let out is to be rated in respect thereof to the
Poor Rate, no matter what the value thereof may be.

---

[1] (1871) L.R 7 Q B 90, 41 L J M C 30, 25 L.T. 696, 20 W R 79
Known as "The Westminster Tontine Case."
[2] (1891) 2 Q.B. 436, 61 L J M.C 27, 65 L T 450, 40 W.R 86,
56 J P 117.
[3] (1909) 1 K B 133
[4] 30 & 31 Vict., c. 102.

The facts of the case as stated were five houses of rate-able values varying from £17 to £55 and each let out in separate apartments or lodgings, in one case to four and in each of the other four cases to two tenants Each tenant had a separate letting and a separate key, and each tenant had the exclusive use and occupation of the room or rooms let to him or her The only parts of each house which were used in common by the tenants thereof were the outer doors passages and stairs and water closets and a room in the basement used as a scullery or wash-house with a copper Each of the tenants in each house used in common the said parts thereof None of the apartments or lodgings in any of the said houses were structurally separated from each other, as in the case of flats There was only one door in each house in the nature of a front door, and the rooms on the several floors were entered by ordinary doors, as in a house occupied by one family only The owners respectively exercised no supervision or control over the said houses *Held*, that the owners of the houses and not the occupiers were rateable. Kennedy, J. said " The whole section, then, may be thus paraphrased . Prior to the passing of this Act [1] there have been cases in which (as, for example, under the Acts of 1819 and 1850 and special local Acts) the owner of a dwelling house or of a tenement has been rated or has been liable to be rated. In all Parliamentary boroughs this state of things shall cease, and thenceforward in respect of all dwelling houses and tenements in such boroughs the occupier shall, and the owner shall not, be the person rated." The only exception shall be this . Wherever a dwelling house or tenement shall be found to fulfil two conditions—(*a*) that it is wholly   out in lodgings or apartments, (*b*) that those apartments or lodgings were not separately rated at the time of the passing of this Act [1]—in

---

[1] The Representation of the People Act, 1867 (30 & 31 Vict , c. 102).

such case the owner and not the occupier shall be rated in respect of such dwelling house or tenement "

On comparing these facts with the facts in the other two cases, it will be noticed that they are in many respects similar to those in the *Westminster Tontine* case, and almost identical with those in the *Hendon* case, and that they answer to the test suggested by Cockburn, C J., in the former case in that the landlord retained no control of the outer door or indeed at all   It is true that in the stated case on which the judgment in the recent case was based it is said the houses were "let out in apartments or lodgings," and that "none of the apartments or lodgings were structurally separated from each other as in the case of flats", but, having regard to the conditions of tenancy, it is somewhat difficult to see what is meant by this last expression except as applying to that description of flats in which there is complete separate occupation, including separate entrances and staircases and nothing in common

In the two earlier cases, however, the effect of the said section was not in issue, and in the recent case the decisions in such earlier cases were not referred to, the main point there in issue being whether or not the said Section 7 had been impliedly repealed or superseded by the Poor Rate Assessment and Collection Act, 1869.[1]

Thus, in not one of the three cases has the point been really judicially determined as to what may or may not be considered "apartments or lodgings" within the meaning and for the purposes of the said section

It, therefore, is not easy to reconcile all these decisions

The probable solution is that where the part of the house let off constitutes in itself a complete dwelling, or where the house or tenement has been specially constructed for occupation in separate dwellings or holdings, the tenants should be rated ; but in other cases, where a

---

[1] 32 & 33 Vict , c 41

house or tenement is let in parts, even though the land-lord retain no control, the provision of the said Section 7 will apply.

It was further decided in *Nokes* v. *Strong*[1] that under the said Section 7 "the owner" to be rated did not mean or include an agent employed to collect the rents but only the true owner

As already stated the question of who is the occupier for rating purposes of flats and chambers was contested and decided in the Westminster Tontine case (*R.* v. *St. George's Union*)[2] The facts were these: There were several blocks of buildings having each a principal entrance to the public street. Each block was divided into two ranges by an internal staircase, and was structurally divided into 117 different sets of rooms distinct from each other, and capable of being let and occupied separately as residences or offices. Each such set had an outer door opening on to one of the internal staircases, and also an inner private hall or passage. There were no means of communication between the sets except the internal staircase. The sets of rooms were let severally, in writing, by the owners to certain tenants for a year, and then on from quarter to quarter, with power to the lessors to enter for certain specified purposes, and to resume possession on non-payment of rent, etc. And under these agreements each outer entrance (locked at night) and the rooms connected therewith were in the charge of a porter (resident in the basement set of each block), who was appointed and was removable by the owners of the building There were duplicate keys to the outer door of every set of rooms, one of which was always in the hands of the porter, the other in the care of the tenant whilst the rooms were in use, and the

Flats and chambers

---

[1] (1909) 2 K B 625
[2] (1871) L R. 7 Q B. 90; 41 L J. M.C. 30, 25 L T. 696, 20 W.R. 179

tenants had the right, free of charge, to the general services of the porter and to special services; the latter to be rendered as the servant of the tenant.

It will be noticed that the outer or street door was kept locked at night; and also that a porter had a key of, and access to, the suites of rooms in the building for the purpose of general superintendence, and therefore as the servant of the respective occupiers, by whom he was in some cases employed and paid for looking after the rooms

The agreement under which these suites of rooms were let is given in full, as it has an important bearing on the decision.[1]

_____

[1] An agreement made and entered into the   day of   , 18 , between the Mutual Tontine Westminster Chambers Association (Limited), by George Sands Sidney, their secretary, hereinafter called the lessors, of the one part, and   , hereinafter called the lessee, of the other part

The lessors hereby let, and the lessee hereby takes, all that   rooms, numbered   , and being on the   floor of the buildings, and numbered   of the Association, called the Westminster Chambers, situate in Victoria Street, in the City of Westminster   Together with the use of the water closet and washing closet attached thereto, and also the use, in common with other tenants, of the entrance hall, and stairs, and lift leading to the same premises for the term of   year   from the day of   , 18 , and so on from quarter to quarter, but determinable at the end of the first quarter, or of any subsequent quarters, by either of the parties giving to the other of them three calendar months' previous notice in writing for that purpose, and under the quarterly rent of £   , payable on the usual quarter days free from all deductions whatsoever, the lessors hereby agreeing to pay all rates, taxes, assessments and impositions, parliamentary, parochial, or otherwise, charged on the premises, but if the premises shall be rendered uninhabitable by fire, not originating therein and not occasioned by the lessee, his executors, administrators, or assigns, or his or their servants, the rent shall be suspended until the premises are rendered habitable   And the lessors and lessee hereby mutually agree as follows —The lessee, his executors, administrators, and assigns, will not do or permit to be done, any damage or waste to the premises, and will, at least once in every two months during the term hereby granted, properly clean the windows of, and belonging to, the said demised premises, and will, as often as occasion requires during the term, repair and maintain and keep the premises in such repair as that the same shall be at all times suitable and ready for

The judgment delivered by Cockburn, C.J., was as follows —

Westminster
Tontine case

"The case is a very clear one, and I entertain no doubt whatever that every one of the occupiers of these distinct tenements, 117 in number, is rateable to the Poor Rate, and to other rates to which occupiers are liable; consequently, a valuation of each of these separate tenements in the assessment list is the right course, and the alteration of the original list was an error which we must set right.

"The question is, whether the occupiers of these tenements or the lessors are rateable in respect of the whole or any part of these blocks? The question in these cases, of course, always is whether there is an occupation of a

the occupation of a tenant, and will it the expiration of the tenancy leave and deliver up possession of the same in such repair unto the lessors, or as they direct, together with all chimneypieces, stoves, windows, doors, fastenings, partitions, locks, keys, and all other fixtures, matters and things which at the time of the entry of the lessee on the premises shall be found thereon, or which at any time during the tenancy shall be added to and so fastened upon the premises by the lessee, his executors, administrators, or assigns, as that the same cannot be removed without damage or injury thereto, but the lessors shall make good all damage to the premises by fire not originating therein and not occasioned by the lessee, his executors, administrators, or assigns, or his or their servants

The lessee, his executors, administrators, and assigns will not, without in every case the written consent of the lessors, pull down or alter or in any manner interfere with the construction or arrangement of the premises, or cut, alter or injure any of the walls, timbers or floors, of the premises, or in any manner deface or disfigure the walls or ceilings thereof, or convert into or use or occupy the premises, or any part thereof, as a shop or warehouse, or for any unlawful or immoral purpose, or for any purpose other than purposes proper for residential, professional or official chambers, or affix any board, placard or notice upon any external part of the premises, or in any of the windows thereof, or have or deposit any stores of coal, or any combustible or offensive goods or materials on the said premises, or permit any of such things to be done

The lessee, his executors, administrators, or assigns, will not, without such consent, assign, underlet or part with the possession of the premises or any part thereof, or any interest therein The lessors or their agents shall at all times during the term hereby granted have liberty to enter upon the said premises for the purpose of painting the outside wood and iron work thereof, and may at all reasonable times enter and view the

distinct and separate tenement by a person who inhabits a portion of a house or building, or whether he is merely an inmate under a landlord.

"It is necessary to establish some criterion It is not always, perhaps, very easy to find one, but the one which has been adopted here, and which is, perhaps, the most convenient and only one, is whether the landlord retains the control of the outer door, and has shown, by his retaining the control of the outer door, that he has control of the whole of the premises, so that although he may be liable to an action upon the breach of his contract

premises and examine the condition and use made thereof, and give notice of defects, and wants of repair and misuses, all of which shall be amended and corrected within one calendar month after such notice, but nevertheless without prejudice to any other right or remedy in respect thereof nothing shall be done or allowed in, upon or with respect to the premises which may annoy or tend to the annoyance of the lessors, or of any of the other tenants or occupiers, or which may injure or tend to injure the character thereof as a place for residential, professional or official chambers In case of non-payment of the rent within twenty-one days after becoming due, and demand made thereof, or on breach of any of the foregoing stipulations and articles, or on the bankruptcy of the lessee, his executors, administrators or assigns, the lessors may without any previous notice re-enter and resume possession of the premises, and put out all persons therefrom, but without prejudice to any right or remedy for any such non payment or breach And it is lastly agreed that the expense of these presents and of a duplicate thereof shall be paid by the lessee In witness whereof the parties hereto have set their hands the day and year first above written

Memorandum —The premises are taken by the lessee subject to the regulations made by the lessors, with respect to the duties of the porter, the supply of coal and other matters for the general convenience of the tenants These regulations are set forth in the schedule to this agreement, and are to be considered as forming part. The lessors, however, reserve to themselves the right of altering and modifying these regulations from time to time, as the convenience of the tenants, or other special circumstances may render desirable

THE SCHEDULE REFERRED TO—THE REGULATIONS.

Memorandum made by the directors in respect of supply of coals, cleaning rooms, etc.

There are seven entrances to the building, and the care of each entrance and the rooms connected therewith will be in the charge of a resident porter appointed and removable by the directors.

to allow the tenant to occupy a portion of the premises so let to him as lodger, yet the tenant could not maintain trespass against the landlord, because the landlord has retained in himself the dominion and control over the whole house

" I think the possession of the street door may be taken as a criterion, because it is only by the landlord opening and shutting the street door, or allowing it to be opened and shut for the ingress and egress of the tenant, that the tenant can have the enjoyment of the premises

---

There are duplicate keys to the outer door of every set of chambers, one of which is to be always in the hands of the porter, the other in the care of the tenant, while the rooms are in use

The tenants have the right free of charge to the general services of the porter, within the scope of his general duties as hereinbefore defined

Tenants have the right to the special services of the porter as hereinafter defined upon the terms hereinafter mentioned

Coals are supplied by the directors at a charge of three pence half-penny per measure of 900 cubic inches, and wood at one penny for each fire lighted, and gas is brought to the entrance of each set of rooms, and may be laid on by the tenants at their own expense if desired

Tenants are not allowed to have stores of coals in their rooms

The general duties of the porter, and which are to be performed free of charge to the tenants, are as follows —

To be constantly in attendance in the section of the building committed to his charge, either by himself or in his temporary absence by some trustworthy assistant

To cleanse every morning before nine o'clock a m the general stairs, passages, lifts and entrances attached to the section, and to attend to the lighting and extinguishing of the gas therein

To receive and deliver to the several tenants all letters, parcels and messages, and to receive the keys of the outer doors of the several sets of rooms from the tenants on their leaving for the night

To attend to the regular and proper supply of coals to the several apartments

The special services of the porter which he is bound to render to the several tenants, if required, at a charge of one shilling and sixpence per week for each such room, and the lighting of the several fires whenever required

Any extra services required of the porter by the tenants, and which are not inconsistent with his general duties, are to be subjects of special arrangement

Any services, whether special or extra so rendered by the porter, will be rendered as the servant of the tenant, and for which, or the consequences thereof, the association will not be responsible " (Vide " Law Journal ")

"If I could see that the landlord here had retained the exclusive possession of the outer door, so that the tenant could only come in and go out with his assent and permission, then I might say that these persons were mere inmates or lodgers, and not the lessees of the respective tenements In order to determine that question it is necessary to look to the agreement , I look to that and nothing else, and I see that all the characteristics of a lease and a tenancy under a lease are contained in the agreement. The landlord has not reserved to himself, directly or indirectly, expressly or by implication, any right to go into the apartments of any of these people

"It is true that, for the common protection and general convenience of all, there is to be a porter, who is to have a key of every one of these tenements in order that, if the necessity should arise, he may be able to get access to them   But the more I look at it the more I am satisfied that the porter is only there for the convenience and benefit of the tenants, the occupiers of the separate and distinct sets of rooms , and that he is not there for the purpose of securing to the landlord the right of entry or control over the whole of these premises, so as to give the landlord the right, at any time, to go upon the premises

Right of land-
lord to enter
premises

"On the contrary, it is expressly stipulated, on the part of the lessors, that they shall, at given times and for given purposes, have access to these different sets of chambers Would there be that stipulation if they already had control or general dominion over the whole of the house, which is thus divided into separate occupations ?

"Then it is said that the porter is to retain the keys when the tenants go away at night, and the porter is bound as their servant, not the servant of the landlord, in addition to receiving their letters and parcels, and handing them over, to receive their keys at night.

"That is for the convenience of the tenants; but if a man likes to take away a key in his pocket, there is nothing to prevent him from doing so   Looking to the whole scope of this agreement, I cannot see that there is anything which makes the porter anything other than the servant of the occupiers.

"It seems to me, therefore, that the case fails in that which is the point upon which many of these cases have been decided, namely, that it does not appear on the whole that the landlords have retained that control, either over the house generally or the front door of it, which would make the tenant liable to be excluded at their will, subject only to a right of action on the contract, if the landlords refused him access   The case fails in that particular, and as that is the criterion, and the acknowledged criterion, it is wrong to say that these houses are to be assessed in blocks, so as to make the lessors liable "

Blackburn, J., said (following) ·

"I am of the same opinion   The duty of the Assessment Committee is to assess each hereditament, which word is expressed in 32 & 33 Vict., c 67, s. 4, to mean 'any lands, tenements, hereditaments. and property which are liable to any rate or tax in respect of which the valuation list is by this Act made conclusive'   If, therefore, each set of rooms is made liable to the Poor Rate, if the occupier is rateable, they ought to put a value upon it, so that the value at which that occupier is to be rated shall be fixed and found in the valuation list.   If, on the other hand, the occupiers of the rooms ought not to be rated, but the owners of the entire block of buildings continue as occupiers of the chambers, so as to be rated for one entire thing, then. doubtless, it would be improper to value each of them separately, but the valuation ought to be for the entire mass; if, for instance, the block was like one of the large hotels—the Palace Hotel at Westminster, for instance—which I believe is partly occupied

Occupation of hotels

in that way, there is no doubt that the landlord occupies the whole hotel, and has as many lodgers as he likes, he would be rateable for the whole hotel, and, therefore, there ought to be a value put upon it   Then comes the question, as to these rooms which are separate.

" I take it that there is no doubt at all, in point of law, that the landlord, or owner of the fee simple of an entire house, may, if he pleases, agree with another that he will let him a portion of a house and a portion only   Whether he does so agree, or not, depends upon the terms of the agreement.   If it is in writing we can judge of the terms of it ; if it is not in writing, and the letting is by parole, we must gather the terms of agreement by the matters of fact given in evidence to show whether or not the agreement was such as to put him in exclusive occupation or merely an agreement to let to him as a lodger or an inmate, the occupation of the whole of the house being retained   If it is in writing that must depend very much on the words of the agreement ; but if not, upon what the Court, or whoever is to judge of the facts, has to collect from the different facts

" I think that the registration cases (and they are very numerous) come simply to this, that where there is not an actual demise in writing which the Court can construe ; as a matter of law, it has to determine the question of

Possession of outer door fact whether or not there was a separate lease, or merely an agreement to allow the tenant to come in, while the occupation remained with the landlord.   I think that in such cases the possession of the outer door is of the highest importance.   I do not think any one of these cases goes any further than that.   But where there is an actual agreement in writing between the parties the construction of that agreement will be for the Court

" Now let us look at the agreement set out in the present case, to see whether it can be contended that it was not the intention of the parties that the appellants, who are the landlords, should part with the exclusive possession of these chambers to the tenants. 'The lessors hereby let, and the lessee hereby takes all' the premises numbered so and so, of the chambers belonging to the association, 'together with the use of the water closet and washing closet attached thereto, and also the use, in common with other tenants, of the entrance hall and stairs and lift leading to the same premises, for the term of' so many years from such and such a day, subject to notice to quit and so on, the rent to be payable free from all deductions.

"Then subsequently in the agreement this power is given—'the lessors or their agents shall at all times, during the term hereby granted, have liberty to enter upon the said premises, for the purpose of painting outside wood and iron work thereof'

"Can it be for a moment contended that the saying 'we let the premises to you for a term of years at a yearly rent, reserving to ourselves the power to enter for the purpose of painting the outside, the tenant having to keep them in order,' does not show an intention that the exclusive possession should be parted with?

"Then it goes on further than that—'in case of non-payment of the rent within twenty-one days after becoming due and demand made thereof, or on the breach of any of the foregoing stipulations and articles, or on the bankruptcy of the lessee, his executors, administrators or assigns, the lessors may, without any previous notice, re-enter and resume possession of the premises. Words cannot be stronger to show that they had agreed to put themselves out of the premises Then it is said that, although that is their agreement and they do all that, and although they had only an easement in the staircase—the fact that there was an outer door which the porter who belonged to the appellants, and who had one key, was to shut, shows they did not mean to part with possession

"It seems to me that it would be monstrous to hold that, and in consequence, taking the true and clear construction of the agreement, I think it clear that there was exclusive occupation of these premises"

House divided, two tenements

In the case of *Allchurch* v. *Hendon Assessment Committee*[1] a house had been divided into two parts, the upper half being let to one and the lower half to another tenant, the house had two floors, each floor had a kitchen, scullery and sink, in conjunction with the living rooms, the only addition wanting to render it a complete residence being a separate water-closet, there being only one water-closet in the back yard to the joint use of which each tenant was entitled. There was one front door. A staircase from the passage, into which the front door opened, was for the *exclusive* use of the upper floor, and there was also an outside staircase from the back yard which the upper floor tenant usually used. There was no structural division between the two floors. *Held*, that the occupants of the upper floor and of the ground floor were respectively each the occupier of a separate tenement, and should be separately rated.

Lord Esher, M R, in delivering judgment in this case, said[1]. "The argument in this case is clearly made to depend upon this, that because there is no structural division in this house, therefore the occupation of each part of the house is to be treated as a joint occupation of the people who do in fact occupy separate parts of the

Structural severance

house. Now the phrase 'structural severance' is not a phrase which has anything whatever to do with occupation at all. It was a phrase invented by the Judges at a time when, in considering the Statute of Elizabeth" (as to the Poor Rate) "and in the Franchise Acts, they were labouring to determine what was to be an occupation

---

[1] (1891) 2 Q B 436, 61 L J M C. 27, 65 L T 450, 40 W.R 86, 56 J P 117

which in one case would give a liability to be rated, and in the other the right to the franchise. The phrase was in use for a long time, and it had so far got into use that the Legislature was obliged to deal with it, and the Legislature has dealt with it, and has, in fact, done away with it, and has determined that when dealing with occupation as the foundation either for a right or for a liability, you must look to the occupation and see what it is that is occupied. Now apply that in this case. The question here is, What is occupation? Because a person to be rated is a person who is occupying something you are to look at his occupation. What do each of these people occupy? The one occupies rooms on the ground floor of a house, and occupies them separately. It cannot be doubted that his occupation is a separate one, because nobody else has any right to interfere with his occupation of that part. That makes it a separate occupation by him. The other occupies another part of the house, and his occupation is a separate occupation, and nobody has a right to interfere with it. Therefore, you have each of them occupying a separate part of something, whether it is a separate part of a house signifies not. If it were a field it would be a separate occupation of a part of a field. They are to be rated in respect of their occupation. How can each of them be rated as the occupier of something into which he has no right to go—in respect of which he has no beneficial right at all, in fact, in respect of something with which he has nothing to do, and with which, if he attempts to do anything, he is a trespasser? The occupation is as clearly separate as can be. It is a misuse of terms—not only a misuse, but an untrue use of terms—to say that they jointly occupy this house. There is no inch of this house which they jointly occupy. With regard to the staircase, if the staircase is the common entrance for both of them, it seems to be obvious that neither of them occupies it; but if there is

What is occupation?

Staircase, common entrance

D

any occupation it is the occupation of the landlord. In the case of this house the landlord occupies no part of it, unless it be the staircase. He has given up the whole occupation, he has given up his right to occupy some part of it, at all events, to each tenant He has given them no right to occupy it jointly. Taking it as I say, the question is really one of occupation, and you have to find out what each man occupies You find each man occupies a something which, whether you call it his house or whatever you may call it, is a thing in respect of the occupation of which he is liable to be rated. If his occupation is a separate one, he is separately occupying something in respect of which he is liable to be rated, and he, in respect of that separate occupation, must be the only person So that the proper way of rating these people was to have rated each of them in respect of that separate part of the house, if you please to call it so, or of the thing which each separately occupies, which thing is not a chattel, but is a thing which makes the person who occupies it liable for rates"

Kay, L.J, in the same case, said "I also agree, and I can only say I am very glad the conclusion seems to be inevitable, because any other would be productive of a very great injustice To make the man who occupies the ground floor of this house liable for the rates of the first floor, the floor above it, upon which he cannot go without committing a trespass, would certainly be a very great injustice. In the same way, to make the occupier of the first floor liable for the rates of the ground floor, into no part of which he can go, except possibly the staircase which leads to one of the outer doors, would be equally unjust That they have a common use of that staircase, if they have such a common use, cannot make the occupation of one the occupation of another, so that each has the joint occupation of both the ground floor and the first floor. I entirely agree with what the Master of the Rolls has said."

The above cases have been dealt with at some length, as, owing to the enormous quantity of flats that have been erected during the past few years, and the importance of the correct method of assessing them, it is desirable that they should be fully comprehended. As it is a common practice to let a flat at an inclusive rent, the owner paying the rates, many Assessment Committees have looked upon a block of flats as one hereditament. The landlord's interest, however, has always been that each occupation should be separately entered in the Rate Book. Thus, a landlord, in the event of one of his suites of rooms being unoccupied, would be entitled to a rebate of the rate; but if the whole block be assessed as one property no rebate could be obtained, as otherwise a precedent might be set up that because a man did not furnish two or three rooms at the top of his house he would be entitled to a rebate, which is wrong in law.[1]

It also follows that, where tenants of this class of property pay a rent to the landlord and under agreement the landlord undertakes to pay the rates, should any default be made in such payment by the landlord, the tenant, as occupier of the flat, would be called upon to pay the rates, and he would have to proceed against the landlord, or probably he would be able to deduct the sum paid from the rent next due.

While it is clear that exclusive occupation or possession is essential to create liability for rating, so also is it necessary that the occupation should be beneficial. Beneficial occupation of property is an occupation for any purpose whatsoever, provided that such property is *capable* of a rental value being placed upon it, that being the basis of all rating.

Occupation must be beneficial

It is not necessary that the occupier should derive a pecuniary profit from the use to which he puts the

[1] See *R. v St. Mary-the-Less (Durham)* (1791) 4 T R 477, 16 R R 811.

hereditament; in fact, there may be an actual loss to such occupier

London sewers case This view is most definitely laid down in *London County Council* v *Erith and West Ham* [1] In this case the London County Council were the owners and occupiers of certain sewers, sewage works, and a pumping station connected therewith, which were necessary to enable the appellants to discharge their statutory duties   The sewers, sewage works, and pumping station, while used as part of the Metropolitan sewage system, were *incapable of yielding a profit*   It was held (by the House of Lords) that, though this hereditament yielded no pecuniary profit to the occupier, yet the occupation was valuable as *capable of yielding a rent*, and therefore rateable

School Board case So also it was held in the case of *R.* v *School Board for London* [2] that, although the School Board could not make any pecuniary profit, yet they had a statutory duty to perform which might conceivably cause them to become tenants and so to pay a rent for the use of the premises.   Lord Esher, M R , in giving judgment, said "The School Board can be tenants.   It is said that the School Board ought to be excluded because it can never obtain any beneficial interest from its tenancy. but it can be a tenant, it has a duty to perform which may induce or force it to be a tenant   It follows, therefore, that it would be wrong to exclude the School Board from the list of possible hypothetical tenants, whether it is in the position of owner or that of occupier."

Empty houses, definition of Empty houses—and by empty houses are meant such as are "to let"--whether occupied by caretakers or not, are not rateable because there is no beneficial occupation

By 6 Geo IV , c 7, s 3, "an empty house shall be deemed to be unoccupied and not liable to the inhabited

---

[1] (1893) A C 562, 63 L J M C 9, 69 L T 725 , 57 J P. 821
[2] (1886) L R. 17 Q B D 738 , 55 L J M C. 169 , 55 L T 384

house duty, although such house or tenement shall or may be left or committed to the care or charge of a person or servant, who shall or may have been placed and shall dwell therein solely for the purpose of airing the same, and of preventing depredation or injury to the premises during the period of their being so unoccupied "

Although this section specially refers to Imperial taxes, yet it provides a definition of what may be regarded as an empty house in the case of the Poor Rate

While, however, a house in charge of a caretaker as such only is not rateable, yet where a landlord put in a caretaker, paying him a small amount in addition to the use of living rooms, the caretaker also being allowed to appropriate the produce of the garden and appurtenances, the owner was held to be rateable [1] The decision seems severe.   There was undoubtedly beneficial occupation by the caretaker, but it is a question whether the landlord could not have obtained a purely caretaking tenant, if such expression be permissible.   The Court, however, held that the owner was rateable as occupier through the caretaker as a servant, and rated him accordingly at the full rateable value.

Liability of owner in respect of caretakers or servants

In the case of *Bertie* v. *Walthamstow Overseers* [2] a builder was erecting a number of new dwelling houses in the same road, and, for the purpose of looking after the houses, and letting them, and generally carrying out the duties of foreman of the works, one house was occupied by the foreman and his family. It was held that the foreman was not only a caretaker, but that there was a beneficial occupation of the house by the foreman as servant of the builder, as distinct from a mere occupation as a caretaker.

---

[1] *Hicks v. Dunstable*, (1883) 48 J P 326
[2] (1904) 68 J P 525

In the case of *Staley* v. *Castleton Overseers*,[1] where a
mill ceased working owing to the depression of trade
caused by the American Civil War, all the employes
were discharged, but a caretaker was installed for the
purpose of keeping the machinery belonging to the mill
in good order so that it could be used again in the event
of revival of trade It was here held that the occupier
was still liable to be rated for the mill, but only to the
extent of its value as a warehouse for the machinery
stored therein

Rateable
occupation a
question of
fact

In a recent case,[2] however, where certain warehouses
were unoccupied and no goods stored, but shafting and
hoists for the use of the warehousing business were left
on the premises, the Justices before whom the case was
brought decided that there was no rateable occupation,
and it was held by the Divisional Court that it was a
question of fact whether there was rateable occupation

Reference must also be made on this point to the more
recent case of *R* v. *Melladew*,[3] decided in the Court of
Appeal in 1906, in which, where a warehouse had been
empty for four months and a bill " to let " placed upon
the premises, it was held that there was no cessation of
rateable occupation of the warehouse and that rates were
payable during the period it was empty; but the decision
in this case was affected by the facts, because it appeared
that the reason why the owners were not using the warehouse was that they had not sufficient goods on hand to
make it commercially remunerative to use it, although
it was admitted in the case that the warehouse was
ready to be re-opened at any time and used by the
owners   During the period referred to all weights, scales
and other chattels had been removed to an adjoining
warehouse belonging to the same owners

---

[1] (1864) 33 L J M.C 178, 5 B & S 505, 10 L T 606
[2] *Bootle-cum-Linacre Overseers* v *Liverpool Warehousing Co*, (1901)
85 L T 45, 65 J P 740, 17 T L R 550
[3] (1907) 1 K B 192, 76 L J. K B 262, 96 L T 189, 23 T L R 207

This decision over-ruled the decision of the Divisional Court, and notwithstanding the express finding in the case stated, that the owners were not in occupation, it was held that the question was one of *mixed law and fact*, so that the Court of Appeal was able to determine whether, as a matter of law, the Justices had correctly decided on the evidence before them that there was no rateable occupation of the warehouse.

Notwithstanding this, in the yet more recent case of *Borwick* v *Southwark Corporation*,[1] the Divisional Court were inclined to the opinion expressed in the Bootle case,[2] that the question of occupation and rateability was a question of fact in each case. Bigham, J., in his judgment, said "Cases of this kind depend much more on fact than on law. Whether a man 'occupies' or not is in each case a question of intention to be ascertained with reference to the particular circumstances, and if there are facts which one way or the other can reasonably support the conclusion at which the Justices arrive, I do not think this Court should interfere with that conclusion. It is a finding of fact. The Bootle case[2] and Melladew's case[2] are said to raise some doubt as to the law, but I do not think they do. Occupation is and must always be a mere question of fact which may involve a question of intention, and the only question of law is whether there is evidence which can reasonably support the finding, whatever it may be. The difficulty, if there be any, in reconciling the two authorities cited arises, not from any doubt as to the law, but from the different conclusions of fact which were arrived at in circumstances which perhaps, at first sight, appear somewhat similar."

In the case[3] where an occupier of a boarding house, held on a three years' agreement, removed her furniture

[1] (1909) 1 K B at p. 84.
[2] See p. 54 *ante*
[3] *Gage* v. *Wren*, (1903) 87 L.T 271, 67 J P 32

from the house during the winter months, and while she was absent from the house it was left entirely empty, with the exception of a few hired fittings, it was held that there was beneficial occupation of the house for the period that it was left, and that the tenant was liable to pay the rate for the whole of the period   It must be noticed in this case, however, that it was admitted that the house was not to let and there had always existed the intention on the part of the tenant to return to the house, and consequently the furniture was merely removed for her own convenience [1] And where a shop-keeper rented premises under similar conditions, and during the winter months of each year he removed his stock, but left on the premises the necessary fittings for the business, although no one resided on the premises, he was held to be liable for the period during which the premises were closed [2]

Empty fur-
nished houses   So if an owner furnishes a house and keeps it ready for habitation. although he may be prevented from residing in it at all, during any period, he is liable to be rated at the full value as an occupied house, and cannot claim abatement on the ground of inability to dwell therein.[3]

And in the case of a lessee of a dwelling house who ceased to reside there, but left it furnished for the use of a possible tenant, the Court of London Quarter Sessions held that it was rateable at its value as a dwelling house

Part occupa-
tion by owner   If an owner of a house occupies part of it he is liable to be rated for the whole , unless, of course, there is a distinct occupation of the rest by some other person.[4]

Property in
course of
construction   Property during construction is not rateable, and although there is occupation of land during the building

---

[1] *Gage* v *Wren*, (1903) 87 L T 271 , 67 J P 32

[2] *Southend-on-Sea Corporation* v *White*, (1900) 65 J P 7 , 83 L T 408, 17 T L R 5

[3] *R* v *St Pancras Assessment Committee*, (1877) 2 Q B 581 , 46 L J M C 243, 37 L T 126

[4] *R* v *St Mary-the-Less, Durham*, (1791) 4 T R. 477, 16 R R 811

of a house there is no " beneficial occupation ", therefore the builder or owner of such incomplete building is not liable.

It, however, frequently happens in large engineering undertakings, the construction of which is spread over many years, such as reservoirs, railways, and the like, that the contractors erect huts for the accommodation of their workmen These huts are capable of being readily moved from place to place, and, in fact, are moved, and usually they are constructed of the lightest building materials and without any sanitary arrangements. Nevertheless they are rateable [1]

Theatres and places of entertainment, even when unlet (that is, no performance being given at such places), are held to be occupied, from the fact that the necessary furniture and appliances are within them Owners, therefore, may be paying considerable rates to the parochial authorities while the establishments are profitless This seems unfair to the owner, and was the subject of a question in the House of Commons a few years ago, but the answer then obtained still leaves his liability unaltered

The liability, however, of the theatre to be closed must therefore be taken into consideration in fixing the total gross and rateable values. It is a matter of common knowledge that frequently, pending productions, theatres are closed temporarily, while the majority of provincial theatres are closed through the summer and also a month before Christmas for the preparation of pantomimes

The occupier of advertisement hoardings for the purposes of rating is the person who shall permit the land to be used for that purpose.[2] This may be the contractor who is erecting buildings on a site not owned by him,

Theatres (margin)

Advertisement hoardings (margin)

[1] *Mitchell Bros* v *Worksop Union Assessment Committee.*) 92 L T. 62 , 69 J P 53 , 21 T L R 156
[2] 52 & 53 Vict , (1889) c 27. s 3

providing he permits the erection of an advertisement hoarding [1] But the advertising contractor cannot be held to be liable, as he is not the person who permits the land to be so used.[2]

Occupation by liquidator

In the event of the winding up of a company the liquidator in occupation of such company's premises is bound to pay the rates in full, where such occupation is with the view of obtaining a better price for such premises as a going concern See the case of the *Blazer Fire Lighter Company, Limited* [3]

See also the case of the *International Marine Hydropathic Company*,[4] where an hotel company was wound up, and the liquidator was ordered to sell the hotel, but with liability to carry on the business until the sale, in order to dispose of it as a going concern. *Held*, that the liquidator was rateable

But where there was " merely possession and occupation " but no enjoyment of beneficial occupation by the liquidator of a company wound up by order of the Court, it was held that he was not liable.[5]

An application for a distress warrant upon a liquidator's goods and chattels for non-payment of the Poor Rate was refused, as the Court held he was not such an occupier as to be liable for the rate in respect of his personal property.[6] But in the case of *Dent* v. *Commondale (Overseers)* [7] the liquidator's name appeared as owner and occupier in the Rate Book; and as he did not appeal against the rate or produce any evidence that there was no beneficial occupation, there was a distress warrant

---

[1] *Chappell* v *Overseers of St Botolph*, (1892) 1 Q B 561, 65 L T 581, 56 J.P 310
[2] *Burton* v *St Giles' and St George's Assessment Committee*, (1900) 1 Q B 389, 69 L J Q B 181, 82 L T 21, 64 J P 213
[3] (1895) 1 Ch. 402, 71 L T. 665
[4] (1885) L R 28 Ch D 470, 33 W R 587—C A
[5] *In re Watson Kipling & Co*, (1883) L R 23 Ch D 500, 52 L J Ch 473, 49 L T 115 See p 59 *post*
[6] (1682) *R* v *Curzon*, 46 L T. 159, 30 W.R. 521, 47 J P. 37
[7] (1892) 56 J P 519.

issued against him This last-mentioned decision would seem to be at variance with the decision in the case of *In re Wearmouth Assurance Glass Company*,[1] as well as with *R v Curzon*.[2]

In the event of liquidators entering into possession of property solely for the purposes of the winding up and not to carry on the business thereof, they are not liable to be rated in respect of such occupation See the case of the *West Hartlepool Iron Company* [3]

The liquidator's duty on entering premises of a company in the process of being wound up is undoubtedly to get the rate reduced but if through any cause he omits to make the necessary application until after the time of appeal against the valuation list, he is not to be held responsible for the full rate, unless the premises are being occupied for the carrying on of the business as a going concern In the case of *Watson Kipling & Co*,[4] Kay J, sitting in the Chancery Division, said: " It was said that the liquidator might have appealed against the assessment and have got it reduced , that he had chosen not to appeal, and as the time had gone by for that purpose they were proper rates fixed by law , and therefore the Courts should have no regard to the amounts at all, but should order them to be paid in full , but would that be equitable as between the persons claiming to be paid the rates and the other creditors of the company ? It seems to me that such an order would be most inequitable as against the other creditors . It is sufficient answer to say that it would not be equitable to allow rates of that amount to be paid in full. Even if there had been default on the part of the liquidator, are the rating authorities entitled to be paid in full rates upon an assessment which it would not be possible to maintain if there were an appeal against it ? "

[1] (1882) 19 Ch D 643, 45 L T 757
[2] See p 58 *ante*
[3] (1876) 34 L.T 568.
[4] (1883) L R 23 Ch D 500, 52 L J Ch D 473, 49 L T 115 See p 58 *ante*

It will be observed that much stress was laid on the point of over-assessment by the rating authorities

Where owner liable

The owner of property is liable to be rated in some cases. The provision in this respect of the Representation of the People Act, 1867, has already been dealt with (see pp 36 *et seq., ante*). The Poor Rate Assessment and Collection Act, 1869 (32 & 33 Vict , c. 41), provides as follows —By Section 3, that in case the rateable value of any hereditament does not exceed £20 if the hereditament is situate in the Metropolis, or £13 if situate in any parish wholly or partly within the Borough of Liverpool, or £10 if situate in any parish wholly or partly within the City of Manchester or the Borough of Birmingham, or £8 if situate elsewhere, and the owner of such hereditament is willing to enter into an agreement in writing with the Overseers to become liable to them for the Poor Rates assessed in respect of such hereditament for any term not being less than one year from the date of such agreement *and to pay the Poor Rates whether the hereditament is occupied or not*, the Overseers may subject, nevertheless, to the control of the Vestry, *agree* with the owner to receive the rates from him and to allow him a commission not exceeding 25 per cent. on the amount thereof

By Section 4, that the Vestry of any parish may from time to time *order* that the owners of all rateable hereditaments to which Section 3 of the Act extends, situate within such parish, shall be rated to the Poor Rate in respect of such rateable hereditament, *instead of the occupiers*, and all rates made after the date of such order, and thereupon and so long as such order shall be in force the following enactments shall have effect —

" (1) The overseers shall rate the owners instead of the occupiers, and shall allow to them an abatement or deduction of fifteen per cent from the amount of the rate.

" (2) If the owner of one or more such rateable hereditaments shall give notice to the overseers in writing that he is willing to be rated for any term not being less than one year in respect of all such rateable hereditaments of which he is the owner, *whether the same be occupied or not*, the overseers shall rate such owner accordingly, and allow him a further abatement or deduction not exceeding fifteen per cent from the amount of the rate during the time he is so rated.

" (3) The Vestry may by resolution rescind any such order after a day to be fixed by them, such day being not less than six months after the passing of such resolution, but the order shall continue in force with respect to all rates made before the date on which the resolution takes effect

" Provided that this clause shall not be applicable to any rateable hereditament in which a dwelling house shall not be included "

It will be noticed, therefore, that if by agreement between the Owners and the Overseers under Section 3 the owners become liable to pay the rates, they are entitled to such abatement, not exceeding 25 per cent, as shall be agreed, and that the rate (subject to such abatement) has to be paid, whether the property is occupied or not; while, if under Section 4 the Vestry make an order the owner becomes liable to pay the rate, whether he wishes it or not, subject to an abatement of 15 per cent, and, in addition, he is entitled to the allowance for empties in the usual way, or if he gives notice to the Overseers that he is willing to be rated, whether the property be occupied or not, the Overseers are to allow him, in addition to the first-named 15 per cent, a further abatement not exceeding 15 per cent

Where, however, a tenant, through excessive poverty, is excused his rates, a landlord cannot be held liable in respect of houses let to such tenant [1]

---

[1] *R v Hull Dock Co*, (1824) 5 D & R 359, 3 B & C 516, 3 L J K B 85.

Non com-
pliance of
owners with
liability to
pay rate

By the same Act, s 12, in the event of the owner becoming liable for payment of the Poor Rates and of non-compliance with that liability, the goods and chattels of the occupier are made liable to be distrained and sold for payment of such rates as may accrue during his occupation of the premises, at any time whilst such rates remain unpaid by the owner, subject to the following provisions —

" (1.) That no such distress shall be levied unless the rate has been demanded in writing by the overseers from the occupier, and the occupier has failed to pay the same within fourteen days after the service of such demand

" (2.) That no greater sum shall be raised by such distress than shall at the time of making the same be actually due from the occupier for rent of the premises on which the distress is made

" (3) That any such occupier shall be entitled to deduct the amount of rates for which such distraint is made, and the expenses of the distraint, from the rent due or accruing due to the owner, and every such payment shall be a valid discharge of the rent to the extent of the rate and expenses paid "

It should be noted that, although the owner may be compelled or may agree to pay the rates under the foregoing Act, it is the duty of the Overseers under Section 19 of that Act, in making out the rate and in preparing the Rate Book, to cause the name of the occupier to be inserted in the occupiers' column, in order to give him the advantage of the qualification for franchise[1] By Section 11 of the Parliamentary and Municipal Registration Act, 1878, it is enacted that the said Section 19 shall not be deemed to apply exclusively to cases within the Poor Rate Assessment and Collection Act, 1869,[2] but shall be of general application.

[1] See also *Barton* v *Birmingham (Town Clerk)*, (1878) 48 L J C P 87 and *Cross* v *Alsop*, (1870) 40 L J C P 53
[2] The Poor Rate Assessment and Collection Act, 1869, 32 & 33 Vict , c 41

The owner of property is also liable to pay the rate where the occupier holds such property on a term which does not exceed three months   See Section 1 of the Poor Rate Assessment and Collection Act, 1869,[1] which enacts as follows   "The occupier of any rateable hereditaments let to him for a term *not exceeding three months* shall be entitled to deduct the amount paid by him in respect of any poor rate assessed upon such hereditaments from the rent due or accruing due to the owner, and every such payment shall be a valid discharge of the rent to the extent of the rate so p   1"

---

[1] 32 & 33 Vict , c 41

CHAPTER IV.

VALUE

Origin of Phrases " Gross Value " and " Rateable Value "—Terms as defined by the Valuation (Metropolis) Act, 1869 – How far Actual Rent has Relation to Value— Present Value only Basis upon which Property is to be Assessed—When Occupier and Owner are One, how Value to be Ascertained.

Origin of
phrases
"gross value"
and "rateable
value"

HAVING dealt with the principles and foundations underlying the present law of rating, and having, it is hoped, made clear the liability and non-liability of persons and property, it is now proposed to consider the question of value   The point to be ascertained is the meaning of the phrases "gross value" and ' rateable value," and to do this the reader is referred to the first of the Rating Acts, viz , 43 Elizabeth, c 2, which was passed in 1601, and provides for the raising by taxation, weekly or otherwise, of a convenient stock of flax, wool, etc , also competent sums of money for and towards the necessary relief of the poor, etc. Although the words " by taxation " are used, there would seem to be much doubt as to the method of taxation actually adopted at that time   A person was rated according to his ability to pay such rates, but the question as to what that ability might be was left to the Overseers of each particular parish to determine   There was thus no uniform rule for levying the rate for the relief of the poor, and the confusion must have been great   A person was rated, originally, according to the profits derived from the sale of his stock-in-trade and of his other property. This was

an obvious difficulty to the Overseer who had to make
the assessment, as he possessed no absolute guide as to
the capabilities of the ratepayer to contribute to the rate,
but had rather to depend on the veracity of the con-
tributor. The liability to be thus rated in respect of
personal property was not in fact acted upon to any
extent, but the provision therefor was repealed only as
recently as 1840[1], but, curiously enough, Parliament,
when exempting the liability of a person in respect of
his stock-in-trade, only did so for one year   Section 2 (a)
enacts that "This Act shall be in force till the 31st day
of December, in the year of Our Lord 1841, and from
the said 31st day of December this Act, and all the
provisions hereinbefore contained, shall absolutely cease
and be of no effect." It is, however, in force at the
present day, for, by the Expiring Laws Continuance
Acts, it has been continued in force from year to year,
and is in force to-day under the last of these Acts, viz.,
the Expiring Laws Continuance Act, 1909[2] It must,
therefore, not be forgotten that the law exempting from
liability to be rated for trade profits is, even at the
present day, only temporary in its form

The Churchwardens and Overseers used to meet once a
month in the parish church, " upon the Sunday in the
afternoon, after divine service, there to consider of some
good course to be taken, and of some meet order to be set
down in the premises."   And, although power was given
to appeal to Quarter Sessions by any person finding
themselves grieved with any cess or tax, or other act done
by the said Churchwardens, it was rarely exercised , and
the mere fact of the passing of such an Act as that
providing for the non-rateability of stock-in-trade *for one
year only* showed that the law as it then stood was *not
clearly defined*; neither did the legislators seem at all
certain as to the best method of taxation for the purpose.

[1] The Poor Rate Exemption Act, 1840 (3 & 4 Vict , c 89).
[2] 9 Edw. VII , c 46

It is difficult to imagine the chaos that would ensue, having regard to the order of the Rate Books kept by each parish at the present day, should Parliament determine to alter the law of rating for one year only   Owing to the large number of public companies and the multifarious hereditaments, a union often requires the attention of a professional valuer for considerably more than twelve months in order to assess every property on a fair and equitable basis.

Pool Rate
Act, 1743

It will be seen, therefore, that by 43 Elizabeth, c. 2, the Churchwardens and Overseers had almost unlimited power ; and that they misused the authority given them is evident from the preamble of the Poor Rate Act, 1743,[1] which reads as follows :—" Whereas great inconveniences do often arise in cities, towns corporate, parishes, townships and places, by reason of the unlimited power of the churchwardens and overseers of the poor, who frequently, on frivolous pretences, and for private ends, make unjust and illegal rates in a secret and clandestine manner, contrary to the true intent and meaning of a statute made in the forty-and-third year of the reign of Queen Elizabeth "[2]

It is apparent, therefore, that there had long been needed a principle which could be made applicable to all classes of property, and which would take out of the hands of the Overseers the power of levying an unfair rate to meet their own ends.   The first Statute that attempts to define such a principle is the Parochial Assessment Act, 1836 (6 & 7 William IV., c. 96), which enacts that " no rate for the relief of the poor in England and Wales shall be allowed by any justices, or be of any force, which shall not be made upon an estimate of the net annual value of the several hereditaments rated thereunto ; that is to say, of the rent at which the same might

[1] 17 Geo II , c 3
[2] (160) 43 Elizabeth, c 2

reasonably be expected to let from year to year, free of all usual tenant's rates and taxes and tithe commutation rent-charge, if any, and deducting therefrom the probable average annual cost of repairs, insurance and other expenses, if any, necessary to maintain them in a state to command such rent."

It has been said that this principle of rating was not first created by this Statute, but that in the case of *R. v Kingswinford*[1] the Court decided that it was to be found in the Statute of Elizabeth. It is submitted that this is an opinion not strictly correct. The principle laid down in the case was apparently that a person should contribute to the relief of the poor according to the *profits* which he derived from the use of the land in his occupation and not as it is submitted it should have been, according to the rental value of the property, although it cannot be denied that the rental value would probably often be determined by the ability to make profits out of the land. This method would, no doubt, have worked satisfactorily had there been only one kind of occupation of land, viz., for the purposes of carrying on a business connected directly with such land, but there are innumerable occupations which may be an actual pecuniary loss to the occupier—a private residence for instance.

Then, on the other hand in the case of assessing a town, there may be two buildings next to one another covering the same quantity of land, and indeed exactly similar in every respect, the one being occupied by a merchant with a large capital returning to him some thousands per annum, and the other by a merchant in a smaller way of business. These two hereditaments, therefore, under the old system would have had different values placed upon them by the Overseers; but, on the passing of the Parochial Assessment Act, 1836,[2] the "net annual

---

[1] (1827) 7 B. & C. 236, 1 M. & R. 20, 6 L. J. M. C. 3
[2] 6 & 7 William IV., c. 96

F 2

value" was defined as "the *rent* at which the same might reasonably be expected to let from year to year," and the landlord erecting these buildings would require the same interest on his money in both cases, and the one tenant would not expect or be willing to pay more than the other   The question of the tenant's profits would not affect the landlord when calculating the rental value of the premises, that is to say, the amount of rent which would repay the outlay of his capital together with the interest upon it, always assuming there was a certain amount of competition for the premises   The net annual value would be the same in each case under this latter Statute ; whilst, under the Statute of Elizabeth, it might vary according to the individual profits of the respective merchants or tenants   That there was no uniform principle before the passing of this Act is obvious from the recital to the Act that "it is desirable to establish *one uniform mode* of rating for the relief of the poor throughout England and Wales '

In the Parochial Assessment Act, 1836,[1] we have the term "net annual value," *i e* , the "rateable value" first

"Rateable value " first defined

defined ; and although the term "rateable value"—and it is clearly synonymous with "net annual value "—is not used in the Act itself, it is mentioned in the Schedule to the same

There is no definition of the term "gross value ' given here , in fact, there was none actually enacted by Parliament until twenty-six years after the passing of the above Act.   Reference to it, however, is made in Section 2, inferentially —"Every such rate made after the said period shall, in addition to any other particular *which the form of making out such rate shall require to be set forth,* contain an account of every particular set forth at the head of the respective columns in the form given in the Schedule to this Act annexed," and one of the columns in the form of rate in such Schedule is headed "gross estimated rental "

---

[1] 6 & 7 William IV , c 96

That the laws were then in a chaotic state is patent to
any investigator, as, on the one hand, trade profits were
rateable (that is, an occupier of land was liable to be
rated according to the profits derived from his stock-in-
trade), yet at the same time, he was only rateable at the
rent at which the property might reasonably be expected
to let from year to year.   This, on the surface, would
seem absurd, but it would appear that the different principles were to be applied according to the different classes
of property they affected   Take, for instance, the case of
a public-house.   An incoming tenant would naturally and
properly desire to know the profits of the said house
before agreeing to any rent proposed by the landlord.
Now the facts respecting the trade done in this case
would practically be the only reliable data available for
the purposes of estimating the rent, and assuming, for
the sake of argument, that instead of a public-house the
hereditament had consisted of a private dwelling-house,
then would the tenant pay as much for his occupation
thereof, or could the landlord expect to obtain as large a
rent ?   Probably not, but there are cases where a license
to a house actually decreases the value of it as compared
with the surrounding property, that is to say, that there
is so little trade that the property used for some other
purpose might return a greater rent   This, however,
will be dealt with in a later chapter on licensed premises.
In the case of the public-house, the profits from the
stock-in-trade regulated the rateable value, whilst, in
the case of the private dwelling, the rent (which also
regulated the rateable value) was governed by the value
of the building and land upon which it stood and the
amount a tenant in competition would be willing to give.

The next important step in rating law was the passing
of the Poor Rate Exemption Act, 1840 (3 & 4 Vict.,
c 89), an Act to exempt the liability of ratepayers in
respect of their ability derived from the profits of stock-

in-trade. It has previously been mentioned in this chapter[1] that, although this Act was only passed for one year, it is, nevertheless, in force at the present day.

We now arrive at the point at which the rent alone can be the standard to go upon in making the valuation. Returning to the case of the public-house, it will be seen that the rent there was governed by the trade profits, nevertheless, it was a rent at which the hereditament might reasonably be expected to let from year to year, and as such was taken into account in estimating the value This is not rating trade profits directly, and must not be confused with the old principle of a tenant having to produce his books year by year, and the Overseers fixing the assessment according to the actual money he received—a rate in the nature of our modern income taxes. Next, in 1862, was passed an Act entitled the Union Assessment Committee Act, 1862 (25 & 26 Vict, c 103) Twenty-six years before, earlier as we have seen, we had in the Parochial Assessment Act, 1836,[2] the term "rateable value" defined, and, curiously enough, though the "rateable value" was apparently to be derived from the "gross value or gross rent," there was no definition given of the term. But here Section 15 is entirely devoted to it. It runs as follows   "The gross estimated rental for the purpose of the Schedule *(Form of Rate)* to this Act shall be the rent at which the hereditaments might reasonably be expected to let from year to year, free of all usual tenant's rates and taxes and tithe commutation rent-charge, if any, provided that nothing herein contained shall repeal or interfere with the provisions contained in the first section of the said Act 6 & 7 William IV., c 96), defining the net annual value of the hereditament to be rated "

I will be observed from the above definition of "gross estimated rental" or "gross value" that there is no

[1] See p 65 *ante.*
[2] 6 & 7 William IV , c 96

principle laid down as to how this is to be arrived at.
The definition starts with the term that the gross
estimated rental shall be the rent at which the hereditament might be expected to let, etc.

In calculating rent there are innumerable factors and
two distincts points of view to be considered, namely,
that of the landlord and that of the tenant

Factors in
calculating
Rent

The first consideration of a landlord in estimating the
rent at which he could afford to let a property would be
the amount of the outgoings, and, on the assumption that
the property was to be let for a short period, he, the
landlord, undertaking to do all repairs or pay the
insurance, and having to provide a sinking fund to replace
the original capital at the end of the life of the hereditament, he would as a prudent business man primarily
estimate these sums as the first factors he would of
necessity require, and in addition he would claim a return
on his own capital sunk in the property in the shape of
interest

From this it would appear that the gross value of rent
cannot be a concrete sum arrived at arbitrarily, but ought
to consist of various items taken together, and, therefore,
although it is commonly said in theory that it is necessary,
—even compulsory by Act of Parliament, to arrive at the
gross rent first before deductions are made to arrive at the
rateable value, the real basis for a valuer to adopt in
arriving at the gross rent from a landlord's point of view,
is to estimate the amount of capital value in the concern,
take this at a reasonable rate of interest which cannot be
a fixed sum, add to such sum the cost of repairs and all
other outgoings which have to be paid, and the total
amount would represent the rent at which a landlord
could afford to let the property to a tenant.

On the other hand the tenant is not concerned with any
outgoings at all, and the first principles of finance would
instil into his mind the fact that he must get the property

for as little as possible.   This is what has been commonly referred to as the "higgling of the market," and whilst

the true test of rent for rating purposes should be that which the tenant is willing to pay and not necessarily that which the landlord would demand, at the same time it is not possible to ignore the fact that rent must have some relation to capital value, and *vice versâ*, and that, if it were not for the fact that in the majority of cases landlords are able to obtain sufficient sums by way of rent after paying all outgoings to render a slightly higher rate of interest than would otherwise be derived by investing money in another kind of security, landlords—from a commercial point of view, would cease to exist. The effect of such a situation would be that a tenant would then have to become his own landlord, and if he were forced under these peculiar circumstances to erect or purchase his own property, it follows as a matter of common sense that the interest he would be losing upon the money invested in the property must be in effect rent, and would represent the rateable value of the premises

It may seem unnecessary to dilate upon this point, but as a matter of fact, it is frequently urged that it is enacted by Parliament that the gross value should be the datum point from which the rateable value is derived, whereas in commerce the practical datum point is the net return to the landlord, and so the rateable value, and to this, in order to ascertain the gross rent, additions have to be made for repairs, etc   There seems to be nothing in the Act which enacts that, in order to arrive at the gross value or gross rent, the various sums which go to make up this amount shall not be first added together and afterwards certain of them subtracted, to fix the net rent or rateable value within the terms of the Act itself

It is submitted, therefore, that it is incorrect to state that in all cases the gross value must be arrived at first and the rateable value directly derived from it. and that whether this should be done or not must be determined by the circumstances of the particular case.

It certainly must not be overlooked that in dealing with a public company, where receipts and expenditure form the basis of a valuation, the net rateable value cannot be arrived at until after the gross value has been settled, because in such a valuation the datum point is the gross receipt.

It is a little curious, however, that the definition of "gross value" in the 1862 Act seems not to have contemplated in terms, such concerns as Railways, Gas and Water Companies, etc, where as a rule the data for the valuation are the accounts

Shortly after the passing of the Act of 1862 the Poor Law Commissioners gave what, in their opinion, was the construction to be placed on the Statutes as to " gross rent" and "net rent," or, in other words, "gross value" and "rateable value."

"Gross rent ' they defined as the rent which would be paid " to a landlord, who himself undertakes to pay all the usual tenant's rates and taxes with which the hereditaments or premises rented by the tenant are chargeable, together with tithe commutation rent-charge, the expense of upholding the buildings in tenantable repair, insurance against loss by fire, and any other expenses (if any shall exist) necessary to maintain such hereditament in a state to command such gross rent " This definition, however, would seem to be hardly correct as rates, taxes, tithes, &c, are excluded by the statutory definition from the "gross" as well as from the "rateable ' value

"Net rent" they defined as "the amount which is received by or which remains clear in the hands of a landlord after all such taxes, charges and expenses as are above enumerated shall have been provided for "

Terms as defined by the Valuation (Metropolis) Act, 1869

Doubts were still existing as to the actual meaning of the terms; and after a lapse of seven years the Valuation (Metropolis) Act, 1869,[1] was passed, defining the terms "gross value" and "rateable value," so that no other construction could be placed upon them; and uncertainty as to the Legislature's meaning was to a large extent set at rest   It will be noticed that, whereas in this Act the term "gross value" is used for the first time, for the purpose of saving confusion the term has been used in the previous pages of this chapter alternatively to the actual term of "gross estimated rental" used in the Statutes prior to the Valuation (Metropolis) Act.   Yet it is a strange coincidence that, although no trace of the present-day expression of "gross value" can be found before the passing of this Act, the term "rateable value" was used as far back as the year 1836   The definitions in this Act of the terms "gross value" and "rateable value" are respectively, of the former, "the annual rent which a tenant might reasonably be expected, *taking one year with another,* to pay for an hereditament if the tenant undertook to pay all usual tenant's rates and taxes, and tithe commutation rent-charge, if any, and if the landlord undertook to bear the cost of the repairs, insurance, and other expenses, if any, necessary to maintain the property in a state to command that rent", and of the latter, "the rateable value of any property is the gross value after deducting from it the probable annual average cost of the repairs, insurance, and other expenses, if any, necessary to maintain the property in a state to command the rent."

Here we have the definitions of both the terms which are in force at the present day   There is, no doubt, still some modification required in the definition of "gross value"; as in the year 1891, when the Tithe Act[2] came into

---

[1] 32 & 33 Vict., c 67, s. 4
[2] 54 Vict , c. 8, s 1

operation, it was enacted that the landlord, and not the tenant, should pay the tithe, whereas it is assumed in the definition that the tenant pays it The consequence is, that a landlord who formerly received a rent from a tenant, who himself paid the tithe, now has to increase his rent to a figure which will leave him, by way of profit, the same amount as before The result of this will be seen at once—the former rateable value will remain the same, because as the tithe is rateable the landlord pays the rates on it, and in the event of the rateability of the property being increased, owing to the raising of the rent through the circumstances as stated above, not only will the landlord pay the rates on the tithe, but the tenant also, an injustice which cannot have been contemplated by Parliament when passing the Act

It must not be imagined that the basis of a valuation of a hereditament is necessarily the actual rent paid by the tenant to the landlord, or that such a rent is conclusive proof of the "gross value." The Act says "the rent at which a property might reasonably be expected to let, taking one year with another." So long as freedom of contract continues, tenants will come to terms with their landlords as to their rents, and this might be altogether misleading if used as the only basis for the purposes of the Poor Rate without other information For instance, a father may let a property to his son at a merely nominal rent, and so on.

How far actual rent has relation to value

Cooke, in his "Notes on Rating," says "As a broad principle rent is *primâ facie* evidence of value, but it is not conclusive evidence, the rent, however, paid by a perfectly free occupier would be a criterion of value difficult to set aside."

This point was clearly laid down in *Hayward* v. *Brinkworth Overseers* [1] Here there were three farms

---

[1] (1864) 10 L T N S. 608

situate in one parish, which were let at a certain sum annually, they might, however, reasonably have been expected to let, and might have let at a larger sum The Overseers assessed the occupiers to the relief of the poor at the rent actually paid by them. *Held*, that they were wrong, that they should have adopted a larger sum, viz., the rent at which the farms might have been reasonably expected to let.

Blackburn, J., in delivering judgment, said: "I think that the case is perfectly clear, and the rate must be amended The Legislature has stated that the estimate according to which the rate shall be calculated shall be, not the actual rent paid, but the rent at which the premises may be reasonably expected to let from year to year. The rent actually paid is no doubt *primâ facie* the estimate, but it is not conclusive Here the premises might have been let at a larger sum than that demanded by the landlords, and the rate, therefore, should have been calculated on that amount "

On the other hand, if a property be let at a rental higher than one which could reasonably have been expected, the value of the property must be assessed at such a sum as it "may be reasonably expected to let from year to year "—see *Clark* v *Alderbury Union*[1] Here there were some refreshment rooms let to a contractor for a term of years at a fixed rent, but his accounts proved that the business was carried on at a loss, and he contended that the rent was consequently too high, and did not represent the value, this view of the case was adopted by the Court

When occupier and owner are one, how value to be ascertained It has also been held that the value of a property where the owner and occupier are one must be ascertained by determining the rent a hypothetical tenant would give for the property[2] As has been said before, it does not

---

[1] (1880) 6 Q B D 139, 50 L J M C 33, 45 J P 358

[2] *London County Council* v *Erith Churchwardens, etc*, (1893) App Cas. 562, 63 L J M C. 9, 69 L T 725, 57 J P 821

matter whether there be an actual monetary benefit from the occupation, but for ascertaining the value of a hereditament all possible occupiers, including the actual occupier, must be taken into account as possible tenants[1] This point is very important, as it will be observed that in certain cases there can only possibly be one occupier, such as, for instance, public sewerage works, workhouses, county lunatic asylums, and the like, and where if the actual occupier were to be excluded as the hypothetical tenant, there would be no other occupier This decision is a far-reaching one, as it has frequently been contended on the part of rich ratepayers that, because they are the owners and occupiers of property, they expend a larger sum of money than is necessary to make the property fit for occupation, and that, in calculating the rent a hypothetical tenant would give, certain luxuries should be excluded from the valuation, but, if the actual occupier may be considered as a possible tenant, it is reasonable to suppose that he at least would give a rent to include such luxuries.

In making a valuation of any property for rating purposes, it must never be made with any consideration of the past, i e, what the property was worth years ago, or upon any estimate of how the said property may increase in value. The *present value* must always be the guide in making the rate. Lush, J, said upon this subject[2] "The rateable quality of property is not to be determined by what it once was, or may hereafter become. If a piece of fertile land were to be covered by the ashes of a volcano or by an inundation, it would have no rateable value so long as it continued in that condition. So also, on the other hand, a barren rock, so long as it remains a barren rock, has no rateable value; but the moment it is

Present value only basis upon which a property is to be assessed

---

[1] *R v School Board for London*, (1886) 17 Q B D. 738, 55 L J. M C 169, 55 L T 384

[2] *Metropolitan Board of Works v West Ham*, (1870) L R 6 Q B 193, 40 L J. M C 30, 23 L T 490

worked as a quarry it becomes rateable   The rateable
quality of property must be determined *by what it is at
the time the rate is made*"

In London, where valuation lists are only made once in
five years, there is provision for altering the assessments
where fluctuations have taken place, and outside the
Metropolis at any time a new supplemental list can be
deposited if alterations in value become apparent.[1] Appreciable fluctuations in value, however, seldom occur in such
a limited time as six months, and therefore, although in
theory valuation lists as a whole should be frequently
altered, in practice it is found unnecessary to do so
except, in the case of individual properties, as occasion
may arise.

---

[1] *See* Part III. Procedure *post*

CHAPTER V.

SPECIAL PROPERTIES

Principles of Rating as applied to Special Properties—Parochial and Mileage Principles — As applied to Canals—As applied to Railways—As applied to Gas and Water Undertakings—As applied to Tramway Undertakings—As applied to Telephone, Telegraph and Electric Light Undertakings—How far Trade Profits enter into the Valuation—Gross Receipts—Terminals — Expenses—Tenant's Capital — Statutable Deductions—Accounts to be taken.

IN the preceding pages the general method of arriving at gross and rateable values respectively has been explained, and in this chapter the application thereof to the rating of special properties will be dealt with

The special properties in question are those which, from their nature or circumstances, are usually occupied by the owners, or either cannot be let or (if at all) are very seldom let, and so very rarely the subject of bargain between Landlord and Tenant, and include Railways, Canals, Docks, Gasworks, Waterworks, Tramways, Electrical Undertakings, Telegraphs, Telephones and Undertakings of a similar nature.

To ascertain the "gross value" and the "rateable value" of such properties, based as such values are on the rent at which the properties may reasonably be expected to let, is a task of considerable difficulty.

The liability of these properties to be rated is beyond question, the occupiers thereof are occupiers of land, and as such they are clearly liable to contribute to the relief of the poor in the several parishes in which the property is situated.   Although trade profits, as we have seen, are not rateable as such, yet receipts and expenses may form the basis of calculation for rating purposes in these special cases, it having been decided that the rent a hypothetical tenant would be willing to pay therefor is the measure of the "gross value," as being the rent at which "the property might reasonably be expected to let, taking one year with another."

A railway or similar trading company is rated as the occupier of certain land, and an incoming tenant, supposing the undertaking were "to let," would first enquire what return he could reasonably expect for his outlay, and practically the only data for settling this upon a fair and equitable basis are the accounts of the company showing its receipts and expenses.

Parochial and mileage principles   The limit of area for rating being the parish an undertaking extending throughout several parishes (whether in one or more unions) is assessed at so much in each parish   A hereditament wholly contained in one parish has a rateable value placed upon it and such value entered in the Rate Book, but in the case of an undertaking (such as a railway, water or gas company), which extends into many parishes, the value of the whole is spread over such parishes, *not* in equal portions, but according to the particular value in each parish   This method of valuation is known as the "parochial principle "

As applied to canals   Possibly the first case in which this principle was raised was that of *R* v *Kingswinford*[1] in 1827.   Here a canal ran through several parishes, and it was decided that to estimate the rateable value for any one parish by making a valuation of the whole property, and then dividing it according to the length of the canal in each parish was incorrect, and that the real rateable value was to be found in proportion to the profits earned in each parish.

[1] (1827) 1 M & R 20, 7 B & C 236, 6 L J M C 3

Bayley, J , in this case said "Where there is a long line of canal extending through different parishes, although the money produced by the tonnage collected in all the parishes constitutes one common fund, out of which all the expenses are to be borne, still the proportion which those expenses may bear to the tolls collected—even in cases where the rates are the same along the whole line of the canal—may vary in different parishes

"The traffic on the canal may be greater in some parishes than others, or the rate may be unequal, and thus the net profits, which constitute the value of the land used for the canal, may vary in different parishes There are twelve miles of length of the canal in the parish of Kingswinford. Assuming that the different branches of the canal had been made under one Act of Parliament, I am of opinion that the company ought to be rated in each particular parish in proportion to the profit which they derive from the land there used by them for the purpose of the canal If a canal runs through six different parishes, and there is the same traffic through the whole line of the canal, every part of the canal will earn an equal proportion of the tolls But it may happen that in that part of the canal situate in one parish there may be double or treble the traffic which there is in any other of the six

' Why are the other parishes to have any part of the tolls earned in that parish ? The land in those parishes contributes nothing towards earning the sum derived in the other parish from the use of the land there The true principle is this a canal company is to contribute to the relief of the poor in each parish through which the canal passes, in proportion to the profit which they derive from the use of their land in that parish. If the profit arising from a given quantity of land vary in different parishes, the rate must vary in the same proportion "

G

As applied to railways

Three important cases upon the same point were decided in 1851,[1] the London, Brighton and South Coast Railway desired to establish the mileage principle, whilst the South Eastern and Midland Railways contended, successfully, for the "parochial principle." The judgment delivered by Coleridge, J , in the three cases was as follows :—"The first question is as to the principle on which the rate was to be imposed, whether upon what has been called the mileage principle, that is by treating the whole line of railway (trunks and branches) as one entire subject matter, and the whole rateable value, however constituted, as entire, and then, for the purpose of rating, dividing it among the several parishes simply according to the distance which the line passes through each , or upon the ordinary principle of ascertaining the actual rateable value of the land occupied by the company in each parish, by the rules which are applicable to any other land occupied by other bodies or persons for other purposes. The judicial decision of this question has hitherto been avoided by agreement and mutual concession : and we have delayed to pronounce our judgment on it, not so much from the difficulty of determining the rule of law as from that which arises on its practical application This presses particularly against what is called the parochial principle How are you by any means now in the power of the parish authorities to ascertain the particulars of profit and outgoings, from a comparison between which the rateable value of the land occupied is to be deduced, both profit and outgoings being affected by circumstances spread through the whole line ? On the other hand, against the mileage principle is to be urged that, although as regards the railway company—an entire body with an entire interest—

<hr/>

[1] R v London, Brighton and South Coast Railway Co , (1851) 15 Q B 313, 20 L J M C 124, R v South Eastern Railway Co , (1851) 15 Q B 344 20 L J M C 137, R v Midland Railway Co , (1851) 15 Q B 353, 20 L J M C 140

it is a matter of indifference how you divide a rate assumed to be entire for the whole line, yet, as the parishes are bodies with separate interests, there is a manifest injustice in attributing to the same space of land the same proportionate share of the whole rate everywhere, the land in the several parishes notoriously earning the profits and occasioning the outgoings in very different proportions, because you cannot do this without depriving some parishes of what they should receive, in order to give to others what they should not If, however, the legal principle be ascertained, it is clear that the difficulties in applying it, or even the practical imperfection which circumstances may occasion in applying it, are not to influence our decision

' It is unnecessary to consider what the force of the argument would be if it could be shown that there was an absolute impossibility of applying it, for nothing like that exists in the present case

" Now upon the legal principles we have no doubt. The Poor Rate and the principles of its assessment are entirely statutory The 6 & 7 William IV , c 96,[1] made expressly with a view ' to establish one uniform mode of rating for the relief of the poor ' prescribes the rule—the rate must be made on an ' estimate of the net annual value of the several hereditaments rated thereunto '— such value to be arrived at in the manner stated in the first section—the subject is parochial, the enquiry is to be conducted by parochial authorities with limited powers, if any matters specified in the section are locally situate without the parish, that is, if any such affect the amount of ' the net annual value or ' rent reasonably to be expected ' they will, of necessity, fall within the range of enquiry, but beyond this the principle does not go This principle, so limited and understood, was not first created by the Statute just mentioned The Court had decided

---

[1] The Parochial Assessment Act, 1836

so early as in 1827, in the case of *R* v. *Kingswinford*,[1] that it was to be found in the original Statute of Elizabeth ; and since that decision it has been uniformly applied to cases where the same party, whether company or individual, occupies in different parishes land forming one entire property, such as a canal : though the profits may be earned in different proportions and with a different rate of outgoings in each, the value which the land occupies in each parish produces, after the due allowance, is that upon which the occupier is to be rated in each

"It is unnecessary to cite more authorities in support of a proposition now become settled ; the decisions will be found to flow in a remarkably uniform current since the case last cited   Whether the circumstances of railways (which were in 1836 a comparatively infant interest) escaped the notice of the legislature or were advisedly thought not to need any special provision, certain it is that none was made ; and as, in its broad principles, the occupation of a railway company does not differ from that of a canal company, a Court of Law has no choice but to apply to it the same general law under which in its terms it certainly falls

"It is to be remembered that the amount of assessment on a particular occupier is a question between that occupier and the rest of the contributors to the whole rate ; and the consideration of that occupier's relation to the contributors to another rate in another parish is irrelevant to this question ; he may be rated in that other parish too high or too low, but this is a matter which does not interest the contributors to the first-named rate ; nor have they interest in the settlement of it   And this suggests the answer to a difficulty raised on the argument in this case   If you give C —— the full benefit of all the earnings made by the railway in the parish, what is to

1 1 M & R 20 ; 7 B & C 236 ; 6 L J M C 3

be done in the case of a parish on some branch line, in which the company may work at a loss ' The answer is, that that case must be decided, when it arises, between the company and that parish on the same principle precisely as the present, without reference to C——— "

The recent decision in *Great Central Railway v Sheffield Union* [1] is interesting in connection with this dictum

The parochial principle is therefore to be adopted in making a valuation, and it is perhaps the best method there could be Supposing, for instance, that a valuation were made of the entire system of the London and North Western Railway, and each parish took as its share of the rateable value the proportion that the length of line in the particular parish in question bore to the whole, the result will be as follows —The company's land would be rated no higher in the thickly-populated towns and cities than in the rural and outlying areas through which the railway passes, and so a hypothetical tenant would in effect be paying no higher rental for land at Euston than he would for the same acreage of land at Harrow. This would be absurd, and emphasizes, it is submitted, the equity of the parochial principle.

As long ago as 1857 the Royal Commission on Railways recommended " That, in order to meet inequalities in the local taxation of railways, some means should be devised by which some public authority, such as the Poor Law Board, should make an assessment for rating the whole railway, and then divide the amount according to an equitable principle, between the several unions or parishes " This suggestion has never been acted upon in England, and the objections to it are manifold The Royal Commission on Local Taxation in their report issued in the year 1901 have also recommended that a valuation should be made of the whole of the system of a railway company, and that after deducting

Recommendation of Royal Commission on Taxation

---

[1] (1908) 1 K B 750 (1909) A C 78

the value of the stations, the amount as representing the value of the permanent way should be distributed according to train mileage in each parish

System in Scotland

This last recommendation is, with a difference, dealt with later, based on the system in Scotland where the railway assessor makes a yearly valuation of the whole of the running line, and the value thereof is then allocated according to the lineal mileage in each area The following statement, however, made by Mr Henry, City Assessor of Glasgow, before the Commission,[1] shows how inequitably the system would work if applied to England and Wales with its many large towns and valuable suburban traffic, viz —" In Glasgow, prior to the amalgamation of the City Union Railway with the North British and the Glasgow and South Western Railways, the value of the City Union Line was £4,413 per mile The entire system of the Union Railway having been practically within the city boundaries, the full earning value of the line, under its separate existence, all fell to Glasgow Under the present law this value, created by the city within its own area, is now spread throughout the hundreds of miles of those companies' systems, and has reduced the city's share of its own value to a fraction, parishes distant, it may be, a hundred miles, draining from Glasgow its fair quota of taxation. '

The inequalities thus indicated would be far greater in England, as there are a larger number of railway centres than in Scotland The construction of railways tending as it does to centralisation of trade, it naturally follows there is greater traffic and greater earning capacity near large towns and in those towns, land is of course of far greater value than in the country or collecting districts through which the railway passes

Recommen dation of Royal Com- mission on Taxation

The Royal Commission to some extent have recognised this inequality in recommending the division of valuation

[1] See page 59 of the Final Report

for the purpose of the parish to be made, not according
to the lineal mileage, but according to the train mileage.
Strong objections to the recommendation still remain
however, as the earning capacities of various trains and in
different areas are so vastly different that grave inequalities as to the value of the line in any particular
parish must result if the recommendation be followed
The difference in the earning capacity of a passenger
train as compared with a goods train or with a mineral
train is so obvious that it would be grossly unfair, for
example, to allocate the same amount per train mile
for the whole of the Great Western system, seeing that
at Penzance there is exceedingly little coal traffic, as
compared with the areas in South Wales, through which
this system passes And again, the earning power of
trains at Penzance, as compared with South Wales, or
Paddington, is so vastly different that it would be most
inequitable to give the same value to the train mileage in
the three districts The ratepayers in the small parishes
of Cornwall, where the rates are exceedingly low, would
be reaping immense advantages from money earned on
various parts of the system, hundreds of miles away, and
the ratepayers in the parish of Paddington would be thus
contributing towards benefits for other parishes in which
they could not in any way participate Then again there
is the coal traffic, which is of a peculiar nature, inasmuch
as the waggons leave the collieries loaded with coal for
their destination and have to return empty It
frequently happens that the empty waggons, for the
purpose of convenience, return on a different route from
the one by which they travelled when loaded Should the
recommendations of the Commission become law, those
parishes through which the empties travel would receive
the same amount per train mile as those where the money
is actually earned Another case in which inequalities
would arise, and one frequently met with all over the

country, is that of a single branch line to a town of some importance situated a few miles from the main line Take for instance a case such as Staines on the Great Western Railway, or Horncastle in Lincolnshire Here practically speaking, one train runs backwards and forwards on the single line from the town to the nearest junction on the main line. The bulk of the passenger traffic goes one way in the morning and the other way at night, yet the train has to run backwards and forwards, one way full and the other empty On the present system of rating, the receipts which the trains earns would be the starting-point of the valuation, and as a set-off both journeys would be allowed in the expenses but under the system recommended by the Royal Commission the parishes through which this train journeyed would receive so much rateable value for each trip of the train, whereas, in point of fact, one line might be working at a loss, and as far as that line *per se* was concerned would have practically no rateable value at all

Parochial principle as applied to gas and water undertakings

The same difficulty immediately arises in assessing a gas or water undertaking as in a railway or canal company, and where the undertaking extends beyond one parish, there is the same question as to division A gas or water undertaking is not only rateable for the works necessary to carry on such undertaking, but for the pipes which form the medium of conveying the produce of the concern to the consumer. This point has been laid down in several cases [1] In the case of *R. v. West Middlesex Water Co* [2] Wightman, J, said "In this case the first question is, whether the company are rateable for their mains, which are laid under the surface of the highway,

---

[1] *New River Co v St Pancras Vestry,* (1880) 45 J P 75, *R v Bath Corporation,* (1811) 14 East 609, 13 R R 333 *R v Rochdale Waterworks Co,* (1813) 1 M & S 634, *R v Brighton Gas Light and Coke Co,* (1826) 8 D & R 308, 5 B & C 466, 29 R R 290, *R v. Shrewsbury (Trustees),* (1832) 3 B & A 216, 1 L J M C 18, 37 R R 409

[2] (1859) 28 L J M C 135, 5 Jur N S 1159, 1 El & El 716 23 J P

without any freehold or leasehold interest in the soil thereof being vested in the company *We think they are* These mains are fixed capital vested in land. The company is in possession of the mains buried in the soil, and so are *de facto* in possession of the space in the soil which the mains fill, for a purpose beneficial to itself. The decisions are uniform in holding gas companies to be rateable in respect of their mains, although the occupation of such mains may be *de facto* merely, and without legal or equitable estate in the land where the mains lie, by force of some Statute "[1]

The difficulty in applying the parochial principle to a gas or water undertaking is at once apparent. A railway, or canal, or tramway company earns money in every parish it passes through, irrespective of where the money may be actually collected, as in the following example —

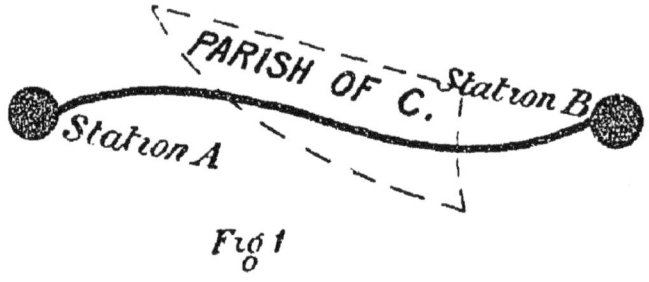

Fig 1.

Here the line of railway runs from station A to station B, through the parish of C Though the fares may be collected at station A, they are really earned by the company along the whole line of route A B, a certain portion being attributable to the parish of C This is the case with any company making the conveyance of passengers or goods its business, and can be readily

---

[1] See also the case of *Holywell Union v Halkyn District Mines Drainage Co*, [1895] A C 117, 71 L T 818 59 J P 566, in which the House of Lords clearly decide that underground pipes are rateable

understood. But compare the case of a gas undertaking
(Fig 2) which manufactures gas at the works A, conveys

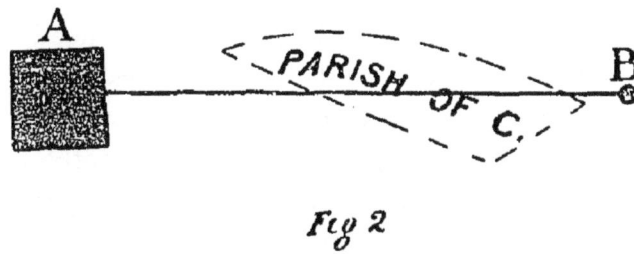

Fig 2

it through the parish of C (the rating of which we
presume is in question) and sells it to a consumer somewhere beyond that parish, say B   Here then, at B, is the
money earned, and the main in C being non-earning is
what is known as a "dead main."   The parish authorities
can only assess the rent of such main based on a percentage of its structural value

In the event of a company (Fig 3) making gas at works

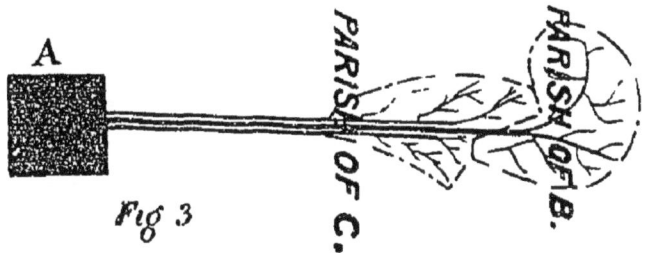

Fig 3

Live and
dead mains

A and then carrying the mains through to parishes C and
B, a further difficulty at once arises in the parish of C
In addition to the mains supplying the consumers in that
parish, there are others carrying gas to the consumers in
the parish of B   therefore, there are two distinct sets of
mains in C which have to be rated separately   These
two sets have been called respectively the "live mains"
and the "dead mains"   There has been a great deal of
contention as to what constitute live and what dead
mains, and it is proposed to deal more fully with this
point in the chapters on "Practice'   Suffice it to say

here, that a valuation is made of the whole undertaking, the value of the dead works (viz, the actual manufacturing works, or, in the case of a water company, the reservoirs, pumping apparatus, etc), and of the dead mains is then subtracted, the result being the rateable value of the entire live works or directly productive mains The next step is comparatively simple. The total receipts of the concern and the actual receipts in the parish in question are obtained and a simple proportion sum is made thus : As the receipts in the parish are to the total receipts, so is the rateable value of that parish to the total rateable value   Then must be added the value of the dead mains or indirectly productive mains and works (if any) in the parish, which as has been said before, is calculated by a percentage of the structural value of such works, and the valuation for the whole parish is complete.

This is the "parochial principle" as applied to gas and water undertakings   Wightman, J , in giving judgment in the before-mentioned case, *R* v *West Middlesex Water Co*,[1] said upon this point   "If an apparatus occupied by one occupier, consisting of several parts. lies in one parish, the rate is on the whole and is received by that parish. If such an apparatus lies in several parishes, the occupier is liable for the same amount of rateable value and no more ; but that amount is to be apportioned among the parishes in which it lies   And the question then arises, as in the present case, what is the principle which regulates such apportionment ?

"It is clear that each parish must rate the part that lies within it, such part becomes a separate rateable subject in that parish. and must be rated, according to the Parochial Assessment Act, 1836,[2] upon an estimate of the

---

[1] (1859) 28 L J M C 135 , 5 Jur N S 1159 , 1 El & El 716 , 23 J P 164
[2] 6 & 7 William IV , c 96

rent which that part would yield after proper deductions
In practice, a tenant of the parochial portion of a canal,
railway, gas works, water works, or the like, has rarely, if
ever, been known   But a hypothetical tenant must be
assumed   and the terms of such a tenancy are not
difficult to be conceived, if in the hypothesis some
necessary incidents are also assumed to be involved   no
one tenant of an essential part being able to stop his
part, secondly, that the title to the required land is
permanent, so that there is no risk of being compelled to
move fixed capital, thirdly, that there is land in the
required quantity and capital to be invested therein, and
occupants ready to take and work parts yielding profits, as
tenants at rack rent, and parts not yielding profit, as
contractors for remuneration, provided any greater profit
can be obtained than is ordinary in such relations   If a
tenancy of each parochial part be assumed according to
this hypothesis, then although each parish rates separately
upon its own estimate of the value of the part lying within
it, and the law gives no power of making all the parishes
co-operate in rating the several parts lying in each, nevertheless this Court is bound to protect the occupier of
such an apparatus from being rated beyond the rateable
value of the whole taken together, and it is in reference
to this protection that the Court must take into its
consideration at once all the separate rates as so many
claims upon one given fund, and must apportion that
fund, bearing in mind that every addition to the rateable
value assigned to one parish must be a subtraction from
the rateable value which might be given to some other
parish   Supposing, then, the apparatus to be apportioned
to several tenants according to the parts in several
parishes, the tenants of the parts directly earning net
profits in a parish would be rated by that parish for all
the profits earned therein, this being the parochial
principle of apportionment which has been unanimously

West Middle-sex Water case

upheld hitherto in respect of all canals, railways, water companies, gas companies, and bridges But the tenants of the parts directly earning no profit would not be liable to be rated in respect of rent in the ordinary sense, which is profit remaining after all deductions have been taken from the receipts But as these parts of the apparatus directly earning nothing, but indirectly conducing to such earnings elsewhere, are assumed to continue in operation, the company, to whose interest such continued occupation is essential, must be assumed to pay adequate remuneration to a contractor for land and fixed capital vested therein, together with the labour and skill requisite for the effective continuance of such operation, and this contractor with the company would stand in the relation of occupying tenant to the parish, and the part within the parish would be the rateable subject, and the local rateable value would be such sum as would pay the rent of the land and the profit on fixed capital therein.

This is a most clear definition of the parochial principle as applied to gas and water undertakings, and is, perhaps, the best we have on this complicated subject. At the conclusion of the case above referred to, the same Judge said "There appears to me, however, so much difficulty in applying the parochial principle of rating, by estimating the rent that a tenant would give for the subject-matter, in such a case as the present, as practically to amount nearly, if not entirely, to an impossibility of doing so satisfactorily. Indeed, the whole subject-matter appears to me to be involved in so much difficulty and uncertainty that I cannot but hope the Legislature may interfere and make some provision adapted to the rating of the property of such companies as that in question, and which may declare the principle upon which such companies are to be rated, and establish some uniform and practical mode of carrying that principle into effect "

This, it is submitted, is an extreme view of the case, but there can be no doubt as to the great difficulties to be overcome, for the companies, in most cases being strong and wealthy bodies, can afford to fight, and where, as in some county Poor Law Unions, there are two parishes adjoining one another, the rates in one being perhaps 1s 6d. in the £, whilst in the other they are as much as 10s in the £, it can be seen that the company is likely to endeavour, when dividing the whole rateable value, to place the larger amount in the parish in which the rates are the lower When once the parochial principle is properly understood, the way of rating is comparatively smooth It is one thing to determine the rent that would be paid for a hereditament, but it is quite a different matter to be able to divide this rent between the several parishes in which the property is situated, to the satisfaction of all parties concerned.

Recommendation of Royal Commission as to rating of gas and water works, etc.

The Report of the Royal Commission on Local Taxation with regard to gas and water companies, electric light and so on can hardly be considered as satisfactory. The Commission sat for several years for the purpose, apparently, of formulating a scheme to reduce chaos to order, and the following extract from the Report (page 60) leaves matters exactly where they were before the Commission was appointed, and indeed suggests few reforms of any practical worth beyond that of recommending a competent authority to hear appeals The extract is as follows "We do not think that it is desirable, or indeed possible, for us to make any recommendations with regard to the actual procedure which should be adopted in ascertaining the annual value of these properties There must always be some difference of opinion among valuers on the question of what a hypothetical tenant might reasonably be expected to pay, but we think that it is of great importance that the valuation of these special properties should be centralised as far as possible, and undertaken by the most skilled class of valuers "

The parochial principle as applied to tramway undertakings is precisely similar to that of a railway or canal company, and there is little further to be said upon the subject. Perhaps no clearer rule could be laid down than that in the judgment delivered in the case of the *London Tramways Co* v *Lambeth*[1] "The tramways laid in the respondents' parish comprise one entire route confined to this parish, and considerable portions of five other service routes, running without break in several parishes, each route forming part of an incorporated system of tramways belonging to the appellants and which extend altogether into eight parishes. In this, as in all cases under the Parochial Assessment Act, 1836,[2] the value to be found has to be determined according to the annual rent that a hypothetical tenant, making the suitable deductions, would give for the rateable property, that is to say, in estimating property of this kind, what amount a tenant of the whole hereditaments would give, upon a fair division of the entire rent, for so much of the rateable property as is situate in the particular parish, and in the endeavour to arrive at this amount we have, conformably with the now well-established rule. been guided, as far as the facts and circumstances of the case admit, by what is called the parochial principle in contradistinction to the mileage principle.

" This amount—the rent which the property would command—or, in other words, the beneficial value of the occupation, must necessarily, therefore, be based upon the receipts and expenses connected with the entire undertaking, so that, accepting the annual gross receipts as the basis of the estimate of the rent, the net receipts in each parish would afford the best criterion of rateable value in each parish "

---

[1] (1874) 31 L T 319
[2] 6 & 7 William IV , c 96

The principle is the same as to telephone, telegraph, and electric light undertakings, and needs no further comment A valuation of the whole is made, and is divided in the proportion —As the receipts in the parish are to the total receipts so is the rateable value of the parish to the total rateable value.

Parochial principle as applied to telephone, telegraph and electric light undertakings

How far trade profits enter into the valuation

As has already been indicated in this chapter, the receipts of a company form the basis of calculation to arrive at the rateable value This may seem rather contradictory, after the Act providing for the exemption of rateability of trade profits, but upon this subject Lord Denman, C.J., in delivering judgment in *R. v. London and South Western Railway Co.*,[1] said "The 3 & 4 Vict., c 89, was referred to in the argument by counsel, but it has in truth little or no bearing upon this question It prohibits the rating of any inhabitant as such inhabitant in respect of his ability derived from the profit of stock-in-trade, or any other property, to the relief of the poor, but it expressly leaves unaffected the liability of any occupier of lands or houses to be taxed under the provisions of 43 Elizabeth, c 2, and 13 & 14 Car 2 Under 6 & 7 William IV., c 96, the rate must be made on an estimate of the 'net annual value, and that value is declared to be 'the rent at which the hereditaments might reasonably be expected to let from year to year, free of all usual tenant's rates and taxes, and tithe commutation rent-charge, if any, and deducting therefrom the probable average annual cost of repairs, insurance and other expenses, if any, necessary to maintain them in a state to command such rent ''

The judgment of the Court in the case was as follows "The rateable value of the land in occupation of a railway company in a parish, such company being carriers on their own line, is to be estimated according to the rent at which the railway might be expected to let from year to year, to a lessee capable of deriving therefrom all the

[1] (1842) 1 Q B 558 11 L J M C. 98, 2 Rail Cas 629, 6 Jur 686

profits which accrue to the company from the conveyance of passengers, cattle and goods, etc , under the powers of their Acts , such lessee finding locomotive power, carriages, etc , and paying the expenses incidental to working the railway, and having the use of the stations, fixtures and appurtenances of the railway , allowance being made for the deduction specified in the Parochial Assessment Act.'[1]

The method to be adopted in arriving at the rateable value of a special hereditament, owned and worked by a company is, therefore, as follows   The gross receipts must first of all be obtained , from these the working expenses, the expenses of management, and the rates and taxes payable by the company, are deducted , the result is the profit accruing from the undertaking   The hypothetical tenant, who has, it is assumed, sunk capital in the concern, requires interest on it in the form of profits, etc these have to be deducted. and the balance left is the amount due to the landlord, in other words the landlord s share (i e., the rent or " gross value").

The deductions to be made from this "gross value to arrive at the "rateable value" of the property are the expenses of insurance, the repairs necessary to keep the property in a state to command the rent, including a depreciation or renewal fund which a prudent landlord would set aside to reimburse himself at the end of the life of the undertaking. It is proposed now to deal with each item separately, taking first the gross receipts

As has been explained, the unit of area for rating *Gross receipts* purposes is the parish for which the valuation is made The receipts. therefore, have to be obtained for the parish in question.   For the objects of this book, it may be assumed that there are two classes of undertakings, and these may be briefly placed under the following heads, viz , undertakings for the purpose of conveying passengers

---

[1] (1836) 6 & 7 William IV , c 96

H

and goods, etc , such as a railway or canal company , and
undertakings for the making of certain commodities, as
gas, water, etc   Taking the first class of undertaking, it
is at once seen that a difficulty arises, which perhaps may
be made clearer by a sketch

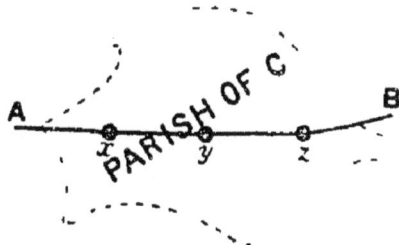

A B is a line of railway running through the parish of
C   There are tolls collected at stations x y z for the
conveyance of passengers and goods to various parts of
the system belonging to the company   It cannot be
contended that the money collected in this way is all
earned in the parish of C, as the building of stations is a
mere matter of convenience   A passenger pays at station
x a fare for the privilege of being conveyed some
distance from his starting-point , the money is earned
by the company throughout the whole length of the route
travelled over, and not all in the parish of C.   Or, again,
a train may run right through the parish of C without
stopping at any of the stations in the parish, yet nevertheless it earns money in that parish, and to this extent is
liable to contribute to its rates   To obtain the parochial
receipts, therefore, is a matter of great difficulty , in fact,
the company themselves are the only persons who can
supply the *actual* figures, and this is rarely done in the
initial stage of a valuation, not owing to any hostile feeling
on the part of the company, but because the expense and
time necessary for an investigation of this character is considerable, the only way to arrive at the correct result being
to find the earnings from station to station throughout the
system, a most laborious and difficult task   To estimate

the amount of receipts in the parish, a task which the
surveyor acting for the parish invariably has to perform,
it is necessary that he should be in the possession of one
of the company's working or "staff" time tables, so that
he can ascertain approximately the amount of "train
miles" run throughout the parish in the year. From the
company's published accounts he can obtain the receipts
over the whole system, also the average price per train
mile for the same, and having obtained the number of
train miles in the parish for which he is making the
valuation, he has then to use his best judgment as to
whether and to what extent the receipts earned there
are above or below the average of those earned over
the whole system.

In addition to the receipts actually earned in the *Terminals*
parishes, there are certain "terminal charges" to be
added. All companies keep at their stations a staff of
officers for the convenience of passengers and also for
receiving, loading, unloading and dispatching goods etc.
This staff's earnings are called terminal charges, and it
was sought [1] to make these charges 'Parochial,' i.e., the
benefit to belong to the parish in which the station was
situated, and in which the money was collected. But it
was held that this view was wrong. Blackburn, J., in
delivering judgment in the case, said "It appears that if
the stations and line in———belonged to different companies, and if the Clearing House system were in force,
certain allowances would be made to the companies
owning the station, by way of remuneration for the
accommodation afforded in receiving, loading and unloading, fetching and delivering the goods, either taken in or
given out at the stations. The appellants contend that
these allowances, which are called 'terminals' are not
part of the earnings of the line, but are to be considered

---

[1] (1863) *R. v. Eastern Counties Railway Co.*, 4 B. & S. 58, 32
L J M C 174, 9 Jur N S 1339, 8 L T 419, 11 W R 694

as earnings of the station   . We think the amount of
these terminals, and the amount of the expenses incurred
in earning them, are parts of the general earnings and
general expenses of the line, and are to be treated in the
same way as any other part of the gross receipts and
outgoings."

The method of estimating the parochial receipts is only
briefly touched upon here, a fuller exposition of the practice, however, will be found in the chapter upon railways,
in the second part of this work

With regard to the other class of undertaking, such as
a gas or a water undertaking, it has been shown that a
valuation is made for the whole as a going concern, and
the rateable value is then divided amongst the parishes in
which it is situate, according to the parochial receipts
To arrive at the receipts of the whole as a going concern
is comparatively simple, the published accounts showing
these

The parochial receipts, however, are earned in the parish
in which the produce is sold, and herein lies the difference between a railway and a gas or water undertaking,
for, whereas on the one hand, the money actually collected
by a gas or water undertaking in a parish is the amount
of receipts upon which basis the valuation is made for
that parish. on the other hand, a railway company may
not, and very often does not, have a station in a parish
through which its line of way runs, and therefore no
money actually passes from the hands of its customers
into the pockets of the company in the parish.

The only possible way of obtaining the parochial
receipts of a gas or water company, etc, is by making
application for the necessary information to such company, as it would be out of the question for a surveyor
to visit each consumer in a parish for the purpose of
ascertaining the amount of gas purchased in order to

arrive at the parochial receipts, and, besides, the law gives no power either to the parochial authorities themselves or their agent to adopt such a course

Returning to a railway company, the expenses are an Expenses item of deduction which is considerably involved, so intricate is the subject that the Court once held over a decision for a considerable time in the hope that the Legislature would alter the law The alteration, however, was not made and is apparently as far off as ever, so it was left to the Court to lay down a principle This was done in the case of *R v Great Western Railway Co*,[1] Lord Campbell, C.J, in delivering judgment, said "The net rateable value' is that which remains of the gross receipts after all just deductions have been made It might seem at first sight that we might confine our enquiry to the two miles and a half" (the length of line, the rating of which was in question), "and that we only encumber the investigation uselessly by introducing into it any consideration of the gross and rateable value of the whole line, but the circumstances of a railway make this absolutely necessary The enquiry may become, and undoubtedly does become, more complicated and difficult thereby, but it would be wholly incomplete, and illusory even, in its result, unless we do so .   Of the outgoings of a railway some are general and have no more connection with or influence on one part of the whole line than any other incurred for the sake of the whole line, and contributing to the profits of everywhere. Of course these must be distributed, and to every mile must be apportioned some share on whatever principle the apportionment is to be settled Some, again, seem merely local, a tunnel here, an inclined plane there—we purposely mention striking and definite peculiarities—yet even these are contributing to the earnings everywhere, without these the traffic on

[1] (1852) 15 Q B 1085 7 Rail Cas 130. 21 L J M C 84

either side would have had no existence. It would be wrong to set these wholly and exclusively against the receipts earned in the same part of the line We need not dwell on this, because in principle some distribution is agreed on all hands to be necessary, the only difficulty is in determining what mode is to be adopted for making it justly, a difficulty, we believe, actually insurmountable in fact, if a strict mathematical accuracy were insisted upon It is our business, however, only to lay down the general rule, and in applying it much must be left, not only to the experience and acuteness, but also to the good sense and good faith and candour of the parties concerned, whose interests will be found, in the end, best consulted by this mode of dealing   .   How, then, are the deductions from total gross revenue, which constitute the difference between it and the total net rateable value, to be apportioned so as to arrive at the actual sum which constitutes the rateable value of the two and a half miles?

" There is no difficulty in giving the first answer : indeed principle and authority leave us no option, it must be done by acting on what is called the parochial principle We are dealing with a parochial question, with one in which the several parishes on a line are quite distinct We are to ascertain what expenses are incurred in earning the gross receipts on the two miles and a half, what charges, parochial or otherwise, they are liable to what is fairly to be deducted for tenant's profits, and so on The same process is to be gone through, with reference to the two miles and a half, as would be with regard to the whole line, if that were all in one parish

" This principle does not preclude a consideration of charges and expenses, whenever arising locally, which are necessary for keeping the subject of assessment at the value which is to make the measure of that assessment, and further, we must add that, whenever it is found that

such charges and expenses do, in fact, apply equally to
every mile of railway, it is a convenient and allowable
mode to arrive by a mileage division at the proportional
part to be assigned to the miles in any particular parish
This is no departure from the parochial principle. If it
be assumed, as to particular charges (general superintendence, for instance), that a separate investigation of them
as they actually arise in, or are referable to, a particular
parish, would lead us to a same result as a mileage distribution of the whole, it becomes, by the hypothesis, but
another mode of arriving at it. In many cases it would
be more convenient and just; in some, perhaps, it may be
the only practical mode.

" The mode adopted by the respondents is now to be
considered The case finds that having ascertained the
rateable value of the whole railway, minus the stations,
they ascertained the gross annual receipts of the appellants in respect of each mile, or portion of a mile, of
railway in their parish, and they assessed the appellants
in respect of the two miles and a half in the ratio which
such annual receipts bore to the gross annual receipts of
the company in respect of the entire Great Western
Railway, trunk and branches, the rateable value of a mile
of railway in the respondents parish being calculated in
the same proportion to the rateable value of the whole
line, exclusive of the stations, as the gross actual annual
receipts in respect of such mile bore to the total annual
receipts of the company

" Before we consider the general principles here stated,
we should notice in passing, the term ' trunk and
branches' in the plural. This is the only place in the
case in which the plural ' branches' is used We do
not know whether this was intentional or not; if it were,
as we are not informed of any circumstances relating to
the other branch or branches, we cannot say whether it
or they ought to have been amalgamated with the trunk

for the present purpose, but, passing this by, it appears
the respondents have taken the deductions at the same
rate for every mile of railway, for they say, as the gross
receipts of one mile are to the gross receipts of the whole,
so the rateable value of one mile is to the rateable value
of the whole   This is, in effect, to strike off from the
gross receipts of a mile an aliquot part of the sum which
is struck off from the gross receipts of the whole, and
assumes, at least, that the expenses are at one uniform
rate throughout the whole line   If the case was silent on
this subject, we might have assumed this to be the fact,
and then there would have been no objection to a mileage
division, but the case, reasonably understood, excludes
this, for it finds that the actual expenses of the company
are not in the proportion of the actual gross receipts,
either on the branch or throughout the entire railway,
nor are either such gross receipts, or such expenses, at
one uniform rate per mile throughout the entire railway.
The counsel for the respondents laboured in vain to
explain away the clear meaning of this passage, and,
failing that, they equally laboured in vain to show that
all the expenses on a railway were necessarily to be distributed in the calculations equally over the whole line "

In the great Haughley case[1] heard in 1866, this same
point was before the Courts. Here the respondents contended that there was an additional portion of the profits
beyond those actually earned in Haughley properly
attributable to the occupation in Haughley, and, therefore, to be taken into account in ascertaining the rateable
value. They contended that, in respect of that portion of
the traffic which passes not only over the line in Haughley but also over other portions of the line, there should
be participation in all the profits earned, and, therefore,
inasmuch as the same traffic is carried at much greater

[1] *Great Eastern Railway Co v Haughley*, (1866) L R 1 Q B 666, 95
L J M C 229, 14 L T 548, 30 J P 438

profit over other portions of the line where traffic is much greater than in Haughley, yet each part of the line may be regarded as contributing to earn those additional profits. The amount of contribution which the respondents insisted upon was based upon the mileage in Haughley, as they contended that in respect of the same traffic passing over any portions of the line, each mile over which it passes must be considered as participating equally in the profits earned by that traffic, or, in other words, as earning a proportionate part of them

Cockburn, C J , in delivering judgment, said

"There is a through traffic from London to Norwich, and beyond Haughley, on the road to London, there is a large accession to this traffic Now it is said by Mr Field that the effect of this additional traffic is to reduce the expenditure with respect to each individual traveller, so that, supposing him to have started from Norwich, the expense of his carriage through the parish of Haughley must be lessened by taking into account the diminished expense of conveying him upon other parts of the line on the way to London But I do not think that the expenses of the line to be rated ought to be calculated with reference to the cost of conveying passengers The working expenses of the whole of the traffic between Norwich and London ought to be ascertained, and a proportionate part of these expenses must then be apportioned to the traffic in Haughley The cost of carrying a passenger may vary upon different parts of the line, but the working expenses may still be after a uniform rate This may be illustrated by the case of the old stage-coaches The expense of running a stage-coach between Norwich and London was so much per mile, with hardly any variation. Sometimes there were five passengers, sometimes fifteen. If there were five passengers. the coach ran at a loss, if there were fifteen, its journey was a profitable one So, also, with

Stage-coach illustration

this railway; when it is being worked from Norwich to
Haughley, the profit is likely to be less than when it is
being worked along those parts of the line beyond
Haughley, where there is received a large addition to the
passengers and traffic, so that the rest of the journey is
lucrative and profitable   There is also this fallacy
in Mr Field's argument, for, according to him, the
working expenses of the line rated are to be got at by
taking into account the profits of the additional traffic
beyond Haughley, and not the mere working expenses of
this traffic   These profits, whether by accident or not,
are acquired without and beyond the parish of Haughley,
and they cannot be rated as belonging to that parish '

There is another leading case on this important subject,
viz., *Manchester, Sheffield and Lincolnshire and Trent,
Ancholme and Grimsby Railway Cos v Caistor Union,*[1]
the judgment in which was delivered as follows   "The
Appleby portion of this company's line is three miles, six
furlongs and three chains long, and its rateable value
is assessed at £1,851, and the Appleby station at £50,
station and line together having been previously rated at
£300   The assessment has been made in the usual
manner by ascertaining the gross receipts of the parochial
portion of line, and after deducting working expenses
and profits and all outgoings allowed by Statute, assuming
the remainder to be the rent or net annual value to let of
the land and buildings   The first question here is whether
the gross receipts have not been understated by the
company by their having deducted in the case of
merchandise traffic the amount charged at each end for
collection and delivery   The receipts for the whole line,
in 1872, averaged £1,855 per mile, but according to the
company, in Appleby parish the average per mile was
only £1,448   We do not see why the receipts in this
parish should have been so considerably below the general

---
[1] (1874) 2 Nev & Mac 53

average As to through traffic, the receipts brought to account half-yearly would be mileage receipts only, and would include no station or cartage terminals due to other companies, and as regards other traffic the company admit that they perform no cartage Every mile may not have equally contributed to the earnings of the whole line, but those earnings seem to us in a case like this a better criterion of the receipts due to the portion in the parish than taking a mileage division of the gross rates, less the amount charged at each end for collection and delivery We also think that whatever part of a goods' rate covers ordinary station work at a terminus should all be taken to be receipts of the line to which the terminal station belongs We understood it to be contended that where less than half the transit is on the local line part of its terminal should, for rating purposes, be deemed to be earned on the foreign line , but we think that what would belong to the local line for other purposes should be treated as belonging to it in a question of rating

Terminals

"The next difference has reference to the deduction to be made from the gross receipts for working expenses and tenant's profits The working stock of this line is provided by the Manchester, Sheffield and Lincolnshire Company, who, until June, 1872, were paid by the rate of 1s 1d per train mile, but since then have been paid by a percentage of $33\frac{1}{2}$ upon the total traffic receipts The amount they received in 1872 was £7,254 The respondents contend that this sum should be taken as the aggregate amount of the expenses for locomotive power, and repairs of carriages and waggons, and relative services, and be divided amongst the parishes according to the train miles run in each, and moreover that, as the hypothetical tenant would not in this case require any capital for working stock, no deduction should be made from the gross receipts for profits on capital The company, on the other hand, would ignore the amount actually paid to the

Deduction for working expenses

Manchester and Sheffield Company, and then multiply the number of train miles run in Appleby by the cost per train mile of the total locomotive expenses, and total carriage and waggon repairs of the Manchester and Sheffield Company as given in their printed accounts, and maintain that the product is the proper deduction to be made for such working expenses. They claim, further, to have it assumed that the tenant would require a capital bearing the same proportion to the number of train miles run in Appleby as the capital of the Manchester and Sheffield Company bears to the train mileage of their entire system, and that the deduction for tenant's profits should be at the rate of 20 per cent. upon the assumed capital. We think as to this difference that the respondents are right. Admitting that the Manchester and Sheffield Company might at any time withdraw their rolling stock, still, during the ten years the line has been open for traffic, it has never been worked in any other way, and we think that the supposed tenant, calculating his probable out-goings in the year commencing with the prospective period for which the rate is made, might reckon that the working of the line would continue to be provided for as before. For the same reason, there should be no deduc-

Distinction between tenant's profits and profits on capital

tion for profits on capital, but as an occupancy should yield profit of some kind, which profit in this case may be calculated either upon the gross receipts or upon the value of the rolling stock, we think there should be a deduction for tenant's profits as distinct from profits on capital, and that the amount should be 5 per cent upon the gross receipts, such percentage to cover outlay on floating capital, stores, furniture and the like.

" The deduction for traffic charges, general charges and compensation should, in our opinion, be what the respon-dents propose. We need not stop to notice the small differences between the parties in the items of government duty, rateable value of stations, law charges and the amount per pound of the rates and taxes in Appleby, and we come to the only remaining difference, which is as to the amount to be deducted for maintenance and renewal of the permanent way and works The respondents at first would only allow £584 for both maintenance and renewal for the whole distance in the parish, but at the hearing they admitted such an amount to be inadequate, and proposed instead that £726 should be allowed for maintenance and £524 for renewal These sums do not differ much from the sums claimed by the company, which are £812 for maintenance and £630 for renewal. The difference is partly due to this, that the respondents calculate the cost per train mile of the repairs to way and works by the amount expended on the whole Trent line as shown in the Trent Company's published accounts, while the company make the calculation by the amount they find by their books to have been expended on the Brigg Union Considering that the whole of this line, except three quarters of a mile, is in the Brigg Union, and that the half-yearly accounts printed and distributed to the shareholders are the only documents to which both sides have equal facilities of access, we think the mode of calculation adopted by the respondents is in this case to be preferred

" We will next proceed to the appeal of the Manchester, Sheffield and Lincolnshire Railway Company from the valuation made of their property by the Caistor Union The main line of this company runs through the parish of Stallingborough for a distance of two miles and eight chains The gross receipts in the parish, ascertained by dividing the gross rates by mileage between the forwarding and receiving stations, after deducting, in the case of merchandise traffic, the amount charged at each end for collection and delivery, come, according to the company, to £4,447 per mile The respondents object to this mode of calculating the receipts from merchandise as too

favourable to the company. We see no objection to it
where a deduction for cartage is made by the clearing
house, but for local traffic it was not shown to us that the
allowance the clearing house make for cartage, as between
different railway companies, is added to the goods rate
and ought to be regarded as an extra, not chargeable to
land, but referable to the trade of a carrier by road, and
we think that, as regards local traffic in Stallingborough,
only what the company expend in carting goods carried at
carted rates, and a reasonable profit thereon, should be
taken off the gross rate. We have no means of knowing
whether that mode of ascertaining the receipts would
make the total sum in Stallingborough differ from the
company's estimate of it.

Working
expenses

" Coming next to the working expenses incurred in the
parish in earning the gross receipts to be credited to it,
we have, in the first place, to consider the difference
between the respondents and the company as to the
expense for carriage and waggon repairs The company
divide their total outlay on that head of charge by the
gross number of train miles run on their own lines, excluding mileage on the lines of other companies, and the
product multiplied by the number of train miles run in
Stallingborough gives the expense, as they estimate it, of
this item in the parish The respondents, on the other
hand, refer to the company's half-yearly accounts, showing the train miles run in 1872, including ballasting and
mileage run for other companies, to have been 6,214,608,
and excluding the same, 4,719,629 only—a difference of
nearly one million and a half, and they claim that the
divisor of the sum expended by the company in 1872,
in repairs to carriages and waggons should be the mileage
of 6,214,608, instead of the smaller one taken by the
company The company admit that the six million and
odd miles are the right divisor to find locomotive cost,
but they say that their engines draw other rolling stock

on the lines of other companies, admitting at the same time that their own carriages and waggons do, to some extent, run on other lines So far as they do, they increase their wear and tear, and, therefore, the miles they run should be added to the divisor ; but as the company could not give the number of these miles, we think the number may be taken approximately at one-fifth of the difference of the two mileage totals 'rent of shops' follows 'repairs of carriages and waggons' as a working expense in the amended schedule of the company The deduction was not insisted upon, and we propose to omit it "

This judgment is given at great length, as it is perhaps the best one dealing with so many various points in the valuation of a railway

It will be seen, therefore, that there are certain expenses which are to be deducted on the parochial principle and others on the mileage principle, the division is briefly as follows —Those on the parochial principle are the locomotive expenses, passenger and goods, which are, to a certain extent, regulated by the number of train miles. and the carriage and waggon expenses, which are also estimated by the same method, and the Government duty, those on the mileage principle (or in proportion to the whole) are the miscellaneous expenses including the general charges—that is, the expenses of management, the law charges, traffic expenses, etc The rates and taxes are deducted as they occur in the parish for which the valuation is made, but care must be taken to deduct the proper amount which the company must pay on the valuation as finally settled These points are more fully explained later on

These deductions having been made, the result will be the "gross profits" of the undertaking So much with regard to the expenses of a railway company

What expenses to be deducted on the parochial principle and what on the mileage principle

With regard to a gas, water, electric power company, etc., the expenditure is briefly as follows

Expenses of
gas, water
company, etc

> The pumping and engine charges, including the cost of coal, wages, etc
>
> Filtration, including the cost of materials and labour.
>
> The manufacture of gas or electric power.
>
> The distribution of gas or electric power.
>
> Salaries of engineers, superintendents, inspectors and clerks, and wages of turncocks.
>
> Salaries of telephone operators
>
> Dues to a river conservancy, if any, from which water is obtained
>
> Rates and taxes, exclusive of income tax.
>
> Allowance to directors
>
> Allowance to company's auditors
>
> Salaries of secretary, accountant and office clerks
>
> Stationery, printing and general establishment charges
>
> Parliamentary and law charges
>
> Auditing

Deductions
for stations
and dead
works

Then to return to the case of a railway company, the rental of the stations has to be deducted, as we are for the present only making a valuation of the line This amount is arrived at by obtaining the gross values of the stations over the whole system, then the same percentage as the total of such gross values bears to the total receipts of the whole system is the deduction to be made in the parish from the parochial receipts. The deduction generally made ranges between 5 and 9 per cent. The rates paid on the stations are also permissible deductions, but, in the absence of the actual figures, which can only be supplied by the company at great trouble and expense, an estimate must be made.

In the case of a gas or water company the corresponding deduction is necessary with regard to the dead works, as it must always be borne in mind that the valuations of the so-called live and dead portions of the undertaking are to be kept separate.

The foregoing deductions having been made the net receipts of the concern are arrived at, these are divisible between landlord and tenant The next item therefore for our consideration is the share of the profits of the undertaking due to the tenant.

In the management of large public companies (such as railway, gas and water, etc.), assuming—as has to be done in making a valuation—that the property could be let to a tenant, there would be two capitals employed, the one belonging to the hypothetical landlord and the other to the hypothetical tenant, or, in other words, the property as owned by the landlord would consist, in the case of a railway company, of the line of railway, the sidings and stations, the tenant having to provide the necessary stock, etc, to work the concern This would include the rolling stock, i e, engines, waggons, carriages, coal-trucks, horse-boxes, etc., tarpaulins and sacks, horses and harness, and the necessary tenant's stores, such as fodder, lamps and oil, etc   Furniture and fittings at stations would also be an item, and the non-rateable machinery and tools A prudent tenant, again, would always have a sum of money at the bank, and this would be an allowable sum to be included in his capital The question of arriving at the value of these various items is one of considerable importance, inasmuch as the chances of a railway company letting its property to a tenant are extremely rare, and one point which would naturally arise in making a valuation on the basis of a hypothetical tenancy would be whether the forenamed constituents of the tenant's capital should be taken at their prime cost, i e, when new, or at their present value as second-hand. This point came before the Courts in 1860,[1] and the following is an extract from the special case

[1] R v North Staffordshire Railway Co, (1860) 3 El & El 392, 30 L J M C 68, 7 Jur N S 363, 3 L T 5   9 W R 235

Tenant's capital

" The rolling stock of the company, which included all the locomotive engines, tenders, passenger-carriages, horse-boxes, carriage-trucks, luggage vans, goods, cattle, and mineral waggons, and all other vehicles of every kind for conveyance of persons, cattle, animals, goods, wares, minerals, merchandise or other articles, matters or things whatsoever on the railway, cost the company the sum of £356,843, and for the purpose of this case it is admitted that this was a fair price at the time the articles constituting the rolling stock were purchased, and also that similar articles would at the time of laying the rate have cost as much

" In addition to this stock, the company has been obliged to provide, at a cost of £52,950, turn-tables, cranes, weighing-machines, stationary steam-engines, lathes, electric telegraph and apparatus, office and station furniture, and gas works used for supplying the stations with gas The turn-tables and some of the weighing-machines are affixed to the freehold by means of an iron bolt inserted in a large stone sunk in the land The lathes and steam-engines are connected with the building in which they are placed by means of iron bolts The electric telegraph consists, *first*, of posts driven into the ground ; *secondly*, of wires passed through sockets annexed to such posts, but which wires may be disconnected from the posts without injury or displacing them ; *thirdly*, of the electrifying machines, which are in no way affixed to the freehold The gas works consist partly of buildings and partly of gasometers, retorts, and the other usual plant for making gas, and of the pipes for conveying the same from the works to the railway stations. The other weighing-machines, which are all used for the purpose, of the traffic on the line, and the office and station furniture are unconnected with the freehold. Beyond these amounts of capital, the company allege—and for the purposes of this case it may be admitted to be the fact—that it has been found necessary, in carrying on the traffic and business of the railway, that the company should have in hand, at command, a sum of money, by way of floating capital, for the purpose of providing surplus stores (such as rails, sleepers, etc) to be used in case of accident on the line or other emergency, and partly in paying the wages of porters pointsmen and others, servants of the company, and in the other current expenses of the line, which are for the most part paid weekly, or at short periods whilst it is found necessary to give credit to some of the goods-traffic customers of the company to a large amount and for various periods

"The traffic over the whole of the company's line of railway is worked under a contract between the company and the contractors, which contract, it has been agreed, shall form part of the case

"The total amount of the deductions made by the company from the contractors, at the time when the rates were made, in respect of the depreciation of the rolling stock and plant in the hands of the contractors was £17,000, which sum would not be more than sufficient to restore the said rolling stock and plant to its original value, but which, it is admitted, has not been expended in such restoration.

"The company have also expended in the erection of their stations, buildings and sidings the sum of £350,000.

"The respondents contend that the deduction to be allowed in respect of interest on capital and tenant's profits ought to be ascertained by taking, as the capital sum upon which such interest and profits ought to be calculated, the actual or depreciated value of the rolling stock at the time the rates were made, and that no allowance for interest and tenant's profits should be made in respect of a floating capital

"The respondents also contend that the deduction to be allowed in respect of the turn-tables, cranes, weighing-

R v N Stamford Railway is to tenant's capital

i 2

machines, stationary steam-engines, lathes, electric telegraph apparatus, gas works, stations, buildings and sidings,
ought to b ascertained by taking the amount at which
they are collectively assessed ¦to the relief of the poor in
the several parishes and townships within which the same
are severally situate, and dividing the nd amount amongst
each parish and township in a certain proportion agreed
upon between the said respondents and the appellants

"The appellants contend that they are entitled to
claim, as the proper deduction in respect of interest on
capital and tenant's profits, the percentage amount of
the said capital sums of £356,843, £52,950, and the
floating capital

"They also contend that the proper deduction to be
allowed in respect of all the stations, buildings and
sidings is £6 per cent per annum (which is a moderate
rate of interest for money invested in buildings) upon the
original cost of construction, and to take the annual
amount so ascertained as the value to be deducted   And
it is agreed, with reference to this head of deduction, that
the original cost of construction of the whole of such
stations, buildings, and sidings was £360,000.

Questions for
the Court as
to deductions
for tenant's
capital

"The questions for the opinion of this Court are —
First, whether the percentage amount to be allowed for
interest on capital and tenant's profits is to be calculated
upon the capital invested in the rolling stock taken at its
cost price, or upon the depreciated value of the rolling
stock as estimated at the time when the rates were made,
or at any other time, secondly, whether the appellants
are entitled to a deduction for interest on capital and
tenant's profits upon the said sum of £52,950, the
additional amount of capital invested in turn-tables,
cranes, weighing machines, stationary steam-engines,
lathes, electric telegraph and apparatus, office and station
furniture and gas works, or upon any and what portion
of such items, and, if so, whether upon the sum originally

invested in the said plant, or upon the depreciated value
of the same, estimated at the time the rates were made,
or at any other time, or how otherwise, a deduction, if
any, should be made in respect of the last-mentioned
plant, or in respect of any part thereof; thirdly, whether
the appellants are entitled to a further deduction for
interest and tenant's profits, or either, upon the said
floating capital"

Cockburn, C J, who delivered judgment, said.—

"The first question is, whether the percentage amount
to be allowed for interest on capital and tenant's profits is
to be calculated upon the cost price of the rolling stock
or on the depreciated value which that stock may bear at
the time the rate is actually made? We are of opinion
that the allowance must be made with reference to the
actual, and not to the original, value

"The point has already been decided by this Court
in the case of R v. The Great Western Railway
Co,[1] in which decision we entirely concur   In addition
to the reasons given in the judgment of the Court in that
case, it may be observed that, under the Parochial
Assessment Act,[2] tenant's profits upon stock must necessarily be calculated with a view to their deductions from
the gross earnings, in order to ascertain what a tenant
would give for the entire property   Nothing could be
more inconvenient than that a different principle should
prevail in calculating the profits in the two cases

"Now the question, when considered under the Parochial Assessment Act,[2] must be looked at, not with reference to the railway company, who may have expended on
the purchase of the stock a much larger sum than such
stock would now realise, but with reference to an incoming tenant, and the amount of capital which such tenant
would have to lay out in the purchase of the rolling stock

[1] (1816) 4 New Sess. Cas. 205, 6 Q B. 179, 15 L J M C 80, 10 Jur 134
[2] (1896) 6 & 7 William IV, c 96

necessary to carry on the undertaking It is obvious that
what it would be worth the while of a person or company
about to embark in a commercial undertaking to give as
rent for the premises in which it was to be carried on
would depend on the amount to be deducted, in addition
to repairs and other necessary outgoings, from the gross
earnings in respect of the profits due to the capital to be
employed in the concern. But it is plain that a tenant
would calculate such profits on the amount of capital
actually required to be expended on the stock, not on
what may have been the value of the stock at some other
time, or in other hands Now it must be assumed that
the stock in its existing condition is sufficiently effective
to produce the earnings which, after the necessary deductions, constitute the improved value of the railway, and
it cannot reasonably be supposed that, if the company
were about to give up the undertaking, they would not be
willing to part with their stock at its actual value, or that,
if they refused to do so, the incoming tenant could not
procure other stock of an equally efficient character, at
its real value, to supply the deficiency In estimating
therefore, under the 6 & 7 William IV, c 96, what a
tenant would pay, the profits must be calculated on the
actual value of the stock. It cannot be supposed that in
exempting profits under the 6 & 7 Vict, c 48, a different
principle of calculation was intended to be acted on

Actual not
original value
of the stock to
be deducted

"The second question is, whether the company are
entitled to a deduction in respect of various articles
therein specified, being things necessary for carrying on
the business of the company? The articles to which such
a question may have reference may be divided into three
classes first, things moveable, such as office and station
furniture, secondly, things so attached to the freehold as
to become part of it; and, thirdly, things which, though
capable of being removed, are yet so far attached as that
it is intended that they shall remain permanently

connected with the railway or the premises used with it, and remain permanent appendages to it, as essential to its working   It is clear that in respect of the first class of articles a deduction should be allowed.   It is equally clear that no deduction should be allowed as to the second   As to the third, the question is finally settled by the decision of this Court in the case of *R* v *The Southampton Dock Co*[1]

" The third question, whether the company are entitled to a deduction in respect to the floating capital therein referred to, is one of considerable nicety, and which, as it appears to us, must depend on whether, on the whole capital employed, a greater delay occurs in realising the returns than is ordinarily incidental to the employment of capital   No doubt, as the rent which the imaginary tenant contemplated by the Parochial Assessment Act could afford to pay would be the difference between the gross earnings (after the necessary deductions) and the amount of profits due (reference being had to the nature of the undertaking) on the capital employed, whatever tends to diminish such profits must go, *pro tanto*, to diminish the rent   Any delay in realising the profits beyond such as is generally incidental to the ordinary employment of capital may, therefore (as it must be presumed that it would be taken into account by the tenant) be fairly taken into account in determining the rateable value   On the other hand, it must be observed that, as a very large proportion of the earnings of a railway company is of a ready money character, it may well be that when the whole of the capital and of the earnings are taken into account, the profits on the whole capital may be realised in a shorter time in this species of undertaking than in the average of commercial enterprises.   If this should be the case, the delay in realising the profits which might

[1] (1851) 14 Q B 587, 6 Rul Cas 128, 15 Jui 268, 20 L J M C 155, 15 J P 145

arise as to a part of the capital might well be considered to be compensated by the more than ordinary quickness of the return of the rest   We have no means before us of determining the question with reference to this view of the case.   We can do no more than point out the principle by which we think it must be determined "

It having been laid down in the above judgment that the actual present value of the rolling stock is to be taken in calculating the tenant's capital and not the prime cost, the next course is to ascertain this value   In the published accounts of a railway company there is a return of the working stock (and from this can be obtained the particulars of the rolling stock) under the three headings — Locomotive, Coaching, and Merchandise and Mineral   Assuming, for the purpose of argument, that this stock is all new, no depreciation would be allowed, but as this would practically never be the case, a certain amount of depreciation has to be allowed.   This varies considerably and must be left to the judgment of the surveyor who undertakes the valuation, but as some guide may be mentioned the case of the *Manchester, Sheffield, Lincolnshire and Trent, Ancholme and Grimsby Railway Cos v. Caistor Union*,[1] where the respondents contended for a reduction of 30 per cent as depreciation, but the Railway Commissioners, who heard the case, were of opinion that the stock would be kept up nearer than this to its original value, and they allowed a reduction of 20 per cent only   This, however, must vary in every case, as evidenced by the fact that in a later case, namely that of the *London and North Western Railway Co v Wigan Union*[2] heard before the same Commission, one of the agreed figures between the litigants was the value of rolling stock, and also the amount of depreciation at 12½ per cent.   Here, again, this amount

Depreciation
of stock

[1] (1874) 2 Nev & Mac 53   See p 108 ante
[2] (1876) Ibid 210

would be wholly insufficient in such a case as the Great Western Railway, where so much of the original capital sunk in the rolling stock was lost by the conversion of the line from the broad gauge to the narrow gauge

With regard to the tarpaulins, horses and harness the *Live stock* same rule would apply, but the question of horses is one which is not easily dealt with, as some stock of this nature must improve in value rather than decrease, whilst, on the other hand, upon the death of live stock the value is gone This, however, is not a big item, and can only be left to the discretion of the parties concerned

Then as to the stores, the published accounts will give *Stores* the stores on hand at the date of the account, generally under the following headings—General Stores, Permanent Way Stores and Locomotive Stores These will include all tools and the like, and it may be fairly assumed that the average amount on hand at the time of the publication of the accounts for a period of any three years would be a fair value to allow, though in many cases only two-thirds of this amount and sometimes only a half is allowed, this, again, is a matter for the discretion of the parties interested A deduction has next to be made for the tenant's furniture and fittings at the various stations *Furniture at* throughout the system, and in several recent cases the *stations* actual cost of these articles has been ascertained so that the true percentage of the gross receipts of the whole system is arrived at, and it becomes only a matter of arithmetic to apply it to any individual parish, it is usually calculated upon a percentage of the receipts

We now come to the amount of capital which a tenant would require to have on hand for any exigencies which might happen, such as long credit, accidents, etc The former in the case of a railway company may be small, in addition to which it always has on hand a certain amount of deposits from season ticket holders.

In the chapters on "Practice" will be found a valuation in full of a railway company, and in it an example of a tenant's capital is fully set out   For the present we will assume that we have arrived at a figure agreed upon by all parties.   The next point for consideration is the percentage to be allowed on this capital, which has to be deducted at the point of the valuation at which we have arrived, namely, the amount divisible between the landlord and tenant   Here is a most important question, and the cases that have been contested upon the subject are very numerous.   A hypothetical tenant having money at his disposal would, of course, if he so chose, be at liberty to invest the same in any Government Stock, or, in other words, any person having money can always obtain a certain rate of interest upon it by lending same to the Government   This having the advantage of being the greatest security possible, a tenant would at least expect to realise an equal, or even a larger amount, from an investment not equally well secured   In addition to this he would expect to make trade profits and also be allowed a sum for the risk which accompanies the financing of a large trading concern, together with a percentage for the insurance and renewal of his stock, which has to be deducted whether the tenant actually insures or not.   There are three percentages, therefore, to be taken upon the tenant's capital, and to be considered as a deduction from the gross receipts   They are, briefly, interest on capital sunk, trade profits from the concern and a sum to cover the risks which would be incurred through accident, strikes, or other contingencies.   The first is more or less regulated according to the current rate of interest for money always having regard, however, to the nature of the security, so that it is difficult to lay down a rule, however, for this purpose we will assume that 5 per cent should be allowed.   The next item is the percentage for trade profits   This also varies, and one cannot lay down an invariable rule, all that can be done is to give the various amounts allowed in a few cases and to recommend the reader to refer to them, so that he can judge for himself the particular bearing which each case has upon the question. Perhaps the first of these cases before the Court of Queen's Bench, was *R v The South London Railway Co*,[1] heard in 1842.

An allowance was here made of 20 per cent for tenant's profits, but this seems to be an exceptionally high rate and cannot be taken as a criterion, as the case was contested altogether on a point of law, the facts being agreed by the parties. In the case of *R v. The Great Western Railway Co*[2] four years later, 10 per cent was the amount allowed by the Court, and a decision by the Railway Commissioners in the year 1874 in the Sheffield and Lincolnshire case[3] placed the amount also at 10 per cent. And again, in the case of *The London and North Western Railway v Wigan Union*[4] 10 per cent was allowed. This case was heard before the Railway Commissioners, and the following is an extract from their judgment: "The next question is what percentage shall be allowed for profit, the railway company claiming 20 per cent, and the respondents contending that 10 per cent. will be quite sufficient, interest, profit and deterioration included. Of the 20 per cent in the company's claim, one-fourth is for deterioration, risk and insurance, to cover any contingent loss of capital from those causes, and against this we think the Union are entitled to a partial set-off in the circumstances that the expenses for locomotive power and for carriage and waggon repairs paid out of revenue provide for additions and improvements to rolling stock,

[1] (1842) 2 G & D 49, 1 Q B 558, 11 L J M C 93, 2 Rail Cas 629, 6 Jur 686

[2] (1846) 2 New Sess Cas 205, 6 Q B 179, 15 L J M C 80, 10 Jur 134

[3] 2 Nev & Mac 53

[4] (1876) *Ibid* 240

the gain from which will compensate the tenant for any loss from deterioration. We infer this from the fact that, while the total charge to capital for working stock to December, 1874, is £6,929,862, the agreed value in 1874 exceeds nine millions. Another matter to be considered in fixing the percentage has reference to the value put upon the rolling stock. That value is a high one compared with the amount at which the stock stands in the capital account, and high also in relation to the earnings of that stock in the Wigan Union, the coal receipts in private waggons forming a considerable part of the gross earnings. While, therefore, we shall allow the company 15 per cent. for interest and profits, we think the further 5 per cent. claimed by the company should be reduced to 2 per cent., making 17 per cent. the total allowance."

The 15 per cent. allowed was made up of 5 per cent. for interest, which we have dealt with in the preceding pages, and 10 per cent. for tenant's profits. This may be taken as a fair guide, although, as has been pointed out before, there can be no rule to govern such a contingency.

The next item is the percentage to be allowed for the insurance of the capital against risks and casualties. As it will be seen in the case just referred to, only 2 per cent. was allowed, but this is rather low, as, notwithstanding the few accidents that actually occur on a railway company, the risk is necessarily great; and in addition to this, there is the risk of loss of trade which is included in the figure, a prudent tenant having to provide for this. It may be taken that $2\frac{1}{2}$ per cent. in the case of a railway company would be a fair sum, and there is less deviation from this figure than in each of the other items.

At the London Quarter Sessions, as far as can be ascertained, the figure of $17\frac{1}{2}$ per cent. as interest to the tenant on his capital sunk in such a concern as a railway seems to have been allowed, as witness the following instances:—

As far back as 1871, in the case of the *South Eastern Railway Co* v *Lewisham*,[1] 17½ per cent was allowed on the whole of the tenant's capital

Then, again, in the case of the *Midland Railway Co* v *St Mary's, Islington*,[2] the same amount was allowed, and again in 1897, in the *London and North Western Railway Co* v *St John's, Hampstead*,[3] the deputy chairman, Mr Loveland-Loveland, K C, in giving judgment, said "We have not departed from the general practice in these Courts of allowing 17½ per cent on what is in our opinion the proper amount of tenant's capital"

In the case of the *South Eastern Railway Co* v. *Dorking Union*,[4] decided before the Surrey Quarter Sessions, the Chairman, delivering the judgment of the Court, said 'It has been the practice hitherto to allow 17½ per cent, and although the figure should not be lightly altered it is not immutable Taking into account all the evidence we have heard, *we* think it right to allow 16½ per cent on tenant's capital all round, including stores, etc We have come to that conclusion after a great deal of consideration, and we are not likely to alter that figure without a good deal more consideration in any future case.' It is interesting to note in this case that the decision was by a Bench of Magistrates where the vote of the majority may or may not have had some effect upon the decision

Another decision on the point, again by a Bench of Magistrates, was that in the case of the *Great Northern Railway* v. *Hitchin Union*[5] His Honour Judge Tindal Atkinson, as chairman of the Court, in delivering

[1] "Ryde's Metropolitan Rating Appeals," p 56
[2] *Ibid*, (1886-1890), p 139
[3] "Ryde and Konstam's Appeals (1894 1904), p 21.
[4] *Ibid*, p 71
[5] "Konstam's Rating Appeals" (1904-1908), p 130

judgment, said upon this point "As to the interest on the capital the majority of the Court are of opinion upon the evidence in the present case that a tenant of the undertaking of the Great Northern Railway is entitled, as against the landlord before he can ascertain what rent he can afford to pay, to a profit of 16½ per cent on his capital   As a matter of business we agree with the evidence of Mr Ryde, and we think that any hypothetical incoming tenant would, as between himself and the landlord, insist on having at least 16½ per cent. on his capital Several reasons may be urged for this conclusion, but in addition to other reasons it may be supported by the facts and circumstances involved in the case now under consideration. The investigation of the figures show that the nett receipts of the line amount to a certain sum, and what, under the circumstances, could the tenant reasonably insist upon and expect to obtain, and the landlord as a reasonable man agree to, as the tenant's share of the profits? The tenant risks his capital, in this case amounting to a very large sum of money viz, £7,180,661. He has to give his labour and skill in the carrying on of the undertaking. He has to face the chances of all kinds of contingencies which might either for a time stop or much impede the profitable working of the line He has to employ an immense number of hands and to bring to bear upon the whole working of a most complicated business great powers of administration and to have sufficient money always available Having once agreed to this rent he has to pay it, whatever may happen, even although for one or more years all profit may be swept away and the line worked at a loss. The embarking of this great amount of money in the working of the line enables the landlord to command a rent incomparably greater than he otherwise could The increased value to the landlord of his land is earned exclusively by the money and labour of the tenant. The landlord is secure of his rent without any appreciable risk. That rent for the land in the Holwell Parish is ascertained by the majority of the Court to be £2,314. What would be the rental value of this strip of land upon an agricultural basis? Then what is the fair division between landlord and tenant? Although competition is an important factor, we have to consider what would be the probable action of an ordinarily prudent person proposing to become tenant of the line, having regard to his own interests and the risks he would have to run. We think any proposed tenant, whoever he might be, would successfully command $16\frac{1}{2}$ per cent., and would refuse to entertain an allowance of only $12\frac{1}{2}$ per cent. on his capital. As we have pointed out, this and a larger percentage has been allowed by most experienced Justices in the country whose knowledge of the world, and rating cases, entitle their opinion to the greatest weight, and it is impossible to suppose they can have arrived at their opinion arbitrarily, and not on any reasonable basis." [1]

It may be again observed that the two decisions referred to with regard to the rating of Railway Companies where the percentage of $17\frac{1}{2}$, practically universally adopted in recent years, has been departed from, have been in appeal cases before a Court of Quarter Sessions where the majority vote of the magistrates may or may not have had an effect upon the decision. Further, a point was urged in the Hitchen case that money could be borrowed at very much cheaper rates than 5 per cent., and that when the $17\frac{1}{2}$ per cent. was fixed, the price of money was considerably more than it was to-day, but this argument would seem to be founded on a fallacy, because the real question to be decided is the amount of interest that would have to be paid when the security offered to an intending lender is not two-thirds of the value

[1] This quotation is from the shorthand notes in the author's possession.

of real estate, as in a mortgage, but consists of chattels, rolling stock, live stock and the like, upon which no margin of security is allowed for depreciation, etc, for it must be assumed that money is borrowed and lent up to the last penny of the total value of the security

In the case of the *North Eastern Railway v. Sculcoates Union*, 16½ per cent was allowed by Sir James Woodhouse who sat as arbitrator in the matter, and gave his decision on 17th February, 1905 [1]

The cases referred to above are all railway cases, and it would seem that the preponderance of opinion is in favour of 17½ per cent, as being the correct amount to apply to tenant's capital

Dealing, however, with gas and similar companies, circumstances are different. Such points as the limitations of dividends enter into the question, but it is sufficient to say here that because 17½ per cent has been applied, with some exceptions, in the case of railway companies, it does not by any means follow that such a sum should be adopted in other trading concerns—it may be more or less as the occasion demands and the facts warrant

Much has been made of a suggestion recently that the London Quarter Sessions are departing from the 17½ per cent hitherto for so long adopted It is founded on a dictum in the judgment of Mr R Wallace, KC, in the case of the *South Metropolitan Gas Co v Woolwich Union, etc* ,[2] where, in delivering judgment to the Court, he said "I want also to say something in regard to the percentage that ought to be allowed on the tenant's capital Again, I decline absolutely to recognise, and I understand that all my colleagues agree, that any percentage is fixed by this Court or any one. The percentage has to be taken into consideration in regard to every particular case, and having regard to all the

From the shorthand notes in the author's possession

2 "Konstam's Rating Appeals" (1904-1908), p 61 .

varying elements which come into each particular case. In a case of this kind, where there is a company, established, progressive, largely receiving its receipts in cash, or within so short a period that it almost amounts to cash, enjoying a monopoly of its own trade by Statute within its district (I do not mean a monopoly against other illuminants, of course), all these are elements to be taken into consideration. We neither name 17½ per cent., nor 15 per cent., nor 12½ per cent., nor any other figure."

This judgment was delivered in the case of a Gas Company, and does not seem to affect the position as already indicated, as it must, of course, be admitted, as before pointed out, that the amount to be allowed a tenant is a question of fact to be determined in every individual case.

With regard to the amount of the tenant's capital of a gas, water, electric power or telephone undertaking, this is not such a difficult item to ascertain; it is made up of the following items, viz., stores, loose plant (i.e., tools, etc.), a certain amount for working expenses, meters, and a cash balance at the bank. With reference to a water undertaking, the rates[1] for water supplied are generally collected in advance, the tenant thus having a certain amount in hand at the beginning of his tenancy, and in the case of a telephone company the subscriptions for the use of the telephone are usually paid in advance. The case is different, however, with a gas or electric undertaking, they having to make the gas or electric current and deliver it to the consumer before obtaining any income, save so far as the introduction of the slot meter system has helped in this respect. To meet these differences, the ratio of the working expenses allowed would be higher in the case of the latter undertakings

Tenant's capital of gas, water, electric power and telephone undertakings

---

[1] The term "rates," commonly used in this sense, is rather a misnomer —it is the sum paid by the consumer to the water company for water bought in the same way that gas or electricity is bought—and has led to a good deal of litigation

than in that of the former. but this will be more fully dealt with in the chapters relating to these undertakings

We have now arrived at the sum which belongs to the landlord as rent for the hereditament, and this in the words of the Act[1] is the "gross value," being the annual rent which a hypothetical tenant might reasonably be expected, taking one year with another, to pay for a property, if the tenant undertook to pay all usual tenant's rates and taxes, and if the landlord undertook to bear the cost of the repairs, insurance and other expenses, if any, necessary to maintain the property in a state to command that rent This being the landlord's share as distinct from that of the tenant, a deduction now has to be made to obtain the rateable value The items of deduction must vary considerably, but the repairs, maintenance and renewal fund would occur under this heading in every case The Act gives a wide scope to the outgoings of the landlord, as in addition to insurance expenses being allowed it provides for other expenses, if any are necessary, to maintain the property in a state to command the rent

It has been seen, in the case of a railway company, that the freehold belonging to the landlord consists of the line of way with its appurtenances, and this part of the property he is required to keep in tenantable repai The statutable deductions in the valuation of a railway company would therefore consist of the maintenance and renewal of the permanent way, and a sum to provide a sinking fund for the landlord's plant. The great difficulty that presents itself is this. The valuation being made for one parish alone, the receipts of that parish may be less than the actual expenditure for maintenance of way, and as the receipts have to be taken on the parochial principle, so must the expenses, we therefore have here an instance of a railway company actually working at a loss. No tenant could be

---

[1] (1896) 6 & 7 William IV, c 96

found for a property of this kind, and at first sight it would appear that there would be no rateable value To carry the parochial principle to its logical conclusion this would be so; but in this case, in practice, an exception to the principle is found, and because of this position it has been argued that the parochial principle is unsound as applied to railway companies Possibly the Royal Commission on Taxation realised this when making the recommendations as dealt with on page 85 ante, but, as stated before, it is not clear that the suggested alteration will work at all equitably. Possibly if the parochial principle as applied to gas and water companies, etc., were applied to railways, viz., that a division of the total rateable value of the whole (except so-called dead works) be made between the various parishes in which the property is situated according to the receipts in each parish, a more equitable result would be obtained, although it has been expressly laid down that this is wrong, but in a very old case This point, however will be dealt with in the special chapter, in Part II, devoted to railways The question of the statutable deductions has been before the Courts many times, but notably in the case of *R. v The London, Brighton and South Coast Railway*[1]

The following is an extract from the special case:— *Deduction for permanent way* " Besides the allowance already made (under the head of ' working expenses ') for the annual cost of keeping the way in a working condition, the appellants further claimed a right to deduct from the amount of the gross earnings of the year such additional sum (besides the annual costs aforesaid) as would countervail the depreciation which takes place in the permanent way (rails, sleepers, etc), so as to maintain the permanent way in a state to command a rent equal to that which the Sessions have assumed to be a fair rent in fixing the assessment The respondents

---

[1] (1851) 15 Q B 313, 6 Rail Cas 410, 20 L J M C 124; 15 Jur 372.

denied the right of the appellants to this deduction   The
Sessions found that the rates in the parish of Croydon
(including the rate which is the subject of the present
appeal) are made in pursuance of the Parochial Assessment Act (6 & 7 William IV , c 96) , that there are in
each rate two columns, one headed 'gross estimated
rental,' the other 'rateable value', and that the sum set
in the latter column opposite to the property rated (being
the sum on which the assessment is made) varies from
that set opposite the same property in the former column,
the sum inserted as the 'rateable value' being that which
the parish officers judge to be the sum which would be
received by the landlord after all the deductions contemplated by the Parochial Assessment Act ; and the sum
inserted as such 'rateable value' in this parish being, on
the average, about one quarter less than the gross estimated rental in the case of buildings, about one-seventh
less in the case of land occupied with farm buildings, and
one-tenth less in the case of land occupied alone   The
Sessions found that the sum of £100 per mile would be
a fit sum to deduct for the purpose of countervailing the
depreciation which takes place in the permanent way, so
as to maintain it in a state to command the rent aforesaid,
supposing the Court should be of opinion that, under the
circumstances, any deduction ought to have been made in
respect thereof.   But, it being proved that the appellants
had never hitherto, in fact, set apart any annual or other
sum out of the earnings of the railway for the purpose of
meeting this depreciation of the permanent way, the
Sessions disallowed the claim of the appellants to this
deduction   If the Court should be of opinion that the
appellants were entitled to this deduction, the Sessions
found that the rate (whether the mileage or the parochial
earnings principle be adopted by the Court) should be
further reduced by the sum of £647 10s "[1]

---

[1] There were three cases before the Court at this time, viz *R* v *The
London, Brighton and South Coast Railway Co* , *R* v *The South
Eastern Railway Co* , and *R* v *The Midland Railway Co* , but only one
judgment was delivered.

Coleridge, L J, in delivering judgment, said "The second question submitted to us is on the right to a deduction from the rateable value, in order to countervail the depreciation which takes place in the value of the permanent way, and to maintain it in a state to command the supposed rent, which is the measure of the assessment. As a general principle, we do not understand the respondents to deny that a deduction for the purpose here stated, and as stated, is proper to be made; the objection which they raise to the particular claim of the company is founded on two circumstances—first, that the proper provision is already made under a head called 'working expenses,' to which we do not agree, secondly, that if more may be at any time necessary, the necessity has not yet arisen, because the company has not yet incurred the expense, nor laid by from their receipts any sum to meet it when it shall arise. This question, under nearly the same circumstances, came before the Court in the case of *R v The Great Western Railway Co*[1] and was decided against the company, but we are desired to review the decision. We there said that we thought such an expense, as distinct from mere annual repair, fell under the same principle, and was an unobjectionable head of deduction when it should either be actually incurred or provided for; but we thought that, as no allowance would be made for annual repairs in any year in which no repairs took place, so none should be made for this annual depreciation in value, unless, at least, there were funds set aside to meet it when it should be thought expedient to do the work of renewal. In that case, too, there was a further circumstance which had some influence on our judgment, and which is not found here, that, whatever expense had been in fact incurred, the company had chosen, rightly or wrongly, at all events conclusively on

---

[1] 2 New Sess Cas , (1846) 6 Q B 179, 203

themselves, to make a charge on their capital, and not on their receipts, converting it therefore into landlord's improvements, rather than tenant's repairs

"The difficulty which we now feel arises from the same fact, that no charge has in fact, either by way of outlay or setting apart, been made on the company's receipts If the depreciation be, as probably it is, both certain and capable of an annual average, though not proper to be, in fact, repaired annually, we think it should be met by laying by a certain sum annually, and that, if the company, in order to swell their dividend, or for any other motive, neglect to do so, they act unlawfully in one or two ways, either they make a dividend which in substance impairs their capital, because they throw a burden on the latter which ought to be deducted from the former (and this is in violation of the 193rd section of their Act), or they cast the whole burden of the heavy restoration of the permanent way on the dividend of some future year, to the manifest injury of the then proprietors and for the unfair benefit of the present body In such case, too, there may possibly arise some difficulty in resisting the claims to be allowed the whole deduction from the rate of the year in which the expense shall be actually incurred, although, it would be manifestly unjust to allow it twice over, first in detail annually and then in the lump This difficulty was met in the argument by instancing the ordinary case of house property, as to which a larger difference is made between 'gross estimated rental' and 'rateable value' than in the case of land, on account of this very annual depreciation of the thing itself, and the necessary prospective restoration, and yet, it was said, you never inquired whether the owner did, in fact, lay by a portion of his annual rent to meet that distant expense.

"We have considered this question with much attention, and upon the whole we think that the company are entitled to a deduction on this head We cannot make a substantial distinction between this and house property, or any other of a perishable nature, which must require renewal And although we think that the company ought to set apart the sum which they claim to deduct, we cannot compel them to do so in this indirect way and we think that, whenever a time shall come for actually making the restoration, they will be stopped from claiming more than that annual deduction which they now insist on, exactly as the landlord could not claim to deduct the expense of restoration made by him of a house The rate, therefore, will be amended by a reduction according to the calculation made by the Sessions in this respect "

There can be no doubt as to the justice of this deduction, but a question arises as to the amount that has to be fixed We have two items, viz , the maintenance of the permanent way and the renewal of the permanent way It must not be forgotten that it is the average annual amount that has to be ascertained, and not the expenses for any one year [1] A case bearing very much upon the question of maintenance and renewal was that referred to in the previous part of this chapter, viz., the *Manchester, Sheffield, Lincolnshire and Trent Railway Cos v Caistor Union* [2] The Railway Commissioners there laid it down that the repairs which would come under the heading of ' working expenses " would not alone be sufficient for maintenance, and as to the amount to be allowed they go on to say " The appellants or company follow a different method as regards at least the items of repairs They have prepared a return of the actual cost of repairs only, excluding renewal, in the Caistor Union, and divide this cost among the twenty-two parishes in the Union in proportion to their train

[1] *R v Hull Dock Co* , (1824) 5 D & R 359, 3 B & C 516.
[2] (1874) 2 Nev & Mac 53

mileage, and as we think this is the better mode in principle, on account of the smaller area, we allow the deduction they claim for repairs of £374 per mile in Stallingborough parish   The company claim in addition a deduction of £168 per mile as the annual cost of renewal, but we are not prepared to allow them a reduction of more than three-fourths of this, or £126 per mile, which we think enough, because repairs and maintenance together did not in 1872 exceed an average of £415 per mile for the company's whole line, and the train miles per mile in Stallingborough, viz, 17,695 were below the average number of train miles per mile for the whole 258 miles of that line "

As a matter of fact, no one could actually gauge the sum of money necessary for the maintenance of any one mile of railway. Cases could be cited without number, but one would be no nearer towards fixing an amount which might be laid down as an invariable rule   The actual expenses, of course, a railway company could give, as the method they have of keeping their accounts would allow this, but then the sum for renewal is so involved with that of maintenance, that it would be almost impossible to separate the two, indeed no one could actually say from an examination of the accounts where maintenance left off and renewal began.   Repair and renewal in point of fact go on simultaneously, and when making a valuation of a railway company an inclusive sum to cover both items is usually estimated.   In ascertaining this amount it must be borne in mind that, although the parochial principle is to be adopted, yet there are certain expenses, such as tunnels and viaducts, which, in spite of being situated in the parish for which the valuation is made, must not be charged wholly to that parish, they are contributing to the earnings everywhere, and, without these, the traffic on either side could have no existence   It will be seen, therefore, that the figure is largely

Where parochial principle not adopted

an estimate, and consequently the amount of train mileage may have considerable bearing upon the question, as where the traffic is heavy the expenses will be greater than where it is light, but not by any means in the same proportion. A rule adopted by some surveyors for finding the sum to be allowed as renewal of way, is to ascertain the cost of the permanent way putting it as lasting for so many years on the 4 per cent table, the life being determined by the amount of traffic passing over it.

With regard to the statutable deductions of a gas, water, electric power or telephone undertaking, there is one difficulty less to contend with than in that of a railway company, for while, on the one hand, in a gas or water undertaking, etc., a valuation must first be made of the whole concern before dividing it into the various parishes of which the assessment is in question, on the other a valuation of a railway company is purely parochial. The items which make up the statutable deductions in the case of a gas undertaking are the repairs and maintenance of the works and plant, including the renewal of retorts, etc., the repairs, maintenance and renewal of mains and services, and a certain sum for a renewal fund of the gasholders, buildings, etc. their value must be obtained, based on the estimate of their average life. The insurance, which is a heavy item has to be calculated on the value of the plant, etc. The statutable deductions attributable to a water undertaking, and indeed, with regard to any similar trading concern, are much the same as those enumerated above, they consist of the maintenance and renewal of the hypothetical landlord's property, i e, the impounding and service reservoirs, filtering beds, works and pipes, the fittings, meters and mains connected with the distribution of the water, and a sum for the renewal and insurance of the buildings, works and plant. These can be invariably ascertained from the company's published accounts, and in

Statutable deductions of gas, water, electric power and telephone undertakings conclusion it is well to call to mind the words of the Judge, who said "It is impossible to be mathematically accurate, but it is my effort only to lay down a general rule, and the applying of it must be left, not only to the experience and acuteness, but also to the good sense, good faith and candour of the parties concerned, whose interest will be found in the end to be best consulted by this mode of dealing", or the recommendation of the Royal Commission on Local Taxation on the subject, that "There must always be some difference of opinion on the question of what a hypothetical tenant might reasonably be expected to pay, but we think it of great importance that valuations of these special properties should be centralised as far as possible and undertaken by the most skilled class of valuers."

Accounts to be taken Assessing undertakings of any kind where receipts and expenses are taken as the basis, the question as to which year's accounts are to be taken often arises. In *R. v. London, Brighton and South Coast Railway*,[1] this point was discussed, and Coleridge, L J, said "Sessions might avail themselves of every light that can be afforded them down to the latest period antecedent to the actual making of the rate in order to bring it to the greatest possible accuracy." It is clear then that the latest published accounts before the making of the rate can be used in evidence. Can those published after the making of the rate but before the hearing of the appeal? This point is not of so great importance outside the Metropolis, where a supplemental valuation list may be made at any time, or the next or any succeeding rate may be appealed against but in the Metropolis, owing to the Quinquennial Valuation it is. In this case, in *South Metropolitan Gas Co v Greenwich Union*[2] in 1893, the last accounts prior to the hearing by the Assessment Committee of the objection were admitted, while in 1906, in the case of the

---

[1] (1851) 15 Q B 313, 6 Rail Cas 410, 20 L J M C 124, 15 Jur 372
[2] "Ryde's Rating Appeals" (1891-1893), p 56

Charing Cross, City and West End Electricity Supply Co v City of London Union,[1] it was decided that the case must proceed on the accounts for the year prior to the valuation, but allowed questions to be put as to the general results of the working of the year of the valuation And in dealing with the Quinquennial Valuation of 1905, in the *South Metropolitan Gas Co v. Woolwich Union and other Assessment Committees,*[2] in which the appellants had based their valuation upon the accounts for the year ending 30th December, 1905, and the respondents the year ending 31st December, 1904, the Court stated they did not limit their view to any particular year.

[1] " Konstam's Rating Appeals " (1904-1908), p 32
[2] Ibid , p 49

CHAPTER VI.

MACHINERY.

PERHAPS there is no subject upon which there has been a greater diversity of opinion than that of the question of the liability of machinery to be rated. The absolute refusal of the Judges of the High Court to lay down a definite method for assessment authorities to follow in taking machinery "into consideration," and the apparently conflicting decisions in some of the cases, largely account for this. Many Bills have been before Parliament having for their object the exemption of all machinery with the exception of the first or primary motive power—that is, engines, boilers, and shafting, and whilst these have repeatedly passed the second reading they have never become law. It is well to trace thoroughly the course of the large number of cases that have been decided before summing up the subject.

First case relating to machinery

The first case relating to machinery would appear to be that of *R* v *St Nicholas, Gloucester*,[1] decided in 1783, where the Corporation of Gloucester were assessed for a weighing machine and office combined, the machine being of a large type for the purpose of weighing carts, etc. It was here held that the machine and house *comprised one hereditament*, and whereas it was sought to exclude the machine and only assess the house, the Court were of opinion that the machine was the important subject of rating and that the house formed only a shelter for it, consequently it was correct to include the value of the machine in the rateable value of the property. This case it is believed has never been overruled, and appears to be

---

[1] (1783) 1 T R 723

most reasonable, for a hypothetical tenant might reasonably say to a hypothetical landlord, " I cannot use this machine to profitable advantage without a machine house ", or on the other hand, " The house would be useless to me without the machine " The case would appear to form the whole foundation of the question of the rating of machinery, although it is submitted that under the Act of Elizabeth machinery would probably be rateable in former times as stock-in-trade, and this up to as recently as the year 1840, when stock-in-trade became exempt.

The next case of importance, four years later, is that of *R* v *Hogg*,[1] in the year 1787, where it was held that a house containing what is known as a carding engine, used for separating cotton in its raw state in the process of its manufacture, which with the house was rented as one entire property, was rateable, although the engine was not fixed in any way and could be worked by hand It is clear in this case that the premises were let as an engine house containing a carding engine, at an inclusive rent Therefore, if the carding engine had been removed the premises would have ceased to be a carding engine house , and although personal property was rateable at this time, this decision now holds good from the fact that the description in the valuation list was " an engine house," and as such it would appear from the case already quoted, of *R* v. *St Nicholas, Gloucester*,[2] that the engine house without the engine would probably have had no value

In 1837, in the case of *R* v *The Birmingham and Staffordshire Gas Light Co* ,[3] in which objection was taken to a rate because in the valuation certain houses in which steam engines and other machines were affixed had been

[1] 1 T R 721
[2] (1783) 1 T R 723
[3] (1837) 6 A & E 634

valued without reference to the steam engines and machinery. Lord Denman, C J, said: " This rate is bad on a ground which makes it unnecessary for us to discuss any other It is expressly found that houses to which machinery is attached are not rated according to the increased value arising from the machinery. Such machinery constitutes a mode of occupying, that really is clear from the beginning to the end of all the cases on the subject This principle has never been called in question, and, even where the machine has not been attached, a house has been held rateable in respect of it, if the value of the house was increased by the machine "

In the case of *R.* v. *Guest,*[1] decided in the year 1838, the machinery in question was that used in connection with the iron industry " The soil was excavated and strong walls of masonry were built, into these walls were introduced baulks of strong timber secured by bolts to an iron platform, upon this were placed frames of wood and iron. The engines and machines were attached to these frames by cotterells, or keys and jibs, so as to be tightened, or slackened, or removed at pleasure without injury to the machinery, buildings, or soil, and without displacing any part thereof.' Lord Denman, C J, in holding this machinery to be rateable, said that " Real property ought to be rated according to its actual value, as combined with the machinery attached to it, without considering whether the machinery be real or personal property, so as to be liable to distress or seizure under a *fieri facias*, or whether it would descend to the heir or executor, or belong, at the expiration of a lease, to landlord or tenant." It must be noticed here, in view of later decisions where it is held that machinery *must be taken into consideration when valuing a property*, that Lord Denman said in the above case that property ought to be

Iron foundry

[1] 7 L J M C 38, 2 N & P 663, 7 A & E. 951.

rated at its *actual value* as *combined* with machinery, without regard, as it were, to the nature of the machinery or to the person by whom it had, in fact, been provided, clearly laying down at this date that machinery must be valued on the same principle as buildings.

The next case in the sequence of cases to which it is important that attention should be drawn is that of *R. v The Southampton Dock Co.*,[1] decided in 1851, after the Act of 1840, exempting stock-in-trade, which was then and still is in force. The machinery here consisted of ponderous derricks, cranes, steam engines, etc., attached to the freehold and essential to the business of the company. Lord Campbell, in delivering judgment, here said "This is a rate upon buildings to which machinery is attached for the purpose of trade, and it has been decided that such real property ought to be assessed according to existing value as combined with the machinery, without considering whether the machinery be real or personal property or whether it go at the expiration of a lease to the landlord or tenant," and added that in *R. v Guest (ante)*, "All the arguments pressed upon us to show such fixtures are stock-in-trade and not to be taken into account in a rate on realty were urged in vain," thus shewing that the same arguments in this respect were used before as after the Act of 1840. A point was emphasized in the argument when his Lordship also said "The question of rating personal property was never suggested in these cases," *i.e.*—the earlier cases. Dock machinery

In the same year, namely 1851, the case of *R v Haslam*[2] was also before the Court. Here the rate was made on chemical works, lands and buildings; part of the works was devoted to the manufacture of sulphuric Chemical works

[1] (1851) 14 Q B 587, 6 Rail Cas 128, 20 L J M C 155, 15 Jur 268, 15 J.P 145

[2] (1851) 17 Q B 220, 15 Jur. 972, 15 J P 642

acid and contained certain plant, which consisted of tanks and vats made of lead, some 50ft long and weighing several tons. Steam was conveyed into these vessels through steam-coils from the boiler ; the tanks, however, were kept in position by their own weight, and were not actually fixed to the land   The Court held that it was plant which would be taken into account in the letting of the premises, which would thus have an improved rental, and that it was therefore rateable. Mr Justice Patteson, in delivering judgment, said "We do not think it necessary in this case to determine whether the chambers erected on the appellants' premises are or are not annexed to the freehold, which is rather a question of fact for the Court of Quarter Sessions to find than for us to decide, because we are of opinion that, according to the principle laid down in the various cases on this subject, the rateable value of the premises is undoubtedly increased by the *use* of these chambers "   And again   "It was urged that the chambers were rather of the nature of movable utensils or machines or of furniture in a dwelling-house than of fixtures   It is, however, plain from the facts stated that they are used as part of the fixed machinery of the works attached to the other buildings for the purpose of being so used and necessarily so attached in the use of them, although capable perhaps of being removed without injury to the other buildings.   Nor can it be denied that, if the appellants were to underlet the premises, they would fetch a higher rent as they now stand, with these chambers upon them, than they would if the chambers were removed."

Cotton mules   In the same year (1851) a case was decided, although not a rating case, which it may be well to consider here   It was that of *Hellawell* v. *Eastwood*,[1] where it was decided that cotton mules used in the process of the

---

[1] (1851) 6 Ex. 295, 20 L J. Ex. 154.

manufacture of cotton, although fixed by screws to the floor, were not liable to a distraint, the Court holding that these mules were not part of the freehold.

Parke, B., said : "The question is whether the machines when fixed were part of the freehold ; and this is a question of fact, depending on the circumstances of each case, and principally on two considerations. First, the mode of annexation to the soil or fabric of the house, and the extent to which it is united to them, whether it can easily be removed *integre salve et commode*, or not without injury to itself or the fabric of the building; secondly, on the object and purpose of the annexation, whether it was for the permanent and substantial improvement of the dwelling, in the language of the civil law, *perpetui usus causa*, or in that of the year book, *pour un profit de l'inhéritance*, or merely for a temporary purpose, or the more complete enjoyment and use of it as a chattel.

"Now, in considering this case, we cannot doubt that the machines never became a part of the freehold. They were attached slightly, so as to be capable of removal without the least injury to the fabric of the building or to themselves; and the object and purpose of the annexation was, not to improve the inheritance, but merely to render the machines steadier and more capable of convenient use as chattels. They were never a part of the freehold, any more than a carpet would be which is attached to the floor by nails for the purpose of keeping it stretched out, or curtains, looking-glasses, pictures, and other matters of an ornamental nature, which have been slightly attached to the walls of the dwelling as furniture, and which is probably the reason why they and similar articles have been held in different cases to be removable. The machines would have passed to the executor. They would not have passed by a conveyance or demise of the mill. They never ceased to have the character of movable chattels."

L

This case has, however, been distinguished on the facts, and the conclusion of facts arrived at has not been approved in a number of later cases, commencing with *Longbottom* v *Berry*[1] in the year 1862, in which Hannan, J., said "It is difficult to conceive that a machine which at all times requires to be firmly fixed to the freehold for the purpose of being worked, could truly be said never to lose its character as a movable chattel" See also the cases of *Holland* v *Hodgson*,[2] *Reynolds* v *William Ashby and Son, Limited*[3] and *Calico Printers' Association* v *Glossop Union* (reported in "The Estates Gazette," April 18th, 1903) These cases really dispose of the case of *Hellawell* v *Eastwood*,[4] and it has only been referred to, as it is sometimes quoted at Quarter Sessions and Assessment Committees in support of the contention that mules in cotton mills should be exempted from rating

Railway machinery

In 1860, in the case of *R* v *North Staffordshire Railway Company*,[5] it was held that things so attached to the freehold as to become part of it, and things which, though capable of being removed, are yet so far attached as that *it is intended that they shall remain permanently connected with the premises* and remain permanent appendages with them, must be taken into account in estimating rateable value

In 1866 the case of *R.* v *Lee*[6] was before the Court, and had reference to the valuation of a gas company, and it was held that gas holders, retorts, purifiers, steam engines, boilers, and other fixtures necessary in the process of the manufacture of gas, were rateable, although in this case the Court held that meters on the consumer's

---

[1] (1869) L R 5 Q B 123

[2] (1872) L.R. C P 328, and see p 149 *post*

[3] (1903) 1 K B 87, 19 T L R 70

[4] (1851) 6 Ex 295, 20 L J Ex 154

[5] (1860) 30 L J M C 68, 3 El & El 392, 3 L T 554, 9 W R. 235, 7 Jur. N S. 363

[6] (1866) L R. 1 Q B 241, 35 L J. M C 105, 30 J P. 132, 12 Jur. N S. 225, 13 L T. 704, 14 W R 311,

premises were not liable to be assessed   Cockburn, C J , in delivering judgment, said : " If the company desired to abandon this undertaking, and to let the gas works to another company or any individual, what the lessee would propose to take and pay rent for would not be land independent of all these articles, all of them essential to the manufacture, viz., gas.   The retorts, purifiers, and gas-holders are all as *essential to the using and occupying these premises as gas works* as any other thing that can possibly be suggested, however permanently attached to the freehold.   They seem, therefore, clearly to come within the principle laid down in *R.* v. *North Staffordshire Railway Co* "[1]   And Lush, J., said   " I agree that it makes no difference at all whether the tenant rents the whole or whether by contract between him and the land-lord he purchases the fixed plant which, if not so purchased, would be part of the permanent premises "

The following is an extract from the judgment of Blackburn, J , in the case   " If you are rating a house let furnished, you will ascertain how much was paid in respect of the furniture, and the things in no way forming part of the rateable premises, and, deducting that from the rent paid for the furnished house, the remainder would be the rent given for the house itself, for which it would be rateable   The question, then, would arise, and must arise, what the things are for which you are to make an allow-ance and deduction, whether they are in themselves part of the premises, or are, like the furniture, not part of the premises   Now, there are some fixtures that are attached to the premises and are part of the premises, although, as between landlord and tenant and heir and executors, there is a right to remove them   Clearly no allowance is to be made for these.   There are other things, such as movable furniture, which are manifestly not part of the house, and for which allowance must be made.   But

Machinery in gas works

---

[1] (1860) 30 L J M C 68 , see p 146 *ante.*

L 2

there are intermediate things, with respect to which it is sometimes very difficult to determine whether they are made part of the premises or not, and upon those the question mainly arises in the present case The rule laid down has been that, where the things are attached to the premises, so as to be part of the premises, although they are removable, still they are part of the premises, although there may be a right to remove them But if things or chattels be fixed to the premises, but so as to be still chattels, being only fixed and steadied for the purpose of use there, they remain chattels altogether. so that they would not be part of the premises at all ; they would never cease—to use the phrase in the case of *Hellawell* v. *Eastwood*[1] — to have the character of movable chattels, although fixed for the purpose of the enjoyment of them, still they remain movable chattels The common illustration is a mirror, which, in the ordinary way, would be screwed to the wall, still it remains a movable chattel, and is no part of the premises. On the other hand, a grate which is built into a chimney, although it is capable of being removed by a tenant, would still be fixed to the premises, so that it would be part of the premises, and therefore part of what would be considered to be let to the hypothetical tenant, and for which he would pay rent."

Silk weaving machines

In 1867, in the case of *R* v *Halstead*,[2] the line of decisions as to the rateability of machinery seems to have been checked, as in this case the machinery consisted of silk-weaving machines, which are of a very great length, sometimes as much as 50ft or 60ft , and of a width of 3ft. to 4ft Although it was admitted here that the machines were fastened to the floor for the only purpose of steadying them whilst in use, the Sessions found as a fact that the machines could be

---

[1] (1851) 6 Ex 295; 20 L J Ex 154, see p 144 *ante*.
[2] (1867) 32 J P 118.

removed without damage to themselves or the buildings, and that they could have been steadied for working by placing heavy weights upon them The Court held they were not rateable, probably following the case of *Hellawell* v *Eastwood*,[1] which had already been dealt with (see p 144 *ante*). A somewhat similar decision was given in 1874 in *Chidley* v *West Ham*,[2] in which certain bricks which formed part of the roof of some sheds and the floors of looms over the same were held to be not rateable But this case was disposed of in *Reynolds* v *Ashby and Son, Limited*, in which Mathew, J., said . " The case of *Chidley* v *West Ham Churchwardens*[2] is an instance of the inflexibility of a special case It was there pointed out by Blackburn, J , that the question which it was probably intended to raise by the special case was not really raised, and that the only question left to the Court was whether the machines could be separately rated as movable chattels, not whether, as annexed, they would enhance the rateable value of the premises "

In the year 1872 the case of *Holland* v *Hodgson*[3] was decided This however was not a rating case, but the opinion of the Court was asked as to whether looms in a cloth mill would pass under a mortgage of the mill, although being steadied in a similar way to those in the case of *Hellawell v. Eastwood*,[1] which was discussed and distinguished The Court held that the machines would pass under a mortgage, and the following is an extract from the judgment of Blackburn, J. "The general maxim of the law is that what is annexed to the land becomes part of the land ; but it is very difficult, if not impossible, to say with precision what constitutes an annexation sufficient for this purpose It is a question which must depend on the circumstances of each case,

Looms in cloth mill

[1] (1851) 6 Ex 313 , 20 L J Ex 154
[2] (1874) 32 L T. 48C , 39 J P 3 0
[3] (1872) L R 7 C P 328 , 41 L J M C 146 , 26 L T 709

and mainly on two circumstances, as indicating the
intention, viz , the degree of annexation and the object of
the annexation.   When the article in question is no
further attached to the land than by its own weight, it is
generally to be considered a mere chattel — *Wiltshear*
v *Cottrell*,[1] and the cases there cited   But even in such
a case, if the intention is apparent to make the articles
part of the land, they do become part of the land—see
D'Eyncourt v *Gregory*[2] Thus blocks of stone placed
one on top of another without any mortar or cement, for
the purpose of forming a dry stone well, would become
part of the land, though the same stones, if deposited
in a builder's yard, and for convenience sake stacked on
the top of each other in the form of a wall, would remain
chattels   On the other hand, an article may be very
firmly fixed to the land, and yet the circumstances may
be such as to show that it was never intended to be part
of the land, and then it does not become part of the land.
The anchor of a large ship must be very firmly fixed in
the ground, in order to bear the strain of the cable, yet no
one can suppose that it became part of the land, even
though it should chance that the shipowner was also the
owner of the fee of the spot where the anchor was
dropped   An anchor similarly fixed in the soil for the
purpose of bearing the strain of the chain of a suspension
bridge would be part of the land   Perhaps the true rule
is that articles not otherwise attached to the land than by
their own weight are not to be considered as part of the
land, unless the circumstances are such as to show that
they were intended to be part of the land, the onus of
showing that they were so intended lying on those who
assert that they have ceased to be chattels , and that, on
the contrary, an article which is affixed to the land even
slightly is to be considered as part of the land, unless the

---

[1] (1853) 1 E & B 674, 22 L J Q B 177
[2] (1866) L R 2 Eq 382, 36 L J Ch 107

circumstances are such as to show that it was intended all along to continue a chattel, the onus lying on those who contend that it is a chattel "

It will be seen, therefore, that the ruling of the Court was clearly that looms in cloth mills are to be considered as part of the freehold, and therefore it is submitted must be taken into consideration for rating purposes.

Following on this is the case of *Laing v. The Overseers of Bishopwearmouth*,[1] decided in 1878 This case had reference to shipbuilding machinery There was certain machinery fixed to the premises by means of bolts, etc., to the roof and floor, and also other machinery kept in position by its own weight. The premises, as they stood, could be used only for shipbuilding purposes, and a particular description of machinery was as follows —

(margin: Shipbuilding machinery)

Boilers	Drilling Machines
Engines	Saw Benches
Shafting	Steam Hammer
Punching and Shearing Machines, with Engines	Shear Legs and Cranes
	Pumps
Planing, Boring and Slotting Machines	Weighing Machines
	Smith's Shop
Riveting Machines	Water Tanks
Punching and Shearing Machines	Grindstone
Lathes	Railway

All the machinery was held rateable Cockburn, C J , in delivering the judgment of the Court, said

"Applying the rule established by these decisions," (i e —those already referred to) "to the present case, it appears to us, after having carefully considered the character of the machinery in question, that the whole of it, though some of it may be capable of being removed without injury to itself or to the freehold, *is essentially necessary to the shipbuilding business* to which the appellants' premises are devoted, and must be taken to be intended to remain permanently attached to them so long as those premises are applied to the present purpose Our judgment must, therefore, be for the respondents," the Overseers

---

[1] (1878) 3 Q B D 299, 47 L J M C 42 37 L   St, 42 J P 309

The next case to be considered is the well known and much discussed *Tyne Boiler* case,[1] decided in 1886, which was undoubtedly stated in order, if possible, to get the Courts to decide that the line of demarcation between machinery which should be taken into consideration and machinery which should be looked upon as personal chattels, should be between those machines that were attached physically to the freehold and those that were not

The importance of this case would seem to justify a somewhat lengthy extract from the special case and judgment, as it is undoubtedly one of the leading cases on the subject at the present day   The special case was as follows —

(1) On the 9th January, 1885, an appeal against a rate was heard by the said Court of Quarter Sessions, in which the Tyne Boiler Works Company, Limited, were the appellants, and the Overseers of the Poor of the parish of Longbenton and the Assessment Committee of the Tynemouth Union were the respondents   The rate against which the said appeal was brought was a rate for the relief of the poor of the parish of Longbenton, in the county of Durham, made the 28th of June, 1884, whereby the appellants were rated in respect of premises in the said parish occupied by them, as hereinafter appears

(2) The valuation assessment and rate in question were as appears from the following extract from the Rate Book .—

Occupier	Owner	Description	Gross Estimated Rental	Rateable Value	Rate at 10d in the £
			£	£	£ s d
Tyne Boiler Works Company, Ltd	Tyne Boiler Works Company, Ltd	Boiler Works Land	} 590	501	20 17 6

(3.) The grounds of appeal were that the appellants were overrated in respect of the said premises.

---

[1] *Tyne Boiler Works Co v Longbenton*, (1886) 18 Q B D 81, 56 L J M C 8, 55 L T 825

(4) All proper notices were given and steps taken to entitle the appellants to raise upon the appeal the questions and objections raised by them herein appearing Tyne Boiler Works case

(5.) The appellants were at all material times, and still are, the tenants and occupiers of the premises in the said parish before referred to, and which are known as the Tyne Boiler Works The said premises comprise upward of 5,100 square yards of land upon the banks of the Tyne, part of which land was, and still is, covered by a large brick building, roofed in, the roof being supported by the walls of the building and by iron columns, and the rest of the said land being, with the exception of certain offices and boiler or engine sheds erected on parts thereof, open and uncovered by buildings

(6) The premises were and are held by the appellants as assignees under a lease from the Corporation of Newcastle-upon-Tyne, which was granted to Joseph Pollard for a term of 75 years from September, 1864. In or about 1868 or 1869, Messieurs Thompson and Boyd, who were then the assignees of the terms created by the said lease, erected the brick building mentioned in paragraph 5, and placed therein the engine in the following list referred to as No. 2, and the boiler in the same list referred to as No 1, and certain of the shafting and machinery still on the premises for the purpose of making boilers and erecting machinery on board vessels, and also for the purpose of making forgings. The appellants have, since they became assignees of the said term and occupiers of the said premises, have purchased and placed upon them other machinery and plant in addition to that put up by Messieurs Thompson and Boyd, and have used the said lands and building together with the boilers, engines, plant and machines thereon, for making boilers and erecting them on board vessels. The proximity of the premises to the Tyne makes them suitable for boiler works, but at successive periods

previous to their being occupied by the appellants *they have been used for manufactures or purposes of different kinds.*

(7) It was agreed and admitted that in arriving at the rateable value £501, at which the said premises are assessed, the machinery and plant hereinafter specified, which were and are upon the said premises, had been taken into consideration as enhancing the rateable value of such premises, viz —

IN THE MAIN BUILDING

Water supplies
1. Boiler
2. Main engine
3. Main shafting
4. Fan blasts
5. Blast pipes
6. Hydraulic accumulator
7. { Pair of hydraulic pumps near end of buildings
    {   do   do   near accumulator
8. Two small open return water tanks
9. Flanging machine
10. Riveting machine
11. Two plate edge planing machines
12. Plate bending rolls
13. Punching machine
14. Punching plate, shearing and angle shearing machine
15. Three wall drills
16. Radial drilling machine
17. Boiler shell drilling machine
18. Grindstone
19. Drilling machine
20. Screwing machine
21. Rivet heating furnace
22. Two hand-power travelling cranes

OUTSIDE THE MAIN BUILDING.

23. Shear-legs with engine and boiler
24. Line of rails from main building to shear-legs
25. Punching and shearing machine
26. Line of rails to middle of yard
27. Jib crane
28. Plate rolls
29. Plate furnace
30. Open smithy fire in yard

It was further agreed between the parties, on the hearing before us, that if the whole or any part of the above-mentioned machinery and plant ought not to have been taken in consideration in assessing the premises, then the rateable value should be reduced by the whole sum of £221, or by a proportionate amount to be afterwards agreed upon between the parties as sufficient to give effect to our decision

Tyne Boiler Works case

Photographs of the more important parts of the machinery were also, by agreement, placed before us, and are afterwards referred to as adjuncts to this case.

(8) Of the above specified machinery and plant, the boiler No 1 (photograph No 8) is, as usual, set on a brick seating in a building or shed outside the main building. The steam from that boiler is conveyed to the main engine (No 2) through iron pipes which pass through the wall of the main building   The main engine No 2 (photograph No. 29) is fixed by iron screw bolts to masonry foundations, in which a well is constructed for the fly-wheel of the main engine.   The hydraulic riveting machine (No 10), the two hand-power travelling cranes (No 22), the plate rolls (No. 28), the flanging machine, the accumulators and the boiler attached to the shear-legs (No 23), are not attached either to the soil or the building, but rest by their own weight

The main standards have an iron bolt passed through them, and through the end walls of the main building

The fly-wheel shaft passes through the wall of the main building, and is carried by a bearing, fixed in an iron box, built into the wall of the main building

The main shafting No. 3 (photographs 22, 23, 27 and 34) runs along the entire length of the main building, and is supported by the main wall of the building by means of bracket bearings on iron plates fixed to the wall buttresses Each bracket is fixed to the wall by six iron screw bolts passing through the main wall

All the machines are driven from the main shafting by means of leather belts.

The fan blast (No 4), for supplying an air blast to the smithy fires, is sunk in a hole in the ground, and is driven from the main shaft

The blast pipes (No 5), for conveying the air, are earthenware pipes laid underground, branches being taken to the various smithy fires

The smithy fires No 6 (photographs 11, 12, 13 and 14) are open hearths and fires built of brick, and having an air blast conveyed to each by means of the fan blast and blast pipes mentioned in the immediately preceding paragraph   The smithy fires are capable of being moved to another place.   They rest on the ground solely by their own weight.   Such removal would necessitate the moving of the air blast pipes along with the fires

The hydraulic plant consists, first, of an accumulator (photograph No. 18), which rests by its own weight on concrete foundations, and secondly, of pumps in connection therewith.   The waterpipes pass underground to the accumulator.

The hydraulic riveting machine No. 11 (photograph No. 15), the plate roller No 28 (photograph 6), the flanging machine, the accumulator, and the boiler for the shear-legs No 23 (photograph 4) rest by their own weight upon cement or stone foundations prepared for them   The boiler (No. 23) is connected with steam pipes with the engine which works the shear-legs

The two hand-power travelling cranes No. 22 (photograph No. 34) are not fixed but run along the whole length of the main building on rails laid on baulks of timber, which rest upon brackets, forming part of the columns which support the roof of the main building

The shear-legs (photographs 1, 2 and 3) are placed on the edge of a timber jetty or quay, built on timber piles, which are driven into the bed of the river, and project beyond the stone quay out into the river. They are worked by means of a separate engine and boiler (photograph 4) A line of iron rails, laid on sleepers for waggons, connects the main building with the jetty.

The wall drills (photograph No. 24) are bolted to iron brackets, which are held in position by iron screw bolts, passing through the main wall of the building, and secured by a plate on the other side

The jib cranes are attached to the iron columns which support the roof of the building, and are worked by steam by means of a steam pipe from the main boiler. With these exceptions the whole of the machinery and plant referred to in this case are held in position in the following manner A foundation of stone, timber or concrete is prepared for the individual machine Into this foundation bolts are let and fastened by lead or cement. When the machine is brought into position it is hoisted by the crane over the foundation and let down in such a manner that the holes pierced in the lower portion (or bed plate) of the machine slides over the bolts fixed in the foundation. A nut is then screwed on to the top of each bolt to steady the machine. All the machines are worked by belts from the main shafting When a machine has to be removed the nuts are unscrewed and the machine is hoisted up over the bolts which remain in the foundation

(9) It was proved that the whole of the above specified machinery and plant were in fact the property of the appellants and not of the Corporation of Newcastle-upon-Tyne, the owners of the freehold, the same having been brought upon the premises either by the appellants or their predecessors in the occupancy of the premises under the lease before referred to

(10) All the said machinery and plant are required for the purpose of boiler making, and are in practice, adapted for use upon the said premises for manufacturing and setting up boilers, and were, and are in practice,

Tyne Boiler
Works case

used by the appellants for such purpose, but further than
appears by this case there was not any intention on the
part of the appellants of making such machinery and
plant part of the soil or hereditaments, or of permanently
annexing them thereto

(11.) The machines constituting the said machinery
and plant are each of them as machines, except so far as
herein appears, separate and distinct from each other, and
can be, and are in practice, from time to time, bought,
sold, renewed and removed as separate and distinct
articles.

(12) The said machines and plant can be and in
practice are, taken down or removed when and as required,
either for repairs or rearrangement, or change in the use
of the premises or for any other purpose, and that without injury to themselves or structural damage to the
hereditaments

(13) The object of the attachment described in the
eighth paragraph of this case is the steadying the
machines in working and the preventing them from being
pulled by the belting by which they are worked.

(14) The above method of attachment does effectually
steady the machines in working and prevent them being
pulled by the belts, and it is also convenient if, and when,
occasion arises for the machines being for any purpose
removed.

(15) The mode in which the rateable value of the
premises was arrived at was by ascertaining the gross
estimated rental which a tenant, from year to year, might
reasonably be expected to be willing to give for the use
of them (*inclusive of the machinery and plant before
specified*), and by making the statutory deductions from
such rental

(16.) The appellants contended that the above specified
machinery and plant were not, any of them, part of the
freehold or hereditaments, but were chattels; and that

they were not, nor were any of them, rateable or to be taken into consideration as enhancing the rateable value of the hereditament.

The respondents, on the other hand, contended that the said machinery and plant were necessary to the beneficial occupation of the premises as boiler works, that being the purpose to which they are appropriated, and ought to be taken into consideration as enhancing the rateable value of the hereditaments to which they are attached

(17.) We considered that at least before us the case of *Laing* v *Overseers of Bishopwearmouth* [1] was conclusive, and in accordance with what we understood to be the principles laid down in that case, we held that the said machinery and plant had been rightly taken into consideration in estimating the rateable value of the premises to which the appeal related.

It being, however, urged upon us by the counsel for the appellants that the special case in *Laing* v. *Bishopwear-mouth* had been agreed upon by the parties themselves out of Court, and that it was desired to test the soundness of the principle alleged to have been enunciated by the decision in that case, by arguments on a special case to be stated by us, and counsel for the respondents not objecting to our doing so, our order dismissing the appeal was made subject to a special case to be stated by us, as this has now been, for the opinion of the Court

(18) Each party is to be at liberty, if and so far as the Court shall permit, to refer to the shorthand notes of the hearing before us, or to the photographs of the machinery produced before us, or to the articles of association of the Appellant Company, by way of supplementing this case upon any point or points which may appear to the Court to require further elucidation.

---

[1] L R 3 Q B 299, see p 151 *ante*

(19) The question for the opinion of the Court is
whether our decision above stated was correct or incorrect, and if incorrect, in respect of what items, matter
or principle.

If the Court should be of opinion that the whole of the
said machinery and plant was properly taken into
consideration as enhancing the rateable value of the
premises to which the appeal relates, our order is to be
affirmed   If otherwise, our order is to be quashed

M. W RIDLEY,
                    Chairman of the Court

The judgment of Lord Esher, M R, in the case was
as follows —

" The first difficulty in this case is to determine what
is the question raised by the special case   We are
confined to that question, and must not be led away if we
think arguments are presented to us which discuss other
questions which are not raised by the special case.   It
appears to me, upon looking at the contentions stated in
the special case, that the dispute, on the one hand, was
that the machinery and plant were chattels and were not
rateable, and that they ought not to be taken into
consideration as enhancing the rateable value of the
hereditament ; whilst, on the other hand, it was contended
that they ought to be so taken into consideration   That,
therefore, as it seems to me, was the dispute between the
parties before the Court of Quarter Sessions, which held
that those things had been rightly taken into consideration in estimating the rateable value of the premises.   It
is, therefore, clear that the Quarter Sessions merely
decided that it was right that these things should be
taken into consideration , and the question for us is not
how all or any of these things ought to be valued, but
whether they ought to have been taken into consideration
at all as enhancing the rateable value of the premises.

"The present case has been stated for the purpose of testing the soundness of the principle said to have been laid down in *Laing v Overseers of Bishopwearmouth* [1] It was argued on behalf of the appellants in the Court below that these machines could only be taken into account as enhancing the rateable value of the premises if they were so affixed as to be part of the inheritance; that it was not sufficient that they should be fixtures in the ordinary sense of the word, for every fixture is not necessarily a part of the premises to which it is affixed, and that the test was whether they are removable *integre salve et commode*, and whether they are intended to be permanently used on the land, and therefore to benefit the inheritance But I cannot help thinking that the argument is not to be confined to that particular question; for the real question is whether these things are to be taken into account at all in determining the rateable value of these premises, and not whether they are to be rated. No question has been here raised whether or not the valuer took them properly into account The argument for the appellants was that Laing's case had gone beyond the former cases, and that that case could not be supported in this Court. That raises the question whether the latter case has gone beyond the former cases If that is not so, the argument must attack not only Laing's case, but also all the former cases I do not think it can be held that the Court ever intended in that case to overrule the former cases; the intention was to adopt and apply them It was said that the former cases are not to be considered as authorities in this case because of the Statute as to rating personalty A doubt had been raised whether personal chattels ought to be taken into consideration in rating the inhabitants of a parish, and that doubt had been removed by the Statute 3 & 4 Vict,

[1] (1878) 47 L J M C 11, L R 3 Q B D 229, 37 L T 781 26 W R 3.1 2 J P 309

Tyne Boiler
Works case:
Judgment

c. 89 ; which, however, did not touch the question how real property was to be rated, or how the value of real property was to be arrived at for the purpose of rating. The question is whether these machines are to be taken into account, not for the purpose of rating, but for the purpose of estimating the value of premises in respect of which the owner or occupier is to be rated ; therefore all the authorities with regard to the mode of arriving at the annual value of real property remain untouched by the Statute. It would be a very strong measure to overrule the many cases which have been decided by a Court more conversant than any other with the subject. We ought, therefore, to look at those cases, not for the purpose of overruling them, but for the purpose of guiding us as to the true principle to be applied to the present case. I think it will be found on looking at the cases that the same idea was present to the minds of the Judges throughout, but there was a difficulty in expressing themselves so as beyond all cavil or dispute to lay down the rule. Although the words used differ in almost every case, yet they were intended to lay down the same rule, and all the cases seem to contain the idea. In *R* v. *Haslam*,[1] Mr Justice Patteson says 'We do not think it necessary, in this case, to determine whether the chambers erected on the appellants' premises are or are not annexed to the freehold, which is rather a question of fact for the Court of Quarter Sessions to find than for us to decide, because we are of opinion that, according to the principle laid down in the various cases on this subject, the rateable value of the premises is undoubtedly increased by the use of those chambers.'

"Then in *R* v *The Southampton Dock Co*,[2] Lord Campbell, after stating the contention as to the

---

[1] (1851) 17 Q B 220, 15 Jur 972, 15 J P 612

[2] (1851) 14 Q B 587, 6 Rail Cas 428, 20 L J M C 155, 15 Jur 268, 15 J P 145

fourth question, says 'This is a rate upon buildings to which machinery is attached for the purposes of trade, and it has been solemnly decided that such real property ought to be assessed according to its existing value *as combined with the machinery*, without considering whether the machinery be real or personal property, or whether it be liable or not to distress or seizure under a *fieri facias*, or whether it go to the heir or executor, or at the expiration of a lease to the landlord or tenant. Now what was the rule which had been laid down by Lord Denman in *R v Guest*,[1] following the decision in *R v The Birmingham and Staffordshire Gas Light Co*[2]? I am aware it is said that real property ought to be rated according to its actual value as combined with the machinery attached to it, but I do not think the phrase 'attached to it' means so attached as to become a fixture in the ordinary sense of the word.

"Then we come to the more elaborate judgment of Mr Justice Blackburn in *R v The Inhabitants of Lee*,[3] which is the very touchstone of the matter. His lordship there cites and intends to follow *R. v The North Staffordshire Railway Co*[4] and *R v The Southampton Dock Co.* (a, above), and says that they contain the same idea as that stated in *Hellawell v Eastwood*,[5] although not the precise words there used, so that he did not think there had been any alteration in the law. Mr Justice Blackburn says 'There the rule laid down for the guidance of Sessions was this. The articles may be divided into three classes, first, things movable, such as office and station furniture. It is clear

Tyne Boiler
Works case
Judgment

[1] (1838) 7 L J M C 38, 2 N & P 663, 7 A & E 951, W W & D 651
(1837) 6 A & E 634, 6 L J M C 92
(1866) L R 1 Q B 241, 35 L J M C 105, 12 Jur N S 225, 13
L T 704, 14 W R 311, 30 J P 132
[4] (1860) 3 El & El 392, 30 L J M C 68, 7 Jur N S 363, 3 L T
951, 9 W R 235
(1851) 6 Ex 295, 20 L J Ex 154

these are not to be included'—he there means personal
chattels, which it was not contended were to be taken
into account or to be rated 'Secondly things so attached
to the freehold as to become part of it It is clear, on
the principle of all the cases, that no deduction is to be
made for them, and they are to be considered as part of
what is let Thirdly, things which, though capable of
being removed, were yet so far attached as that they
were intended to remain permanently connected with the
railway or the premises used with it, and to remain
permanent appendages to it as essential to its working'
Here, no doubt, the language differs from that used by
other Judges, but the idea was the same, namely, that
things annexed, though but slightly, with a view of
enhancing and permanently improving the inheritance,
are to be considered as part of it and rateable Then
dealing with the things in the case before him he says
'Nevertheless, I think it is clear that they all are in fact
attached to the premises with the view of enhancing the
benefit of the premises' No doubt Mr. Justice Blackburn
there spoke of the things as being attached, but I do not
think he intended to overrule what had been said in
the previous cases Then Mr Justice Lush says 'I
apprehend that the premises to be rated are to be taken
as they are with all their fittings and appliances by which
the owner has adapted them to a particular use, and
which would pass as a part of the premises by a demise
of them to a tenant, wherever the things have become
so far a part of the premises that they would pass by a
demise of these premises, they would form a part of the
rateable subject of the inheritance for the purpose of
rating When we have to apply the test to any particular
thing, the question is not what a tenant might remove,
nor what might be taken in execution, but what as
between landlord and tenant would pass as a part of the
premises which he would let and the tenant would take'

Tyne Boiler
Works case
Judgment

The rule is then applied to the case before him, and although he said, 'All these things are fixed and so far annexed as to be intended to be permanent and as really necessary for the use of the premises as gas works,' yet he certainly did not mean that they were fixed in the sense of being 'fixtures' The same rule, therefore, seems to have been laid down in that case as in the other cases, although precisely the same words were not used Then there is the case of *Laing v The Overseers of Bishop-wearmouth* (as above), where all the cases are gone through and adopted, and where Chief Justice Cockburn says 'Applying the rule established by these decisions to the present case, it appears to us, after having carefully considered the character of the machinery in question, that the whole of it, though some of it may be capable of being removed without injury to itself or to the freehold, is essentially necessary to the shipbuilding business to which the appellants' premises are devoted, and must be taken to be intended to remain permanently attached to them so long as those premises are applied to their present purpose' Now does the word 'attached there mean attached by some physical fastening, such as screws or bolts? If it does, a thing weighing tons, which cannot be and never was intended to be lifted, would not be taken into account if not fastened to some part of the building, whereas if it were fastened it would That, as it seems to my mind, would be a monstrous consequence I do not think the word attached does there mean 'physically fastened,' so as to determine whether the thing is to be taken into account or not It is, therefore, only from the difficulties of expression that the argument can be brought forward that these things must be physically fastened to the buildings in order to be taken into account As that cannot be the meaning of the word it becomes necessary to consider what it does mean The test now laid down, which will leave out the words

'attached' and 'fixed,' may, I think, be put thus —
Things which are on premises for the purpose of making,
and which, in fact, make those premises fit as premises
for the particular purpose for which they are used, ought
to be taken into account in order to ascertain the rateable
value of the premises   It therefore follows that directly

What
machinery
passes is
between
landlord and
tenant

things can be brought into that category they would as a
matter of law pass by a demise (unless expressly excluded
by its terms) as between landlord and tenant   This test
is identical with that enunciated by Mr Justice Lush,
because, in his opinion, the things which come within
the definition would pass on a demise between landlord
and tenant   Taking that to be the proper principle, and
applying it to the question asked in this case, I say,
considering what is the question here and without considering whether these things are physically fastened,
that I am of opinion that they all come within the
principle   They are all on the premises, they are all
there for the purpose of making, and do make, these
premises fit for the particular purpose for which the
premises are used, namely, as boiler works, and, therefore, I think they ought to be taken into account in order
to arrive at the proper rateable value of the premises
The mode in which the valuer has treated them in
bringing them into account is not the question for this
purpose. With regard to the case of *Chidley* v. *The
Overseers of West Ham*,[1] I agree with the Divisional
Court   I do not say that the Court in that case were
incorrect in the view which they took on the question
which they had before them, but I am unable to understand, if the right question had been put to them, how it
could be said that the things there in question ought not
to have been taken into account in order to arrive at the
rateable value   The case of *R* v *The Overseers of*

[1] (1874) 32 L T 486, 39 J P 310

Halstead[1] is of no importance, as I do not think it lays down any principle. The question asked by the Quarter Sessions *must* be answered in the affirmative, and the appeal be dismissed.

Lindley, L J, following, said. "The first question to be ascertained is, what is the property to be rated, and how ought it to be described? It is, in fact, described in the Rate Book as 'boiler works and land', a great deal depends upon whether that description is right or is not correct, but no one quarrels with it. I do not think the Courts have ever departed from the construction originally put upon 6 & 7 William IV, c 96, and I agree with the contention of the appellants that we must look at the Statute and also see in what way it has been construed. That Statute says that the Poor Rate is to be made on an estimate of the net annual value of the several hereditaments rated (that is to say, of the rent at which the same might reasonably be expected to let from year to year), and then it goes on to state what deductions are to be made. Then comes a proviso, the wording of which is a little obscure —'Provided always that nothing herein contained shall be construed to alter or affect the principles or different relative liabilities, if any, according to which different kinds of hereditaments are now by law rateable. We must, therefore, first look at the hereditaments to be rated, and find out as best we can the rent at which they might reasonably be expected to let from year to year. Now that shows that the property is to be taken as it is found, and not as mere land. If the land is covered with buildings, it must be taken as it is found and not as being only so much land. Here the premises must be looked at as they are described, that is, as boiler works. It is said that in ascertaining the rateable value of these works the machinery, or a great part of it, ought not to be taken into account. I do not agree with that. nothing that

---

[1] (1867) 31 J P 373. 32 J P 118.

has been included here could be described as loose
machinery which a tenant would not take if he were
hiring the works from year to year. The machinery
seems to me to come within the same category as mill-
stones in a mill, which would pass by a demise of the mill.
It appears to me that all these things are part of the
works taken as a whole. Physical annexation, so far as
I can discover, never has been taken as the test either
before or after the Act—see *R v Hogg*[1] and *R
v Haslam*[2] *Per contra*, there are many cases where the
things were physically attached to the land, but where
the physical annexation was disregarded. There are,
therefore, two lines of cases, one where attachment is *not*
taken as being conclusive, and the other where it was
held *non*-attachment was *not* conclusive. We are asked
to hold that only those things are to be taken into account
in arriving at the rateable value which are so physically
attached to the land as to become part of it. If we were
to do so we should be departing from the Act itself and
the previous decisions. The only case which is at all
puzzling is that of *Chidley v. The Churchwardens of West
Ham* (see above). The true view of that decision is that
the articles in question, being mere personal property, could
not be rated. I do not understand that case to decide
that the articles there described could not be taken into
account in ascertaining the rateable value of the premises.
The true test is that which the Master of the Rolls has
laid down."

Lopes, L J also said "The question here is whether
certain articles of machinery are to be taken into account
in ascertaining the rateable value of these premises, those
articles not being physically attached to the freehold in
the sense of being either landlord's or tenant's or trade
fixtures. *Prima facie* such things as machinery are not

[1] (1787) 1 T R 721 Caldecott 266
[2] (1851) 17 Q B 220, 15 Jur 972 J P 612

rateable, but if they are attached to the premises, whether as *landlord's or tenant's or trade fixtures*, it is clear they must be taken into consideration in ascertaining the rateable value of the premises Some things are so placed on premises, and are so much intended to be used with the premises, as to become part of the premises, and I am of opinion that in such a case they ought to be taken into consideration A number of cases have been cited which clearly establish this   The only one which at first sight appears to be inconsistent is that of *Chidley v The Churchwardens of West Ham*, but if it is closely looked at, it is clear that the ground of the decision was that the articles there were separate from the premises, and being personal property were not rateable I think that the articles of machinery in this case ought to be taken into consideration, and I adopt what was said by Mr Justice Mathew in the Court below, that the land and machinery here combined are used for carrying on the business, and that there seems no reason *why the combination which is essential to this use of the land should not be rateable* It was said that, although that might be the rule deducible from a long line of cases yet the Court of Appeal ought to overrule them   I can see no ground for so doing It seems to me those decisions are founded upon both good sense and good law   The appeal must therefore be dismissed '

This case, which has designedly been given in full, clearly determines that all machinery and plant that make premises fit to carry on any particular trade must be taken into consideration when ascertaining the rateable value, and moreover, that where the combination of machinery and buildings is essential to the use of the land, the whole is rateable. It should also be observed that the machinery in this case was of itself for the most part of a very small and valueless character, the rateable value appealed against being only trifling

The next case was that of *Gifford, Fox & Co.* v *The Chard Union,*[1] which referred to bobbin net machines used in a lace factory, and was carried to the Court of Appeal, by whom it was decided that such machines must be taken into account as enhancing the value of the hereditament, although it was proved that the machines were only fixed to the floor to steady them, and could be removed without injury to themselves or the building

The importance of the subject of the rating of machinery fully justifies the following long extract from the special case in this appeal, and as it is believed that the special case is not set out in any published book, it is given at length below, together with some extracts from the shorthand notes on the case, which it is hoped will be found useful, as it is important to consider the judgment in conjunction with the special case upon which it was founded

The special case is as follows —

1. On the 3rd July, 1889, the said appeal was heard by the said Court of Quarter Sessions (County of Somerset), against a Poor Rate made the 13th day of October, 1888, whereby the appellants were rated in respect of premises in the said borough, occupied by them as hereafter appears

2 The valuation assessment and rate in question were as appears from the following extract from the Rate Book which was in accordance with the valuation list —

No	Name of Occupier	Name of Owner	Description of Property	Name or Situation of Property	Estimated Extent	Gross Estimated Rental	Rateable Value
						£	£
128	Gifford, Fox & Co	Gifford, Fox & Co	Lace Factory, Workshops, and Gasometer	Holyrood Street		1,642	1,097

[1] (1890) 63 L T 249 6 T L R 431

3   The grounds of appeal were —

(1) That the rate or assessment was unequal and unfair, because the appellants were assessed and rated therein at a greater sum than they ought to be assessed and rated at in respect of the said property

(2) That the rate or assessment was unfair and incorrect for that it was not made upon an estimate of the rent at which the said property might reasonably be expected to let from year to year, free of all usual tenant's rates and taxes, and tithe commutation rent-charge (if any), and deducting therefrom the probable average annual cost of the repairs, insurances and other expenses (if any) necessary to maintain them in a state to command such rent, according to the Statutes

(3) That the principle on which the annual value of the premises occupied by the appellants in the said borough was estimated was erroneous

(4) That personal property had been taken into consideration as enhancing the rateable value, which should not have been so treated

(5) That if such personal property ought at all to have been taken into consideration as aforesaid, it was taken into consideration for that purpose in a wrong mode, and its effect incorrectly estimated

4   The appellants are the owners and occupiers of the said premises, which comprise an area of about 3,000 square yards of land, upon which the said factory, workshops and gasometer are erected

5   The appellants have in the said factory certain
boilers, engines, and shaftings, bobbin net and other
machines, and have used the said land and buildings
together with the boilers, engines, shaftings and machines
for weaving cotton or silk into plain bobbin net, which is
used as a groundwork for lace and embroidery, and is
also used for millinery and ball dresses, and some of the
coarser qualities for mosquito curtains   The factory, and
others of this class, are commonly known and styled as
" lace factories "

6   It was admitted that, in arriving at the rateable
value at which the said premises were so assessed, the
machinery specified in the following schedule, together
with the boiler, engine, and shafting, which were and are
upon the said premises, had been taken into consideration as enhancing the rateable value of such premises

SCHEDULE OF BOBBIN NET MACHINES

No of Machines	Dimensions
1	10 4 = 2½ yards
71	12 4 = 3 ,,
3	14 4 3½ ,,
6	16 4 = 4 ,,
16	18 4 = 4½
4	24 4 = 6 ,,
101	

7   It was stated in evidence, on the part of the
respondents, that the sum of £1,097 rateable value was
made up of £297, the rateable value of land, buildings,
and fixed motive power, and of £800 the amount by
which the value of such land, buildings, and fixed motive
power was enhanced by the machinery mentioned in the
last paragraph   The rateable value was reduced by us to
£895, being £295 in respect of the land, buildings, and
fixed motive power, and £600 in respect of such enhanced
value as aforesaid   We found that the sum of £895 was

such rateable value calculated upon the rent at which *Gifford, Fox and Co. v Chard Union* the said premises, including the said machinery, might be reasonably expected to let from year to year, free from tenant's rates, taxes, and tithe rent-charge, and after deducting from such rent the costs of repairs, insurance, and expenses necessary to maintain such rent

8   Photographs of bobbin net machinery, initialed by the chairman and marked (M), which are similar to those in the said factory, accompany and are to be taken as part of this case

9   The buildings are well arranged and substantially built   The main block is a fire-proof building containing the principal machines

The following is a description of the buildings —

Entrance Lodge and Carpenter's Shop (2 storeys)
Store with Loft (2 floors)
Fitting Shop (1 floor)
Blacksmith's Shop and Loft over.
New Weaving Shed
Boiler House
Store
Factory (main block, 5½ floors)
Store Shed
Offices and Warehouses etc
Ditto   ditto
Chimney Shaft.
Gas Works and Plant

The machinery is driven by a condensing beam engine with 24in cylinder, 5ft stroke   The steam is supplied by two Lancashire boilers

The machinery on the various floors is driven by bands from the main and counter-shafting, and is of the most modern description and comprises —

Lace machines, winding machines, engines
Warping machines or mills
Lathes, punching, planing, slotting, drilling, screwing, and shaping machines

10   The bobbin net machines stand on the floors of the factory, the upper floor being supported by pillars and

the flooring substantial, the machines stand on legs and are of the dimensions stated in the schedule to paragraph 6. Some of them weigh as much as two tons; some are fastened to the floor by means of screws through the feet of the machines, others are not fastened through the feet, but are attached to the floor above by iron rods screwed to such floor and to the top of the machines, others are not fastened at all, their own weight being sufficient to steady them The machinery is driven from the main shafting by means of belts.

11. All the machinery mentioned in the said schedule is required for the purpose of making bobbin net, as mentioned in paragraph 5, and is arranged and adapted for use upon the premises for that purpose, and is in practice so used by the appellants, but there was no evidence of any intention on the part of the appellants to make such machinery part of the soil or hereditament, or further than appears by this case to annex them permanently thereto.

12 The machines constituting the said machinery are each of them as machines separate and distinct from each other, and are in practice from time to time bought, sold, renewed and removed, as separate and distinct articles

13. The said machines can be and in practice are taken down and removed, when and as required, either for repairs or rearrangement, which is frequently necessary, and such removal can be effected without injury to either the machines or structural damage to the hereditament.

14 The machines have not been removed by the appellants except for the purposes of repair or rearrangement It was stated to be not unusual in Nottingham for a tenant to take a space or standing in a factory by the week or month, and to put thereon machines of a similar character to those in Chard Union, and to remove them at the end of the tenancy, the steam power for working

such machines being supplied by the landlord, but no such practice had ever been known to exist in Chard or in the West of England.

15 The building on the premises in question is about sixty-five years old, and has been continuously used for its present purpose, and there was no evidence of any intention of any change in the manufacture as now carried on there

16 Machinery of this description is essential to the use of the premises so long as they are used as a bobbin net lace factory The premises, however, although especially adapted for that purpose, might be used without structural alteration as a sail-cloth factory or for stocking-making machinery, or other such like purposes.

17 The appellants contended that the said bobbin net machinery mentioned in the schedule was not, any of it, part of the freehold or hereditament, that it was not, nor was any of it, permanently attached thereto, that it was not essential to the use of the premises, that it was not, nor was any of it, rateable, and that such bobbin net machinery ought not to be taken into consideration as enhancing the rateable value of the hereditament

18 The respondents, on the other hand, contended that the said bobbin net machines were necessary to the beneficial occupation of the premises as a lace factory, that being the purpose to which they were appropriated, and for which they had been always used on the premises, and that such machinery, therefore, ought to be taken into consideration as enhancing the rateable value of the hereditaments, and that the extra rent which a tenant would pay on account of its being there was the sum by which it enhanced the value of the hereditament

19 We considered that the freehold hereditament had been originally erected as a bobbin net or (so-called) lace factory, that the bobbin net machinery was essential to the user of the premises for the purpose of such bobbin

Gifford, Fox
and Co v
Chard Union
net lace manufacture, and that such machinery had been always, and still was, on the premises for such purpose, and that, in accordance with the decisions in the *Laing v Bishopwearmouth* case and the *Tyne Boiler Works* case, and more especially, having regard to the judgment of the Master of the Rolls in the last-mentioned case, the said machinery had been rightly taken into consideration in arriving at the rateable value of the premises as enhancing such rateable value; and that the premises were accordingly assessable to the Poor Rate at the amount at which they would let to a tenant from year to year as a going concern of a lace factory, *equipped with such machinery as was essential to its user as such factory*, the rateable value calculated upon which amount, after making the statutory deductions we found to be £895.

20   The questions for the opinion of the Court are —

> (1) Whether the bobbin net machinery mentioned in the schedule to paragraph 6 is to be taken into consideration as enhancing the rateable value of the premises?

> (2) Whether, assuming such machinery is to be so taken into consideration, it has been taken into consideration on the proper principle?

21   If the Court should be of opinion that it was right to take the said bobbin net machinery into consideration as enhancing the rateable value of the said premises, and that it was taken into consideration on the proper principle, our order is to be affirmed If, however, the Court should be of opinion that the said bobbin net machinery ought not to have been taken into consideration as enhancing the rateable value of the premises, or that it has not been taken into consideration on the proper principle, then our order is to be quashed

THOS E ROGERS,

Chairman of Court

It will be noticed in paragraph 7 that the Sessions there arrived at the sum for the land and buildings altogether irrespective of any enhancement by reason of the presence of machinery. To this they added a sum which they considered to be the proper amount by which the land and buildings were enhanced by the machinery. Notwithstanding this and the fact that the decision of the Sessions was upheld in the Court of Appeal it has been sought to contend that because in the case of *Crockett and Jones* v *Northampton Union*,[1] Lord Alverstone, L C J, held that there was to be no separate valuation of the machinery from the buildings in the *ultimate result*, there should be no separate valuation whatever of the machinery. To any such contention it is submitted the *Chard* case is a complete answer, and further that the decision of the Lord Chief Justice is quite consistent with such case. It is to be observed, too, that in the case of *Gifford, Fox & Co* v *Chard Union*, neither in the Divisional Court nor in the Court of Appeal were the respondents, the Assessment Authorities, called upon to reply to the case of the appellants, and Lord Esher (Master of the Rolls) in giving judgment, said · "There were things which had to be taken into consideration, because they were part of the freehold, but there was an intermediate case where the machinery was not so fixed as to form part of the freehold, but the question was, were the things requisite to make the premises suitable for a particular business? and so long as they were used for that purpose *they would be rateable*"

So that the decisions of the Courts would clearly seem to be that not only such machinery as would in fact become a fixture, and therefore part of the freehold, should be rated as part of the freehold, but also, all

[right margin: Gifford, Fox and Co v Chard Union]

[right margin: Separate valuation of machinery]

[right margin: Judgment in Chard case]

---

[1] (1902) 18 T.L R 451, and see p 178 *post*

Gifford, Fox and Co v Chard Union that machinery which was not fixed but became essential to the carrying on of any particular trade, and made the hereditament fit for that trade, is also rateable.

Travelling cranes in docks

In the comparatively recent case of the *London and India Docks v Poplar Union*[1] there were certain cranes for facilitating the lading and unlading of vessels in the docks and which were able to travel upon iron rails up and down the dock, being worked by hydraulic power communicated to them by means of mains laid in the surface of the quays and securely attached by a flexible tube capable of resisting the hydraulic pressure. It was held that these cranes must be treated as enhancing the rateable value of the dock undertaking. Kennedy, J, said, in giving judgment "We feel ourselves unable to satisfactorily distinguish the character of these cranes, with regard to the subject of rating, from the character of the portable engine and boiler mounted on cast iron wheels so that it could be moved from place to place, in *Laing v The Overseers of Bishopwearmouth,*[2] or from the character of the traversing crane weighing thirty tons carried on a pair of wrought iron girders bolted to the iron columns supporting the roof mentioned in page 302 of the same case, and apparently held by the Court to be properly included as part of that which enhances the value of the hereditament "

Crockett and Jones case

Boot and shoe machinery

A later case on the subject of machinery is that of *Crockett and Jones v Northampton Union*[3] which partly referred to very small machines used in the manufacture of boots and shoes The Assessment Committee had included in their valuation of the premises all the machines which were in any way fixed or rested by their own weight, and the contention of the appellants was that such machines were chattels In stating the

[1] (1900) 83 L T 371, 64 J P 820
[2] (1878) 37 L T 781, 17 L J M C 41, L R 3 Q B D 229, 26 W R 351, 42 J P 309
[3] (1902) 18 T L R 451

case for the High Court, the Recorder divided the Crockett and Jones case machines into two classes, No 1 comprised gas engines, shafting, etc, and No 2 the machines used in the process of the manufacture of the boots. During the course of the case for the appellants it was admitted at Quarter Sessions that they had taken into consideration the presence of the machinery in arriving at the figure which they contended was the fair rateable value, and, moreover, they gave an alternative figure for the assessment excluding the machinery in class No 2   The respondents on the other hand had adopted the same principle, but they had arrived at the valuation by first determining the value of the buildings, the machinery No 1, and adding thereto a sum representing the enhancement of the premises by reason of the No 2 machinery   The Recorder, however, neither adopted the contention of the appellants nor the respondents, but in the special case which he settled he stated his findings as follows

"(A) That upon the authority of the *Tyne Boiler Works* case,[1] the whole of No 2 machinery must be taken into consideration in valuing the premises for the purposes of parochial assessment, and the real test is the value of the buildings as fitted with machinery

"(B) That the only reasonable way to do this, if it has to be done, is by valuation of such machinery, that the mere fact of its being in the manufactory is not enough, or the suitability of the building to it

"(C) That such valuation must be separate from the buildings "

This last finding was entirely foreign to any contention on behalf of the respondents during the course of the case, and as Lord Alverstone, L.C J, during the hearing of the case in the Divisional Court, said: "More depends upon the stating of the case than anything"   It was this paragraph that introduced some confusion with

---

[1] (1886) 18 Q B D 81, 56 L J M C 8, 55 L T 825, 51 J P 420.

Crockett and Jones case   regard to the method in which machinery, which has admittedly to be taken into consideration, is to be treated   The Court found that the appellants had taken the machinery into consideration, in the correct way, and, as a matter of fact, the respondents had adopted precisely a similar principle, with this exception, that, in arriving at the enhancement of the buildings by reason of the machinery, the appellants estimated a figure, but the respondents arrived at it by making a valuation of the actual machinery and taking this capital sum at 5 per cent, and so fixed the amount   Later on in the chapter the question of how machinery should be taken into account will be dealt with, but before doing so it would be well if the judgment in this case of *Crockett and Jones* were considered

Judgment   The Lord Chief Justice said[1]   " I think that perhaps the questions before us might have been narrowed had I noticed that which I had not noticed with sufficient care until a few minutes ago, namely, the way in which the question is stated by the learned Recorder in paragraph 22   It was not read to us yesterday by Mr Boyle, and perhaps, if I had seen and appreciated before the actual way in which he had stated the question, one could have directed the attention of the learned counsel more to the actual point to be decided.

" The Recorder states the question in this way   ' The questions for the opinion of the Court are whether the whole of No. 2 machinery, or any and what part thereof, ought to be taken into consideration '—I will deal with the question of ' any or what part thereof ' presently, which, of course, is not a matter which we can deal with— ' as enhancing the value of the premises for the purpose of assessment, and if so whether such machinery is to be taken into consideration upon the principle adopted by me, or according to the contention of the appellants as

[1] From the original shorthand notes in the author's possession

stated in paragraph 17 hereof, or to the contention of the respondents as stated in paragraphs 15 and 16 hereof, or upon what other principle'

"Therefore it does seem to me that the learned Recorder has *adopted* advisedly *the main contention of the respondents, which is for a separate valuation of the machinery,* and has therefore stated his findings and his figures in accordance with those findings fairly in paragraphs 19 and 20, in order to enable the question to be raised That clears up the difficulty which I had in my mind, that I did not understand why, having adopted, as I think that he must adopt, the principle laid down by the Court of Appeal in the *Tyne Boiler Works* case, he had followed it out in a way which did not seem to be in accordance with that principle I think that, taking the findings of the Recorder, he has not properly applied the principle which, after a great many years of discussion and debate, was, at any rate as far as this Court was concerned, so settled in the *Tyne Boiler* case

' Mr Ryde and Mr Latham have been travelling with skill through paths in which some of us wandered for a great many years with more or less advantage to ourselves, and Mr Ryde has endeavoured to get the Court first, I think, to lay down a rule which would have been inconsistent, with the test laid down by the Court of Appeal in the *Tyne Boiler* case For a great many years there had been two contentions on two sides strenuously debated—the manufacturers were attempting to get all the machinery excluded ; the rating authorities were attempting to get all the chattels which were of any permanent character at all included (I do not mean spades, barrows, and things of that kind), but they even went so far as sewing machines at one time There is no doubt that each side contended for a great deal too much from their point of view ; and it is perfectly true, as Mr Ryde pointed out in his argument, that one difficulty in these

Crockett and Jones case Judgment

cases is that you may take the judgments in some of these cases, and in terms, if they are to be taken without consideration of the subject-matter before the Court, they would have a much wider scope and operation than they were intended to have. I quite agree with him that to take the gas meter case and the judgment of the Court in the case of *R. v Lee*,[1] and to apply it to similar machines or different machines, may lead to a result quite contrary to what the Court intended, but I think that at any rate in this Court—probably anywhere short of the House of Lords—it is now settled that once you get machinery in a building, making that building fit for a particular trade or manufacture—a particular purpose—and you get that machinery intended to remain there permanently, then it is a question of fact whether the presence of the machinery intended to remain there permanently does or does not enhance the rateable value assessed upon the basis of the Parochial Assessment Act, or in other words, the rent which the hypothetical tenant would pay one year with another, making the deductions that were indicated in that Act

"In the *Bishopwearmouth* case the finding (I think it was in paragraph 23 of the case, if I remember rightly) stated that the machinery was intended to remain there permanently, and to be permanently used for the purpose of a ship-repairing yard, and the Court without discrimination following that schedule (there were a great many things that were quite as movable as the things referred to here) held that they were all to be taken into consideration Then came the *Tyne Boiler* case, which, (as quite correctly stated in the judgment), was intended to be stated in order to get the Court of Appeal to decide that the *Bishopwearmouth* case had gone too far I am able to say (as I know quite well how it came about) that the *Tyne Boiler Works* case was most carefully stated. It

[1] (1866) L R 1 Q B 241 ; 35 L J M C 105 , 12 Jur N S 225 , 13 L T. 701 , 14 W R. 311 , 30 J.P. 182

was stated in order to endeavour to make the question of attachment to the freehold the crucial test, and the Court were asked to find (it being brought prominently to notice that many of the machines were not attached either to the soil or building, but rested by their own weight on the ground or on stone foundations especially prepared for them) that the object of attachment to the machines was to steady them, and it did steady them in the working, and that the method of attachment was convenient if occasion arose for their removal. An attempt was made to get the Court to say that, unless you have the machines so attached that they become part of the freehold, they are not to be taken into consideration at all as enhancing the rateable value. Now that the Court of Appeal, whatever else they decided, distinctly declined to do. I will not go over the matter at length, but they said that in their opinion the *Bishopwearmouth* case had not, when properly understood, gone further than the earlier cases. Lord Esher dealt with the question of mere attachment, and pointed out, with his usual very good sense in such matters, that where you got a machine heavy enough into the warehouse which was intended to remain there, it ought not to make any difference because there happened to be a screw which was not wanted for the moment and which was used to attach the machine to the soil. Then he stated the rule which has been acted upon ever since. 'I believe the rule really to be that things which are on the premises to be rated, and which are there for the purpose of making, and which make the premises fit as premises for the particular purpose for which they are used, are to be taken into account in ascertaining the rateable value of such premises. Of course, it is not all things on the premises, or that are used on the premises, which are to be taken into account, but things which are there for the purpose of making, and which do make them fit as premises for the particular purposes for which they are used'

Crockett and Jones case
Judgment

What machinery to be taken into account

Crockett and Jones case
Judgment

" That case was not taken further It was considered to be at any rate a final enunciation of the law, and be it right or be it wrong, or be it subject to appeal or review ultimately, it is binding upon us, and for the purposes of this case of course I adopt it. It is to be noted the Master of the Rolls did not say how they are to be taken into account

" I think that the subsequent decision in the House of Lords, not, I admit, upon the same matter, but upon a kindred matter, in the *Mersey Docks* case, shows that, once that question is put to the Court of Sessions by itself, it becomes a question of fact, and that it is a question of fact which the Court of Quarter Sessions have to answer for themselves, giving the best light and obtaining the best information they can It is in that connection, and in that connection only, that the nature of the machinery, *its value, its life, and things of that kind*, may become material , because, of course, it is self-evident that machinery which will last a very short time—machinery which is replaceable in a day or two—is in a very different position, as far as making premises fit for the trade which is carried on in them, as compared with machinery which is of a large and heavy description and which will require considerable trouble to take in and out, and which could not be replaced except with considerable derangement of the premises as such Therefore, there are elements, when you come to apply the test, which are really questions of fact.

" Now, having at some length, because it is of some importance, endeavoured to explain what I understand to be the true view of the law, which has now been in force I think for something like fifteen or twenty years or even more, one has to consider which side, as far as the question is concerned, has adopted the true view The appellants, I think substantially in the earlier part of paragraph 17, have stated the contention correctly. I do not adopt all that they have said, and I do not intend to send the case back in order that the question may be answered in exactly the same way, but I think that part of their contention in paragraph 17 was right. They said this. 'The appellants, on the other hand, in agreeing the figures of £275 as the rateable value of the buildings, stated that they had taken into account the No 2 machinery so far as the law allows or requires it to be considered as enhancing the value of the premises. That is to say, they had taken into account the suitability of the premises to receive such machinery, and the fact that such machinery was to be found on the premises. Had they not so taken it into account their estimate, as stated in evidence, of the valuation of the building was £185.'

"Of course, I express no opinion as to whether the £185 was the right figure or whether it ought to be increased to as much as the Recorder has increased it to or not, but I think that that contention of the appellants is in substantial conformity with the rule laid down by the Court of Appeal in the *Tyne Boiler* case, and the latter part of the contention, which I do not adopt, is really only a discussion of the way in which the Court should inform its mind in arriving at the particular estimate they will form of the enhanced value of the premises by reason of the presence of the machinery. Therefore, I do not adopt, nor do I think it necessary to criticise further, the last part of paragraph 17. My adoption of it, as expressing in other words the rule of the *Tyne Boiler* case, stops short at the passage I have left off at, ending at the words, 'the valuation of the buildings was £185.'

"Now, by the other side, it was contended 'No, you are to have a separate valuation of the machinery, you are to rate it as though you were, so to speak, rating the machinery as a rateable hereditament, and you are to add that to the value of the building.' The learned Recorder,

Crockett and Jones case Judgment

Crockett and Jones case
Judgment

in order to raise the question, has adopted that contention,[1] and he has said that the valuation must be separate from the buildings, and that such valuation should be based upon the actual cost of the machines as applied to the purpose for which the premises are intended In my opinion that is adopting a principle which is inconsistent with the rule that I have read from the *Tyne Boiler* case

Valuation of machinery necessary to determine enhancement

I think that the valuation ought not be separate in its *ultimate result   That you may have to enquire into value in order to get at the figures may be possibly true, but the valuation ought to be an answer to the question put by Lord Justice Brett, of how much is the rateable value of the premises enhanced by the presence of this machinery, as it is there and intended to permanently remain there* Therefore, in reducing the £275, which has been agreed, down to the £202, excluding all the machinery, and in treating the machinery as a separate item to be valued by itself, taking up the total to £329 as compared with £275, the Recorder has adopted a wrong basis

"Therefore I think that the case must go back to the learned Recorder in order that he may answer the question in his own way and assess the amount of the enhanced rateable value, if any, upon the bases laid down by the Master of the Rolls and Lord Justice Lindley in the *Tyne Boiler* case, and in accordance with that he will amend the valuation list. But I think that the separate valuation of machinery, for which he has contended, is not one which is in accordance with the decision I have only to say this We are asked to say what part of No 2 machinery should be included Now that I absolutely decline to do. Over and over again, to my knowledge, a similar attempt has been made by appellants and respondents to get the Court to go through this kind of case and say, ' This

---

[1] This can scarcely be said to have been the contention of respondents, see p 179 *ante*

machine does enhance and that machine does not enhance' That is just where the question of fact comes in.
As was pointed out in the course of the argument by my
brother Channell, which was founded on an observation of
Mr Ryde's, there may be things which, if they were taken
out and were not there, would render other things in the
place not only of less value, but, it might be, actually
worthless. Therefore it is not for the Court, sitting to
decide questions of law, to go through a long schedule and
say, 'This machinery does enhance and the other does
not' Otherwise, as has been pointed out, we should have
to lay down some absolutely arbitrary rule, such as was
attempted to be laid down with reference to the attachment, which, as has been pointed out, is not conclusive in
any way in the matter The Court of Sessions, or the
tribunal of fact, must decide for itself upon the principle
which I have referred to Therefore our answer is that,
understood by the light which I have endeavoured to
explain, the contention of the appellants is right, founded
upon the judgment in the *Tyne Boiler* case and that the
contention of the respondents adopted by the Recorder is
wrong."

The contention of the respondents, however, did not
go as far as the Recorder, and nowhere had they asked
for a separate valuation of the machinery in the *ultimate
result*, a contention wrong in law, which in itself, it is
respectfully submitted, was sufficient to justify the course
taken by the Divisional Court in sending the case back
for revision

Having traced thus far the course of the cases, in the
history of rating, with respect to machinery, it would
seem impossible to come to any other conclusion than
that all machinery used in a factory or works, whether
attached or unattached, for any reason incidental to the
peculiar machine or factory, must be taken into account
when fixing the gross and rateable values of a heredita-

Crockett and Jones case Judgment

Conclusions in other cases

ment containing machinery, where it can be shown that such machinery makes a hereditament what it is, that is to say, a brewery ceases to be a brewery when the mash tuns, fermenting vats and other vessels necessary for the manufacture of beer, are taken away, or a cotton mill ceases to be a cotton mill when the carding engines, mules and other machines have been removed, and so on That this conclusion is correct is strikingly evident from the many Bills that have been before Parliament, having for their object the exemption from rating of all machinery save the first motive power, namely, engines, shafting, although, why the promoters do not go so far as to exclude these it is difficult to say, but in a work of this nature it is not desired in any way to deal with the moral or economical side of the question, but rather to attempt to elucidate the difficulties in the way of Assessment Committees in applying the principle   It is, however, a well-known fact that a large number of Unions in many parts of England do not even take into consideration the presence of machinery at all, and this has the effect of relieving the manufacturer at the expense of the other ratepayers of the Union, an illegality which might have the effect of upsetting the rate.[1]   It is also a fact that much confusion seems to have been occasioned — unnecessarily, it is submitted — by the decision in *Crockett and Jones* v *Northampton Union*,[2] with the result that two Quarter Sessions, presided over by most eminent King's Counsel, have since given decisions on the question of taking machinery into consideration in directly opposite ways.   The cases in question are the Clarendon Press at Oxford, reported in the "Oxford Chronicle," June 20th, 1902, (also "Estates

---

[1] See *R* v *Birmingham and Staffordshire Gas Light Co*, (1837) 6 A & E, p 634, 6 L.J M C 92 (referred to at p 141 *ante*), and also the evidence of Mr P R Smith before the Royal Commission on Local Taxation (1898), Vol I. at p 415

[2] (1902) 18 T L R 451

Gazette," May 3, 17, 24 , June 21 and 28, 1902), and the
" Devon and Exeter Gazette' Printing Works, reported
in " The Estates Gazette," January 10th, 1903. In the
Oxford case, the Hon. A. T Lyttelton, K C , is reported   Oxford case
to have said, in giving judgment " I am satisfied that,
in this case, the witnesses for the University have
insufficiently considered the presence of the tenant's
machinery, which makes the premises fit for the purpose
of publishing and printing, and so enhances their rateable
value   Mr Humphreys Davies, the first witness called
for the University, went so far as to assert that, in his
opinion, it was immaterial whether machinery of this
nature, worth £40,000, or £20,000, was on the premises,
and admitted that the £250, the sum which, he computed,
measured the enhanced value of the premises, had been
arrived at as he stood in the witness box   On the
hypothesis, which was not controverted, that the tenant's
machinery was necessary and had been installed in
a prudent manner, and that the presence of the tenant's
machinery did enhance the value of the premises,
I am unable to understand why a large quantity of
useful machinery does not give a greater enhancement
'o the value of the premises than a small. It was said
that the machinery, being the tenant's, there was no
difference in the rent which the landlord could exact
owing to its presence. This proves too much, for it
leaves the witness without reason for adding anything
to the value of the premises owing to the presence of
the machinery, although he conceded an enhancement
to the extent of £250.   It fails also to recognise the
increased rent which premises can command by reason
of their fitness to carry on at once a going concern
Justification was further sought for this position in
the judgment of the Divisional Court in the case of
Crockett and Jones v *The Northampton Union*
(unreported, but a transcript of the judgment in which

case was furnished to me)   But though that case decides
that, in the ultimate figure arrived at as the rateable
value, no separate valuation of machinery should be given
as distinct from the hereditament to be rated, I can find
nothing in the judgment which entitles a witness, when
seeking that ultimate figure, to blindfold himself as to the
amount and value of the machinery which enhances the
value of the hereditament   On the contrary, the Lord
Chief Justice in this case emphasises once more
the well-known proposition of the *Tyne Boiler*[1] case,
in which it was held that machinery and plant
placed in a manufactory for the purpose of making the
premises fit as premises for such a manufactory are to be
taken into account as enhancing the value of the hereditament, although such machinery and plant remain personal
property, and are not physically attached to the premises.
The Chief Justice nowhere asserts that it is illegitimate
to arrive at the ultimate figure of the rate by a process
which (*inter alia*) may include a valuation of the
machinery and the placing of a percentage on that
value "

Exeter Case   In the *Exeter* case, however, on similar facts as far as
the principle and the class of machinery were concerned,
Mr J. A Foote, K C, gave judgment as follows " In
what sense is it correct to say that when the tenant brought
the machinery on the premises and installed it there he
increased or enhanced the yearly value of the hereditament? Using language in its ordinary sense, is it true
that he increased that value by an amount equivalent to
interest on the capital value of the machinery—machinery
for which he pays rent, so to speak, to himself, and which
he could remove at his own will and pleasure? I am
unable to accept this view, which is the only one presented to me on behalf of the respondents, and I believe
the real enhancement of value must be measured in a

---

[1] (1886) 18 Q B D 81, 56 L J M C 8, 55 L T 825, 51 J P 120

very different way. The present, or any person proposing to carry on the same business and able to hire machinery from him, would give the landlord something more for the premises than other people would do, because they are adapted to receive the machinery and because the machinery is there installed and ready to hand. I can see no other enhancement of the value of the hereditament, and I am strongly of opinion that it would be wrong to take this machinery into account in the same sense as the plant of a gasworks or a railway. In the *Northampton* case last year, as in the case of *Chidley v West Ham*,[1] the valuing authority had done exactly what the respondents ask me to do here. and it was held that they were wrong in both cases. If they were wrong in substance, and not merely in form, I ought not to follow them in either. For these reasons I decline to consider the rateable value of the premises as enhanced by a percentage on the value (either cost value or present value) of the machinery.'

The judgment in the *Oxford* case confirms the views already submitted on p 189 *ante*, while that in the *Exeter* case controverts it, and both arguments were claimed to be based on the case of *Crockett and Jones v The Northampton Union*,[2] so that it is evident that that case was not by any means a final settlement of the much-vexed question, and it is to be noticed that, throughout the list of cases referred to, the *crux* of the whole matter seems to lie in the answer to the question " Does a machine for the time being become part of the freehold when so annexed in a factory—whether by weight, bolts or otherwise—as to make it essential to that factory in order to enable an incoming tenant at once to carry on the business of that factory with the machines planted there ? " This question would entirely seem to have been decided

Machinery part of freehold

---

[1] (1871) 32 L T 486 39 J P 310, see also p 119 *ante*
[2] (1902) 18 T L R 151

in favour of the parochial authorities. This view is further strengthened by the case of *Reynolds* v *William Ashby and Son*[1] decided in 1903 in the Court of Appeal The facts of the case, as reported in The Times Law Reports, were as follows The lessee of a factory mortgaged it *with the fixtures* Subsequently the lessee hired, on a hire-purchase agreement, certain carpenters' machines, which were worked by steam power, and which were fixed to the land by bolts and screws to prevent them vibrating By the hire-purchase agreement, the property in the machines was to remain in the vendor of the machines until all the hire instalments were paid, when the property would then vest in the hirer The vendor was to be at liberty to determine the hiring and to retake possession of the machines on the happening of certain events. The lessee of the factory committed some default and the mortgagee took possession of the premises under the mortgage deed, whereupon the vendor of the machinery sought to recover the machinery, but the mortgagee detained it, contending that it had been so fixed to the freehold that it became part of the hereditament and passed under the mortgage. The vendor of the machinery thereupon brought an action, and, at the trial of the action, Mr Justice Lawrance held, upon the authority of *Hobson* v *Gorringe*,[2] that the articles in question were fixtures and passed under the mortgage There was an appeal from this to the Court of Appeal, and the Master of the Rolls, in dismissing the appeal and holding that "the machinery had become part of the freehold, said that the machinery consisted of a number of solid and weighty machines, which were all actuated by power—he understood steam power—and which constituted one system of machinery   . The plaintiff contended that the machines never lost their character as movable chattels,

[1] (1903) 1 K B 87, 19 T L R 70
[2] (1897) 1 Ch 182

and never became fixtures in the true sense, namely, something that had become annexed to the freehold, but was removable by the tenant for life as against the remainderman or the tenant as against his landlord Unless the plaintiff could carry his position that far, he could not succeed upon this part of the case . There was a long series of decisions in which it had been treated as an inference of law that chattels attached as these were to be regarded as fixtures . With regard to the case of *Chidley* v *Churchwardens of West Ham,*[1] that was a rating case, and it had been commented upon in this Court in *Tyne Boiler Works Co* v *Overseers of Longbenton,*[2] and if it could be sustained it could only be upon the ground on which it was distinguished in that case, namely, that the chattels there had been rated as personal property "

From the extracts from the Master of the Rolls judgment above, it would consequently appear that the majority of machinery in all factories, directly it is put there and intended to remain permanently there, becomes part of the freehold property, and thus is brought within the decision of the *Tyne Boiler Works* case,[2] namely, that it must be considered as passing by a demise from landlord to tenant, and there is nothing in the case of *Crockett and Jones* v. *Northampton Union*[1] that overrules or could overrule the decision in the Court of Appeal, the main point of the latter case being that a separate valuation in the ultimate result is wrong, although it was stated by the Lord Chief Justice in that case that a valuation might have to be made at some time to answer the question of the amount of enhancement to the value of the buildings *qua* buildings by reason of the presence of the actual machinery. In fact, therefore, the only

[1] (1874) 32 L T 486 , 39 J P 310
[2] (1886) 18 Q B D 81 56 L J M C 8, 55 L T 825, 51 J P 420
[1] (1902) 18 L T R 451

question that has to be answered is, What rent a fitted factory would realise if a hypothetical landlord let it to a tenant? and the rent a tenant would give under such circumstances could only be based on the value of the hereditament offered him, and therefore he could not exclude from his mind the capital value (as distinct from cost) of the machinery, any more than he could exclude the capital value of the land and that of the buildings

It is satisfactory to find that a further attempt has been made by the Assessment Committee of the Hunslet Union (Leeds)[1] to get a final settlement of the matter, if possible, and for the first time in the history of machinery rating cases a decision of the House of Lords has now been obtained which, it is submitted, sets the conflict at rest, but it is more than curious that the Earl of Halsbury, L C., in delivering judgment in that case, said "It is enough for me that a long series of decisions for certainly half a century have established the bald proposition which is all I am insisting upon, namely, that although the machinery may not be part of the freehold it yet is to be taken into account, and in saying that I do not want to muffle it in a phrase, but what I mean by that is, that to increase the amount of the rate which is exacted from the tenant you may enter into that question and form a judgment upon it, although as a matter of fact the machinery may not be attached to the freehold "

It is obvious that in the opinion of the Lord Chancellor the bald proposition that machinery was to be taken into account in a way that increased the amount of the rental value of the premises had been established for fifty years and was no new proposition.

This case is so important that it is deemed desirable to set out at length below the judgment of the Recorder, Mr. Tindal Atkinson, K C —a judgment clearly stating

---

[1] *Kirby v Hunslet Union*, (1906) A C 43, 75 L J K B 129, 94 L T 36, 70 J P. 50, 22 T.L R 167.

the issues and the principles involved and upheld by the Divisional Court, the Court of Appeal and the House of Lords, the respondents only being called on to argue the case in the Divisional Court.

It is also interesting to compare this judgment with those of Mr Foote and Mr Littelton respectively, in the *Exeter*[1] and *Oxford*[2] cases because the state of the law was exactly the same in both these cases as when Mr Tindal Atkinson came to give his judgment at Leeds

The judgment is also valuable as dealing with the mode in which machinery can be taken into account, not only the question of whether or no it is to be taken into account, but the proper method to apply.

Mr Tindal Atkinson's judgment[3] is as follows "The appellant in this case is an occupier from year to year, under an expired tenancy, of some engineering works at Hunslet, at a rental of £28 per annum, and he is appealing against an assessment of £67 gross and £45 rateable, the previous assessment being £29 gross and £22 rateable The importance of the case is certainly not in the amount involved, but it has been fought at considerable length for the purpose of settling an important principle, upon which the assessment of a large number of much more important works in the Hunslet Union will depend

"The question involved is the settlement of the mode in which machinery, such as this is admitted to be, can be made available for the purposes of Poor Law Assessment Machinery by itself is not the subject of rating If fixed to the freehold, either as the landlord's or as the tenant's fixture, it is, for the purpose of being rated, a part of the freehold, and no difficulty arises Where the plant and

---

[1] "Ryde's Rating Appeals" (1894-1904), p 101 "The Estates Gazette," January 10th, 1903

[2] *Ibid*, p 96 "Oxford Chronicle," June 20th, 1902

[3] From the shorthand notes in the author's possession

machinery are not affixed to the freehold, but have been placed on the premises to be rated, for the purpose of making, and do make, the premises fit for the particular purpose for which they are used (to use Lord Esher's words), they then 'are capable of being taken into account in ascertaining the rateable value of such premises' In this case the machinery belonging to the tenant, and which is at present on the premises in question, is admitted to come within the above category, and it is common ground between the parties to this appeal that this machinery has, in some way, to be taken into account in arriving at the rateable value The point that has been so strenuously fought in this case is In what way is it to be made available ? The appellant contends that the value of the user of this machinery connected with the occupation of the premises ought not to be considered, but that the question of benefit must be limited to the advantage derived from the fact that the machinery affords proof of the convenience of the building for the purpose of the business, and a possible value from the tenant being able to take it *in situ* The respondents, on the other hand, say that the only way in which you can properly take machinery into account is by taking the hereditament as you find it, furnished and equipped with the necessary machinery, and ascertaining what is the rent which the tenant from year to year will give for such premises as they stand, including, of course, the right to use what he finds there.

"It is extraordinary how little decisive authority there is on the point. The earlier authorities which have been quoted are of little or no assistance in this regard, although exceedingly valuable on the point as to what sort of machinery may be treated as adding to the rateable value, and, in the leading authority on the above point. the Court of Appeal, in the case of the *Tyne Boiler Works*

Co.,[1] carefully and deliberately refrained from expressing any opinion on the method by which the value was to be ascertained   In the case of *R v Haslam*,[2] in dealing with the case of large chambers placed upon the premises used as chemical works, Mr Justice Patteson said . 'We do not think it necessary to determine whether the chambers erected on the appellant's premises are, or are not, annexed to the freehold, because we are of opinion that, according to the principle laid down in the various cases on the subject, the rateable value of the premises is undoubtedly increased by the use of those chambers,' showing that that learned Judge was of opinion that the additional value of the hereditament was in respect of the user of the plant in question and not merely in consequence of its existence   The only case which can be called a direct authority on this point is the case of *Gifford, Fox & Co v Chard Union*,[3] in the Court of Appeal.   I have, however, been furnished with a print setting out the case as stated by the Quarter Sessions, the proceedings in the Divisional Court, and in the Court of Appeal   It is most important to see what was the contention adopted by the Sessions and what were the questions submitted to the Court   In paragraph 19 of the case there are set out the findings of the Sessions They found, first that the machinery had been rightly taken into consideration in arriving at the rateable value, and, secondly, 'that the premises were accordingly assessable to the Poor Rate at the amount at which they would let to a tenant from year to year as a going concern of a lace factory, equipped, with such machinery as was essential to its user as such factory.'   There were two questions submitted to the Court, first, whether the machinery was to be taken into account at all; second,

---

[1] (1886) 15 Q B 81, 56 L J M C 8, 55 L T 825 51 J P 120
[2] (1851) 17 Q B 220, 15 Jur 972, 15 J P 612
[3] (1890) 63 L T 249, 6 T L R 431

whether, assuming it was, it was taken into consideration
upon the proper principle. Now it is clear that not one,
but both of these questions would have to be answered,
if the first question was answered in the affirmative.
The only point argued was the first one.   The Divisional
Court and the Court of Appeal answered that question in
the affirmative, and as they affirmed the order of the
Sessions, it must be taken that they answered the second
question in the affirmative also, that the Sessions had
taken into account the machinery on the proper principle,
namely, of a rent which would be paid for a factory
equipped with such machinery   The observations in the
judgment of Lord Esher in this case in the Court of
Appeal, as reported in the ' Times Law Reports,' namely,
' that machinery, whether fixed to the freehold or not, if
necessary to the use of the premises as such and going to
make up the value for which the rent was paid, might
be taken into account,' show clearly to my mind that he
was referring to the user of both premises and machinery
as the factor in the production of the rent

   " Two main objections which have been urged by
Mr. Boyle to the principle adopted by the respondents
are, first, that in adopting it you will be rating
machinery, secondly, that the tenant buys the
machinery, and yet has to pay the landlord rent
for it

   " As to the first objection, I think the answer is, that
to take the value which machinery may add to the
letting value of the premises is not to take the value of
the machinery, the added rent has no fixed relation to
the value of the machinery   It is quite true that you
may have cases where the added value to the rent may
very closely approximate to the hiring value of the
machinery: where, for instance, the machinery is new
and the building is such that every advantage is gained
from the machines by the construction and character of

the building itself—in such case you might arrive at the
added value by taking the hiring value of the machinery
on a percentage basis. But in most cases it would not
at all be the fact that the two things would be the same
If new machinery is put into old and inconvenient
buildings, where the full benefit of the machinery could
not be gained, no tenant would give as an addition a
5 per cent rental on the value of the machinery or
calculate the rent he offered on such basis. Indeed, the
premises in this case afford an illustration of what I
mean Evidence has been given that, owing to the
lowness of the room, full power cannot be obtained to
drive the machinery, which has the effect of detracting
from the value of the machinery as applied to this
building The vice of the way in which the Recorder
dealt with the valuation in the case of *Crockett v The
Northampton Union*[1] was, that he had not considered
what was the rental value of the premises with the
addition of the machinery, but had arrived at the value
of the latter independently of any connection with the
premises themselves

"The second point urged by Mr Boyle was that the
tenant buys the machinery, and yet has to pay the landlord rent for it I think this involves the consideration
of the facts of the particular tenancy in question, which
I think is fallacious The question is, not what this
tenant has done in the purchase, or whose property, in
this case, the machinery is. For rating purposes you
must take the premises as you find them, permanently
equipped as engineering works, with all the necessary
appliances and machines as it stands, what is the rent?
and the answer to this question shows you what is the
rateable value. I am of opinion, therefore, that the principle by which the rateable value is to be ascertained in
this case is that contended for by the respondents,

[1] (1902) 18 T L R 451

namely, that in ascertaining the rent you must take into account the value of the user of the machinery as contributing to the rental value of the freehold, but in saying this I am far from saying that such value is to be arrived at by taking the cost or value of the machinery, putting a percentage on such value, and adding it to the rent   The increase of value due to the machinery may and will vary in each case, owing to a number of causes, such as I have indicated.

"I have now to apply these principles to the case before me   I find the net rental value of the land, buildings and landlord's fixtures, without the rest of the machinery, at £21.   To this has to be added what a tenant would give, by way of additional rent, for these premises, equipped as they are with the machinery in them, including the right of user   This I estimate roughly at £10 a year, making the net rateable value £31.   For the purposes of an appeal I may say that if the appellants' contention should be found to be correct, the rateable value should stand at £26 "

When the case was before the Divisional Court it was twice sent back to the Recorder for explanations on the judgment.   On the first occasion in the Divisional Court the Lord Chief Justice (Lord Alverstone) asked the Recorder for a further explanation of the passage which reads as follows —

" I am of opinion therefore that the principle by which the rateable value is to be ascertained in this case is that contended for by the respondents, namely, that in ascertaining the rent you must take into account the value of the user of the machinery as contributing to the rental value of the freehold."

In answer to this question, Mr. Tindal Atkinson signed a memorandum to the following effect —

" I desire to add that what I meant and what I thought I had expressed was that the proper basis of assessment is the rent which a hypothetical tenant would give for the premises already equipped with the necessary machinery, as included in the demise—a rent which would be something more than the rent which would be given for the bare premises without the machinery The value of the machinery was only taken by me into account as enhancing to some degree the rent of the premises, and I have put no separate rent or value on the machinery as such."

It will be observed here that Mr Atkinson had not followed what was done in the case of *Crockett and Jones \ Northampton Union*,[1] and therein the two cases are easily distinguishable.

On the case being heard a second time before the Divisional Court, it was again sent back to Mr. Tindal Atkinson for a further explanation, and an addendum was added by the Recorder as follows —

"I held that in enquiring what was the gross estimated rental and the rateable value, the basis of the problem was to ascertain what was the rent which a hypothetical tenant would give for the engineering works as a combination of land, buildings and scheduled machines, on a demise which included the right to use the scheduled machines, that is to say, on the assumption that the hypothetical tenant would get as part of the consideration for the hypothetical rent the right to use such machines upon the premises during his tenancy, and that in this way the scheduled machines were properly being taken into account as enhancing the rental and rateable value of the freehold. I also held that the value of the user of the machinery was not necessarily to be arrived at by taking the cost or value of the machinery, and putting a percentage on such value as had been done by the respondent's valuers '

---

[1] (1902) 18 T L R 151

It is submitted, therefore, that in valuing a factory—
i e , a hereditament that is a combination of land and
buildings and machinery used thereon and therein—for
assessment purposes there are three factors.   First, land ;
secondly, buildings, and, thirdly, how much these two are
enhanced by the actual machines that are *in situ* on the
premises, or, in other words, how much will a hypothetical
tenant give in addition to the rent of the buildings and
land for the right to use the machines?   It clearly follows,
that to adequately answer this third factor a valuation of
the machinery is as essential as a valuation of the land or
the buildings, as it is the combination of the three factors
that is rateable (Lopes, J , in *Tyne Boiler* case), and to
value only the suitability of the premises to receive
machinery is obviously not sufficient.   Indeed, the rent
paid for premises which are suitable to receive particular
machines is only a part of the rateable value, as this sum
would not vary whether costly or cheap machines were
laid down   In the case even of *Crockett and Jones
v Northampton Union*,[1] where the Recorder at Quarter
Sessions held that it was necessary to make a separate
valuation of the machinery in the *ultimate* result, the
Lord Chief Justice, in giving judgment in that case, said
that, although it was wrong to have a separate valuation
in the *ultimate* result, yet to get at the figures of how
much the rateable value of the premises would be
enhanced by the presence of machinery, the value of the
machinery would have to be inquired into, and this might
be an answer to the question, " How much is the rateable
value of the premises enhanced by the presence of
machinery ? "

It has been argued that this method of taking
machinery into consideration virtually amounts to the
rating of machinery *per se*, and indirectly this may be so,
but clearly the principle must be right if the rule laid

---

[1] (1902) 18 T L R 451

down by Lord Esher that the machines are to be considered as part of what is let as between landlord and tenant, is to be followed, for in a competitive market a hypothetical tenant would pay a hypothetical landlord rent for the machines, based on the principle of capital value and interest thereon, in exactly the same way that the rent of a building would be ascertained, although it must be borne in mind that the whole concern is to be looked on as a going concern, and in the *ultimate* result, which can only mean the Rate Book, only one figure is to be inserted for the concern as a going concern, and this rule has now been endorsed and confirmed by the House of Lords in the *Hunslet* case

In concluding this chapter—the question is often asked, why should 5 per cent. be taken on the capital value of machinery for the rateable value? The answer briefly is this, that it is on the assumption that a tenant would willingly give to a landlord not less than 5 per cent per annum on its capital value for the use of machinery, he, the tenant, repairing same and keeping same in working order. The gross value may be very much in excess of the rateable value, as the statutable allowances may be very heavy where machinery is concerned, but the machinery should be treated in the same manner as the buildings and the land, although the percentage may vary, and thus the decisions in the various cases be applied, but when the ultimate result of the valuation is arrived at the figures must not be separated in the valuation list. It would be equally absurd to separate in the valuation list the buildings and fixtures of a house, and as in all houses there are certain landlord's fixtures which are included in the rent of the house, so machinery in a factory—when intended permanently to remain there— must be considered as a landlord's fixture and so let with and part of the factory for rating purposes

Why machinery taken at 5 per cent on capital value

PART II.—PRACTICE.

CHAPTER I.

LAND.

Introduction — Unoccupied Land — Unenclosed Land — Common Land—Incorporeal Hereditaments—Sporting Rights — Woodlands — Coprolites — Tithes — Farms — Agricultural Rates Act—Nursery Grounds and Market Gardens— Sewage Farms —Tolls— Lighthouse Tolls — Market Tolls—Lairages—Moorings—Race Course

IN order to present the subject of Rating in as clear and Introduction intelligent a manner as possible, it has, so far, been attempted to deal only with the leading principles which underlie and govern the actual practice, the principles which must be fully appreciated before any step is taken in the actual making of a valuation for rating purposes. In this the second part of the book— Practice—it is assumed that the preceding Part I has already received attention

It has been shewn that the occupier is liable, and that the Poor Rate is not a tax upon land itself, as is generally understood, but a personal charge in respect of a beneficial occupation of land [1]

Where land is vacant therefore—that is, not being Unoccupied used in any capacity, but merely having upon it a board land announcing that such land is "to let"—it is not rateable The land, however, should not be cultivated, but should

---

[1] *Rews v Gells*, (1778) Cowp 452, 1 Dougl 301.

cattle stray upon it (without the permission of the owner) for the purpose of grazing, it has been held that there is no liability on the part of the owner to be rated [1]

Unenclosed land

Where land is let in its natural and uncultivated condition, it could command but a very small rental, and the difference between the gross and rateable values would be practically nothing, as there would be no repair and no insurance, and practically no expenses to keep the property in a state to command a rent. It could apparently be let only for the purpose of grazing; and that the risk which a tenant would run in allowing his stock on the land would be very great, owing to the probability of the cattle straying

A right of common is, however, not rateable. That is to say, where certain burgesses of a town, who were consequently occupiers of ancient messuages within it, had a right to turn cattle at certain periods on to the land, the owners of the land, for the time, being excluded, it was held that such occupation was a mere right of common for which the burgesses were not rateable.[2] See also upon this point the case of *Lincoln (Mayor of)* v *Holmes Common*[3] and that of *R* v. *Tewkesbury*.[4]

Incorporeal hereditaments

The value of land is often very much improved by certain rights of fishing or shooting, and with regard to this the Rating Act, 1874,[5] enacts that " Where any right of fowling, or of shooting, or of taking or killing game or rabbits, or of fishing (in the Act hereinafter referred to as a right of sporting) is severed from the occupation of the land, and is not let, and the owner of such right receives rent for the land, the said right shall not be separately valued or rated, but the gross and

---

[1] *Smith* v *New Forest Union* (1890) 61 L T 670, 54 J P 324, 6 T L R 31—C A

[2] *R* v *Churchill*, (1825) 4 B & C 750 6 D & R 635

[3] (1867) L R 2 Q B 482, 16 L T 731 36 L J M C 73 15 W R 786

[4] (1810) 13 East 155

[5] 37 & 38 Vict, c 54, s 6

rateable value of the land shall be estimated as if the said right were not severed." And again, " Where any right of sporting, when severed from the occupation of the land, is let, either the owner or the lessee thereof, according as the persons making the rate determine, may be rated as the occupier thereof " It will be seen, therefore, that a tenant renting a property, in respect of which there is a right of sporting reserved by the landlord, is liable to be rated, but the Act further provides that unless he has specially contracted otherwise, he may deduct from his rent such portion of any poor or any other local rate as is paid by him in respect of such right Subject to these provisions, the owner of any right of sporting when severed from the occupation of the land (e g a tenant of land with right of sporting who lets the same) may be rated as the occupier thereof, and for the purposes of the Act the person who, if the right of sporting is not let, is entitled to exercise the right, or who, if the right is let, is entitled to receive the rent for the same, shall be deemed to be the owner of the right and therefore rated for it. There have been several cases decided upon this point, notably the one of *Rogers* v. *St. Germans Union* [1] Here the landlord of a hereditament consisting of a dwelling-house, out-buildings, etc., let his property on lease to a tenant with certain exceptions, amongst which were the liberty of hunting, fowling and fishing over and through the premises at all times during the term It was held that this right of sporting was severed from the occupation of the land and owned by the landlord, consequently that it was rateable as such

It frequently happens that sporting rights are not assessed as prescribed by this Act, and there can be no denying the inconvenience that would be occasioned if the Act were literally followed in the actual preparation of Valuation Lists The position under the Act is briefly as follows :—

Sporting rights

---

[1] (1876) 35 L.T 332

A is the owner of certain lands in a parish, which he lets to B , a tenant, but reserves to himself the right of sporting and does not let it to a third party. Strictly under the Act this right, whatever it is worth (say, two shillings per acre), is not to be separately valued but is included in the Valuation List in the gross and rateable values of the land itself The rates would be collected from the ter ., but he is entitled to go to the Assessment Com .,.ee and obtain a certificate of the amount of the increase of rates due to such sporting right and to deduct the same from his rent

Assume, therefore, that in a certain parish there is an estate of 2,000 acres owned by one person, but let to tenants in twenty different holdings of 100 acres each. twenty certificates would have to be obtained from and given by the Assessment Committee in respect of each rate as it fell due With a large estate running into two or three thousand acres, and possibly in more than one parish, and the value of the sporting rights possibly not being uniform, the labour entailed upon the tenants, the Assessment Committee and the estate agent would be enormous

Practice in assessing sporting rights

The practice, therefore, generally speaking is to assess sporting rights when severed from the occupation of the land separately to the owner, with the result that there is only one assessment in each parish in respect of the sporting rights on the estate in question, although that right may extend over a large number of farms occupied by several tenants

The passing of the Agricultural Rates Act[1] has introduced a further difficulty into an already inconvenient system. as under the Agricultural Rates Order, 1896, Section 2, it is directed that " where any right of sporting is severed from the occupation of the land, but is not let, and the Assessment Committee have

[1] (1896) 59 & 60 Vict. c 16

certified the amount by which the rateable value of the land is increased by reason of its being estimated as if the right of sporting were not so severed, such amount (according to the certificate of the Assessment Committee) shall be included in the rateable value of the buildings and other hereditaments for the purpose of the Agricultural Rates Act, 1896, so that the value of the sporting right will not benefit by the Agricultural Rates Act."[1]

From this direction it would appear that the value of the sporting right is to be added to the value of the building where relief is given under the Agricultural Rates Act for land, but as it not infrequently happens that land is let without any buildings at all thereon, according to this Order a separate entry would have to be made in the column for buildings and other hereditaments in respect of the value of the sporting right, and assessed direct to the tenant, although he would not ultimately pay the rate, and this is the opinion of the Local Government Board.[2]

It follows therefore that the practice in question is not legal, and might afford an owner the opportunity of raising the technical objection that he was wrongly rated, and such an objection might be sufficient to upset a rate Such an objection has been taken within the knowledge of the author, but was not proceeded with beyond the Assessment Committee The object of the objection as stated by the objector was to use the technical point for the purpose of getting the assessment reduced.

That the practice, however, is general may be deduced from the case of the *Alton Urban District Council v Spicer*,[3] where an occupier of sporting rights severed

[1] Agricultural Rates Order, 1896, s 2
See Decisions of Local Government Board by W A Casson
[3] (1904) 1 K B 678, 20 T L R 296 68 J P 256, 90 L T 576, 73 L J K B 280

P

from the occupation of the land claimed to be rated
under the Public Health Act, 1875, Section 211,[1]
as one-fourth part only of the net annual value under
the provision in this section of the Act, but it was
held in that case that the occupier was not entitled to
be assessed in the proportion of one-fourth part only
It is suggested that this case could not have matured
in the way it did had the assessment been made on
the tenant and the tenant paid the rates thereon and
claimed the deduction from the landlord

Difficulty in
valuing
sporting
rights

There is great difficulty in valuing sporting rights,
and assessments of this nature may fluctuate at a very
rapid rate   Moreover, it often happens that the
smaller the area over which the right extends the
greater is its value. For example, two large estates
are divided by a small estate   The advantages gained
by the small estate from the close proximity to these
larger estates have often the effect of making the right
more valuable per acre than that of the larger estates
Care must be taken—when assessing a sporting right,
if actually let—to ascertain whether the landlord or
tenant pays the rates   Under the Assessment Acts it
is clearly the occupier's liability to pay same, but it is
generally the fact that sporting rights are let at so
much per acre, and the landlord undertakes the liability.
When this is the case the gross value would be something less than the rent actually paid—see *R* v. *Smith* [2]
Inasmuch as, under the Rating Act, 1874,[3] the persons
making the rate may determine whether the owner or
lessee of a shooting right, when such right is let, shall
be rated as occupier, it might appear that this deduction would not have to be made from the actual rent if
the landlord was called upon to pay same, but this

[1] 38 & 39 Vict , c 55
[2] (1885) 55 L J M C 49 , 54 L T 431 , 50 J P 215
[3] 37 & 38 Vict , c 54.

is obviously not so, as the tenant who had to pay
the rates in addition to the rent would not be willing
to pay to the landlord so much rent as if this liability
did not devolve upon himself. There are no deductions
to be made in the case of sporting rights from the
gross value to arrive at the rateable value, it being
clear that there are no repairs, insurance, etc, necessary
to such incorporeal hereditaments

By the Rating Act, 1874,[1] the gross and rateable value   Woodlands
of any land used for a plantation or a wood, or for the
growth of saleable underwood, shall be estimated as
follows —

1 If the land is used only for a plantation or a wood,
the value shall be estimated as if the land, instead of
being a plantation or a wood, were let and occupied in its
natural and unimproved state.

2 If the land is used for the growth of saleable underwood, the value shall be estimated as if the land were let
for that purpose

3 If the land is used both for a plantation or a wood
and for the growth of saleable underwood, the value shall
be estimated either as if the land were used only for a
plantation or a wood, or as if the land were used only for
the growth of the saleable underwood growing thereon, as
the Assessment Committee may determine

This provision appears to be contrary to the principle
of rating, that a property shall be rated at its value as it
at present exists, for it enacts that the value of land
used for a plantation or a wood shall be estimated as if
the land were in its natural and unimproved state This
could only be a nominal rental, such as would be
received if the land were let for grazing purposes
The Statute, therefore, while admitting that the property
is in an unproved state, yet only allows that it shall be

---

rated at something under the present value   With this exception it may be taken as a rule of rating that every hereditament must be rated at its value at the time when the assessment is made

But with regard to the provision that a plantation or wood is to be rated as if it were let and occupied in its natural and unimproved state, the question immediately arises, What is the state contemplated by the Act ? Land in a natural state would presumably be entirely uncultivated, such as common land, for immediately a fence is placed round it an improvement and consequently an enhancement in value of the land is effected. But if the land were cultivated, and, as has often occurred, the owner has afterwards planted a wood thereon, a point of difficulty, in arriving at the assessment, is whether the natural and unimproved state means the value of the land before the wood was planted, and not such value as the land might have possessed in its so-called natural state, that is, before it was cultivated by man, and this it is submitted is the meaning.   In the case of *Westmorland (Earl)* v. *Southwick and Oundle*,[1] some woodlands were assessed at their value as unimproved land, and that notwithstanding the fact that by converting the natural land into that of woodland it had materially increased its value   The assessment was upheld on appeal as being a correct one under the Rating Act, 1874,[2] s 4, although in the course of the case it was stated that the original value of the unimproved land was only about 6s. per acre, whereas in its improved condition it was worth more than 20s per acre   It may be well to mention here that woodlands are rated, for the purpose of the General District Rates, in the proportion of one-fourth part only of their rateable value,[3] but there is no relief given to

Where woodlands partly exempt

---

[1] (1877) 36 L T. 108
[2] 37 & 38 Vict , c. 54
[3] 38 & 39 Vict , c 55, s 211

this class of property by the Agricultural Rates Act, 1896,[1]
If land be let for the growth of saleable underwood, then
the rent which one might reasonably expect to pay for it
would be the gross value, but in the event of land being
used for a plantation or a wood in addition to the growth
of saleable underwood, the discretion lies with the
Assessment Committee as to whether it shall be assessed
as a plantation or wood, or as a hereditament used
wholly for the growth of saleable underwood It must
not be forgotten, however, that in the event of a sporting
right being attached to lands used as woods or plantations,
whether used for the growth of saleable underwood or not,
the right enhances the value, and such sum must be
added to the rateable value[2] The test to be applied as
to what are and what are not " saleable underwoods ' is
not whether the tree is held as timber, but whether the
land is managed in such a way that a profit will be derived
from it, although several years may elapse before the
profit accrues.[3] The fact as to what constitutes or does
not constitute " saleable underwood " is one to be found
by the Court of Quarter Sessions[4] In a case which came
before the Courts in 1882, a number of young oak and ash
trees were planted, and to protect these in their growth a
certain number of larch and fir trees were placed round
them to act as a screen As the young trees grew the firs
were cut and sold, and it was sought to increase the
rateable value of the property owing to this circumstance,
but the Court held that the object of planting them was
not for the purpose of profit, but to protect the other

---

[1] 59 & 60 Vict , c 16, s 9

[2] *Eyton* v *Mold (Overseers)*, (1880) 6 Q B D. 13 , 43 L T 472 , 29
W R 122, 15 J.P 54

[3] *Fitzhardinge (Lord)* v *Pritchett*, (1867) L R 2 Q B 135 , 36 L J M C
49 , 15 L T 502, 15 W R 640 , 8 B & S 216

[4] *R* v *Narberth (North)*, (1839) 1 P & D 590 , 9 A. & E 815 ,
8 L J M C 46

tees, and so they were held not rateable [1] It is to be observed that a difficulty may arise in placing the value upon " saleable underwood," as more often than not a sale may only take place at periods many years apart, but in this event their annual value is to be estimated at the rent they would reasonably fetch per annum the manner of ascertaining this being to estimate the amount that would be received at the time of the sale, and, after deducting the expenses and other charges, to spread the result over the number of years intervening between the periodical sales.[2]

The value of land is enhanced by the power to dig for coprolites A piece of land was let with the privilege to the tenant to dig and search for coprolites, but he was required to fence in the land and to leave the surface in a good condition at the end of the term. It was held that in rating the land a higher value must be put upon it than if it were mere farm land, because of this privilege [3]

Tithes

Tithes have been assessed to various rates since the Act of Elizabeth, and they have to be valued on the basis laid down in the Parochial Assessments Act, 1836,[4] at their net annual value from year to year Tithes can hardly be let on the ordinary basis of a tenancy, in which the tenant seeks to secure a fair rate of interest on capital invested, undertaking to provide for the necessary services and duties incidental to the holding of a benefice The Courts have admitted the difficulty of applying the Act, and consequently there has been much legislation on the subject of the assessment of this class of rateable property Probably there is no other class of property

[1] R v Ferrybridge, (1823) 2 D & R 634, 1 B & C 375

[2] R. v. Mirfield, (1808) 10 East 219

[3] Roads v Trumpington, (1870) L R 6 Q B 56, 40 L J M C 35, 23 L T 821

[4] 6 & 7 William IV , c 96

where the basis of assessment results in the contribution of so large a proportion of income towards local taxation, and in consequence of this, the Royal Commission on Local Taxation published a report dealing solely with the subject of the taxation of tithes, and, amongst other conclusions arrived at, were the following —

I That the representations made to the Commission on behalf of the owners of tithe rent-charge not severed from the benefice have shown that the burden of local taxation upon such owners is unduly onerous, and that sufficient allowance is not made for the fact that the persons entitled to the rent charge are under a legal obligation to render services and to perform duties in return therefor

II That the case of the owners of tithe rent charge not severed from the benefice is based on the ground, which we consider to have been fully established and the present law, as interpreted by the Courts, works unjustly, and places those owners in a much less favourable position than other owners who are also occupiers of rateable property

There was an addendum to the recommendations signed by three members of the Commission as follows —

We desire to add that, in our opinion, the inequality which exists to the detriment of the owners of tithe rent-charge not severed from the benefice is due to the fact that, in ascertaining the rateable value of such tithe rent-charge, sufficient deductions from the gross value have not been allowed, and that it is necessary, in order to place the owners of such tithe rent-charge on a footing of equality with the owners or occupiers of other rateable property, to provide by legislation for the allowance of further deduction from the gross value, and in such deductions to recognise the liability which is imposed on the owners of such tithe rent-charge to render certain services as a condition of enjoying their emoluments

(Signed)   C A Cripps
            John T Hibbert
            C H Murray

This addendum goes to the root of the matter, as there is little doubt that the deduction allowed from the gross to the rateable value, in some Unions, often as low as 5 per cent., is a very small figure These recommendations have not yet become law, but they may be useful to Assessment Committees in dealing with tithes before any fresh legislation takes place, although, of course, until such legislation takes place, however unequal and unfair to the tithe owners, the decisions in the cases upon the subject must be followed.

It is not proposed here to deal with the various Acts on the subject of tithes, as no useful purpose would be served.

The Tithe Act of 1891,[1] may, however, appear to come into conflict with the statutory definition of "Rateable Value,"[2] wherein the tenant is presumed to pay the tithe rent-charge, inasmuch as the above named Act enacts that "Tithe rent-charge, as defined by this Act, issuing out of any lands shall be payable by the owner of the lands, notwithstanding any contract between him and the occupier of such lands, and any contract made between an occupier and owner of the lands, after the passing of this Act, for the payment of the tithe rent-charge by the occupier shall be void", and further "Any rate to which tithe rent-charge is subject shall be assessed on and may be recovered from the owner of the tithe rent-charge, in the like manner and by the like process as on and from any occupying ratepayer and so much of any Act as authorises any rate on tithe rent-charge to be assessed on or recovered from the occupier of any lands out of which the tithe rent-charge issues is hereby repealed." An exception to the rule that the occupier of the hereditaments is to be rated is thus found in the case of the assessment on the tithe, which can only be recoverable from the landlord At first sight it might appear that, owing to the owner paying the assessment upon the tithe rent-charge, the rateable value of the land would be increased, as there would be less expense to the tenant, but this is not so, because Section 15 of the Union

---

[1] 54 Vict, c 8
[2] The Parochial Assessments Act, 1836 (6 & 7 William IV), c 96

Assessment Committee Act, 1862,[1] defines the gross estimated rental of any hereditament as "the rent at which
the hereditament might reasonably be expected to let from
year to year, free of all usual tenant's rates and taxes,
and tithe commutation rent-charge, if any", that is to say,
the rent at which the hereditament might be expected to
let if the tenant bore those burdens   It follows therefore
that, although the actual rent of the land may be raised in
consequence of the owner having to pay the tithes instead
of the occupier, the rateable value of the land will not
thereby be increased [2]   Great care must be exercised in
ascertaining the amount of the tithe, together with the
rates thereon, in the valuation of a hereditament, as
these must first be deducted from the rent which the
tenant pays, and then the necessary statutable deductions
must be made before arriving at the rateable value   It is
believed there are many cases where even now the rates
on the tithe rent-charge are collected by the parochial
authorities twice over, that is, from the owner of the land
and from the tenant in the manner described above The
rateable value of a tithe is the amount at which it would
let from year to year, free from all tenant's rates and taxes
and other expenses (if any) necessary to maintain the
property in a state to command the rent   These deductions
are, perhaps, set out in the best form in E F Studd's
"Law of Tithes and Tithe Rent-charge,' page 116, and
are as follows —

(1)   All expenses of collection, including legal expenses

(2)   Losses by ultimate non-payment

(3)   Ecclesiastical dues, first-fruits and tenths

(4)   The hypothetical tenant's profit

(5)   The tenant's rates and taxes, these would consist
of—

<hr>

[1] 25 & 26 Vict , c 103
[2] See Circular of the Local Government Board in relation to this Act
30th April, 1891

(i.) Poor Rate—including County, Highway and School Board Rates.

(ii.) Income Tax under Schedule B.

(iii.) General Rate under Metropolis Local Management Act

(iv.) Lighting Rate

(v.) General District Rate under the Public Health Act, 1875.

(vi.) Rate for public libraries and museums

In a case[1] where the vicar of one benefice, which included three parishes, was rated in respect of the tithe commutation rent-charge, and for two of the parishes, for the purpose of assisting him in his duties, he engaged the services of two curates, and performed the necessary duties of his office in the third one himself, he endeavoured to claim, as a deduction, the stipends which would have been paid had a curate been appointed for each of the three parishes   The Court held that this was not an allowable deduction. It has also been held that a curate's stipend is not an allowable deduction[2] There is no deduction to be made for Land Tax or Landlord's Property Tax.[3] There is also no deduction to be made with respect to any sum paid as interest for, or any sum for, the purpose of reducing the principal of money borrowed by an incumbent from the Governors of "Queen Anne's Bounty," for the purpose of building a vicarage.[4]

No deduction can be made for repairs to a chancel,[5] although it must be observed in this case that the Court

---

[1] *R v Sherwood*, (1867) L R 2 Q.B 503, 36 L J M C 113, 16 L T. 663, 15 W R 1035, 8 B & S 596

[2] *Wheeler* v *Burmington*, (1861) 1 B & S 709, 31 L J M C 57, 8 Jur N S 304, 5 L T 345, 10 W R 57

[3] *R* v *Goodchild*, (1858) 27 L J M C 233 El Bl & El 1

[4] *R* v *Hawkins*, (1858) 27 L J M C 248, 22 J P 148

[5] *Dean and Chapter of St Asaph* v *Llanrhaiadr-Yn-Mochnant*, (1897) 1 Q B 511, 76 L T 42, 61 J P 213

of Appeal held that the hypothetical tenant would be under no obligation to do the repairs to the chancel It was also held that an incumbent was not entitled to claim a deduction with respect to money voluntarily given to endow a district parish for spiritual purposes out of part of his own parish, by granting the minister of such new parish certain funds out of the tithe rent-charge [1]

To recover the rates by distress warrant full power is given under Section 6 of the Tithe Act of 1891 [2]

The owner of any tithes, or of any tithe commutation rent-charge, is only assessable to the General District Rates [3] in respect of one-fourth of the rateable value of such tithe

By the Tithe Rent-charge (Rates) Act, 1899,[4] the owner of tithe rent-charge attached to a benefice is relieved during the continuance of the Agricultural Rates Act, 1896, from the payment of one-half of the amount of any rate other than a rate to which tithe rent-charge attached to a benefice was already assessed at one-half or less than one-half the rate in the £ leviable upon buildings

When making a valuation of a farm the same rule Farms has to be borne in mind that is, the rent at which it would let must be ascertained, and there is no other way of doing this (with the exception of the gratuitous information of the farmer as to the rent actually paid, which even then is only a guide to the value, and not necessarily to the rent at which the property might reasonably be expected to let) than by a " field valuation," i.e , a valuation made by ascertaining the various numbers of fields on the

---

[1] *Lawrence v Tolleshunt Knights*, (1862) 31 L J M C 148 2 B & S 533

[2] 54 Vict , c 8

[3] The Public Health Act, 1875 (38 & 39 Vict , c 55), s 211

[4] 62 & 63 Vict , c 17

land, dividing them into arable and pasture land, and then approximately estimating the value of each of them by taking as a guide the rents received for similar property in the neighbourhood There are other items which must be borne in mind, such as the development of the farm, the distance from a railway or town, and the market there is for the products of the particular hereditament in question Should a landlord let a piece of land to a tenant at a low rental, and thereafter the tenant by cultivation improve and so add to the value of the land, although he may be in possession of a long lease at a low rental, the rateable value would thereby be increased, as it might reasonably be expected that the tenant would have been willing to have given a higher rent for it in its more cultivated state. This from a financial point of view would be the same to the tenant as giving a low rent and sinking a certain amount of capital in the property to improve it   In the case *R* v *Hall Dare*[1] there were certain lands in which a Commission of Sewers carried out some improvements ; the tenant had to pay the taxes in connection therewith, and these he claimed as a deduction from the gross value. The Court upheld the claim, taking the view that, as the law obtains, the landlord has to bear the cost of maintaining the improvements made by the sewer authorities   In making a valuation of a farm it is not correct to insert the rateable value of each field in the Valuation List, one figure for the entire hereditament only is required[2]

Agricultural Rates Act The passing of the Agricultural Rates Act, 1896,[3] renders it necessary, however, in the event of there being buildings on any farm land, that the value of such buildings shall be separately entered in the Valuation List

---

[1] (1864) 5 B & S 785, 34 L J M C 17, 11 Jur N S 59, 11 L T 301, 13 W R 70

[2] *Rawlence* v *Hursley Union*, (1877) 3 Ex D 44, 47 L J M.C 31, 37 L T 503, 42 J P 24, 26 W R 81

[3] 59 & 60 Vict, c 16, s 5

By this Act[1] every occupier of agricultural land
in England and Wales is, in respect of such land,
relieved from the payment of one-half of the rate
in the £ payable in respect of buildings and other hereditaments for a period of five years, which ended 31st
March, 1902   The Act has since been continued under
the Expiring Laws Continuance Acts   Land used as
arable, meadow or pasture ground only is also relieved
under the Public Health Act of 1875[2] to the extent of
three-quarters of the net annual value for the General
District Rate levied under that Act, and all rates levied
on a similar basis under Public or Local Acts

The term " agricultural land ' is defined in Section 9
of the Agricultural Rates Act[1] as " any land used as
arable, meadow or pasture ground only, cottage gardens
exceeding one-quarter of an acre, market gardens, nursery
grounds, orchards or allotments,' but the term does not
include " land occupied together with a house as a park,
gardens other than as aforesaid, pleasure grounds, or any
land kept or preserved mainly or exclusively for purposes
of sport or recreation, or land used as a racecourse "

A point of doubt arises in the application of this Act in
such cases as county asylums or private asylums where
agricultural land is within the curtilage of the property,
and, inter alia, is used for the purpose of setting the
patients to work as a remedy in the shape of physical
exercise for any particular malady from which they may
be suffering   No case has been decided upon this point,
but it would appear that the Act was not framed to relieve
this class of property, and it would seem to be safe to
consider that such land is not agricultural within the
meaning of the Agricultural Rates Act,[1] and that therefore rates should be charged on its full value   For the

Land
attached to
asylums, etc

---

[1] (1896) 59 & 60 Vict , c 16
[2] 38 & 39 Vict , c 55, ss 211 and 230

purpose of the Agricultural Rates Act[1] two columns headed respectively "Rateable Value of Agricultural Land" and "Rateable Value of Buildings and other hereditaments not being Agricultural Land," are now inserted in the Valuation List in lieu of the column "Rateable Value." Consequently, at the present day, although no separate valuation is to be given of a farm, the buildings and land have to be divided and inserted in separate columns

In this division in the Valuation List certain conditions are to be followed according to the Agricultural Rates Order, 1896, issued in pursuance of the Act. The instructions are contained in Section 3 of the Order and are as follows —

"Upon such division the minimum rateable value of the buildings and other hereditaments shall, subject to the proviso hereinafter contained, be as follows —

(a) If they include a house, then the minimum rateable value shall be one-eighth of the rateable value of the undivided hereditament as previously stated in the Valuation List

(b) If the said buildings or other hereditaments do not include a house, then the minimum rateable value shall be 5 per cent. of the rateable value of the undivided hereditament, as previously stated in the Valuation List

(c) Provided that—

(1) If in any special case it appears to the Overseers or Assessment Committee that by reason of the character or condition of the house or buildings or other exceptional circumstances the minimum rateable value fixed by the above regulations is higher than the rateable value would be if ascertained in the ordinary way, they may,

---

[1] (1896) 59 & 60 Vict , c 16, s 5

subject to the consent of the Surveyor of Taxes, fix a rateable value below the minimum fixed by the above regulations, and the rateable value so fixed shall be substituted for the minimum rateable value fixed by the above regulations;

(ii) If the said minimum rateable value of the house, buildings, and other hereditaments would otherwise be less than three pounds, it shall, notwithstanding any such consent of the Surveyor of Taxes, be three pounds;

(iii.) If the house is assessed to the inhabited house duty, and the said minimum rateable value for the house, buildings and other hereditaments together would otherwise be less than the annual value of the house as so assessed, it shall, notwithstanding any consent of the Surveyor of Taxes, be the annual value of the house, as so assessed."

The rating of nursery grounds is on the same principle, namely, the amount at which they would let, and under the heading of Nursery Grounds may be included market gardens, orchards, poultry farms, watercress beds and allotments Probably the most profitable form of use to which arable land can be put is that of market gardens and nursery grounds, and in the rating of such property, although it cannot be denied that the ability to earn profits must be an element in the rent a hypothetical tenant would give, care must be taken not to let actual profits influence the valuation The point to be ascertained is the rent the hereditament would fetch if it were on the market, therefore the locality of such property must have a great bearing upon the assessment. Vegetables, and the like, would be of little value if they could not be transported to the consumers expeditiously Consequently a

Nursery grounds

market garden in or near a large town must be more valuable than one in a remote part of the country. Nursery grounds are only assessed at one-fourth of their value for the purpose of the General District Rates,[1] and at one-half of their value for the rates to which the Agricultural Rates Act, 1896,[2] applies. Nursery grounds are often enhanced in value by the fact that greenhouses are erected thereon but it was held in the case of *Purser* v *Worthing Local Board*[3] that land with greenhouses upon it is nursery ground within the meaning of the Public Health Act of 1875,[1] and is only liable as regards the General District Rates to one-fourth of its value. In the case of *Smith* v *Richmond*,[4] however, glasshouse and greenhouses on market gardens were held to be buildings under the Agricultural Rates Act,[2] and consequently liable to pay the full rate in respect of such buildings and the land upon which they stand. It therefore follows that, when dealing with a large market garden, all the land and greenhouses for the purpose of the General District Rate are only liable to one-fourth of their value, and for the purpose of the Agricultural Rates Act[2] a division must be made between the land occupied by the glasshouses which would be considered as part of the glasshouses and be inserted in the Valuation List as buildings, and the land used solely for gardening purposes and inserted in the Agricultural Land column.

The Agricultural Rates Act, 1896,[2] with the Order by the Local Government Board making regulations for the purpose of the said Act, will be found fully set out in the Appendix.

---

[1] The Public Health Act, 1875 (38 & 39 Vict., c 55), s 211
[2] (1896, 59 & 60 Vict., c 16, s 9
[3] (1887) 18 Q B D 818 56 L J M C 78
[4] (1899) A C 448 68 L J Q B 899, 81 L T 269, 15 T L R 523

A form of property that has not infrequently to be dealt with by Assessment Committees are Sewage Farms, and the difficulties that arise from the assessment of them are generally caused by the incidents of the holding   In many cases Local Authorities are the freeholders of several acres of land which are primarily used for the disposal of sewage, they let to tenant farmers for agricultural pur- poses the surface of the land, reserving to themselves certain rights of entry in order to cleanse out channels, tanks and other appliances, so that in fact exclusive occupation can hardly be said to rest with the tenant farmer.

It has, however, been held[1] that in rating such a here- ditament the agricultural tenant should be considered the occupier, but that in addition to the rent paid by the tenant, or the value of the land for agricultural purposes, the Rating Authority are bound to take into account the additional value or benefit accruing to the Sewerage Authority in respect to the facilities afforded them in carrying out their statutory obligations

In other words, although only one person is to be rated, namely the agricultural tenant, there are two factors which go to make the total value of the land in question for rating purposes, and in a great number of cases the second factor is larger than the first.

Although the point has not been decided, it is presumed that the agricultural tenant, while paying the full rates, would be able to recover from his landlord (the Sewerage Authority) the amount payable by reason of the additional value to the purely agricultural interest

Another point in the assessment of Sewage Farms, alike when exclusively occupied for sewage purposes and when the surface is let for agricultural purposes, is whether relief should be granted under the Agricultural

¹ Davies v Scisdon Union, (1908) H L, 25th May, 1908, (1905) A C 315

Q

Rates Act.[1] It is believed that there has been no case decided upon the point, but there is very little doubt that no abatement should be claimed or allowed, as the Agricultural Rates Act expressly defines agricultural land to which the Act applies to mean any land used as arable, meadow or pasture ground *only* The italics do not appear in the Act, but inasmuch as it was primarily passed for the relief of the agriculturist, and the principal use to which land is put in the case of a Sewage Farm is the disposal of sewage, it is difficult to see the justification for granting to such land the relief it was intended should be granted to purely agricultural land by the Act

Tolls   The next class of hereditament to be considered is that of tolls, which however, if detached altogether from real property, cannot be rateable *per se*[2]. but, at the same time, if the subject-matter out of which the tolls arise can be rated, then the tolls, which constitute its profits, would enhance the value of the subject-matter and should thus indirectly contribute to the rates[3] In the case of *R.* v. *North and South Shields Ferry Co*[4] the facts were briefly as follows —The company had landing stages in two parishes on opposite sides of the River Tyne, one in North Shields and the other in South Shields The tolls were collected at the landing place in South Shields, but in the parish of North Shields the company were rated as occupiers of "a ferry, landing and tolls" at a figure which represented half of the net profits of the ferry The Sessions held that this was the correct method to deal with the matter, but the Court of Queen's Bench decided that the tolls could not be rated *per se*, but

---

[1] (1896) 59 & 60 Vict, c 16, s 5
[2] R v Nicholson, (1818) 12 East 330
[3] R v Kingswinford, (1827) 1 M & R 20 7 B. & C. 236
[4] (1852) 1 E & B 140, 22 L J M C. 9

they went on to state that the rateable value of the land occupied by the landing stage, toll-houses, etc., must be determined according to its value as enhanced by being available for the purpose of earning tolls

The following is an extract from the judgment of Lord Campbell, C J.:—

"We think that in the present case, in rating the landing place, the profit of the tolls cannot properly be brought into the calculation as the profits of the occupation of the landing place, which is in effect done by the rate. On the other hand, the existence of the tolls cannot be wholly excluded from consideration, but the land should be rated, not as land in that situation without reference to the tolls at all, but the value should be taken not as the value of the land merely but as the value of land as enhanced by being available for the purpose of earning the tolls. This appears to be the true principle according to the test laid down in the Parochial Assessment Act, 1836,[1] as it would be the rent that could be obtained, and which the company would have to pay for the land for the purpose for which it is available under the circumstances "

Lighthouse tolls *per se* are also not rateable—*R v. Coke*[2] It is difficult to reconcile the judgment in this case with that in *R* v. *North and South Shields Ferry Co.*,[3] for in the former case it was decided that tolls of a lighthouse could not be taken into account at all, but the point seems to be wholly a question of fact as to whether the ability to earn tolls is secured by any particular lighthouse In the case of *The Commissioners of the Port of Lancaster* v *Barrow-in-Furness*[4] it was held on the facts that, as the Commissioners could take

Lighthouse tolls

---

[1] 6 & 7 William IV , c 96, s 1
[2] (1826) 5 B & C 797
[3] (1852) 1 E & B 140 22 L J M C 9
[4] (1897) 1 Q B 166

another piece of land and erect for themselves an equally suitable lighthouse elsewhere, the rent they would pay for such lighthouse could only be calculated on the structural value and not according to the amount of the tolls earned   Certain lighthouses are exempt from rating (see Chapter II , Part I).

Markets tolls   With regard to market tolls, the case of the *Duke of Bedford* v. *St Pauls Covent Garden Overseers*[1] is perhaps the leading decision upon the point, and it was here held that, as certain persons under the provision of an Act of Parliament had the right of user of certain stands and paid tolls for same to the Duke of Bedford, the payment was in respect of that convenience, and therefore fell within the class of tolls which enhance the value of the occupation of the soil, but where a toll is paid for the right merely to enter a market, and no specific portion of that market is allocated by way of stallage to the person paying the same, it has been decided that the toll in that case is not rateable—see *R* v *Caswell*,[2] also *Mayor of London* v *St. Sepulchre*[3] But in the case of the *Mayor of London* v *Greenwich Union*[4] it was held that tolls paid in respect of the user of a certain market built for the reception of cattle, prior to the disposal of same, were tolls paid in respect of the occupation of the soil of such market and were therefore to be taken into consideration in assessing the rateable value.

In the case of *Horner* v *Stepney Assessment Committee*[5] it was held that franchise tolls not connected with the occupation of land were not to be taken into account as enhancing the value of a market place for rating purposes.

---

[1] (1881) 45 L T 646, 51 L J M C 41
[2] (1872) L R. 7 Q B 328
[3] (1871) L R 7 Q B 333
[4] (1883) 48 L T 437, 47 J P 420
[5] (1908) 98 L T 450, 72 J P 262, 24 T L R 500.

With regard to tolls earned by bridges, it has been Bridge tolls
decided that the rateable value should be apportioned
between the parishes into which the bridge extends,
according to the length of the bridge in each parish [1]
As to the tolls earned by bridges, see also the case of
R v Blackfriars Bridge Co.[2]

Where certain lairages were used for the slaughter of Lairages
foreign cattle, as it was stated to be impossible to
ascertain the rental value of such by comparison, it
was held that the evidence of receipts (otherwise tolls)
and expenditure might be properly considered in order
to determine the rateable value of the lairages—*Mersey
Docks and Harbour Board v Birkenhead Union
Assessment Committee* [3]

Moorings in a river are in certain cases liable to be Moorings
rated where it can be shown that there is exclusive
occupation of part of the soil of the bed of a river, and,
although the occupation might be a wrongful one, the
person found in occupation would appear to be liable [4]
In the case of *Grant v Oxford Local Board,*[5] it was,
however, held that a houseboat moored to posts driven in
the bed of the river was not rateable, but it is doubtful if
this case is good law after the decision in the House of
Lords in *Cory v Bristow,*[6] where it was held that it
would be possible for a person to be in occupation of
part of the soil of the bed of a river where a hulk of a
vessel was moored, and that the occupier should be rated
in respect of the profit derived by him from the occupation.
In the case also of *Forrest v Greenwich Overseers*[7] it was
held that a barge or floating-pier used for embarking in

---

[1] *R v. Hammersmith Bridge Co.*, (1849) 18 L J M C 85
[2] (1839) 9 A & E 828
[3] (1900) 1 Q.B 143, 69 L J Q B 260
[4] *Cory v Bristow*, (1877) 2 App Cas 262
[5] (1868) L R 4 Q B. 9
[6] (1877) 2 App Cas 262
[7] (1858) 8 E & B 890, 27 L J M C 96, 22 J P 130.

steamboats, or so moored to the bed of a river that it became an occupation of land in the bed of the river, was rateable. Where, however, only a license was granted to use a certain mooring it was held that there was not exclusive occupation and therefore that it was not liable to the Poor Rate.[1]

Racecourse   The valuation of a racecourse for rating purposes may be based upon the receipts and expenditure, and the evidence of such is of assistance when preparing a valuation, but it by no means follows that it is the only data an Assessment Committee should rely upon.

In the case of *R v Verrall*[2] the Sessions refused permission for the respondents to call upon the appellants to produce their books, but the Court of King's Bench found that as a matter of law it was wrong to exclude such evidence. It, however, does not necessarily follow that the true rental value of a racecourse could be obtained by having regard only to the receipts and expenses for a few years. The business is a most hazardous one; for the principal courses, dates of meetings are usually arranged and licenses granted by the Jockey Club, and there are many courses where only one meeting is held during the year—at other courses two or more meetings may be held—therefore it will be readily seen that a variety of causes might operate to prevent a successful financial year from the point of view of the tenants of the course; whereas, on the other hand, an incoming tenant would not give as rent a figure based upon the profits only of a successful enterprise without taking into consideration the fact of the extremely precarious nature of the business. Good weather is a very great factor in the success of a course. It is common knowledge that many meetings have to be postponed, or

---

[1] *Mathias v Mitton-next-Gravesend Overseers*, (1868) 37 L J M C 73, 18 L T 601

[2] (1875) 45 L J M C 29, 1 Q B D 9, 33 L T 379, 40 J P 550

even cancelled altogether, by reason of frost, fog, etc, and in the event of a postponement it is possible that the adjourned date may clash with another meeting in the country, or the entire cancelling of the fixture might be occasioned, both of which eventualities would mean a heavy loss to the proprietors

For these reasons it is probable that in the case of *Sandown Park v Epsom Union*[1] the Surrey Quarter Sessions, whilst admitting as evidence the profits earned by the company, founded their decision upon the rent actually paid under a lease, presumably on the ground that in fixing the rent the probable profits were taken into account both by the landlord and the tenant The observations of Mr Ryde upon this matter is much in point "The thing to be ascertained is the yearly rent which may reasonably be expected, the actual profits may be evidence of that rent, but cannot be better evidence than a rent recently fixed with the expectation (founded on experience) that those profits will continue to be made'

It frequently happens that racecourses are let for other purposes during the times when they are not actually occupied as a racecourse The most common form of letting is for grazing, although there are courses which are used for sports, such as golf, cricket, football, etc If this letting is in addition to the letting to the racecourse tenant the added value of the land must be taken into consideration

Racecourses are not exempt under the Agricultural Rates Act.[2]

---

[1] Reported on page 171 of the Second Edition of " Ryde on Rating '
[2] (1896) 59 & 60 Vict, c 16, s 5

CHAPTER II.

BUILDINGS

Houses—Country Mansions—Small Tenements—Where Premium Paid—Public-houses and Hotels—Schools—Shops—Theatres—Hospitals, Convalescent Homes, Asylums and Workhouses—Hotels

Houses   PERHAPS the description of property most frequently met with in making a valuation of almost any parish is that of the private house. In ascertaining the gross and rateable value of a house, it must be looked at as if it were let unfurnished, and although the rent which the tenant gives is *primâ facie* evidence of value, yet it cannot be held as conclusive[1]. In the third Schedule of the Valuation (Metropolis) Act, 1869,[2] there is a maximum rate of deduction from the gross value or rental value to arrive at the rateable value, and notwithstanding that the Act says that the rate of deduction shall not be more than it provides for, it nowhere says it shall not be less. There are three classes of houses and buildings which are liable to Inhabited House Duty, and these, with the deduction allowed by the Valuation (Metropolis) Act, are as follows —

	Maximum rate of deductions Per cent or proportion
Class I.—Houses and buildings, or either of them, without land other than gardens, where the gross value is under £20	25, or 1-4th

---

[1] *Hayward v Brinkworth Overseers*, (1864) 10 L. T. N S 608
[2] 32 & 33 Vict, c 67

	Maximum rate of deductions. Per cent or proportion
Class II.—House and buildings without land other than gardens and pleasure grounds valued therewith for the purpose of Inhabited House Duty, where the gross value is £20 and under £40 ...	20, or 1-5th
Class III.—Houses and buildings without land and other gardens and pleasure grounds valued therewith for the purpose of Inhabited House Duty, where the gross value is £40 or upwards	16⅔, or 1-6th

The most simple case of assessment to be met is where a tenant occupies a dwelling house at a rent, say, of £19 per annum, the landlord doing the repairs and paying the insurance. In this case the gross value would be £19. Then under Schedule III., Class I., of the Valuation (Metropolis) Act the maximum deduction must not be more than £4 15s. This would be about £4 10s. for the repairs and renewal fund, and 5s. for the insurance, leaving a rateable value of £14 5s.

Supposing, in another case, that a tenant takes a house at a yearly rental of £39, the landlord doing repairs and paying insurance as above, then the gross rent would be £39. The maximum deduction under Schedule III., Class II., of the Valuation (Metropolis) Act would be 1-5th (£7 16s.), the rateable value being £31 4s.

It must not be overlooked that in the two examples given the tenant has no expense of repairs, etc., the landlord bearing these charges; but if the tenant undertake them, then the rateable value would be the rent paid, with the exception of a small amount for the renewal fund, as it could hardly be expected that a tenant should raise a sinking fund in order to restore to the landlord the property intact at the end of the term

A tenant takes a house on a yearly agreement at a rental of, say, £600 per annum. The average annual cost of repairs are, say, £60 per annum, and the landlord pays about £12 insurance: then the gross value would be £600. The following deductions would have to be made to arrive at the rateable value. Repairs, £60, insurance, £12, renewal fund, say about, £15, any other expenses, if necessary, nil—£87, leaving a rateable value of £513.

This house would come under Schedule III., Class III., of the Valuation (Metropolis) Act, and although the maximum deduction allowable would be 1-6th, in the instance given above it does not quite amount to this. Had the full deduction been made as allowed by the Act, the rateable value would have been £500.

A tenant takes a house at a rent of £100 per annum, and agrees to do the internal decorative repairs, as distinct from structural repairs (that is, repairs to the walls, etc.), at a cost, say, of £3 per annum: the landlord agrees to do the other repairs and pay the insurance, in addition there is the renewal fund to be provided, which is a legal deduction. Supposing for the sake of argument these amounted to £13, then the gross value would be £100, plus £3—£103. Deduct from this the sum of £16 for repairs, renewal and insurance, the rateable value would be £87.

This may not appear clear at first sight, but it is accounted for in the following way:—A landlord would expect to make as net rent £87, and to do this the rent would be, under the most usual form of tenancy, £103, but because the tenant agrees to do the internal repairs, the landlord can afford to let it at £100. Here is a case, then, where the gross value is not the same as the rental value, because the rent which one might reasonably expect to obtain for such a property would be £103, and this would consequently be the gross value.

Again, a tenant takes a house at a rent of £100 per annum, and agrees to do all the repairs and pay the insurance, which would amount to, say, £13, then the rateable value would be £100, less, say, £3 for the renewal fund, or, £97. To arrive at the gross value as defined by the Act there would have to be added to this £97 the £3 for renewal fund and £13 for repairs which would make £113.

From these examples it will be seen that the following is a short and concise rule to obtain the rateable value. Ascertain the net amount which accrues to the landlord from the hereditament, fter the aforenamed expenses have been deducted, and then add, according to the tables, something for the gross value. The following tables may be found useful in assessing this class of property :—

CLASS I (Maximum deduction equals 25 per cent)		CLASS II (Maximum deduction equals 20 per cent)	
Gross Value	Rateable Value	Gross Value	Rateable Value
£	£	£	£
4	3	20	16
5	4	21	17
6	5	22	18
7	6	23	19
8	6	24	20
9	7	25	20
10	8	26	21
11	9	27	22
12	9	28	23
13	10	29	24
14	11	30	24
15	12	31	25
16	12	32	26
17	13	33	27
18	14	34	28
19	15	35	28
		36	29
		37	30
		38	31
		39	32

It will be noticed that in the above the deduction from the gross value to arrive at the rateable value never exceeds the maximum amount allowed by the Valuation (Metropolis) Act, 1869 [1] It is sometimes less it is true,

CLASS III					
(Maximum deduction equals 16½ per cent)					
Gross Value	Rateable Value	Gross Value	Rateable Value	Gross Value	Rateable Value
£	£	£	£	£	£
40	34	70	59	105	88
41	35	71	0	110	92
42	35	72	60	115	96
43	36	73	61	120	100
44	37	74	62	125	105
45	38	75	63	130	10J
46	39	76	64	135	113
47	40	77	65	140	117
48	40	78	65	145	121
49	41	79	66	150	125
50	42	80	67	155	130
51	43	81	68	160	134
52	44	82	69	165	138
53	45	83	70	170	142
54	45	84	70	175	146
55	46	85	71	180	150
56	47	86	72	185	155
57	48	87	73	190	159
58	49	88	74	195	163
59	50	89	75	200	167
60	50	90	75	205	171
61	51	91	76	210	175
62	52	92	77	215	180
63	53	93	78	220	184
64	54	94	79	225	188
65	55	95	80	230	192
66	55	96	80	235	196
67	56	97	81	240	200
68	57	98	82	245	205
69	58	99	83	250	209
		100	84		

but for the sake of convenience the amounts are not worked out to shillings, etc , and although this Act applies especially to the Metropolis, and the tables are worked

---

[1] 32 & 33 Vict , c 67

out on the basis of the law as therein laid down, it is submitted that they would not be entirely useless for Unions not situated within the metropolitan area, although, for reasons given later on in the chapter. they are not always applicable, especially in small towns and country districts.[1]

Cooke, in his "Notes on Rating,' p 28, gives the following rule To make these tables applicable to houses let on lease (the occupier doing repairs and paying insurance premium), deduct from the rent paid a renewal fund, approximately as follows —

For a rental up to £50			.	..	£2
,,	,,	,, 100	...	.	3
,,	,,	,, 150			5
,,	,,	,, 200		..	6
,,	,,	,, 250			7
,,	,,	,, 300			9

For example, take the case of a tenancy on the above terms. The rent is, say, £200, then the rateable value would be £200 less £6=£194, and the gross value according to the table would be £235

In rating a large mansion not likely to let on a yearly *Country* tenancy, it has to be assessed on its probable value if let *mansions* for a term of years[2] The difficulty experienced in rating large country mansions is very great The hypothesis that such establishments would let unfurnished from year to year is a fallacious one, and indeed it is seldom found that a letting of any sort takes place But being owned by the occupiers, handed down from one generation to another, or built by millionaires for their own occupation, it is exceedingly difficult to determine values for assessment on this class of property The capital value or selling value of the property may be a guide Quarter Sessions have

---

[1] But see complete tables in Appendix
[2] *Clue v Foy (Overseers),* (1875) 39 J P 774

occasionally adopted the principle of taking 3 per cent. on the capital value as representing the gross value The evidence of high-class estate agents, however, is invaluable in dealing with hereditaments of this nature, as the cost of up-keep is generally very large, consequently a large deduction from gross to rateable value is acquired—see *West* v *Guardians of Exeter Union*, reported in "The Estates Gazette," October 25th, 1902

Small tenements

Under the Poor Rate Assessment and Collection Act, 1869[1] (as set out in p. 60, *ante*), hereditaments the rateable value of which does not exceed in the Metropolis £20, or if in Liverpool £13, or if in Manchester or Birmingham £10, or if elsewhere £8 may be assessed to the owner instead of to the occupier; but as shown in the foregoing examples, the method of ascertaining the rateable value does not differ here   In the case of artisan's dwellings, however, each tenement must be regarded as a separate hereditament for assessment purposes, and in converting weekly and monthly tenancies into hypothetical yearly tenancies for the purpose of arriving at the gross value, the annual payment for rates (including water) and House Duty should be deducted from the annual amount receivable by weekly or monthly payment, these deductions are calculated according to the rates in the £, and vary in each parish as the rates vary   The reason of this is because the rent of such a tenement usually includes the rates, which are paid by the landlord instead of the tenant, and so have to be deducted as they occur.

In the Appendix will be found tables worked out showing the gross and rateable values of properties let at from one shilling upwards, with rates ranging from one shilling to twelve shillings in the £, which would be applicable to

Water Rate

all parishes outside the Metropolis   In the case of *Smith* v. *Churchwardens of Birmingham*[2] the property in question

---

[1] 32 & 33 Vict, c 41
[2] (1889) 22 Q B D 703, 58 L J. M C 161, 53 J P 787

was of the character and description known as artisans' or workpeople's dwellings They were let by the week, and the appellant as landlord paid all the outgoings in respect of Poor Rate, Water Rate, and other local rates It was held by the Sessions that the deduction claimed by the landlord (the appellant) of the property. before ascertaining the gross value, on account of the Water Rate, was permissible, as the amount received from the tenants, although included in the rent they paid, was not received from them on account of rent for the buildings but for the commodity of the water The Court of Queen's Bench upheld this decision

In this case another point raised by the appellant is one commonly met with and is of importance. Owing to the constant change of occupation in many small dwellings, a prudent person in buying property of this description would make allowances for this fact, and it is a very common practice to allow two weeks' rent as the probable average loss that would accrue to the landlord This loss, the appellant contended, he was entitled to deduct before commencing the valuation, so that instead of reckoning fifty-two weeks in a year, the rent per week, it was contended, should be only multiplied by fifty The Court refused to uphold this view, probably on the ground that the gross value is defined by the Statute as the rent that a property would let at for a year, and, although possibly a landlord would be willing to make two weeks' abatement of rent to a tenant who occupied the property for a whole year, as far as the writer's knowledge goes this is never done, for the reason that an agreement with a tenant of this class would be of little value and very difficult to enforce When paying the rate, however, the number of weeks the property has been empty should be given to the rate collector, and he will make an allowance for this cause

Allowance for empties in weekly properties

The above case also decided that expenses of collection of rent from weekly property was not an expense necessary to maintain the property in a state to command the rent, and therefore was not a proper deduction to be made from the total rent paid.

In the case of *Pullen v St Saviour's Union Assessment Committee*[1] it was held that, where tenants of a block of tenement flats paid, in addition to the rent of the premises, a further weekly sum to a third party for cleaning, watching and lighting of the common staircase, such further sum should be added to the rent before determining the gross value of each hereditament under Section 4 of Valuation (Metropolis) Act, 1869.[2] This decision is rather unsatisfactory, but such an expense would clearly be a statutable deduction

Where a composition is made for the rates between the parochial authorities and the owner of the property, the owner is entitled to deduct from the gross rent received the full amount of the rates that would have to be paid if no compounding agreement were in force[3], but whatever arrangement be made between the Overseers and the owner of small property with reference to the payment of rates, the full gross and rateable values must be inserted in the Valuation List[4] In the assessment of a row of houses similar in every respect (that is to say, containing the same number of rooms and alike as to accommodation), but let at varying rentals, the correct method of assessing these houses would be to ascertain the average of the rents and assess them all at a similar sum, not at a different figure according to the amount of rent paid by each individual tenant[5]

Row of
similar
houses

[1] (1900) 1 Q B 138, 69 L J Q B 139, 81 L T 588

[2] 32 & 33 Vict, c 67

[3] *R v Dodd*, (1865) 35 L J M C 97, 6 B & S 903 13 L T 327

[4] *Sunderland Overseers v Sunderland Union*, (1865) 34 L J M C. 121, 13 L T 239

See judgment of Lord Ellenborough in *R v Hull Dock Co*, (1816) 5 M & S 394

In many cases, a house may be taken on an ordinary repairing lease, and a premium paid to the landlord on entry. A premium is only rent in advance, and it would have to be distributed over the whole term of the lease, either on the 4 per cent or 5 per cent tables; this done, 10 per cent should be added for repairs, etc, and the figure arrived at would be the gross value To give an example it is necessary to append the following table — Where premium paid

INTEREST CALCULATED AT FIVE PER CENT

No of Years	Percentage	No of Years	Percentage
1	105	17	8¾
2	53¾	18	8½
3	36¾	19	8¼
4	28¼	20	8
5	23	21	7¾
6	19¾	22 and 23	7½
7	17¼	24	7¼
8	15½	25 and 26	7
9	14	27 to 29	6¾
10	13	30 and 31	6½
11	12	32 to 34	6¼
12	11¼	35 to 39	6
13	10½	40 to 45	5¾
14	10	46 to 60	5½
15	9½	61 to 100	5¼
16	9¼	Perpetuity	5

Case No 1.—A house is let on lease as above for 7 years at a rental of £200 per annum, the lessee paying £500 premium ...	£200	0	0
This £500 has to be spread over the term of 7 years, and on referring to the table above it will be seen that the percentage to be taken upon it is 17¼ This is	86	0	0
	£286	0	0
10 per cent. should be added for repairs .	28	0	0
Gross value ...	£314	0	0

This £31¹ will be the gross value, and, as the property comes under Class III. of the Valuation (Metropolis) Act, the deduction from the gross value to obtain the rateable value would be 16⅔ per cent The assessment would therefore be entered in the Rate Book as gross value £314 and rateable value £262. The reason 10 per cent. is added to the rent to ascertain the gross value is because, under the lease, it is assumed that the tenant does the repairs', but as the insurance and sinking fund are theoretically paid by the landlord, a greater deduction from the gross value is necessary than 10 per cent. in order to include all the statutables

	£	s	d
Case No 2 —A house is let on lease for 21 years at a comparatively small rental of per annum . ..	£100	0	0
There is a premium paid of £2,000. Spreading this £2,000 over 21 years on the table as given above, the percentage to be taken upon it is 7¾ This equals	155	0	0
	£255	0	0
Add 10 per cent as before	25	0	0
Gross value	£280	0	0

The assessment will therefore be £280 gross and (Class III) £234 rateable value

Rating of new houses where occupied by owner

	£	s	d
To find the rateable value of a house built on a plot of ground let on lease for, say, 99 years, at a ground rent of per annum	£15	0	0
The same principle as that applied to where a premium is paid would be adopted The house costs say, £1,000 to build, and according to the table this would be taken at 5¼ per cent ..	52	0	0
Add 10 per cent as before	5	0	0
	£72	0	0

This £72 is the gross value, and **the rateable value** would be £60.

The question of the valuation of a public-house is one *Public-houses* upon which there are many opinions. Very often the actual rent which passes between landlord and tenant is only a nominal sum. but the net amount which goes to the landlord has to be ascertained, following out the principle which has already been laid down We have seen that trade profits are not rateable *per se*, but at the same time it is patent that the rent which a hypothetical tenant would be willing to give for property of this description must solely rest on the position of the house, the nature of the trade done in the neighbourhood, and the capacity of the particular house for doing trade, etc. On taking over a public-house a tenant usually has to pay a premium, part of this may be for goodwill which is not rateable, and part of it may be rent in advance. This latter portion would have to be spread over the term in a similar way to that explained in a preceding part of this chapter (see p. 241), and added to the rent. In making a valuation of a public-house the tenant often informs the assessor that on his entering the premises there was no premium paid This may be so in point of fact, but the landlord (frequently the brewer) lends him a certain sum by way of premium as a mortgage, which sum the tenant never actually receives in cash, although he has to liquidate the liability during his term together with interest This amount must be reckoned as premium and spread over the term as before

When valuing a " tied house " it must always be valued irrespective of the tie, as obviously a brewer would let a house at a lower rental if the tenant were compelled to purchase his stock-in-trade from him than if he (the tenant) were at liberty to go to the cheapest market for his stock A good rule for the valuing of a freehold public-house is to ascertain the value of the site,

R 2

and to take it at 4 per cent , then to add 6 per cent on the value of the building, and these two sums together may be assumed as the rent exclusive of the value of the license , the premium which is given for public-houses of a similar class in the same neighbourhood must then be ascertained , 5 per cent is taken of half this and added to the estimated rental value, and the result will be the estimated gross value   The reason why only half the premium is taken is because it is assumed that in a premium given for a public-house there is a certain sum set aside for goodwill, and this is commonly reckoned at about one-half   Where a lessee of a public-house makes any structural alterations, or improves the premises in any way, the sum spent in such work must be spread over the term as before   In the event of a license being obtained for a house after the lessee has entered into an agreement to take it for any term, the fact of the license being attached to the premises must be taken into consideration when the property comes up for assessment, as it obviously increases the value of the hereditament , and if the lessee had power to sublet the premises, he could obtain a higher rental for them than that which he had agreed to pay   The following is an example of a valuation of a public-house —

A public-house is let on lease for 21 years at a rent of per annum	£50	0	0
The lessee pays a premium on entering the premises of £1,000			
Then £500 spread over the 21 years on the 5 per cent table would be taken at 7½ per cent	38	0	0
	£88	0	0
To this must be added 10 per cent. as before	8	0	0
Gross value	£96	0	0
Deduct one-fifth ...	19	0	0
Rateable value	£77	0	0

With regard to the weekly takings of a public-house and their admissibility as evidence, there are two very important cases upon the point which it would be well to discuss here The first is that of *Dodds v South Shields Union Assessment Committee.*[1] When this case was before the Court of Quarter Sessions, a witness for the appellant, having completed his examination-in-chief, was cross-examined by respondents counsel as to the takings of the house in question ; this was objected to, and upon request of the parties a case was stated for the High Court It was there held that in the absence of special circumstances, that is to say, where there would be no other guide as to the value for rating purposes of a public-house, evidence of the takings should be excluded

Evidence of takings of public-house

Wills, J , in his judgment, said "I think in this case we cannot interfere with the decision of the Court of Quarter Sessions Upon the facts stated I have little doubt that this was the first step to get at the profit of public-houses in the district Counsel contradict each other as to the practice at Sessions in ordinary cases of assessment of public-houses, but from my own experience whilst at the bar, which was considerable in such cases, I think it is a novelty, and a dangerous novelty, to enter upon an enquiry of this sort The proper subject of enquiry is what would be the rent, calculated according to Section I of the Parochial Assessment Act, 1836, with reference to similar hereditaments used in the same way in the neighbourhood. I gather from the cases that enquiry into takings is always excluded, except in cases where the rateable value cannot be got at in any other way, *e g ,* the cases of railways, docks, etc Then 'unfortunately' as Blackburn, J., said in *R* v. *London and North Western Railway Co ,*[2] you are obliged to enter into this enquiry for the purpose of excluding

---

[1] (1895) 59 J P 452.

[2] (1874) L R 9 Q B 134 , 43 L J M C 51

profits from the only sum available for estimating the
rateable value, viz, the gross takings, with which the
profits are mixed up   In such cases there is no standard
of comparison, the circumstances differ as to each
particular railway, or dock, or whatever it is.   But in
the case of the great majority of public-houses, there is no
difficulty whatever in resorting to the ordinary method of
assessment   The takings in the case of a public-house are
often mixed up with personal considerations peculiar to
the licensee, which would render them a most unsafe
guide   I see nothing in this case as stated to justify entry
into such an enquiry "

Wright, J   ' I agree, but on rather different grounds
The Court of Quarter Sessions has asked us a question
which we cannot answer without knowing a great deal
more than they have told us   The takings might, perhaps,
have been gone into to test the credit of the witness.
But we do not know for what purpose the evidence was
tendered   We have no materials for deciding, but we
cannot send back the case to the Quarter Sessions   It
is enough to say that, if the takings were asked for
in order to get at the profits, the evidence was not
admissible "

It will be seen, however, that in this case the Judges,
for different reasons, refused to alter the decision of
Quarter Sessions   Mr Justice Wills on the ground that
in the great majority of public-houses there is no difficulty
in resorting to comparison, and also because of the fact
that there are various considerations, possibly personal,
which have to be taken into account when ascertaining the
gross receipts   Mr Justice Wright, however, although
he agreed with the judgment, stated that, as insufficient

Dodds' case
considered
reason had been given in the special case for the purpose
for which the evidence was proposed to be given, the
Court of Quarter Sessions had asked a question it was
impossible to answer without more information.

In the abstract the judgment in the above case, no doubt, would work equitably if the conditions which were evidently in the mind of Mr Justice Wills were found to exist largely in practice He assumes that it would be, in the majority of cases, comparatively simple to compare one public-house with another, and by such comparison to ascertain the value for rating purposes. He had apparently overlooked the important point, that although a house may be let with all sorts of encumbrances, obligations, etc , the rating authorities have to sweep all these aside and value the house from the standpoint that the tenant from year to year would be a man of such position as to be able freely to purchase beers, wines and spirits from whatever market he chose.

That these incumbrances exist is a matter of common knowledge, in fact there are a large number of towns and villages where what is known as a free public-house cannot be found , the tenants also are very often men of little or no financial position Brewers, who have bought public-houses so largely of late years, are compelled to let their houses to this class of tenant and, whereas the rent which passes between the tenant and the brewer may be only a nominal sum, there is invariably a contract whereby the tenant has to purchase his beers, wines and spirits from the brewer at a very much higher price than the fair market value of the articles This system is known as the "tied system,' the contract is of Tied system a purely personal nature between the landlord and the tenant and must be ignored when assessing the property The point then arises, how is the value of such a house to be arrived at ? If comparison can be made with a free house, it is clear that such comparison should be made, but for comparison to be of any value a similar house must be found. It is impossible to compare public-houses at any great distance apart, because local conditions are the only factors which influence rents.

A public-house almost entirely depends for its well being
upon the inhabitants in the immediate neighbourhood
It is admitted that there are many houses which do what
is known as a "call-trade," that is to say, there are half-
way houses between certain fixed places where people
when driving, riding, etc, pull up, but it cannot be
denied that the vast majority of public-houses depend
upon their local trade.   Now, if comparison is to be
made, the house proposed as a standard must be within
a reasonable distance and have a similar class of trade
as the house under consideration, and great care must
be exercised to ascertain that all the conditions are on
the same level   For instance, in many parts of the
country, what is known as a "long pull" is given, that
is something more than the imperial measure, to customers, although the customer only pays for the nominal
measure   Where this condition prevails it must readily
be seen that, if comparison is to be made, the conditions
must be similar   Again, the "long pull" varies as to
quantity, which is another important factor.

The question of comparison, it is submitted, can only
amount to this, that a public-house, which is a tied
house—or where it is admitted that the rent that actually
passes between landlord and tenant is not a fair criterion
of the value —can only be compared, in order to ascertain
its value, with a similar house, but entirely free, let at a
rent fixed by the higgling of the market   It has been
argued that a comparison can be made, upon the hearing
of a rating appeal, with the assessment of other public-
houses ; there can be no objection to this if the ground of
appeal is inequality, but for the purpose of arriving at the
value of any individual public-house it is entirely wrong
to argue, "Because A is assessed at £100, B is a similar
public-house and should be assessed likewise at £100."
This contention has been brought forward at Quarter
Sessions, but the obvious objection to it is, that unless

one can inquire into all the circumstances of how the assessment of £100 was arrived at upon A, the standard of comparison is absolutely valueless. It has also been contended that you can compare a public-house with the assessment of another one twenty miles away in another Union. This is equally fallacious, and if such a principle were permitted there would be no finality to it. The very first essence of comparison is to have a correct standard, and the only correct standard is a perfectly free house under exactly similar circumstances, but let on an annual tenancy in competition. This proposition itself gives rise to the following question, "What rent would a free tenant give in competition for a public-house?" Now the first question a prospective tenant would ask himself is, "What is the trade of the house I propose to take?" Indeed, it may be said, that a public-house has never been let, unless of course it be an entirely new one, without this question being asked and answered; for it is apparent that this would be the only datum upon which a tenant could fix his rent. What would be the best guide to the incoming tenant of a public-house? The only answer is, the trade that the house has done in the past. It is not for one moment suggested that the prospective tenant might not say to himself, "I can increase the trade of this house, and therefore I am willing to give more rent than I should be justified in so doing if the trade of the past could not be exceeded," or, on the other hand, "the outgoing tenant is a man whose personality in the district commands a larger trade than I could command", but practically the only element that can possibly form the groundwork of ascertaining the rental value of the future would be the actual business done in the past. It is admitted that the ability to carry on trade, the situation of the house, the convenient arrangement of the house, the personality of the late tenant, are all elements of the greatest import-

Trade the only datum of actual letting of a public house

ance, but, having taken all these into consideration, the
question must resolve itself into this, "What business
can be done in the future?" and the best evidence of
that is what has been done in the past.

Now in the case of *Dodds* v. *South Shields*,[1] the
presumption of Mr. Justice Wills can only have been
that there are many standards of comparison to be found
when assessing a public-house   Indeed, he says " In the
case of the great majority of public-houses there is no
difficulty whatever in resorting to the ordinary method
of assessment, ' namely, that of ascertaining the value by
comparison , but at the present day, with regard to the
great majority of public-houses it is quite impossible to
obtain any reliable standard of comparison, and therefore
other methods have to be resorted to   This difficulty, no
doubt, brought about the case of *Cartwright* v *Sculcoates
Union*,[2] where it was endeavoured, and successfully, to
show that the case of *Dodds* v. *South Shields*[1] was wrong
as applied to the majority of public-houses, inasmuch as
evidence as to the trade done was excluded, but in *Cartwright's* case it was held successfully, from the arbitrator
to the House of Lords, that such evidence was permissible
and, indeed, was necessary to ascertain the real value
The case, however, did not decide that it is compulsory for
a publican to produce his books when appealing against
his assessment, but the inference to be drawn from the
refusal on the part of the appellant to give this information is so obvious as hardly to need comment   The
judgment, in the Court of Appeal, of the Lord Chancellor
(Lord Halsbury) in the *Cartwright* case was as follows —

Cartwright
case

" I am of opinion that this appeal must be dismissed
The problem is to ascertain, according to the Statute,

---

[1] (1895) 59 J P 152

[2] (1899) 1 Q B 667, (1900) A C. 150 69 L J Q B 103, 48 W R 894,
64 J P 229, 82 L T 157

what a tenant from year to year might reasonably be expected to give as rent. That is the problem, and for the solution of that problem it appears to me that, apart from the decisions, as to which I will say a word presently, all that could reasonably affect the mind of the intending tenant ought to be considered. There have been a series of decisions with which I do not mean to quarrel, but I think this general observation might be made about them— that sometimes, giving advice and directions to the Justices in Quarter Sessions, before whom this question more commonly and almost invariably comes, phrases have been used by learned Judges which might seem at first sight to be decisions upon the law of evidence, but I think it would be a mistake so to consider them. They are rules (if they are to be called rules) which the Court of Queen's Bench, in administering that form of jurisprudence, have given as advice to the Justices in considering what should and what should not form topics for their consideration, and the mode by which those topics should be brought before them. I should hesitate, speaking generally—not individualising any particular case—to assume that, when a Judge says that this or that is not evidence on such a question, he intends to express by that, that according to the ordinary rules of evidence such and such a topic might not be approached. I do not think that is the meaning of it. But very often the judgment comes upon a case reserved by the Sessions, which asks practically for advice in what way the problem is to be solved; and it is intelligible enough, I think, that under those circumstances the Judges, in giving the advice and the decision at which they ultimately arrive, have used phrases of the kind that I referred to. They are not intended to be laid down as abstract propositions on the law of evidence, but as applicable to the subject-matter with which they are dealing, and to their advice as to the mode in which such and such a fact is to be ascertained.

And nothing could be more appropriate, I think, to a
consideration of that character than to point out to the
Justices that they should not allow, for instance, a roving
commission over a man's books, in the nature of an
income tax commissioner's, to find out what he is making.
That would be, I should say, inexpedient, and, I think,
the late Master of the Rolls uses the phrase that it would
be mischievous and oppressive. I think in that sense that
those decisions to which I have referred are very good and
sound sense. Fortunately, I think it is not necessary to
consider the effect of those decisions here, as if they were
to be treated as matters of absolute decision on the
question of what is the law of evidence in this country,
because in this case, in accordance with all the evidence
that has been given, and in pursuance, I think, of a long
line of decisions on this question, the evidence here was
properly received—such evidence as there was—and
properly acted upon by the arbitrator. I am not aware
that, as one test in ascertaining whether a house is capable
of doing a good business or not, it would be inappropriate;
whether it is a public-house or a shop of any other kind,
that somebody or another should be called as a witness to
say, 'Why, I saw every day the house quite full of
customers.' There is no decision which to my mind
justifies the proposition that that would not be legitimate
evidence. It would be to my mind one of the most
extraordinary things in the world if you could give expert
evidence that such and such a house would be likely
to command such and such a business, and yet not be able
to verify that *à priori* opinion by proof of the fact that it
did command such a business. That is a totally different
proposition from saying that you can go into a question
of profit and loss, and ascertain whether a man has made
so much money by conducting the business in the house.
So, here, whether it is by proof that a great number of
persons brought drays of beer from time to time to this

house, or whether it is by saying that a great number of
people were in the house drinking, both these topics of
enquiry seem to me to point to the same thing, that it
was a good house for business. It is not that you are
ascertaining the exact quantity of business done, but that
it is a good house for business, and that, therefore, if you
want to know whether such and such a rent is appropriate
to any house for business in the neighbourhood, that is
legitimate evidence to ascertain whether it is a good house
for business or not.

' That, I think, would be the law, quite independently Dodds' case
reviewed in
Court of
Appeal
of *Dodds'* case, upon which reliance has been placed,
but if I am to take the strictest view of *Dodds'* case as
applicable to the question now under debate, it appears
to me that the arbitrator has in terms found that *Dodds'*
case is not applicable Because what was said in *Dodds'*
case was this—Where there are no exceptional or
peculiar circumstances, and where you can ascertain
what is the rateable value of a house by looking at the
houses next door or houses similarly situated in the
immediate neighbourhood, then you have no right to go—
and again I say those words have to be reasonably understood with reference to the canon of construction to
which I referred just now—you have no right to go into
a man's profit or loss, to look at his books, and so on.
You must take the ordinary case of the market value of a
house such as this or of other houses similarly situated in
the neighbourhood, and if you have these materials you
have no right to go beyond that That is all that *Dodds'*
case decided, but they said in the case of a railway
refreshment room and the case of the racecourse, where
you have not the same power of comparing one subject
of rating with another, you must, of course, go into the
question more minutely—what money can be made out
of it That is the effect of the decision. Now what
does the arbitrator say here? He may be right or he

may be wrong, as a matter of fact, but what he says is
I cannot find out the proper rateable value from materials
of that character, the houses are so far apart, free houses
are so few, they are in such distant parts of the neighbourhood with which we are dealing, that I cannot find
that out unless I am entitled to consider the amount of
business   Having done that, is it possible to contend in
the face of his own specific finding that this is not
within the exception created by *Dodds'* case?   It seems
to me to be hopeless, and under those circumstances,
therefore, it appears to me that, without interfering with
any decisions which have been arrived at, and without
laying down any other rule by which the thing is to be
ascertained, the broad proposition is whether this arbitrator has improperly—that is what it comes to—taken
into consideration something that he ought not to have
considered.   I am of opinion, on the other hand, that he
has very properly considered that this was a house which
would probably do a certain amount of business—the
exact amount is not before us—and that the rateable
value that he has affixed to this house is the rateable
value which he has fixed on taking into consideration all
the circumstances of this case.

"However, the result of this is, that I am of opinion
that this appeal should be dismissed   I think the
arbitrator has properly arrived at a conclusion at which
he was entitled to arrive. So far as the quantity is
concerned, that question is not before us, but only
whether he was entitled to arrive at the conclusion he
has done by the materials he has enumerated as the
materials upon which he formed his judgment "

It will be noticed from the above judgment that the
Lord Chancellor was of opinion that the case of *Dodds*
v. *South Shields*[1] was not altogether on the same footing,
because it was found as a fact in that case that there were

---

[1] (1895) 59 J P 452

no exceptional or peculiar circumstances to prevent the
value of the house being ascertained   Lord Justice
Collins, in delivering judgment in the same case, made
use of very powerful arguments in support of the
question of the admissibility in evidence of the trade
done at a house.   His judgment is as follows: " I think
when the *Mersey Docks* and *Liverpool* case,[1] which
the Master of the Rolls says is the foundation of the
judgment in *Dodds'* case, is looked at, it merely is a
decision that profits are not to be rated.   That is the
decision   Then comes the explanation of why they are
not to be rated, and in that explanation given by Mr
Justice Blackburn I find the authority for what has
been done in this case   This is what he says about it
' Though the profits which may be reasonably expected
to arise from such a business no doubt form an element
in estimating the enhanced value of the occupation of the
premises, the actual profits made do not form any element,
except in so far as they afford evidence of what might be
reasonably expected to be made from the occupation of
premises affording facility for carrying on such a business '
If the evidence is used and applied in the proper direction
for that purpose, it is an authority that it is clearly
admissible.

"It seems to me that this rule, as to what evidence is
admissible, and what not admissible, is really a rule of
convenience.   The principle at the bottom of our law of
evidence simply is, I think, a principle of convenience.
We exclude a great many elements that might affect the
judgment of ordinary persons, because, as a matter of
convenience, it would be impossible to sift and examine
and qualify all those different elements of evidence so as
to give them their exactly adjusted position in the investigation   It is not practicable, and therefore we do
not do it   Therefore we make a rule that you admit the

---

[1] (1873) 43 L J M C 33, L R 9 Q B. 84.

best evidence and not the second-best evidence. But in
a great many given cases, that which I call the second-
best evidence is the most direct evidence on the matter,
and, as a matter of practice, when you are dealing with
the rateable value of inhabited houses, it is, as an ordinary
accepted rule of convenience (as the late Master of the
Rolls says), admitted that, in dealing with inhabited
houses as ordinary business premises, you may determine
the question by inquiring what rent is given for similar
premises in a similar position in the same place It is
obvious, where you have a simple standard like that ready
to your hands, it is undesirable to embark upon an investigation as to the special circumstances in which the
individuals occupying those particular houses carried on
their work Although it would be wrong to say that, as a
matter of law, it is to be excluded, because it will have no
bearing, still it is right to say that, as a matter of convenience, its bearing is subject to so much discussion and
to so many qualifications that it is much better, as a
general rule of convenience, to reject that class of evidence,
and take that which is ready to your hand and is so easily
applied I do not think the decision in *Dodds'* case goes
beyond that. It seems to me that to say, as a matter of
law, you are to shut your eyes to that which must be a
factor, if not the dominant factor, in governing the decision
of any would-be tenant, namely, what possibility of
making profits out of it there is, would be to shut our
eyes to the purpose for which evidence is admissible
It seems to me in this case, when you exclude altogether the profits from the subject-matter of the rate,
but admit evidence as to the special facilities incident
to this particular hereditament, that you are simply
using the most obvious and important factor in determining the intention of the tenant whether he would
or would not give a certain rent for those premises The
facilities incident to the hereditament itself are absolutely

germane to the matter. One way of arriving at these facilities—probably the best way—is to enquire how far they have been efficacious in the past. What inference are we to draw from what we know as to what business can be done on those premises by an ordinary tenant? Why, the business that has been done seems to me the most important factor in arriving at that decision. Of course it has to be qualified by any special circumstances.

Business done most important factor when valuing public house

The House of Lords upheld the decision, and Lord Macnaghten said: "My Lords, notwithstanding the able argument on the part of the appellants, I think this is a very simple case. To my mind it is a question of common sense, and not a question of law. It is a question of common sense having regard to the plain language of the Act of Parliament. What your Lordships have to consider is whether the learned arbitrator proceeded on the lines on which the Act of Parliament directs or fairly indicates that he ought to proceed.

" Now, what has the learned arbitrator done? He has found that in this particular case there does not exist the ordinary basis of commutation, and he has excluded any inquiry into profits. In that I think he was perfectly right, not that the profits, if they could be ascertained, would not be an element in arriving at the rent which a tenant might reasonably be expected to pay, but that any further inquiry into profits should be avoided, because it would be oppressive. There is nothing that a tradesman so much dislikes as any inquiry into his profits. In some cases, possibly, it cannot be avoided, and then, according to the decided cases, it may be done; but in this case there has been no enquiry into profits. What the learned arbitrator has done is, he has taken into consideration the amount of business which this public-house was doing. Was he wrong in that? Surely the very first thing that a tenant who was

8

going to offer for a house of this sort would do would be to consider (roughly if he could not do it accurately) what amount of business he was likely to do there? It appears to me that the volume of business done in a public-house, as apparent to the man in the street—if I may use such an expression—is the very first thing that a tenant proposing to make an offer for such a house would take into consideration"

Lord Morris also said "My Lords, I concur, and I especially concur in the opinion that this is a very plain case

"The Act of Parliament states very concisely that the question to be solved by the Quarter Sessions, or by the arbitrator selected by the parties and approved, is, what would it be reasonably expected that the premises would let for to a tenant? That has been paraphrased (and personally I do not object to it) into, what would a hypothetical tenant pay? Now, there does not appear to me to be any law at all in the question. I am told that two great divisions have been made by those who have built a superstructure of law upon that rather simple line in the Act of Parliament, into what are called 'exceptional cases' and 'ordinary cases' I can find no such distinction in the Act of Parliament. The Act of Parliament leaves it general The tribunal that has to assess is to decide what the premises would be reasonably expected to let for. That may, in certain cases, like railways, gas companies, docks, etc, be most difficult to ascertain, because there is no probability—I might almost say no possibility—of considering that there a tenant would ever arise to take it Therefore, in that case, the tribunal is obliged to resort to a discussion as to the amount of profits that have been made, and to deduce some sort of estimate, in a rough way, from that, to solve the problem of what the hypothetical tenant would pay.

"The present case relates to a public-house, which I presume is at a corner —they generally are, so as to capture two streets—and it is said that it was not competent for the arbitrator, as a matter of law. to take into consideration the amount of profits, or to weigh that in his mind, largely or lightly I am sure I do not know which, because this case has been rather dealt with as if appeals could be made to the Court of Queen's Bench, the Appeal Court, and this House, as to whether the arbitrator came to a right conclusion, not in point of law, but in point of fact? What error did he make in point of law? He asked himself almost the very first question that the hypothetical tenant would ask, namely, Is this a house doing a good business or a bad business? Is it a house with what is popularly called a roaring business, or is it a house that is going down for some reason or other, such as there being other houses in its neighbourhood? That is the very first question that a hypothetical tenant would put to himself What have been the profits that have been made in it? Because that is the best proof as to whether it is doing a good business or not True, it is said A B might make good profits, but C D might lose All that, it is to be presumed, the arbitrator would consider; he would not value it on the principle that it was always to have superlatively good occupiers or the worst of occupiers. I suppose he would, as a sensible man, take a sort of average between them The contention, as I understand it, is that the arbitrator, in deciding that question as to what a hypothetical tenant would pay, is to be precluded, as a matter of law, from entering upon the very question which, as I have said, in my opinion is almost the first question that the hypothetical tenant would put It is true that the best way of ascertaining what the trade was which was going on would be the production of the books of the then tenant, but

How profits of public house affect hypothetical tenant

that was objected to   It is suggested that the case
of *Dodds* v *The South Shields Union*[1] decided that that
is improper evidence   If it so decided, I can only say
that I entirely disagree with it, and not being bound
by it here, as the Lord Chancellor was when sitting
in the Court of Appeal, if it goes that length—I have
not had the opportunity of looking into it—I am entirely
of an opposite opinion

"It is said that this would be an inquisitorial inquiry,
a mischievous one, and several other adjectives are
applied to it   I do not see how it is inquisitorial if
the parties themselves are ready to bring the evidence
forward   There is no force put on a publican to produce
his books, he is not in this inquisition threatened
with the screw, and if he chooses not to bring forward
his books he need not do so, and the arbitrator is then
obliged to forage about for the purpose of ascertaining,
in the best way he can under the circumstances, what
the profits would be   As I have said, that question, in
my opinion, is one of the most important factors in
arriving at a conclusion as to what a sensible man would
pay as rent for the premises'

Judgment in
Cartwright's
case   House
of Lords

Lord Shand said 'My Lords, I am of the same
opinion   The simple question which had to be answered
by the arbitrator, and which this House has now to
consider in dealing with his award, is   At what rent
would the premises be reasonably expected to let for from
year to year ? I am of opinion, with your Lordships,
that the arbitrator has taken the proper elements into
view in deciding that question

"It may be that, in a case of this class, it is not
competent to prove, as the Courts have held in the case
of *Dodds*, the amount of the actual detailed profits made
by the tenant in the particular house in bygone years
The true ground for so holding is, I think, that such

---

[1] (1895) 59 J P 452

proof is, or might be, of an inquisitorial character I can very well understand that on the part of the tenants it may be a very reasonable objection for them to make to evidence of that kind that it would rip up affairs, which they are not bound to disclose to the public in questions of this kind. If it were not so, it seems to me that such evidence would be admitted as an important element in ascertaining what trade has been done in the house for really it appears to me that this would be the element of all others which a tenant might be expected to take into view in fixing the rent he ought to give for the premises In this case the arbitrator made the trade actually done the main element in ascertaining the trade which might be expected to be done and in reaching the rent which might reasonably be expected In doing this, I am of opinion that he was right '

Since the decision in this case it has been the writer's experience that the majority of appellants lay open their books for perusal by the assessment authorities, and the point now to be considered is how the information is to be dealt with when obtained It has been said that the question of profits shall not be considered, although, on the other hand, the trade done at the house is to be inquired into and it is very difficult to see where the line of demarcation is, for it is clear that any practical man who knows the trade or gross takings of a public-house could not fail to realise that a certain profit would be derivable from such takings, and it is also necessary, before a hypothetical tenant could fix his rent, to ask himself what would be the probable profits out of the gross takings It is also clear that certain public-houses are worked very much more cheaply than others, that is to say, it is repeatedly found that certain houses are built very much in excess of the requirements for the trade that is actually done at the premises, and consequently are more expensive to work in the matter of assistants,

etc, than smaller houses doing the same amount of
business.   Then again, as all houses have to be looked
upon as being free, the distance from a brewery might
have the effect of the tenant having to pay cart go
There are also several other elements to be considered, so
that it will be at once seen that when the trade of a
public-house is obtained, there can be no hard and fast
rule to apply in dealing with such trade   It is, however,
certain that a tenant would be willing to pay a rent
having a foundation on a percentage of the gross takings
but the percentage must vary enormously, and it would
also vary according to the amount of trade done, for a
tenant would certainly pay a higher percentage if the
returns were high than he would if they were comparatively small, or, in other words, if the takings of a
public-house amounted to, say, £2,000 a year, a tenant
might be disposed to give £200 or possibly more for the
house, but if the takings only amounted to £200 per
annum, it is obvious that he might not be able to afford
to pay £20 rent.

These remarks may give some idea as to how the
takings are to be dealt with, but it is quite impossible to
say more, each individual case necessarily having to rest
on its own merits   As the question of the trade of a
public-house is admissible evidence, it would be quite
legitimate to put in as evidence the cost of management
of the house and other equally potent factors which must
affect a tenant's mind. There is also nothing to prevent a
tenant, if he so chose, going into the question of profits.
In the case of *Clark* v. *Alderbury Union*[1] there were
certain refreshment rooms at Salisbury Station, and on an
estimate made by the tenant of the trade to be done, he
agreed to pay a rent of £1,000 per annum for five years
The estimate proved to be incorrect, but the committee
in assessing the property took as a basis for the rateable

[1] (1880) 6 Q B D 139 50 L J M.C 33, 45 J P 358, 29 W R 314

value the above figure   On appeal to Sessions, the tenant
in the course of his evidence produced his accounts, and
it being held that they were admissible evidence, in the
result the assessment was reduced.   The case was taken
to the Queen's Bench, and during the proceedings it
was stated by the appellant that he had made a mistake
in his lease with regard to his estimate of the rent which
he could afford to give, he having offered the sum in
question in the expectation that the number of passengers
and trains would be increased, but this event not
happening he had incurred considerable loss   Field, J,
in delivering judgment, said ' The case is, in my judgment, free from doubt   The appellant is the occupier of
a rateable hereditament, and the question raised by the
appeal is, whether he was properly assessed on the annual
value of the premises   The facts of the case are shortly
these   Mr Clark is a refreshment contractor on the
London and South Western Railway, and acted in that
capacity at the Salisbury Station.   In 1878 a second
refreshment room was added at that station, of which the
appellant obtained the lease by open tender   The rent
which he agreed to pay was, as it turned out, considerably
larger than he could afford to pay   At the hearing of the
appeal, evidence was tendered of the loss which had been
sustained, by showing the receipts and expenditure for
provisions, salaries and other expenses, and also to prove
what was really the amount which a tenant could afford
to pay his landlord for these premises, after making the
usual allowances and deductions   This evidence was
objected to by the respondents on the ground, first, that
the appellant having offered a particular rent for these
premises was estopped from saying that the annual value
was less than the rent offered, and, secondly, that the
price annually paid for provisions, etc, could not be
evidence against the respondents' objection.   The Sessions

Where tak-
ings admis-
sible evidence

overruled the respondents objection and admitted the evidence, and we have now to decide whether the ruling of the Sessions was correct.

"Now I am of opinion that the decision of the Sessions was perfectly right Mr Wills admitted that the actual rent was not the criterion on which the question before us must be determined. The only question, therefore for us is whether certain evidence was admissible The appellant proposed to show that by reason of the price of provisions, etc , it was impossible to carry on business at a profit. It was put thus 'I'll show you what I have to pay I buy as cheap and sell as dear as I can, but I cannot afford a higher rent than £100' Now is evidence of this kind inadmissible? In *R* v. *Venall*,[1] the very point was raised, and evidence of the profits derived from the use of certain land as a racecourse was held admissible, not as an absolute test, but as a material element in determining the value of such land That was the converse of the present case, but the same principle applies It seems to me that *R* v *Venall* in no way conflicts with the decision in *R* v *The Guardians of North Aylesford*,[2] where all that was held was that evidence of a particular mode of carrying on business was inadmissible to show the value of the premises On those grounds I think our judgment must be in favour of the appellant "

This case, taken in conjunction with *Cartwright* v *Sculcoates Union*,[3] makes it clear that an appellant can offer evidence of expenses as a set-off against the receipts

The question of the large prices which were paid in past years by brewers for the possession of public-houses, and also the enormous rents paid by brewers in order to tie the trade, cannot be taken into account, as brewers cannot be considered as ordinary tenants

---

[1] (1875) 45 L J M C 29 , 1 Q B D 9 , 33 L T 379 , 40 J P 350
[2] (1872) 26 L T N S 618 , 37 J P, 148
(1899) 1 Q B 667

of a public-house. In the case of *Bradford-on-Avon v White*,[1] the Sessions found that if brewers were to be excluded as possible tenants of the public-house in question, although they did not intend themselves to occupy the premises, but to convert them into a tied house, the rent at which the premises might be expected to let would have been considerably higher than if the brewers were excluded from this competition; and they went on to find that it was the hereditament independently of the personal advantage to the brewers that had to be assessed, although they did not exclude brewers as competitors, but treated them like ordinary tenants. This decision was confirmed by the Court of Queen's Bench, Channell, J, saying, in the course of his judgment · "I do not think that the competition of brewers should be wholly excluded from consideration, but the special prices which they may give owing to personal considerations, and not on account of the value of the premises, should be excluded, except so far as the possibility of such special prices being obtained raises the market value generally '

Since the passing of the Licensing Act, 1904,[2] an endeavour has been made to deduct from the gross value, in estimating the net annual value, the amount of the annual compensation payable under Section 3 of that Act, but it was held by the Court of Appeal that such a deduction was illegal [3]

It, however, does not follow that when obtaining the gross value of a house, by a process involving the deduction of the expenses from the receipts and the allocation of the balance as between landlord and tenant, that any sum payable such as this should not be considered an expense of the house

---

[1] (1898) 2 Q B 630, 67 L J Q B 643, 62 J P 548

[2] 4 Edward VII (1904), c 23

[3] *Baddle v Sunderland Union*, (1908), C A, 23rd January, 1908, 1 K B 642

In dealing with large hotels belonging to public companies they should be treated rather in the nature of a special property, as it is impossible to conceive that a public company would pay a rent for a large hotel unless there was a reasonable prospect of a profit being made, and in the event of an occupation being profitless or a very small profit being made, as in the case of *Clark* v. *Alderbury Union*,[1] the books showing the business of the hotel would clearly be admissible evidence during the hearing of a case if the appellant so desired, and therefore the following figures may serve as a guide as to how the accounts might be dealt with :—

ESTIMATE OF THE VALUE OF THE —— HOTEL, YEAR ENDING 31ST DECEMBER

RECEIPTS

	1900	1901.	1902
From business done at hotel	£24,003	£27,321	£30,005
			27,321
			24,003
Striking an average .. .			3)£81,329
Average annual receipts .			£27,109

EXPENSES.

	1900	1901	1902
Provisions, wines, spirits, mineral waters, ales, cigars, fuel, and cleaning materials	£11,235	£13,298	£12,704
Wages, salaries, and liveries .. .	2,957	2,655	2,139
Gas, electric light, water, etc	800	1,080	1 100
Laundry materials, etc . .	223	326	370
Printing, stationery, etc ..	209	498	423
General charges .	472	564	583
Horse and carriage hire .. .	413	346	451
Law expenses	41	33	52
Carried forward ..	£16,350	£18,800	£17,822

[1] (1880) 50 L J M.C. 33, 6 Q.B.D 139

	1900.	1901.	1902
Brought forward ...	£16,350	£18,900	£17,822
Manager's Salary	160	150	150
Director's fees	175	175	200
Repairs and renewals to tenant's effects, say .	1,400	1,400	1 400
	£18,085	£20 525	£19,572

	£18,085
	20,525
	19 572
Taking the average	3)£58,182
Average annual expenditure	£19,394

AVERAGE ANNUAL RECEIPTS	£27,109
AVERAGE ANNUAL EXPENSES	19,394
NET RECEIPTS	£7,715

NET RECEIPTS (including rates, which have to be deducted on the rateable value of the hereditament) .	£7,715
Deduct rates at 5s. in the £ on an assessment of £2,241 ..	561
	£7 154

TENANT S SHARE

17½ per cent on tenant s capital as per details (see below) £18,300	3,202
	£3,952

DETAILS OF TENANT'S CAPITAL

Cash at bank ...	£2,000
Present value of furniture and working stock .	14 000
Stock of wines, etc. ...	1,700
Book debts etc	600
	£18,300

Carried forward	£3,952

Brought forward	...		£3,952

STATUTABLE DEDUCTIONS

Repairs and renewals as charged in accounts

1900			..	£1,010
1901	..			1,156
1902	.	.	.	1,874
			3)£4,040	

Average per annum	.	£1,346
Extra repairs are done every seven years which amount to £2,000—say, per annum ..		285
Insurances say . ..		80
		1,711

Rateable value of hotel	£2,241

The application of the principle of percentages on the structural value and on the value of the site of a hotel has been shown to be wrong in several cases, it being obvious that the rent could not be affected by mere structure only

It, however, does not follow that there are certain special cases in which evidence of the structural value of an hotel is not admissible It cannot be denied that in order to ascertain the rent of any property anything or everything which would affect the mind of a tenant cannot as a matter of law be excluded from evidence, but how far that evidence is relevant to each particular case is a question of fact to be dealt with only as cases arise

It is, however, interesting to note that in the appeal of the *Great Eastern Railway Co* v *City of London Union*[1] the London Quarter Sessions admitted evidence both as to receipts and expenses and as to structural value. The gross receipts of the hotel amounted in round figures to £72,000, and the rateable value contended for by the appellants was £2,086 The respondents presented to the Court a valuation based on the contractor's principle,

---

[1] Reported on Page 63 of Vol 1 'Konstam's Rating Appeals ' (1907)

and taking $3\frac{1}{2}$ per cent on the capital value of the
buildings, added to the estimated annual value of the
land, obtained a rateable value of £14,450 The Court,
however, fixed the rateable value at £5,800, which in
effect was about 8 per cent. of the gross receipts. It is
submitted that if the method of the contractor s principle
had been correct, 5 per cent., and not $3\frac{1}{2}$ per cent would
have been the more correct figure to apply, which would
have had the effect of making the rateable value of the
hotel nearer £18,000 than £5,800 the amount decided by
the Court

Although it is true that the Court fixed the rateable
value at a considerably higher figure than that arrived at
by the appellants on a basis of profits, the ultimate
decision of £5,800, as compared with the valuation of the
respondents of £14,450, is sufficient evidence that the
Court must have abandoned the contention of the
respondents in its entirety and simply modified the
valuation of the appellants Upon their basis a total
rateable value of £2,086 was arrived at as the landlord's
share, the amount claimed for the tenant being £11,101,
and there can be little doubt from observations which fell
from the Bench during the course of the case, although
not reported, that the Court were of opinion that while
the allowance claimed for the tenant was too high, the
principle of structural value advanced by the respondents
was incorrect

In making a valuation of a school the prosperity of it Private schools
must not be taken into account, what has to be
ascertained is the rent at which it would let, and the
aptitude which one man might have for filling his school
as compared with another must not enter into the calculation There might be two schools adjacent to one
another having exactly the same accommodation, and
indeed alike in every particular, at the head of one there
is a master whose capabilities permit him always to keep

his school full, whilst as regards the other the reverse is the case. It would be obviously unfair to assess the one higher than the other, so that some other method than the basis of the prosperity of the school has to be adopted. In the case of *R. v London School Board* [1] the rateable value was arrived at by calculating the annual value of the land, that is, by putting the present value to purchase at 4 per cent, and adding to that 5 per cent on the estimated cost of the buildings. This is a satisfactory method as to the principle of arriving at the value of the hereditament, and may be applicable to any school in any part of the country

Contractor's theory defined

The principle of taking a percentage upon the structural value to arrive at the gross and rateable values of hereditaments not likely to be let in the ordinary sense, and therefore the possibility of comparison with similar properties being nil, is commonly known as contractor's rent, or, in other words, the rent or interest that A would give to B, if B erected for A buildings suitable to A's requirements. The question, however, of the percentage to be applied to the capital value is a very difficult one, for it cannot be denied there are many considerations to be dealt with when fixing the rate of interest in a particular case. In the case above referred to, the interest was fixed at Sessions presumably upon the ground that it is a very common form of interest to apply to private property in London, and therefore the Court were of opinion that, notwithstanding the fact that the School Board by reason of their position and ability were able to borrow money at smaller rates than those allowed, they should therefore not be assessed on a basis to the disadvantage of the other ratepayers. In other words, it would appear that the decision was arrived at because the

---

[1] (1886) 17 Q B D 738, 55 L J M C 169, 55 L T 384, 34 W R 583, 50 J P 419—C A See also *London School Board v Wandsworth and Clapham Union*, (1900) 16 T L R 137.

Court had the anomaly placed before them of two rate-payers in a parish, the one able to borrow money at a far less rate of interest than the other, and on this account an appeal brought, asking that the rent of the ratepayer, able to borrow money more cheaply, should be reduced proportionately. Of course it would be unreasonable to suppose that, if there were two houses side by side, not let but owned and occupied by two individuals, the credit of the one being good and of the other bad, the rate per cent on the structural value to ascertain the rateable value of the two houses should vary owing to this, because when assessing the two houses the question that has to answered is What rent would a hypothetical tenant pay altogether irrespective of the structural value of the houses? But where it is impossible to ascertain that, by means of comparison, another method has to be found, and the most reasonable one may be that of the contractor's rent; but it must be assumed that the hypothetical tenant is a man whose position is an average one without any extraordinary conditions, which might occur in exceptional cases.

With regard to the occupation of a large building such as the School Board were compelled to occupy, however, it would seem that the most reasonable way of fixing the percentage on the capital outlay would be to take the interest which is actually being paid by the Board in question, for it is clear that the actual amount of rent that is being paid by such a Board is in effect the interest they are paying on the capital outlay, for if any public body are able to borrow money at, say, 3 per cent and with that money erect buildings which they themselves occupy, it is tantamount to asking a capitalist to erect such buildings for them, they agreeing to pay by way of rent such interest on the outlay.

It is to be observed that there is great distinction to be made between capital outlay and structural value; for if the rate of interest which is payable by a public body is to be regarded as the basis of rent, the whole of the capital outlay incurred in erecting premises would apparently be the starting point of the valuation,[1] although in many cases it is found that money has been recklessly and wantonly spent in the erection of buildings —here the discretion of the assessor must come in   In the writer's opinion there is no analogy between the letting of ordinary premises and the letting of premises occupied by public bodies for public purposes   The whole system of rating is to ascertain the rent that would be paid by the probable hypothetical tenant, therefore it is only reasonable to take into consideration the conditions of the hypothetical tenancy and the probable rent that would be paid if, instead of erecting buildings and occupying them, an actual letting took place   For it must be obvious that the School Board for London for instance, could not afford to say to a contractor, "If you will erect us a school we will pay you 5 per cent on your outlay by way of rent," if they were in a position to borrow money and erect a school themselves and only pay 3 per cent. for the money which was sunk in the erection of the building and purchase of the land   This theory was borne out by Lord Herschell when delivering judgment in the case of the *London County Council v. Erith and West Ham*[2]   He said that, although a practice prevailed of taking 5 per cent of the cost in the case of buildings as a basis for arriving at the rental, such a rule of thumb would be all very well where the premises would be likely to find competing tenants, but it is by no means always practicable. It would often be obvious that an owner, who was also an occupier, would never be willing to pay rent arrived at in such a fashion   He went on to say " In all cases of the

---

[1] *Mayor of Liverpool v Llanfyllin Union*, (1899) 2 Q B 14
[2] (1893) A C. 562

description of which I am speaking, the whole of the circumstances and conditions under which the owner has become occupier must be taken into consideration and no higher rent must be fixed as the basis of assessment than that which it is believed the owner would really be willing to pay for the occupation of the premises "

In valuing a building for assessment purposes, in the event of its being highly decorated, the decoration should not be assessed at its full value, as a building used for the purpose of a school, for instance, need not necessarily be highly decorated, and a hypothetical tenant would give no more rent for it than if the building were in a less ornamented state   This is self-evident, as decoration is not necessary for education, and in a case of this sort a hereditament could not obtain any higher rent from the mere fact of there being unnecessary ornamentation

Where ornamentation not rateable

A certain amount of decoration, however, is necessary according to the class of school. It could not be imagined that a building erected by the School Board for London would be equally suitable to be used as a college at Oxford, and *vice versa*, but it is against excess of ornamentation that allowance has to be made in valuation

In a very important case decided at Oxford Borough Quarter Sessions,[1] the Hon A. T Lyttelton, K.C., sitting as Recorder, adopted the view that, in ascertaining the capital value of the Universities of Oxford for rating purposes, it was wrong to take into account the whole of the vast amount of capital that had been spent in superb decoration, although he stated that the University authorities, regarded merely as managers of a business, were wise to consider, within reason, architectural beauty as essential to their buildings. He pointed out that Oxford was not the only university in the kingdom, Birmingham, Manchester and London were in the field and

---

[1] *Oxford University* v. *Mayor, etc, of Oxford*, " Oxford Chronicle," June 20th, 1902

had in modern times added their youthful forces to the competition of ancient institutions like Cambridge and Durham Universities. In such a competition the beauty and stateliness of her buildings were of real value to Oxford, and in this matter he said that the authorities in studying sentiment without extravagance would follow sound business principles

Shops

The principle to be followed in valuing a shop is the same, viz, to ascertain the rent which it would fetch if it were in the market to be let. The position of the shop has an important bearing upon the question; as, although there might be buildings well adapted for the purposes of a shop, supposing it not to be in a good thoroughfare no tenant would be found to take it at the same rental as if it were favourably situated. If a premium be given on entering the premises, that portion of it not attributable to goodwill would have to be spread over the term, either on the 4 per cent or 5 per cent table, as explained in the earlier portion of this chapter. Provided there were no particulars forthcoming as to the rent, etc., which the property might be expected to command, in most large towns the value of the land at 4 per cent and the value of the building at 5 per cent may reasonably be taken, and then something added by way of a premium if the position justifies it

Theatres

When assessing a theatre there are several important points to be borne in mind. The first of these is, that for the purpose of the rate the owner is deemed to be the occupier, and secondly, that a theatre is held to be occupied whether there be any performance at the time or not, but in making an assessment (and more particularly in London, where it is only done once in every five years) the liability of the theatre to be empty is a contingency which must be taken into consideration. Where a private box in the theatre was held on lease for a number of years, it was held by the Court that the box

must be separately rated to the lessee[1]   In the event of
such an occurrence happening when making a valuation
of a theatre, the rateable value of such box or boxes
would have to be deducted from the whole and separately
entered in the Valuation List, as otherwise the owner of
the theatre and the lessee of the box in question might
both be paying rates on the same assessment to the local
authorities

Hospitals are rateable to the poor under 43 Elizabeth, *Hospitals and convalescent homes*
c 2, and the method to be adopted when valuing the
same is to take a percentage upon their structural value,
and a percentage on the value of the site   It may be
thought that hospitals as charitable institutions are only
liable to be rated at a nominal sum, but this is not so
Convalescent homes and the like would come under this
heading, and the following are a few cases which may
be useful for reference   *R v St Giles*[2], *St. Thomas's
Hospital (Governors) v Stratton*[3], *R v Baptist
Missionary Society*[1]   With regard to lunatic asylums *Lunatic asylums*
the Lunacy Act, 1890,[5] provides for the rating of
such hereditaments   Section 263 enacts that "lands
and buildings already or to be hereafter purchased or
acquired for the purposes of any asylum, and any
additional building erected or to be erected thereon, shall,
while used for those purposes, be assessed to county,
parochial, district and other rates, made after the commencement of this Act, on the same basis and to the same
extent as other lands and buildings in the same parish,
township or district."

---

[1] *R v St Martins-le-Grand*, (1842) 2 G & D 426, 3 Q.B. 204;
11 L J M C 112

[2] (1832) 3 B. & Ad 573

[3] (1875) L R 7 H L 477, 45 L J M C 23, 23 W R 882

[4] (1849) 3 New Sess. Cas 555, 10 Q B 884, 18 L J M C 194;
13 Jur 748

[5] 53 Vict, c 5

Private lunatic asylums are amongst the most valuable properties that have to be dealt with by assessment authorities It is very difficult, if not impossible, to obtain licenses such as were granted some years ago to doctors and others who became proprietors of such establishments, and therefore the value of the license of a private asylum is an exceedingly important factor when making the assessment, and to the writer's knowledge the prices that have been paid for institutions of this sort have been exceedingly high, competition being very keen in the rare cases of such hereditaments finding their way into the market It very often happens that in a private asylum of any size there is a chapel for the use of the patients solely, and where this is so it must be treated as part of the lettable property, and is apparently not exempted under the Poor Rate Exemption Act, 1833 [1] Land belonging to the asylum may or may not be considered as agricultural land, but this has been dealt with in the preceding chapter on land.

In the case of county lunatic asylums and other public lunatic asylums, the rate of interest to be applied to the structural value on the contractor's theory should certainly be less than the ordinary rate of interest for private property, for reasons fully discussed in the present chapter in the paragraph on schools and buildings in the hands of local bodies

Workhouses　　Workhouses are also rateable　The Guardians of a Union having constructed a workhouse for the occupation of the poor in the parish, under 4 & 5 William IV, c 76, s 23, were held to be rateable as occupiers of the workhouse. Notwithstanding that, in this case the workhouse was built on land which, from the nature of its previous occupation, had not been assessed to the Poor Rate [2]

---

[1] 3 & 4 William IV , c 30
[2] *R* v *Wallingford Union (Guardians)*, (1839) 10 A & E. 259, 2 P & D 226, 8 L.J M C. 89.

There have been several cases upon this point, notably those of the *Holborn Union (Guardians)* v *St. Leonard's (Vestry), Shoreditch,*[1] and the *Bedford Union (Guardians)* v. *Bedford Improvement (Commissioners).*[2]

The interest to be adopted in calculating the value, on the contractor's theory, in the case of workhouses, is probably the chief point of difficulty in the valuation of this class of property   The point arises, which also arises in other cases, more particularly perhaps with regard to workhouses, cottage homes, etc , as to whether the rate of interest in adopting the contractor's theory should be calculated on the original cost or structural value.   A large number of workhouses throughout the country have been built at various times, added to, and are consequently badly arranged, and, for their accommodation, may have cost a considerably larger sum than more modern houses with the same capacity   In the case of the *Mayor of Liverpool* v. *Llanfyllin Union*[3] the Corporation of Liverpool had constructed an enormous reservoir, under a special Act, in connection with their water scheme and in so doing certain buildings were entirely demolished , but by the provisions of their Act these buildings had to be erected elsewhere, and various roads and bridges constructed to give access to same.   It was contended on behalf of the Assessment Committee before the Sessions that, in calculating the value of the reservoir, the capital value of the concern should include the cost of the erection of the buildings, roads and bridges as mentioned above, presumably on the ground that the Corporation of Liverpool were in fact paying interest or rent on the capital employed in these works, in addition to the capital employed in constructing the reservoir, in order to have the advantage of the use of the reservoir.   The

---

[1] (1873) 28 L T 106 , 21 W R 541
[2] (1852) 7 Ex 777 , 21 L J M C 225
[3] (1899) 2 Q B. 14

appellants, on the other hand, contended that all that
could be rated was the reservoir itself, and therefore the
rateable value should be a percentage on the value of the
reservoir *per se*, excluding the value of the additional
works occasioned by the erection of the reservoir and the
submersion of the buildings, which included a school,
church, etc., etc.   The Sessions decided that the percentage should be applied to the total capital expended on
the reservoir and the reinstatement of the buildings, and
the Court of Appeal held this to be the correct method,
although it should not be overlooked that the decision in
the Court of Appeal reversed the decision of the Queen's
Bench, who in their turn had reversed the decision of
Quarter Sessions.   A. L. Smith, L.J., in giving judgment,
said "If a person buys a piece of land, and spends so much
in erecting a building upon it, the amount so expended by
him forms some criterion of the rent which he would give
if he had to rent the hereditament so created   I agree
that a certain rate of interest on the capital expended in
creating the hereditament is by no means to be taken as
necessarily equivalent to the rent which a hypothetical
tenant would give; but I think the amount of capital
expended is admissible in evidence as a criterion by which
to estimate that rent in the case of works like these which
are incapable of being compared with other hereditaments
which form the subject of letting. .   The Corporation
must be taken into consideration as possible tenants of the
works   They could not construct the works which they
desire to construct, as necessary for the purposes of the
water supply to their city, without coming under the
obligation to provide a new church, vicarage and schools,
in lieu of paying a pecuniary compensation for those which
would be destroyed by the works   I cannot see why, as a
matter of law, that expenditure was not properly taken
into account by the Sessions in arriving at the rateable
value. .   The same considerations appear to me to

apply to the amount expended in providing roads and bridges, as to that expended on the new church, vicarage and schools"

This judgment should be very carefully considered, together with the subject-matter of the appeal, for the question that had to be answered was the rent that the tenant would give for the reservoir, and, if it would be impossible to obtain that reservoir without carrying out the alterations on the site and the reinstatement of the demolished buildings—and it was still worth the while of the intending tenant to pay for this to be done—it is clear that, in fixing the rent of the reservoir, he would have been willing to have given such a sum to the hypothetical landlord as would have represented interest on the capital outlay necessary to achieve the object, although such outlay would have had nothing to do ultimately with the thing let.

On the other hand, where excessive reservoir accommodation had been provided, the Court of King's Bench, in the *Mayor of Bradford* v. *Keighley Union*,[1] held that the Quarter Sessions were right in making a deduction on this account in arriving at the cost of the reservoir This case may very usefully be compared with the *Liverpool* case in considering what may be reckoned effective cost.

When applying this principle to a building in the nature of a workhouse, which may have been standing for fifty or sixty years, altered from time to time, possibly pulled down and re-erected, it would be dangerous to lump the whole cost, including alterations from the inception of the hereditament, and assume it to be the landlord's capital to-day, and that a tenant would be willing to pay interest or rent on money which ceased to be represented in any tangible form, for it would be open to a Board of Guardians to say to the landlord, if it could be conceived that they could become tenants of a

---

[1] " Konstam's Rating Appeals " (1904-8), p 517

workhouse, that, rather than pay interest on capital
unwisely spent, they would erect for themselves a modern
structure where every penny of capital spent would be of
value and for which they would be willing to give rent.
It therefore follows that, in dealing with such properties,
the question largely becomes one of fact as to the rent that
could be paid, and although the contractor's theory may be
applied, the question as to the capital value is one requiring grave consideration, as in the case of *R* v *Mile End
Old Town*[1] it was distinctly held that capital expended on
plant which had become superseded could not be taken
into consideration in arriving at the rent.

---

[1] (1847) 10 Q B 208, 16 L J M C 184, 11 Jur 988.

CHAPTER III.

MANUFACTORIES

Breweries—Chemical Works—Iron Works—Silk Works—Distilleries—Cotton Mills, etc

WHEN making a valuation of a manufactory for rating purposes a difficulty frequently to be overcome is where the property is owned by the tenant, and there is absolutely no guide to the rent it would command if placed upon the market In but very few instances would there be any possibility of comparing the property in question with manufactories of the same nature, therefore apparently the right principle to adopt is the principle laid down in the *London School Board* case,[1] namely, to proceed to ascertain the structural value on the assumption that a tenant would be willing to pay interest on capital useful to him in his business rather than supply the hereditament himself Manufactories are included under Class VIII. of Schedule III of the Valuation (Metropolis) Act, and the maximum deduction allowed in this class to arrive at the rateable value is $33\frac{1}{3}$ per cent from the gross value The large deduction (which, by the way, is not necessarily to be allowed, although it must not be exceeded) will give some idea of the wear and tear to property of this nature ; and this is of the utmost importance when the item of machinery is in question, as the cost of a machine would in many cases be little, if any, guide to its present value We have seen before that property must only be rated as it exists at the time the rate is made, and that the then value is the figure to be adopted in the Valuation List.

---

[1] *London School Board v St Leonard's, Shoreditch*, (1886) 17 Q B.D. 786, 55 L.J M C 169, 55 L T 384

The invariable rule to be applied to the valuation of a factory and all other properties is to ascertain the rent the factory would let at , by adopting the contractor's theory the result would be fallacious in many cases, if the structural value of the premises to be rated, without regard to the purpose for which the premises are used, was the only datum upon which the rate is to be based   It is within the knowledge of everybody that during the last hundred years factories containing machinery have rapidly sprung up all over the kingdom, and that, with the continual and rapid changes in the method of producing various perfected articles, manufactories quickly become antiquated if not altogether obsolete in design and methods. For this reason it is very essential that great care should be exercised in considering the adaptability of premises to the trade for which they are used and this should be carefully taken into consideration by the valuer when making the assessment   Speaking broadly, it may so happen that twenty years ago a factory had been erected containing certain machinery, which, without to-day having become useless, has been superseded by modern machinery, and which, if erected in another building with the same power of production as the old machinery, would occupy far less space and therefore require smaller buildings and probably reduce the wages bill of the old factory by a considerable amount   It therefore follows that the value of the old factory would be less than the new one with the same power of production, as it would be impossible to find a tenant who would give the same rent for both concerns, it being clear that, in the case of the new buildings, he would be able to work more cheaply than in the old ones   It is consequently entirely wrong, as is done in a great many cases, to take all the buildings and machinery that are found *in situ*, and deduce a value without having regard to the all-important question of whether they would be worth to a hypothetical tenant the same amount as a more conveniently arranged hereditament. The fact that factories are only occasionally let—indeed fitted factories are seldom let—makes the application of the rule very difficult; because, where it is found that the tenant and occupier are one, if he spent money in erecting his premises and putting machinery therein—although new methods may be adopted in building new factories—it is very evident that as long as the machinery lasts and does its work, although possibly many improvements exist, it cannot be expected that he would demolish the factory whilst it still continued to be productive and return interest to him. But the assessment authorities, on the other hand as long as there is a beneficial occupation, have to assess the works at some figure having regard to all the facts of the case, and it is therefore very important that the assessor should take into most careful consideration the respective advantages and disadvantages of any particular hereditament when ascertaining the capital value for the purpose of applying the contractor's theory. For example, in the case of a brewery there are six distinct processes —

1 Grinding
2 Mashing and Sparging
3 Boiling
4 Cooling
5 Fermenting and Cleansing
6 Racking

In a well-designed brewery it is necessary that the plant for these processes should follow each other in rotation, and be so arranged that the wort will gravitate from one vessel to another in order to reduce the cost of pumping to a minimum. Therefore the grinding apparatus and mash tuns should be at the top of the building; from here the wort would gravitate to the coppers and again to the hop backs. It is then pumped to the coolers, which should be at the top of another building, and thence gravitate through the fermenting squares to the racking vats. It is, however, frequently found in old breweries that, during the manufacture of the beer, the wort has to be pumped on two or possibly more occasions, and it is very obvious that the cost of the manufacture of the article is consequently increased, and, although it may not be increased to such an extent as to make it impossible to work the brewery at a profit, or to justify replacement on modern lines, it is certain that any tenant in fixing the rent that he could give for the property would take into consideration this defect in the brewery, and it would have the effect of reducing the rent he would be willing to pay for the use of the concern. In the assessment of a brewery, another exceedingly important factor is the ability to obtain water, and the class of water obtainable by the particular concern. It may happen that a brewery has been erected on a particular site, and the well from which it derived the water necessary for the business has given out. It then becomes necessary to purchase water from other sources, the quality of which may be inferior, but even if it is equal in every respect to the former supply it would have to be paid for, and the cost might be greater than formerly, on the assumption that the well was on the property and formed part of the hereditament under discussion. Then, again, in certain districts water is especially valuable because of its particular properties, and so a brewery in that district exactly similar in every other respect would be worth more to a hypothetical tenant than one situated in a district where the water had to be chemically treated or dealt with in other ways necessary for the trade.

Value of water rights

This question of water is an exceedingly important one to the printing, dyeing and bleaching works which are found in the North of England. In some cases an unlimited supply of water is absolutely essential to the business carried on, and inasmuch as sites with these advantages are becoming more scarce every day, it consequently follows that the value of water rights is increasing very much, and is a considerable feature in such undertakings

The same general remarks apply as to arrangements, etc , Foundries in the case of an iron foundry, it being very advantageous for a foundry to be near to a railway or canal   The main principle in the arrangement is to erect the various buildings so that the metal in its various stages can be transferred from one building to another with the least amount of haulage and with as little delay as possible

Taking another instance, viz., that of a cotton mill, the Cotton mills machines through which the raw cotton passes before it arrives at the loom are usually in the following order :—

Bale Breaker	Intermediate Frame.
Opener	Roving Frame
Blowers and Lap Machine	Mule
Carding Engine	Cop Winding Frame
Drawing Frame	Beaming Frame
Slubbing Frame	Slasher, and Loom

As the cotton has to be carried by hand during the process from one machine to another, it will be at once observed that in a well-designed cotton mill the machine rooms should fall in rotation as far as possible to avoid undue labour

Whilst on the subject of cotton mills it may be mentioned that many Unions in the North of England have scales for the assessment of the mills, which are applied in some cases according to the number of spindles in the mill and also according to the amount of floor space in each mill   This latter principle of valuing mills according to their floor space is very much to be condemned, and it is alike unsatisfactory to the owners and to the assessment authorities   Very severe criticism was passed on the principle in the case of the *Calico Printers' Association* v *Glossop Union*[1] at the Derby County

---

[1] Reported in "The Estates Gazette," April 18th, 1903

Quarter Sessions on April 7th, 1903 The system of
valuing cotton mills according to the number of spindles
has more to be said in its favour, although the number
of classes that mills must be arranged into, that is to say,
modern, old, fire-proof, non-fire-proof, etc , makes the
application of the scale a matter of considerable difficulty,
as it is a common thing to find in a mill certain machines
of modern design together with older machinery, and also
a mill may contain buildings which are fire-proof and
others not so

All these conditions point strongly to the advantage of
valuing each individual hereditament on the basis of
its effective capital value, when each individual building
and machine has to be duly considered, for no rough-
and-ready guide, as all scales must of necessity be,
ought to be applied indiscriminately.

To the above instances may be added the multifarious
trades and their processes, but sufficient examples have
been given, it is hoped, to show the force of the argument, viz , that in considering the capital value of any
particular manufactory the adaptability of the premises
to the purpose to which the same are applied is, perhaps,
the most important point in ascertaining the answer to
the question, " What rent would a hypothetical tenant
give ? "

Depreciation
in factories

The question of depreciation in factories, slightly
touched upon previously, is another very difficult point
which the valuer has to cope with, and two theories
are at various times advanced with reference to this In
fixing the gross and rateable values the difference
between the two should include, inter alia, a sinking fund
to replace the hereditament at the end of its life, and it
has, therefore, been argued that a tenant would give as
much twenty years hence for a concern as he would
to-day, on the ground that the hypothetical landlord
would first of all be required to keep the hereditament

in an efficient order in twenty years' time as when new
This is theory only, however, for in practice it is found
that factories depreciate in value very rapidly unless new
machinery replaces the old   In the majority of trades
new inventions are so rapid that machinery quickly
becomes out of date, and although the theory is that the
difference between the gross and rateable value would,
if the hypothesis were correct, deal with this deficiency,
it is in most cases not in fact dealt with , and, as the
letting has to be assumed from year to year, the rent of
most places would probably decrease owing to the
contingencies mentioned   Therefore, when assessing a
factory, the condition of things at the time of making
the rate should be the sole factor in determining the
value , although if a machine be old, and if removed and
sold as second-hand, it might realise less than when it
was new, provided it will do its work as economically and
as ably as when it was new and there is no machine to
supersede it   The rateable value should be calculated on
the capital value as though the machine were new ,
because in this instance, and this instance alone—and be
it remarked that it is very rarely met with—the tenant
would be prepared to give as much rent year by year for
an old machine as he would for a new one, as he could
get the same amount of work out of it without extra cost
for motive power on account of its age, the sole question
being, as far as he is concerned, the capacity of the
machine at work.

The necessity for revision in the definitions of gross
and rateable values is evident, when factories and other
buildings containing machinery have to be dealt with   The
Acts of Parliament appear to assume that the gross value
would be arrived at first and a deduction made therefrom
for the average annual cost of repairs, and insurance,
and a sinking fund to replace the property, as it exists
when the rate is made, at the end of its life. As has

Difference
between gross
and rateable
values in
factories

been stated before, in London under the Valuation (Metropolis) Act, 1869,[1] there are certain maximum deductions from gross to rateable, but, although these deal somewhat hardly with ratepayers of this class, as will be shewn later on in the chapter, for the moment it is desired to deal with the district outside the Metropolis where no scale exists, but where it is clear that the actual expenses incurred in providing for these items must be allowed and constitute the difference between gross and rateable value. It is often argued that, under the authority of the Acts of Parliament, the gross value *must* be arrived at in the first instance, and after the proper deductions have been made the rateable value would be ascertained, but there seems to be nothing to justify this contention. On the other

Is gross or rateable value to be first ascertained?

hand, in the Parochial Assessment Act, 1836, the rateable value is defined as the rent that a property would reasonably be expected to let at from year to year free of all usual tenant's rates and taxes, etc, and deducting from the rent the probable average annual cost of repairs and other expenses, etc, so that it is obvious that the rateable value is the main thing to be ascertained, inasmuch as in this Act it is provided that no rate shall be allowed which shall not be made upon an assessment of the net annual value, that is to say, the rent less the above expenses. At the date of the passing of this Act factories in their present form were probably not contemplated, and in applying the Act to a factory clearly the important figure that has to be obtained is the net annual value. It may also be remembered that no definition of "gross value" was given by Act of Parliament until the passing of the Union Assessment Committee Act of 1862,[2] twenty-six years after the Act[3] defining net annual value or rateable value. If the

---

[1] 32 & 33 Vict c 67.

[2] 25 & 26 Vict, c 103

[3] 6 & 7 William IV, c 96.

contention is right that the gross value of rent should be arrived at first, there is absolutely nothing in the Act that states how the gross rent is to be arrived at, and it is therefore only reasonable that a hypothetical landlord and a hypothetical tenant should receive and pay, as the first important item in the rent, the necessary sum for repairs, renewals, insurance, and in addition a sinking fund and be it observed that it cannot be contended that a hypothetical tenant would be unwilling to pay this, as if he refused the landlord could not possibly let the factory to him without a certain loss on the other hand, the tenant would have to provide the factory, and out of his profits make an allowance for these expenses It therefore follows that in arriving at the rent of a factory, if an actual letting took place, the very first items to be considered would be these Then, in addition, the hypothetical landlord would require interest for himself on his capital sunk in the hereditament, and the tenant would be willing to pay the same Of course, it does not follow that he would be willing to pay on all the capital sunk by the landlord if injudiciously spent, but for the purpose of the argument the case of an entirely new factory with perfectly modern machinery is assumed, and in this case the tenant would be willing to pay, in addition to repairs, sinking fund, etc., as above, interest to the landlord, or he would have to provide the factory for himself, and his capital, which in that case he would have to sink, would be lying idle, which is equivalent to the same thing.

Therefore, it would seem there is nothing incorrect, when valuing a factory, in ascertaining the effective capital value (*a distinct figure from the cost*), and taking a percentage upon this, to arrive at the rateable value. To this figure, for the purpose of the Rate Book, as a gross value has to be shown, should be added the cost of repairs, renewals, insurance, etc , and the gross value will be arrived at, which is exactly the same thing as arriving at the gross value first by adding together the net interest received by the landlord to the cost of repairs, etc, and then taking from this total sum the cost of repairs, etc., in order to arrive at the rateable value.

A large number of appeals are brought on the ground that the deduction from the gross to rateable is insufficient, and Assessment Committees may, in this respect, be placed in an unenviable position owing to the wording of a very old Act. The gross value is accepted by the appellant and he comes to Court with the actual cost of repairs etc, and thereon claims to succeed and have his rateable value reduced, so that it is most desirable that the difference between the gross and rateable values should be large enough to cover all the contingencies that may arise Indeed, a careful overseer endeavours to first ascertain these expenses in arriving at the figures of his valuation It cannot be overlooked that in some factories the gross value may be three times or even more than that of the rateable value—see *Calico Printers' Association* v. *Glossop Union* [1] It is neither in the interest of the ratepayer or of the Rating Authorities that there should be so large a difference in individual instances of assessment between the gross and the rateable value.

In the case of *Horton* v *Wallsall Union*,[2] the appellants at Quarter Sessions accepted the gross value, and in order to arrive at the rateable value, claimed to have statutory deductions made, which, while being admitted to be reasonable, in fact, far exceeded the amount which had been allowed The assessment authorities endeavoured to prove that the gross value as entered in the Valuation List was too low, but the Court of Queen's

---

[1] Reported in " The Estates Gazette " April 18th, 1903

[2] (1898) 2 Q B 237 , 67 L J Q B 801 , 78 L T 684 , 46 W R 607 , 62 J P 437

Bench decided that the respondents could not give evidence to show, that the gross value was too small in order to prove that the rateable value was correct, if the gross value had been larger than in the Valuation List. Although this case applies to places under the Union Assessment Committee Acts, it is difficult, if it is good law, to see the result of it with regard to property in London affected by the Valuation (Metropolis) Act, 1869 [1] In this Act there is a maximum scale of deduction to be allowed from the gross value to arrive at the rateable value, and if it is to be assumed that the gross value is to be ascertained first, although the actual repairs, insurance, etc , may far exceed the maximum allowance under the Act, the tenant would have to pay rates upon a rateable value which would be far higher than the net rent the property would command, which is an anomaly. It has been the practice of London Quarter Sessions, where the objection of insufficient deduction has been taken, to permit the respondents to give evidence as to the real gross value when it was alleged that it should have been higher than stated in the list [2], but it seems doubtful now whether this procedure is correct after the decision in *Horton* v *Wallsall Union* [3] The result of this decision may affect the position of manufacturers in the Metropolis very seriously, as the definition of gross value under the Valuation (Metropolis) Act, 1869, being the gross rent which the hereditament would command, on the assumption that the landlord does all the repairs, such value must be a fixed amount, and if from this amount a deduction of only 33⅓ per cent can be made, when in many cases the actual repairs may amount to 50 per cent or even more, the rateable value in such case might exceed the definition of

---

[1] 32 & 33 Vict , c 41

[2] *Middle Class Dwellings Co. v St George's Union* and *Chappell v St George's Union* " Ryde's Rating Appeals," 1891 to 1893, p 61. (1898) 2 Q B 237, 67 L J Q B 804, 78 L T 684.

the term in the Act itself, so that by fixing a maximum
scale of deduction the definitions of the terms gross and
rateable values would be defeated, and the difficulty to
assessment authorities on the one hand and to ratepayers on the other insurmountable. It is a question, however, whether the case of *Horton* v. *Walsall Union*[1] may not
in many cases be distinguished on the ground that it was
admitted by the assessment authorities that the amount
sought to be deducted was necessary to maintain the
premises in a state to command the rent Anyhow, under
the present state of things, a remedy available to an
Assessment Committee outside the Metropolis is in such
a case to immediately bring in a fresh Supplemental List
increasing the gross value to its proper amount

In the event of a factory (owing to depression of trade,
or for other reasons) ceasing to work for a time, but
meanwhile the owners maintaining the machinery in a fit
state to recommence working on the revival of the trade,
the factory is not rateable at its full value, but only as a
warehouse for the machinery contained therein—see
Staley v *Castleton (Overseers).*[2] Another case on somewhat similar lines was that of *Harter* v *Salford (Overseers).*[3]
Here the owner of a silk mill retired from business with
the intention of never resuming it   He, however, was
not content to lose the rent which the hereditament might
Mill to let
continuing
machinery
fetch, so he advertised it as being "to let" The
machinery, etc, of this mill was essential for the trade
carried on within it, namely, that of silk manufacture,
there was also a caretaker of the property to protect it
against thieves, etc   It was held that although the mill
was not then being used as a manufactory, yet the build-

---

[1] (1898) 67 L.J Q B 804, 79 L.T 684

[2] (1864) 5 B & S 505 33 LJ M C 178, 10 Jur N S 1147, 10 L T
606, 12 W.R. 911

[3] (1865) 6 B. & S. 591, 34 L J M.C 206 11 Jur N S 1036,
13 W R 861

ings were a shelter for the machinery, which was in working order and consequently were to be rated as a warehouse.

The case of *Hoyle and Jackson* v *Oldham Union*[1] is also of importance as affecting the question of a rate made on certain factories which were not working on account of a general strike. In this case the appellants sought to have their factories assessed only as warehouses for machinery, but the Court of Appeal held that the mills must be assessed at their full value, probably on the ground that it was impossible for the authorities to say that the strike would last long enough to affect a possible tenant who would take the factory from year to year.

---

[1] (1894) 2 Q B 372, 63 L J M.C. 178, 70 L T 741, 58 J P. 669, 10 T L R 315

CHAPTER IV.

RAILWAYS

Specimen Railway Valuation—Each Item considered separately—What constitutes a Station—Signal Boxes —Advertisements—Refreshment Rooms—Total Sum to be inserted in Valuation List—Contributive Value— Branch Lines—Running Powers—Railways in Course of Construction—Railways and General District Rates

Railway
valuation

IN this chapter it is proposed to trace the course of a valuation of a railway company in an imaginary parish, as shown on the sketch-plan given below.

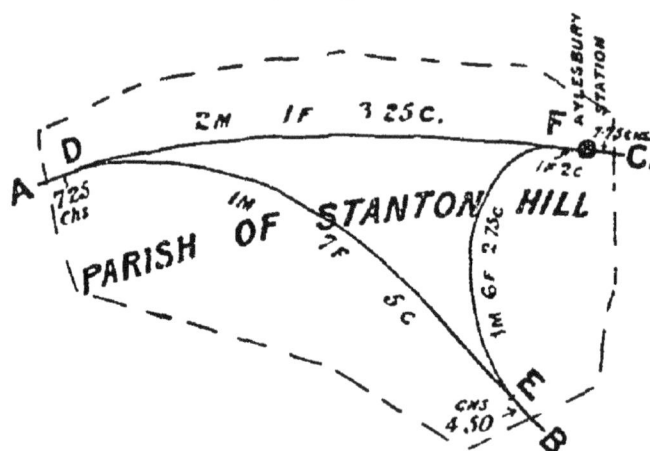

It will be seen that there is a line of railway running from A to B, another from A to C and another from B to C   These three lines of railway join at the respective junctions D E and F, and between the points A D, E B and F C there is a double quantity of traffic, that is to say, trains coming from some point beyond A and which are travelling to either B or C must pass over the way between A and D, and in the same manner trains from B travelling to either A or C must pass over the part B and E, and so on with regard to C F   Supposing that the appointment to make the valuation has been made, the first step on the part of the valuer would be to obtain the Ordnance plans of the district, and carefully scale off the respective lengths from centre of station to centre of station (if there were more than one station in the parish), from centre of station to parish boundary, from centre of station to point of junction, etc. This having been done his next step would be to request that a statement of receipts, together with a statement of train mileage (goods and passengers to be separately stated), be furnished to him by the company between the following points —From parish boundary next A to junction D, from junction D to junction F, and from junction F to centre of Aylesbury station, and from centre of Aylesbury station to the parish boundary next C. So much for the traffic upon line A C. The next particulars he would require would be as to the traffic upon D E and F E, bearing in mind that between the points E and B the traffic would be the addition of that upon D and E and F and E. Generally in the preliminary stage of a valuation the railway company are unable to supply these figures, and an estimate therefore has to be made[1] The surveyor's task would be a comparatively easy one should all the information which he requires from the company itself be forthcoming; but in actual working this is not often the case, and it is with a view of furnishing some guide as to the method to be adopted when the valuation has to be made upon an estimate that this chapter is written. The lengths of line are agreed upon without much trouble, as the Clearing House lengths may be replied upon as generally correct. These are in the possession of the company, but it is advisable to check them from the Ordnance Survey, as there is, of course, always a possibility of, at least, a clerical error. The next

[1] See upon this point the evidence of P R Smith before Commission on Local Taxation (1898), Vol. I , p. 416

step would be the preparation of a general statement of the company's receipts, earnings, etc, and this should be done by obtaining the published accounts of the company for the last two half-years. It might possibly be found advisable to make a general statement on the accounts of the last three years, so as to take that average as a working basis.

The following, based upon the accounts of a railway company, might conveniently be used as a model in similar valuations:—

GENERAL STATEMENT FOR THE YEAR ENDING DECEMBER 31ST, 1900

TRAIN MILEAGE

	Half year, June, 1900.	Half year, December, 1900	Total
Passenger trains	9,693,782	8,973,632	18,667,414
Goods and Mineral trains	9,224,865	8,784,940	18,009,805
	18,918,647	17,758,572	36,677,219

GOVERNMENT DUTY.

Half-year ending June, 1900 ...	£34,681
Ditto December 1900 ..	29,450
	£64,131

Equals 1 52 per cent on (£4,200,469) gross passenger receipts

RECEIPTS

	Half-year, June 1900.	Half-year December, 1900	Total
Passengers, season tickets, parcels, horses, carriages, etc, and mails	£2,287,234	£1,913,235	£4,200,469
Merchandise (less expenses of collection and delivery) live stock and minerals . .	2,381,212	2,240,889	4,622,101
	£4,668,446	£4,154,124	£8,822,570
Less mileage and demurrage of rolling stock	969	612	1,581
	£4,667,477	£4,153,512	£8,820,989

Passenger . $\dfrac{\pounds 4,200,469}{\text{T M} \quad 18,667,414}$ = $\overset{s}{4} \cdot 5$ (4/6) per train mile

Goods .. $\dfrac{\pounds 4,620,520}{\text{T M} \quad 18,009,805}$ = $\overset{s}{5} \cdot 13$ (5/1½) per train mile

LOCOMOTIVE EXPENSES.

Half-year, June, 1900   £675,317

Ditto, December, 1900 .   646 122

$$\underline{\pounds 1\,321,439} = \overset{\text{Pence}}{317,145\,360}$$

Passenger T M   Goods T M.

$\quad 18,667,414 \quad + \quad 18,009,805 \quad = \quad 317,145\,360$

Goods train miles $\times$ 2½d.   =   45,024,512

$$\overline{272,120,848}$$

$\dfrac{272,120,848}{\text{Total T M.} \quad 36,677,219} = \overset{d.}{7} \cdot 42$ per passenger train mile.

The difference between passenger and goods is 2½d .. .. = 2 50

$$\overline{9 \cdot 92} \text{ per goods train mile.}$$

CARRIAGE EXPENSES.

Half-year ending June, 1900 ... .. . £103,091

Ditto   December, 1900 .. .. 93 000

$$\overline{\pounds196\,091}$$

$\dfrac{\pounds 196,091}{\text{T M} \quad 18,667,414} = \overset{d.}{2} \cdot 52$ per passenger train mile

WAGGON EXPENSES.

Half-year ending June, 1900 .. .. £102,721

Ditto   December, 1900 114,372

$$\overline{\pounds 217,093}$$

$\dfrac{\pounds 217,093}{\text{T M} \quad 18,009\,805} = \overset{d}{2} \cdot 89$ per goods train mile

MISCELLANEOUS EXPENSES

	Half-year, June, 1900.	Half-year, December, 1900	Total
Traffic expenses ..	£729,452	£699,718	£1,429,170
Less dock, harbour and coal tipping expenses, etc ...	24,925	22,067	46,992
	707,527	677,651	1,382,178
General charges .	91,940	84,112	176,052
Law ditto ...	11,417	12,271	23,688
	£807,884	£774,034	£1,581,918

£1,581,918 equals 17.93 per cent on £8,820,989 gross receipts

This is a general form for the whole company, based upon published accounts, and the headings used are those usually adopted in the accounts of railway companies The first item in the statement is the train

Train mileage

mileage over the whole system, and there is little to be said under this heading except that it is necessary that it should be extracted, for it is by dividing the train mileage into the gross receipts that the average amount of receipts per train mile in any particular parish may be estimated

Government Duty

The next item is the Government Duty This duty was first levied by the Railway Passenger Duty Act, 1842,[1] and was in respect of all passengers conveyed for hire upon or along any railway, and a duty was charged at the rate of £5 per cent upon all sums received or charged for the hire, fare, or conveyance of all such passengers. This section of the Act was, however, repealed by the Cheap Trains Act, 1883,[2] which is as follows —"After the commencement of this Act the duties now payable in respect of passengers conveyed for hire on a railway shall, subject to the provisions of this Act, be varied as follows —(1) Fares not exceeding the rate of

[1] 5 & 6 Vict., c. 79, s 2
[2] 46 & 47 Vict , c. 34, s 2

1d. per mile shall be exempt from duty[1], but fares for return or periodical shall be exempt from duty only where the ordinary fare for the single journey does not exceed that rate (2) Duty shall be payable at the rate of 2 per cent. on fares exceeding the rate of 1d per mile for conveyance between the railway station within one urban district certified so to be in manner provided in this section Having extracted from the accounts the receipts, it is a simple matter to find the percentage of the Government Duty to the gross receipts In the case with which we are dealing it is 1·52 per cent —a very small sum and seldom, if ever, a matter for dispute between parties

With regard to the gross receipts of the company, that is an item which can be extracted without the slightest difficulty from the accounts Briefly the sources of it are — Passenger Traffic—which is often the largest item in the account—mails parcels, horses and carriages, merchandise, live stock, minerals (the expenses of collection and delivery in the case of merchandise being deducted, as it is the gross receipts of the railway *per se* that have to be obtained) and terminal charges, *i e* charges for receiving, loading. unloading. dispatching, etc , at stations[2] Having ascertained this gross sum, the mileage and demurrage of the rolling stock paid out to other companies has to be deducted, and the result will be the gross receipts of the railway company over the whole system It will be noticed that, in the general statement of account as given, the passenger receipts are kept separate from those of the goods, this is most essential, as the two classes of traffic are distinct in every particular, and from the fact that Government Duty is only paid on passenger

Receipts

---

[1] That is to say third class fares

[2] *R v Eastern Counties Railway Co*, (1863) 32 L J M C 174. See also upon the point, *Buckfastleigh and Totnes Railway Co v South Devon Railway Co*, (1874) 1 N & M 321, and *M S & L Railway Co v Castor and Glandford Unions* (1874) 2 N & M 54

traffic   The two sums are then divided by the passenger
train mileage and the goods train mileage respectively,
and in this way the average sum received per train mile
over the whole system is ascertained

Locomotive expenses

We now arrive at the locomotive expenses, these must
vary according to the traffic with which the engine is
engaged, but in the item in the accounts an aggregate
sum only is given.   It includes, however, the salaries,
office expenses, and general superintendence, the running expenses (which are the wages connected with
the working of locomotive engines), coal, coke, water, oil,
tallow and other stores, and repairs and renewals   The
difference of cost of the locomotive power of a passenger
and of a goods engine per train mile varies considerably,
and it may be taken as without exception that the locomotive cost for running a goods train is more than that for
a passenger train   This difference varies between 2d and
4d., although 4d is a high figure   In the example-
valuation it has been assumed that the locomotive
expenses for a goods engine per train mile are $2\frac{1}{4}$d.
more than those for a passenger engine running over
the same distance   In the accounts the total locomotive
expenses (passenger and goods) are given together in one
sum, and the way to divide this is briefly as follows —
Reduce the sum for locomotive expenses given in pounds
for both passenger and goods train miles to pence ; next,
multiply the goods train miles by the difference it has
been decided to adopt (in this instance $2\frac{1}{4}$d), and deduct
the result from the total locomotive expenses ; then divide
the difference by the total number of train miles, and the
price per passenger train mile is ascertained.   The price
per goods train mile will, of course, be the price per
passenger train mile plus $2\frac{1}{4}$d.

Carriage and waggon repairs

Then as to the carriage repairs : this item also includes
salaries, office expenses and general superintendence,
wages and material, and by dividing the amount so

expended by the passenger train miles, the cost per train mile is ascertained. The same method is adopted in the case of the waggon repairs and renewals.

We next have to consider the miscellaneous expenses. *Miscellaneous expenses* These comprise first, the traffic expenses, which consist of —Charges in connection with the conveyance of passengers and goods, etc , being the salaries and wages of the permanent staff, fuel, lighting, water and general stores, clothing, printing, stationery and tickets, wages of shunters, waggon covers, ropes and other expenses, such as hydraulic hoists, and the necessary working and repairing of same, etc , second, the general charges, which include directors' fees, auditors' fees, salaries of secretary, general manager, accountant and clerks, office expenses, advertising, the Railway Clearing House and general expenses, etc. It was originally held that the allowance of fees to directors and auditors was not a legitimate deduction from the gross receipts [1] Patteson, J., said, *Directors fees* with regard to this point "The question has turned on the propriety, or otherwise, of deductions for the general expenses, including payments to the directors and auditors. We are of opinion they ought not to be allowed." But this question was again before the Court in the case of *R. v. Southampton Dock Co.*,[2] and directors fees were allowed as a reasonable expense to maintain the property in a state to command the rent Lord Campbell, C J , said, during the course of his judgment, with particular reference to this question "We cannot say there ought not to have been an allowance for management, which might be stated as a reasonable remuneration to the lessee of the company." Directors' fees were also allowed in the case of the *London*

---

[1] *R. v. St Giles, Camberwell* (1850) 14 Q B 571, 19 L J M C 122, 14 Jur 519

[2] (1851) 14 Q B 587, 20 L J M C 155, 6 Rail Cas. 428, 16 L T O S. 460, 15 J P 145

Tramways Co v. *Lambeth* [1] The total sum of miscellaneous expenses equals a certain percentage of the gross receipts and is easily obtainable.

Having now ascertained the figures which would partly constitute a valuation of the company in the event of the company's property being contained in one parish, the next step is to apportion these where, as is invariably the case, the property extends through many parishes, and to do this the parochial tram miles must be ascertained

Parochial
tram miles

Anyone conversant with the working of staff time-table will have little difficulty in obtaining these figures The easier method is to make per-mile valuation, and where fractional parts of this unit occur a proportionate part only of the mile-rate is to be used for the purposes of the valuation. Supposing that the train miles, for instance, are 50,000 per mile on the portion A D, then, assuming that they run equally to C and B, there would be 25,000 passenger train miles per mile on the portion D F and D E, and again, if there were 30,000 goods train miles on the portion A D, running equally to C and B, there would be 15,000 on D F and D E, and for the sake of illustration, assuming that there are the same number of train miles on F C as there are on A D, there would be 80,000 train miles on the portions A D, E B and F C, and 40,000 train miles on D F, E F, and D F, so that it would be necessary upon the basis of this train mileage to make two valuations of the line of railway per mile for these two different classes of traffic. Of course an occurrence such as this would be extremely improbable, and these figures are given only as an extreme case and for example only It might so happen that the train miles on the six different sections would all be different, and consequently a separate valuation would have to be made for each portion of the line, in addition to which the portion between F

1 (1874) 31 L T 319

and the parish boundary next C might have to be divided
into two parts, as it is quite possible that the traffic might
be very much heavier on one side of a station than
another. Take, for instance, the case of the London,
Chatham and Dover Railway at Margate. A train leaves
London for Ramsgate. Supposing 50 per cent. of its
passengers alight at Margate, assuming the train stops
only at this one station, then the traffic on the London
side of Margate would be 100 per cent more than that on
the Ramsgate side, and although the train miles would be
the same, the receipts would be only half. In the
example-valuation (of the parish of Stanton Hill) we will
assume that it is an average portion of the line of the
system, that is to say, the receipts over the whole
system yield, in the case of the passengers, 1s 6d. per
train mile, and in that of the goods 5s 1¼d. per train
mile, then (working out the portion A D first) we have
50,000 train miles at 1s 6d., which equals £11,250, and
30,000 train miles at 5s 1¼d., which equals £7,687,
therefore the receipts per mile per annum on the portion
A D equal £18,937, and those upon the portion D E,
working it out on the same principle, would equal £9,468.
We now proceed to the valuation of one mile of railway
on the figures ascertained.

GROSS RECEIPTS PER MILE IN PARISH .. £18,937

WORKING EXPENSES

Locomotive Passenger	50,000 @ 7.42	1,545	
Locomotive Goods	30,000 @ 9.92	1,240	
Carriage	50,000 @ 2.52	525	
Waggon	30,000 @ 2.89	361	
Miscellaneous, 17.93 per cent on £18,937		3,395	
Government Duty, 1.52 per cent on £11,250		171	
Rates and Taxes, 5s in the £ on an assessment of £5,365		1,341	
			8,578

NET RECEIPTS DUE TO LINE AND STATIONS ... £10,359

Carried forward . £10,359

Brought forward	.	£10,359

GROSS ESTIMATED RENTAL OF STATIONS

5 per cent on £18,937	£946	
Add Rates thereon estimated at	236	
	——	1,182

NET RECEIPTS DUE TO LINE OF RAILWAY	**£9 177**

OCCUPIER S SHARE

Interest 5 per cent on £18 937 .. . ⎫	
Trade Profit 10 per cent on £18,937 . . ⎬	3,312
Risks and Casualties 2½ per cent on £18,937 . ⎭	

GROSS ESTIMATED RENTAL OF LINE	**£5,865**

STATUTABLE DEDUCTIONS

Maintenance and Renewal of Way, say £400 Maintenance and £100 Renewal.	500

Rateable value per mile	**£5,365**

The rateable value per mile for the portions A D, E B and F C would thus be £5,365

There are one or two points to be noticed with reference to this valuation, which are as follows : The working expenses, viz , those of the locomotive, carriage and waggon, are taken at the average cost per train mile over the system These expenses are deducted on the parochial principle, and, although the receipts in the parish may be the same average per train mile as those over the whole system, it does not follow that the same will be the case with regard to the expenses—indeed in practice it will be found that this is very seldom so The above is only an example of how a valuation is made, and it must be patent that it is not possible to give particulars as to the peculiarities of a line of railway in any hypothetical parish. The miscellaneous expenses and the Government Duty are invariably deducted on the principle of their relation to the whole

Working expenses

system   The rates and taxes are the next items, and
it will be noticed that this deduction is made upon the
net rateable value after the rates and taxes themselves
(in addition to the other working expenses) have been
deducted

A case upon this point was before the Court in 1863,[1]
and Cockburn, C J , in the course of his judgment, said
" The only practical way of treating the rates and taxes
is to treat them as other outgoings   The tenant contemplated by the Parochial Assessment Act[2] would consider
the rates which he would be obliged to pay before he could
see what return he would get for the capital invested by
him   He could not tell what amount of rent would be
proper till he knew the amount of the rates, and he is
entitled to deduct the amount of the rates which are to be
assessed upon the net rateable value   Those who make
the rates would get into a difficulty if they were merely
to strike a balance for profits, and then to make an
assessment upon the balance.   The allowance should be
upon the rateable value " The sum to be allowed for
rates and taxes is not necessarily the actual amount
that is paid, for, in the case of *R v South Staffordshire
Waterworks Co*,[3] it was held that the deduction to be
made in respect of the rates and taxes was the sum at
which a property ought to be assessed, and not the rates
based upon the assessment of the property in the existing
Valuation List.   There are several methods of obtaining
this amount, but the one here given is perhaps the most
simple.   From the gross receipts in the parish deduct all
the allowances, including working expenses, the allowance
for stations, tenant's capital, maintenance and renewal

---

[1] *Tyne Improvement Commissioners v Chirton (Churchwardens)*, (1863)
32 L J M C 192 , 6 L T 489

[2] (1836) 6 & 7 William IV , c 96

[3] (1886) 16 Q B D 359, 55 L J M C 88, 54 L T 782, 34 W R 242,
50 J P 20—C A

X

of way; multiply the result by 240, and divide this by 240 plus the number of pence that there are in the rate in the £ for the parish

Example

GROSS RECEIPTS IN PARISH.   .   £18,937

WORKING EXPENSES

Locomotive Passenger		£1,545
Locomotive Goods	. .	... 1,240
Carriage .	. .. .	... 525
Waggon ..	. .	. 361
Miscellaneous .	. ..	3,395
Government Duty		. 171
Allowance for Station ..	..	.. 1,182
Occupier's Share	.. .. .	3,312
Statutable Deductions ..	. ...	500

                                                                    12 231

                                                                     6 706

$$6,706 \times 240 = 1,609,440$$

$$\frac{1,609,440}{240 + 60} = 5,365$$

£5,365 is the rateable value of the line of way in the parish, and the rates at 5s in the £ on this assessment are £1,341

Income tax

Income Tax payable by a railway or other company must not be deducted in ascertaining the gross and rateable values [1]

Deductions for stations

The next item to be considered is the deduction for the rental of the stations, as they are rated separately from the line, and it must be understood that this sum is not ascertained on the parochial principle Undoubtedly the correct way of obtaining the figure would be to find the relation which the total rental value of the stations over the whole system bears to the gross receipts of the railway, allowing a sum in the parish for which the

[1] *R* v *Southampton Dock Co*, (1851) 14 Q B 587   20 L J M C 155, 6 Rail Cas 428, 15 J P. 145

valuation is made at the same proportion of the total
rental of stations that the gross receipts in the particular
parish bear to the whole gross receipts of the railway.

This task involves a considerable amount of work, in
fact in the recent case of a large railway company it
required the undivided labours of several clerks for some
six or more weeks

In the case of the *Great Northern Railway Co.
v. Hitchin Union* [1] the sum under this heading proved by
the company as being the actual amount of gross rent
payable by them for the use of their stations amounted
to 81 per cent. of the gross receipts, but the Court,
apparently not allowing certain of the items, fixed the
amount at 72 per cent. including rates and taxes.

It must be recorded, however, that this amount may
vary in every railway company in the kingdom, and that
although in the specimen valuation 5 per cent. is taken,
this is only a figure by way of example

This deduction for stations in the valuation for assessment of a railway line is sometimes not fully understood,
and it is perhaps convenient to explain here that the
reason of the deduction is as follows —The valuation
that we have hitherto been dealing with is a valuation of
the running lines of the company, and, in order to ascertain the rent that a tenant would give for such lines, the
whole expenses necessary for the proper working of the
railway have to be deducted.   It will be readily conceded
that it is impossible to conduct passenger traffic without
railway stations, platforms and their usual appurtenances,
and goods traffic without goods sheds, etc, and therefore
a tenant of the line *per se* would have to provide for the
rents he would have to pay a contractor or landlord for
the use of the railway stations, always assuming the
hypothesis (which must be assumed) that the landlord of
the stations may be a different party from the landlord of

---

[1] Reported in " Konstam's Rating Appeals " (1906), Vol I , p 116

x 2

the line, and therefore, in order to earn the net receipts of the line of railway, a rent must of necessity be paid for the use of the stations. Further, it frequently happens that in many parishes there are no stations at all, but to earn the gross receipts in those parishes services are rendered by the railway company in the way of stations, and therefore from the gross receipts in those parishes must be deducted the portion of the cost of the stations.

Stations are of course assessed at their full and proper value in those parishes where they actually exist, and, in order to further explain the matter, the following example is given:—

A passenger travels from King's Cross to Newcastle, and pays, for the sake of argument, £3 for his fare. He uses the station at King's Cross and that at Newcastle, and the company, in order to earn this £3, are compelled to provide a station at each of the two termini. Each of the stations is assessed at its value in the parish in which the station is, i e, where the station service is performed, but in rating the whole of the line from London to Newcastle a deduction from the £3 in respect of the station service must be made in every parish through which the line passes, as the service performed by the line is not the whole service for which the £3 is paid, there being the additional obligation on the part of the company to provide stations.

Out of the receipts of the line the hypothetical tenant would have to pay, in addition to a rent for the use of the stations, the usual tenant's rates and taxes. A sum should be allowed for this, which in this instance has been estimated at one-fourth the rental value, although this is a high figure in certain cases, but it is used for the purpose of convenience in working out the valuation.

Tenant's capital

Coming now to the tenant's capital, enough perhaps has been said in Chapter V, Part I, as to the several items which go to make up the total, and it may be thought that taking a percentage upon the gross receipts in the parish is contrary to the principle laid down in that chapter. This is not necessarily so, however, for the average amount of capital that would be necessary for a hypothetical tenant to have would be, in the case of many railway companies, the gross receipts for one year. That is to say, if a tenant take possession of a line of railway where the gross receipts for one year are £1,000,000, it might be necessary for him to sink in rolling stock, etc, about the sum named This, of course, is not by any means an invariable rule, as some railways might require a much heavier rolling stock than others, and therefore the capital needed to carry on such an undertaking would be greater than in the case where the rolling stock was of a lighter description Appended is a form of a tenant's capital of a railway company where the amount works out at 100 per cent. of the gross receipts

Engines—

		£	£
489 with tenders at £2 400	.. .	£1,173,600	
336 without tenders at £1 500	.. ...	504,000	
			1,677,600

Coaching—

		£	£
14 First Class Saloons at £700	..	9,800	
7 Mails at £350 ...	.	2,450	
366 First Class Carriages at £500	.	183,000	
476 Composites at £450	.. ..	214,200	
406 Second Class Carriages at £400	.	162,400	
1,061 Third Class Carriages at £350	...	371 350	
308 Third Class Comp Brakes at £300		92,400	
322 Horse Boxes at £180	. .. .	57,960	
20 Cattle Boxes at £180 ...	..	3,600	
134 Carriage Trucks at £125	..	16,750	
224 Break Vans at £250	.. . .	61,000	
11 Milk Vans at £129	.. . .	1,419	
74 Fish Vans at £120	.. . .	8 880	
52 Yeast Vans at £100	... . .	5,200	
9 Tram Cars at £300	... ..	2,700	
23 Omnibuses at £150	... ..	3,450	
1 Invalid Carriage at £300	.. ...	300	
			1,196,859

Carried forward . £1,196,859

Brought forward .. £1,196,859

Merchandise and Mineral Stock—

10,573 General Goods Waggons (covered and uncovered) at £80 ...	845,840	
2,446 Sheep and Cattle Trucks at £100 ..	244,600	
740 Timber Trucks at £80 ..	59,200	
1,048 Loco Coal Trucks at £70 . .	73,360	
375 Goods Breaks at £150 .	56,250	
324 Ballast Waggons at £70	22,680	
24 Ballast Breaks at £100 .	2,400	
853 Waggons and Carts at £70	59,710	
		1,364,040

	£4,238,499
Less, say 25 per cent for depreciation ..	1,059,624
Estimated present value of Rolling Stock .. .	£3,178,875

Tarpaulins and Sacks—

10,573 General Goods Waggons at £2	21,146

Machinery and Tools (non-rateable)—

2½ per cent of £3,171,800 estimated value of Rolling Stock	79,470

Horses and Harness—

327 at £70	22,890

Furniture and Fittings at Stations—

4½ per cent of Coaching Receipts, viz, £2,087,555, as per accounts	93,940

Stores and Materials on hand, as per accounts—

General Stores in Hand	£315,319	
Permanent Way Stores in Hand ...	93,481	
Locomotive Stores in hand .	45,818	
Two thirds of	£454,618	303,078

Cash Balance at Bankers (say)	80,000

N B —The Company would always have on hand a large sum as Deposits on Season Tickets

Estimated Total of Tenant's Capital . ..	£3,849,399

Gross Receipts = £3,814,382

$$\frac{3,849,399 \times 100}{3,814,382} = 100 \text{ per cent of gross receipts.}$$

Although in the above example the tenant's capital equals 100 per cent of the gross receipts, it is a matter of common knowledge at the present date that in the majority of the important companies tenant's capital is far in excess of the gross receipts. This has been caused to a large extent by modern competition, with its consequent improved facilities for the travelling public for which no extra charge is made. The race from London to Scotland between those companies owning the East and West routes is an example of this competition, with the direct result that modern locomotives are compelled to carry greater loads at greater speeds than was the case ten or fifteen years ago. The accommodation also, given on many of the main lines, has advanced at a very rapid rate, and the luxury of travelling to-day as compared with a decade ago has entailed upon railway companies large expenses for which there is no direct return, and with which the increase in gross receipts is not commensurate. On certain of the lines where dining cars are provided practically two seats are allowed for many of the passengers in each train, one in the dining saloon and one in the ordinary compartment. The introduction of corridor trains has reduced the seating accommodation in each compartment, and modern requirements with regard to heating and lighting are such that the cost of a railway carriage to-day, as compared with the cost comparatively few years ago, is nearly double, whereas its capacity for carrying passengers is less.

It follows that a larger and more expensive stock is required than formerly, and not only for the above reason, but modern competition has the effect of a large number of trains running with a small complement of passengers. This obtains more particularly where two or more companies are serving the same town. The third-class fare, however, was fixed by Parliament many years ago, and has not been increased ; indeed the tendency is to decrease fares.

It may, therefore, safely be said that with regard to the principal railway companies the tenant's capital must be largely in excess of 100 per cent of the gross receipts, and it is worthy of note that in the case of the *North Eastern Railway Co v Sculcoates Union*[1] the Arbitrator, Sir James Woodhouse, M P, in delivering judgment on February 17th, 1905, allowed 147 per cent of the gross receipts as tenant's capital, and that in the case of the *Great Northern Railway Co v Hitchin Union*[2] the amount allowed by the Court was 144 8 per cent

It will be observed in the example valuation that the deduction for tenant's capital has been made on the assumption that the average of the tenant's capital necessary to carry on the work in the particular parish is equal to the average over the whole railway

Tenant's capital parochial

Although it is conceded that the hypothetical tenant of a railway system in a particular parish must be considered as an imaginary person who would take the railway not only for that parish but for parts extending beyond, at the same time it may be argued, and has been argued with considerable effect that certain items in the tenant's capital are more or less governed by parochial circumstances and that in estimating the tenant's capital for any particular parish, regard should be given to this point

It will be readily seen that on a large number of branch lines no heavy locomotives, dining cars, sleeping carriages or heavy stock is ever run   Further, there are a number of lines in the kingdom devoted exclusively to goods traffic upon which passenger stock is not used, and there are similar instances of extraordinary use of tenant's capital in certain districts which will have the effect of varying the amount to be allowed

---

[1] From the shorthand notes in the author's possession (1905)
[2] Reported in "Konstam's Rating Appeals" (1906), Vol 1 , p 116

In the recent case of the *London and North Western Railway Co* v *The Penrith Union,*[1] it was claimed on behalf of the company that owing to the peculiar nature of the traffic over the line from Penrith to the South through the mountainous district of Westmoreland, particularly traversing Shap, it was necessary that the bulk of the trains should be drawn by two locomotives. Further, it was contended on behalf of the company that no local traffic passed over the line and therefore the tenant of this section would be compelled to provide himself with rolling stock far in excess of the average over the whole system of the London and North Western Railway, and he was, therefore, entitled to consider upon this section of the line a tenant's capital above the average of the whole

The Court by a majority decided in favour of the contention of the company, but it is only fair to add that one member of the Bench was opposed to the principle of the judgment. It was contended by the Magistrate in question that the principle was new and the difficulty of applying it was very great

This view, however. was not shared by the majority of the Court, and it can hardly be claimed as a new principle As far back as the year 1899 the point was raised on behalf of the Parochial Authorities in the case of the *London and North Western Railway Co* v *The Llanrwst Union*[1] Here the proposition was put forward by the Parochial Authorities that because, on this particular branch line, heavy traffic did not exist, a deduction should be made in the tenant's capital The Arbitrator in giving his judgment reduced the tenant's capital of the particular branch below the average over the whole of the London and North Western Railway system, thereby accepting the principle which it has been suggested was raised for the first time only in the *Penrith* case

[1] From the shorthand notes in the possession of the author

The last item is the maintenance and renewal of way, which has been inserted at the sum of £500. In making a valuation of a railway company this is the last deduction that should be made, and in the event of the sum being worked out on the principle of the train mileage (that is to say, the expenses for the maintenance and renewal of way being divided by the train mileage over the whole system and thus ascertaining an average) the result would be of little practical use, as the difficulty in ascertaining whether the particular parish in question is below or above the average is almost insuperable, not to mention the fact that certain expenses under this heading are deducted upon the parochial principle, whilst others are deducted upon the mileage principle Take, for example, the case we are now dealing with. Here we have traffic going from A to B, and from A to C, over the portion A D there is just twice the amount of traffic that there is over D F and D E but it could not be contended that the maintenance and renewal of way should be double on this portion of the line Of course there are cases where it might be advisable to extract this figure from the accounts, but care must be exercised in so doing, as there are certain items which refer to the maintenance of way, whilst on the other hand there are items which refer to the maintenance of works, etc What we have to deal with and distinguish is solely the maintenance and the renewal of the permanent way It must also be noticed that in working this figure out in the general statement the maintenance is not separated from the renewal, and the cost per train mile is for both these sums, by the other method of estimating the expense of repairs and renewals in any one particular parish the two items are kept separate This was fully explained in Chapter V., Part I

Although no sum is actually set aside by a railway company on account of a renewal fund for the permanent way, it is clear that a sum for this expense must be allowed for in the valuation.[1]

The rateable value of the line of railway per mile on the portions A D, E B, and F C, as worked out, is £5,365. and assuming that the portions on D E, E F, and D F are half this amount,[2] the rateable value for these portions per mile would be £2,682   The actual rateable value of the hereditament in the parish would work out in the following manner :—

	£	s
From Parish Boundary next A to D	7	25
From Junction E to Parish Boundary next B .	4	50
From Junction F to Parish Boundary next E	1 9	75
	3 1	50

As 80   5,365   31 50 to the rateable value of this portion of the line in the parish

$$\frac{5\,365 \times 31\,50}{80} = £\ 2\,112$$

	M	F	c
From Junction D to Junction E .	. 1	7	5
From Junction E to Junction F	1	6	2 75
From Junction D to Junction F .	2	1	3 25
	5	7	1

As 80   2,682   5 7 1   to the rateable value of this portion of the line in the parish

$$\frac{2\,682 \times 471}{80} = £15,790$$

The rateable value therefore for the portions A D, E B, and F C is £2,112 and for the lengths of line between the junctions D E and F is £15,790 , these two together equal £17,902.

---

[1] R v London, Brighton and South Coast Railway, (1851) 15 Q B. 313, 20 L J M C 124, 15 Jur 372 6 Rail Cas 440

[2] The possibility of the rateable value of this portion of line being half that of the other is almost out of the question owing to the maintenance and renewal of way, but it is taken as such in order that the example may be made as intelligible as possible

Having arrived at the rateable value of the six sections
of line in the parish, the next step would be to make a
valuation of the station, and this brings us to the question
" What is a station ? " It is often very difficult to decide
where the line of demarcation should be drawn as between
the line of railway and the station itself, but it has been
held that where a station is situated, all the land and
buildings and sidings the   should be rated as a station,
with the exception of th   ne of railway on which the
through traffic passes, and so much of each side of the
line as to allow of the passage of the rolling stock[1] It
has been suggested that the case of the *Great Eastern
Railway Co   v. The Churchwardens and Overseers
of the Parish of Fletton, and the Guardians of the Poor of
the Peterborough Union*[2] overrules this case   This
contention it is submitted is no sound, as what the Court
then said was that where good   traffic was diverted on
approaching a station, so as to avoid the passenger traffic,
such lines were not to be considered as sidings, but as
lines of railway which would be included in the receipts
The above case is so important that no work on rating
would be complete without a full report of it   It was an
appeal on the 6th July, 1880, against a Poor Rate made
for the parish of Fletton, in the county of Huntingdon
From the special case stated for the opinion of the Queen's
Bench Division of the High Court of Justice, it appeared
that the questions in dispute between the parties arose
with reference to the principles adopted by the Assessment
Committee and the railway company respectively, in
valuing nine parts of lines of railway passing through
Peterborough Station

[1] *London and North Western Railway Co v Wigan Union (Guardians),*
(1876) 2 Nev & Mac. 240

[2] The author is indebted to " Browne on Rating " (Second Edition),
p 631, for the report of this case. A full report also appears in ' Boyle
and Davies on Rating," and in " Castle on Rating "

Besides the Great Eastern Railway Company, the Great Northern, the Midland, and the London and North Western Railway Companies had lines of railway running to Peterborough and communicating with the line of the appellants

Sidings were used in the ordinary way for loading and unloading, shunting and marshalling the traffic, and storing and repairing rolling stock, and certain sidings and buildings were occupied exclusively by the Midland and London and North Western Railway Companies

By arrangement between the companies the appellants conveyed all the traffic to and from the Great Northern Company's station, the Midland and the London and North Western Companies delivering and receiving their own traffic, the engine of the delivering company being detached from, and the engine of the receiving company attached to, the trains upon the lines in question The traffic consisted chiefly of coal brought from the North by the Midland and the Great Northern Railways, but also to some extent of minerals and goods traffic brought by the London and North Western Railway In order to accommodate this increasing traffic the appellants' station had been from time to time enlarged by taking additional lands in the parish, and several sets of lines had been successively added including the lines in question

Other lines passed through the station for the accommodation of passenger trains of the Great Eastern, London and North Western, Midland, and Great Northern Companies, and for no other purpose

The nine pairs of lines in question were used for the
following purposes.
G E R
Fletton

    1, 2 —Solely for through goods traffic of the Great Northern and Midland Companies—viz, traffic consigned on the one hand from stations on the Great Northern and the Midland Railways to stations on the Great Eastern Railway, and on the other hand from stations on the Great Eastern line to stations on the Great Northern and the Midland lines

3, 4.—For the London and North Western traffic. Trains from the Great Eastern system going to the North Western system passed over No 4, and trains from the North Western system to the Great Eastern over No. 3.

5.—For through traffic coming off the Great Eastern to the Great Northern line only, in small trains

6.—For empty coal waggons travelling from Great Eastern stations to stations on the Midland and the Great Northern Railways, and sent there for the purpose of conveying coal to be used in the locomotives of the Great Eastern Company

7, 8.—For the Midland traffic only, and for empty waggons of all sorts passing between the Midland and the Great Eastern systems

9.—For through trucks loaded with goods travelling from the Great Eastern line to the Midland line

No shunting or marshalling of traffic was done upon these lines. If it became necessary to divide a train before it passed from the Great Eastern system to the railways of any of the other companies, it was done upon the other sidings of the appellants; and similarly, if a portion of a train intended for the Great Eastern system had to be detached, it was detached upon the private sidings of the company from which it came

The whole of the goods and passenger traffic passing through the parish of Fletton was brought into and conveyed from the parish by a double line of railway, consisting of one "up" and one "down" line of rails only, and the Assessment Committee, in arriving at the value of the appellants' railway in the parish for rating purposes, took the mileage proportion of the receipts and tolls for passengers and goods traffic, calculated upon fifty-eight and one-tenth chains of such double line, and

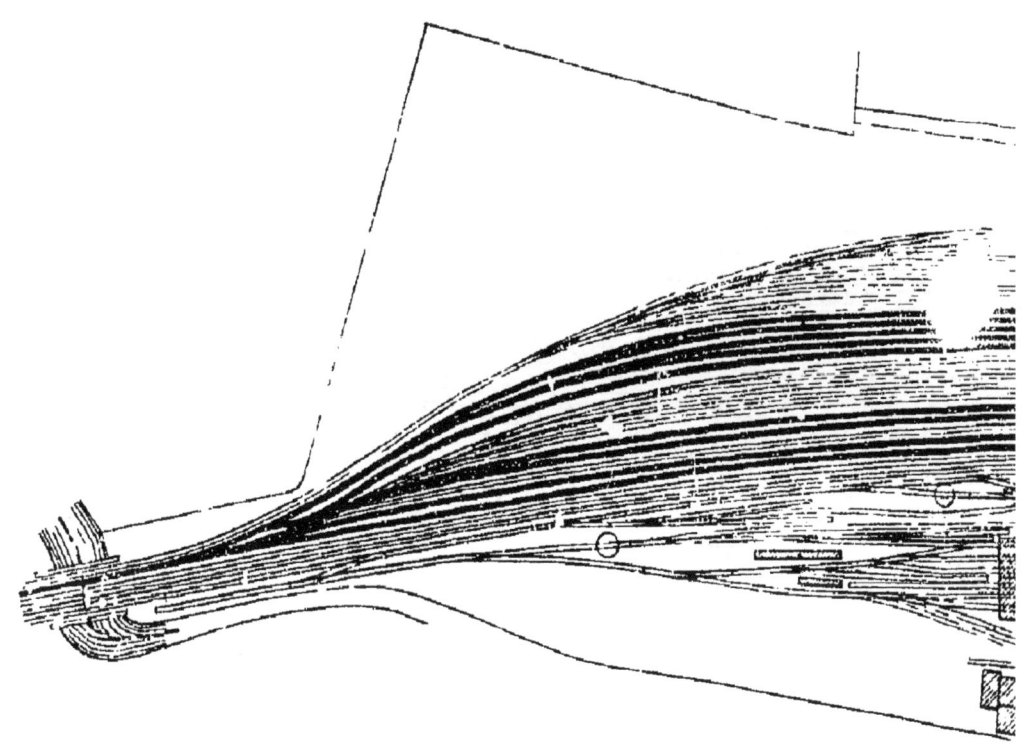

G.E.R.

PARISH OF FLETTON.

PETERBOROUGH STATION

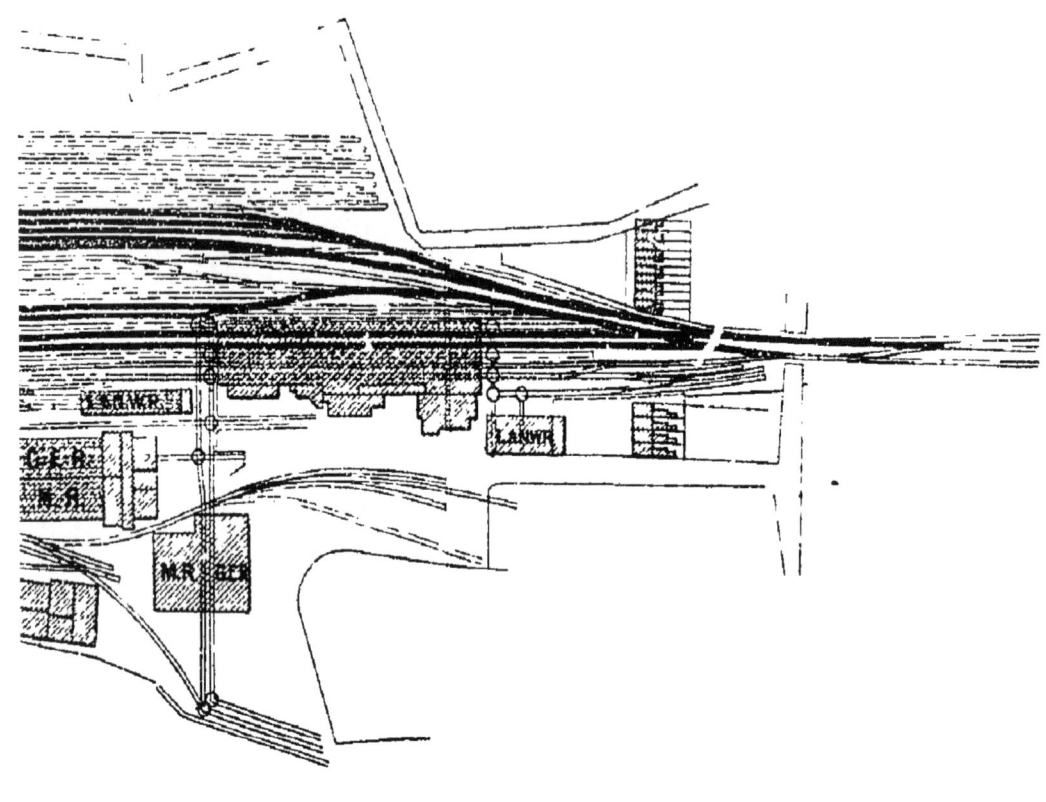

Plan referred to in Case G.E.R Company V Churchwardens of Fletton and Guardians of Peterborough Union, November 6th, 1882

from this they made the usual deductions, including the
maintenance and renewal of fty-eight and one-tenth
chains only The traffic receipts of the line east of the
station were an equal mileage proportion of the rates
calculated on the tolls and rates charged for carrying
passenger and goods tra ic from station to station. The
traffic receipts of the line west of the tation e lso
equal mileage proportions of the traffi receipts; 1 ading
the mileage proportion of the tolls paid under le e by
the London and North Western Ra way Company fc
their use of the line, and the mileage oportion of the
traffic interchanged with the Midland and the Great
Northern Railway Companies. In valuing the station
and appurtenances, th Assessment Committee estimated
the annual value upor he present value of the land and
structural value of the bu 'ings, workshops, platforms,
fixed machinery, and sidings, nd the lines in question

Terminal charges were in   respect of the use of   Terminals
the station, station sidings a v rks, they were however not included in the rece ts for the parish, but were
treated as part of the general receipts of the railway

The appellants contended at the lines in question, as
they were used only for the nveyance and haulage of
through traffic and as relief lines to the main passenger
lines passing through the station buildings, should be
treated as part of the railway directly earning profits,
and that while the gross traffic receipts were calculated
on fifty-eight and one-tenth chains only, the actual
expense of maintaining and repairing the two miles
twenty-six and one-tenth chains of double line in the
parish should be deducted from such receipts—calculated
as aforesaid—in ascertaining the rateable value.

The respondents contended that, as one double line of
railway would have been sufficient for the conveyance of
all the traffic passing through the parish if the appellants'
station had not been in the parish, the lines in question

should be treated as station appurtenances, and should be included in the valuation of the station as not producing direct profits, or that, if treated as part of the railway directly earning profits, the proportion of the traffic receipts in the parish should be calculated upon two miles twenty-six and one-tenth chains of double line and not upon fifty-eight and one-tenth chains only.

The appellants also contended that all the receipts from traffic passing over the lines in question were, in the Assessment Committee's valuation in fact included in the gross receipts, and that they were therefore entitled to deduct the cost of maintaining and repairing the lines in question, and that, if the lines in question were included in the valuation of the station and sidings, they would be twice rated—first, as directly contributing to the earning of the gross receipts, and secondly as part of the station sidings

Questions for the Court

The questions for the opinion of the Court were — Whether, for rating purposes, the nine pairs of lines in question, or any and which of them, ought to be treated as part of the line of railway directly contributing to the earnings of the company, or as station directly contributing to the earnings of the company, or as station appurtenances indirectly contributing to profits, and rateable in the same manner as the station itself? And, if as the former, whether the mode of calculating the gross receipts and the expenses of maintenance and repairs contended for by the appellants, or that contended for by the respondents, was correct? The Court delivered the following judgment :—

Judgment of Field, J

Mr. Justice Field "I think this is a very clear case There is no doubt about the law The only question is the application of particular facts Now the law is very clear. The Statute prescribes that land is to be rated, or rather the occupier of land is to be rated, in respect of profit at the annual sum for which the land is agreed to be let from year to year. Where the occupation of the land is separate from the ownership there is not much difficulty in arriving at the result, but in the case of railway companies, water companies, and so on, where the owner and occupier are the same, you have not the ordinary means of ascertaining at how much the land is let, you have, therefore, to arrive at some other mode of ascertaining it. Take a railway company, which is what we have to deal with. You first of all have to find what is the gross sum which the occupier receives in respect of the land over which he earns profit. That is where the matter is a direct source of profit. The alternative is where the occupier is in the occupation of land which does not directly earn profit, such as shunting stations, the mains of a water company, or anything of that kind, which are a burden on the company, and not earning a profit. Under those circumstances it is to be rated, but not to be rated as was contended in the *Middlesex* case,[1] according to the gross receipts and earnings, but according to what is now known as the contractor's rate, that is, at such a sum as the person who wishes to contract to undertake all their shunting and station business would be willing and able to pay for the land to be used for this purpose. Therefore, of course, when you come to deal with a line of railway without a station, there is no difficulty at all about the matter. It is as simple a thing as possible. You find what is the sum which that land has produced in gross to the occupier, and for that purpose you take what is the sum of money which people have paid to go over and have the use of the land. Having got the gross sum received, you may deduct all the expenses incurred in earning that, and you must deduct the trade profit which a trader will expect to make in carrying on the business. That will then

Contractor rate

---

[1] *R v West Middlesex Water Co*, (1859) 28 L J M.C 135, 5 Jur N S 1159, 1 El & El 716, 23 J.P 164

Y

leave a sum which is estimated to be a sum a tenant would fairly and reasonably give for the land   But when you have got the rateable hereditament, if I may use that word, which consists not only of land directly earning profit, but also of land which, as I said just now, does not earn profit at all, but is a charge upon the occupier, still you have got to divide the two portions of the hereditament, and resolve them into their separate elements   What do you start with first of all ? You start with, first of all, that which directly earns profit   It is the land in this case which directly earns profit   What are the facts on that point ? They seem to me as clear as any facts can be   The Great Eastern Railway Company have a station at Fletton where they carry on their business as carriers of passengers and goods. Where it passes through the parish of Fletton they have got two yellow lines which they reserve for that particular purpose, and the parish have got all the fares calculated on the number of people who have been carried over the two yellow lines that those fifty-eight chains occupy Besides that, the Great Eastern Railway Company use this land for another purpose, namely, their through mineral traffic which is very large, I think, and, rightly or wrongly, they think it most convenient and most useful to themselves, and most desirable, that instead of mixing their passenger trains, which stop at Fletton with their goods trains, which have to go right through when you come into the parish of Fletton you should divide the traffic into separate streams   Accordingly, for that

Relief lines for through traffic, not sidings

purpose they have nine lines which are through lines They are not sidings in the sense which ' siding ' has a meaning, because they are through lines for the purpose of carrying the through traffic. The parish have got in their account the receipts of every ton of goods or truck load of goods charged for and credited, so that they have got in their fifty-eight chains all the direct gross receipts arising from the use of the land there, they have got the nine red lines and the two yellow lines, and it is not suggested that the company have not given credit for everything they ought to have given. On that point I am now asked to say that they are to be charged with two miles and a certain number of chains That would be, to my mind, an entire fallacy. As I said just now, it would be true enough if the through trains travelled up and down and round the yellow, red and blue lines, they might then pass over two miles and twenty-six chains; but as they are not guilty of that waste of labour and time, or wear and tear of metals, it is not done. I, therefore, have not the smallest doubt in the world that fifty-eight chains is the correct sum on which that rate ought to be based, and that is the sum on which the appellants contend it should be settled Having got all the gross receipts accurately down, we have now got to find what is the residue value of the land, and the first thing we have to do is to ascertain what are the expenses incurred by the company in earning these gross receipts on the red and yellow lines But it is said, 'You must not conduct the cost of maintenance of the red lines at all ' Therefore, although there are lines, and they have to be renewed and maintained, and all the expenses incurred, yet all that is not to be deducted Why? What reason is assigned for it? I am at a loss to discover any legitimate reason If any shunting were done upon these two lines, and it was found that they had been used for shunting, then the result would have probably gone into the other assessment, namely, the assessment of the station[1], but they are not used for that They are simply through lines directly earning profit. Then Mr. Smith says what is perfectly true He suggests that this is all an expense because there is a station there, and that

---

[1] See judgment in *London and North Western Railway Co v Stockport Union* (1898) 78 L T 180, 67 L J Q B 335

therefore (I do not follow the reasoning), somewhere or other, the expenses ought to be apportioned. I hold no doubt whatever upon the matter. It is well understood that there are certain things in a parish which are not a subject of deduction in that parish, but which are the subject of deduction over the whole line, and a proportion of which is charged in a particular parish. The expense is all in the parish. It would be inconsistent with the *Haughley* case[1] that the expenses in a parish of that particular thing which, in point of fact, does earn the money, and which the parish are entitled to in the receipts, are not to be deducted. I think, therefore, the appeal must be allowed, with costs."

Mr. Justice Stephen: "I am of the same opinion. I have nothing very much to add to what my brother Field has said, but it seems to me that Mr Lumley Smith's argument comes altogether to this, that if, by reason of there being a station in this parish, the parish is chosen as the place where the goods traffic is to be carried past the passenger traffic, then that which *primâ facie* is line is suddenly to be changed into siding. I cannot follow that."

From the above it is evident that, in making a valuation of a station, all the land is to be included which is not actually occupied by the running lines. We will assume that we have a station consisting of an "up" and a "down" platform with the necessary offices, and that there are a certain number of sidings, turn-tables, signals, etc. The assessment of the buildings, sidings, etc., is based on their structural value.

Part of the above judgment was commented upon in the case of the *Stockport Union* v *London and North Western Railway Co*,[2] which referred to certain lines in

---

[1] *Great Eastern Railway Co* v *Haughley*, (1866) L R 1 Q.B 666, 35 L J. M.C. 229, 12 Jur. N.S 596, 14 L T 515, 14 W R 779

[2] (1898) 78 L T 180, 67 L J Q B 335

connection with their station at Stockport Some of the lines were laid direct to warehouses and coal yards, whilst others were used for through goods trains when the main lines were occupied, although at other times they were occasionally used for standing waggons and carriages The main question, as before, was whether these lines were running lines or sidings, and in giving judgment in this case, A L Smith, J., said "Now, before going into the facts of this case, I wish just to refer to the decision of Field, J. (which was cited during the argument) in *Great Eastern Railway Co* v *Fletton*[1] In this case, Field, J , is reported to have said that, 'if any shunting were done upon these two lines, and it was found that they had been used for shunting, then the result would have probably gone into the other assessment.' that is to say, the two lines would be assessed as appurtenant to the station. I think it is impossible that that can be correct, and for this reason Take any one of the four principal passenger lines at Stockport on which express trains run, and which are, beyond all question, running lines ; it could not possibly be argued that if any shunting were done upon that line, the line would be thereby converted into a siding. They (the other lines) run into what have been called dead ends, but they were made and are used for the purpose of running passenger and goods traffic from the main line into the different towns to which the various branches go It is true that carriages when not in use are left standing upon these lines in the day-time and sometimes at night, but how are the lines thereby converted into being other than running lines ? They were constructed for the express purpose of running traffic from one terminus to another, not merely to be used for the purpose of standing carriages " From the above it would seem to be clear that the test whether a line of

Shunting not a test whether line is siding or not

---

[1] See "Browne on Rating" (Second Edition), p 631

railway is a running line or a siding is entirely a question of fact to be decided in each, and everything depends upon the user of the line in question.

This point was further amplified in the case of the *Great Northern Railway Co.* v *Edmonton Union*[1] The facts here were rather exceptional The Great Northern Railway, in addition to having a large goods station at King's Cross, their London terminus, have a large station in the City, and depots on the Metropolitan and other railways, but owing to the heavy passenger traffic on the Metropolitan Railway it was only permissible for goods to be carried on that system at certain times It consequently followed that trains arriving from the North on the Great Northern system were shunted on to certain relief lines in the parish of Hornsey to await transit over the Metropolitan Company's system, and the Parochial Authorities sought to treat these lines as sidings and not as running lines, or running lines used in the transit of the goods to their destination The effect of the two processes will be readily observed as far as any particular parish is concerned, for the gross receipts in the parish being a fixed sum, the deductions for expenses would vary, according to the number of running lines in the parish, in two ways, first, the parish would benefit by having a small number of running lines and therefore less deduction for expenses, and, secondly, the parish would benefit from the fact that such lines are capable of an additional assessment if they are in fact sidings, and, therefore, part of a station.

The Court, however, held in this case that the lines were primarily and principally used for the purpose of transit, and were properly regarded by the railway company as directly productive of running lines, and

[1] (1905) (K B D , 2nd March and 1st July) 69 J P 179, 316, 21 T L R 638

should be assessed on such basis, notwithstanding that the lines in question might be used, in addition to their primary use, for shunting or marshalling of traffic

The principle of law is therefore clearly laid down that a line used primarily for transit is to be treated not as a siding but as a running line, although it may be put to other uses, and in each case the question of fact as to the use to which the line is put is the material evidence to decide how it is to be rated

This was borne out in the case of the *Taff Vale Railway Co v. Cardiff Union Assessment Committee*,[1] in which certain lines were used for the relief of the main lines on which waggons proceeded to and from the docks   It frequently happened that waggons containing coal were required to wait for considerable periods until certain ships were ready to receive the coal, and it was held by the Arbitrator in this case that the lines were substantially used for the carriage of coal traffic and that they must be treated as directly producing profit and not as sidings

A signal box should be assessed upon the same principle as a station,[2] and not included in the working expenses of the line

Although signal boxes (that is, the mere structure of the signal box) have been held not to be part of the line but part of a station for the purpose of assessment, an important case before the London Quarter Sessions as to levers and signals cannot be overlooked, but there is no decision of the High Court upon the point

The case in question is that of the *South Eastern and Chatham Railway Co v St Saviour's Union*[3]   Mr Cyril Dodd, K.C., the valuer appointed by the Court, appended the following note to his report —

---

[1] (1907) (K B D., 6th July, 1906) 95 L.T 455, 70 J P 534

[2] *Midland Railway Co v Pontefract Union*, (1901) 2 K B 189, 84 L T 586, 17 T L R 439

[3] (1901) Reported in " Ryde and Konstam's Rating Appeals," 1894 to 1904, p 57

"A question arose as to how the levers and signals ought to be dealt with, the appellants contending that they should be treated as part of the running line and as directly productive property, whilst the respondents contended that they were indirectly productive property and analogous to stations, and should not be treated as part of the running line, but as local and parochial The signal boxes contain levers which work simultaneously with the points or crossings and the signals. I treated the boxes themselves as indirectly productive property, and not as part of the running line, and in doing so took into consideration their use for containing the levers and protecting them and for protecting the signalmen I treated the levers and signals themselves as part of the running line. I found that the signals were necessary for the safe working of the line, just as much as the points and crossings, and that the trains could not be run without them any more than they could without lines "

The point was argued before the Court on the finding of Mr Dodd, and his view of the case was upheld on the ground that it was a question of fact

Advertisement hoardings and refreshment rooms

With regard to advertisement hoardings on railway stations, it is clear that under the Advertising Station (Rating) Act, 1889,[1] the railway company granting the right are liable for the rates As to refreshment rooms, it would appear to depend upon the facts of each case, viz, whether or not the railway company are the occupiers

Total sum to be inserted in Valuation List

We will suppose that a valuation of the station has been made, and that it resolves itself into £827 rateable value The rateable value of the line was £18,623, and this added to the valuation of the station, viz, £827, gives a total result of £19,450, the figure that should be inserted in the Valuation List The point as regards the total sum or sums to be inserted is very often raised, but

[1] (1889) 52 & 53 Vict , c 27

the law upon the subject seems clear It is sometimes
contended that it is incorrect to insert in the Valuation
List one total sum, to include the stations, the main,
and the branch lines in the parish. The Act of
Parliament which bears on this point was passed
in 1864, viz , the Union Assessment Committee Act,[1]
which enacts "That a valuer who is appointed by the
Assessment Committee shall make his valuation in
writing, showing the particulars of the several hereditaments comprised therein, and the amounts at which he
has valued the same respectively, and shall sign such
valuation, which shall be open to inspection in like
manner and with the same incidents with respect to the
taking of copies or extracts as the minute books of the
Committee " It will be seen that all that is necessary is
a valuation of the several hereditaments , and the point
to be decided is whether the property owned by a railway
company in one particular parish, consisting of main
lines, trunk lines and stations, is one hereditament or
several, that is to say, should any part of the property
be separately entered in the Valuation List ? This would
appear not to be so, the decision in the case of *Rawlence
and others* v *The Guardians of Hursley Union*[2] is to
the point   Here the appellants had been engaged by the
Guardians of Hursley Union to make a valuation of
certain properties in the Union. On delivering their
valuation the defendants objected to it, owing to the
fact that there were certain hereditaments consisting of
several fields which were valued in one sum. To the
appendix of the special case was annexed an extract from
the Valuation List for the parish of Farley Chamberlavne
(*see following page*)

The opinion of the Court was asked on the following
question, viz , Whether the Valuation List as furnished by

---

[1] 27 & 28 V ct , c 39, s 4
[2] (1877) 3 Ex D. 44, 47 L J M C 31, 37 L T 503, 26 W R 81

the plaintiffs to the defendants was complete under the
section of the Act above referred to, or whether the

No on Ordnance Map	Name of Occupier	Name of Owner	Description of Property	Name or Situation of Property	Estimated Extent a r p	Gross Estimated Rental £ s d	Rateable Value £ s d
2	Heathcote Sir Wm	Heathcote Sir Wm	Arable	Berrydown Farm	40 1 7	440 15 0	396 13 6
4	Ditto	Ditto	Ditto	Ditto	18 3 34		
5	Ditto	Ditto	Rough Pasture	Ditto	163 0 2		
6	Ditto	Ditto	Ditto	Ditto	6 3 9		
40	Ditto	Ditto	Arable	Ditto	42 0 5		
42	Ditto	Ditto	Ditto	Ditto	28 1 39		
43	Ditto	Ditto	Ditto	Ditto	28 3 23		

defendants were entitled to have a separate valuation of
each field? Kelly, C.B., in giving judgment, said · "I
think that the Valuation List, as shown in the appendix

to the case, gives at least as much information as is required by the Act of Parliament What the Act requires is a valuation of each hereditament within the Union. The question is whether it is proper to treat the whole of a farm, or the like, in one occupation as constituting only one hereditament? The defendants contend that the surveyor is bound to value each field. In support of this contention it is said that the valuer himself has given much fuller particulars than on the plaintiffs' view of the case would be necessary, but it is sufficient to say, in answer, that the valuer has, as I think, given unnecessary and even inconvenient details. It is further said, in support of this contention of the defendants, that there might be a severance of occupation, but the utility in such a case of the information desired by the defendants is mere matter of speculation. The information might be of some use, but it might be of none at all. The value might have altered I think it is infinitely more convenient, as well as more in conformity with the letter of the Act, that each farm and the like should be valued in its entirety The purpose of the Valuation List is to enable the Union to assess each occupier within the Union The Acts, no doubt, allow a park and a farm, although in one occupation, to be assessed separately. but a farm should, I think, be valued in its entirety."

Cleasby, B., following " I am of the same opinion, I do not feel the least difficulty in deciding this case. Such a process as is contended on the part of the defendants to be requisite would make the Valuation List inconveniently large, and innumerable challenges would arise The Act of Parliament does not encourage any such thing It says that the valuer ' shall make his valuation in writing, showing the particulars of the several hereditaments comprised therein, and the amounts at which he has valued the same respectively.' That does not mean, as has been contended, that he is to specify each field and the value of each field   No question would probably have arisen if the valuer had not given unnecessary particulars "

All contention upon this point has, however, been finally set at rest by the case of the *North Eastern Railway Co. v. York Guardians*,[1] where the assessment of the whole of the railway company's property in one parish in the York Union was inserted in the Valuation List in one lump sum, and consisted of the running lines, sidings, York station, locomotive sheds and shops, cattle docks, electric light works, yards, refreshment rooms, etc , etc   The whole of the premises were completely fenced round, except, of course, the running lines, which were continuous through other parishes   Altho obvious parts of the property could have been occupied separately —and indeed it was admitted by the respondents that the refreshment rooms should have been rated separately—it was, on the other hand, found as a fact that as the premises were laid out they were only adapted for use by the railway company themselves.   It was held that it is a question of fact, having regard to the actual mode of occupation and the purpose for which they are occupied, whether premises are rateable as one or more hereditaments, and that in this case the decision of the Court of First Instance was correct.   For the purpose of the General District Rate a division must be made between the running lines and the stations, etc , as under the Public Health Act of 1875 [2] a railway company are only liable for one-fourth of the rates for the purpose to which this Act applies   See also upon this point of an inclusive valuation the case of the *Corporation of Kingston-upon-Hull v Sculcoates Union*,[3] where the same point affects a dock company as far as regards land covered with water.

---

[1] (1900) 1 Q B. 733 , 69 L J Q B. 376, 64 J P. 437

[2] 38 & 99 Vict , c 55

[3] (1890) 54 J P 281

The case was very different, however, in the appeal of the *Mersey Docks* v. *Birkenhead (Overseers)*,[4] where certain warehouses adjacent to the docks, but having the same owner, were separated in the Valuation List, as undoubtedly such hereditaments were capable of a separate occupation Perhaps a small extract from the judgment of Quain, J., in the case referred to will make further reference to this point unnecessary "The question is, What would a tenant give for these warehouses by the year, making the usual deductions? The case distinctly finds that such a tenant could be found, and that there would be a rateable value for these warehouses. Therefore it seems to me on that ground these items are rateable The fact that they belong to a concern which, as a whole, is carried on by a dock company at a loss, is no answer to the question as to their rateability"

Having traced the course of a valuation of a railway Contributive value company in an imaginary parish, it is now proposed to deal with what is known as contributive value. On the system of a large railway company we usually find one main or trunk line with several branches Many of these branches are worked at a loss, but they are the means of bringing traffic to the main line, they are feeders of the trunk line, and as such are material sources of wealth to the company. Should the whole system of a railway company be contained in one parish, the difficulty of the assessment of such would be easily surmounted, but the parochial principle having to be adopted in the case of a company extending throughout many parishes, the local receipts and expenses are those only which can be taken into account The question has been before the Courts on many occasions, and former decisions are conflicting It is necessary to thoroughly understand the principle of contributive value for the purpose of estimating the receipts in any given parish, and to put this before the reader clearly the diagram below is used

---

4 (1873) L.R. 2 Q B. 445; 42 L J. M C. 141, 29 L T 454, 21 W R 913

From each of the stations *c, d, e* and *f* a train runs to
the station B   Each train has twenty passengers, and

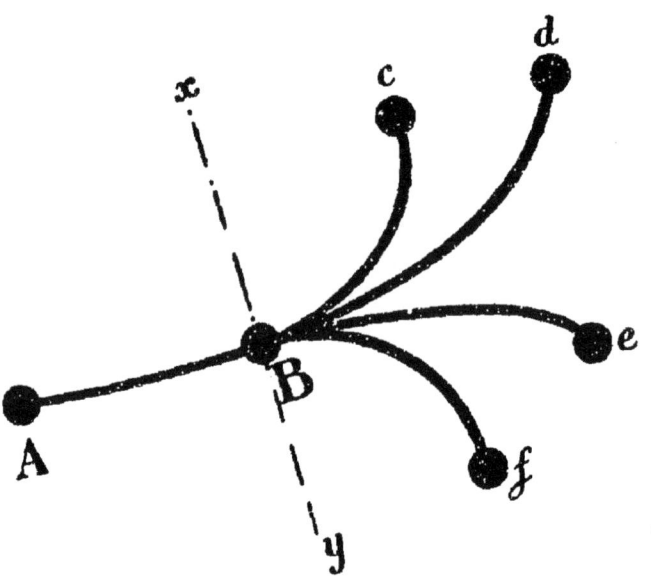

they are all bound for A   From B to A one train is
forwarded containing all the passengers, viz , eighty from
the four branch lines, and although the working expenses
on the four branches B *c*, B *d*, B *e* and B *f* exceed the
amount of receipts on those branches, yet the profit made
on A B is sufficient to cover the expenses over the whole
system and still leave a balance to go to the proprietor of
the railway. Supposing, for the sake of argument, that
this railway is in two parishes, the parish boundary
coming through the centre of the station B, shown by the
line *x y* , then the four branches are usually rated in the
parish in which they are situated only at the value of the
land, because by adopting the receipts and expenses
principle a minus quantity would result (but see p 335
post), but in the other parish the assessment is fixed on
the principle of receipts and expenses in the same method
as the example-valuation given before   This is following
out the parochial principle as explained in Chapter V.,
Part I. A very important case upon the point was that

of *Great Western Railway Co. v. Llantrisant*[1] Here the question of the assessment of the Ely Valley Railway and branches were under consideration The appellants, the Great Western Railway Company, held the lease of the line for 999 years at a rental of £4,000 per annum This high rental was because of the mineral traffic which this part of the railway brought to the main system, and it was to the benefit of the company to pay a higher rental than the line was absolutely worth *per se* The Assessment Committee rated the company on the basis of the rent paid, but on the receipts and expenses principle (which the appellants contended was the correct method) the rateable value would have been very much less The respondents relied upon the case of *The London and North Western Railway Co v The Overseers of Cannock*,[2] where Cockburn, C.J, said in the course of his judgment " Rent is *prima facie* evidence of value Suppose at this moment there were no lease and the appellants wanted to take it, what is the rent they would give? ' But Mellor, J, said, in reply to this " The rent of the branch lines does not show its real value The appellants may have rented it as a mere speculation I think there has been some confusion between the value of the line to an ordinary tenant and its value to a special tenant."

The judgment of Mellor, J, in this case is very clear " I am of opinion that our judgment should be for the appellants It is extremely difficult to reconcile everything which has been said as to the mode in which railways ought to be assessed to the Poor Rate I think, however, that in this case it is immaterial whether the line to be rated is a branch line or a portion of the main line What is to be done is to ascertain the value of the railway in each particular parish through which the line passes, that is, what would the hypothetical tenant give

---

[1] (1869) L R 4 Q B 354, 38 L J M C 93, 20 L T 364
[2] (1863) 9 L T 325

for this portion of railway ? And I think that it would be very unsafe to disturb the recent decisions by introducing a different principle, and deciding that the fact that the railway in Llantrisant contributes to the traffic upon the main line ought to be taken into account in ascertaining the rateable value. For my own part I adhere to the opinion which I expressed in the *Great Eastern Railway Co* v *Haughley* [1] With regard to the observations attributed to the Court in the *London and North Western Railway Co* v *Cannock* [1] I think that the Lord Chief Justice must be taken to have reconsidered them in the *Great Eastern Railway Co* v *Haughley* [2] for, to the best of my memory, he fully concurred in that decision, and there was not the slightest difference of opinion upon the Bench. I repeat what I said in that case, the value must depend upon the actual earnings of the railway within the parish, deducting the expenses

Actual rent a guide only to value

which properly belong to this part of the line. The rent which would be paid by the hypothetical tenant, and not that which is paid by some particular tenant, must decide the value. There is nothing to enable us to take into consideration the value of the line as a feeder to other lines in different parishes The simple question is whether, because traffic comes from Ely Valley Railway to the Great Western, any addition ought to be made to the rateable value of the Ely Valley Railway in the parish of Llantrisant ? To this question there can be but one answer, that no such addition ought to be made to the value, and therefore the order of Sessions must be confirmed."

Branch lines

From this it will be seen that, when rating a branch line, no consideration must be given to its value as a feeder to the main line, because, as the main line is

---

[1] (1866) L R 1 Q B 666, 35 L J M C 229 12 Jur N S 596, 11 L T 548

[2] (1863) 9 L J 325

rated at something higher owing to the traffic which is brought to it by the branch, if the branch were to be rated at its value as a feeder to the main line, this value would be rated twice over This opinion is a mere generalization of the judgment The rent paid was some £4,000, and assuming that the branch was rated on the basis of the rent paid, then something would have to be deducted on the assessment of the main line, because certain of the traffic had been rated upon the branch It is not proposed to go more deeply into this subject of contributive value, but some of the cases bearing upon the point it may be well to study, viz —The *Haughley* and the *Cannock* cases already referred to, the *South Eastern Railway* v *Dorking (Churchwardens)* [1] and the *Cornwall Railway Co* v *Lisheard Union* [2]

It is submitted that seldom, if ever, is a rent of a line agreed upon several years ago of any value in determining the assessment of the line in question to-day,[3] and, further, that the cost of construction of a branch line (or, indeed, as a matter of fact, of any line) is evidence of the rateable value of the line.

In the case of the *London and North Western Railway Co* v *Ampthill Union* [4] a small line of railway had been constructed in 1845 by a company which was subsequently worked under an agreement by the London and North Western Railway Company, they (the London and North Western Company) agreeing to pay a rent equal to 4 per cent. on the cost of the construction, but it was held by the Court of Appeal that evidence as to the cost of construction in 1845 was too remote to be of value, and as it had been proved that there was no competitive value in the line, the proper mode of assessment was according to the receipts and expenses.

[1] (1854) 7 Rail Cas 877 3 E & B 191, 23 L J M C 64, 18 Jur 672.
[2] "Browne's Law of Rating" (Second Edition), App II, p 623
[3] *East London Railway Joint Committee* v *Greenwich Union Assessment Committee,* (1907) 97 L.T 404, 71 J P 460
[4] (1908) (C A 16th November, 1907) 97 L T. 869, 71 J.P. 545

z

A later and more important decision upon this point is that of the House of Lords in the case of the *Great Central Railway Co.* v. *Banbury Union.*[1] The facts, briefly, were as follows —

In 1900 the Great Western Railway Company, in order to connect their system with the Great Central Company and thus create a main line route from the North to the South and West of England, advanced to the Great Central Company a sum of money for the purpose of constructing the line in question at an agreed rate of interest, namely, $3\frac{1}{4}$ per cent per annum. The questions presented to the House of Lords were whether the Parochial Authorities were entitled to take into account in ascertaining the rateable value the fact that the Great Central Company paid $3\frac{1}{4}$ per cent interest on the cost of construction, or whether the line ought to be assessed only on its actual net earnings within the parish

The judgment of the Lord Chancellor is most important in this case and confirms the principle very clearly, and, therefore, the quotation below is given *in extenso* viz

" My Lords, I naturally look for guidance to the authorities, but some of them, or at all events some of the opinions which they contain, are irreconcilable one with the other   I t'ink the best course is to apply the principles on which those decisions are founded, which, as I am obliged to make a choice, seem to me preferable as authorities

" The chief source of difficulty was foreseen long ago It is this   A railway is an undertaking extended through a multitude of rating areas   Generally no section of it situated in any rating area would be rented by any tenant except as a component part of the system. Yet the governing Statute requires the rateable value of every such

---

[1] (1909) A C 78, 25 T L R 148

section to be ' the rent at which the same might reasonably be expected to let from year to year ' after making the prescribed deductions Obviously a natural way of ascertaining the rateable value of such a section in obedience to the Statute is to consider at what rent it would be hired by the railway company to which the entire system belongs , usually no other tenant is conceivable In such a state of things the railway company might be willing to pay almost any rent for a section of the main line, without possession of which its whole business might be dislocated and half ruined. But the Statute speaks of a rent which might ' reasonably ' be expected, and this excludes the idea of an oppressive demand fixed upon imagined necessities

"It follows that the rent must be fixed in accordance with the real value of the section to the company concerned because that is the footing on which a tenant would base his offer of rent if he be not exposed to extortion And the method usually adopted for arriving at that real value is to ascertain the net earnings of the section by allocating to it a mileage proportion of all rates and fares received for the whole journey in respect of all traffic passing over the section, after making from the receipts proper allowances for working expenses, Government duty, rental of stations separately assessed, trade profits, interest on tenants' capital and the statutory deductions This is for present purposes a sufficient description of the usual method I do not pretend to define it No doubt this method is not ordered by the Statute It is, to use Lord Watson's phrase, a ' formula ' Nevertheless, though Courts of Law have never said that it must be adopted, it is in ordinary cases a sound way of fixing the true value When adopted by Quarter Sessions, the proper judges of this question of fact, Courts of Law, have repeatedly allowed it

"It does not treat all the miles on the line as of equal value. On the contrary, The measure of the value is the sum which is, in fact, earned by each mile, so that a much-used mile will pay more, exactly according to its profit-earning use. Without saying that this formula is imperative, or usurping a right to decide on questions of fact I do not think it has been so long and so constantly applied that the tribunal which decides the fact would not depart from it without good reasons

"On the hearing of this appeal before your Lordships, it was not disputed that the formula to which I have referred is applicable to ordinary cases But, it was said, the present case is out of the ordinary, because this particular line, including the portion of it within Wardington Parish, has a value apart from the actual net profits earned on it, and either the Great Central Railway Company or the Great Western Railway Company might reasonably be expected to give a greater rent for it as a means of connecting their systems, which otherwise could not be effected And so it was argued, interest on the cost of construction is an element which might properly be taken into account in ascertaining the rateable value, for it shows what the railway company would give as rent.

"Now, I cannot assent to these contentions

"If there be a special value in the Banbury branch line, it must arise because this line is indispensable for through traffic from the North of England to the South and West, and therefore a railway company or companies occupying the other portions of the through line would give a great rent in order to occupy this also. No doubt that is true It is also true of all other sections of the through line from the beginning to the end of it No single mile could be spared. The Statute says the rateable value is what a tenant might 'reasonably' be expected to give as rent. That is not to be arrived at by assuming that the hypothetical tenant already controls all the rest of the line he requires, and is driven by his necessities to pay excessively for the single link that he does not control. It would be equally reasonable for the railway company to say, 'Here is a mile of railway line, you are to isolate it from the rest of the system, for all you are to rate is this single mile, no one would give a sixpence for an isolated mile of railway, therefore, the rateable value is nil.' When the method I have described is applied the true view seems to lie between these extremes. Each section is regarded as a profit-earning part of the system to which it belongs. Each section is indispensable to the working of the system. And I think the resulting inquiry is: If the whole system were to be let at once, though it be in separate sections, how much of the rent that a tenant would give for the whole is applicable to the particular section which is to be assessed? That depends on profit-earning.

"Even if there were a special value in this Banbury branch line which could be considered in making the assessment, I do not see how it can be proper to measure that special value by the cost of construction or its annual equivalent, the interest payable on that cost. It is not merely that the rate of interest will depend on the financial position of the borrowing company and the security it can offer. Possibly that criticism might be met by a correction so as to assume an ordinary commercial interest. The real objection is that cost is not a measure of rent. Many houses constructed at enormous expense notoriously fetch very moderate rents. Many portions of a railway cost immensely more than the average, where, for example, there are tunnels or bridges or embankments. If a railway company were considering what rent it could pay for an entire line offered for letting, the cost of construction would not be considered either of the whole or of its parts The company would simply consider what rent it could pay so as to have a profitable concern

"It would be practicable, though I think it would be wrong, to rate every section of a line on the annual equivalent of its cost   But I do not think it is practicable to adopt a mixed calculation based partly on profit-earning and partly on cost. As Mr. Justice Wightman said in *R v Middlesex Waterworks*,[1] the Court is bound to protect the occupier from being rated beyond the rateable value of the whole apparatus taken together. And that could not be done under the mixed method adopted in this case

"Accordingly, I think evidence of the interest on cost of construction was inadmissible

"I will only add that there may be exceptional cases, as for example where a railway company rents an auxiliary line, not really a part of its system, or a number of railway companies occupy in common a piece of line I do not wish to say anything in regard to such cases, unless and until they come to be argued before this House, feeling the danger of general rules beyond the need of the case under consideration

"I respectfully advise your Lordships that the appeal should be allowed, and the assessment fixed at £102."

This principle was also applied by the House of Lords in the case of the *Great Central Railway Co v Sheffield Union Assessment Committee*[2]

Branch lines   In valuing a branch line it is submitted from the foregoing that the receipts actually earned in the parish for which the valuation is made are the only ones to be taken into calculation   The hereditament in that particular parish has to be rated as though it could be separated

---

[1] (1859) 1 E & B 716, 28 L J M C 135, 5 Jur N S 1159, 23 J P 164.

[2] (1909) A C 97

from the whole, and as if it constituted one independent rateable property When assessing a railway it should be rated according to its value *qua* railway; and the valuation should be in no way affected by the assessment of adjacent land used for any other purpose[1] It will be seen that there are many cases where the expenses of a portion of railway are far greater than the receipts, so that legally the railway has no rateable value at all Upon this point Castle, in his "Law of Rating" (3rd edition), p 226, says "It is true that, where a railway is worked at a loss, it is often put at 40s an acre, as representing agricultural value, but, in reality, there is no reason for this being done, except to prevent the property appearing in the Rate Book without any value attached to

It would appear that in a parish where there is a main line worked at a profit and a branch line worked at a loss, when considering the valuation of the whole of the company's property in the parish, it would be reasonable for the company to claim the loss sustained on the working of the branch line from the profits earned on the main line, for, if the assessment is to be in one lump sum, as in the case of the *North Eastern Railway Co.* v *York Union,*[2] the question that has to be answered is the value of the property in the parish as a whole, and therefore all the lines would have to be looked at from a hypothetical tenant's point of view, if it were possible to conceive a tenant being found for any such property in one parish only. The effect of branch lines being worked at a loss in a parish where there is no main line has been discussed But in the case of *R.* v *Great Western Railway*[3] it was held that in considering the value of a main line it was wrong to deduct the losses on a branch line situated in another parish

[1] *R* v *Manchester and Altrincham Railway*, (1848) 15 Q B 395, n
[2] (1900) 1 Q B 733, 69 L J Q B 376, 64 J P 437
[3] (1846) 3 Q B 179, 15 L J M C 80, 2 New. Sess Cas 205, 10 Jur 134

In the event of a railway company having running
powers over the system of another company, there is no
legal occupation, and the company in possession of the
running powers are not liable to be rated for them—
see *Midland Railway Co v Badgworth (Overseers)* [1]
There is no doubt, however, that the rateability of the
line would be increased owing to this circumstance, as a
company allowing another running powers would not do
so without some compensation, and it is evident that a
hypothetical tenant would be willing to pay more rent for
a line of railway where a certain income was secured by a
lease or concession to another company—see *R. v Grand
Junction Railway Co* [2] An interesting point arose in
the *Badgworth* case. There a line of railway ran between
Cheltenham and Gloucester, both the Midland and Great
Western Companies owned half of it, not jointly, however,
but they each had reciprocal running powers over the
respective portions In the parish of Badgworth the part
of the railway which was next to Cheltenham and
belonged to the Great Western Company was the portion
in question Previous to this appeal both companies had
been rated in that parish, but the Midland contended that
this was incorrect, and the Court of Queen's Bench on a
special case for their opinion upheld this view [3] It so
happened that the traffic of the Midland Railway Company over this portion of the line was more profitable
than and very much exceeded that of the Great Western
Company, but it was agreed that neither of the two companies was to pay any toll to the other in respect of the
use of the half of the railway belonging to the other The
Great Western were the legal occupiers; and in fixing

---

[1] (1864) 34 L J M C 25, 11 Jur N S 14, 11 LT 303, 13 W R 202

[2] (1844) 4 Q B 18, 4 Rail Cas 1; D & M. 237, 13 L J M C 94,
8 Jur 508

[3] *Great Western Railway v Badgworth*, (1867) L R 2 Q B 251, 31
J P 261, 36 L J M C 33, 15 W R 579

the amount of the assessment the Committee adopted the following plan, viz. —They made a valuation of the Great Western Company's traffic, that is to say, a valuation on the receipts and expenses principle, and to this they added a sum three times the amount of that assessment, as representing the rateable value in the parish in respect of the sum which the Midland Railway Company would have to pay to the appellants if they had not been in possession of running powers on the terms that existed It was held by the Court that this was incorrect, and that the value of the land ought to be assessed to the Great Western Company only according to their own profits Cockburn, C J , in delivering judgment, said " I do not think it necessary that I should do more than say this, that I think the appellants are rateable in respect of their property in the parish according to the profit they make of it, plus the increased value by reason of their having the right of running, not only over this part and the rest of their own line, but also the right of running over the Midland line , and I do not think it would be at all a sound principle to go on to say that they are liable in respect of the profit which the Midland Company make. I think the Sessions would be well warranted in assuming that, whatever profit the Midland Company make on this part of the line, the appellants make a corresponding profit on the portion of the Midland Railway. But if that *prima facie* case is disposed of by evidence of the fact that the Midland Railway Company make a great deal more by the line than the appellants, I think the Sessions must get at the value in the best way they can , they must ascertain what is the value to the appellants, what would be the value to anybody who came as an incoming tenant from year to year, in their place, of this property, enhanced by the easement of running free over the other half of the line. I do not see any other way in which, with due regard to the Parochial

Assessment Act,[1] and to the decisions upon it, we can say that this rate ought to be made '

Where a railway company pays tolls to another company in respect of running powers over the system of the other company, the amount of such tolls has to be deducted from the receipts of the company paying the same before the gross receipts of such company are arrived at for rating purposes—see *R.* v *St Pancras Vestry.*[2]

Railways in course of construction

A railway company having obtained Parliamentary powers to construct a line of way, there can be no beneficial occupation established during the course of construction, but the company are usually made liable to make good the deficiency in the rates of the parish caused by the operations   A common clause in an Act is as follows   That if and while the company is possessed under this Act of any lands assessed, or liable to be assessed to any sewer's rate, consolidated rate, poor rate, police rate, main drainage rate. church rate, or other parochial or ward rate, they shall from time to time, until the railway or the works thereof are completed and assessed, or liable to be assessed. be liable to make good the deficiency in the assessment for such rates by reason of those lands being taken or used for the purposes of the railway or works, and the deficiency shall be computed according to the rental at which those lands with any buildings thereon are now rated   Directly the railway is completed, that is, open for the conveyance of passengers and goods, this liability ceases, and the principle of assessment as already laid down must then be applied—see the case of the *East London Railway Co.* v. *Whitechurch* [3]

---

[1] (1836) 6 & 7 William IV , c 96

[2] (1863) 3 B & S 810 32 L J. M C 146 , 9 Jur N S 1102, 8 L T 273 , 11 W R. 615

[3] (1874) L R 7 H L 81 43 L J M C 159 , 30 L T 412 22 W R. 665 38 J P 484

But in the case where, under a private Act, a railway company during the construction of a railway were bound to pay rates in respect of all lands and buildings acquired by them for that purpose, and the company acquired certain lands which at the time they took them had no buildings thereon, the buildings having been pulled down prior to possession having been obtained by the company, it was held that the company were not liable to pay the rates on the property described in the Valuation List as " shop, offices and warehouse," as the buildings had been pulled down and the land was vacant land prior to possession [1]

The lines of a railway, that is to say, the lines of way used for through traffic, sidings, etc., are assessed for the purpose of the General District Rates (as embodied in the Public Health Act, 1875[2]), at only one-fourth of the net annual value thereof   This would not apply to stations, nor indeed to any other class of railway property   In the case of the *Midland Railway Co. v Birmingham* [3] the local authorities sought to rate certain property belonging to the railway company, consisting of sidings and turn-tables, occupying some ten acres of land and used for loading trucks and carriages with goods, and also as a standing place or siding for carriages and for goods waggons both loaded and unloaded , it was held that the land was rateable at only one-fourth of its net annual value for this rate.   *R v South Wales Railway Co.* [4] is, perhaps, the leading case upon this subject, and the following is an extract from the special case stated for the opinion of the Court of Queen's Bench :—

General
District
Rates

---

[1] *City of London Churchwardens and Overseers of St Stephen v Great Northern and City Railway Co* , (1902) 86 L T 390 , 66 J.P 373.

[2] 38 & 39 Vict , c 55

[3] (1865) 13 L T. 404 , 30 J P 197

[4] (1854) 24 L J M C. 30 , 4 El & Bl. 189 , 1 Jur N.S 326

On the 26th of August, 1853, a rate for the relief of the poor of the town and franchise of Swansea was made by the churchwardens and overseers of the said town and franchise of Swansea, and the said company were assessed in respect of the land within the said town and franchise, forming the site of the main or through line of railway, consisting of a double line of rails (exclusive of the stations, platforms, offices, engine-sheds, warehouses, sidings, turn-tables, tanks, waterworks, cranes and other fixed plant, buildings, machinery and works) at the sum of £100, and in respect of the said stations, platforms, offices, engine-sheds, warehouses, sidings, turn-tables, tanks, waterworks, cranes and other fixed plant, buildings, machinery and works at the sum of £500. It was not disputed that the aggregate net annual or rateable value of all the aforesaid rateable property of the said company, within the said borough and franchise, was correct, and such value was, for the purposes of the case, admitted.

On the 7th of September, 1853, the Local Board of Health for the borough and district of Swansea made a rate, for the purposes of the Public Health Act,[1] upon all the rateable property in their district, and the appellants, as occupiers of the said railway, were, by the said Local Board, assessed at one-fourth part of the full net annual or rateable value of the land forming the site of the said main or through line of railway, but in respect of the said stations, platforms, offices, engine-sheds, warehouses, sidings, turn-tables, tanks, waterworks, cranes and other fixed plant, buildings, machinery, and works, they were assessed at the whole of the full net annual or rateable value of such last-mentioned property.

The question for the decision of the Court was, whether under Section 88 of the Public Health Act, 1848,[2] the

---

[1] (1875) 38 & 39 Vict, c 55

[2] 11 & 12 Vict, c 63

appellants were rateable in respect of the said stations, platforms, offices, engine-sheds, warehouses, sidings, turntables, tanks, waterworks, cranes and other fixed plant, buildings, machinery and works, upon the whole of the full net annual or rateable value, or on only one-fourth of such value, or upon the whole of the full net annual or rateable value of such portion only of the station as was appropriated and used for the temporary deposit of goods, and for which a charge was made for demurrage as aforesaid? If the Court were of opinion that the appellants were rateable upon the whole of the full net annual or rateable value of the said stations, platforms, etc, the rate so made upon the appellants was to stand confirmed, otherwise the said assessment upon the appellants was to be amended, and the appellants were to stand rated in such manner and on such portion or portions of the said stations, platforms, etc, as the Court should direct, and in either case the judgment of the Sessions was to be entered accordingly

Erle, J, in delivering judgment, said —

"The object of the proviso in Section 88 was to distinguish between property deriving the full benefit from the works done by the Local Board, and which is to be rated at its full annual value, and that which derives little or no benefit from these works, and which is to be rateable at a smaller amount   This being the principle, we have to apply the Statute, with the exceptions specified therein, to the property here assessed   Land used only as a railway is to be rated at a fourth of its net annual value, and I think the whole Court agrees that the line of railway, according to judicial interpretation, includes everything on each side of the central line to the extent of twenty-five feet   If an embankment or cutting is required, a still greater width would be included   All this, I consider, would be rateable at the lesser amount, as 'land used only as a railway'   I do not mean to say that the same partial exemption could necessarily be claimed if the land were turned into a warehouse, or otherwise used for profit Possibly in that case the company would be rateable for it at its full value   But here that is not so.   Therefore, the line of railway, and everything which constitutes the side of the railway, is rateable at the reduced amount   I think also that the sidings having rails laid upon them and the turn-tables, are land used as a railway orly   Then we come to the offices and warehouses, as to which I am clearly of opinion that they are not entitled to the exemption   They are proximately used for the purpose of habitation   The station here is in the middle of a large town, and used for the arrival and departure of passengers and goods.   These buildings have been erected under the powers of the Act for taking additional land besides that required for the line of railway, and such buildings ought not to be exempted as part of the railway   I believe that the principle upon which we are now acting has been put into practice upon many railways, viz, that buildings ancillary to the transit of passengers are rateable upon a different principle from the railway itself   It has never been judicially determined at what point that which is ancillary begins or ends, but the practice of rating may be referred to on this point, and that practice has treated stations, offices and warehouses as different from the railway   Therefore, on the materials now before us, I think it better to hold that, where additional land has been taken and buildings erected upon it, the company should be rateable for it at its full annual value '

But in the case of *Williams* v *London and North Western Railway Co.*[1] a provision in a local Act directed that land used as railway should only be liable for one-fourth part of the rateable value, and it was held that, under the definition of the word " railway " in addition to the sidings the platforms used for the purpose of loading

---

[1] (1899) 2 Q B 197, 80 L T 803, 15 T L R 409

and unloading railway waggons, although situated some distance from the main line, should be only liable as railway at one-fourth net annual value, so that for the purpose of the General District Rate platforms must be considered as railway, not as part of the station

In *London and North Western Railway Co* v *Llandudno Improvement Commissioners*[1] it was held that a railway company should be assessed at one-fourth part only of the net annual value for so much of the station as was necessary for the use of the railway, as a railway, for the conveyance of passengers, viz, the lines of rails, platforms and sidings, roofed and uncovered (consequently the roof itself must be allowed abatement), signal boxes and turntables. But cab drives and adjoining buildings, such as waiting rooms, booking offices, etc, were held not to be "railway," and therefore must pay the full rate

---

[1] (1897) 1 Q B 287, 61 J P. 55 See also *North Eastern Railway Co* v *Scarborough Local Board*, (1868) 4 Q.B 163, 38 L J M C 65

CHAPTER V.

CANALS.

WITH regard to the rating of canals, a great similarity exists between this class of property and that of railways The object of both is the conveyance of passengers and goods over various systems, and their revenue is altogether derived from these sources The owners of canal property (including the canal towing-path and warehouses, etc, necessary for the carrying on of the undertaking) are to be rated upon the same principle as the occupiers of land[1] That is to say, the rent at which a canal would let to a hypothetical tenant in any one particular parish is to form the basis of the gross and rateable value Formerly it was held that land over which a canal passed should be rated as other hereditaments supposing such hereditaments were not applied to the purposes of a canal but remained in the hands of individual owners, and that the land were used for ordinary agricultural purposes[2] The principle on which canals are now rated is, to ascertain the gross receipts and to deduct the expenses and a sum as profit on the tenant's capital, etc., the buildings, reservoirs, etc., belonging to the canal company being assessed on a percentage of their structural value—the same principle practically, as that adopted in the case of a railway undertaking *The Birmingham Canal Co v. The Overseers of the Parish of Birmingham*[3] is a case in which arose most of the questions likely to occur in practice, and a full report of it is here appended The special case was as follows —

[1] *R v Bridgewater Trustees*, (1829) 4 M & R 143 9 B. & C (

[2] *R v Grand Junction Canal*, (1818) 1 B & A 289, also *R v Grand Junction Canal*, (1859) 7 W.R 597

[3] (1868) 19 L. T. 311

1.—This is an appeal against a rate made for the relief of the poor of the parish of Birmingham, in the county of Warwick, on the 27th September, 1862, in which the appellants are rated as follows —

For their offices, weighing machines, engine-houses, steam engines, machinery and works, wharves, and land covered with water, towing-path, reservoir, and feeders, and other land, buildings and premises within the parish, £20,779 gross and £17,277 net

What included in canal rating

2.—The grounds of appeal are sufficient to raise all the questions to be determined in this case.

4.—The appellants were originally incorporated by an Act of Parliament passed in the 8 Geo III. By an Act passed in the 5 William IV,[1] which, as well as every other Act relating to the appellants, may, if necessary, be referred to as part of the case, the Act of 8 Geo III and various other Acts relating to the canal company were repealed, and the company was dissolved and re-incorporated under the style of the Company of Proprietors of the Birmingham Canal Navigations, and the canals and property of the old company were vested absolutely in the new company, the appellants Several other Acts of Parliament have since been passed, authorising new works and extensions, and amalgamating other companies with the appellants, who are now the owners and occupiers of numerous canals in the counties of Stafford, Worcester and Warwick These canals pass through many parishes and townships, and are altogether about one hundred and sixty-two miles in length, of which about five and a-half miles are within the respondent parish The canals are on three different levels First, the level of the canal at the said company's wharf in Paradise Street, Birmingham, called the Birmingham level, secondly, the Walsall level, and thirdly, the Wolverhampton level, and are supplied with water

---

[1] 5 William IV, c 34

A A

principally by means of large reservoirs, into which water is brought by conduits or feeders, and by means of pumping engines. There are altogether five of such reservoirs, and a portion of one of them, known as the Rotten Park reservoir, is situate within the respondent parish. This reservoir is supplied with water, partly by a feeder running from Titford Pool, distant about six miles from the respondent parish to the said reservoir known as the Titford feeder, a portion of which feeder is in the respondent parish, and partly by flood water pumped up by means of engines from a feeder running out of the Wolverhampton level, called the Smethwick feeder, and a part of which latter feeder is also situate within the respondent parish.

5.—The appellants also occupy in the respondent parish a building hereinafter called the "engine-house," in which are erected the steam engines and machinery used for pumping water out of the Smethwick feeder into the Rotten Park reservoir. These engines, etc, are necessarily kept in a continual state of repair and ready to work at any moment, but are only actually used when water is required in the Rotten Park reservoir, which is on an average about twenty days in each year, dependent chiefly upon the state of the rainfall

6.—The canals are carried over numerous valleys, by means of embankment and aqueducts, and through several hills by means of tunnels and cuttings. There are also many flights of locks on various parts of the canals, some of which are within the respondent parish. These reservoirs, feeders, engines, embankments, aqueducts, tunnels, cuttings, locks and works have been constructed at great cost, and are necessary for the working of the canal; considerable outlay is also required for the repair and proper maintenance of the canal and works. Previous to the Act of 4 William IV, the canal in many places pursued a winding course, but that Act authorised the appellants to make certain short cuts, which have since been made

7.—The appellants are not themselves carriers, but their profits are derived from certain tolls (herein called tonnage), which are authorised by their several Acts of Parliament, and are paid to them by persons using the canals for goods, etc, passing along the canals, and also from certain other tolls for wharfage and weighing, which are demanded and paid under 5 William IV., c 34, s 129

12.—The appellants have the following public wharves situate within the respondent parish (1) The wharf in Paradise Street, mentioned in the 128th section of the Act of 5 William IV, commonly known as and herein called the Old Wharf (2) The Bordesley Street Wharf (3) The Oozel Street Wharf. (4) The Nile Street Wharf. (5) The Shadwell Street Crescent Wharf. (8) The Icknield Port Road Wharf, and also a private wharf, called Summer Row Wharf

13.—The following is a description of the Old Wharf

It is surrounded by a wall, and contains altogether an area of 26,494 square yards This wharf is bounded on the east by Suffolk Street, and on the west by Bridge Street The water enters the wharf at the westerly end thereof, under the street called Bridge Street. There is a towing-path along each side of the canal up to and on the west side of the bridge under Bridge Street, at which point the towing-path ceases, and there is no towing-path on the east side of that bridge ; for the sake of distinction the canal on the west side of this bridge is hereinafter called "canal proper.' Directly after the water passes under the bridge into the wharf it expands from about 25 feet (the width of the bridge) to about 150 feet It is then divided into two waterways or basins, running in an easterly direction parallel to and at a distance of about

AA 2

30 yards from each other, and each extending from west to east, a distance of about 200 yards, where the water ends, at about 40 yards from the easterly end of the wharf   In these waterways or basins, boats, after passing over the "canal proper," are moored for unloading or loading.

14—In setting up the mile-stones and fractional distance posts, required by the Act of William IV , s. 128, these waterways or basins in the Old Wharf have always been treated and considered as part of the "canal proper," and the distances have been measured from the easterly end of such waterways, so as to include them as part of the "canal proper," and "tonnage" always has been and is calculated and charged accordingly   The boats are drawn along the canal by horses, and when the boats have arrived at the bridge, at the entrance of the Old Wharf, the horses are detached and the boats pushed into and forced along these waterways or basins by hand power and poles to and are moored at convenient places along either of these waterways or basins for unloading, subject to certain restrictions made by the appellants for the public convenience for the purpose of preventing any boat remaining at the wharf for more than eight hours

15 —Divers coal dealers (who are large traders over the canal) are allowed by the appellants to have the use of certain defined spaces of the Old Wharf, called " Stacking Grounds " for the purpose of stacking and storing their coals, when unloaded from their boats, until required for delivery to their retail customers.   Many of them have offices erected there for the transaction of their business   No lease has ever been granted of these stacking grounds, nor has any rent ever been paid to the appellants for the use of them beyond the sums paid for tonnage

16.—A gangway or path, averaging about 6ft. wide, is, by another regulation of the appellants, required to be at all times kept clear and unobstructed round and adjoining the two above-mentioned waterways or basins, for the convenience of business, as required by Section 117, 5 William IV., c. 34. The occupiers of "Stacking Grounds," however, occasionally encroached, and the foregoing regulations, as to the remaining of the boats, and as to the gangways, are not always enforced. Certain other spaces in the Old Wharf always have been, and necessarily are, also kept clear and unobstructed as carriage and other ways, and for passages for the convenience of business

19 —The assessment upon the wharves has been made by the respondents upon the whole area, each taken as a whole as wharf land, and buildings, with fixtures and machinery attached, and deriving some additional value from the capacity of being applied to such purposes as those of a canal company.

The appellants contend that they are only liable to be rated in respect of the wharves at a sum having regard to the amount of the wharfage tolls actually taken by them in respect of the use of the wharves, or at all events, that the assessment should not exceed the amount authorised to be taken, either as demurrage tolls, or by way of rent, if the wharves were leased or demised under the authority of Section 177 of 5 William IV, c 34.

The assessment made by the respondents has not been limited to the sum actually taken for wharfage tolls, nor to the sum to which the wharfage and demurrage tolls authorised by the Acts of Parliament as hereinbefore mentioned would amount if actually taken, nor to the sum to which the maximum rent would amount if the whole of the ground of the said wharves were leased or demised under the authority of Section 177 of 5 William IV, c 34.

20 —It is admitted that in the following table A, column No 2 shows the assessment that ought to be

made in respect of the said wharves, if the principle contended for by the respondents is correct   Column No. 3 shows the amount at which the same wharves ought to be assessed if the appellants are correct in contending that they are only liable to be rated in respect thereof at a sum

TABLE A

No 1	No 2	No 3	No 4	No 5
Name of Wharf	Net Assessment if the principle contended for by the respondents is correct and if no deduction from the total area is allowed	Amount of net assessment if on amount actually taken	Amount to be added to column No. 3 if the amount of demurrage tolls authorised to be taken is to be included	Amount of net assessment, if on amount of maximum rent of lease
	£ s d	£ s d	£ s d	£ s d
1 The Old Wharf	2,758 0 0			510 14 x
2 The Bordesley Street Wharf	644 0 0			331 4 x
3 The Oozel Street Wharf	440 0 0			323 6 x
4 The Nile Street Wharf	29 0 0			14 10 x
5 The Shadwell Street Wharf	147 0 0	458 13 0		66 9 4
6 The All Saints or Soho Wharf	100 0 0		220 0 0	99 10 x
7 The Crescent Wharf	66 0 0			86 6 x
8 The Icknield Port Road Wharf	76 0 0			178 9 1
	3,880 0 0	458 13 0	220 0 0	1,500 14 x

having regard to the amount of the wharfage tolls actually taken in respect of the use of the said wharves.   Column No. 4 shows the amount, in addition to column No 3, at which the same wharves ought to be assessed, if the amount authorised by the said Act of Parliament to be taken, and not in fact taken, ought to be included, and column No 5 shows the amount at which the said wharves ought to be assessed if the assessment ought to be limited to the maximum amount of rent authorised to be charged under Section 177 of the above Act, if the whole of the ground of the said wharves were demised or leased.

21.—If, however, the contentions of the appellants mentioned in paragraph 19 are erroneous then the appellants contend that, having regard to the circumstances hereinbefore stated, the total area of the waterways or basins as to each of the said wharves (except the Shadwell Street Wharf), and the total area of the several gangways or paths and spaces for carriage and other ways hereinbefore mentioned as to each of the said wharves, ought not to be included or taken into account in the valuation, but should be deducted from the number of square yards which form the area of the whole of each of the said wharves, and the appellants ought only to be assessed as upon the residue after making such deductions

24.—With regard to the portion of the Rotten Park reservoir in the respondent parish, and the portions of the Titford feeder and the Smethwick feeder in the same parish, the net apportionment, if the principle contended for by the respondents is correct, will be as follows, that is to say The Rotten Park reservoir, £559, the Titford feeder, £35, the Smethwick feeder, £380 Whereas the appellants contend that these works have no assessable value beyond what is dealt with in rating the other parts of the undertaking.

25 —With regard to the engine-house, this has been Engine-house assessed at the rent which it is considered by the respondents reasonable for the company to pay as a tenant from year to year. The appellants contend that they ought to be assessed according to the value of the power

involved in the actual pumping work performed during
the year by the engines. According to the mode adopted
by the respondents the annual value of this engine-house
is £445 gross and £360 net. According to the mode
contended for by the appellants the annual value is £35
gross and £25. The appellants also contend that the
rateable value of the buildings ought to be ascertained for
the non-pumping periods, as of a warehouse or storehouse
for machinery, upon the principle of the late cases as to
cotton mills. Upon this principle the annual value of the
engine-house both for pumping and non-pumping periods
will be £150 net.

Canals—how
assessed

26.—With regard to the canal proper, the respondents
have assessed the appellants as follows:—From the total
of the gross receipts along the whole line of the canals
the following amounts have been deducted. 1 Repairs,
ice breaking, salaries, expenses of engines, feeders,
reservoirs, incidental and other charges from the company's accounts of the description usually called
" working expenses." 2. A deduction of the estimated
annual value of all the appellants' works, such as
reservoirs, feeders, buildings, steam engines, machinery,
wharves, etc., which are usually rated separately.
3. Tenant's profits on the estimated amount of tenants'
capital and depreciation on his stock. 4 A reproduction fund. The residue is then taken as the total
rateable value of the whole line of canal proper (but
including rates and taxes), and a part of it is apportioned to the respondent parish in the proportions of
the local to the general receipts, to which mode of
apportionment the appellants do not object. From the
part so apportioned a further deduction is made for the
rates and taxes payable by the appellants in the respondent parish; the balance is then treated by the
respondents as the net rateable value of the said
tonnage and weighing tolls in the respondent parish.

Treated in this way it is agreed that the net rateable value of the appellants' tonnage and weighing tolls in the respondent parish is £8,500, and it is also agreed that the rateable value of the Summer Row Wharf is £313.

27.—To the net rateable value of the said tolls, so ascertained, is added a sum equal to the total annual value of such of the works (deducted under the second item of deductions) as are situated in the respondent parish, and the aggregate amount of these two sums is taken to be the net rateable value of all the appellants' property in the respondent parish. The last-mentioned works (viz, those that are deducted under the second item of deductions) are the engine-house, the eight public wharves before mentioned, the portion of the Rotten Park reservoir in the respondent parish, and the portions of the Titford feeder and the Smethwick feeder in the same parish.

The opinion of the Court of Queen's Bench is requested upon the following questions :—

1.—Is the principle upon which the wharves are assessed by the respondents correct? Or is any and which of the principles contended for by the appellants the correct one? Questions for the Court

2.—Is the principle of assessing the engine-house adopted by the respondents correct? Or is that contended for by the appellants the proper one to apply?

3.—Is the principle of assessing the reservoirs and feeders adopted by the respondents correct? Or have they no assessable value beyond what is dealt with in rating the other parts of the undertaking?

And it has been agreed that the rate upon the appellants, in respect of the matters aforesaid, shall be altered or amended in accordance with that opinion, and upon any principle the Court may consider correct, and that the case may be sent back to the Sessions to make the alteration or amendment.

Cockburn, C J , in delivering judgment, said "You cannot give the whole canal, or those who travel the whole length of the canal, and use parts of the canal, a benefit at the expense of the parish   The parish is entitled to a rate upon the property of the canal for what occurs in Birmingham, and for the profits which might be made in Birmingham, that is to say, not only in respect of the profits which the company do make, but in respect of the profits which the company might make, but which they are pleased to forego, from, no doubt, a very wise policy, namely, that by foregoing those profits in Birmingham they may make a greater profit upon the whole area of the canal   Therefore, Mr Keane's contention is right, that whatever might be the value of this property in Birmingham, the company—which is to make the value that they might extract from it with respect to that—to that extent would be rated. I have expressed my opinion before that as to the reservoir the rate is right   With regard to the ' engine-house ' it has a certain value by reason of the land or the building erected upon it, and of the machinery attached to that building, all of which is necessary for the purpose of the canal   It is situated in Birmingham , it is only made available and put to a particular use on certain occasions, or, if you like, in certain contingencies, nevertheless it must always be there ; it has a certain value with respect to the land and buildings upon it, and the machinery permanently affixed to it, and in that respect I think it ought to be rated, whether it is used all the year or not."

Although it will be seen from this that canals are assessed on the basis of receipts and expenses, it must be remembered that it does not touch the question of rating tolls collected by the proprietors of the canal   Tolls *per se* are not rateable [1]

[1] *R* v *Milton*, (1819) 3 B & A 112, also *R* v *Palmer*, (1823) 1 B & C 516, 2 D & R 793, also *R* v *Oxford Canal Co* , (1829) 5 M & R. 100 , 10 B & C 163.

In estimating the rateable value of a canal, the private Canals under private Acts Act of Parliament granting the owners permission to construct and occupy the same should be carefully studied, as in most cases special reference is made to the parochial rates and taxes to be paid by the owners.[1]

With regard to the deduction to be made under the Working expenses heading of working expenses, the expense of collecting the tolls, of repairing the banks of the canal, of supplying it with water, and the rates and taxes paid by the canal proprietors are legitimate deductions[2], but with regard to the expenses necessary to maintain the locks in good working order, these are to be distributed over the whole system on the mileage principle, and the expense of maintaining any lock is not to be deducted from the receipts in the parish in which the lock is situated[3]

In concluding this chapter on canals, it would be well to point out that a canal company is only rateable for artificial cuts, and that where a company made use of a natural river course, it was held that they only possessed an easement.[4] Canals are only assessable at one-fourth General District Rates of their annual value for the purposes of the General District Rates. Section 211 of the Public Health Act, 1875,[5] enacts that " The occupier of any land covered with water, or used only as a canal or towing-path for the same, shall be assessed in respect of the same in the proportion of one-fourth part only of such net annual value thereof "

---

[1] See with regard to this the following cases —*R v St Peter's the Great, Worcester*, (1826) 5 B & C 473, *Regent's Canal Co v St Pancras Assessment Committee*, (1877) 3 Q B D 73, 47 L J M C 37, 37 L T 637, 26 W R 281, *Warwick and Birmingham Canal Co v Birmingham (Guardians)*, (1860) 27 L T 487, *R v Glamorganshire Canal Co*, (1860) 3 El & El. 16, 29 L J M C 238, 6 Jur N S 1146, *R v Grand Junction Canal Co*, (1818) 1 B & A. 289, *R v Chelmer and Blackwater Navigation Co*, (1831) 2 B & A. 14, *R v Leeds and Liverpool Canal Co*, (1804) 5 East 325

[2] *R v Oxford Canal Co*, (1829) 5 M. & R 100, 10 B & C 163

[3] *R v. Coventry Canal Navigation Co*, (1859) 1 El & El 572, 28 L J M C 102, 5 Jur. N S 862

[4] *Manchester, Sheffield and Lincolnshire Railway Co. v Doncaster Union*, (1894) 71 L T 585, 10 T L R 567, 6 R. 280 H.L.

[5] 38 & 39 Vict, c. 55.

CHAPTER VI.

TRAMWAY UNDERTAKINGS.

THE method to be adopted in valuing tramway under-takings is similar to that already given as applicable to either railways or canals

A tramway company, however, unlike a railway company, has not exclusive occupation of its line of way, sets of rails are laid down in the roadway, and although by the Tramways Act, 1870,[1] exclusive right is given to the use of the tramway for carriages with flange wheels, or other wheels suitable only to run on the prescribed rail, and Section 54 of the same Act imposes a penalty upon persons who may use the tramways with carriages with flange wheels, or other wheels suitable only to run on the prescribed rail, yet by Section 57 of the same Act it is enacted that the company shall not acquire, or be deemed to acquire, any right other than that of user of any road along or across which their tramways are laid, and by Section 62 it is enacted as follows —" Nothing in this Act, or in any bye-law made under this Act, shall take away or abridge the right of the public to pass along or across every or any part of any road along or across which any tramway is laid, whether on or off the tramway with carriages not having flange wheels or wheels suitable only to run on the rail of the tramway "

Sections 29, 30, 31, 32 and 60 of the Act preserve the right of certain public and other authorities to alter and divert the road, and Section 32 further provides—" That the authorities shall not be liable to pay to the appellants any compensation for injuries done to the tramway by

---

[1] 33 & 34 Vict , c 78

the execution of the work for which the section provides, or for loss of traffic occasioned thereby, or for the reasonable exercise of the powers so vested in them as in the section provided " It was the construction of these Acts that formed the chief questions before the Court in the case of the *Pimlico, Peckham and Greenwich Tramways Co* v. *The Assessment Committee of the Greenwich Union* [1]; but it was, however, held that tramway companies were rateable, as they had an occupation of the soil of the road like the occupation of gas and water companies

Blackburn, J, in delivering judgment, said "When once we understand the facts of the case, I think there is no difficulty in saying that the promoters are the occupiers of property rateable under the Statute. I perfectly agree in what Mr. Giffard laid down as his first proposition, that in order to be liable to be rated the parties must be shown to be in occupation of some portion of the road, but I do not agree with him in limiting the land to what is, in the popular sense, the 'earthy' part, if I may call it so I think, if they are occupiers of land in the sense that they are in the exclusive occupation of any portion of it, whether above or below, they are liable to be rated, but they must be shown to be occupiers. I also agree with what was decided in the case of *R* v *Jolliffe* [2] Where a person merely enjoys a right to go across land in the sense of a right of way or wayleave, he is not in the occupation of land and is not rateable It may be that the actual occupier, if he takes payment, may have the value of his occupation enhanced in consequence of that, or it may be otherwise, but a person who has no more than a mere easement to go across the land, or drive over it, would not be an occupier of the land, and would not be rateable.

Occupation of land by a tramway company

---

[1] (1873) 43 L J M C 23, 29 L T 605

[2] (1787) 2 Term Rep 90

"But then, when we come to look at what the present case is, we find this, that under the Tramway Act authority is given to the promoters, under certain conditions which I need not at present enumerate, to lay down along the roadway a tramway, and to make it in such a way that along that tramway there may be room for a carriage which has a flange going into a groove or a space, which keeps it upon the way, and the tramway is laid down solely and entirely for the purpose of facilitating the use of such carriage with these flanges along that portion of the ground over which the tramway is made That being so, we have to see, taking the whole Act together, and not any one particular word of it, whether the object and intention of the Act is not this, that the promoters, who have laid down the tramway for that purpose, are to have the occupation of that portion of the land upon which they lay the tramway, so as to make them the occupiers of land and liable to be rated It seems to me, I think, looking at the whole Act, they are clearly liable for that occupation, the value of which is enchanced, not by the carriages that run upon it, or the horses that draw, or anything of that kind, but by the power of carrying on the traffic upon it It seems to me they are the occupiers of land to the same extent and in the same manner as in the cases which are now perfectly well established, and, indeed, of every-day occurrence, where a gas company or a water works company lay in the road their main pipes and carry them along the road under the surface of the road instead of above it These pipes, which carry the water from the supply to the place where they are to distribute it, are held liable, inasmuch as the company are occupiers of so much of the land as the pipe fills, the beneficial value of which land is increased because it facilitates their carrying gas or water from the point of supply to the point of distribution I am, therefore, of opinion that the promoters of the tramway are occupiers of land in the same sense that the layers of the pipes are. There is a considerable resemblance between the iron tram metal or artificial tramway here and the pipe which is laid down, though there is this difference, undoubtedly, that in the case of the pipe (I do not know that it would be absolutely necessary it should be so) it is generally buried in the soil some way below the causeway, pavement or macadam, which forms the thing actually supporting the carriages upon it. But I do not think that makes any difference. We have it, by the 34th section of the Act, pointed out that when the tramway is laid down, then the promoters of the tramway authorised by the Act may use, on their tramways, carriages with flange wheels, suitable only to run on the rail prescribed by such Act, and subject to the provisions of such Special Act and the Tramway Act, the promoters and their lessees shall have the exclusive use of their tramways for carriages and flange wheels or other wheels suitable only to run on the prescribed rail. Clearer words can hardly be used than these for the purpose of saying that the rails are laid down entirely to facilitate that purpose, and for that purpose the appellants are to have the exclusive right of user. The Act proceeds to say in various sections which have been referred to and quoted, that notwithstanding that the public shall still have all the right of way over the road just as if the trams had not been laid down, and they may drive across it, and may use the rights of road everywhere over it, but they must not use it for the purpose for which it is laid down. Further, it is provided that, notwithstanding the trams are laid down, and notwithstanding the promoters are given the exclusive right of using them, yet the way shall be considered a road, and the appellants shall be subject to pay tolls if they should happen to pass through a turnpike These matters do not seem to me in the slightest degree inconsistent with their being occupiers of

Only tramway company have exclusive right to use rails

that land which is *de facto* occupied by the tramway, laid down for a particular purpose, namely, for their benefit, the user of which for that particular purpose is, by the terms of the Act, given exclusively to them. It seems to me, therefore, that they are occupiers and liable to be rated , judgment must be given for the respondents '

Lush, J , following " The Act of Parliament enables the proprietors of a tramway to appropriate to their own purpose a given portion of the public road for the purpose of laying down the rails or trams which are requisite for the conveyance of their carriages along the line of road The trams occupy a portion of the soil , they are exclusively used by the tramway company for the purpose of the tramway, and that, I think, makes them occupiers of that portion of the soil   I do not think they are the less occupiers because the public still have the right of passing over the surface of their iron road   The road as a tramway is in their exclusive use and used for their exclusive benefit , therefore, I agree in thinking they are occupiers, and must be held to be rateable "

Quain, J , following " I am unable to distinguish this case from the cases which have been decided upon the occupation of land by water companies and gas companies The principle upon which those pipes are rateable is laid down in the case of *R v The West Middlesex Waterworks Co* [1] by Mr Justice Wightman. ' In this case the first question is, whether the company are rateable for their mains, which are laid under the surface of the highway, without any freehold or leasehold interest in the soil thereof being vested in the company ? We think they are these mains are fixed capital vested in land. The company is in possession of the mains buried in the soil, and so are *de facto* in possession of the space in the soil which the mains fill, for a purpose beneficial to itself

[1] (1859) 1 E & E 716, 28 L J M C 185

The decisions are uniform in holding gas companies
to be rateable in respect of their mains, although the
occupation of such mains may be *de facto* even, and
without any legal or equitable estate in the land where
the mains lie by force of some Statute' It appears to
me that no difference can be pointed out in this case and
those of gas and water mains, except that the gas and
water mains are deeper in the soil than this iron tramway.
According to the 25th section of the Act of Parliament
the upper surface of the iron tram must be on a level
with the road; therefore, there is the difference that the
one is placed deeper in the soil than the other. But I am
unable to distinguish the iron tram from the gas and
water pipes, both physically occupy the soil, one is
somewhat deeper than the other, the tram having the
upper service level with the road, but they both occupy
the soil of the road physically and in exactly the same
manner   I do not see either in the 57th or 62nd section
of the Tramway Act any provision which in any way
interferes with that principle, they only preserve the
rights of the public to or over the surface as before, but in
no way is it stated that the tramways so made and the
baulks of timber upon which they are laid are a part of
the road, in the sense of being the property of the public
authorities   They remain the private property of the
tramway company, who by means of that iron tramway
and its foundations, the baulks of timber, are occupying
the soil of the road in the same manner exactly as it is
occupied by gas pipes and water pipes, and I think are
rateable also "

The parochial principle, as applied to railway companies, is the correct method to be adopted in valuing
tramway companies. The total gross receipts over the
whole system must form the basis of the rent, and, therefore the gross receipts in the parish are the basis of the

rateable value in the parish.[1]   But upon this point difficulties arose in the case of the *London United Tramways* v *Brentford Union*, see *post*, p 371

In ascertaining the gross receipts of a tramway
company, the money received from advertisements on the
cars must be considered as part of the gross receipts of
the line [2] This is obvious from the fact that the tramcars
earn money by carrying and exhibiting advertisements in
exactly the same way as money is earned by the carrying
of passengers.

Tramways are assessed for the purpose of the General
District Rate at the full value—see *Swansea Improvement
and Tramway Co* v *Swansea Urban Sanitary Authority* [1]

A large number of modern tramways, however, are
constructed under the Light Railways Act of 1896,[3]
and it has been held that they are entitled under
Section 211 of the Public Health Act of 1875[4] to
claim the advantage of that Act and be rated at one
quarter of their net annual value [5] See also the case of
the *Blackpool and Fleetwood Tramroad Co* v *Thornton
Urban District Council* [6]

Electric
tramways,
light rail-
ways, etc.

With regard to electric tramways, light railways, etc.,
although there is no reported case as far as the writer
can ascertain, it is clear that they should be assessed in
the same way as horse tramways, steam or cable tram-

---

[1] *Swansea Improvement and Tramway Co* v *Swansea Urban Sanitary
Authority* (1892), L R 1 Q B 357, 61 L J M C 124, 56 J P 248,
also *London Tramways Co* v *Lambeth Assessment Committee*, (1875)
31 L T 319.

[2] *North Metropolitan Tramways Co* v *St Mary's, Islington*, (1874)
" Ryde's Metropolitan Rating Appeals," 112

[3] (1896) 59 & 60 Vict., c 48

[4] (1875) 38 and 39 Vict., c 55

[5] *Wakefield and District Light Railway Co* v *Wakefield Corporation*
(H L, 8th May, 1908), A C 293, 77 L J K B 692, 99 L T 1

[6] (1907) (C A, 23rd January), 1 K B 568, 76 L J K B 492,
96 L T 209

ways, on the basis of the receipts and expenditure, duly applying the parochial principle and considering any special provision that may exist in the company's Act.

In the case of the *London United Tramways (1901) v Brentford Union Assessment Committee*[1] the difficulty of applying the parochial principle arose because the tramway company alleged that it was impossible to ascertain the gross receipts in any particular parish. Fares were chargeable between fixed points in such a way as to make it impossible to do this. The Court of Quarter Sessions therefore adopted a method which consisted of ascertaining the rateable value of the running lines of the whole system, and in order to determine the value of the parts in the various parishes a system was adopted of dividing the total assessment by the total number of car miles run over the system, thus ascertaining a value per car mile, and an assessment was allocated to each parish according to the number of car miles in that particular parish, which was information easily obtained

This principle was held by the Court of Appeal not to be wrong, as the circumstances prevented the ascertaining of the gross receipts in the parish

The variation of the parochial systems, where it was found impracticable, was also permitted in the case of the *City of London Union v. Metropolitan Water Board*,[2] dealt with more fully in Chapter VIII.

Variation of parochial principle

---

[1] (1907) (C A , 13th March) 96 L T 528 , 71 J P. 249

[2] (1907) " Konstam's Rating Appeals," 1904-8, p. 33

CHAPTER VII.

GAS UNDERTAKINGS

Valuation of a gas undertaking

PERHAPS the property most often dealt with by rating authorities, with the exception of railway companies, is that of a gas undertaking. The principle which is to be adopted in the rating of such a concern has been dealt with in Chapter V., Part I., and it is now proposed to give a specimen valuation and to treat it by methods similar to those adopted in the case of a railway company, viz., to explain each item.

RECEIPTS

	Half-year June £	Half year December £	Total £
By Sale of Gas	14,050	15,235	29,285
By Rental of Meters	364	375	739
By Ditto, Stoves	77	83	160
	£14,491	£15,693	£30,184

WORKING EXPENSES

	Half-year June £	Half-year December £	Total £
MANUFACTURE OF GAS			
To Coals, including Carriage and Labour ...	9,009	9,788	18,797
Purifying Materials and Labour . ..	292	181	473
Total Value of Coals carbonised during the year, and of Purifying Materials and Labour			£19,270
Less Residual Products Sold—Coke, Ashes, Tar and Sulphate	£5,000	£4,852	9,852
Net cost of Coal and Purifying Materials and Labour ..			£9,418
Salaries	£200	£200	
Wages at Works	1,246	1,236	
	£1,446	£1,436	2,882
Carried forward			£12,300

	Half-year June £	Half-year December £	Total. £
Brought forward			£12,300
DISTRIBUTION OF GAS.			
Wages, etc	£134	£129	
Repairing and Renewing of Meters, Tools, etc	427	234	
	£561	£363	£924
MANAGEMENT			
Directors' Allowance	£180	£186	£366
Salary of Secretary	72	96	167
Collectors' Commission and Clerks ...	362	340	702
Stationery and Printing	40	53	93
Incidentals	27	24	51
Auditors' Allowance	22	22	44
Working Expenses, less Rates and Taxes			£14,647
GROSS RECEIPTS			£30,184
WORKING EXPENSES, less Rates and Taxes			14,647
NET RECEIPTS, plus Rates and Taxes .. .			£15,537

TENANT'S ALLOWANCES

Interest 5 per cent, Trade Profit 10 per cent	on	£16,061	2 811
Risks and Casualties 2½ per cent .			
GROSS VALUE of Entire Undertaking, plus Rates and Taxes £12,726			

STATUTABLE DEDUCTIONS

Repairs, Maintenance of Works and Plant, including Renewal of Retorts and Labour, half-year June	£1,099
Ditto Ditto half-year December .	1,339
Repairs, Maintenance and Renewal of Mains and Services, half-year June	734
Ditto Ditto half year December ..	222
	£3,394

INSURANCE

Say	50	3 444
RATEABLE VALUE of Entire Undertaking, plus Rates which must be deducted as they occur		£9,282

The principle of receipts and expenses is adopted, as will be seen by this valuation, it having been held by the Court that the rateable value of the mains and service pipes of a gas company is the rent which a hypothetical tenant would give, a sum that can only be ascertained by estimating the amount of profit that would be derivable from the undertaking.[1]

The gross receipts are first ascertained from the company's published accounts; the working expenses are then deducted, and the result will be the net receipts of the concern. Interest has then to be allowed on the tenant's capital, which, being deducted from the net receipts, leaves the annual rent at which it might be expected the whole hereditament would let to a hypothetical tenant; this is the gross value, or, in other words, the gross amount which a landlord would receive as rent. The statutable deductions have then to be made, and the result will be the rateable value of the entire undertaking. Proceeding to take each item more in detail:—" Gross receipts "—these include, in addition to the receipts from the sale of gas, the receipts from the rental of meters and of stoves. In the event of any bad debts having been contracted by the company it would be only equitable that these should be deducted. It will be seen that the valuation is based upon the accounts for one year; this point was brought up in the Gas Light and Coke Company appeal, heard before Sir Peter Edlin at the London Sessions in 1891 (and reported in "Ryde's Rating Appeals," 1891-93), where it was decided that the calculation of the rateable value may be based on the accounts of the year immediately preceding the date on which the valuation is delivered; that is, should the Valuation List be signed in February, the last half-yearly account

Gross receipts [margin note]

[1] See *R v The Cambridge Gas Co*, (1838) 8 A & E 73; 7 L J. M C. 50; 3 N & P 262; also *Sheffield United Gas Co v Sheffield (Overseers)*, (1863) 4 B & S 135; 32 L J M C 169; 11 W R 1064

published before that date may be taken, together with the one immediately preceding it.   Outside the Metropolis the last account published before the date of the rate apparently should be the datum for the valuation   Most gas companies make up their accounts in June and December, and in such circumstances the accounts to be taken would be those of the year ending the 31st December, if the rate is made in April.   It was, however, held in the case just referred to that accounts could be put in as evidence to show whether or not the profits were increasing or decreasing, and it would be advisable, therefore, when making a valuation of a gas company (and for the matter of that of any company where the principle of receipts is adopted), that the last three financial years' accounts should be taken into consideration, not necessarily for the purpose of directly using the average, but as furnishing criteria whereby a more satisfactory result would be arrived at, both in the interests of the parochial authorities and of the occupiers of the hereditaments in question

What accounts to be adopted for valuation

The " Working Expenses " have next to be deducted, and it is convenient to divide them into three classes, viz —(1) the working expenses in connection with the manufacture of gas, (2) those in connection with the distribution of gas, and (3) those connected with the management of the company   With regard to the expenses in connection with the " Manufacture of Gas "—these include the cost of the coal and the purifying ·material, with the necessary cartage and labour connected with the same   A gas company has also a further source of revenue to those already mentioned, inasmuch as after gas has been extracted from the coal the residue is not useless, and can be sold in the shape of coke, ashes, tar, etc   These are called residual products, and it is perhaps a simpler method to deduct the amount received for them from

Working expenses

the total amount paid for coal, instead of including them under the heading of the "Gross Receipts"—by this means the net cost of the coal is ascertained (see example-valuation). The "Salaries" and "Wages" at works are the next two items, and need no comment With regard to the expenses incurred in the "Distribution of Gas"—these comprise the wages in connection with the distribution, and the repairing and renewing of meters, tools, etc   Then as to the "Management Expenses"—these include the directors' allowance, the salary of the secretary, collectors' commission, and clerks' wages, stationery and printing, incidentals and fees to auditors. Only one of these items calls for remark, viz, the directors' allowance; but it has already been pointed out in a previous chapter that the case of *R v Southampton Dock Co*[1] appears to be conclusive upon the point, and this, notwithstanding that it was brought up again in the *Gas Light and Coke* case, to which reference has also already been made

Tenant's capital

The next item that we have to deal with is the "Tenant s Capital" The amount estimated in the example-valuation is £16,061, and is made up as follows —

DETAILS OF TENANTS CAPITAL

	£
Five months Working Expenses, $\frac{5}{12}$ of £14,647	6,103
Eight weeks extra Allowance Stock of Coals, $\frac{8}{52}$ of £18797	2,891
Stock of Residuals on hand —Coke, Ashes, Oxide, Sulphate and Tar	317
Cash at Bank	1,800
Tenant s Tools and Chattels at Works	850
Stock of Stoves on Hire and in Store	1100
Present value of Meters on Hire	3,000
	£16 061

---

[1] (1851) 14 Q B 587, 20 L J. M C 155, 6 Rail Cas 428 17 L T O S 460, 15 J P 145

There is no item in any valuation which gives rise to more contention than that of the "Tenant's Capital." For example—supposing certain gas works to be taken at a given rent, and the occupier proceeds to work the same for the purpose of making a profit, to do this it is readily seen that he would require a certain amount of working capital, and the point to be settled is What portion of the works belongs properly to the landlord and so is included in the rent paid for the hereditament, and what amount of money (or capital) would the tenant have to find to provide the necessary articles for the purpose of carrying on the undertaking, in addition to the other working and management expenses, which would include the cost of coal and the distribution of the gas? That which constitutes the freehold belongs to the landlord, and it will be well to refer to the chapter on machinery, with particular reference to the *Tyne Boiler* case[1] and other decisions, so that it may be perfectly clear as to what constitutes, on the one hand (with regard to a machine), a chattel and not part of the freehold, and on the other, what would be considered so to belong to the hereditament that it would constitute part of it and therefore be included in the rent paid. The first item in the tenant's capital is the working expenses   A tenant entering upon the management of an undertaking of this description would require a certain sum, which he would have to disburse in cash ; the occupation would continue for at least three months before any accounts would be rendered to his consumers, so that, with the exception of certain receipts, chiefly derived from the sale of residual products, or from the slot meter system, no money would be received by the tenant at least for that period.   It would be necessary, therefore, to allow a certain sum to meet this contingency. In the example given, five months' working expenses are allowed, but

[1] (1886) L R 18 Q B D 81, 56 L J M C 8, 55 L T 825

this amount may often be less than this   The reason for this allowance is that a tenant of a gas company, in the same way as any other trading concern, would have to allow a certain amount of credit   In the *Gas Light and Coke* case before referred to various amounts were taken by the several witnesses engaged in the case   Mr. J. W Field, the accountant of the company, allowed five months of the net amount of working expenses, the late Mr Edward Ryde, surveyor, who was a witness for the respondents, likewise allowed five months' working expenses, whilst two other surveyors, also for the respondents, allowed four and a-half months' working expenses as sufficient allowance for the hypothetical tenant

Slot
installations   Of recent years the introduction of what is known as " slot installations " on the part of gas companies has had, however, the effect of reducing the allowance of five months' working expenses to the tenant   It has been observed that the ordinary consumer receives an account quarterly, but the introduction of the penny-in-the-slot machines brings revenue to the company which is practically a cash transaction   The consumer who has a slot installation upon his premises virtually pays in advance, because before he can obtain a supply of gas he has to put into the slot receiver a penny, or other coin, as the case may be

The collection of this money is made at frequent intervals, and it therefore follows that the reason for allowing so much as five months' expenses to a tenant disappears where a company's revenue is largely made up of sales under this heading

In the case of the *South Metropolitan Gas Co.* v *Woolwich Union*[1] Mr T Dinwiddy, who gave evidence on behalf of the respondents, the Woolwich Union, in

---

[1] (1907) Reported in " Konstam's Rating Appeals " (1904-1908), Vol I, p 48

estimating the tenant's capital of that company, allowed four and a-half months' working expenses, but from this sum he deducted four average months' automatic receipts (slot meters) and he also deducted the average consumers' deposits, which amounted to a considerable sum, and, although there is no dictum in the judgment sanctioning such a course, the fact remains that the appeal was dismissed with costs and the rate upheld, thereby justifying the principle that Mr Dinwiddy adopted

It will be seen that an allowance is made for an extra stock of coal; this is because a prudent tenant would have to keep a certain amount of coal on hand to provide for strikes, temporary increase in the price of coal, or similar contingencies There can be no doubt that the quantity allowed in the example, viz, eight weeks' consumption, is a large amount but in a debateable question, such as this is, the example must not be considered as an invariable amount

The stock of residuals on hand can be obtained from the accounts published by the company, and having added to the amount of rates and taxes payable by the company an estimated sum for cash at bank, we next come to the question of "Tenant's Chattels.' It will be seen that the stoves and meters are included in the tenant's capital, and it has been held that these, *inter alia*, constitute the necessary tools or chattels with which a tenant would have to supply himself. In the case of *R. v. Overseers of Lee* [1] it was sought to include the retorts as part of the tenant's capital. The sum as stated by the appellants was as follows —

Working Capital	£50,000
Present value of Meters ..	35,000
Present value of Retorts	18,000
Present value of Fixtures and Utensils	97,000
	£200,000

In the course of the case (*vide* Law Journal) it was contended on behalf of the respondent that deductions of a percentage of £5 per cent for interest, £10 per cent for tenant's profits, and £2 10s per cent for risks and casualties upon present value of meters, present value of retorts, and present value of fixtures and utensils, should not be allowed, inasmuch as the matters in respect of which the deductions were claimed, and which are more particularly described hereafter, were fixed to or connected with the land, and, instead of diminishing, increased its value for the purposes of rating.

Meters

Meters, in all cases, were placed on the premises of the consumers They were not in any way connected with the manufacture, nor were they indispensable, although used for the distribution of gas and the earning of profits They were maintained in their position by being soldered to the service-pipes, which were made of lead. Meters were taken off when they required repair or renewal, or for other causes, and were replaced by others, and when repaired were frequently placed in a different house and in a different parish

Description of retorts

Retorts are the instruments in which the coals are carbonised and the gas produced, and they consist not merely of the circular pieces of clay to which the heat is applied, but also of the arches which contain them, the pipes which permit the gas to ascend from them, the iron faces of them, and the pipes over the arches which convey the gas from them through the purifiers to the tanks, where it is received by the gas-holders All the parts which are above the floor level are included in the term "retorts," and the whole of these parts are distinct and separable from the foundation or basement floor, and are not attached to it by mortar or cement, but are packed with fire-clay, which hardens by the action of the heat and holds them in their place The parts of the retorts above the floor-level are very perishable. By wear and

tear caused by the action of the heat and other processes
of the manufacture of gas, they are soon rendered useless,
and require to be renewed every two years   They are,
therefore, so constructed as to be removable without
difficulty and without injury to the basement on which
they rest

Purifiers are massive iron vessels, standing on a brick   Description
base, but not fixed thereto   They are, however, con-   of purifiers
nected, on the one side, with the pipes passing through
the soil from the retorts in which the gas is produced, by
screwed bolts fastened into the plates of the purifier, and
on the other with main pipes, similarly attached, passing
through the soil to the tanks and gas-holders, where the
gas is stored for use   The purifiers may be described as
groups of hollow cylinders or columns of iron, perpen-
dicularly set up parallel to each other on the brick base,
closed at the top by movable lids, retained in their place
by their own weight, and rendered gas-tight only by
means of their edges resting in a water lute or circular
channel containing water, and running round the top of
the cylinder   The gas passes from the retorts through
the purifiers to the tanks and gas-holders, and in its
passage is purified by a chemical process

Gas-holders or gasometers are hollow vessels of plate   Description
iron, cylindrical in form, open to the bottom, but roofed   of gasometers
in with the same materials, and are used for storing the
gas until required for consumption   They are not fixed
in any way, but are so placed that as they fill with gas
they rise, or as they are emptied they fall into circular
tanks excavated beneath the surface of the soil, into
which the gas passes through the purifiers from the
retorts   Around the edges of these tanks are placed
irons columns   Gas-holders are fitted on their upper
rim or edge with wheels, which run on the columns,
and guide the gas-holder in its ascent   In some cases,
also, chains are attached to gas-holders, and pass over

the top of the columns. To the other end of these chains can be attached weights, by which the weight and pressure of the gas-holder can be at pleasure regulated. They do not last more than twenty years

The balance of the £97,000 referred to in the tenant's capital, as set out above, after deducting the then present value of the purifiers, steam engines and boilers, and of the movable part of the gas-holders, represented the then present value of various trade fixtures, such as pumps and exhausters, which are fixed to the freehold, but under such circumstances and in such a manner that, under the law governing the right to remove fixtures, a tenant who during his term had erected and fixed them for the purposes of his trade would during his term have the right to sever and dispose of them. The original cost to the company of the property valued at £97,000 exceeded this sum by £25,000

Questions for the Court

The question for the opinion of the Court in the case of *R* v. *Lee*[1] was, whether it was competent for the Court of Quarter Sessions to allow a deduction by way of tenant's profits in respect of any, and, if any, of which of the matters and things comprised under the heads "meters," "retorts," "tenant's trade fixtures" and "utensils"—*i e*, purifiers, gas-holders, etc. ?

R v. *Lee*

Cockburn, C J, in delivering judgment, said "I am of opinion that the appellants are not entitled to the substantial deductions from the rateable value of their property which are claimed by them. Whatever doubt hung over the case at the commencement has been entirely removed by the arguments which we have heard I entirely agree with the proposition that we must look not at the position of the actual tenant and the fact that he has had to pay down an additional sum for machinery and fixtures which are necessary for the working of the gas establishment, but that we ought to

_____

[1] (1866) L R 1 Q B 241

consider what would be the rent, taking the whole concern as it stands, that an imaginary tenant would be ready to pay Everything which is merely a chattel, and would not pass under a demise from the actual to an imaginary tenant, should be of course excluded from our consideration This being the case, there is really no difficulty in saying what, if any, are the deductions which the company are entitled to have made from the rateable value of their premises In the first place, I think that the counsel who have last addressed us have entirely failed in showing that meters are anything more than common chattels With regard to the rest of the articles, they may, I think, be ranged under two classes, both of which may properly be taken into account as enhancing the value of the building I am satisfied that the retorts are so permanently attached and annexed to the freehold as to become part of it, and that they must not be dealt with as removable fixtures They are, therefore rateable as the entire freehold would be As for the other items, they seem to me to fall within the principle cited in the argument, those of *R* v. *The Southampton Dock Co*[1] and *R* v *The North Staffordshire Railway Co*[2] In the latter case the Court, in a considered judgment, laid down this rule, ' that where things which, though capable of being removed, are yet so far attached as that it is intended that they should remain permanently connected with the purposes of the undertaking as a railway, or the premises connected with it, and to remain permanent appendages to it as essential to its working, these must be taken to be things increasing the rateable value of the land, and in respect of which the company were not entitled to have a deduction made ' That principle

Retorts rateable

---

[1] (1851) 14 Q B 587 , 6 Rail Cas 426, 20 L J M C 155, 15 Jur 268, 15 J P. 145

[2] (1860) 30 L J M C. 68 , 7 Jur N S 363 , 3 L T N S 554, 9 W R 235

applies directly to the present case No one can doubt
that the purifiers and the gas-holders are part of the
works which are absolutely necessary for the manufacture
of gas, which is the purpose of the undertaking, and that
it was intended that they should remain permanently
connected with the premises. Now, if the company
proposed to abandon their undertaking and to let their
premises, the gas works, which the lessee would propose
to take and to pay rent for, the land would not be stripped
of purifiers, retorts and gas-holders These articles are
as essential to the manufacture of gas as any fixture upon
the premises, however firmly it may be attached to the
freehold There is also another rule which applies to
these articles, that in *Walmsley* v *Milne*.[1] There the
owner of land mortgaged it, and afterwards erected
buildings upon it for the more convenient use of the
premises in his business of an innkeeper, brewer
and mill proprietor He affixed a steam engine and
boiler, a hay-cutter, a malt-mill or corn-crusher, and a
pair of grinding-stones The lower grinding-stone was
fixed on to the floor of part of the premises by means of a
frame screwed to it, the upper one being fixed in the
usual way, and the steam engines and other articles,
except the boiler, were fastened by means of bolts and
nuts to the walls or the floors for the purpose of steadying
them, but were all capable of being removed without
injury either to themselves or to the premises (It is
possible that some of the articles here, such as the steam
engine, the purifier, and the gas-holders may be removed
without injury to themselves or the premises) The
Court, after saying that it appeared as a matter of fact that
all these articles were firmly annexed to the freehold for
the purpose of improving the inheritance, and not for any
temporary purpose, and that the owner who had
mortgaged the premises, after having attached these

---

[1] (1859) 7 C B N S 115, 29 L J C P 97

articles to the freehold in the manner described, proposed to take them away as belonging to him and not passing under the mortgage, go on to say ' When the mortgagor (who was the real owner of the inheritance), after the date of the mortgage, annexed the fixtures in question for a permanent purpose, and for the better enjoyment of his estate, he thereby made them part of the freehold which had been vested by the mortgage deed in the mortgagee, and consequently the plaintiffs, who were the assignees of the mortgagor, cannot maintain the present action ' So here we cannot doubt that when these purifiers and gas-holders, and the steam engine and boiler, which are absolutely essential to the working of the manufactory were erected, it was intended that they should remain where they were for the benefit of the inheritance I therefore think that upon both the grounds which I have specified, the articles in question are so connected with the freehold as to show an intention that they should remain permanently attached, and that the Sessions were wrong in allowing deductions in respect of them These deductions must be disallowed, and the rate *pro tanto* increased."

Following this judgment Blackburn, J, said "I am of the same opinion. By the Parochial Assessment Act [1] the rateable value of premises is to be determined according to the rent which a hypothetical tenant, making all suitable deductions, would give for the rateable property. The Sessions very properly endeavoured to ascertain the amount of that rent. Now the property in this particular parish is a portion of a larger property belonging to the gas company in this parish and in others The first thing, therefore, which the Sessions had to do was to ascertain the rateable value of the whole property of the company, and afterwards to find out what portion of it belonged to this parish In this endeavour they

[1] 6 & 7 William IV , c 96

could not ascertain the ordinary rent, as it is not usual in practice to let out such property, and they were therefore obliged, as is commonly the case, to ascertain for themselves the elements which a tenant from year to year would take into consideration if the premises were let to him. Now it was admitted early in the case that the question which we have to decide is, What rent would a hypothetical tenant give for the whole value of the rateable property? and although the person who actually did occupy would not pay rent for portions of the property which are fixed to the premises so as to become part of them, although capable of removal, because instead of paying rent for these portions he would purchase them, yet it is allowed that we are to consider what is the rent which a hypothetical tenant would pay looking at the premises with these articles of manufacture annexed to them It was in applying this principle that the Sessions were wrong. I take it to be clear that what the cases have laid down is

Example of a furnished house

this: If you wish to know for how much a furnished house is rateable, you must ascertain what is the rent of the house, and what is the rent for the furniture and fixtures; deduct what is paid for the use of the furniture and those things which form no part of the rateable premises, and the remainder will be the rent for which the house is rateable A question will then arise whether those things in respect of which you purpose to make a deduction are in themselves part of the premises, or, like the furniture, no part of them. Some things are attached to the premises so as to be part of them, although as between the landlord and tenant, and the heir and executors, there is a right to remove them, and of course no allowance can be made for these Other articles, such as movable furniture, are manifestly not part of what is let, and are the subject of an allowance But there are intermediate things with respect to which it is sometimes very difficult to decide whether they are part of the premises or not, and to this class the articles in the present case belong The rule laid down has been that where things are attached to the premises so as to become part of them, although there may be a right to remove them, they are to be looked upon as part of the premises. But if anything is fastened to the premises so as still to remain a chattel, although fixed and steadied for the purposes of use, it never ceases, to use the phrase in the case of *Hellawell* v *Eastwood*,[1] to have the character of a movable chattel, although fixed for the purpose of having the enjoyment of it The ordinary illustration is the case of a mirror, which is screwed to a wall, but still remains a movable chattel, and is no part of the premises. On the other hand, a grate which is built into a chimney, although it is capable of being removed, would still be fixed to the premises so as to be part of them, and, therefore, part of what would be considered as let to the hypothetical tenant, and for which he would pay rent In *Hellawell* v *Eastwood* the Court were dealing with machinery which was fixed, screwed and attached to the premises, and they laid down the rule as being a matter of fact depending upon the circumstances in each case, but principally upon two considerations First, the mode of annexation to the soil or fabric of the house, and the extent to which it is united to them—whether it can be easily removed, *intégre, salve et commode*, or not without injury to itself or the fabric of the building ; secondly, and this is worthy of attention, on the object and purposes of the annexation, whether it was for the permanent and substantial improvement of the dwelling in the language of the Civil law, *perpetui usus causa*, or in that of the Year Book, *pour un profit de l'inhéritance*, or merely for temporary purposes, or the more complete enjoyment and use of it as a chattel. In the case before

---

[1] (1851) 6 Ex R 295

them the Court thought that the articles in question were only put up and fastened for the temporary use and enjoyment of them as chattels; but they clearly and distinctly pointed out two important elements for consideration : first, the degree of annexation ; and, secondly, the object of the annexation. Was the article attached for the improvement of the inheritance or for the enjoyment only of the article itself ?

"In the case of *Walmsley* v *Milne*,[1] which was similar in its facts to *Hellawell* v *Eastwood*,[2] the Court of Common Pleas laid down the same rule, and thought that the machinery attached to the inheritance for the purpose of improving it, became part of it. So also in the case of *R* v *The Southampton Dock Co*[3] the same idea is conveyed. There the articles were cranes, turn-tables, and other machinery, which were, in some sense, attached to the premises of the company by being screwed down, some of them firmly attached, and some not The Court said that an allowance must be made in respect of those articles which were not attached to the freehold, but that no allowance ought to be made for those things which were affixed to the freehold. The rule laid down for the guidance of the Sessions was this —' The articles may be

Three classes of machinery divided into three classes first, things movable, such as office and station furniture, secondly, things so attached to the freehold as to become part of it; thirdly, things which, although capable of being removed, are yet so far attached as that they were intended to remain permanently connected with the railway or the premises connected with it, and to remain permanent appendages to it as essential to its working ' This phrase, as it seems to me, contains the same idea as that in *Hellawell*

---

[1] (1859) 7 C B N S 115, 29 L J C P 97

[2] (1851) 6 Ex R 295

[3] (1851) 14 Q B. 587, 6 Rail Cas 428 15 Jur 268, 20 L J. M C 155 15 J P 145

v *Eastwood*, where, quoting from the Year Book, it is said that one consideration is whether the annexation was *pour un profit de l'inhéritance*, and in the case in the Common Pleas, where the question is stated to be whether the articles are for the enjoyment of the inheritance. The idea is throughout the same. The articles may be but slightly annexed, but if this is done for the permanent improvement of the inheritance, they are rateable. Keeping this principle in view, I was at first disposed to think that some of these articles belonging to gas works were not rightly included in the rate. With the exception of the meters, they are all, although but slightly, attached to the premises. And I think it quite clear that they are, in fact, attached with the view of enhancing the benefit of the premises to which they belong, so as to come within the principle laid down in the cases of which I have spoken. With reference to the meters the case is different. The meters are themselves chattels, except so far as they are attached to the houses in which they are put up. They are attached to the houses by means of a pipe which comes through the wall, and is joined to the meter. If they were attached to the house for the purpose of improving it, they would become fixed property; but it is obvious that the meters are kept as the company's meters, to be used as their chattels for measuring the gas, and were never intended to be for the benefit of the house to which they are attached at all. They are, therefore, no part of the inheritance of the company. Mr. White, indeed, endeavoured to show that a meter occupies part of the space of a house, and therefore the company, by means of the meter, occupied part of the house. But, although the meter is firmly fixed to the house, and steadied by being fixed, it does not make the company the occupier of any part of the house any more (as I observed during the argument) than Mr. Broadwood can be said to occupy

Meters to be allowed

houses by means of pianos which are hired from him   I therefore think that meters were properly made the subject of a deduction, and that a proportionate sum ought to be deducted in respect of them."

After which Lush, J., said "I am of the same opinion   The sum to be arrived at is the net annual value of these premises, that is, the rent at which they might reasonably be expected to let from year to year, free from all usual tenant's rates and taxes, and deducting the expenses necessary for their maintenance in their present condition.   What is the rateable subject which is comprised within the premises to be rated here?   Now, I apprehend that the premises to be rated are to be taken as they are, with all fittings and appliances by which the owner has adapted them to a particular use, and which would pass as part of the premises if they were demised to a tenant.   That seems to me to express what is laid down in two cases which have been referred to   Wherever such fittings and appliances have become so far a part of the premises as to pass by a demise of these premises, they form a part of the rateable subject of the inheritance for the purpose of rating   When we have to apply this test to any particular state of circumstances, the question is not what a tenant might remove, nor what might be taken in execution under a writ against the owner, but what, as between the landlord and tenant, would pass as a part of the premises.   In applying this rule I cannot entertain a doubt that, with the exception of the meters, all the articles which have been the subject of the present discussion would pass as necessarily belonging to the premises   Without the retorts, purifiers, steam engines and gas-holders, the premises would be worthless for the purpose for which they were erected, and could not be used as a gas manufactory   They are all of them fixed and so far annexed to the freehold as to make it plain that they are intended to be permanently placed for

Articles passing by a demise are rateable

the use of the land and buildings as gas works. The meters are on a different footing. They are not a part of the gas works, as they are neither upon land occupied by the company nor fixed in such a manner as to be part of the freehold. I was struck in the early part of the argument with the finding in the case that, according to the practice and courses of business in letting and hiring gas works, the tenant would have to take to and find capital for all the property comprised under the head meters, retorts, tenant's fixtures and utensils, and would have to provide £15,000 for that purpose, and that a deduction in respect of such outlay was to be made in estimating, according to the provisions of the Parochial Assessment Act,[1] what rent a tenant from year to year would give. I sought at first that, as the tenant would take the premises without making outlay by purchasing those articles, the rent he would have to pay would be so much less, and would represent the rateable value of the property. But, upon consideration, I agree with my lord and brother Blackburn that this is not a right view of the case. If the landlord agrees that the tenant should pay down a price for part, that is, purchase part of the freehold, it would be absurd to say that its rateable value is diminished. It makes no difference whether the tenant occupies the whole, or whether, by contract between him and the landlord, he purchases the fixed plant, which, if not so purchased, would be part of the permanent premises. I entirely agree in the opinion that, with the exception of the meters, all the rest of the enumerated articles are rateable, and that no deductions in respect of them ought to be allowed."

Where tenant purchases fixed plant and pays rent for buildings, the rent paid may be less than rateable value.

This judgment is perhaps the most important decision on the vexed question of tenant's capital, and on the subject of machinery its value cannot be over-estimated. Mr Justice Blackburn, in using the simile of a private

----

[1] 6 & 7 William IV, c 98

house, made it quite clear that that which has to be
decided is, what article on any premises is of such a
character that it constitutes part of them? and, on the
other hand, what is the furniture necessary for the
profitable occupation thereof? not necessarily meaning
profit in a pecuniary sense

In the case of the *Ipswich Gas Light Co. v Ipswich
Union*[1] the gas company included in their tenants'
capital, in addition to meters and stoves, the whole of
the cost of the installation where slot meters had been
introduced ; that is to say, they had included the cost
of the pipes throughout the houses where the installation was made and the gas fittings in addition, and
this was held by the Court of King's Bench to be
correct.

Immediately the pipes in the carcase of the house had
been fitted they would, as a matter of law, cease to
belong to the gas company and would be part of the
freehold of the house in question, and they could not
be taken away by the company   It is difficult, therefore,
to reconcile this decision, and it is probable, but for the
findings of the special case, that the decision as to these
pipes would have been different

Portable gas stoves and meters are in a different category, although it may be urged that if the decision in the
Ipswich case is to stand, gas engines which may be
the property of gas companies and let on hire to consumers, should also be included in the tenant's capital,
and, carrying this a step further, the principle would be
identically the same with regard to motors the property
of electric light companies, which are hired to consumers of current.

An answer to this may perhaps be found in this   That
gas engines and motors take the place in factories of

[1] (1907) Reported in " Konstam's Rating Appeals " (1904-1908), Vol II ,
p 699.

steam engines and boilers, and that from the beginning of a long line of cases there has been no other decision than that such articles as steam engines and other plant constituting motive power are part and parcel of the realty and must be rated as such, whereas there has been no such decision with respect to meters, or otherwise the claim in respect of tenant's capital might conceivably so reduce the rateable value of the gas works and mains as to leave it a minus quantity, while, on the other hand, if the gas company had not in fact provided these articles, the rateable value of the same gas undertaking might have been of a considerable amount

What has to be ascertained is the rent at which a gas company would let to a proposed tenant, and, in order to answer this question, a form of valuation has existed based upon the old case of *R* v *Lee*,[1] which form might answer the question very properly as to the amount of rent a tenant could afford to give, but, applying the form to modern conditions, it is found that competition has been so great that gas companies have entered into a field of business which previously was not contemplated, and in addition to being makers and vendors of gas, they have in many cases become financiers to their consumers and have provided them with articles such as gas engines, ornamental stoves for heating living rooms, complete installations of gas fittings and carcase pipes in private houses, etc. An extra charge has been made to the tenant for this convenience, and the company are not the losers thereby, but the effect of adopting the old form of valuation used in the case of *R.* v *Lee*[1] has been to swell the tenants' capital to such an extent that by allowing $17\frac{1}{2}$ per cent thereon, or other rate of interest, the rate-

---

[1] (1866) L R 1 Q B D 241, 35 L J M C 105, 12 Jur N S 225, 13 L T N S 704, 11 W R 311, 30 J P 68

able value may be reduced to a minus quantity, notwithstanding that maximum dividends are paid to the shareholders and the company is in a flourishing condition

It is an anomaly to suggest that a tenant could not be found to give a rent for a hereditament under such conditions, when he is in a position to earn dividends up to 10 per cent. or more, therefore, *primâ facie*, the method of valuation must be wrong if such an absurd result is arrived at, for it does not require an expert to determine that any hypothetical tenant would give a very considerable rent for a concern out of which he can make 10 per cent on his capital invested, although it may be necessary for an expert to determine the exact amount he could afford to pay

In this connection, as has been referred to in Part I (see page 128), the Courts in the case of gas companies have indicated a possible alteration in the $17\frac{1}{2}$ per cent, which has been fixed for so many years, and which, as stated in the judgment in the *Hitchin Railway* case,[1] "has been allowed by most experienced Justices in the country whose knowledge of the world and rating cases entitle their opinion to the greatest weight." In addition to the dictum of Mr Robert Wallace, K C, in the case of the *South Metropolitan Railway Co v Woolwich Union*,[2] it is important to note that Mr Justice Channell, in delivering judgment in the case of the *Ipswich Gas Light Co. v. The Ipswich Union*,[3] stated, in giving his reasons for the inclusion in the hypothetical tenant's capital of the fittings of the slot installations, that "if too much is taken out in this way (that is too

[1] *Great Northern Railway Co v Hitchin Union* (1906), reported in "Konstam's Rating Appeals" (1904-1908), Vol I, p 116

[2] (1907) Reported in "Konstam's Rating Appeals" (1904-1908), Vol I., p 48

[3] *Ibid*, Vol II, p 699

great a deduction by reason of the swelling of the tenants' capital) that must be because the 17½ per cent. which has been applied to the tenants' capital is too high "

A further important consideration is the restriction that Parliament places upon gas undertakings in the shape of the limitations of dividends, and it is difficult to reason why a tenant should be allowed, in addition to 2½ per cent for risks and casualties and 5 per cent. for interest on money, 10 per cent for trading profit for money invested in the company when Parliament have fixed the amount of profit and interest at, say, 10 per cent

In assuming a hypothetical tenant it has been laid down in the case of *Sculcoates Union* v *Hull Dock Co* [1] that the restrictions to which any particular tenant is subject must be taken into consideration when assessing the property in question, therefore to set up the hypothesis that a tenant should be entitled, in addition to a sum for risks and casualties, 15 per cent upon his capital sunk in the concern, when in fact he could not possibly derive more than 10 per cent., is inconsistent

The Legislature have fixed the remuneration of a tenant in the case of most gas companies, and the consumers of gas of any company are virtually taken into partnership with the shareholders of the concern to the extent that it is compulsory upon the company to reduce the price of gas when they reach certain maximum dividends In the case of the *Cannock Gas Co* v. *Cannock Union*, reported in "The Estates Gazette," May 29th, 1909, the amount of the percentage upon tenant's capital was practically the only point in dispute between the parties and the only point seriously raised before the Court For the purpose of that case the

---

[1] (1895) A C 136, 64 L J M C 49, 71 L T 642; 43 W R 623, 59 J P 605

witnesses of the respondents accepted the gross receipts, the working expenses, and the amount claimed as tenant's capital, but they only allowed a tenant's share at the rate of 12½ per cent upon the capital, as compared with the appellant's claim of 17½ per cent   The difference was sufficient to support the assessment and was the practical difference between the respondents and the appellants The Court dismissed the appeal with costs, and although they gave no reason, as this was practically the only point before them, it is suggested that their decision was come to on the basis of 12½ per cent interest to the tenant, made up as to 10 per cent for trade profits and 2½ per cent for risks and casualties

A few weeks later the Peterborough Gas Company appealed to the Peterborough Quarter Sessions. In this case the same point was raised, the company claiming 17½ per cent. and the respondents 12½ per cent   As in the previous case the appeal was also dismissed with costs, and as the respondents' figures could not be justified if 17½ per cent had been applied to their tenants' capital, it is only fair to assume that again in this case 12½ per cent was the amount fixed by the Court

Many years ago at Dover Mr Harry Poland, as Recorder of Dover, in an appeal by the Dover Gas Company, also allowed only 12½ per cent in the case of this company.

Lastly, reference is again made to the case of the *South Metropolitan Gas Co.* v *Woolwich Union*,[1] where the appeal of the gas company was dismissed with costs, although the Court in delivering judgment declined to name any figure which they had applied to the tenant's capital.

In the gross receipts of a gas company there are generally included the rents that are received from gas

---

[1] "Konstam's Rating Appeals" (1904-1908), p 61

stoves, engines, installations, etc., and if these items
were eliminated, in order to ascertain the gross receipts
from the sale of gas, it would be found that the sum
actually received for the hire of these articles would
be considerably less than the amount claimed
by the tenant as interest on the capital sunk, for
it is a common thing for gas companies to invest
money in such chattels, hiring them out to consumers at a percentage to cover a reasonable wear and
tear and interest on money sunk, but when the claim is
made against the rating authorities it is done by a process
which, *inter alia*, includes these chattels as part of the
tenant's capital and a claim thereon of 17½ per cent

It is therefore suggested that in order to arrive at the
value to a hypothetical tenant of a gas company *per se*,
that is to say, at the value to a tenant of making gas and
selling it, the extra business ought to be eliminated, and
from the gross receipts the receipts from hiring out these
chattels be deducted so that they may be omitted from
the tenant's capital, because although the *Ipswich* case
is authority for their inclusion in the tenant's capital, it
was apparently only because in that case the gross
receipts included the hire of these articles

With regard to the deduction of the rates and taxes it
will be noticed that they have to be deducted in the
parish for which the valuation is made, and although some
surveyors deduct them under the heading of "Working
Expenses," perhaps the better method is the one already
suggested

The statutable deductions, that is to say, the expenses
necessary to keep the property in a state to command the
rent, would be the next deduction, the items consisting of
the repairs, maintenance and renewal of plant, mr and
service pipes, will be ascertained from the publis   accounts of the company, and to these should be added a
sum for the insurance of the works, etc., which must be

Statutable
deductions

estimated by taking a percentage on the structural value of them as they exist   There has now been ascertained the rateable value of the entire undertaking, including both dead and live mains, and the rateable value of the works.   It is, therefore, necessary where the property extends to several parishes to obtain the rateable value of the dead works, and this is ascertained upon a basis of their structural value, the value thus arrived at is deducted from the value of the whole. the result being the rateable value of the live mains of the entire undertaking. A simple proportion sum is then made as follows   As the receipts in a parish are to the whole receipts, so will the rateable value of the live mains of a parish be to the rateable value of the whole of the live mains, but from the value so arrived at must be deducted the rates to be allowed in a particular parish in the method set forth in the chapter on railways, then the sum attained will be the rateable value of the mains in the parish.

Live and dead mains   Now as to the question what constitutes " live mains " and what "dead mains"   The definition of these two classes of mains was given in Chapter V., Part 1, under the heading of the side note "Parochial Principle as applied to Gas Companies."   In the case of *R.* v *The West Middlesex Waterworks Co.*[1] the questions before the Court were, Whether the company was rateable for a main which conveyed water for distribution and consumption in parishes other than the one in question ?   And also on what principle the company was to be rated ? Wightman, J , in delivering judgment, said   "In this case the first question is, whether the company are rateable for the mains, which are laid under the surface of the highway, without any freehold or leasehold interest in the soil thereof being vested in the company ? We think they

[1] (1859) 1 El. & El 716, 28 L J M.C 135, 5 Jur N S 1159, 32 L T O.S. 888, 23 J P. 164.

are   These mains are fixed capital vested in land   The
company are in possession of the mains buried in the
soil, and so are *de facto* in possession of the space in the
soil which the mains fill, for a purpose beneficial to themselves   The decisions are uniform in holding gas
companies to be rateable in respect of their mains,
although the occupation of such mains may be *de facto*
merely, and without any legal or equitable estate in the
land where the mains lie, by force of some Statute

" To the second question, requiring the principle to be
stated on which the company are to be rated in respect of
the plant, engine-houses, cottages, buildings, wharves,
mains, land and premises, we answer, in the words of the
Mile End Town case,[1] that it is to be rated as for
' mere land and buildings with fixtures and machinery
attached, and deriving some additional value from their
capacity of being applied to such purposes as that of a
water company '; and we add, such additional value is
derived from an increase of demand beyond supply,
according to the principle regulating exchangeable value,
and not by reference to receipts earned in another parish,
beyond assuming that they are sufficient to pay for all
outgoings, including profits on capital   If an apparatus
occupied by one occupier, consisting of several parts, lies
in one parish, the rate is on the whole and is received by
that parish   If such an apparatus lies in several parishes,
the occupier is liable for the same amount of rateable
value and no more , but that amount is to be apportioned
among the parishes in which it lies , and the question
then arises, as in the present case, What is the principle
which regulates such apportionment ?   It is clear that
each parish must rate the part that lies within it ; such
part becomes a separate rateable subject in that parish,
and must be rated, according to the Parochial Assessment

Gas mains, etc , extending into several parishes

---

[1] *R v Mile End Old Town,* (1874) 10 Q B 208, 16 L J M C 184,
11 Jur 988

Act,[1] upon an estimate of the rent which that part would yield after proper deductions. In practice a tenant of a parochial portion of a canal, railway, gas works, water works, or the like, has rarely, if ever, been known; but a hypothetical tenant must be assumed; and the terms of such a tenancy are not difficult to be conceived, if in the hypothesis some necessary incidents are also assumed to be involved, such as, first, that each part of the apparatus is to continue in joint co-operation, no one tenant of an essential part being able to stop his part; secondly, that the title to the required land is permanent, so that there is no risk of being compelled to move fixed capital; thirdly, that there is land in the required quantity, and capital to be invested therein, and occupants ready to take and work parts yielding profits, as tenants at rack rent, and parts not yielding profit, as contractors for remuneration, provided

Contractor's theory explained

any greater profit can be obtained than is ordinary in such relations. If a tenancy of each parochial part be assumed according to this hypothesis, then, although each parish rates separately upon its own estimate of the value of the part lying within it, and the law gives no power of making all the parishes co-operate in rating the several parts lying in each, nevertheless this Court is bound to protect the occupier of such an apparatus from being rated beyond the rateable value of the whole taken together; and it is in reference to this protection that the Court must take into its consideration at once all the separate rates as so many claims upon one given fund, and must apportion that fund, bearing in mind that every addition to the rateable value assigned to one parish must be a subtraction from the rateable value which might be given to some other parish. Supposing, then, the apparatus to be apportioned to several tenants according to the parts in several parishes, the tenants of the parts

---

[1] 6 & 7 William IV, c 96

directly earning net profits in a parish would be rated
by that parish for all the profits earned therein · this
being the parochial principle of apportionment which has
been unanimously upheld hitherto in respect of all canals,
railways, water companies, gas companies and bridges
But the tenants of the parts directly earning no profit
would not be liable to be rated in respect of any rent in
the ordinary sense, which is profit remaining after all
deductions have been taken from the receipts   But as
these parts of the apparatus directly earning nothing, but
indirectly conducing to such earnings elsewhere, are
assumed to continue in operation, the company, to whose
interest such continued operation is essential, must be
assumed to pay adequate remuneration to a contractor
for land and fixed capital invested therein, together with
the labour and skill requisite for the effective continuance
of such operation, and this contractor with the company
would stand in the relation of occupying tenant to the
parish, and the part within the parish would be the
rateable subject, and the local rateable value would be
such sum as would pay the rent of the land and the profit
on fixed capital therein

"It is said in the *Mile End* case[1] that the parts
indirectly conducing to produce profit are to be rated as
mere land, etc , with some additional value from their
capacity of being applied to such purposes as those of a
water company   The meaning of those words would be
exemplified in this case, if it be supposed that the bank
of the Thames and the underground of the highways in
Hampton were heretofore of no rateable value, but that
when a wharf on the bank was required to raise water
from the Thames, and when the underground of the
highway was required for laying the mains giving transit
to such water, the owners of the soil of the bank and of

---

[1] *R* v *Mile End Old Town,* '847) 10 Q B 208, 16 L J M C. 184, 11
Jur 988

the highway could get some payment for allowing the use
of their soil.   Thus, land which before produced nothing
would produce something, and so have some rateable

How value
derived

value, which would be an addition arising solely from its
capacity for being used for a water company   Value is
derived entirely from the relation of demand to supply,
and if a water company comes into competition with a
mere agriculturist for land for water works an addition is
made to the value of such land by the additional competition   This principle might raise land worth nothing
into being worth something, as above supposed, and land
worth something into higher value, in the case of a site
for a steam engine with yard and shed and cottages
attached, or a site for a reservoir or filtering-bed and the
like   Upon the common principles regulating value, it is
enhanced in proportion to the scarcity of the thing in
demand , so that if a few levels only were suitable for the
required transit, or a few sources of water alone were
accessible, the price would be higher   In this sense, the
words cited above from the *Mile End case*[1] are applied
to the mains in Hampton in their ordinary meaning, and
in the meaning in which they are applied to stations,
warehouses, yards, workshops and the other premises
appertaining to railways and canals, rated on the principle
of indirectly conducing to the direct earnings of railways
and canals   On this principle the company contended
that the rateable value of the part of the apparatus in the
parish of Hampton was to be ascertained ; and we are of
opinion that the company is right

" The parish contended for a higher rateable value : and
it remains to consider on what ground   It was argued
that every part of the apparatus was equally essential for
the delivery of water from Hampton to the consumers in
other parishes, and that therefore the rate should be on

---

[1] *R v Mile End Old Town,* (1847) 10 Q B 208 , 16 L J M C 184   11
Jur 988

the quantity of apparatus in Hampton The answer is two-fold In the first place, all the apparatus is not equally essential. The subject of purchase by the consumer is water delivered at the required place. It matters not to him whether the water has passed from the east or the west, or been raised on the spot from a well Transit of water is not the subject of demand, as in the case of goods or passengers to be conveyed by railways and canals, but the water itself is brought to the service-pipe of the consumer, the junction of such pipe with the main being the source of profit Such delivery is the one indispensable requisite for purchase, whereas the course of transit might be varied in manifold directions, according to convenience, without affecting the value of the water to the consumer. In the next place no definite meaning was, and, as it appeared to us, could be given to 'quantity of apparatus,' for apportionment of rateable value Quantity must be ascertained by some measured, lineal, superficial, or solid, and if any of these measures were applied to steam engines, reservoirs, filtering beds, cottages, mains, and the like, and the rate upon the sum-total of earnings appropriated accordingly, the sum-total would be disposed of upon a principle not more rational than a lottery.

'The cases relating to apportioning the rateable value on water companies are worth consideration In *R* v *New River Co*[1] the question was, whether Amwell should rate Chadwell Mead at £5, or £300 The case stated that no profits arose in Amwell, that the land alone without the spring was of the value of £5 but, if the advantage which the company derive from the use of the spring may by law be included in the rate upon the land, the land and the spring together are of the annual value of £300 The judgment was for the rate on £300 This case has been supposed to sanction the notion that the parish of Amwell

---

[1] (1813) 1 M & S 503

was entitled to rate land in Amwell by reference to profits made in Islington or elsewhere Probably, the parish officers and Sessions may have included a reference to those profits in the amount , but the Court entirely ignores any such reference, and takes the question to be whether the rate is to be on two acres of mere land according to the value of the land of that kind in Amwell, or with reference to its value in the occupation of the company with the power of using it for their purposes, and with capital laid out on it making it fit for those purposes. Lord Ellenborough confines his judgment expressly to the local value in Amwell, for he says 'The water has a certain ascertained local value at the fountain-head.'   'If it has, it is rateable for that value, irrespective of profits which may or may not be derived elsewhere from distribution through pipes'

"In *R v Mayor of Bath*[1] the question of apportionment was also approached, but left undecided , there the Corporation had collected springs in the parish of Lyncomb and Widcomb into reservoirs, and distributed the water there and in Bath, making £50 profit by the sale of water in that parish and £550 in Bath The parish rated for £600, claiming the whole profit, because all the water was derived from the fountain-head ; but the rate was quashed, 'because a large portion of the apparatus and the soil in which the pipes are laid, producing eleven-twelfths of the water rent, is situate in Bath, therefore Lyncomb and Widcomb is wrong in rating for the whole water rent' The source of water, not being rateable for all the profits of the supply, the Court decides that the profit from the water ought to be apportioned, but give no rule for apportioning

Profits to be apportioned

"In *R v Mile End Old Town*[2] the principle of apportionment above mentioned was adopted It has

---

[1] (1811) 14 East 609
[2] *R v Mile End Old Town*, (1847) 10 Q B 208 , 16 L J M C 184 ; 11 Jur. 988

been said to be inaccurate in laying the rate for the direct
source of profit on service-pipes, which belong to the
consumers, because the rate must be on real property
in the occupation of the party rated   The principle of
the judgment is that the direct source of profit from water
or gas is the delivery of the article to the consumer, and
that the instrument of delivery should be rated for the
net profits, and if the service-pipe belongs to the
consumer, the junction of the service-pipe with the main
is in the occupation of the company, and is rateable
Our judgment here is founded on that case, and we have
thus endeavoured to apply the principle there laid down
to the rating of the premises here in question

This judgment is valuable as laying down the method
which must be adopted in assessing "dead mains, and
it now remains to be decided what are 'dead mains '
and what are " living mains " in a parish where both are
situated   In the Gas Light and Coke Appeal before
referred to (see " Ryde's Rating Appeals," 1891-93, page
204), one of the questions before the Court was—On
what principle is the rateable value of directly and
indirectly productive mains to be distributed ? In the
course of the case Mr. H E Jones, the engineer of
the Commercial Gas Company, advanced a theory
that a sum estimated at £19 would be the value of
the mains necessary to supply a parish with one million
cubic feet of gas per annum   he then calculated the
structural value of all the mains situated in the parish,
and, after ascertaining the amount of gas consumed in
that parish, for every million cubic feet of gas sold he
deducted £19 from this total value, the remainder being
the estimated value of the dead mains in the parish. The
witnesses in the case put forward various methods of
distinguishing between the live and dead mains, but the
one ultimately adopted by the Court was the late Mr
Ryde's system of treating all mains with a diameter of

What are
dead mains

24ins and upwards as being unproductive, or dead mains
Of course the size of the dead mains must vary, as it is
easily understood that a gas company supplying only one
parish and having works in another would not need such
large mains for the purpose of conveying gas as a company which might have to carry gas throughout many
parishes, and in larger quantities.

Limitation of dividends Many gas companies have clauses prohibiting a higher
dividend being paid than 10 per cent. or some other figure,
and two very difficult points arise in rating such concerns,
firstly, as to whether the actual receipts and expenses are
to be the only data upon which the valuation is to be
made, and secondly, whether, in the event of the profits
exceeding the amount required to pay the dividends, such
excess of profits over the amount legally divisible should
be considered in making the valuation   Both the points
have been before a Court of First Instance, but neither
has been decided as such   The first point was discussed
in the case of the *Northampton Gas Co* v. *Northampton
Union*,[1] and the second point in the *Gas Light and Coke
Co.* v *City of London Union*, reported in " Ryde's Rating
Appeals " (1891-1893)   It will readily be seen that where
such a limitation of dividends exists it would be possible,
and indeed it actually occurs in several instances, for a
gas company to charge to revenue account items properly
attributable to capital account, that is to say, the profits
so far exceed the amount required for dividends that
new plant and other landlord's property are purchased, and even land, to extend buildings, without
increasing the nominal capital or issuing more shares
The following position then occurs, which to the writer's
knowledge has happened.   So successfully has a gas
company been managed that the works have been more
than doubled since the formation of the company, fresh
land has been bought, and, although the nominal capital

---

[1] " The Estates Gazette,   October 26th, 1901

of the company, which, in the first instance, stood at, say, £60,000 had not been increased, the structural value of the works alone, without considering mains, had been raised to some £150,000, and if 4 per cent. upon the structural value of the works had been taken to represent the value of the dead work in the parish in which they were situated, it would have exceeded the value of the whole concern based on a valuation of the receipts and expenses and thus have left nothing for the many parishes which contained live mains, although in fact the company was so prosperous that it was able to pay a 10 per cent dividend, and the value of its works alone, as stated above, was over twice the value of its nominal capital. The proposition therefore resolves itself into this: if the actual accounts of a company are to be the only data upon which to make a valuation, notwithstanding the extreme prosperity of the company, the parishes in which are situated the live mains will receive nothing in rates, or, in other words, have no value, because in the division of the total value of the concern the assessment on the dead works will swallow up all the value. This is an anomaly, because if the Rating Acts alone are to be considered, it is perfectly clear that the rent a hypothetical tenant would give for such a concern, even admitting that the hypothetical tenant would only be allowed to make 10 per cent net profit, would in practice be found by some other method than the one usually adopted, namely, that of receipts and expenses, owing to the fact that each year so much had been expended out of the revenue account to increase the works, and also that, although only a certain amount was charged to the consumer for the gas, power was given to charge a far higher sum. Moreover, if a landlord were letting such works *de novo*, his capital would amount with the mains very possibly to £200,000, and it would only be reasonable that he should expect a fair percentage on his outlay, and there is no doubt whatever that a hypothetical tenant could afford to pay the same   Under these circumstances, it is very difficult to decide how the live mains should be assessed, and, although there has been no decision in the High Court on the matter, it cannot be suggested that there would be no rateable value to such mains, the cause being the excessive prosperity of the company itself, and while the company, in fact, could pay a very much greater   nt than the accounts *per se* might show, they would   ll be able to pay 10 per cent dividend, although when new works were required fresh capital would have to be issued in the ordinary way

The second point is very much involved in the first, as in cases where the profits in one year exceed the amount required to pay a 10 per cent. dividend, for instance, and are carried forward to a less prosperous year, the point as to whether in the years when the surplus is made it can be taken into consideration for rating purposes as against those years where there is a deficit in the required amount is one of equal difficulty   All these points must be considered as having some bearing on the annual rent a tenant could afford to pay in each individual case

CHAPTER VIII.

WATER UNDERTAKINGS.

As water undertakings bear, in many respects, features identical with those of gas undertakings, many of the books on Rating deal with these two classes of property together, but it seems better to separate them, possibly more for convenience than for any very material points of difference in the method of assessing them for rating purposes.

FORM OF VALUATION OF A WATER UNDERTAKING.

GROSS RECEIPTS

From Water Rents *less* empty Houses, Bad Debts, Overcharges and Rebate ...   £

EXPENDITURE.

Pumping and Engine Charges, including cost of Coal, Wages, etc ...
Filtration, including the cost of Materials and Labour ...
Salaries of Engineers, Superintendents, Inspectors and Turncocks ..
Fees (if any) for obtaining Water .
Allowance to Directors ..
       „ „ Auditors ...
Salaries of Secretary, Accountant and Office Clerks
Commission to Collectors .
Stationery, Printing and General Establishment Charges

£

GROSS RECEIPTS . . . . . . £
LESS EXPENDITURE ...

NET RECEIPTS . .. . £

Carried forward ... £

Brought forward .. £

DEDUCT TENANTS CAPITAL

Say —twelfths of Working Expenses . ⎫
Stores, Implements, etc   ..   ⎪ 17½%
Meters   ..   ..   .. ⎬ thereon
Rates payable in advance   ..   ⎪
Cash at Bank ...   ...   ⎭

Gross Value   ...   £

STATUTABLE DEDUCTIONS

Maintenance and Repair of Impounding and Service
  Reservoirs, Filtering Beds, Works and Pipes for
  obtaining and storing Water, including the cost of
  Materials, Labour, etc   ..   ..
Maintenance and Repair of Mains, Pipes, Fittings,
  Meters and Works connected with the Distribution of
  Water, including the cost of Materials, Labour, etc
Insurance, etc   .   .

Rateable Value of entire undertaking .. £

In an examination of this form of valuation, it will be
noticed that the titles of the various items are similar to
those of a gas company.

Tenant's capital — The sum to be allowed for tenant's capital would be,
in most cases, the chief cause of difference between the
parties. It has been seen in the case of a gas undertaking that the amount of working expenses to be allowed
as part of the tenant's capital must vary considerably, and
it is certain that no definite amount can be used. At the
same time, in making an assessment of a water undertaking, some consideration must be given to the fact that
it is usual for the water rates to be collected in advance
from their customers, while a gas undertaking has to
manufacture gas and then supply it to the consumer,
who pays for it according to the quantity used. This, of
course, has a very important bearing on the question
of the tenant's capital.

In some cases, in valuing water undertakings, owing to
the tenant's capital being so small, and to the probability

that no hypothetical tenant could be found to take the responsibility for so slight a remuneration as $17\frac{1}{2}$ per cent upon such capital, a sum of 10 per cent upon the gross receipts has been allowed, and this has frequently been accepted by both sides as representing a reasonable share to attribute to the tenant in respect of his obligations

The case of *R v West Middlesex Water Co*[1] (ante p 398) is perhaps the leading one on the question of the rateability, and the method to be adopted in ascertaining the rateable value, of water companies Wightman, J, said in the course of his judgment "We answer in the words of the *Mile End Old Town* case[2] that it is to be rated as for mere land and buildings with fixtures and machinery attached, and deriving some additional value from their capacity of being applied to such purposes as that of a water company."

The judgment of Lord Denman, C J, in the *Mile End* case referred to, was as follows —"In this case the rateable subject, being the apparatus for supply of water situate in twenty-one parochial districts, and the rateable value (that is, £30,800), being the residue of the gross receipts, after making all the deductions to which the company are entitled, have been correctly ascertained by the award The principle for dividing that sum among those districts is the matter to be decided The company contend that the division should be according to the amount of fixed capital in each district But the rule of law laid down by Act of Parliament for ascertaining the rateable value of any subject refers to an estimate of the rent it should yield The outlay of capital might furnish no such criterion, since it may have been injudiciously expended, and what was costly may have become worthless by subsequent changes As our

*Mile End
Old Town
case*

---

[1] (189, 111 & 16; 28 L J M C 135, 5 Jur N S 1159, 32 L T O S 388 23 J P 16.

[2] *R v Mile End Old Town*, (1847) 10 Q B 208, 16 L J. M C. 184.

opinion is against the company upon the objection relied on the argument on their behalf, it follows that the rate should be affirmed. But as the award suggests different methods of apportioning the rateable value, and so arriving at the same rate, it would be convenient if we also stated our view of those methods for applying the above rule of law to such rateable subjects as the present. The first step in apportioning has been in effect to divide the whole apparatus, constituting the rateable subject, into two portions, of which one is directly productive of rateable value, being the service-pipes which deliver the water to the consumer, the other indirectly conduces to such production, being the rest of the works, bringing the water to the service-pipes. The second portion has been first rated in the ordinary way by valuing the land with the buildings and fixtures thereon, and the amount of rate so ascertained has been deducted from the sum of rateable value, and distributed to the districts in which the parts of this portion are situate. An analogous course appears to have been adopted for railways in *R.* v *The London and South Western Railway Co.*,[1] *R.* v. *The Grand Junction Railway*,[2] and for gas companies in *R.* v *The Cambridge Gas Co.*[3] Also, the spring, which indirectly conduced to the ultimate profit by water-rate, was held rateable in the parish where it was situate in *R.* v *The New River Co.*,[1] the quantum of such rate being left for the Sessions. As this course was acquiesced in by both parties in the three latest cases, we may presume that it can be applied without practical difficulty, and we see no objection to it.

The remaining step has been to apportion the residue of the rateable value among the districts in which the

Directly productive portion and indirectly productive portion

---

[1] (1842) 1 Q B. 558, 11 L J M C 93, 2 Rail Cas. 629, 3 G. & D. 49.

[2] (1844) 4 Q B. 18, 13 L J M C 94.

[3] (1838) 8 Ad & El 73, 7 L J M C 50

[1] (1813) 1 M & S 503

directly productive portion of the works is situate, in the ratio either of the net profits or of the gross receipts, or of the quantity of mains and pipes and of the land occupied by them in each district. Each ratio in the present case gives the same result. If they differed, it would be necessary to select between them, and that ratio should be preferred which would best show the rent to be expected, if the part of the work situate in the district was let separately. It is clear that the net profits in each parish would be the best criterion of such rent, and they would therefore give the proper ratio. It is also clear that the ratio of the gross receipts or earnings in the several districts to each other will be the same as the ratio of the net profits in those districts to each other, in all cases where the total of expense is taken to be common to the whole of the apparatus, and is deducted from the total of receipts in the progress of ascertaining a rateable value. For, in such case, the net profits in each district would be ascertained by distributing the expense among the several districts, and it would be distributed in the ratio of the gross receipts in each; and if a proportional deduction should be made from the gross receipts in each, the ratios of the remainders to each would be the same as the ratio of the gross receipts. As any attempt to ascertain the net profits in each district in any other way would lead to minute and inconvenient inquiries in practice, the ratio of gross receipts should be adopted as being an index of the net profits, when the rateable value is ascertained in the way stated in the case. We think that an apportionment in this sense, according to the gross receipt, is in accordance with the decisions which have apportioned the sum of rateable value from a railway or canal according to the length of line in each parish—*R.* v. *Kingswinford*,[1] *R.* v. *Woking*.[2] Where the

Net profits : best criterion

Gross receipts in parish data for valuation

---

[1] (1827) 7 B & C 236, 6 L J M C 3

[2] (1835) 4 Ad & El 40, 5 L J M C 17

profit arises from the transit, the line of the canal or railway is directly productive of the profit, and the reservoirs, warehouses, stations, etc, indirectly conduce to such production. Each portion of the line earns an aliquot portion of the profit, and if equal portions of one line carrying at one rate could be conceived to be let separately, no one portion would be let at a higher rate than the other, and an apportionment of a sum of rateable value according to the length of line in each parish is according to the rent to be expected for that part of the line. In the case of water companies, where the profit arises from the delivery of the water at a given place, the previous transit being immaterial to the consumer, the service-pipes immediately produce the profit, and the agency by which the water reaches those pipes indirectly conduces to such production. If the service-pipes in each parish could be let separately, the water being assumed to be sold at the same price throughout, the criterion of the rent would be found in the gross receipts, which would depend on the number and diameter and level of the service-pipes in each parish, and an apportionment according to the gross receipts in each district would be according to the rent to be expected from the part of the rateable subject situate in such district. This apportionment is not at variance with the grounds of the judgment in *R. v The Cambridge Gas Co*[1] There the Court decided that the parishes in which the profits are received are not entitled to all the amount produced by the rate, but that the parishes in which parts of the apparatus indirectly conducing to produce profit are situate are entitled to a proportion. The Court also declared that the principle upon which the sum of rateable value from the rates of all the parishes should be apportioned is the same as that which had been applied to canals. By the method adopted in this case the

Apportionment of rateable line

---

[1] (1819) 8 A & E. 73, 7 L J M C 30

rateability of the portion of the apparatus indirectly conducing to produce profit is provided for, and the residue of the sum of rateable value is apportioned to those parts of the apparatus directly producing profit, in analogy to the mileage proportion for canals and railways. We have thus endeavoured to show that the rule for ascertaining the value for separate rating ought to be applied, as far as practicable, to apportioning among separate districts a sum of rateable value arising partly in each. '

In the case of the *Metropolitan Water Board* v. *The City of London Union*,[1] a case described by the Bench as an unique case, the respondents contended that to apportion the rateable value of the whole concern upon the principle laid down in the case of *R* v *Mile End Old Town*[2] was unfair to them.

It is a matter of common knowledge that the water rate is raised by means of a levy, at the present time amounting to 5 per cent. on the rateable value of the hereditament served. In the City of London, where rateable values are higher than anywhere and the consumption of water considerably less per acre of buildings, owing to the fact that the bulk of the property is non-residential, so that while there is an enormous day population there is a comparatively small night population, it was contended that the value of the occupation within the City boundaries was far in excess of the value of the Board's property in other districts for two reasons. first, the gross receipts from the sale of water, owing to the high rateable value, were infinitely larger per million gallons than elsewhere, and, secondly, the expenses of delivering the water were very much less, but although this was conceded as a fact by both sides, the Water Board contended that it was impossible to ascertain the

---

[1] (1907) Reported in "Konstam's Rating Appeals" (1904-1908) Vol I., p 38

[2] (1847) 10 Q B. 208, 16 L J M C 184.

consumption of water within the area, and therefore the cost of supplying same could only be estimated and no accurate figure could be determined

The Court found that this was so in fact and therefore the valuation of the whole undertaking was apportioned on the assumption that the expenses in each parish bore the same proportion to the gross receipts, according to the judgment of Lord Denman in *R v Mile End Old Town* [1] The result of this decision was that the City of London Union lost several thousand pounds in rateable value from an assessment that had been in force for five years previously, although the gross receipts were increasing in the Union The reason of this was entirely due to the amalgamation of the seven companies which formerly existed into the Metropolitan Water Board.

The decision unquestionably caused a great injustice to the ratepayers within the City of London Union, and it further goes to prove that the method of valuation must be wrong if the result is to decrease the assessment on an increasingly valuable property, the decrease being the result of losses caused elsewhere, but had it been possible to ascertain the expenses within the City of London Union, in proportion to the mileage of pipes, for instance, or the consumption of water, the allocation of the total rateable value of the whole concern would probably not have been based upon the gross receipts in each parish, but upon the net receipts in each parish, as is done in the case of a railway and other similar properties

Where a water company under statutory powers takes water from a river upon payment to the conservators, the premises upon the river bank forming the "intake" must be assessed, having regard to their enhanced value in respect of the special fitness for taking water from the

---

[1] (1847) 10 Q B 208 16 L J M C 184

river and the uses made of it, but the actual payment to the conservators cannot properly be taken into account as determining the value of the premises [1]

If, as it frequently happens, water undertakings are in the hands of local governing bodies, corporations and the like, and, because so provided by Act of Parliament or for other reasons, they make no pecuniary profit, they are nevertheless liable to be rated [2] It has been considered, owing to the case of *Mayor, etc, of Worcester v. Droitwich Union* [3] followed by the *Mayor, etc, of Peterborough v Stamford Union* [4] and *Merthyr Tydfil Local Board v Merthyr Tydfil Union,* [5] that where no profits were made under such arrangements there could practically be no rateable value, but this cannot be regarded as a settlement of the question The incongruity resulting is seen by a comparison of the last-named with *Dewsby and Heckmondwike Water Board v Assessment Committee Penistone Union.* [6] In the latter case it was held that a public works rate levied in aid of a works undertaking was to be regarded as income of the undertaking, but not so in the former case, because the aid from such rate was received on terms as to the repayment out of possible future balances. Indeed, all these cases are inconsistent with the principles laid down in such cases as *West Bromwich School Board v Overseers of West Bromwich* [7] and *R. v School Board for London,* [8] and approved by the House of Lords in the *London County Council v Erith and West*

[1] *New River Water Co v Hertford Union Assessment Committee,* (1902) 2 K B 597, 87 L T 880, 71 L J K B 827

[2] *R v Longwood,* (1849) 13 Q B 116, 18 L J M C 65 also second case *R v. Longwood,* (1852) 17 Q B 871.

[3] (1876) 2 Ex. D 49, 36 L T 186, 41 J P 355

[4] (1883) 31 W R 949

[5] (1890) 1891 1 Q B 186

[6] (1886) 17 Q B D 394.

[7] (1884) 13 Q B D 929

[8] (1886) 17 Q B D. 738

Ham,[1] where it has been held that pecuniary profit is not necessarily the standard of value for rating purposes. Is it not clear that, if, for instance, a local authority say to their ratepayers, "We will undertake the control of the water supply for you and charge only so much as will be necessary to cover the expenses," such an undertaking is of great value both to the corporation and the ratepayers, and ought to be assessed? The true rule, it is submitted, is that when the conditions of a water undertaking are wholly different from those applying to similar undertakings, in respect of which there have been judicial decisions, those decisions can no longer be said to apply, and the principles adopted in the later cases, in relation it is true to different undertakings, but undertakings in which the conditions are similar to those in the cases in question must be regarded as the more sound and the more equitable test.

In the case of *Liverpool* v. *West Derby*,[2] the Commissioners erected water works for the supply of water to be employed for public purposes, that is to say, for watering the streets and for use in cases of fire. There was no competition with other water companies for the supply of water to private consumers in the town of Liverpool, and indeed the local Act prohibited the supplying of water by other companies for this purpose. These works were held to be rateable.

The most equitable way to value undertakings where no profit is made, but which are of considerable value for other reasons, is on the basis of the capital value, for it is clear that, if a corporation borrow money in order to provide a water undertaking, the interest that is paid on the borrowed money is in effect rent. In determining the percentage to be taken upon the capital value, reference should be made to the chapter on buildings,

---

[1] (1893) A C 562, 63 L J M C 9
[2] (1856) 25 L J M C 112 C E & B 704

where this matter has been fully discussed, both as to the amount of the percentage and whether original cost or capital value should form the datum of the valuation

In the case of *R* v. *South Staffordshire Water Works Co* [1] the water works were constructed for the supply of water in a district where the population was expected to increase, and the works of the company were therefore much in excess of those which would be necessary to supply the district as it was then populated , but as the whole of the works were used for the distribution of water, and, notwithstanding that they were capable of a very much larger distribution, it was held that the whole capital expenditure must be taken into account, and not so much as would have been necessary had only a small system been constructed

Works larger than at present necessary

If all of the works had not been in use however, that is to say, if there had been a pumping station erected, or even a reservoir for future requirements, and at the present time they were not being used, it is clear that they would not be assessed upon the same principle as if they were being used—see *Liverpool Corporation* v *Llanfyllin Union.* [2] This case and the *Mayor of Bradford* v *Keighley Union* [3] may both very usefully be referred to with reference to what is to be considered effective capital value (see page 271 *ante*).

An artificial in addition to a natural reservoir of a water company is, for the purpose of the General District Rate (see Section 211 of the Public Health Act, 1875), [4] land covered with water, and is therefore liable to be assessed at only one quarter of the net annual value. See also upon this point *Hampton U. D C* v *Southwark and Vauxhall Water Co* [5]

---

[1] (1885) L R 16 Q B D 359 , 55 L J M C 88 , 54 L T 782
[2] (1899) 2 Q B 14 , 66 L J Q B 762 , 80 L T 667 , 63 J P. 452
[3] " Konstam's Rating Appeals " (1904-1908), 517
[4] 38 & 39 Vict , c 55
[5] (1900) A.C 3 , 69 L J Q B 72 , 64 J P 260 , 81 L T. 547.

CHAPTER IX.

TELEPHONE AND ELECTRIC LIGHT UNDERTAKINGS.

Telephone undertakings

ALTHOUGH there can be no question as to the rateability of telephone undertakings, a considerable amount of uncertainty exists as to the method to be adopted in estimating their rateable value, and, so far as we can ascertain, there is no specific judicial decision upon the rules to be followed in making such an assessment. Telephone undertakings, as establishments for the maintenance of telephonic communication between the subscribers, have, *inter alia*, a head office or exchange, from which wires are erected to the residence or the office of every subscriber, who is thus enabled to communicate with any other person connected with the exchange. For the purpose of this business the undertakers have to erect wires between their own offices and those of their subscribers, such wires being carried overhead, supported and steadied, sometimes by poles fixed in the ground, but more generally attached to the roof, chimneys, or walls of some of the buildings over which they pass. Such attachments can be moved easily, without damage to the building. The undertakers have to obtain the consent of the owners or occupiers of the land into which poles are fixed or buildings to which attachments are made, agreements have thus to be made between the owners or occupiers, whereby the undertakers usually pay a small

Wayleaves

annual rent. These agreements are called "wayleaves" In the case of the *Lancashire and Cheshire Telephone Exchange Co. v. The Overseers of the Township of Manchester,*[1] the questions for the opinion of the

---

[1] See the Law Journal Report, Vol 53, p 195, of the Magistrates Cases, (1885) 14 Q.B.D. 267, 54 L J. M C 68

Court were.—(1) Are the appellants' telephone posts, standard ridge saddles, and other attachments and supports for wires, and the wires thereto attached, or any and which of them, rateable to the poor? and, if so, who is liable for the rate? (2) If the telephone posts, and the attachments and supports for wires, and the wires thereunto attached, or any of them, are rateable, do they or any of them constitute a separate rateable tenement, or do they add to the rateable value of the premises respectively to which they are attached? (3) If the appellants are rateable to the poor in respect of any land, telephone posts and wires in the respondents' township, how is the proper amount at which they ought to be assessed to be ascertained?

Mathew, J., in giving judgment, said "We do not think that the third question is one which we ought to advise upon; we therefore decline to answer it.

"As to the first and second questions, the case, in our judgment, is governed by the decision in the *Electric Telegraph Co v The Overseers of Salford*[1] The question in that case was whether a liberty to place posts on the land of another person was an occupation of land capable of being rated under 43 Elizabeth, c 2, s 1—and it was held that it was. That case is really undistinguishable, for here it is sought to assess a whole system of wires used for a purpose analogous to which the wires were used in the *Salford* case. It has been argued by Mr. Webster that there was no permanent occupation, but that such occupation as existed was enjoyed by virtue of a quasi-easement by license; but, in our judgment, there was an exclusive occupation, limited in character I admit, but exclusive in each case as distinguished from a mere user by license. When a wire is attached to a roof, that part of the roof where the wire is attached is used exclusively for the purpose of the support, just as where the wire is upon a post—the post and land in which it is fixed are used exclusively for supporting that wire. The use is not merely temporary, but exclusive and permanent The case of *Watkins* v. *The Overseers of Milton-next-Gravesend*[1] is distinguishable, the *ratio decidendi* in that case being that the owner was the real occupier, a distinction being drawn between the owner and the person who had a mere license to use In *Smith* v *The Lambeth Assessment Committee*[2] it was decided that there was no legal right to exclusive occupation, and on that ground the occupation was held not to be rateable Here, as it seems to me, there was both an exclusive occupation and a permanent user with which it was not intended that the owners or tenants of the houses should have power to interfere It has been said that the only right of user was by wayleaves, but the question is not so much as to the contents of the documents as to what is going on under them, and the conclusion I have come to is that what is going on under these documents is that there is an exclusive occupation of an entire system for the purpose of conveying telephonic messages, and that our judgment ought to be in favour of the respondents.'

It will be seen from this that there is no question as to the rating liability of telephone undertakings, but the Court unfortunately would not answer the questions as to how the amount at which they are to be assessed is to be ascertained

There seems no reason why telephone undertakings should not be assessed on the basis of the receipts and expenses in exactly the same way as any other undertaking is now rated, but unfortunately, owing to the difficulty of ascertaining the parochial receipts, a system has been largely adopted of assessing the wires at a rate

---

[1] (1868) L R 3 Q B 350, 37 L J M C 73 18 L T 601, 16 W R 1059.
[2] (1882) 10 Q B D 327, 52 L J M C 1, 18 L T 57, J P 244—C.A

per mile   This arises from the unwillingness of Assessment Committees to contest the point, although the amount lost to the ratepayers is enormous, and to the writer's knowledge, in a case where an Assessment Committee did venture to make a valuation upon this plan, although the National Telephone Company lodged notice of appeal to Quarter Sessions, they failed to put in an appearance and allowed judgment to go by default Little can be gathered from this, however, except the inference that, rather than have the case brought before the public, the company submitted to paying the Union referred to on a very much higher scale than the surrounding Unions

As, however, the National Telephone Company is shortly to be purchased by the Government, telephones will either be exempt, or a similar clause to that in the Telegraphs Act [1] may apply

The receipts and expenses would appear to be the basis for making a valuation for rating purposes of electric lighting undertakings. There has been no judicial ruling as to the method of assessment to be followed with regard to these particular hereditaments, but they would appear to come under the same category as trading concerns of a similar character, i e , gas and water works. The following is a form of valuation based on one given in Messrs Boyle and Davies's "Principles of Rating," second edition, p 511 :— *Electric lighting undertakings*

GROSS RECEIPTS

Sale of Current

Sale of Current under Contract   ..

Public Lighting   ...   .

Rental of Meters on Consumer's Premises

Discounts   .   ...

Sale of Materials, Stores, etc   ..   .

£

[1] (1868) 31 & 32 Vict , c 110

WORKING EXPENSES.

GENERATING AND DISTRIBUTION OF
  ELECTRICITY

 Coals and other Fuel .. ..

 Oil, Waste, Water and Engine Room
  Stores .. ..

 Salaries of Engineers and Officers

 Wages at Generating and Distributing
  Stations ... ...

 Miscellaneous Expenses . .

MANAGEMENT EXPENSES

 Directors' Remuneration ... .

 Salaries of Secretary Clerks, etc .

 Stationery and Printing ..

 General Establishment Charges .

 Auditors ... .

 Law Charges . .. ...

 Rates in the £ on £ rateable
  value .. ..

            £

OCCUPIER'S SHARE Tenant's Capital £

 Interest on Capital employed . ...

 Trade Profits

 Risks and Casualties

    GROSS VALUE ... £

STATUTABLE DEDUCTIONS

Maintenance and Renewal of Mains and
  Works . . ...

Insurance .. ..

    RATEABLE VALUE . £

As has been explained previously, the working expenses
and occupier's share are deducted from the gross receipts,
and this will give the gross value, from which the usual
statutable deductions are to be made to ascertain the
rateable value

CHAPTER X.

DOCKS, HARBOURS AND PIERS

WHEN valuing a dock company, the gross receipts have to be ascertained and the working expenses deducted, in addition to an allowance to the hypothetical tenant by way of interest on his capital—a method already fully explained as the one applicable to railway companies and similar properties [1] In the event of the expenses exceeding the receipts of a dock company (so that, strictly speaking, there would be no rateable value at all attached to the dock), it will not prevent the warehouses and sheds on the quays, which are capable of separate occupation, from being rated. In the case of the *Mersey Docks and Harbour Board* v *Birkenhead*[2] it was held that the separate rating of warehouses, etc., where they were capable of beneficial occupation, was correct, notwithstanding the connection they had with the docks, which were worked at an actual loss It must, however, be borne in mind that such warehouses are to be capable of distinctly separate occupation, or, in other words, they *must* be so occupied as to be capable of being separately rated [3]

Docks and harbours

Warehouses capable of separate occupation

The chief difficulty met with when assessing dock property is where the docks extend throughout many parishes The principle to be adopted in apportioning the rateable value has been the subject of much litigation, and although the Courts lean towards the

---

[1] See *Mersey Docks and Harbour Board* v *Birkenhead*, decided in H L. 25th April, 1901, (1901) A C. 175, 70 L J K B 584, 84 L T. 542, 65 J P 579

[2] (1873) L R 8 Q B 445, 42 L J M C 141, 29 L T 454.

[3] See *Allan* v *Liverpool*, (1874) L R 9 Q B 180, 43 L J M C 69, 30 L T 93, also *Rochdale Canal Co* v *Brewster*, (1894) 64 L J Q B 37; 71 L T 243.

Parochial
and acreage
principles
applied to
docks

parochial principle as applied to railway companies, where it has been found impossible to divide the rateable value in this manner, it has been laid down that the division shall be according to the acreage of the dock. In the case of *R v Hull Docks Co.*[1] where the question for the opinion of the Court was as to the manner in which the rateable value of the whole of the docks was to be apportioned among the different parishes in which they were situate, Lord Campbell, C J., said: "This Court has, in rating undertakings of this nature, adopted what is called the parochial earnings principle wherever it can be adopted. But can it be adopted in the present case? If it cannot, I see no other principle applicable except that of acreage. Here there is one single source of profit lying in different parishes, and the profit is earned in respect of the whole concern indiscriminately; we can, therefore, only look to see how much lies in one parish and how much in another. The tolls are paid in respect of the use of the land in all the parishes. They may be received in any one of the parishes, but the land in all is equally the meritorious source of the profit. This case entirely differs from a railway, where the toll is paid for the power of travelling over a particular portion of the whole line; whereas, in these docks a person who has paid the toll has the right of taking his ship to any other of the docks just as much as he has to take it to that into which the ship first entered. There is, therefore, only one single meritorious cause of the toll, and that being situate in different parishes the parochial earnings principle cannot be applied; we must see how much of the docks lie in each parish."

Second Hull
Dock case

In 1894 the assessment of the Hull Docks Company was again the subject of litigation.[2] When the

---

[1] (1852) 18 Q B 325, 21 L J M C 153, 5 M & S 394

[2] *Hull Docks Co v The Guardians of the Sculcoates Union*, (1894) 2 Q B 69, 63 L J. M C 279, 70 L T 742, affirmed on appeal to House of Lords, 64 L J M C. 49, 71 L.T. 642

question of the apportionment of the rateable value was first before the Courts there were certain docks not completed; these docks when completed did not communicate with the others, and as they belong to the same company it was sought to rate them on the following principle, viz —A valuation was made of the whole concern and the rateable value was divided among the several parishes in which the property was situated, on the principle laid down in the case above referred to, that is to say, according to the acreage, but the Court of Queen's Bench held that the rateable value of the docks which communicated with each other must be divided in proportion to the acreage of the water area of each dock; and that the docks which did not so communicate must be separately rated (see "Ryde's Rating Appeals," 1891-93, p. 318) This was afterwards affirmed by the House of Lords In the case of the *Mersey Harbour Board* v *The Liverpool Overseers*[1]—which appears to have influenced the decision in the second *Hull Docks* case—it was stated that on each side of the Mersey there were two distinct sets of docks constructed, owned and worked by the same company It so happened that one set of docks was more frequently used by vessels than the other, consequently receipts were higher in one case than the other The fact that the River Mersey separated the two parts of the property may have affected the decision that these docks were to be rated upon the parochial principle, that is to say, according to the receipts in each parish and not according to the acreage Cockburn, C J, said, in delivering judgment "The *Hull Docks* case[2] undoubtedly establishes this, that where there is a series of docks all lying contiguous to one another, and forming part of one entire concern, and toll is taken for the right to

Mersey Docks case

[1] (1872) L R 7 Q B 643, 41 L J M C 161, 26 L T 868
[2] This, of course, referring to the case o. *R* v *Hull Docks Co*, (1852) 18 Q B 325, 21 L J M C 153

enter into and have the benefit of any of that series or general system of docks and dock accommodation, you cannot apply the parochial principle of rating, but you must have recourse to the acreage principle; but the language of all the Judges in that case, I think, goes entirely to this, that you are not to resort to the acreage principle, except *ex necessitate*, where you really cannot apply the other   If this case were on all fours with the *Hull Docks* case, I do not know, as it has stood for eighteen years, that it would be right to overrule it, certainly not without further consideration   But this case appears to me to be plainly distinguishable, as the docks on the one side and the other of the Mersey do not appear to me to come within the designation of one series or system of docks.   It is true that by the Act of Parliament these docks, which are essentially distinct and separate, are to be treated as one for the purpose of general management, and for the financial operations connected with this property, but that does not appear to me to alter that which, in the very nature of things, is separate and distinct   Although for certain purposes they may be treated as one estate, in truth they are two estates, and the docks on the Cheshire side of the water can no more be said to be the same estate as the docks on the Liverpool side than two private estates, though under one management, can be said to be one estate   The people in Liverpool have a perfect right to the contribution of the local burthen of this property according to the value of the property on the Liverpool side   The docks extend, it appears, into more than one parish on the Liverpool side . and so far as the docks on the Liverpool side are concerned, the principle in the *Hull Docks* case

Acreage system only to be used in cases of necessity

may apply.   But it seems to me that we are not, in the present case, called upon to resort to the acreage system, which is an objectionable one, and only to be resorted to in case of necessity   There is no occasion to apply it here

Although there might be some difficulty in detail, yet there is no insuperable difficulty in ascertaining what proportion of the earnings of these two docks is due to the docks on the one side of the river, or due to the docks on the other side of the river. Therefore, there is no necessity to have recourse to the acreage principle "

In the case of the *Swansea Union Assessment Committee and Overseers* v. *Swansea Harbour Trustees*[1] the harbour authority had constructed a floating dock and basin, and it was held that although the authority were entitled to charge harbour rates on shipping and goods whether the vessels entered the dock or not, such harbour rates were in the nature of tolls and were not to be taken into consideration in assessing the docks

In the case of *Smith's Dock Co* v *Tynemouth Corporation*[2] part of the dock company's property consisted of pontoons which were originally on land not covered by the river, but the company had excavated and dredged it and each pontoon was attached to piles driven into the ground and was always afloat, although they could be detached and taken away at any time A large part of the business of the company was repairing ships, which, being too large for their dry docks, were dealt with on the pontoons It was held, first, that the excavated ground was in the occupation of the company and that such occupation was enhanced by the presence and use of the pontoons , and, secondly, that, notwithstanding the presence of the pontoons, the property must be considered as land covered with water within the meaning of Section 211 of the Public Health Act, 1875,[3] and, as such, liable to be rated to the general district rate in the proportion of one quarter of the rate

[1] (1907) (H L , 30th July), 97 L J 385 , 71 J P 497

[2] (1908) (C A , 13th March) 1 K.B 948 , 77 L J. K B 560 , 72 J.P 201 , 99 L T 136

[3] 38 & 39 Vict , c 55

Public
property

Certain docks have claimed exemption from rating on the ground that they are public property, but this contention has not held good.   By certain local Acts the Commissioners were authorised to build and work docks on the river Tyne   The rates levied on the ships using these docks were applied to the repayment of the capital borrowed and the interest on such capital   There was a sinking fund formed for the renewal of the docks, and the whole concern was carried on on strictly business principles.   As the rate of interest on the money borrowed was fixed, there was a possibility of a surplus after all payments had been made under the Act, and in such an event the Commissioners had to reduce the rates and tolls levied on the vessels, but it was held that the Commissioners were rateable, as there was proved to be a beneficial occupation, there being nothing in the Acts forbidding the payment of Poor Rates in the event of a surplus arising as stated [1]

Piers

When rating a pier, what has to be ascertained is the rent at which it would let to a hypothetical tenant   The principle of the "receipts and expenses" has to be adopted, as previously explained   With regard to piers on the seashore a peculiar point arises from the fact that the pier is built out into the water, and in most cases the foundations, even at low tide, are in the sea itself.   It has been held that the land beyond low-water mark is not extra-parochial within the meaning of the Poor Law Amendment Act, 1868,[2] therefore that part of the pier stretching out into the sea beyond low-water mark is

[1] *Tyne Improvement Commissioners* v *Chirton*, (1859) 28 L J M C 131, 1 El & El 516, see also *Mersey Docks and Harbour Board* v *Cameron*, (1865) 35 L J M C 1, 11 H L Cas 443, 12 L T 643, 13 W R 1069, *London County Council* v *Erith, West Ham and St George's Union*, (1893) A C 562, 63 L J M C 9, 69 L T 725, 57 J P 821, and *R* v *London School Board*, (1886) 17 Q.B D 738, 55 L J M.C 169, 55 L T 384

[2] 31 & 32 Vict, c 122, s 27

not rateable [1] This would not apply in the case of a tidal river, or indeed in the case of any river, as it has been held that where a parish extends to the bank of the river there is *prima facie* evidence that the parish boundary is not the bank, but the middle of the river [2]

[1] *Blackpool Pier Co.* v *Fylde Union,* (, 46 L J M.C. 189, 36 L T. 251, 41 J P. 344.

[2] *M'Cannon* v *Sinclair,* (1859) 2 El & El 53, 28 L J M C. 247, 33 L.T. 221

CHAPTER XI.

MINES, BRICKFIELDS AND CEMETERIES

COAL mines are the mines most frequently dealt with by rating authorities, and the assessment of them is fraught with no little difficulty

In many districts agreements have been entered into between the colliery owners and the Rating Authorities for assessments based on the tonnage output of the mines   These agreements have various conditions, both as to price and other matters, which it is not necessary to go into here, but the agreements are frequently open to objection on legal grounds—as, e g, the possibility of inequality, a point that may be taken by any ratepayer—although it cannot be denied that for convenience they are often very useful

A recent case on the assessment of coal mines is of considerable value to the surveyor from many points of view, but care must be taken not to fall into the error of laying too much emphasis on an isolated judgment on a specified point arising out of certain defined facts as conclusive in all cases

The case referred to is that of the *Denaby and Cadeby Colliery Co v. Doncaster Union*,[1] where it was held that it was not necessarily wrong to adopt a similar principle in the case of a coal mine to that applied in fixing an assessment of a gas or water company   That is to say, that from the gross receipts for the sale of coal certain expenses should be deducted, and, having allowed a certain sum to the tenant as interest upon his capital sunk in the concern, the gross value would be ascertained, from this a deduction for repairs, renewals, and insurance would leave the amount of rateable value of such mine.

Coal mine valued on receipts and expenses principle

[1] (1899) 78 L T 388, 62 J P 443, 14 T L R 347

On referring, however, to the special case upon which the decision was given in the Court of Queen's Bench, it will be observed that the arbitrator found as a fact that there were no means of comparing the particular colliery in question with others for the purpose of ascertaining the rent that a tenant would give from year to year   The custom that existed in that district was for the freeholder to grant a long lease at so much per acre for a mine and the arbitrator found that the price paid for the coal under such a lease was not sufficient evidence to answer the question propounded by the Act of Parliament, namely —What rent would a tenant give for the property from year to year, taking into consideration the prospect of a continuing tenancy"

Such were the conditions in that case that the arbitrator in fact used the best means available to ascertain the true rateable value, but to the author's knowledge the facts are different in a great many districts, and the decision (as in so many rating cases) amounts to little else than an expression of opinion of the Court of Queen's Bench that in order to find the true rateable value the evidence of receipts and expenses, where every other method had failed, is not inadmissible before the Courts, in which questions of fact are of primary importance

Mr Justice Day, in delivering judgment in that case, said   "What value the Arbitrator will attach to it (the evidence of accounts) I am sure I do not know, but it seems to me it is clearly admissible "

In support of the view that the decision in the *Denaby* case[1] merely amounted to what evidence it is right to admit or to exclude, reference may be made to the judgment of Mr Justice Blackburn in the case of *R. v North Aylesford Union*,[2] where, dealing with a similar

[1] (1898) 78 L T 388 , 62 J P 343 , 14 T L R 347.
[2] (1872) 37 J P 118 , 26 L T 618

class of property, namely a chalk pit, he said   "No
tenant gives all he could afford to give, and the true test
is not what he could afford to give but what a tenant
would be likely to give who took the pit from year to
to year   It is not the profits a man makes that make
the difference, for whether he gains or loses in his
trade the rateable value is the same '

This dictum of Mr Justice Blackburn, that the rateable
value is the same whether a man loses or gains in his
trade, can clearly be followed in such cases as a private
house or shop, but if the facts be such that letting must
depend on profits which may be made, so that a valuation
is to be based upon receipts and expenses, as distinct
from merely admitting such evidence in the Courts, it is
clear that the rateable value must go up or down according
to whether large or small profits are made

Coal mines
let on
royalties

Where coal mines are not owned by the occupiers
an exceedingly common form of letting is one based on
the tonnage of coal actually raised to the surface, and
in such a case it is difficult to say that the best evidence
of the rent is not that which is actually paid   Indeed,
although coal mines have been rated since the Act of
Elizabeth, it was not until the Rating Act, 1874 [1]
that tin, lead and copper mines became indisputably
rateable, and in that Act the method of valuation is also
prescribed, therefore it is not unreasonable to suppose that
the Legislature adopted the method that had probably
been in operation for many years, viz , that of basing the
rateable value upon the dues payable in respect of
the occupation of a mine where it is occupied under a
lease granted without fine, and the amount at which the
mine might be reasonably expected to let without fine in
a lease of ordinary duration according to the usage of
the country.

---

[1] 37 & 38 Vict , c 54, s 7

It seems to follow that as a matter of law it is wrong to exclude any evidence which would go to prove what, as a fact, a tenant would give as rent for an occupation from year to year, but the application of the evidence must be determined by the Rating Authorities in each particular case

Where it has been decided that no comparison can possibly be made, the receipts and expenses principle, as briefly referred to on page 97, would be applicable, and applying that principle care must be taken to distinguish on the one hand moneys spent upon the concern which are in the nature of landlord's expenses, and those which are purely expended by the tenant in working the mine For instance, all the cost of the surface plant, machinery and the sinking of shafts on a virgin coal field are clearly expenses which should be charged to the capital account of the hypothetical landlord and not taken into consideration in the early stages of the valuation which is based on the revenue account of the colliery as a working concern

Having arrived at the gross value by deducting the working expenses from the receipts a further deduction has to be made to obtain the rateable value, which, though appearing in the revenue account of the company, would not be considered in arriving at the gross value These expenses are those incurred by the hypothetical landlord, and consist of the cost of maintaining and repairing the permanent roads and airways, haulage plant, if any, and the surface plant [1] There is, however, no allowance to be made for a sinking fund in arriving at the statutable deductions from gross to rateable value in the case of a coal mine from the fact that, as the subject-matter is worked out, it would be impossible to replace it at the end of its life, it being a natural commodity

---

[1] *Brown & Co, Limited v Rotherham Union*, 83 L T 193, 64 J P 580

which has ceased to exist and cannot be artificially produced A sinking fund to replace all plant, however, would be a permissible deduction

Having by the above method arrived at the rateable value of the colliery, it will frequently happen that the property extends into several parishes, and the division of the assessment between the parishes will have to be made In many cases the shaft and surface plant is in one parish and the actual seam of coal in a parish some distance away, with the possibility of a further complication for rating purposes from the fact that the actual coal may be mined in parish A, brought underground by means of a permanent roadway through parish B and come to the surface by means of the shaft in parish C

As far as the author is aware there is no decision as to how the rateable value of the whole concern ascertained upon this principle is to be allocated to the three parishes, and it would appear that no better method could be adopted than, with some modification to meet the different circumstances, that followed in the case of a water company, where a reservoir in parish A supplies consumers in parish C through what is termed a "dead main" running through parish B. In this last case, as has been explained in the chapters on gas and water companies, the value of the reservoir and carrying main, commonly called "dead works," is estimated by a process involving the ascertainment of the structural value, and taking a percentage thereon to represent the rateable value, and when the total value of the "dead works" has been thus ascertained, it is subtracted from the whole, leaving the remainder as the assessable value of the live works or directly supplying mains in the parishes in which they are situate and in which the water is supplied for consumption

Such a principle as applied to a coal mine would work as follows —The structural value of the shaft, surface and haulage plant and main roadways could be ascertained comparatively easily, and having deducted the rateable value of these from that of the whole, the balance would be attributable to these parishes where the coal is mined, not the parish where it is brought to the surface and sold[1]; and in the event of the coal being recovered in more parishes than one, no more equitable principle could be adopted than by dividing the rateable value for the coal *per se* amongst the various parishes according to the actual tonnage mined per annum in each parish, taking into consideration the quality of the coal in a mine where there might be more than one seam of varying values

In the case of *R v Foleshill*[2] it was held that an Assessment Committee could not assess the owner of a mine in the parish where the surface plant was situated for coal mined in another parish

With regard to the case of a surface plant near the seashore where the coal was actually worked from under the sea, although the coal mined in this case would come from land which was extra-parochial and therefore not liable to be rated, it is obvious that a tenant would give a higher rent for the surface plant and shaft when this was the only way to obtain the coal from the extra-parochial ground

It would consequently follow that a valuation of the colliery, whether the valuation be based upon the receipts and expenses, or of a royalty or tonnage, the rent thus fixed would include, indirectly, at all events, some part of the value of the coal from under the sea

There are, however, objections to the method of assessing coal mines according to expenses and receipts, especially in its entirety The first of these is, that, owing to the fluctuations in the price of coal, it would only be equitable to the colliery owner, the Assessment Committee

Objections to profits principle of rating mines

[1] *R v Foleshill*, (1835) 4 L J M C 631, 2 A & E 593, 4 N & M 360

[2] (1835) 4 L J M C 631, 2 A & E 593, 4 N & M 360

and the other ratepayers for a revaluation of the collieries to be made at least once every year, and a complicated valuation upon this method would be exceedingly expensive Then, again, such varying conditions exist in several collieries that it is impossible for one form of valuation to apply in every case. For instance, for the haulage in one colliery ponies are used, which are clearly the property of the tenant, and should be considered tenant's capital, but in an adjoining colliery it may be that the haulage is done by electric power, the generators for which are at the surface this constitutes part of the hypothetical landlord's capital, and it is not difficult to see that there are many points that would be peculiar to each colliery in adopting such a principle Further, the principle carried to its ultimates must inevitably, in certain cases, result in the anomaly of there being no rateable value at all, as it is quite possible to conceive the expenses and the interest on the tenant's capital absorbing the whole of the gross receipts ; whilst the alternative case might be that owing to a very profitable year the rateable value of the colliery would be an enormous figure

Further, the principle assumes that the tenant makes a fixed profit on his capital whatever the conditions of the trade may be, and it allocates to the landlord all the profits or losses of the working of the mine The author ventures to suggest that in practice this is never the case where an actual letting takes place Hundreds of collieries are let throughout the country on the basis of a fixed royalty for a fixed number of years, on the actual coal mined, and it is impossible to conceive a tenancy under better conditions, for as the landlord has no voice in the management of the concern, although he would be permitted under the lease to measure the coal taken, the actual possession of the mine would be given up to the tenant.

Another objection arises to the system It is a well-known fact that many collieries in certain years actually work at a loss, whereas the profit in other years compensates for that loss, and therefore the rateable value in the bad years would be nil, while for good years it might be a very large figure, and, therefore, given a large mine in a particular parish the total rateable value in that parish might be altered by a very large sum, with the result that in a good year the poundage might be as low as 1s for all the other ratepayers, owing to the contribution of the colliery, but in a bad year the rates for the other ratepayers and the colliery owners might be increased to any figure, and the unfortunate owners of small property who may have compounded for their rates would find their income partially if not wholly absorbed by the extra rates payable by reason of a depression in the coal trade

It will therefore be seen that where possible the above system of valuation should not be adopted. By this it is not suggested that the receipts and expenses over a number of years of a colliery should not be fully considered, and a valuation based on an average thereby obtained would obviate excessive valuation from year to year, but it is obviously desirable that a more equitable method of assessment should be adopted, not only with regard to the colliery occupier, but for the benefit of the community at large

Further, there is the case of *R v. Parrot*[1] to be considered, where it was held that the occupiers of a mine were still liable to be rated, although the rent they had agreed to pay absorbed all the profits of the mine, and it is at once seen that if the principle, which the Bench decided was not wrong in the case of the *Denaby and Cadeby Colliery Co*,[2] were applied in some cases to-day,

---

[1] (1794) 5 T R 593, 2 R R 454
[2] (1898) 78 L T 388, 62 J P 343, 14 T L R 317

the result might be in conflict with the decision in *R* v *Parrot*,[1] although this last decision merely amounted to the proposition that if a profit were made it was sufficient to create liability for rating, the amount at which it should be rated not being dealt with

Mines assessed on their output The other method which is very commonly used is to assess mines annually on the basis of the output for the preceding year, that is to say returns are made in January from the various ratepayers showing the operations of the previous year, and upon this basis the assessment is fixed for the subsequent year   This is a very equitable method of dealing with the assessment and is highly to be commended, as it is fair alike to the assessment authorities and to the owners of the mines   Moreover, if an annual tenancy of a mine could be conceived it would be very reasonable to suppose that the rent a tenant would give would be based upon the preceding year's output at so much per ton

This principle of rating a coal mine however, only applies to the coal actually recovered, and the result must be considered as a net rent paid to the landlord and constitutes part of the rateable value of the whole concern

In practice the majority of leases of mines are based upon this principle, that is to say, a price per ton is paid to the landlord for the actual coal mined, but although this is the practice, the hypothesis is that the landlord also sinks the shaft, erects the service plant and lets the whole as a going concern   In addition, therefore, to the rent or royalty actually paid, an estimated sum, usually based on interest on capital value, must be added to the figure of royalty already determined in order to obtain the total rateable value of the mine [2] This figure, together with the cost of the repairs, renewals and insurances of the

[1] (1794) 5 T R 593
[2] *R* v *Voleshill*, (1835) 4 L J M C 631   2 A & L 593   4 N & M 360

surface plant and the cost of maintaining permanent roads and airways underground, will give the gross value [1] The assessment for the surface plant, etc., unless alterations were made, would remain permanently until such time as actual alterations were made in it, but each year the assessment on the coal mine might vary according to the output

It has been observed that the commonest form of letting a coal mine is upon a royalty for a fixed number of years, the obvious reason being that no person or company would sink a shaft to get coal for one year only, and the general practice is for the proposed tenant to agree with the proposed landlord for a fixed amount of royalty extending over the whole period

It would, therefore, seem that this is the best possible evidence that could be obtained as to the value of the mine, and is the best basis upon which to assess it Of course, there are many factors appertaining to individual mines, which afford evidence sufficiently strong to justify an authority in assessing the coal obtained at a less or greater price per ton than was actually paid For instance, assume a lease for, say, 50,000 acres granted 20 years ago, and that the royalty then fixed was considerably less or considerably more than that paid under leases in the same neighbourhood granted in recent times, in either case there is justification for alteration of the actual amount paid when taken as a basis of present rateable value

Again, a shaft is sunk and the seam of coal is found to be 8ft thick, but the mine, after being worked some few years, exhausts the 8ft seam and has to depend say on a 4ft seam. It may be that the cost of getting the coal is so much increased that although the tenant is bound under his old lease to pay the original royalty, it is obvious that if a fresh agreement were entered into at the present time a less royalty would be agreed upon between the landlord and tenant.

Assessment of surface plant

---

[1] *Brown & Co v Rotherham Union*, (1900) 64 J P 580

A further instance requiring alteration of a royalty fixed under a lease granted several years might be the distance from the shaft of the face of the coal   It is a matter of common knowledge that coal may have to be brought underground two miles or more in many old collieries

The above and many other factors may arise and so have to be considered by the valuer in determining the assessment, but by adopting the principle of a price per ton for coal mined there will be some assessable value, and it is only reasonable to suppose that the landlord would always get something for his property, the *corpus* of which was being worked out, whereas the other principle, as has been shown on the previous pages, may result in no rateable value at all.

A difficulty that presents itself in rating coal mines, which is equally patent to both principles, is the fact that the rate or assessment is made in advance, and as in both principles evidence of the value of the concern is not forthcoming until the previous year's workings are known, it is quite possible to conceive that a mine could be worked out in one year and have no beneficial occupation in the second year   Theoretically, therefore, in the second year there would be no assessment and there would certainly be nothing to distrain upon for rates, whereas in the first year, from the absence of any evidence at all as to the value of the concern, it would be equally impossible to assess the mine except at a nominal figure

It may be suggested that this instance is very extreme, and although it is admitted that such a case would be very rare, on the other hand it is quite an ordinary experience for the whole of the coal in a particular parish belonging to a colliery company to be wholly worked out in one year.

For instance, a colliery has its shaft in parish A, and its workings extend into parishes B, C, and D   In the year 1908 it extends its workings to parish E   In the year 1909 it takes 100,000 tons out of parish E   In the year 1910 the whole of the coal having been worked out of parish E, no further operations in that parish take place

Obviously no assessment can be made in 1908 because there is no beneficial occupation in parish E   It is not the practice on any principle to assess the colliery owner for parish E in 1909, because no evidence whatever of the coal got is forthcoming, the whole matter being regulated by supply and demand, and it is quite possible that in 1910 the colliery proprietors would object to pay rates in parish E, on the ground that they occupy no property within the parish, but it is a little difficult to see how an Assessment Committee could defend their position should such an objection be taken

It therefore follows that an arrangement is most desirable between the colliery owners and the Rating Authorities, although such an arrangement may not be free from objections on legal grounds   This shows a defect in the law that has to be dealt with by the good sense of both parties.

When a coal mine is unproductive it is not assessable to the Poor Rate   In a certain case, a mine being flooded the coal company erected machinery for the purpose of pumping the water out of it, and laid metals on land (taken by them for that purpose), to convey coal to the boilers necessary for their pumping operations   All the machinery erected was used for the purpose named, and only during the time of the pumping operations   It was held by the Court that the company were rateable only for the surface of the land they occupied, and were *not* rateable for the buildings, boilers, engine, plant and railway, as they constituted only a part of a valueless colliery, and could not be said to have any value apart from such colliery [1]

Coal mine unproductive

---

[1] *Tyne Coal Co v Wallsend Parish Overseers* (1877) 46 L J M C 185, 35 L T 854, 41 J P 375

Where a mine is worked out and a rent is payable under an old lease, it was held that the occupier could not be rated for the mine, it having become exhausted, and that the subject-matter of the rating was gone—see *R v Bedworth* [1]

As has already been stated the fact of coal mines being specially mentioned in the Act of Elizabeth led the Courts to determine that it was the intention of the Legislature to exclude other mines (not being mines where royalties were payable in kind) from liability to be rated and it was not until 1874, when the Rating Act of that year [2] was passed, and it is thereby enacted that mines of other kinds not mentioned in the Act of Elizabeth should be subject to be rated in like manner as if they had been so mentioned The Act of 1874 goes further, and provides the rule to be followed in assessing a tin, lead or copper mine For the exact provisions in this respect reference should be made to the Act itself (see Appendix), but shortly stated they are these —That where a mine is occupied under lease without a fine on a reservation, wholly or partly on dues or rent, the amount of dues or rent payable during the year ending the 31st December preceding the date of valuation, with the addition of the amount of any fixed rent reserved which may not be satisfied by such dues, is to be the gross value, and the rateable value is to be the same as the gross value, except that where an owner of the mine is liable for repairs, insurance, or other expenses necessary to maintain the mine in a state to command the rent the average cost of these last mentioned items is to be deducted from the gross value to ascertain the rateable value That where any such mine is occupied under a lease granted wholly or partly on fine or is occupied and worked by the owner, the gross value and annual value thereof is to be the annual amount of the dues and

Tin, lead and copper mines

---

[1] (1806) 8 East 387
[2] 37 & 38 Vict , c 54

rent at which the mine might be reasonably expected to let without fine on a lease of the ordinary duration according to the usage of the country if the tenant undertook to pay all tenant's rates and taxes and tithe rent-charge, and also the repairs, insurance, and other expenses necessary to maintain in a state to command such annual amount of dues or dues and rent

Although this Act [1] was passed ten years later than the last two Union Assessment Committee Acts,[2] it is curious that, notwithstanding the fact that gross and rateable values had been defined years before, it should be enacted with regard to copper, tin and lead mines that the gross value should be the same as the rateable value where a tenant undertook to do the repairs, insurance, etc   As this clause exists in the case of repairing leases of private property and of the majority of coal mines, iron mines, stone quarries, and a vast number of other classes of property, it is again evidence showing the desirability of abolishing the gross value altogether

The Rating Act of 1874 [3] provides that nothing in the Act shall apply to a mine of which the royalty or dues are for the time being wholly reserved in kind as to the owner or occupier thereof   Persons receiving such royalty in dues or kind had already been held to be and still are rateable [4]

It is a little curious that coal mines are specifically mentioned in the Act of 1601,[5] and that copper, tin and lead mines should be referred to in the Act of 1874,[3] whereas such mines as ironstone, manganese, clay, slate, and under this heading one might almost class chalk pits,

---

[1] (1874) 37 & 38 Vict , c 54

[2] (1862) 25 & 26 Vict   c 103 , (1864) 27 & 28 Vict , c 39

[3] 37 & 38 Vict , c 54, s 13

[4] *The Van Mining Co v Llanidloes*, (1876) 45 L J M C 198, 1 Ex D 310, 34 L T 692

[5] 43 Eliz , c 2

gravel pits, sand pits, and the right to dig for copiolites, have never been referred to specifically in any Act of Parliament   Unquestionaoly the occupiers thereof were rateable under the Act of Elizabeth, 1601,[1] as occupiers of land, and it would appear that the earlier cases of *R* v. *Pomfret*[2] and *R* v *Bishop of Rochester*[3] were decided upon the question of fact as to the occupation

There were other cases exempting mines, but these are now overruled , reference is not made to them

Ironstone mines   The rating of an ironstone mine does not differ in principle from that of a colliery   Mines are frequently let at a royalty per ton on the amount taken , but here the valuer must take into consideration not only the question of the rent payable under the lease, if any, but also whether that rent is fair, because it frequently happens that the cost of getting the ironstone varies owing to flaws in the stone or unexpected depth of "baring," all of which would affect the mind of an intending tenant

There may be similar peculiar conditions existing with regard to the other mines mentioned above, all of which are elements to be considered in arriving at the rateable value

Brickfields   With regard to the valuation of brickfields, it is difficult to see how the case of the *Denaby and Cadeby Colliery Co.* v *Doncaster Union*[4] could not be held to apply although it must be remembered, as has been previously stated, that receipts and expenses are only evidence and not necessarily conclusive evidence of the rental value of such an undertaking.

It is clear that a brickfield, and for the matter of that a chalk pit, stone quarry or gravel pit, etc., is of the same

[1] 43 Eliz , c 2

[2] (1816) 5 M & S 139

    (1810) 12 East 353.

[4] (1898) 78 L T. 388 , 62 J P. 343 , 14 T L R 347

class of property as a coal mine, the land being worked for the mineral it contains.

In the case of *R* v *Westbrook*[1] it was stated that Westbrook held the land (about 10 acres) for which he had to pay a rent of £20, or £2 per acre, in any event, in addition he had to pay a royalty of 1s 6d for every thousand bricks moulded in any one year. The Overseers estimated the rent on the full capacity of the plant, from that they made a deduction for bricks wasted, and inasmuch as the factors of a brick consist, in addition to the clay, of breeze, ashes, etc., a further deduction was allowed in order apparently to arrive at the actual amount of clay got from the earth, and the assessment was based thereon.

This is in effect the royalty principle, for in fact the Overseers had assessed the property by adding to the actual surface rent of £2 per acre 1s 6d for every thousand bricks which could be made in the yard, after making the deductions referred to. The Sessions held in this case that this was the correct method, namely, a rating based on the royalty paid, but they also alternately found that an incoming tenant would be willing to give £10 per acre for the land with liberty to consume the clay and apparently no more. Upon these two alternative findings, the assessment in the one case being £159 10s 0d and in the other £100, the case went to the Court of Queen's Bench, where it was held, and very properly, because no doubt of the finding in the special case, that the latter amount was the true assessment.

This case illustrates how questions of law and fact are involved and the difficulties of the valuer enlarged, for undoubtedly the Sessions were in favour of, and in fact found, that the correct method was to apply a price per thousand bricks in order to obtain the rateable value, but at the same time, having found as a fact the answer to

---

[1] (1847) 10 Q B 178 16 L J M C 87

the question propounded in the Act of Parliament as to
what rent a tenant would be willing to give at £10 per
acre only, the Judges in the Queen's Bench Division had
no alternative but to assent to a finding of fact, although
it is impossible to conceive how such a finding could have
taken place without evidence as to what was paid for
similar land, which apparently was not given in the
case

Advantage of   This case shows the advantage of entering into an
arrangement, such as was referred to in the early part
of this chapter with regard to coal mines, between the
assessment authorities and the owners of brickfields, chalk
pits, and kindred subject-matters, because it is obvious
that it is to the interest of the ratepayer to be assessed
upon his actual sales   Lack of orders might occur, in
which case a prudent tenant of a brickfield would not
make more than a certain number of bricks, but if no such
agreement has been entered into, it may well be that,
although at the end of any one year the lessee had made
so many bricks that he could afford to pay, for instance,
£150 as royalty to his landlord, he could not prudently at
the beginning of any one year when the rate is made
contract at all events to pay more than £100   and as this
case decides in that event that the £100 is the full
measure of the rate for the ensuing year, it would probably
happen that in fact higher royalties or rent would be paid
to the landlord than the local authorities could assess the
occupier upon, for the simple reason that it would be
impossible to prove at Quarter Sessions the likely make of
any brickfield for the ensuing twelve months because orders
are not given twelve months in advance, and there could be
no possible evidence to show the certainty of the make in
the future   The probability of the make in the future would
not be sufficient, because it might be exceeded or not
reached, and in either case an injustice would occur either
to the ratepayer or the local authority

It would appear, therefore, that the soundest method, under the existing conditions, which are admittedly most conflicting, is to rate such a property for the ensuing year on the evidence of the previous year, or in other words to presume at the beginning of any one year that the rent for the ensuing year will be the same as was actually paid in the last year, and if all sides agreed to this proposition comparatively little injustice could arise

In the case of *R* v *The Abney Park Cemetery Co* [1] Mr Justice Blackburn is reported to have said "No injustice will be done if the company are rated in every year according to the value which a hypothetical tenant would give for the occupation in the preceding year, and according to this rule the company's receipts in one year will govern the rateable value of the cemetery in the next" but this dictum was discredited as a statement of law by Collins, LJ, in the case of the *Farnham Flint and Gravel Co* v *Farnham Union* [2] It is obvious that the dictum of the learned Judge could not amount to a statement of law, but for all that the utility of the method is endorsed, and while such a practice may be illegal in the strict sense, the convenience and the desirability of it is confirmed by the adoption of it with regard to copper, tin and lead mines in the Rating Act, 1874, [3] and the practical reasons and advantages in the case of these mines is no less in other similar subjects of rating

The cases of *R* v. *Whaddon* [4] and the *Farnham Flint and Gravel Co* v *Farnham Union* [2] are two interesting cases, the one in connection with a coprolite field and the other in connection with a gravel pit, but they are not

---

[1] (1873) L R 8 Q B 515
[2] (1901) 1 Q B 273
[3] 37 & 38 Vict., c 54
[4] (1875) L R 10 Q B 230

comprehensively dealt with here, as in the author's opinion they do not assist the valuer by laying down any new rule to be applied when rating such concerns

Cemeteries

There have been certain companies formed, and, indeed, others are at the present time in formation, with the object of purchasing land to be used as burial grounds These are known as cemetery companies, and they are rateable to the Poor Rates, etc   A curious point arises in the valuation of such companies, as obviously their property is decreasing in value owing to the fact that as the burial ground is continually being filled up there is less space, as time proceeds, for the construction and selling of graves. In one case, viz, *R v St Mary Abbotts, Kensington*,[1] the company contended that, as some parts were sold to persons to be used as vaults in perpetuity, and other portions were disposed of to be used as family graves, the occupation could not be held to be with them (the company), but the Court, however, held that the occupiers of the vaults and family graves were the cemetery company, and, therefore, the company was liable to be rated as such.   There are three important cases upon this subject, including the one already mentioned,[2] and one case (*R v Abney Park Cemetery Co*) stated somewhat *in extenso*, may be found useful   There were nine paragraphs to the special case —

1 —The Abney Park Cemetery Company is a co-partnership duly formed and constituted by and under a deed of settlement, bearing date the 11th of September, 1839, which deed was executed by all the partners of the said co-partnership   Under the provisions of the said deed the company has purchased lands and laid them out as a cemetery, and has erected buildings and catacombs

---

[1] (1840) 10 L J M C 25

[2] (1850) The other two cases being *R v St Giles, Camberwell*, 14 Q B 571, 19 L J M C 126, and *R v Abney Park Cemetery Co*, L R 8 Q B 515, 42 L J M C 20, L T 174, 37 J P 822

and vaults therein for cemetery purposes, and has enclosed the same. The company carries on there the business of a burial company for profit in connection with the said cemetery.

2.—The company charges and receives fees or sums of money for the interment of bodies in graves, and the deposit of bodies in vaults and catacombs, for the re-opening of the same for the proprietors thereof, and making further interments therein, and for the performance of divine worship.

The company also from time to time sells plots of ground for family graves. A copy, marked "A," of the conveyance of one of such plots of ground accompanies and forms part of this case, and it is to be taken that all the other conveyances are in the same form, *mutatis mutandis.*[1]

3.—For the year 1869, £2,333 was received by the company as purchase money for divers plots so disposed of and conveyed.

4.—The company was rated as the occupier of the said lands, buildings, catacombs and vaults, and upon the principle that the company was liable to be rated for,

---

[1] The following was the form of conveyance

"A"

This Indenture made the   day of   , A D 18   ,
Between   the Trustees and Directors of the Abney Park
Cemetery Company of the first part
of the second part, and the said
the Chairman of the Board of Directors of the said Abney Park Cemetery
Company of the third part   Witnesseth that in consideration of
to the said (trustees and directors) paid by the said   (they, the
said trustees and directors) do by the presents (made in pursuance of the
Act for rendering a release as effectual for the conveyance of freehold
estates, as a lease and release by the same parties) release and confirm
unto the said   and his heirs, all that plot of ground numbered
in square No   in the Abney Park Cemetery, in the parish of St
Mary, Stoke Newington, in the County of Middlesex, containing   feet
in length and   feet in width   To hold the said plot of ground unto the
said   , his heirs and assigns, for ever, but nevertheless, upon

inter alia, the receipts derived by them from the sale of
the plots of ground so disposed of and conveyed, the said
sum of £2,333, so received as purchase money for the sale
of the said plots of land, was treated by the respondents
as part of the annual value of the occupation of the
cemetery by the company in the year 1869

5 —The company are bound to keep in good order the
said plots of ground for the purchaser thereof, the doing
of which entails on the company various outlays, which
form part of its working expenses   A duty is moreover
cast upon the company to keep in order in perpetuity all
the grounds of the cemetery, not only during the period
which the company shall continue to realise a revenue
from the burials taking place, and shall receive the sums
of money from time to time as payments for the fee
simple for the plots of land sold as aforesaid, but after
they shall, by selling and using the ground for burials,
have exhausted the land for the above purposes

6 —The gates of the cemetery are closed at half-past
four o'clock p.m. and opened at seven o'clock a m. during
the winter months, and closed at six o'clock p.m and
opened at six o'clock a m during summer months, and

---

trust, and to the intent that he the said   his heirs and assigns
may (subject, nevertheless, to the rules and orders for the time being of
the said company, for the management and regulation of the said
cemetery, and the catacombs and vaults therein) erect or construct a vault
or mausoleum in or upon the same and may use the said plot of ground
(vault or mausoleum) as and for a place of burial for the body or bodies of
such persons only as he or they shall, for the time being, think proper to
permit or suffer to be buried there, and for no other purpose whatsoever
And subject to the intent aforesaid, in trust of the said (trustees and
directors), their heirs and assigns, for ever, as part of the property of the
said company   And the said   doth hereby for himself, his
heirs, executors, administrators and assigns, covenant with the said
(trustees and directors), their heirs and assigns, and also as a separate
covenant with the said (chairman), his heirs, executors, administrators
and assigns, that he the said   , his heirs, and assigns, shall and
will, from time to time, and at all times hereafter, and at his and their
own costs and charges as often as occasion shall require, well and
sufficiently repair the grave, gravestone, mausoleum or vault to be erected

during the intervals, according to the regulations of the company, no admission is allowed even to a purchaser of a vault or catacomb

7—The appellants contended that the company was entitled, in calculating the rateable value which a hypothetical tenant would give, to exclude the sums received for the purchase of the said plots of ground sold and conveyed in fee simple during the year from the gross receipts of the company.

8.—If the Court should be of opinion that the respondents were right in calculating the rateable value of the property as being that set forth in the rate, without deducting therefrom the sums received as purchase money for the said plots, then the rate to be confirmed.

9—But if the Court should be of opinion that the appellants were entitled to deduct the said sum of £2,333 then the Valuation List to be sent back to the Sessions to fix the amount.

Blackburn, J, delivered the following judgment "There can be no doubt that the Court of Quarter Sessions was right in this case. There are two questions, the first of which arises upon the mode in which the

---

or made in or on the said plot of ground hereby released or intended so to be, and observe, perform and abide by all and singular the rules and orders which have been, or shall from time to time hereafter be made, by the said company, for the management and regulation of the said cemetery and the catacombs and vaults therein. Provided always, and it is hereby agreed and declared, and in case the said _____ his heirs or assigns, shall at any time or times hereafter without the consent of the said company, make any erection or erections other than a mausoleum, gravestone or vault, as the case may be, on the said plot of ground or any part or parts thereon, or use or permit to be used the said plot of ground, or any part or parts thereof, or any erection or erections thereon, otherwise than as a place of burial, or in case default shall be made in performance of all or any or either of the covenants or stipulations hereinbefore contained, then and in such case it shall be lawful for the said trustees and directors, their heirs and assigns at any time thereafter, into the said plot of ground or any part thereof, in the name of the whole, to re-enter, and the same to have again, hold, possess and enjoy, as in their first or former estate IN WITNESS, etc

company disposes of plots of land for family graves" His Lordship here read part of the conveyance, and then continued "There is, therefore, a conveyance of the fee simple in the plot which is sold to the purchaser upon trust, and to the intent that he may use it for a place of burial, but subject to the rules and orders for the time being of the appellants for the management and regulation of the cemetery Subject to the said intent the purchaser is to hold the plot in trust for the trustees and directors, their heirs and assigns, for ever, as part of the property of the appellants The effect of this is, that the legal estate is outstanding, but there is an occupation by the defendants as *cestui que trusts*, and they have an equitable right in the land. Does it make any difference in respect to their liability to be rated as occupiers that the legal estate is outstanding? I think not The rate is to be made upon the occupiers, and it is immaterial whether the actual occupation is by them in their legal or in their equitable right Upon the question whether or not they are occupiers, *R. v St Mary Abbotts*[1] is precisely in point.

"I think that Mr Poland principally relied upon the second point as to the manner in which the quantum is to be got at Now, the Parochial Assessment Act[2] provides that no rate shall be allowed which shall not be made upon an estimate of the rent at which the hereditament 'might reasonably be expected to be let from year to year' In some cases, perhaps, it would have been better to have said 'to be let for a reasonable number of years, but the Legislature has not said so Here the Assessment Committee find that in the year 1869 the appellants received a sum of £2,333 in respect of the lots which were sold, and the question is, whether the Committee is entitled to take that as part of

---

[1] (1840) 12 A & E 824
[2] (1836) 6 & 7 William IV, c 96

the annual value of the occupation of the cemetery I think that there is a fallacy in Mr. Poland's contention that the sum received is not to be treated as part of the annual value of that year, but ought to be spread over a number of years; for if not then a *multo fortiori*, it could not be so treated in subsequent years. This point is really also decided in *R v St Mary Abbotts* In that case Sir William Follett made no such objection as is now made, and I am loth to depart from that decision I think that if we should adopt Mr Poland's construction we should be repealing the Parochial Assessment Act In *R. v. Everist*,[1] which was a case of a brickfield, the Court said 'A case was supposed of a brickfield worked out in less than a year, to meet the demand of some enormous contract for a public work the consequence would be that the land would have a very much increased value for the year, and it would be only reasonable that it should bear an increased rate for that year In the following year its value might sink almost to nothing and the rate ought to fall proportionately, even to nothing, if the brick-earth being exhausted, the land, like an exhausted coal mine, should become entirely unproductive If this were not so an obvious injustice would be done to the other rate-payers Suppose two brickfields of the same size, which, if worked so as to be consumed in ten years, and by equal working in each year, would produce £1,000 each, on which the rate should be £10, in ten years each will contribute £100 to the parochial burthens Let one be exhausted in the first year, the produce will have been £10,000 but the rate only £10 for that year, according to the appellant's argument, and it may be nothing afterwards but whatever it be afterwards, it is clear that there will have been a valuable occupation in one year escaping as to nine tenths the rate entirely. But no injustice would be done if in every year the occupier could be

Brickfields exhausted in one year

---

[1] (1847) 10 Q B 178, 16 L J M C 87

assessed according to the actual value in that year, and it is the duty of the Overseers to arrive as nearly at this as they can' A different mode has been adopted in the anomalous case of saleable underwoods *R.* v *Mufield*[1] was a case of that kind, and the Court held that although such underwoods be cut only once in twenty-one years, they were liable to be assessed every year, and Lord Ellenborough, C.J., said 'We are of opinion that it is not necessary that any of the profits should have been actually reaped or taken from the property during the period for which the rate is made, but that the property is at all times rateable according to the improvements in its value, or in the rent which might fairly be expected from it. . . . Underwoods are annually improving in value, and the rates the occupier pays are for that improvement This may possibly be hard upon the tenants for life, but if the law have thrown this burthen upon the property, they take it with that burthen' That principle is quite exceptional, and in the present case it is much better to suppose that what was the annual value in one year would be a guide to the probable annual value in another year "

Quain, J, following "*R.* v *St Mary Abbotts*[2] really decides this case, for the only difference is that there the occupiers had a legal right to the land, while here, as to these plots, they have only an equitable right In *Jones* v *The Mersey Dock*[3] it was pointed out that the question was, Who are the occupiers of the land ?—no question being raised as to legal and equitable rights In this case the company are clearly the occupiers, and the only other question is, what rent a tenant from year to year would give for the cemetery? It is obvious that the money received for the sale of the plots is part of the income of

Margin notes:

Anomalous case of saleable underwoods

Rent a tenant would give

[1] (1808) 10 East. 219
[2] (1840) 12 A & E 824 10 L J M C 25, 5 Jur 170
[3] (1865) 35 L J M C 1

the appellants. Mr Poland says that it ought to be apportioned, but that is answered by the passage which has been read from *R* v. *Everist* According to him, if the whole of the plots were sold in one year, the amount would have to be extended over a number of years In estimating the rent which a tenant from year to year would give, the amount of the purchase money must be considered as part of the annual profits '

Archibald, J. " 1 am of opinion that this rate has been correctly made, and that the rule must be discharged Mr Poland has failed to point out any real distinction between this case and *R* v *St Mary Abbotts*. As far as the question of occupation is concerned, the cases are substantially the same An easement is conveyed to the purchaser, but the occupation of the whole cemetery is in the appellants Upon the second question I think that it is right to treat the sum of £2,333 as the profits of the last year '

Easement not an occupation

There are certain burial grounds which are partially exempt. Section 15 of the Burial Act, 1855,[1] enacts as follows —

" No land already or to be hereafter purchased or acquired, under the provisions of any of the Acts herein-before recited[2] for the purpose of a burial ground (with or without any building erected or to be erected thereon), shall while used for such purposes be assessed to any county, parochial or other local rates at a higher value or more improved rent than the value or rent at which the same was assessed at the time of such purchase or acquisition "

[1] 18 & 19 Vict , c 128
[2] 15 & 16 Vict , c 85, 16 and 17 Vict , c 134, and 17 & 18 Vict , c 87

PART III.—PROCEDURE.

CHAPTER I.

OUTSIDE THE METROPOLITAN AREA

Scope of Part III.—Origin of Rating—Parish—Overseer —Inhabitant—Union of Parishes—Union Assessment Acts—Appointment and Powers of Assessment Committees—Valuation Lists—Objections to Valuation Lists —Assessing, Levying and Collection of Rates—Appeals against Rates—Quarter and Special Sessions—Arbitration—Case Stated

IN this part of this book—" Procedure "—it is intended only to deal with the processes and formalities requiring to be complied with in the effective making of the Valuation List on which the Poor Rate is based in the assessing, levying and collecting of such Rate, and in the Appeals which lie against the Valuation List and the Poor Rate, and with the statutory and other provisions with respect to these matters. With this view it is hoped to trace as concisely as may be, and as far as practicable in consecutive narrative form, the whole of such processes, formalities and provisions, in this Chapter I as affecting districts outside the metropolitan area, and in Chapter II. as affecting districts within such area, reference of course being made from time to time to the principal cases, but it is not proposed to attempt to treat the case law in any great detail.

Rating had its origin in the provisions of the Act 43 Eliz.,[1] c. 2, passed in the year 1601, and known as "The Statute of Elizabeth," and there can be no greater tribute to the foresight and capacity of the framers of that measure than the fact, that those provisions, after the lapse of upwards of three centuries, are still in force, and still provide the foundation in practically all questions of rating

Scope of Part III

Origin of rating

---

[1] The Poor Relief Act, 1601

13 Eliz., c. 2,
s. 1
Provision of

By the first section of such Act it was enacted that the Churchwardens of every parish and four, three, or two substantial householders to be nominated by the Justices in Easter week or within one month thereafter shall be the Overseers of the Poor of the parish; and that it shall be their duty " to raise weekly or otherwise by taxation of every inhabitant, parson, vicar and other, and of every occupier of lands, houses, tithes impropriate or propriations of tithes, coal mines or saleable underwoods[1] in the parish," competent sums of money for and towards the necessary relief of the poor as therein defined.

By this means, the parish was first made, as it still is, the unit for rating; the Overseers of the parish were first created and constituted, as they still are, the primary authority for rating; and the subjects of rating were first and indeed still are defined.

Main points
in later
legislation

All these matters, however, have to be considered in the light of later legislation, especially as regards such questions as the constitution and method of appointment of Overseers in certain cases, the " Union " of parishes, the Assessment Committee of the Union, the making and regulation of Valuation Lists, and the assessing levying and collection of rates

Definition of
" parish "

A " parish " by the Poor Law Amendment Act, 1834,[2] is to " be construed to include any parish, city, borough, town, township, liberty, precinct, vill, village, hamlet, tithing, chapelry or any other place or division or district of a place maintaining its own poor, whether parochial or extra-parochial ", and the Interpretation Act, 1889,[3] provides that in every Act passed after the year 1866 " the expression ' parish ' shall, unless the contrary intention appears, mean a place for which a separate Poor Rate is or can be made, or for which a separate overseer is or can be appointed '

---

[1] As to underwoods and other woods, see The Rating Act, 1874 (37 & 38 Vict., c 54), ss 1 and 14
[2] 4 & 5 William IV., c 76, s 109
[3] 52 & 53 Vict, c 63, s 5

Where a parish adjoins a river it has been held there is *prima facie* presumption that the parish boundary extends to the centre of the river.[1]

The Overseers of the parish are still appointed under the Statute of Elizabeth,[2] subject to further enactments as follows:—The Poor Law Relief Act, 1662,[3] authorised the appointment of Overseers for townships and villages forming parts of a parish. but this power is by the Poor Law Amendment Act, 1844,[4] confined to any township, village or other place for which separate Overseers had been lawfully appointed before the passing of such last-named Act. The Poor Relief Act, 1743,[5] enables Overseers in every township or place where there are no Churchwardens to perform all acts relating to the poor in like manner as Churchwardens and Overseers. The Poor Law Amendment Act, 1866,[6] provides that if Justices are satisfied in any parish that two overseers cannot be conveniently appointed from the inhabitant householders in such parish, they may appoint one overseer only, and if in such parish there is no householder liable or fit to be appointed, they shall appoint some inhabitant householder of an adjoining parish, willing to serve, to be such overseer, with or without salary, and the Local Government Act, 1894,[7] enacts that in *every rural parish* the Churchwardens are to cease to be Overseers, that to replace them an additional number of overseers may be appointed, and that the power and duty of appointing

Appointment of Overseers

---

[1] *McCannon v Sinclair*, (1859) 2 El & El 53, 28 L J M C 247, also *Forest v Overseers of Greenwich*, (1858) 8 El & Bl 890, 27 L T M C 96, 4 Jur 480 also *Cory v Bristol*, (1877) 2 App Cas 262, 46 L J M C 273, 36 L T 595, 41 J P 709

[2] (1601) 43 Eliz, c 2, s 1

[3] 14 Car II c 12, s 21

[4] 7 & 8 Vict, c. 101, s 22

[5] 17 Geo II, c 38, s. 15

[6] 29 & 30 Vict, c 113, s 11

[7] 56 & 57 Vict, c 73, s 5

overseers and the power of appointing and revoking the appointment of an assistant overseer, and also the power of the Vestry (other than in ecclesiastical matters) shall be vested in the Parish Council, or in parishes where there is no Parish Council, in the Parish Meeting [1] Further, that in a rural parish having a Parish Council, the powers, duties and liabilities of the Overseers with respect to appeals or objections by them in respect of the Valuation List or appeals in respect of the Poor Rate or County Rate, or the basis of the County Rate are transferred to such Council,[1] and in a rural parish not having a Parish Council a similar transfer to the Parish Meeting may be made by order of the County Council [1] It is also provided by the same Act that powers similar to those above enumerated or any of them *may*, by order of the Local Government Board, and upon the application of such Council, be vested in *the Council of a Municipal borough or of an Urban district* [1]

Therefore it is only in those parishes (not being townships) which are urban, and in which no order of the Local Government Board has been made that Churchwardens *ex-officio* are still Overseers, and it is only in urban parishes and urban townships in which such last-mentioned order has not been made that Overseers are still appointed by the Justices, and whenever the expression "overseer" or "vestry" is used the same must be considered in the light of the above-mentioned provisions of the Local Government Act, 1894 [1]

"Inhabitant" defined

An "inhabitant" is anyone who resides, or who is in occupation of any hereditament, in a particular parish [2]

The subjects for and of rating, as defined in the Statute of Elizabeth, have been to some extent amplified by the Rating Act, 1874,[3] and the Advertising Stations (Rating) Act, 1889 [4] (as to which see Part I., Chapter I *ante*)

---

[1] 56 & 57 Vict., c 73, ss 5, 6, 19, 33, 34
[2] *R v North Curry*, 7 D & R 424, 4 B & C 953
[3] 37 & 38 Vict., c 54
[4] 52 & 53 Vict., c 27

There are also certain exemptions from rating which have to be considered (as to which see Part I, Chapter II. *ante*)

Further, it is to be remembered that by the Poor Rate Exemption Act, 1840,[1] the liability of the inhabitant, as such, to be rated, and so the liability of personal property to be considered in rating, which, though little acted on, had existed under the Act of Elizabeth, has been abolished

As time went on, also, it was found convenient for parishes to unite in the matter of the administration of Poor Law relief, and statutory provisions were passed for facilitating and regulating this. Parishes so united constitute what is known as the "Union," with a governing body called "The Board of Guardians of the Union," the election of the members to such Board being now regulated by the provisions of the Local Government Act, 1894[2] This is important from a rating point of view, as it is with the "Union" as a foundation that "An Act to amend the Law relating to Parochial Assessments in England," and called "The Union Assessment Committee Act, 1862,'[3] was passed, to make (to quote the recital of the Act) "more effectual provision for securing uniform and correct valuations of parishes in the Unions of England"

By this Act, s 2, the Board of Guardians of every Union are required in every year at their first meeting after their annual election to appoint from among themselves not less than six nor more than twelve,[4] to be called the Assessment Committee of the Union for the investigation and supervision of the valuations to be made within such Union, and in Section 3 there is

Union" of parishes

Union Assessment Committee Act, 1862

Appointment of Assessment Committee of Union

---

[1] 3 & 4 Vict , c 89, s 1

[2] 56 & 57 Vict , c 73, s 20.

[3] 25 & 26 Vict , c 103

[4] The section originally contained provision as to a proportion of the committee being *ex-officio* Guardians, but such provision has been repealed by the Local Government Act, 1894 (56 & 57 Vict , c 73), s 89

provision, in the event of a Union being coterminous with a Municipal Borough, as to the possible representation of the Council of such borough upon the Assessment Committee

Meetings and Minute books of Assessment Committee

To constitute a quorum of the Committee not less than three, and not less than one-third of the whole number of the Committee, must be present, the Chairman has a second or casting vote, and the Committee are required to keep a Minute of their proceedings in books to be provided for that purpose, and every entry is to be signed by the presiding chairman of the meeting to which it relates, and purporting to be so signed is to be received as evidence in all Courts until the contrary be proved, and all such books are to be open, at all reasonable times, to inspection without fee, to all ratepayers[1] It is well to note this last provision, as sometimes there is a reluctance to produce the books

Assessment Committee may require particulars in writing and production of books of assessment of taxes, rates and valuations

The Committee may require from Overseers and other persons having the custody of books of assessment of any taxes or rates, parliamentary or parochial, or of valuations of any parish, or having the collection or management of any such taxes or rates, returns in writing of particulars thereof, and may require the production of parochial and public books and documents, and may examine persons attending before them, but this provision is not to apply to any valuations or assessments not suffered to be made public[2]

Valuation List for parish to be made by overseers

The Overseers of each parish within three months of the appointment of the Committee are to make a list of all rateable hereditaments in the parish with the annual value thereof in the form annexed to the Union Assessment Committee Act, 1862,[3] or in a parish where

<hr>

[1] The Union Assessment Committee Act 1862 (25 & 26 Vict, c. 103), ss 9, 11

[2] Ibid, s 13

[3] 25 & 26 Vict, c 103, s 14

there is agricultural land, in the form set out below,[1] and unless such Overseers think that the valuation then last acted upon in assessing the rate for the relief of the poor correctly shows such full annual value, they are to revise the valuation[2] The list so made is to be signed by the Overseers and to be styled "The Valuation List"[2]

THE FORM referred to above —

VALUATION LIST for *(the parish or place for which the List is made),* in the County of

Name of Occupier	Name of Owner	Description of Property	Name or Situation of Property	Estimated Extent	Gross Estimated Rental	Rateable Value of Agricultural Land	Rateable Value of Buildings and other Hereditaments not being Agricultural Land
1	2	3	4	5.	6	7	8
				A R P	£ s d	£ s d	£ s d

Signed this   day of

A B } *Overseers of the Poor of*
A C } *the Parish aforesaid*

This form is given as being the one usually used, and it is to be pointed out that it is not usual to make an annual list, but to rely on the provision of Section 24 of the Union Assessment Committee Act, 1862, that every Valuation List approved by the Assessment Committee and delivered to the Overseers of the parish to which it relates, with and subject to the alterations and additions for the time being made therein and thereto by any Supplemental List, is to be the Valuation List in force for such parish until a new Valuation List, in substitution for the same, be approved and delivered in like manner.[3]

The Agricultural Rates Order (1896) Act, Article xvi
[2] The Union Assessment Committee Act, 1862 (25 & 26 Vict., c 103), s 14
[3] *Ibid*, s 24

Supplemental Valuation List, when to be made

A Supplemental Valuation List is to be made by the Overseers when and so often as any property not included in the Valuation List in force in any parish becomes rateable, or where, by reason of any alteration in the occupation of any property included in such lists, such property becomes liable to be rated in parts not mentioned in such list as rateable hereditaments and separately valued therein, or it shall appear to the Overseers that any rateable property included in such list has been increased or decreased in value since the valuation thereof, whether by building, destruction of building, or other alteration in the condition thereof or otherwise, and it is to be with respect to such properties only [1]

Assessment Committee may direct new or Supplemental Valuation List to be made

The Assessment Committee may further from time to time direct a new valuation of all or any of the rateable hereditaments in a parish, and a new Valuation List in substitution for the Valuation List in force for such parish, or a Supplemental List, in substitution for any part thereof or in addition thereto, to be made by the Overseers, or the Committee may, with the consent of the Board of Guardians of the Union, after notice thereof to every guardian, in any case appoint a person for such purpose, and may direct him to make and sign such list instead of the Overseers, and the same when so made and signed is to be delivered by him to the Overseers of the parish to which it relates [2]

The Guardians upon application of the Assessment Committee, and after notice as above, may appoint a valuer to assist the Committee at a salary or other settled remuneration to be paid out of the common fund [3]

---

[1] The Union Assessment Committee Act, 1862 (25 & 26 Vict , c 103), s. 25

[2] *Ibid* , ss. 26, 16

[3] The Poor Law Amendment Act, 1868 (31 & 32 Vict , c 122), s 32

All the provisions with respect to the making, the form, and the signing of, and indeed all other the provisions with respect to a Valuation List, apply equally to a Supplemental or new Valuation List, and the expression "Valuation List" must therefore be taken to include all such lists

"Valuation List" includes Supplemental or new Valuation List

All rateable hereditaments whether occupied or not are to be included in the Valuation List, but not exempted properties, and in the case of partially-exempted properties such values only should be inserted as will give effect to the partial exemption, save in the case of agricultural land, as to which it is provided by the Agricultural Rates Act, 1896,[1] that the partial exemption thereby given is to be effected by levying one-half only of the rate "in the £," payable in respect of buildings and other hereditaments It is, however, also to be noted that where a contribution is paid in aid of the Poor Rate in respect of Government property within any parish there must be entered in the Valuation List the figure representing the annual value of such property, so that the same may be added to the rateable value of the parish in computing the contribution to the common fund of the Union.[2]

Properties to be included in Valuation Lists

The definitions of "Gross Estimated Rental" and of "Rateable Value" respectively, and the methods of and considerations arising or likely to arise in arriving at the amounts thereof in relation to the various classes of hereditaments liable to be rated, as well as the exemptions and partial exemptions from rating, are dealt with in Part I., Chapter IV

Gross estimated rental' 'Rateable value"

The expenses of making a Valuation List by a person appointed for the purpose may be charged on the Poor Rate of the parish or on the common fund of the Union[3];

Expenses of Valuation List, how to be met

---

[1] 59 & 60 Vict , c 16, s 1

[2] The Union Assessment Committee Act, 1862 (25 & 26 Vict , c. 103), s 30 See p 473 *post.*

[3] *Ibid* , s 39

or if such valuation be of all the hereditaments in a parish, the Guardians, with the consent of the Local Government Board, may borrow money for the expenses [1]

Any expenses which may be incurred by the Overseers in making out any list, or in revising or valuing any rateable hereditaments in the parish, may, with the consent of the Vestry,[2] given by express resolution after due notice, be charged on the Poor Rate, or if no Vestry Meeting be held or no decision be arrived at, then the said expenses may be so charged to the extent to which the Assessment Committee shall allow   But, if any such expense be in respect of the valuation of property, it can only be charged on the Poor Rate, if the consent of the Assessment Committee to the procuring of such valuation by the Overseers has been given previously to the same being made.[3]

The valuation of a valuer appointed by the Assessment Committee is to be in writing, showing the amount of each valuation, and signed, and to be open to inspection [4]

As to deposit of Valuation List when made and signed, and notice thereof and transmission of list to Assessment Committee

A Valuation List, when signed by the Overseers or delivered to them by a person appointed to make the same, is to be deposited in the place in the parish in which Rate Books are deposited or kept, and a copy of such list is to be forthwith delivered to the Board of Guardians, and the Overseers are to give public notice of the deposit of such list on the Sunday next following the deposit of such list   This notice is to be given in the same manner, and all persons assessed or liable to be assessed to the relief of the poor of the parish are to have the like right of inspecting and

---

[1] The Union Assessment Committee Amendment Act, 1864 (27 & 28 Vict , c 39), s 8

[2] Subject to the provision of the Local Government Act, 1894   See pp 461-2 ante

[3] The Union Assessment Committee Amendment Act, 1864 (27 & 28 Vict., c 39), s 7

[4] Ibid , s 1, and see *Rawlence* v *Hursley Union*, (1877) 3 Ex D 44

demanding and taking copies of and extracts from such list, as in the case of a Poor Rate (see p 477 *post*)   At the expiration of fourteen days from the time of the notice being given of the deposit of the list, the Overseers must transmit the same to the Assessment Committee [1]

After the list has been transmitted to the Assessment Committee any overseer or other ratepayer in the parish is entitled to inspect and take copies from any list so transmitted [1], and within fourteen days after such transmission the Committee must give notice to every railway, telegraph, canal, gas and water company named in the list, and not having any office or place of business in the parish to which the list relates, of the sum or sums set down as the rateable value of the property purporting to be occupied by such company or companies [2]

Subsequent right of inspection, etc , of Valuation List and notice to certain rail way and other companies

Any overseers of any parish in the Union who shall have reason to think that such parish is aggrieved by the Valuation Lists of any parish in the Union, or any person who may feel himself aggrieved by any Valuation List on the ground of unfairness or incorrectness in the valuation of any hereditament included therein or on the ground of the omission of any rateable hereditament from such list, may at any time after deposit as aforesaid of such list, and before the expiration of twenty-eight days after the notice of deposit as aforesaid, give to the Committee and the Overseers a notice in writing of his objection, specifying the grounds thereof, and where any such ground is unfairness or incorrectness in the valuation of any hereditament in respect of which any person other than the person objecting is liable to be rated, or the omission of such hereditament, notice of the objection and of the grounds thereof must also be given

As to objection to Assessment Committee against Valuation List

---

[1] The Union Assessment Committee Act, 1862 (25 & 26 Vict , c 103), s 17

[2] The Union Assessment Committee Amendment Act, 1864 (27 & 28 Vict , c 39), s. 5

to such other person [1] This power of objection and the
obligations on the Committee to hold meetings next
referred to are enlarged by the provisions of Section 1
of the Union Assessment Committee Amendment Act,
1864,[2] dealt with later (see p 484 *post*) If, however,
it be desired in any case to exercise this power of
objection against the Valuation List, it is to be noted
that (*a*) notice must be in writing, (*b*) all grounds of
objection desired to be taken must be specified, and
only those specified can be considered by the committee or be supported should it afterwards be determined to appeal to Quarter Sessions against a rate
based on such lists, (*c*) notice must be given to the
Assessment Committee and the Overseers, and in the case
of objection on the ground of unfairness or incorrectness
in the valuation, or of the omission, of a hereditament
for which a person other than the person objecting is
liable to be rated, then to such other person also   It is
further to be noted that in place of the Overseers, for the
purposes of objection by them under the powers now under
consideration, there is substituted in a rural parish having
a Parish Council, the Parish Council, and that in the case
of a rural parish not having a Parish Council or of a
municipal borough or urban district, an order may be in
force under which the Parish Meeting, or the Borough or
the Urban District Council, as the case may be, may have
been similarly substituted [3] In any such case it will be
safer to serve both the Overseers and the Parish Council
or other Body, even though for this purpose it may be
questionable whether there has been a transfer of the
power.

Meetings of
Assessment
Committee
to hear and
determine
objections

If objection be taken to a Valuation List, and notices
duly given aforesaid, the Assessment Committee must
hold such meetings as they think necessary for hearing,

---

[1] The Union Assessment Committee Act, 1862 (25 & 26 Vict c 103), s 18
   For general form of objection see Appendix III *post*

[2] 27 & 28 Vict , c 39

[3] See the provisions of the Local Government Act, 1894 pp 161-2 *ante*.

and thereat hear and determine the same, and of any such meeting (other than a meeting by adjournment) they must cause at least twenty-eight days' previous notice in writing to be given to the Overseers of the parish affected and such Overseers are required on the following Sunday to publish the notice in the same manner as a notice of rate allowed by Justices[1] (as to which see p 477 *post*) It is to be noted that this meeting cannot be held earlier than twenty-eight days after the public notice of deposit of the list by the Overseers,[2] or earlier than would allow of an effective notice to be given to any limited companies as provided by the Union Assessment Committee Amendment Act, 1864,[3] but the notice of the meeting may be given, it would seem, so that the publication thereof may be either with or subsequently to the public notice of deposit of the rate.

The Assessment Committee, whether objection be or be not made and either before or after any meeting for hearing objections, may make such alterations in the valuation of any hereditament included in a Valuation List, and insert in such list any rateable hereditament omitted therefrom, and make such corrections in names, descriptions and particulars, and upon such information as to them may seem sufficient, and thereafter the Committee are to approve the list under the hands of three members present at the meeting when the same is approved, with the date of such approval. Before, however, thus approving a Valuation List, if any alteration in the valuation of any hereditament as aforesaid be made, or any rateable hereditament omitted be inserted, the Committee are required to cause the list, with such alteration or insertion, to be deposited in the same manner

As to alteration and approval of Valuation List by Assessment Committee

---

[1] The Union Assessment Committee Act 1862 (25 & 26 Vict c 103) s 19

[2] *Assessment Committee Reigate Union v South Eastern Railway Co,* (1894) 1 Q B 411

27 & 28 Vict, c 39, s 5

as a Valuation List made by or delivered to the overseers (see p 468 *ante*), and are to cause the like notice of such deposits to be given as in the case of a Valuation List made and delivered as aforesaid (see p. 468 *ante*), and also to appoint a day not less than seven nor more than fourteen days from the re-deposit of the list for hearing any objections thereto as so altered, and to hear and determine any such objection [1] The power of alteration thus given extends to the increase of the amount of the assessment, and is to be distinguished from the position of the Committee in respect of an objection under the Union Assessment Committee Amendment Act. 1864, Section 1 (see p 184 *post*) in which case they are bound by and cannot increase the amount of the assessment [2] but on the other hand, in this latter case, they have no need to re-deposit the list if alteration be made [3]

Copy of Valuation Lists to be kept by Guardians for inspection

The Committee are also to cause the Valuation List for the time being in force for every parish in the Union (with the totals therein of "Gross Estimated Value" and "Rateable Value" respectively entered at the foot thereof) to be deposited in the Board Room or other convenient place in the custody of the clerk and to be open at reasonable times to the inspection of any Guardian, or to any Overseers of any parish without charge, or to any ratepayer on payment of one shilling [4]

Valuation List when approved to be delivered to overseers

A copy of the Valuation List when approved by the Committee is to be delivered to the Overseers of the parish to which it relates, and to be preserved at the like place and in the like custody, and be subject to the like resort thereto, and be delivered over from time to time in like manner as the Poor Rate books (see p 177 *post*), and it

---

[1] The Union Assessment Committee Act, 1862 (25 and 26 Vict , c 103) ss. 20, 21

[2] *Horton v Walsall Union* (1898), 2 Q B 237 ; 67 L J Q B 804 , 62 J P 437

[3] *R v Edmonds* (1874), L R , 9 Q B 598

[4] The Union Assessment Committee Act, 1862 (25 & 26 Vict , c 103) s 31, and Poor Law Amendment Act, 1868 (31 & 32 Vict , c 122), s 30

is to be produced by the Overseers before the Justices upon application for allowance of rates, and at the Special, General or Quarter Sessions, when any appeal is to be heard, and also at such times or places as the Committee may from time to time direct.[1]

The totals of the gross and rateable values of the Valuation List for each Parish (distinguishing the values of Agricultural land) are to be sent by the Clerk to the Assessment Committee to the Clerk of the Peace in December each year.[2]

Totals to be sent to Clerk of Peace

For the purpose of computing the contribution to the common fund of the Union, the annual rateable values of each of the parishes in the Union is to be taken from the Valuation Lists for the time being in force, the addition being made, in the case of there being any Government property, of the annual value thereof on which, if a contribution be made, the same is calculated.[3]

Contributions to common fund of Union to be based on Valuation Lists

Against the decision of the Assessment Committee on objection to the Valuation List there is no appeal by the ratepayer until after a rate has been laid on the basis of the list, a point dealt with later (see pp 181 *et seq post*)

For the purpose, however, of testing the fairness of the valuation of one parish as compared with another there is provided a power of appeal by the Overseers of any parish. who, with the consent of the Vestry[4] specially summoned for the purpose, may appeal to the Quarter Sessions to be holden after the expiration of one calendar month from the allowance and deposit of the Valuation List on the ground that the rateable hereditaments comprised in the Valuation List of such parish are valued at sums beyond the annual value thereof, or on the ground that the rateable hereditaments comprised in the Valuation List for another parish are valued at sums less than the annual value

Appeals to Quarter Sessions by overseers against Valuation List of parish

---

[1] The Union Assessment Committee Act, 1862 (25 & 26 Vict c 103), s. 23, and the Poor Law Amendment Act, 1868 (31 & 32 Vict, c 122) s 30

[2] The Union Assessment Committee Amendment Act, 1864 (27 & 28 Vict, c 39), s 9, The Agricultural Rates Act, 1896 (59 & 60 Vict, c 16), s 5 (b)

[3] The Union Assessment Committee Act, 1862 (25 & 26 Vict, c 103), s 30

[4] See the provisions of the Local Government Act, 1894, p 462 *ante*

thereof   In either of such cases fourteen clear days'
notice in writing previous to the Sessions is to be given
to the Guardians of the Union of the intention to appeal
and the grounds thereof, and in the latter of such cases a
similar notice is to be given to the Overseers of the parish
of which the valuation is objected to[1]   This power is
seldom used, but when put into operation the before-
mentioned provisions of the Local Government Act,
1894   must be remembered[2]

Making of
Poor Rate

As provided by the Statute of Elizabeth,[3] the Rate for
the Relief of the Poor is to be made by the Overseers of
the parish, but no longer under the bare provisions of
that Statute   Under the Parochial Assessment Act,
1836,[4] s 1, every such rate must be made upon an
estimate of the net annual value of the several hereditaments rated thereunto, as therein defined, and by Section 2,

Particulars
to be shewn
on rate

every rate must also, in addition to any other particulars
which the form of making out such rate shall require to
be set forth, contain an account of every particular set
forth at the head of the respective columns in the form
given in the Schedule to the said Act, or, in the case of
any parish in which there is agricultural land as defined
by the Agricultural Rates Act, 1896,[5] in the form set
out in Schedule Y to the Agricultural Rates Order, 1896
(see Appendix II., *post*).

Rate to be
based on
Valuation
List

The Union Assessment Committee Act, 1862,[6] s 28,
provides that every poor, or other rate required to be
based thereon, shall be in accordance with and based on
the values in the Valuation List in force for the time
being, and the Overseers are required to sign a declaration

---

[1] The Union Assessment Committee Act, 1862 (25 & 26 Vict , c 103)
ss 32 to 34

[2] See pp 461-2 *ante*

[3] (1601) 43 Eliz , c 2

[4] 6 & 7 William IV , c 96

[5] 59 & 60 Vict , c 16

[6] 25 & 26 Vict , c 103

to this effect in the form set out in the Schedule to the Act (see Appendix I, *post*), provided always that where it happens that the conditions with respect to any rateable hereditament included in the Valuation List as a whole have become so changed that it is liable to be rated in parts, such parts, where not dealt with by a Supplemental List, may be rated according to such amounts as shall be fair apportioned parts of the annual rateable value in the said list. In any such case, however, it is better to deal with the matter by means of a supplemental Valuation List.

By the Poor Law Amendment Act, 1868,[1] s. 38, it is further provided that where any person shall occupy any new house or other building in any parish where the Poor Rate is not made under the provisions of a Local Act, which house or building was incomplete or not finished for occupation, or was not entered as such in the Valuation List in force for the time being, at the time when the current rate for the time being was made, the Overseers may enter such house or building with the name of the occupier thereof, and the date of the entry in the Rate Book, and require the occupier to pay such amount as they shall consider the proper sum, having due regard to the rateable value of such house or building and the time which shall have elapsed from the making of the current rate to the date of such entry, and the person so charged shall be considered as actually rated from such date as fully and effectually, and with the same power of appeal, as if he had been assessed when the rate was made. In any such case, however, the Overseers when they so enter the house or other building, are to forward to the Assessment Committee a Supplemental Valuation List in respect of such house or building, to be dealt with in the ordinary way. When it is desired to enforce this power it is necessary to consider whether the heredita-

Rate may be levied in certain cases when property not in Valuation List

---

[1] 31 & 32 Vict., c. 122.

ment in question comes within the description "house or other building," as such words seem only to contemplate a house or building of like kind, and not to extend to rateable hereditaments in general, and care must be taken to comply with all the requirements of the section concurrently, or the omission of any one of such requirements may afford ground for objection to the ratepayer It should also be noted that from the wording of the section it is clearly intended that the rate shall operate only from the time that it is allowed by the Justices

Title of rate
In the title to the rate there must be set forth the period for which the rate is estimated, and if the same is payable by instalments the amount of each instalment and the date at which each instalment is payable , but notwithstanding, if the necessities of the parish so require, another rate may be made before the expiration of the said period [1]

Rate payable by instalments
If the rate be for a period exceeding three months it may be declared to be payable by instalments at such time as shall be specified, and thereupon each instalment is enforceable as and when it falls due [2]

Occupier's name to be entered in rate in all cases
The Overseers are also required (under penalty) in making out the rate to enter in the "Occupier's" column the name of the occupier of every rateable hereditament, and this whether the owner or the occupier is liable for the payment of the rate, and also where the occupier occupies so as to entitle him to the service franchise [3]

Rate to be allowed by Justices
The rate having been written out in accordance with the foregoing requirements, it is to be submitted by the Overseers to the Justices in Petty Sessions for allowance

[1] The Poor Rate Assessment and Collection Act, 1869 (32 & 33 Vict., c 41), s 14

[2] Ibid., s 15

[3] Ibid , s 19, the Parliamentary and Municipal Registration Act, 1878 (41 & 42 Vict , c 26), s. 14, and the Representation of the People Act, 1884 (48 Vict , c 3), s 9 (8).

by them, and is to be deemed to be made on the day when so allowed[1], and the production of the rate so purporting to be made is to be *prima facie* evidence of due making and publication[2]

When the rate has been thus allowed, notice thereof must be given on the next Sunday. This notice must be reduced into writing, and copies thereof, either in writing or print, or partly in writing and partly in print, must, previously to the commencement of divine service in the morning or the evening, be affixed at or near to the principal door of every church or chapel of the Established Church in which divine service is performed in the parish[3] In any parish in which there is no church or chapel of the parish the said notice is to be affixed in some public and conspicuous place or situation within the parish[4]

Notice of rate

Every inhabitant of the parish is entitled at all seasonable times on payment of one shilling to inspect the rate, and the Overseers must on demand give copies of the same or any part thereof to any such inhabitant on payment of sixpence for every twenty-four names[5], and the Overseers are also bound under penalty to allow any person rated to the relief of the poor in any rate at all seasonable times to take copies of or extracts from such rate without any payment[6]

Inspection and copies of rate

If an occupier assessed in the rate when made ceases to occupy before the rate shall have been wholly discharged he is liable for so much, and no more, of the rate as is proportionate to the time of his occupation within the period for which the rate was made; and if

Apportionment of rate in certain cases

---

[1] The Poor Rate Assessment and Collection Act, 1869 (32 & 33 Vict., c. 41), s. 17

[2] *Ibid*, s. 18

[3] The Poor Rate Act, 1743 (17 Geo. II., c. 3), s. 1, and the Parish Notices Act, 1837 (7 William IV., and 1 Vict., c. 45), ss. 1 and 2

[4] The Poor Rate Assessment and Collection Act, 1869, Amendment Act, 1882 (45 & 46 Vict. c. 20), s. 4

[5] The Poor Rate Act, 1743 (17 Geo. II., c. 3), s. 2.

[6] The Parochial Assessments Act, 1836 (6 & 7 William IV., c. 96), s. 5

during such period an occupier enters on a property he is liable for so much of the rate as shall be appropriate to the time between the commencement of his occupation and the expiration of the said period [1]

It has been stated that *R. v. Tempest* [2] and *Davis v. Woodfield* [3] have decided that the period for the purpose of this provision must be taken to begin on the day when the rate was made   It is submitted that this is not so, as in the former case it was expressly stated that Section 16 of the Poor Rate Assessment and Collection Act, 1869, [4] did not apply , and in the latter case the period of the rate was not set forth in the title of the rate further than that it was to defray expenses to be incurred up to a named date, subsequent to the levying of the rate   Therefore, in fact, there has not been decided more than this —that when the period for which the rate is made is not stated in the title to the rate, the period must be taken to begin when the rate is allowed

Demand of rate   The rate having been duly made allowed, and published, demand for payment thereof must be made by the Overseers or Assistant Overseer or by any person duly authorised in that behalf [5]   This is usually done by means of a printed demand note   The exact sum due must be demanded, and no more," but if less be demanded the authorities may correct the mistake by a fresh demand for the balance, and this though the amount of the first demand has been actually paid. [7]   If the

[1] The Poor Rate Assessment and Collection Act, 1869 (32 & 33 Vict , c 41), s 16, and the Poor Rate Assessment and Collection Act, 1869, Amendment Act, 1882 (45 & 46 Vict , c 20), s. 3

[2] (1898) 14 T.L R 199

[3] (1900) 81 L T 782 , 64 J P. 215.

[4] 32 & 33 Vict , c 41

[5] See the General Orders of the Local Government Board, 1875

[6] *Hurrell v Wink*, (1818) 2 Moore 417 , 8 Taunt, 369.

[7] *R v Blenkinsop*, (1892) 1 Q B 43 , 61 L J M C. 45, 66 L T 187

occupier (or the owner if he be liable to be rated) of the rated hereditament be not living thereon, nor in the parish for which the rate is made, demand of the rate in writing delivered to the person having custody of the hereditament, or if no such person can be found, affixed to some conspicuous part thereof, is to be deemed a sufficient demand[1], while in the case of any corporation aggregate, joint stock or other company, or any conservators or other public trustees, a demand for payment either by letter addressed to or made personally upon their clerk or secretary or other principal officer at their office, is to be deemed a sufficient demand[2]. In the case of a rate payable by instalments one demand in writing for the whole rate is sufficient[3].

If a rate having been duly demanded be not paid or appealed against, proceedings may be taken for recovery thereof before a Court of summary jurisdiction, and for this purpose a complaint must be laid before a Justice and a summons taken out to show cause why the rate has not been paid. If the person liable to be rated does not live on the premises rated or cannot be found, the summons may be served as, in similar circumstances, a demand note may be served as stated above. At the hearing of the summons, to quote the words of Blackburn, J., in *ex parte May*,[4] 'If the rate is good on the face of it, and has been duly made, allowed and published, and there is jurisdiction to make a rate on the person charged, the duty of the Justices becomes ministerial," and a distress is to be granted—as of course. The production of the book purporting to contain a Poor Rate, with the allowance

Recovery of rate by distress

[1] The Poor Law Amendment Act, 1868 (31 & 32 Vict, c 122), s 39
[2] *Ibid*, s 40
[3] General Order of Local Government Board, 1875, *Overseers of Walton-on-the-Hill v Jones*, (1893) 2 Q B. 175, 62 L J M.C. 123.
[4] (1862) 31 L J M C 161

thereof by the Justices, and made in the form prescribed by law, is to be *prima facie* evidence of the due making and publication of the rate.[1] The Justices, however, can clearly entertain evidence by the ratepayer to show that the rate has not been duly made or duly allowed or duly published[2] The Justices are also entitled to enquire, where the owner is rated instead of the occupier, whether any power therefor existed, and to state a case for the opinion of the High Court.[3] On proceedings to recover where the ratepayer has been in occupation for a part only of the period covered by the rate, the Justices may determine the amount due, and forthwith issue a distress warrant for such amount.[4] In the case of a rate payable by instalments, proceedings for recovery thereof can only be taken in respect of such instalments or instalment as shall have actually fallen due.[5] If a number of local rates and taxes whether of the same or different kinds are due from the same person, then under the Poor Rates Recovery Act, 1862,[6] the proceedings for the recovery thereof may be consolidated

Payment of rate pending appeal
Pending an appeal against a rate the ratepayer can be compelled to pay no greater sum of money in respect thereof than that on which he was rated in the last effective rate preceding the rate under appeal, and if he pay a greater sum than that ultimately decided to be due, the Court are required to order the repayment of the excess.[7]

---

[1] The Poor Rate Assessment and Collection Act, 1869 (32 & 33 Vict, c 41), s 18

[2] *Beeson* v. *Derby*, (1903), " Ryde and Konstam's Rating Appeals " 1894-1904, p. 328

[3] *Tower City Mutual Building Society* v *Churchwardens of East Ham*, (1892) 1 Q.B. 661

[4] *Mansel* v *Itchen Overseers*, (1906) 1 K B 221.

[5] Poor Rate Assessment and Collection Act, 1869 (32 & 33 Vict , c 41), s. 15

[6] 25 and 26 Vict , c 82, s 1

[7] The Poor Rate Act, 1801 (41 Geo III , c 23), ss 2, 8

From the time of its inception by the Statute of Elizabeth, there has always been a power of appeal against a Poor Rate to Quarter Sessions, and in Section 5 of that Act[1] it is provided that any person being aggrieved it shall be lawful for the Quarter Sessions "to take such order therein as to them shall be thought convenient, and the same to conclude and bind all the parties." The Poor Relief Act, 1743,[2] s 4, provides that in case any person shall be "aggrieved by any rate or assessment for the relief of the poor, or shall have any material objection to any person being put in or left out of such rate or assessment, or to the sum charged on any person therein, or shall have any material objection to such account as aforesaid or any part thereof," or shall be aggrieved by any neglect, act or thing done or omitted by the Churchwardens or Overseers, such person giving reasonable notice to the Churchwardens or Overseers of the parish may appeal to the next General or Quarter Sessions, and require the Justices there assembled to receive such appeal and to hear and finally determine the same, but if reasonable notice be not given, then the appeal is required to be adjourned to the next Quarter Sessions, and then and there finally heard and determined and power is given enabling the Justices to award costs to the party for whom the appeal shall be determined

On the construction of this section it is to be noted it has been decided that it is obligatory on the Justices to enter and respite an appeal on application at the next practicable Sessions, not only where there has not been sufficient time to allow of reasonable notice being given, but also when there has been sufficient time, and yet the appellant has failed to give either reasonable or even any notice [3]

Appeal against rate

To Quarter Sessions

[1] The Poor Relief Act, 1601 (43 Eliz , c 2)

[2] 17 Geo II., c 38

[3] R v Justices of London, (1840) 9 Q B 41 , R v. Eyre, (1856) 6 E & B 992.

In the Poor Rate Act, 1801,[1] after reciting the last-mentioned Act, it is provided by Section 4 that all notices of appeal against a rate shall be in writing and signed by the person giving the same, or his attorney, and shall be delivered or left at the place of abode of the Church-wardens and Overseers[1] or any two of them, and that the particular causes or grounds of appeal shall be stated and specified in the notice, and that only the grounds as specified shall be considered at the hearing of the appeal, provided, however (Section 5), that by consent of the parties interested the Court may hear and determine an appeal although no notice be given, or may consider grounds not stated or mis-stated in the notice

By Section 6 of the same Act it is required, that if the appeal be on the ground that some other person in the rate in question is or is not rated, or is rated at a greater or less amount than is right, or that some alteration ought to be made with respect to such other person, then notice of appeal is to be given to every such other person as well as to the Churchwardens and Overseers[2], and such other person is entitled to be heard at the appeal

In *R.* v *Eyre*,[3] before referred to, it was decided that the said Acts of 1743 and 1801 must be construed together as forming one Act, and that the position as before stated with respect to entry and respite in the case of insufficient notice (see p 481 *ante*) equally applied under both of such Acts.

By the Quarter Sessions Act, 1849,[4] the before mentioned "reasonable notice" is made "fourteen days at least," and again, notice in writing is required to be given of an appeal to Quarter Sessions, and it is further provided that it shall not be lawful for the appellant at the trial to

---

[1] 41 Geo III , c. 23

[2] See the provisions of the Local Government Act, 1894, pp 461-2 *ante*.

[3] (1856) 6 E & B 992

[4] 12 & 13 Vict , c. 45

go into, or give evidence, on any ground other than those set forth in the notice, it is therefore now a question whether even a consent of the parties can enable this to be done legally There is a further provision that no objection on account of defect in the form of setting forth any ground of appeal, or to the reception of legal evidence offered in support thereof, shall prevail unless the Court shall be of opinion that such ground of appeal is so imperfectly or incorrectly set forth as to be insufficient to enable the party receiving the same to enquire into the subject thereof, and to prepare for trial, and a certain power of amendment by the Court is given.[1]

The Parochial Assessment Act, 1836[2] (ss 6 and 7), provides for the holding, in each Petty Sessional division, four times each year of Special Sessions for the hearing of appeals against rates at which the Justices " shall hear and determine all objections to any rate on the ground of inequality, unfairness or incorrectness " in the valuation of any hereditament, and it is expressly further provided that they shall not " inquire into the liability of any hereditaments to be rated, but only into the true value thereof and into the fairness of the amount at which the same shall have been rated." Of any such objection to Special Sessions, at least seven days' notice in writing under the hand of the complainant must be given to the person by whom the rate is made The Justices, for the purposes of such appeal, are to have all the powers of amending or quashing the rate and awarding costs that a Court of Quarter Sessions has in an appeal against the rate This power of appeal is in addition to that to Quarter Sessions but from the decision of the Special Sessions an appeal lies to Quarter Sessions if, within fourteen days after such decision, notice of intention to appeal be given to the persons in whose favour the decision was given, and the appellant, within five days after giving the notice, enters into the necessary recognizances.

Special Sessions, appeal to

[1] See p 489 post
[2] 6 & 7 William IV, c 96

Provisions of
Union
Assessment
Committee
Amendment
Act, 1864,
restricting
appeal
against rate

The next Statute to be considered is the Union Assessment Committee Amendment Act, 1864,[1] Section 1 of
which provides, that before any appeal shall be heard by
any Special or Quarter Sessions against a Poor Rate, the appellant shall give twenty-one days' notice thereof in writing
previous to the Special or Quarter Sessions, and the ground
thereof to the Assessment Committee, and further enacts
that there shall be *no appeal* to any Sessions against a Poor
Rate made in conformity with the Valuation List, *unless*
the appellant shall have given to such Committee notice of
objection against the said rate, and shall have failed to
obtain such relief as he deems just, and such objection,
after notice given in the manner prescribed by the
Union Assessment Committee Act, 1862[2] with respect
to objections,[3] the Committee are to hear, with full
power to call for and amend the list, although it may
have already been approved, and if it be amended, notice
is to be given of the amendment to the Overseers, who
are thereupon to alter the then current rate accordingly.

The Committee, however, cannot in this case increase
the amount of the gross estimated value as they can
when dealing with an objection under Section 18 of the
Union Assessment Committee Act, 1862,[2] but are bound
by the amount of such value.[1]

If in pursuance of this section the Committee amend
the list it need not be re-deposited as in case of alteration under Section 21 of the Union Assessment Act,
1862.[5]

Effect of
provision

This Act clearly makes notice of objection to the
Valuation List to, and failure to obtain relief from, the
Assessment Committee a condition precedent to any

[1] 27 & 28 Vict., c 39
[2] 25 & 26 Vict., c 103
[3] See p 169 *ante*
[4] *Horton* v *Walsall Union*, (1898) 2 Q B 237, 67 L J. Q.B 801,
62 J P 437, and see p 472 *ante*
[5] *R* v *Edmonds*, (1874) L R 9 Q B 598, and see p. 472 *ante*.

appeal against a rate. There has, however, been much controversy as to whether the further twenty-one days' notice to the Assessment Committee of appeal to Sessions is also a condition precedent, and to be strictly complied with as such, or merely an additional notice in the same category as those to the Overseers and third persons already dealt with[1] The latter was held to be the true view in *Denaby Overseers v. Denaby and Cadeby Main Collieries, Limited,*[2] in which case the House of Lords decided that an appellant was entitled at the next practicable Quarter Sessions to enter and respite an appeal to the following Sessions in accordance with the practice existing under previous Statutes by which notice was required, i.e., although there had been time to give the twenty-one days' notice and it had not been given

To sum the position up, there may be an appeal to Special Sessions on the ground of the amount of the valuation, or to Quarter Sessions on any ground of objection against a Poor Rate, but in either case there must have been notice to the Assessment Committee of objection to the Valuation List on which such rate is based, and failure thereafter to obtain relief from such Committee, such appeal must be to the next practicable Sessions, and, of the appeal, previous notice in writing stating the grounds thereof, must be given of not less than.

> Twenty-one days to the Assessment Committee whether the appeal be to Special or to Quarter Sessions,
>
> Seven days to the Overseers if appeal be to Special Sessions, and
>
> Fourteen days to the Overseers, and to third parties (if any interested) if the appeal be to Quarter Sessions

[1] See pp 481-2 ante
[2] (1909) A C p 247

As to service of notice on Overseers

The powers of the Overseers with regard to appeals in respect of the Poor Rate in rural parishes having a Parish Council being now transferred, by the Local Government Act, 1894, to such Council, it is the safer course in any such case, to serve both the Parish Council and the Overseers.[1] It is also desirable, in any other case, to see whether any order under the said Act with respect to the Overseers and their duties has been made, and if so to take care that in the service of any notices the terms of any such order are fully complied with, and to avoid any possibility of question it is better to serve both the Overseers and the body to whom their powers (or any of them) may purport to have been transferred.[1]

Notice of objection to Assessment Committee to be given in respect of each appeal

The notice of objection to the Assessment Committee must be given in respect of each rate desired to be appealed against, and an objection in respect of one rate, though such notice be still pending and awaiting decision when a further rate is made, will not suffice in respect of such further rate.[2] If, however, objection has been made to the Valuation List and relief has not been obtained from the Assessment Committee, an appeal lies against a rate made and based on such list, without a further objection and notice thereof to such Committee,[3] but whether this goes beyond the first effective rate so made and based would in the view of Lord Alverstone, C.J., seem doubtful.[4]

Next practicable Sessions

The next practicable Sessions are the first Sessions to be held after failure to obtain relief from the Assessment Committee and for which the before-mentioned notices can be given, after allowing for the lapse after such failure,

---

[1] See pp 461-2 ante

[2] R v. Great Western Railway Co, (1869) L R 4 Q B 323, 38 L J M C. 89, 33 J P 598, 10 B & S 318 20 L T 481, R v. Justices of Essex, (1902) 1 K B 180, 71 L J K B 148

[3] R v. Justices of Denbighshire, (1885) 15 Q B D 451, 54 L J. M C 142, 53 L.T 389, 49 J P 788

[4] See R v. Justices of Essex, (1902) 1 K.B 180 71 L J K B 148

of a sufficient time for consideration as to whether to appeal or not   What is a sufficient time is a question to be determined in each case   Two days were held to be in one case [1] sufficient, and in another case [2] not so   The case of the *Liverpool Gas Co* v *Everton* [3] may be usefully referred to in this connection   Having regard, however, to the position already dealt with as to entry and respite after insufficient notice, the point as a practical question is now not likely to arise

As soon as appeal is contemplated it is desirable to at once ascertain the dates fixed for the Special or Quarter Sessions, as the case may be, so that the position as to " the next practicable Sessions," and the dates for giving the necessary notices, may be ascertained   At the same time enquiry should be made as to whether there are any, and if so what, rules of the Sessions applicable to rating appeals.   So long as such rules do not conflict with any rules of law it may be necessary, and in any case it will save trouble, to comply with them , *e g* , see the case of *R* v. *Justices of Suffolk.* [4]   Any such rules, however, as requiring an appeal to be entered a given number of days before the Sessions at which it is to be heard,[5] or requiring an additional notice of appeal to be given,[6] have been held to be *ultra vires*, but in the former case, Blackburn, J , stated that while it was clear that the Justices were wrong in refusing to enter, possibly they had jurisdiction to refuse to hear and to adjourn the case

(margin: Rules of Sessions)

In any appeal the Assessment Committee, with the consent of the Guardians of the Union, after notice shall have been sent to every Guardian, may appear

(margin: Assessment Committee as respondents)

[1] *R* v *Herefordshire Justices*, (1789) 3 T R 504

[2] *R* v *Essex Justices*, (1817) 1 B & Ald 210

[3] (1871) L R 6 C P 414, 40 L J M C 104 , 23 L T 813

[4] (1817) 6 M & S 57

[5] *R* v *Paulett*, (1879) L R 8 Q B 491   42 L J M C 157, 29 L T 390

[6] *R* v *Bird*, (1898) 2 Q B 340 , 62 J P 422

as respondents to the appeal, but in the name of the Guardians [1] Such consent need not be in writing, nor need the notice be of any specified length of time [2] Having regard to the judgment of Lord Herschell in *West Ham Union* v. *Justices of Essex* and *London County Council*,[3] the notice would clearly seem to require to be explicit in its terms, and in this last-mentioned case it was decided that separate notice and consent must be given in the case of each rate appealed against, even though it had been given in one case, and while such case was still pending further rates were made and based on the same list, and appealed against in the same terms.

The costs an Assessment Committee may incur in consequence of becoming respondents to an appeal, or of having received notice thereof, if not recovered from the appellants, as well as any costs the Committee may be ordered to pay to the appellants, are to be paid out of the common fund of the Union, unless the Court order the same or any part thereof to be charged to the parish, the rate of which is appealed against

Powers of Sessions on appeal

With respect to the powers of Sessions on appeal those of Special Sessions have already been stated (see p. 483 *ante*). It is to be noted that while the appeal to Special Sessions may afford a cheaper method of determining the issue so long as there is no further appeal, yet, there is always the risk to be run of such further appeal to Quarter Sessions at the instance of the party—be it the ratepayer or the Assessment Committee—against whose contention the decision is given. And it will be remembered also that the jurisdiction is limited to the question of value.

On the other hand, there is no such limit of jurisdiction in the case of the Quarter Sessions, at which any

[1] Union Assessment Committee Amendment Act, 1864 (27 & 28 Vict c 39), s 2

[2] *Smith* v *Leigh Union*, (1904) 1 K B 484.

[3] (1896) A C 443, 65 L J M C 231, 60 J.P 756

ground of objection may be heard and determined, the appeal being to "any person aggrieved" by any rate or assessment, or on the ground of objection of any person being put in or left out of such rate or to the sum charged on any person thereon [1]

As, has already been pointed out, both the Poor Rate Act, 1801 [2] (see p. 182 *ante*) and the Quarter Sessions Act, 1849 [3] (see p. 482 *ante*), require the grounds of appeal to Quarter Sessions to be stated in the notice of appeal, and such grounds are also required by the Union Assessment Committee Amendment Act, 1864 [4] (see p. 184 *ante*), to be stated in the notice to the Assessment Committee, whether of objection or appeal, and it is only the grounds so stated that can be considered at Quarter Sessions

A general and comprehensive form of notice of objection will be found in Appendix III (*post*).

The position as to the extent to which, at the hearing at Quarter Sessions, objection on the ground of defect in setting forth any ground of appeal in the notice of appeal is to prevail has been shown (see p. 483 *ante*) It is further provided by the Quarter Sessions Act, 1849, [3] s 3, that where the Court shall be of opinion that any such objection ought to prevail it shall be lawful for such Court, if it shall think fit, to cause any such ground of appeal to be forthwith amended by an officer of the Court or otherwise, on such terms as to payment of costs to the other party, or postponing the trial to another day in the same Sessions, or to the next subsequent Sessions, or both payment of costs and postponement, as to such Court shall appear just and reasonable This power would not, however, appear to extend to the

[1] The Poor Law Relief Act, 1601 (43 Eliz , c 2), the Poor Law Relief Act, 1743 (17 Geo II , c 38), and see p 481 *ante*

[2] 41 Geo III , c 23.

[3] 12 & 13 Vict , c 45

[4] 27 & 28 Vict , c 39

notice of objection to the Assessment Committee under Section 1 of the Union Assessment Committee Amendment Act, 1864 [1]

Costs at Quarter Sessions

Section 4 of the same Act provides that if any grounds of appeal be frivolous or vexatious the Court may order the appellant raising the same, to pay the costs incurred by the respondent in contesting any such ground of appeal; and Section 5 provides that in any appeal the Court may order and direct the party against whom the same shall be decided to pay to the other party, just and reasonable costs, such costs to be recoverable in the manner provided for recovery of costs upon an appeal against an order or conviction by the Summary Jurisdiction Act, 1848 [2] The Poor Relief Act, 1713,[3] s 4, also enables the Justices to award and order to the party for whom the appeal be determined, reasonable costs.

These provisions, it is submitted, only enable costs to be given to a successful party, so that if a party be in any measure successful he cannot be ordered to pay costs, except in respect of a frivolous or vexatious ground of appeal, and, in any case, it is at the discretion of the Court whether costs be granted at all

On an appeal to Quarter Sessions from Special Sessions, however, the Court, it would seem, may order costs to be paid by either party at their entire discretion, the Parochial Assessment Act, 1836,[4] s 6, providing that, in any such appeal, the Court may award costs to the party appealing or appealed against as they shall think proper, the like power of awarding costs as a Court of Quarter Sessions, however, conferred on the Justices in Special Sessions by the next section of the said Act, would appear to refer, not to the power conferred on the Quarter Sessions under the Act just mentioned, but to the powers first referred to

[1] 27 & 28 Vict , c. 39

[2] 11 & 12 Vict., c 43.

[3] 17 Geo II , c 38

[4] 6 & 7 William IV , c 96

Any order for costs must be made by and at the Sessions at which the appeal is heard, or at an adjournment thereof, but cannot be made by a subsequent Sessions, further the amount of the costs must be settled by the Court at which the order is made, it having been decided that the ascertaining of costs is a judicial act, and unless a consent be given, the Clerk of the Court has no authority to entertain the question. It is, however, usual to consent to taxation out of Court, and in any such case, the amount so allowed becomes the amount allowed by the Court, and the amount to be paid and received.

If an order be made against the Overseers to pay costs, and be not complied with, an application should be made under Section 18 of the Quarter Sessions Act, 1849,[1] for removal of the order into the King's Bench Division, and thereafter for a mandamus to the Overseers ordering payment

Recovery of costs against Overseers

By the Poor Relief Act, 1743,[2] s 6, it is provided as to alteration of rate by Sessions that upon all appeals from rates and assessments, the Justices are required to amend the same in such manner only as shall be necessary for giving such relief as they think just, without altering such rates or assessments with respect to other persons mentioned in the same, and that if upon appeal from the whole rate it be found necessary to quash the same, the Justices shall order a new equal rate or assessment to be made By the Poor Rate Act, 1801,[3] the Court is to amend the rate or assessment, by inserting therein, or striking out, the name of any person, or by altering the sum charged on any person in any other manner necessary to give the relief, and without quashing or wholly setting aside the rate and there is a provision

Amendment of Rates it Quarter Sessions

---

[1] 12 & 13 Vict , c 45

[2] 17 Geo II , c 33

[3] 41 Geo III , c 23

enabling the Court to quash the rate, but in such case the rate is required to be paid, and allowance of such payments made as on account of the next effective rate

It is to be noted, that the power of alteration of the Sessions does not extend to enable them to increase the assessment appealed against, it having been held that the Rating Authority is bound by the amount of the gross estimated rental as it appears in the rate, and are not entitled to call evidence to show that it is too low [1]

Effect of appeal of General District Rate

The allowance of an appeal against a Poor Rate operates in respect of a General District Rate in an urban district based upon the Valuation List on which such Poor Rate was based, and entitles the ratepayer to a corresponding reduction in the General District Rate.[2] If such rate has been levied in instalments, a reduction in respect of the whole rate may be claimed from the later instalments, though the earlier ones have been paid [3] and the reduced amount of the rate may be recovered within six months, not from the making of the rate, but from the making of the alteration [4]

Appeal may be referred to arbitration

At any time after notice of appeal to Quarter Sessions against a rate, the parties thereto may themselves, by consent and by order of a Judge of the High Court, submit the matter in question to arbitration, and in such case the award is to be as binding and effectual as if it had been a regular judgment of the Court of Quarter Sessions, and either party may require it to be enrolled among the records[5], or the Court of Quarter Sessions may, with the consent of the parties to an appeal before them, refer such appeal to arbitration to

---

[1] *Horton v Walsall Union*, (1898) 2 Q B 287, 67 L J Q B 801, 62 J P 437. See pp 472 and 481 *ante*

[2] *Sheffield Waterworks Co v Mayor of Sheffield*, (1885) 50 J P 6, 55 L J M C 40, 54 L T 179

[3] *Hastings Corporation v Queen's Hotel Co, Ltd*, (1907) 71 J P 369, 97 L J. (N S) 310, 5 L G R. 1158

[4] *Keeton v. Sheffield Coal Co*, (1901) 2 K B 20, 84 L T 387 65 J P 341

[5] The Quarter Sessions Act, 1849 (12 & 13 Vict, c 45), s 12

such person, and on such terms, as the Court shall
think reasonable and proper, and in such case the
award, on the application of either party, at the
Sessions next, or next but one, after such award shall
have been made and published or after the decision
of the High Court on any motion for setting aside the
same, may be entered as the judgment of the Court of
Quarter Sessions, and shall be as binding and effectual
to all intents as if given by the said Court [1]

The order for reference should provide as to the costs,
as to the making of any amendment in the rate that
may be found to be required, as to the repayment of
over-payments (if any), and as to any other specific
points on which questions are likely to arise

If the case is one of difficulty the Court of Quarter Case stated
Sessions may state a special case for the opinion of
the King's Bench, and this is generally done by
judgment being given subject to such opinion   The
question, however, as to whether the case is one of
difficulty is to be determined by the Sessions and is
wholly within their discretion   The whole question is
fully discussed in *R v Overseers of Walsall*,[2] a case
which may very usefully be referred to   The case
should be asked for during the hearing, or when judgment is given, though possibly it would be sufficient to
ask for it at any time during the continuance of the
Sessions at which the judgment was given, but not
after such Sessions have concluded. Rule 34 of the
Crown Office Rules, 1886, requires a special case to be
filed at the Crown Office within six calendar months
from the making of the Order of the Sessions, except
by leave and Rules 36 and 38 require recognizances to
be entered into

The powers of the King's Bench on a special case
so stated are regulated by the Supreme Court of
Judicature (Procedure) Act, 1894,[3] ss 1 and 2

---

[1] The Quarter Sessions Act, 1849 (12 & 13 Vict , c 45), s 13

[2] (1878) 3 Q B.D 457

[3] 57 & 58 Vict , c 16.

CHAPTER II.

Metropolitan Area—Procedure within and without Metropolis compared— The Valuation (Metropolis) Act, 1869 —Assessment Committee—Valuation and Provisional Lists—Procedure as to Valuation Lists—Appeals to Special and Quarter Sessions—Alterations on Appeal— Costs of Appeals—Special and Quarter Sessions, who may appeal to, extent of jurisdiction, powers of—Rules of Quarter Sessions as to proceedings on appeals— Proceedings at Quarter Sessions—Special Case—Provisional List, how to be made and effect of—Inspection —Poor Rate—London Government Act, 1899—General Rate—City of London

Metropolitan Area defined THE Metropolitan Area is the area within the Administrative County of London and includes the City of London

"Metropolis" was first defined by the Valuation (Metropolis) Act, 1869,[1] to mean "the unions and parishes not in union which are for the time being either wholly or for the greater part in value thereof respectively situate within the jurisdiction of the Metropolitan Board of Works appointed under the Metropolis Management Act, 1855"[2] The Local Government Act, 1888,[3] s 100, provides that "the expression 'metropolis' means the City of London and the parishes and places mentioned in Schedules A, B and C to the Metropolis Management Act, 1855,[2] as amended by subsequent Acts", and by Section 40 of the same Act the "metropolis" is made an administrative county

---

[1] 32 & 33 Vict , c 67, ss 3 and 4
[2] 18 & 19 Vict , c 120
[3] 51 & 52 Vict , c 41

The procedure outside the metropolitan area dealt with in the last chapter, so far as it existed before the year 1869, applied equally until that year within the metropolitan area   Some of such procedure still applies within that area   There are, however, important differences created in and since the year 1869, relating principally to the procedure with respect to valuation and appeal, to the constitution of Overseers, and to the form and levying of the rates

This change commenced with the Valuation (Metropolis) Act, 1869,[1] which, with some amendment by later Acts, provides a complete system of valuation for the metropolitan area, the main features of which are periodical valuations, the association of the Surveyors of Taxes with such valuations, and appeals *not* against a rate *but* against the Valuation List.

The scope of the differences in question will perhaps be best appreciated by setting out, by reference to the marginal notes thereof, certain statutory provisions which, while still applying outside the metropolitan area, were repealed as regards such area, and thereafter referring to the provisions which specially apply within the Metropolis

The provisions so repealed (which, except where otherwise stated, are repealed in their entirety) are as follows

Marginal notes:

Procedure " outside " and "within" metropolitan area

Provisions repealed as to metropolitan area

THE PAROCHIAL ASSESSMENT ACT, 1836

SECTION   (6 & 7 William IV c 96)

1   " All rates to be made on the net annual value of the property '

2   " Rates to be made on a given form   Nothing herein to prevent owners from compounding "

6   " Justices acting in Petty Sessions to hold Four Special Sessions in the year to hear appeals "

7   ' Justices may act with all the powers of Justices in Quarter Sessions '

---

[1] 32 & 33 Vict , c 67

THE UNION ASSESSMENT COMMITTEE
ACT, 1862

THE UNION ASSESSMENT COMMITTEE
(AMENDMENT) ACT. 1864

SECTION   (27 & 28 Vict , c 39)

1   "Notice of appeal against Poor Rate to be given to the
      Assessment Committee of Union, 25 & 26 Vict ,
      c 103   No appeal against rate made in conformity
      with Valuation List unless objection has been made
      to list.   Assessment Committee to hear objections "

9   "Totals of rental and rateable value of property
      included in lists to be sent to Clerks of the Peace "

11   ' Penalty on Overseers "

THE POOR LAW AMENDMENT ACT, 1868

(31 & 32 Vict., c 122)

30   "Fair copies of approved Valuation Lists to be given to
      Overseers instead of originals "

31   "Certified copy of Valuation Lists rendered available
      where original or copy sent to Overseers is lost "

32   "Guardians may appoint a paid valuer to assist the
      Assessment Committee "

38   "Provisions for rating of new houses or buildings "

The Valuation (Metropolis) Act, 1869[1] (subject to the repeal of the before-mentioned sections, and so far as consistent with the tenor of the Act itself) incorporates the Union Assessment Acts, 1862[2] and 1864[3]

The Assessment Committee is to be appointed under the provisions of the Union Assessment Committee Act of 1862,[2] except where the provisions of Section 5 of the Valuation (Metropolis) Act, 1869,[1] as amended by Section 13 of the London Government Act, 1899,[4] apply , that is to say, by the Board of Guardians, except where the whole of a Poor Law Union is within one borough, or in the case of a parish not included in a Union and not having a Board of Guardians, but formerly having a Vestry elected

(Marginal notes: The Valuation (Metropolis) Act, 1869 — Appointment of Assessment Committee)

[1] 32 & 33 Vict , c 67
[2] 25 & 26 Vict , c 103
[3] 27 & 28 Vict , c 39
[4] 62 & 63 Vict , c. 14

KK

under the Metropolis Management Act, 1855,[1] in which cases the appointment is by the Borough Council, and in any such case the town clerk is to act as the clerk to the committee

In the City of London "the City of London (Union of Parishes) Act, 1907 "[2]—a local Act obtained by the City Corporation—s. 14, provides that the Assessment Committee for the City shall be appointed by the Common Council

Definition of "Year" "Year" is defined to mean "the twelve months commencing with the 6th of April and ending with the succeeding 5th of April "[3]

There are three distinct lists to be made —two Valuation Lists and a Provisional List—as follows —

1   A new Valuation List[4] to be made every fifth year · that is, in every year ending with "0" or "5,' commonly known as "The Quinquennial Valuation List "

2   A Supplemental Valuation List[4] in each of the intervening years, in which are to be shown *all the alterations which have taken place during the preceding twelve months in any of the matters*—and only those—*stated in the Valuation List*

Each of these two lists is included in the expression "Valuation List," and each such list is to come into force at the beginning of the year succeeding that in which it has been made[5]

3   A Provisional List,[6] which may be made at any time between a Quinquennial and a Supplemental List or between two Supplemental Lists *if in the course of*

---

[1] 18 & 19 Vict , c 120

[2] 7 Edward 7, ch cxl

[3] The Valuation (Metropolis) Act, 1869 (32 & 33 Vict , c 67), s 4

[4] *Ibid* , s 46

[5] *Ibid* , s 43

[6] *Ibid* , s 47

the year the value of any hereditament is from any cause increased by the addition thereto or erection thereon of any building or is from any cause increased or reduced in value, and is to take effect from the time it is approved by the Assessment Committee until the next Quinquennial or Supplemental List comes into force. The procedure is distinct and separate from that relating to a Valuation List, *i.e.* a Quinquennial or Supplemental List, and is dealt with separately later (see pp. 517-9 *post*).

The conditions, however, which justify the making of either a Supplemental or a Provisional List—marked by italics in the short descriptions of such lists above set out —have been held to have the same meaning. The alteration necessary in either case is not merely an alteration in value, but must be assignable to some definite cause affecting especially the value of the particular hereditament in question[1] and must have taken place within the preceding twelve months. Any such alteration will justify the making of a Provisional List followed by a Supplemental List or of a Supplemental List alone,[2] and whether such alteration be or be not dealt with in the Supplemental List to be made next following the alteration appeal will lie to Quarter Sessions as hereinafter set out. *Conditions precedent to Supplemental and Provisional Lists*

The Valuation List in force for the time being is to be the Quinquennial list last made, subject to any alteration therein by any subsequent Supplemental or Provisional List, and is to be conclusive evidence of the gross and rateable value of the several hereditaments included therein for the purposes of the rates levied in the Metropolis, for the purposes of the property tax, and the inhabited house duty, and for determining the value of *Valuation List in force for time being and effect and evidence thereof*

---

[1] *R v New River Co.*, (1879) 4 Q B D 309, *R v Poplar Union*, (1884) 13 Q B D 364, 49 L T 363, 53 L J M C 97, *Ellis v Camberwell Assessment Committee*, (1900) A C 510

[2] See *British Equitable Insurance Co v City of London Union*, "Ryde's Rating Appeals," 1886-1890, p. 229

any hereditament included therein for the purposes of the Acts relating to the sale of excisable liquors, and to the qualification of a juror or of an auditor of accounts under the Metropolis Management Act, 1855,[1] or of a guardian [2]   The list may be proved by the production of a duplicate or copy thereof purporting to be certified by the Clerk of the Assessment Committee [3]

Valuation list for parish to be made by OverseersThe Overseers of each parish are to make and sign a Valuation List of their parish in duplica

There is a form of list set out in the Valuation (Metropolis) Act, 1869,[5] and also one in the Agricultural Rates Order, 1896, Schedule W. 2 (see Appendix II. *post*).   The latter must be used in the case of any parish where there is agricultural land, and is now the one usually used, and is the form of List set out on the opposite page

Every hereditament in the parish (not being Ecclesiastical dues, manors or other royalties, fines and other profits from lands charged according to Rule 2 in Section 60 of the Income Tax Act, 1842[6]), and tithes and payments in lieu of tithes, are to be included in the list, and the same considerations apply as without the Metropolis (see p 467 *ante*), but they must be entered in accordance with the classes mentioned in the Third Schedule to the Act[7] set out on pp 501-2 *post*

The definitions of "gross value" and "rateable value" have been dealt with in Part 1, Chapter III, and, while slightly differing in form, are substantially the same as the corresponding definitions outside the Metropolis, and the same methods and considerations in

---

[1] 18 & 19 Vict , c 120
[2] The Valuation (Metropolis) Act, 1869 (32 & 33 Vict , c. 67), ss 43 & 45
[3] *Ibid* , s 64
[4] *Ibid* , s 6
[5] 32 & 33 Vict , c 67
[6] 5 & 6 Vict , c 35
[7] The Valuation (Metropolis) Act, 1869 (32 & 33 Vict , c 67) s 51

arriving at the amounts thereof equally apply Subject to this difference, however that the rate of deductions to

VALUATION LIST for [*the parish or place for which the List is made*] in the Metropolitan Union or [*or not being in Union*] in the County of

Number	Name of Occupier	Name of Owner	Description of Property	No of Class	Name of Situation of Property	Extent	Gross Value as Estimated by Overseers	Gross Value as Estimated by Surveyor of Taxes	Rate of Reduction, per cent	Gross Value as finally determined by Assessment Committee	Rateable Value as finally determined by Assessment Committee	Rateable Value of Agricultural Land	Rateable Value of Buildings, and other Hereditaments not being Agricultural Land
1	2	3	4	5	6	7	8	9	10	11	12	13	14
							£ s d	£ s d		£ s d	£ s d	£ s d	£ s d

Signed this   day of

{ A B } Overseers of the Poor of the
{ C D }   parish aforesaid

be made from the gross value to ascertain the rateable value must not exceed the amounts in the Third Schedule to the Act,[1] which are as follows :—

Maximum rate of deductions

Class 1 —Houses or buildings, or either of them,
    ,,   without land other than gardens where
        the gross value is under £20 .. ..   25, or ¼th

    ,, 2 —Houses and buildings without land, other
        than gardens and pleasure grounds, valued
        therewith for the purpose of inhabited
        house duty where the gross value is £20
        and under £40 .. ...   20, or ⅕th

[1] The Valuation (Metropolis) Act, 1869 (32 & 33 Vict , c 67), s 52

Maximum rate of deductions

Class 3 —Houses and buildings without land, other than gardens and pleasure grounds, valued therewith for the purpose of inhabited house duty where the gross value is £60 or upwards . ... $16\frac{2}{3}$, or $\frac{1}{6}$th

,, 4 —Buildings without land which are not liable to inhabited house duty, and are of a gross value of £20 and under £40   20, or $\frac{1}{4}$th

,, 5 —Buildings without land which are not liable to inhabited house duty and are of a gross value of £40 or upwards ..   .. $16\frac{2}{3}$, or $\frac{1}{6}$th

,, 6 —Land with buildings not houses   ..   10, or $\frac{1}{10}$th

,, 7 —Land without buildings   .   ..   5, or $\frac{1}{20}$th

,, 8 —Mills and manufactories   . $33\frac{1}{3}$, or $\frac{1}{3}$d

,, 9 —Tithes, tithe commutation rent-charge, and other payments in lieu of tithe

10 —Railways, canals, docks, tolls water-works and gasworks

,, 11 —Rateable hereditaments not included in any of the foregoing classes

To be determined in each case according to the circumstances and the general principles of law

The maximum rate of deductions prescribed in this Schedule shall not apply to houses or buildings let out in separate tenements but the rate of deductions in such cases shall be determined as in classes 9 10 and 11

In every year in which a Quinquennial List is made, or in the month of March preceding any such year, every person who is liable to be charged with a rate has, when required, to make to the Overseers of his parish such statement or return as can be required under the Income Tax Acts.[1]

For this purpose the Surveyor of Taxes in the preceding month of February is to supply notices and forms to the Overseers of each parish, the Overseers are to serve the same within a month after receipt thereof, and the person required to make the return must make it within twenty-one days after such service[2]

Occupier to make returns to Overseers for Quinquennial list

---

[1] The Valuation (Metropolis) Act, 1869 (32 & 33 Vict , c. 67), s 55
[2] *Ibid* , s 56

The Assessment Committee may by order require the owner or occupier, or reputed owner or occupier, of any hereditament in the Union to send them a return in writing of the rent receivable or payable for the hereditament, $\frac{and}{or}$ of the person entitled to or paying any tithe rent-charge charged thereon, $\frac{and}{or}$ of the amount thereof, $\frac{and}{or}$ any other particulars required for the purpose of the Act, and such order is to be obeyed within fourteen days after service thereof [1]

Assessment Committee may require returns from owner or occupier

If any such return as aforesaid be not made liability to penalty not exceeding £5 is incurred, and if a false return be made the penalty is to be not exceeding £10, and in either case to be recovered summarily.[2]

Penalty for not making returns

The same proceedings apply within as without the Metropolis with respect to the deposit of a Valuation List for inspection and afterwards transmission thereof to the Assessment Committee (see p 468 *ante*), objections to the List (see p 469 *ante*), the Committee to hold meetings to hear objections (see p 470 *ante*), the powers of Committee to correct the List, and when corrected to approve the same (see p. 471 *ante*), and to the Valuation List, when altered, being deposited for inspection (see p 472 *ante*), subject to alterations made by the Act,[3] as follows

Procedure to be followed after Valuation List made

> *Deposit of Valuation List* [4]—To be made before the 1st of June in each year; and at the same time that one copy of the Valuation List is deposited by them the Overseers are required to send the other copy to the Surveyor of Taxes of the district, together with, in the case of a Quinquennial List, the returns made under Section 55 of the Act.[5]

---

[1] The Valuation (Metropolis) Act, 1869 (32 & 33 Vict., c 67), s 57
[2] *Ibid*, s 58
[3] *Ibid*, s 7.
[4] *Ibid*, s 42
[5] *Ibid*, ss 8 and 56

Transmission of Valuation List to Committee.—To
be made not less than fourteen nor more than
seventeen days after notice given of deposit.[1]

Objections.—May be made on the ground of the
unfairness or incorrectness of the valuation of
any hereditament, or of the insertion or incorrectness of any matter in or omission of any
matter from the Valuation List, or of such a
List as is required not having been transmitted
to the Committee.[2] The notice of objection
must specify the correction desired to be made,[2]
and must be given by any person (other than
the Surveyor of Taxes and the Overseers) before
the expiration of twenty-five days after the
deposit of the List and by the Surveyor of Taxes
or the Overseers not less than seven days before
the date of meeting of the Committee to hear
objections. Of objections after re-deposit of the
Valuation List seven days' notice are to be given
by the objector [1]

Revision by Assessment Committee —To be made
before 1st of October in the same year [3]

Meetings of Committee to   Objections —To be
held before the 1st of October, but not less than
sixteen days after transmission of the List to
them, and of such meeting sixteen days' notice
is to be given.[3]

Re-deposit of Valuation List —The Committee are
within three days after it is approved by them
to send the List to the Overseers for re-deposit,
and to appoint a day not less than fourteen nor
more than twenty-eight days after such re-
deposit for hearing objections to the alterations,
of which objections seven days' notice are to be
given by the objectors [1]

[1] The Valuation (Metropolis) Act, 1869 (32 & 33 Vict   c 67), s 42
[2] *Ibid* , s 11
[3] *Ibid* , s 42

*Certain Notices to be given by Overseers —*Where in any Valuation List the Overseers or the Assessment Committee insert a hereditament not previously assessed, or raise the gross or rateable value of any hereditament above the value stated in the Valuation List in force, the Overseers are also required, after deposit or re-deposit of such List, as the case may be, to serve on the occupier of such hereditament a notice of the gross and rateable value so inserted [1]

The notice of deposit and re-deposit of the List is to state the times at which, and the mode in which objections are to be made [2]

Any notice required to be published by the Overseers is to be published by them on the Sunday next following the receipt of the notice, or the receipt of the document to which the notice refers, and the two following Sundays, in the manner in which notice of a rate allowed by Justices is required to be published [3] (as to which see p 477 *ante*).

Publication of notices by Overseers

The Surveyor of Taxes is required to insert in the List the amount in his opinion of the gross value of any hereditament where his opinion differs from that of the Overseers, and to transmit the List (together with any returns which may have been sent to him) to the Assessment Committee within twenty-eight days from receipt thereof by him [4]

Duties and powers of Surveyors of Taxes

A Surveyor of Taxes is to have the same right of inspecting, copying, taking extracts from, or objecting to any Valuation List relating to his district as is given to any other person [5]

---

[1] The Valuation (Metropolis) Act, 1869 (32 & 33 Vict , c. 67), s 9.

[2] *Ibid ,* s 10.

[3] *Ibid ,* s 66.

[4] *Ibid.,* ss 8 and 56.

[5] *Ibid.,* s 12

When a Surveyor of Taxes gives notice of objection or of appeal, the amount specified in the notice as being in his judgment the gross value of any hereditament is to be inserted in the Valuation List by the Assessment Committee or Sessions (Special or Quarter), unless it be proved to the satisfaction of such Committee or Sessions that such amount ought not to be so inserted[1], the burden of such proof being thus put on the person rated

If the Overseers of any parish fail to transmit a Valuation List as required by the Act, the Assessment Committee are to appoint some person to make the list, and his remuneration and expenses are to be charged to the parish[2]

The Guardians, upon the application of the Assessment Committee, after notice sent to every guardian, may appoint some competent person to assist the Committee in the valuation of the hereditaments in the Union for such period as they see fit, at a salary or other settled remuneration to be paid out of the common fund[3]

The Valuation List is to be finally approved by the Assessment Committee, and transmitted, as hereinafter stated, before the 1st day of November in the same year, and, being finally approved, the Committee are to cause the gross and rateable value in such list to be ascertained and inserted in the list, and three members of the Committee present at the meeting at which it is finally approved are to sign at the foot thereof declaration of approval and certificate (for form see Part I of Second Schedule to the Act)[4]   One duplicate so certified is to be sent and deposited at the office of the London County Council, who are to print the totals of the gross and rateable values of all the Valuation Lists, and before the

Failure of Overseers to transmit Valuation List

Guardians may appoint paid Valuer

Final approval of Valuation List by Assessment Committee

[1] The Valuation (Metropolis) Act, 1869 (32 & 33 Vict., c 67), s 53
[2] Ibid, s 13, and see p 488 ante
[3] Ibid, s 61
[4] Ibid, s 14   See Appendix I post.

31st December in the same year, are to send a copy of such print to every Assessment Committee and to the Overseers of every parish affected and to certain other bodies named in the Act, and to return the list to the Committee not sooner than fourteen nor later than twenty-one days thereafter.[1] The other duplicate is to be sent to the Overseers of the parish to which it relates, and is to be deposited in the place where the Rate Books of the parish are kept and the Overseers are to publish notice of such deposit and of the time and mode of making appeals and of the ground on which an appeal is allowed.[2]

Deposit of Valuation List and notice thereof

Against a Valuation List—quinquennial or supplemental —there is an appeal to Special Sessions on the question of value only, and to Assessment Sessions, now the Quarter Sessions of the Mayor of London,[3] in any and all cases in which an appeal lies, and from Special Sessions. There is, however, no such appeal against either a provisional list or a rate. Unless, therefore, an alteration takes place in a hereditament which justifies the making of a Supplemental List, the assessment thereof as settled at one must stand until the next Quinquennial Valuation without question, and any such alteration, as already pointed out, must be not merely an alteration in value, but must be assignable to some definite cause affecting the value of the particular hereditament in question.[4] And even so, only the effect of the alteration in value in the year can be taken into account, as apart from such

Appeal against Valuation Lists

---

[1] The Valuation (Metropolis) Act, 1869 (32 & 33 Vict., c 67), ss 14, 16 & 42, and 51 & 52 Vict., c. 41, s 41

[2] The Valuation (Metropolis) Act, 1869 (32 & 33 Vict., c 67), ss 14 & 15

[3] See the Local Government Act, 1888 (51 & 52 Vict., c 41), s. 42 (10), by which it is also provided that upon the hearing of any appeals in relation to property in the City of London, such two members of the Court of Quarter Sessions of the City of London as may be appointed by that Court for the purpose, shall be entitled to attend and sit as members of the Quarter Sessions for the County of London.

[4] *Ellis v. Camberwell Assessment Committee*, (1900) A C 510, and see p. 499 ante

alteration and the value thereof, the list in force at the commencement of the year must be taken to be correct [1]

The Special Sessions are to be held by the Justices in every Petty Sessional Division each year at such time, after the 30th November as will enable them to determine all appeals before the next ensuing 1st January,[2] and notice thereof is to be given to the Overseers of the Parish affected, and they are to publish it as soon as received.[3]

For the purpose of appeals to the Quarter Sessions, meetings of such sessions are to be held at such time after the 1st February as will enable them (save where a Valuation List or valuation is ordered) to determine all appeals before the next ensuing 31st March [4] Notice at least ten days before the first Court is held, of both the time and place of hearing, is to be given by advertisement in a newspaper circulating in the Metropolis, and by sending a copy thereof to every Surveyor of Taxes in the Metropolis, to every Assessment Committee having the right to appeal to such Court, to the Overseers of every parish to which any appeal relates, and to all the parties to the appeal [5] The Overseers are to publish such notice as soon as received [5]

Notice in writing of appeal, specifying the correction desired, is to be given, in the case of appeal to Special Sessions, on or before the 21st November following the making of the list, and in the case of appeal to Quarter Sessions on or before the following 14th January, and must be served—

> (1) On the Assessment Committee which approved the list sought to be questioned

[1] R v Poplar Union (East and West India Dock case) (1884) 13 Q B D 364

[2] The Valuation (Metropolis) Act, 1869 (32 & 33 Vict , c 67), ss 18 & 42.

[3] Ibid , s. 22

[4] Ibid , ss 23 & 42

[5] Ibid , s. 30

(2.) On the Surveyor of Taxes of the district, save where the appeal relates only to rateable value

(3) If in the appeal it is sought to raise any question as to the assessment of a person other than the appellant, then on such person, and

(4.) If the appellant be an Assessment Committee or a Surveyor of Taxes, then also on the Overseers of the parish to which the appeal relates

The Clerk of the Assessment Committee on receipt of notice of appeal is forthwith to serve notice thereof on the Clerk of the Special or County Sessions as the case may be.[1]

One notice of appeal may include appeals by the same appellant in respect of two or more hereditaments separately assessed and comprised in one Valuation List [2]

If from accident or mistake the notice of appeal has not been given, or if an additional notice appears to be required, the Court may order such notice to be given [3]

All appeals are to be heard and determined in open Court, and upon any such appeal the Valuation List may be confirmed or altered   The Clerk to the Assessment Committee or some deputy allowed by the committee is to attend the Court with the Valuation List, and any alteration is to be made and initialled by the Chairman of the Court.[1] *Hearing appeals at both Special and Quarter Sessions*

Notice of any alteration in the Valuation List, whether in consequence of a decision on any appeal to the Special or Quarter Sessions or the High Court, is to be sent by the Clerk of the Assessment Committee to the Overseers *Notice of alteration in Valuation List on appeal*

---

[1] The Valuation (Metropolis) Act, 1869 (32 & 33 Vict , c 67), s 33

[2] The Valuation (Metropolis) Amendment Act, 1884 (47 & 48 Vict , c 5), s 3

The Valuation (Metropolis) Act, 1869 (32 & 33 Vict , c 67), s 34.

and Surveyor of Taxes affected, and the alteration is to be entered by such Clerk and the Overseers on the duplicate lists deposited with them. Of any such alteration in the total of the gross and rateable value of any valuation notice is also to be given by the said Clerk to the Clerk to the London County Council, who is to send in writing such altered total to every person or body of persons who has power to make or levy any rate or assessment or contribution based on such total.[1]

Costs of appeal at Special or Quarter Sessions

The costs of an appeal are in the discretion of the Special or the Quarter Sessions as the case may be, and are to be awarded to be paid by such parties to the appeal, and in such proportions, as they think fit. The discretion, it is to be noted, is an absolute one. It has, however, been decided that to justify an order for costs against an Assessment Committee, such Committee must have appeared as respondents, and have obtained the consent of the Guardians or Borough Council, after notice sent to every Guardian or Councillor, as the case may be, to so appeal.[2] Costs ordered to be paid as aforesaid may be recovered as if awarded by a Court of Quarter Sessions, and where ordered to be paid by parties other than a ratepayer are to be paid as in the Act mentioned.[3]

"Ratepayer" defined for purposes of appeals

"Ratepayer" means every person who is liable to any rate or tax in respect of property entered in the Valuation List,[4] and it is expressly provided[5] that for the purpose of appeal either to Special or Quarter Sessions, the term shall include the owner or lessee of any hereditaments liable to be assessed for any rate or tax in the

[1] The Valuation (Metropolis) Act, 1869 (32 & 33 Vict., c. 67), s. 41.

[2] R. v. London, S. J., etc., Mayor, etc. of Westminster (1907) "Konstam's Rating Appeals," 1904 8, p. 587.

[3] The Valuation (Metropolis) Act, 1869 (32 & 33 Vict., c. 67), s. 39.

[4] Ibid., s. 4.

[5] The Valuation (Metropolis) Amendment Act, 1884 (47 & 48 Vict., c. 5), s. 2.

place of the occupier or tenant, or who does in fact pay any such rate or tax in his place under any contract or arrangement with him

Any ratepayer, and any Overseers of a parish so far as respects the Valuation List of such parish or any Surveyor of Taxes, who may feel aggrieved by any decision of the Assessment Committee, on an objection made with respect to the unfairness or incorrectness of the valuation of a hereditament in such list, may appeal to Special Sessions.[1]

It is to be noted that objection must first be made to the Assessment Committee, and be with respect to a hereditament included in the list, so that appeal to Special Sessions only lies after such objection has been made and does not lie on the ground of omission of any hereditament from the list, and as shewn later it is limited to the question of value.

The right of appeal to Special Sessions is not to deprive a person of any other right of appeal,[1] and from any decision of Special Sessions there is right of appeal to Quarter Sessions.[2] The Special Sessions, moreover, cannot hear any matter in respect of which notice of appeal to the Quarter Sessons has been given, or deal with any question other than the one of the value of the hereditament the subject of appeal, nor does any decision by Special Sessions of itself alter the totals of the gross and rateable value of the whole list though it may form reason for appeal against such totals to the Quarter Sessions.[3]

The Justices in Special Sessions are to have with respect to the attendance and examination of witnesses, the taking of evidence, the keeping order in Court, the enforcing their orders and all matters necessary for the

---

[1] The Valuation (Metropolis) Act, 1869 (32 & 33 Vict., c 67), s 19
[2] Ibid, s 32
[3] Ibid, s 20

execution of their duties under the Act, the same powers and jurisdiction as if they were assembled in Petty Sessions.[1] This provision, however, would not seem to be sufficient to constitute them a Court of summary jurisdiction or to enable them to state a case for the opinion of the High Court

Recognizances to be entered into or deposits made by appellants Special Sessions

Under the orders made in pursuance of Section 27 of the Valuation (Metropolis) Act, 1869,[2] the appellant (other than an Overseer or Surveyor of Taxes) is required within seven days after giving notice of appeal, and by way of security for costs, to enter (with one surety) into recognizances in the sum of £20 each, or to deposit £20 with the Clerk of the Special Petty Sessional Division.[3] The fees payable on such appeals in pursuance of Section 28 of the same Act are also prescribed in the same orders.[3]

Quarter Sessions, who may appeal to, extent of jurisdiction

Any ratepayer and any Surveyor of Taxes and any Overseers (with the consent of the Vestry of his parish) who may feel aggrieved by any decision of the Assessment Committee on an objection made before them to which he was a party, or by any decision of Special Sessions, whether he was a party or not, may appeal against such decision to the Quarter Sessions.[4]

An appeal also lies to Quarter Sessions by any of the said persons or by any Assessment Committee or by any body or persons authorized by law to levy rates or require contributions payable out of rates in the metropolitan area on the ground of the total of either the gross or the rateable value being too high or too low, or of there being no approved Valuation List for some parish.[4]

[1] The Valuation (Metropolis) Act, 1869 (32 & 33 Vict., c. 67), s 21
[2] 32 & 33 Vict, c 27.
[3] See the Orders of County of London Quarter Sessions made thereunder and set out in Appendix II
[4] The Valuation (Metropolis) Act, 1869 (32 & 33 Vict, c 67), s 32

The last-mentioned appeal is the only means by which the totals of the gross and rateable values of any parish, as settled by the Assessment Committee, can be altered, and is strictly limited in its scope, it having been decided that alterations, on appeal to Quarter Sessions, of the valuation of one or more hereditaments in a parish (*a*) does not of itself alter the before-mentioned totals, and that such totals can only be altered by appealing against them,[1] and (*b*) does not of itself even afford any ground for an appeal against totals, Lord Herschell expressing the further opinion that, possibly, if some wrong principle had been adopted, throughout the parish, for arriving at either the gross or the rateable value, which would affect the valuation generally, the appeal in question might lie[2]

It is a little curious to note that in the case last referred to, the provisions of Section 20 of the Valuation (Metropolis) Act, 1869, which provides that alteration of the value of a hereditament by Special Sessions may form a reason for appeal against totals,[3] does not seem to have been considered or even quoted

Under the provisions of Sections 27 and 28 of the Valuation (Metropolis) Act, 1869,[4] the Quarter Sessions are empowered with the approval of the Secretary of State to make orders regulating proceedings in appeals under the Act and determining recognizances and a table of Court fees.

The Orders now in force are set out in Appendix II, and under such Orders ·

    (*a*) Appellants (other than an Assessment Committee, Overseers or Surveyor of Taxes) are by way of security for costs, within seven

---

[1] *R v Woolwich Guardians* (1891) 2 Q B 712

[2] *London County Council v Assessment Committee of St. George's Union*, (1894) A C 600

[3] See page 511 *ante*

[4] 32 & 33 Vict , c 27.

days after giving notice of appeal, to enter
(with one surety) into recognizances in the
sum of not less than £50 each, or, after obtaining from the Clerk to the Court a *præcipe*
therefor, to pay into the London and Westminster Bank (Head Office), in the joint
names of the Chairman and the Clerk of the
Court, the sum of £50, and to deposit the
receipt with such Clerk. It is desirable that
the security should be given within the time
specified, but the failure to do this would not
necessarily prevent the case from being heard

(b) Appeals are to be entered by lodging with the
Clerk of the Court, on or before the 14th
January, a copy of the notice of appeal. If
the notice be not given, upon motion for
leave to enter the appeal, such leave is
usually granted, subject to payment of the
respondent's costs

(c) Respondents are to deliver to the Clerk of the
Court and to serve on the appellant, on or
before the 28th January, notice of their intention to appear, and stating whether they intend
to appear separately or jointly with other
persons.

Any person omitting to give this notice is not
to be heard, save by special leave of the
Court, until he shall have given such notice
or complied with such terms as the Court
shall impose, and the time may be extended
by the Court upon such terms and conditions
as to costs and otherwise as they may think
fit.

(d) Both appellants and respondents in an appeal in
which the total rateable value appealed against
is £300 and upwards, on or before the 1st

February, are to state their respective cases and the facts to be proved, and the points of law (if any) to be argued, and to deliver ten copies thereof to the Clerk of the Court and to serve one copy on each of the respondents or on the appellant as the case may be.

The facts sought to be proved need not be set out in full detail, but the case must be so stated so that the opposite party may know what the case against them is[1]

(e) Where terms of an order are agreed, particulars thereof, signed by the parties or their solicitors, are to be filed with the Clerk of the Court, and upon motion made by either party an order may be made at the next or some subsequent sittings in accordance with such terms

(f) Of any motion two clear days' notice is to be given, and a copy of the notice to be filed with the Clerk of the Court.

(g) All applications are to be made, and all consents are to be given, in open Court by counsel One counsel only for each party to an appeal is (except by special leave) to be heard Counsel for the appellant is to begin, except when the Surveyor of Taxes is the appellant, and then counsel for the respondent begins

(h) No order involving an alteration in the gross value of a hereditament is to be made, until proof, orally or by affidavit, is given that the Surveyor of Taxes has been served with notice of the appeal

The Justices in Quarter Sessions may appoint one of their number to act as chairman, and he is to have a second or casting vote, and they may determine a

Chairman of, and hearing of appeals at, Quarter Sessions

---

[1] (1908) *Artizans, Labourers and General Dwellings Co, Ltd* v *Holborn Union* "Konstam's Rating Appeals," 1904-8, p 73.

quorum, so that it be not less than three. The Deputy Chairman has not a casting vote[1] The Court may adjourn from time to time, and is to have with respect to the attendance and examination of witnesses, the evidence, the keeping order in and contempt of Court, the enforcement of their orders, and all matters necessary for the execution of their duties under the Act, the same powers and jurisdiction, and to be in the same position, as an ordinary Court of Quarter Sessions[2]

Quarter Sessions may appoint person to make Valuation List

If the Quarter Sessions are of opinion on any appeal that there is no approved Valuation List for some parish, they may appoint to make such list, some proper person who is to have for such purpose the same powers and duties as Overseers, and the list is to be deposited and made known to the persons interested in such manner as the Court may direct   The cost of making any such list is to be paid by the Assessment Committee who failed to approve the list[3]

Quarter Sessions may order valuation of hereditament

The Quarter Sessions on the application of any of the parties to an appeal and upon such party giving such security as the Court think proper to pay the costs of the valuation of the hereditament in question, may in their discretion appoint some proper person to make such valuation[4]

In either of such last mentioned cases the Court may fix some subsequent day, either before or after the last day for hearing appeals, to receive the Valuation List or valuation, and may adjourn the hearing to that day[5]

Any person so appointed is to make his valuation in writing, signed by him, and showing the particulars of the hereditaments comprised therein, and the amounts at which the same are valued.[6]

---

[1] (1906) Grund and Kendal v City of London Union   " Konstam's Rating Appeals," 1904-08, p 20

[2] The Valuation (Metropolis) Act, 1869 (32 & 33 Vict , c 67), s 26

[3] Ibid , s 35

[4] Ibid , s 36.

[5] Ibid , s 37

[6] Ibid , s 38

The same proceedings may be had by special case, and *certiorari* or otherwise for questioning any decision of the Justices in Quarter Sessions, as may be had for questioning any decision of the Justices in General or Quarter Sessions, provided that every such *certiorari* shall be sued out within three months after the decision is given [1]

Special case stated by Quarter Sessions

At any time after notice of appeal, and by consent of the parties, and by order of a Judge of the High Court, the facts of the case may be stated for the opinion of such Court The decision may, on the application of either party, be entered by way of judgment at the Sessions next, or next but one, after such decision Notice in writing of such decision is to be served by the Clerk of the Sessions on the Assessment Committee which approved the list questioned on appeal [1]

Special case by consent

The conditions under which a Provisional List is to be made have already been discussed

Provisional List, how to be made, and effect of

The provisions with regard to such list are wholly contained in Section 47 of the Valuation (Metropolis) Act, 1869 [2]

The Overseers of a Parish may, and on the written request of the Assessment Committee, or of any ratepayer, or of the Surveyor of Taxes of the district, are required to, send to the Assessment Committee a provisional list containing the gross and rateable value of any hereditament of which the value has increased or decreased

A copy of the requisition for this purpose is to be sent by any person making it to the Clerk to the Assessment Committee, and if within fourteen days after the requisition has been served on the Overseers they fail to send the list to the Committee, the Committee are to appoint a person to make the list.

[1] The Valuation (Metropolis) Act 1869 (32 & 33 Vict , c 67), s 40.

[2] 32 & 33 Vict , c 67

On receipt of the list, the Clerk to the Assessment Committee is to serve a copy thereof on the Surveyor of Taxes for the district, and a copy of so much thereof as relates to a hereditament, on the occupier of such hereditament The copy is to be accompanied by a notification of the date, not less than fourteen days after service thereof, on or before which objection may be made, and of the mode in which such objection is to be made From the date of such service of the copy list and notice, the list, after it has completed its later stages, is to operate.

Objection to the Provisional List may be made by the occupier or Surveyor of Taxes by notice in writing served on the Clerk to the Assessment Committee and the Overseers, and, as the case may be, on the Surveyor of Taxes or the occupier.

Thereupon a meeting of the Committee is to be forthwith summoned, and notice of the time and place thereof is to be given to the Overseers, the Surveyor of Taxes and the occupier, and any objection to the list is to be heard and determined by the Committee in the same manner as if it were an objection to a Valuation List

Upon the expiration of the time for objection, if no objection be made, or so soon as they have determined it if objection be made, the list and a copy thereof (with any alteration made by the Committee) is to be dated and signed by the Clerk to the Committee and returned to the Overseers The list is then to take effect from the date of the service by the Clerk to the Assessment Committee of the copy of the list and notice as aforesaid on the occupier of the hereditament, and to continue in force until the Valuation List next made comes into force

The Overseers are to alter the annual rate to accord with the Provisional List thus settled and are to enter the date when it is to come into operation and to charge the rate accordingly. This entry is to be made "upon the list coming into operation " This, it is submitted, means, when the list is returned to the Overseers by the Assessment Committee, although the date from which it is to "have operation" is the earlier date of the service of the list and notice as before mentioned.

It is to be noted that there is no appeal from the decision of the Assessment Committee on a Provisional List, but on the other hand, if when the next Valuation List (Quinquennial or Supplemental) comes into operation a smaller value is put on the hereditaments than in the provisional list, the amount of tax or rate thus shown to be overpaid in consequence of the larger assessment is to be repaid or allowed, so that by means of appeal against such Valuation List there is in effect, though not directly, an appeal against the assessment in the Provisional List

A Provisional List is not in any way to affect the totals of the gross and rateable values of a parish

The Valuation List in force for the time being[1] is for all purposes to be deemed part of the rate books of the parish, and to be produced by the Overseers before the Justices upon application for allowance of any rate, and on any appeal, or other occasion when they are bound to produce rate books[2] The duplicate Valuation List is to be kept at the board room or other convenient place appointed by the Guardians and to be deemed to be in the possession of the Assessment Committee

Valuation Lists to be equivalent to rate books of parish

Inspection may be made and copies and extracts taken:

Inspection of documents.

> (1.) By any ratepayer, Overseer, Clerk of an Assessment Committee, or Surveyor of Taxes in the Metropolis, without payment, of and from all Valuation Lists and documents in the control of the Clerk of the London County Council or of the Clerk of the Quarter Sessions.[3]

---

[1] See p 499 *ante*

[2] The Valuation (Metropolis) Act, 1869, (32 & 33 Vict , c 67) s. 68.

[3] *Ibid*, s. 69.

(2.) By any Surveyor of Taxes and any Guardian and any Overseer in a Union without payment, and by any ratepayer in a Union on payment of a fee not exceeding 1s., of and from any Valuation Lists, notices of objection, returns and other documents in the possession or under the control of the Assessment Committee of the Union [1]

(3) By any Clerk of an Assessment Committee of and from any Valuation Lists in the possession or under the control of the Assessment Committee of any other Union [1]

Poor Rate

A Poor Rate in the Metropolis is subject to the same provisions as without the Metropolis, subject to some differences hereinafter referred to

Amendment of error in rate

Any clerical or arithmetical error in a rate may be corrected by the Justices upon application by the ratepayer, after notice to the Overseers." [2]

The name of a person liable to be rated at the time a rate was made, but omitted therefrom, or the name of a person described in the rate by a wrong name, may on the application of the Overseers, after seven clear days' notice of their intention to make such application, be corrected by the Justices or a Police Magistrate [3]

Particulars to be shewn in rate

Every Poor Rate is to contain the particulars specified in the Fourth Schedule to the Valuation (Metropolis) Act, 1869 [4] (see Appendix I) or in any parish in which there is agricultural land as defined by the Agricultural Rates Act, 1896, [5] in the form set out in Schedule Y. 2 to the Agricultural Rates Order, 1896 (see Appendix II)

London Government Act, 1899

Under the London Government Act, 1899, [6] the powers of the Vestry, the Overseers, and the rates to be levied are dealt with in one comprehensive scheme

---

[1] The Valuation (Metropolis) Act, 1869 (32 & 33 Vict, c 67) s 69
[2] Ibid, s 71
[3] Ibid, s 72
[4] Ibid, s 73
[5] 59 & 60 Vict, c 16.
[6] 62 & 63 Vict, c 11

Section 1 of such Act provides for the division of the whole of the Administrative County of London (exclusive of the City of London) into metropolitan boroughs

Metropolitan Boroughs

By Section 4 of the Act the powers and duties of every elective Vestry and District Board are transferred to the Councils of such metropolitan boroughs; by Section 11 (1) of the same Act it is enacted that each such Council shall be the Overseers of every parish within such borough, and that any documents requiring to be signed by the Overseers shall be signed by the Town Clerk of the Borough; and Section 23 (3) of the Act provides that the Churchwardens of every such parish shall cease to be Overseers.

Transfer of powers of Vestry to Borough Councils

Borough Councils to be Overseers

With respect to the rate, Section 10 of the same Act [1] authorises a scheme to provide for all the expenses of a Borough Council to be paid out of one General Rate, and directs that such General Rate and the Poor Rate shall be assessed, made and collected together by the Borough Council as one rate, to be termed "the general rate," and as if it were the Poor Rate, and that all enactments applying to the Poor Rate shall (subject to the provisions of the Act as to audit) be construed as applying and referring also to the General Rate   If a borough comprises more than one parish the amount required to be raised to meet the expenses of the Borough Council (subject to any provisions required for adjustment of local burdens) is to be divided between the parishes in proportion to rateable value

One rate for all purposes

Under Section 11 (2) and (3) of the same Act [1] every precept issued by any authority for the purpose of obtaining money to be ultimately raised out of a rate (other than a precept sent to Guardians by the Local Government Board or by a body containing representatives elected by the Guardians) is required to be sent to

---

[1] The London Government Act, 1899 (62 & 63 Vict , c 14)

the Borough Council, and all rates collected in a metropolitan borough by the Council are so far as practicable to be levied on one demand note, in a form to be approved by the Local Government Board, and stating

(a) the rateable value of the premises in respect of which the rate is levied; and

(b) the rate in the £; and

(c) the period for which the rate is made; and

(d) the several purposes for which the rate is levied; and

(e) the approximate amount in the £ required for each purpose (including so far as practicable the proportionate amount of the estimated costs of and loss in collection); and

(f) any matter required by Section 2 of the London Equalisation of Rates Act, 1894, or any other enactment, to be stated in the demand note.

Following this Act the London (Rating Scheme) 1901 (see Appendix II post), makes provision as to the levying of one rate, on which in the case of exemptions (either by way of reduced assessment or by levying a differential rate or in any other manner) then existing, an abatement of the rate in the £ is to be made corresponding to the value of such exemption.

City of London

The City of London, which had been excluded from the provisions of the London Government Act, 1899,[1] has since been dealt with by a local Act, promoted by the City Corporation, and entitled "The City of London (Union of Parishes) Act, 1907."[2]

By this Act provision has been made whereby, as and from the 1st April 1908 —

(1) All the parishes in the City of London—some 112 in number—have been united in one parish, "the Parish of the City of London"

[1] 62 & 63 Vict., c. 14.

[2] 7 Edward 7, c. cxl

(2) The Common Council of the City are made the Overseers of such parish

(3) Every precept issued by any authority for the purpose of obtaining money which is ultimately to be raised out of a rate within the said parish (other than a precept sent to the Guardians of the City of London Union by the Local Government Board, or by a body containing representatives elected by such Guardians) is to be sent to the Common Council

(4) The powers, duties, and liabilities of every Vestry within the City are transferred to the Common Council

(5) One rate, to be called " The General Rate," is to be levied for all City purposes

(6) The General Rate and the Poor Rate are to be made as separate and distinct rates, but the Common Council may order the Poor Rate to be made at the same time and entered in the same book as the General Rate

(7) All rates collected by the Common Council are, so far as practicable, to be levied on one demand note, which is to contain the same particulars as already set out with respect to the metropolitan boroughs (see p 522 *ante*)

APPENDICES.

APPENDIX I.

pp 527 to 639

STATUTORY ENACTMENTS RELATING TO PAROCHIAL ASSESSMENT AND RATING

———

APPENDIX II.

pp 640 to 654

STATUTORY ORDERS RELATING TO PAROCHIAL ASSESSMENT AND RATING

———

APPENDIX III.

pp 655 to 668

TABLES AND FORMS

APPENDIX I.

STATUTORY ENACTMENTS

RELATING TO

PAROCHIAL ASSESSMENT AND RATING.

NOTE —The provisions of the Acts, as hereinafter set out, are taken
from "The Statutes Second Revised Edition," the dots
indicating the omission of words which have been repealed,
and the asterisks sections or parts which have been omitted.

THE POOR RELIEF ACT, 1601

(43 Eliz, cap 2)

AN ACT FOR THE RELIEF OF THE POOR

BE it enacted by the authority of this present Parliament, that the
churchwardens of every parish and four, three or two substantial
householders there as shall be thought meet, having respect to the
proportion and greatness of the same parish or parishes, to be
nominated yearly in Easter week, or within one month after Easter,
under the hand and seal of two or more justices of the peace in the
same county, whereof one to be of the quorum, dwelling in or near
the same parish or division where the same parish doth lie, shall be
called Overseers of the Poor of the same parish; and they or the
greater part of them shall take order from time to time, by and with
the consent of two or more such justices of peace as is aforesaid, for
setting to work of the children of all such whose parents shall not by
the said churchwardens and overseers or the greater part of them be
thought able to keep and maintain their children, and also for setting
to work all such persons, married or unmarried, having no means to
maintain them, use no ordinary and daily trade of life to get their
living by, and also to raise weekly or otherwise, by taxation of every
inhabitant, parson, vicar and other and of every occupier of lands,
houses, tithes impropriate or propriations of tithes, coal mines or
saleable underwoods,[1] in the said parish in such competent sum and
sums of money as they shall think fit, a convenient stock of flax,
hemp, wool thread, iron and other necessary ware and stuff to set the
poor on work, and also competent sums of money for and towards
the necessary relief of the lame, impotent, old, blind, and such other
among them being poor, and not able to work, and also for the putting
out of such children to be apprentices, to be gathered out of the same
parish according to the ability of the same parish, and to do and

Side notes:
Church wardens and others shall be yearly named overseers of the poor

To set poor children to work

And to raise a stock for that purpose

And money for relief of impotent poor and for apprenticing children

---

[1] Repealed as to taxation of occupiers of saleable underwoods, 37 & 38 Vict,
c 54, s 14

execute all other things as well for the disposing of the said stock as otherwise concerning the premises as to them shall seem convenient

* * * * * *

Appeal against rates, etc., to the quarter sessions

5 Provided always that if any person or persons shall find themselves grieved with any sess or tax or other act done by the said churchwardens and other persons, or by the said justices of peace, that then it shall be lawful for the justices of peace at their general quarter sessions, or the greater number of them to take such order therein as to them shall be thought convenient, and the same to conclude and bind all the said parties

THE POOR RATE ACT, 1743
(17 Geo II, cap 3)

AN ACT TO OBLIGE OVERSEERS OF THE POOR TO GIVE PUBLIC NOTICE OF RATES MADE FOR THE RELIEF OF THE POOR, AND TO PRODUCE THE SAME

Preamble reciting the Act 43 Eliz, c 2

WHEREAS great inconveniences do often arise in cities, towns corporate, parishes, townships and places by reason of the unlimited power of the churchwardens and overseers of the poor who frequently, on frivolous pretences and for private ends, make unjust and illegal rates in a secret and clandestine manner contrary to the true intent and meaning of a statute made in the forty and third year of the reign of Queen Elizabeth, intituled "An Act for the relief of the poor" For remedy whereof, and preventing the like abuses for the future, be it enacted by the King's most excellent Majesty, by and with the advice and consent of the lords spiritual and temporal, and commons, in this present Parliament assembled,

Poor rates to be published in the church

and by the authority of the same, that from and after the first day of May which shall be in the year of our Lord one thousand seven hundred and forty four, the churchwardens and overseers, or other persons authorized to take care of the poor in every parish, township, or place, shall give or cause to be given public notice in the church of every rate for the relief of the poor, allowed by the justices of peace, the next Sunday after the same shall have been so allowed, and that no rate shall be esteemed or reputed valid and sufficient, so as to collect and raise the same, unless such notice shall have been given

The rates to be inspected by any inhabitant and copies taken

2 And the churchwardens and overseers of the poor or other persons authorized as aforesaid, in every parish township, or place, shall permit all and every the inhabitants of the said parish, township, or place to inspect every such rate at all seasonable times, paying one shilling for the same, and shall, upon demand, forthwith give copies of the same, or any part thereof, to any inhabitant of the said parish, township, or place, paying at the rate of sixpence for every twenty-four names

3 And   if any churchwarden or overseer of the
poor or other person authorized as aforesaid shall not admit any
inhabitant or parishioner to inspect the said rates, or shall refuse or
neglect to give copies thereof as aforesaid, such churchwarden or
overseer or other person authorized as aforesaid, for every such
offence shall forfeit and pay to the party aggrieved, the sum of
twenty pounds, to be sued for and recovered by action of debt, bill,
plaint, or information, in any of His Majesty's courts of record,
wherein no essoin, protection, or wager of law, or more than one
imparlance shall be allowed

Penalty on not permitting any inhabitant to inspect, etc

THE POOR RELIEF ACT, 1743

(17 Geo II, cap. 38)

AN ACT FOR REMEDYING SOME DEFECTS IN THE ACT MADE IN
THE FORTY-THIRD YEAR OF THE REIGN OF QUEEN ELIZABETH
INTITULED "AN ACT FOR THE RELIEF OF THE POOR"

4 And .   in case any person or persons shall find
him, her, or themselves aggrieved by any rate or assessment made for
the relief of the poor, or shall have any material objection to any
person or persons being put on or left out of such rate or assessment
or to the sum charged on any person or persons therein, or shall have
any material objection to such account as aforesaid, or any part
thereof, or shall find him, her, or themselves aggrieved by any
neglect act, or thing done or omitted by the churchwardens and
overseers of the poor, or by any of his Majesty's justices of the
peace, it shall and may be lawful for such person or persons in any
of the cases aforesaid, giving reasonable notice to the churchwardens
or overseers of the poor of the parish township, or place, to appeal
to the next general or quarter sessions of the peace for the county,
riding, division corporation, or franchise where such parish, township
or place lies, and the justices of the peace there assembled are
hereby authorised and required to receive such appeal, and to hear
and finally determine the same, but if it shall appear to the said
justices that reasonable notice was not given, then they shall adjourn
the said appeal to the next quarter sessions and then and there
finally hear and determine the same, and the said justices may award
and order to the party for whom such appeal shall be determined,
reasonable costs, in the same manner that they are empowered to do
in case of appeals concerning the settlement of poor persons, by an
Act made in the eighth and ninth years of King William the Third
intituled ' An Act for supplying some defects in the laws for the
' relief of the poor of this kingdom ' '

Persons aggrieved may appeal to quarter sessions

Proviso for corporations, etc

5 Provided always, that in all corporations or franchises who have not four justices of the peace, it shall and may be lawful for any person or persons, in any of the cases aforesaid where an appeal is given by this Act, to appeal, if he or they shall think fit, to the next general or quarter sessions of the peace for the county, riding or division wherein such corporation or franchise is situate

6 And whereas it hath been held, that upon appeals from rates and assessments, the justices of the peace may not only quash the old rates, but make new rates and assessments from which no appeal can

How far justices shall give relief on appeals

be had Be it enacted by the authority aforesaid, that upon all appeals from rates and assessments, the justices of the peace (where they shall see just cause to give relief) shall and are hereby required to amend the same, in such manner only as shall be necessary for giving such relief, without altering such rates or assessments with respect to other persons mentioned in the same, but if upon an appeal from the whole rate, it shall be found necessary to quash or set aside the same, then and in every such case the said justices shall and are hereby required to order and direct the churchwardens and overseers of the poor to make a new equal rate or assessment, and they are hereby required to make the same accordingly

Clause relating to warrants of distress

7. And for the more effectual levying money assessed for the relief of the poor, be it enacted by the authority aforesaid, that the goods of any person assessed, and refusing to pay, may be levied by warrant of distress, not only in the place for which such assessment was made, but in any other place within the same county or precinct and if sufficient distress cannot be found within the said county or precinct, on oath made thereof before some justice of any other county or precinct (which oath shall be certified under the hand of such justice on the said warrant) such goods may be levied in such other county

Appeal to quarter sessions

or precinct by virtue of such warrant and certificate, and if any person shall find him or herself aggrieved by such distress as aforesaid, it shall and may be lawful for such person to appeal to the next general or quarter sessions of the peace for the county or precinct where such assessment was made, and the justices there are hereby required to hear and finally determine the same

Succeeding overseers to levy arrears to reimburse the former

11 And   in case any person or persons shall refuse or neglect to pay to such overseers as aforesaid any sum or sums of money that he, she or they shall be legally rated or assessed to, it shall and may be lawful to and for the succeeding overseers and they are hereby required to levy such arrears and out of the money so levied to reimburse their predecessors all sums of money which they have expended for the use of the poor, and which are allowed to be due to them in their accounts as aforesaid

Copies of rates to be enter'd in a book

13 And .   .   true and just copies of all rates and assessments hereafter to be made for the relief of the poor, be fairly wrote and entered in a book or books to be provided for that purpose

by the churchwardens and overseers of the poor of every parish, township or place, who shall take care that such copies be wrote and entered accordingly within fourteen days after all appeals from such rates are determined, and shall attest the same by putting their names thereto and all and every such book or books shall be carefully preserved by the churchwardens and overseers of the poor for the time being, or one of them, in some public or other place in every such parish, township, or place whereto all persons assessed, or liable to be assessed, may freely resort, and shall be delivered over from time to time to the new and succeeding churchwardens and overseers of the poor as soon as they enter into their said offices to be preserved as aforesaid, and shall be produced by them at the general or quarter sessions, when any appeal is to be heard or determined. *to be kept for public perusal*

14 And   if any churchwarden, overseer of the poor, or other officer of any parish, township, or place shall neglect or refuse to obey and perform the several orders and directions of this Act, or any of them, where no penalty is before provided by this Act, or shall act contrary thereto, every such churchwarden, overseer of the poor, or other officer so offending in the premises, shall for every such offence, on oath thereof made within two calendar months after the offence committed, before any two or more of His Majesty's justices of the peace, forfeit, for the use of the poor of such parish, township, or place, a sum not exceeding five pounds, not less than twenty shillings, to be levied by distress and sale of the offender's goods, by warrant from such justices, which sum shall be paid to some churchwarden or overseer of the poor of such parish, township, or place, for the purpose aforesaid *Penalty on parish officer not obeying this Act*

15 And   overseers of the poor within every township, or place where there are no churchwardens, shall from time to time do, perform, and execute all and every the acts, powers, and authorities concerning the relief of, and other matters and things relating to the poor, as churchwardens and overseers of the poor may do, perform, and execute by this Act, or any former statute concerning the poor, and shall lose, forfeit, and suffer all such pains and penalties for neglect, abuse, or non-performance thereof, as churchwardens and overseers of the poor are liable to by virtue of this or any former statute concerning the poor. *Power of overseers who there in to churchward as*

THE POOR RATE ACT, 1801
(41 Geo III, cap. 23)

AN ACT FOR THE BETTER COLLECTION OF RATES MADE FOR THE RELIEF OF THE POOR   [18th April, 1801]

WHEREAS by an Act of Parliament, made and passed in the seventeenth year of the reign of his late Majesty King George the

Second, intituled "An Act for remedying some defects in the Act," made in the forty-third year of the reign of Queen Elizabeth, intituled " An Act for the relief of the 'poor,'" power was given to justices of the peace, upon appeals from rates and assessments, where they should see just cause to give relief, to amend the same in such manner only as should be necessary for giving such relief, without altering such rates or assessments with respect to other persons mentioned in the same   And whereas the quashing or setting aside of rates or assessments made for the relief of the poor is attended with grave inconvenience , and it hath happened in consequence of the rate or assessment being quashed or set aside or of notice of appeal against the whole rate being given, the churchwardens and overseers of the poor have not had any money in hand for the relief and maintenance of the poor   For remedy whereof, may it please your Majesty that it may be enacted, and be it enacted by the King's most excellent Majesty, by and with the advice and consent of the lords spiritual and temporal, and commons, in this present Parliament assembled, and by the authority of the same, that from and after the passing of this Act, upon all appeals from any rate or assessment made for the relief of the poor of any parish, township, vill, or place, the court of general or quarter sessions of the peace shall and such court is hereby authorised and required (in all cases where they shall see just cause to give relief) to amend such rate or assessment, either by inserting therein or striking out the name or names of any person or persons or by altering the sum or sums therein charged on any person or persons, or in any other manner which the said court shall think necessary for giving such relief, and without quashing or wholly setting aside such rate or assessment   Provided always that it the said court shall be of opinion that it is necessary, for the purpose of giving relief to the person or persons appealing, that the rate or assessment should be wholly quashed, then the said court may quash the same , but nevertheless, all and every the sum and sums of money in and by such rate or assessment charged on any person or persons, shall and may be levied and recovered by such ways and means, and in such and the same manner as if no appeal had been made against such rate or assessment   and all and every the sum and sums of money which any person or persons charged in such rate or assessment shall pay, or which shall be levied upon or recovered from him, her, or them shall be deemed and taken as payments on account of the next effective rate or rates, assessment or assessments, which shall be made for the relief of the poor of the same parish, township, vill, or place

2 And   from and after the passing of this Act, all and every the sum and sums of money at which any person or persons is or are or shall be rated or assessed, in any rate or assessment made for the relief of the poor of any parish, township, vill, or place, shall and may be levied and recovered by distress, and all other

lawful ways and means, notwithstanding the person or persons so rated, or assessed, or any other person or persons, shall have given notice of appeal from or against such rate or assessment, for any cause whatsoever. Provided always, that if any person, rated or assessed in any rate or assessment made for the relief of the poor, shall give such notice of appeal as hereinafter mentioned to the churchwardens and overseers of any parish, township, vill or place, or any two of them, then, from and after the giving of such notice, and until the appeal shall have been heard and determined no proceedings shall be commenced or carried on to recover any greater sum or sums of money from such person or persons, than the sum or sums at which he, she, or they, or any occupier of the same premises, shall have been rated or assessed in the last effective rate which shall have been collected in such parish, township, vill or place

greater than that assessed in the last effective rate

3 And . . in the case of the said court of general or quarter sessions of the peace shall upon appeal order any rate or assessment for the relief of the poor to be quashed, it shall be lawful for the said court to order that any sum or sums of money, in and by such rate or assessment charged on any person or persons, or any part of any such sum or sums, not to be paid, and then and in every such case no proceedings shall, after making such order, be commenced, or if any proceedings have been previously commenced such proceedings shall be no further prosecuted or carried on for the purpose of levying or enforcing the payment of any sum or sums which shall be so ordered by the said court not to be paid as aforesaid. Provided always that no justice of the peace, constable, or other officer of the peace or other person shall be deemed a trespasser, or liable to any action, for any warrant, order, act, or thing which such justice, constable, or other officer or person shall have granted, made, executed or done for the purpose of levying or enforcing the payment of any such sum or sums of money before he shall have had notice in writing of the order for the non-payment of such sum or sums of money which the said court is hereby authorized to make as aforesaid

Quarter sessions having ordered a rate to be quashed, may order the sum charged on any person not to be paid, and stop proceedings for the recovery thereof, etc

4 And from and after the passing of this Act all notices of appeal from or against any rate or assessment made for the relief of the poor, or from or against the account of the churchwardens and overseers of the poor of any parish, township, vill, or place shall be in writing and shall be signed by the person or persons giving the same, or his, her, or their attorney on his, her or their behalf, and such notices of appeal shall be delivered to or left at the places of abode of the churchwardens and overseers of the poor of the parish, township, vill, or place, or any two of them, and the particular causes or grounds of appeal shall be stated and specified in such notice; and upon the hearing of any appeal from or against any such rate or assessment, or account the court of general or quarter sessions to which such appeal shall be made, shall not examine or

Notices of appeal to be given to churchwardens and overseers of the poor, etc, and grounds of appeal stated in such notices

enquire into any other cause or ground of appeal than such as are or is stated and specified in the notice of appeal

5 Provided nevertheless . that with the consent of the overseers signified by them or their attorney in open court, and with the consent of any other person interested therein, the said court of sessions may proceed to hear and decide upon such appeal, although no notice thereof shall have been given in writing, and also that with the like consent such court may hear and decide upon grounds of appeal not stated or misstated in such written notice where any notice shall have been given in writing

6 And from and after the passing of this Act, if any person or persons shall appeal against any rate or assessment made for the relief of the poor, because any other person or persons is or are rated or assessed in such rate or assessment or is or are omitted to be rated or assessed therein, or because any other person or persons is or are rated or assessed in any such rate or assessment at any greater or less sum or sums of money than the sum or sums at which he, she or they ought to be rated or assessed therein, or for any other cause that may require any alteration to be made in such rate or assessment with respect to any other person or persons, then and in every such case the person or persons so appealing for the causes aforesaid or any of them, shall give such notice of appeal in writing as hereinbefore mentioned, not only to the churchwardens or overseers of the poor, or any two or more of them but also to the other person or persons so interested or concerned in the event of such appeal is aforesaid, and such other person or persons shall, if he, she, or they shall so desire, be heard upon the said appeal, and it shall be lawful for the court of general or quarter sessions of the peace, on the hearing of such appeal, to order the name or names of such other person or persons to be inserted in such rate or assessment and him, her, or them to be therein rated and assessed at any sum or sums of money, or to order the name or names of such other person or persons to be struck out of such rate or assessment or the sum or sums at which he, she, or they is or are rated or assessed therein, to be altered in such manner as the said court shall think right, and the proper officer of the said court shall forthwith add to or alter the rate or assessment accordingly

7 And if upon the hearing of any appeal from or against any rate or assessment, the said court shall order the name or names of any person or persons to be inserted therein and him, her, or them to be rated or assessed at any sum or sums of money, or shall order the sum or sums at which any person or persons, is or are therein rated or assessed to be raised or increased, then and in such case all and every the sum and sums of money, at or to which such person or persons shall be so ordered to be rated or assessed or to be raised or increased, or so much thereof as shall not have been already

paid shall and may be recovered in such and the same manner and by such and the same means, as if he, she, or they had been originally named in such rate or assessment, and rated or assessed therein at such sum or sums of money

8 And . . if upon the hearing of any appeal from any rate or assessment for the relief of the poor the court of general or quarter sessions of the peace shall order the name or names of any person or persons to be struck out of such rate or assessment, or the sum or sums rated or assessed on any person or persons to be decreased or lowered, and if it shall be made appear to the said court that such person or persons hath or have, previously to the hearing of such appeal, paid any sum or sums of money, in consequence of such rate or assessment, which he, she, or they ought not to have paid or been charged with, then in every such sum and sums of money to be repaid and returned, by the said churchwardens and overseers of the poor, to the person or persons having paid the same respectively, together with all reasonable costs, charges, and expenses, occasioned by such person or persons having paid or been required to pay the same , and all and every the sum and sums of money so ordered to be repaid or returned by the churchwardens and overseers of the poor, or any of them, shall and may together with all such costs, charges, and expences as aforesaid, be levied and recovered from them, or any of them, by distress and all such other ways and means as the money charged, rated, or assessed on any person, by any rate or assessment made for the relief of the poor, can or may be by law levied or recovered.

In case in the rate the name of any person shall be struck out, or any sum lowered, the quarter sessions shall order any sums paid in excess to be repaid

---

THE POOR RELIEF ACT, 1814

(54 Geo III, cap 170)

AN ACT TO REPEAL CERTAIN PROVISIONS IN LOCAL ACTS FOR THE MAINTENANCE AND REGULATION OF THE POOR, AND TO MAKE OTHER PROVISIONS IN RELATION THERETO.

[*30th July, 1814*]

11 And it shall and may be lawful for any two or more of His Majesty's justices of the peace acting for the county, riding, division, or jurisdiction, in which any district, parish, township, or hamlet shall be situated, in petty sessions assembled, on application made to them by any person rated to any rates or cesses within any such district, township, parish, or hamlet to be discharged therefrom and proof of his or her inability through poverty to pay such rate or cess, with the consent of the churchwardens and overseers of such district, parish, township, or hamlet, or of such other person or

Justices in petty sessions with consent of parish officers may discharge poor persons from the payment of parish rates

persons as is or are competent to act under the authority of any Act or Acts of Parliament for the ordering, management, controul, or direction of the poor of any such district, parish, township, or hamlet to order and direct that such person shall be excused from the payment of such rate or cess, and to strike out his or her name therefrom, and the sum at which such person was so rated in such rate or cess shall not thereafter be collected or any person or persons charged therewith, or in any manner called or liable to account for the same, or for omitting to collect or receive the same.

Goods of persons neglecting to pay poor rate etc, may be distrained in other parishes of the county, and for want of sufficient distress in the county, in another county

12 And   the goods and chattels of any person or persons neglecting or refusing to pay any sum or sums of money legally assessed on and due from him, her, or them in respect of any rate for the relief of the poor, church cess, or highway cess of any district, parish, township, or hamlet, for the space of seven days after the same shall have been legally demanded of him, her or them, shall and may be distrained, not only within such district, parish, township, or hamlet, but also within any other district, parish, township, or hamlet within the same county, riding, division, or jurisdiction and if sufficient distress cannot be found within the same county, riding, division, or jurisdiction, then upon oath thereof made before any one or more justice or justices of the peace of any other county, riding, division, or jurisdiction in which any of the goods or chattels of such persons shall be found, which oath such justice or justices are hereby required to administer and certify by indorsing, in his or their respective handwriting, his or their name or names on the warrant granted to make such distress, the goods and chattels of the said person or persons so neglecting or refusing to pay as aforesaid shall be subject and liable to such distress and sale in such other county, riding division, or jurisdiction where the same shall be found and may by virtue of such warrant and certificate be distrained and sold in the same manner as if the same had been found within the district, parish, township or hamlet in or for which such rate or cess had been made or was due

THE POOR RATE EXEMPTION ACT, 1833.
(3 & 4 William IV, cap. 30)

AN ACT TO EXEMPT FROM POOR AND CHURCH RATES ALL CHURCHES, CHAPELS AND OTHER PLACES OF RELIGIOUS WORSHIP

[24th July 1833]

No persons shall be rated to church or poor rates for churches or places

1 No person or persons shall be rated or shall be liable to be rated or to pay to any church or poor rates or cesses, for or in respect of any churches, district churches, chapels, meeting houses or premises or such part thereof as shall be exclusively appropriated to public

religious worship and which (other than churches, district churches and episcopal chapels of the established church) shall be duly certified for the performance of such religious worship according to the provision of any Act or Acts now in force   Provided always that no person or persons shall be hereby exempted from any such rates or cesses for or in respect of any parts of such churches, district churches, chapels, meeting houses or other premises which are not so exclusively appropriated, and from which parts not so exclusively appropriated such person or persons shall receive any rent or rents or shall derive profit or advantage   *exclusively appropriated to public religious worship and duly certified*

2 Provided always that no person or persons shall be liable to any such rates or cesses because the said churches, district churches, chapels, meeting houses or other premises or any vestry rooms belonging thereto or any part thereof may be used for Sunday or infant schools or for the charitable education of the poor   *Persons not to be liable to rates because premises are used for Sunday schools, etc*

THE PAROCHIAL ASSESSMENT ACT, 1836
(6 & 7 William IV, cap 96)

AN ACT TO REGULATE PAROCHIAL ASSESSMENTS

[*19th August 1836*]

[PREAMBLE]

[1 No rate for the relief of the poor in England and Wales shall be allowed by any Justices, or be of any force, which shall not be made upon an estimate of the net annual value of the several hereditaments rated thereunto, that is to say, of the rent at which the same might reasonably be expected to let from year to year free of all usual tenant's rates and taxes, and tithe commutation rent-charge, if any, and deducting therefrom the probable average annual cost of the repairs, insurance and other expenses, if any necessary to maintain them in a state to command such rent   provided always, that nothing herein contained shall be construed to alter or affect the principles or different relative liabilities, if any, according to which different kinds of hereditaments are now by law rateable]   *Repealed as regards Metropolis. All rates to be made on the net annual value of the property*

[2 .   Every such rate made after the said period shall, in addition to any other particular which the form of making out such rate shall require to be set forth, contain an account of every particular set forth at the head of the respective columns in the form given in the schedule to this Act annexed, so far as the same can be ascertained ; and the churchwardens and overseers, or other officers whose duty it may be to make and levy the said rate, or such a number of the said churchwardens and overseers or other officers as are competent to the making and levying of the same, shall, before the rate is allowed by the Justices, sign the declaration given at the foot of the said form ; and otherwise the said rate   *Repealed as regards Metropolis. Rates to be made in a given form*

Nothing herein to prevent owners from compounding for rates

Power to order new survey and valuation

Power for surveyors to enter and examine lands etc, for purposes of survey and plans

Power to take copies or extracts of rates gratis

shall be of no force or validity . provided always, that nothing herein contained shall be construed to prevent the owners of tenements from compounding for the rates to be assessed on the same, in such manner as they were by any statute or statutes enabled to do before the passing of this Act, so that the gross estimated rental of the hereditaments compounded for be entered on the rate in the proper column]

3   When it shall be made to appear to the Poor Law Commissioners by representation in writing from the Board of Guardians of any union or parish under their common seal, or from the majority of the churchwardens and overseers or other officers competent as aforesaid to the making and levying the rate, that a fair and correct estimate for the aforesaid purposes cannot be made without a new valuation, it shall be lawful for the Poor Law Commissioners where they shall see fit, to order a survey, with or without a map or plan, on such scale as they shall think fit, to be made and taken of the messuages, lands, and other hereditaments liable to poor rates in such parish, or in all or any one or more parishes of such a union, and a valuation to be made of the said messuages, lands, and other hereditaments according to their annual value, and to direct such guardians to appoint a fit person or persons to make and take every such survey, map or plan and valuation, and to make provision for paying the costs of every such survey map or plan and valuation either by a separate rate or by charge on the poor rates as they may see fit , but in case of such charge being made, then provision shall be made for paying off not less than one fifth of the sum charged on the rates and such interest as may from time to time be payable in respect of such charge, or any part thereof, in each succeeding year till the whole is repaid

4   .   .   For the purpose of making every such survey, map or plan, and valuation, it shall be lawful for the person or persons so to be appointed for making the same respectively together with their and every of their assistants and servants, at all reasonable times, until the same respectively shall be completed, to enter, view and examine, survey and admeasure, all and every part of the messuages, lands and other hereditaments aforesaid, and to do or cause to be done any act or thing necessary for making such survey, map or plan, and valuation   provided always, that any map, survey, plan, or valuation made previously to the appointment of such person or persons which shall be tendered to him or them, and which shall be in his or their judgment, and to his or their satisfaction a just and true map or survey, proper for the purposes aforesaid, may be used for such purposes

5   It shall be lawful for any person or persons rated to the relief of the poor of the parish in respect of which any rate shall be made at all seasonable times, to take copies thereof, or extracts therefrom without paying anything for the same,

anything in any Act of Parliament to the contrary notwithstanding, and in case the person or persons having the custody of such rate shall refuse to permit, or shall not permit such person or persons so rated as aforesaid to take copies thereof, or extracts therefrom, the person or persons so refusing or not permitting such copy or extract to be made shall forfeit and pay any sum not exceeding five pounds, to be recovered in a summary way before any Justice of the Peace having jurisdiction in the parish or place *Penalty for refusal to permit*

[6 . . The Justices acting in and for every Petty Sessions Division, shall four times at least in every year hold a Special Sessions for hearing appeals against the rates of the several parishes within their respective divisions, and shall cause public notice of the time and place, when and where such Special Sessions will be holden to be affixed to or near to the door of the parish church of the said parishes, twenty-eight days at the least before the holding of the same, and such Special Sessions shall, and may be adjourned from time to time by the Justices there present, as they may think fit, and at such Special or adjourned Sessions the Justices there present shall hear and determine all objections to any such rate on the ground of inequality, unfairness, or incorrectness in the valuation of any hereditaments included therein, which decision shall be binding and conclusive on the parties, unless the person or persons impugning such decision shall within fourteen days after the same shall have been made cause notice to be given in writing of his, her, or their intention of appealing against such decision, and of the matter or cause of such appeal, to the person or persons in whose favour such decision shall have been made and within five days after giving such notice shall enter into a recognizance before some Justice of the Peace, with sufficient securities conditioned to try such appeal at the then next General Sessions or Quarter Sessions of the Peace which shall first happen, and to abide the order of and to pay such costs as shall be awarded by the Justices at such Quarter Sessions, or any adjournment thereof; and such Justices upon hearing and finally determining such matter of appeal, shall and may, according to their discretion, award such costs to the party or parties appealing or appealed against, as they shall think proper and their determination in or concerning the premises shall be conclusive and binding on all parties to all intents and purposes whatsoever   Provided always, that unless no such objection shall be inquired into by the said Justices in Special Sessions unless notice of such objection in writing under the hand of the complainant shall have been given, seven days at least before the day appointed for such Special Session to the collector, overseers, or other persons by whom such rate was made   provided also, that the said Justices in Special Session shall not be authorised to inquire into the liability of any hereditaments to be rated, but only into the true value thereof, and into the fairness of the amount at which the same shall have been rated]

Repealed as regards Metropolis

Justices acting in Petty Sessions to hold four Special Sessions in the year to hear appeals

Seven days notice to be given of objections

Justices not to inquire into liability of the property

Repealed as regards Metropolis

Justices may act with all the powers of Justices in Quarter Sessions

[7.   The Justices present at any such Special or adjourned Sessions shall for the aforesaid purpose have all the powers of amending or quashing any such rate so objected to of any parish or other district within their division, and likewise of awarding costs to be paid by or to any of the parties, and of recovering such costs which any Court of Quarter Sessions has upon appeals from any such rate, except as herein excepted provided always, that no order of the said Justices shall be removed by certiorari or otherwise into any of His Majesty's Courts of Record at Westminster provided also, that nothing in this Act contained shall be construed to deprive any person or persons of the right to appeal against any rate to any Court of Quarter Sessions provided also, that no order of the said Justices in Special Session shall be of any force pending any appeal touching the same subject-matter to the Court of Quarter Sessions having jurisdiction to try such appeal, or in opposition to the order of any such Court upon such appeal]

Act confined to England and Wales

8 This Act shall extend only to England and Wales

SCHEDULE TO WHICH THIS ACT REFERS

Form of Rate

An Assessment for the Relief of the Poor of the parish of Merton in the county of Surrey and for other purposes chargeable thereon according to Law, made this Thirtieth day of March in the year of our Lord One Thousand Eight Hundred and Thirty seven after the rate of sixpence in the pound

No	Arrears due or if excused	Name of Occupier	Name of Owner	Description of Property rated	Name or Situation of Property	Estimated Extent			Gross Estimated Rental			Rateable Value			Rate at 6d in the Pound		
	£ s d					A R P			£ s d			£ s d			£ s d		
1		James Smith	John Green	Land and Building	Whiteacre Farm	10 0 0			60 0 0			50 0 0			1 7 0		
2		Ditto	Ditto	House and Garden	In West Street	0 1 0			30 0 0			25 0 0			0 12 6		
3	Excused	John Poot	Ditto	House	In Brick Lane				1 10 0			1 5 0			0 0 7½		
etc	etc	etc	etc	etc	etc	etc			etc			etc			etc		

Declaration of Overseers and Churchwardens

We, , do declare the several particulars specified in the respective columns of the above rate to be true and correct, so far as we have been able to ascertain them, to which end we have used our best endeavours

THOMAS JONES, Overseer.

JOHN THOMAS [Churchwarden, etc, etc]

THE PARISH NOTICES ACT, 1837
(7 William IV and 1 Vict, cap 45)

AN ACT TO ALTER THE MODE OF GIVING NOTICES FOR THE HOLDING OF VESTRIES, OF MAKING PROCLAMATIONS IN CASES OF OUTLAWRY AND OF GIVING NOTICES ON SUNDAYS WITH RESPECT TO VARIOUS MATTERS

[12th July, 1837]

Notices not to be given in churches during divine service, etc

[1]   .   No proclamation or other public notice for a vestry meeting or any other matter shall be made or given in any church or chapel during or after divine service or at the door of any church or chapel at the conclusion of divine service

Notices heretofore usually given during or after divine service, etc, to be affixed to the church doors

2 All proclamations or notices which under or by virtue of any law or statute or by custom or otherwise have been heretofore made or given in churches or chapels during or after divine service shall be reduced into writing, and copies thereof either in writing or in print or partly in writing or partly in print shall previously to the commencement of divine service on the several days on which such proclamations or notices have heretofore been made or given in the church or chapel of any parish or place or at the door of any church or chapel be affixed on or near to the doors of all the churches and chapels within such parish or place, and such notices when so affixed shall be in lieu of and as a substitution for the several proclamations and notices as heretofore given as aforesaid and shall be good, valid and effectual to all intents and purposes whatsoever

THE POOR RATE EXEMPTION ACT, 1840[†]
(3 & 4 Vict, cap 89)

AN ACT TO EXEMPT UNTIL THE THIRTY-FIRST DAY OF DECEMBER, ONE THOUSAND EIGHT HUNDRED AND FORTY-ONE THE INHABITANTS OF PARISHES, TOWNSHIPS, AND VILLAGES FROM LIABILITY TO BE RATED AS SUCH, IN RESPECT OF STOCK-IN-TRADE OR OTHER PROPERTY, TO THE RELIEF OF THE POOR

[10th August 1840]

(PREAMBLE RECITES 43 ELIZ, c 2, 14 CHAS II, c 12)

Stock-in-Trade, etc not to be rated

[1] It shall not be lawful for the overseers of any parish, township, or village to tax any inhabitant thereof as such inhabitant, in respect of his ability derived from the profits of stock-in-trade or any other property, for or towards the relief of the poor Provided always that nothing in this Act contained shall in anywise affect the liability of any parson or vicar, or of any occupier of lands, houses tithes impropriate, propriations of tithes, coal mines, or saleable underwoods, to be taxed under the provisions of the said Act for and towards the relief of the poor

† This Act is continued from time to time by the Expiring Laws Continuance Act, 1909 (9 Edw VII, c 46)

THE SCIENTIFIC SOCIETIES ACT, 1843

(6 & 7 Vict. cap 36)

AN ACT TO EXEMPT FROM COUNTY, BOROUGH, PAROCHIAL, AND OTHER LOCAL RATES, LAND AND BUILDINGS OCCUPIED BY SCIENTIFIC OR LITERARY SOCIETIES

[*28th July, 1843*]

[PREAMBLE]

[1] No person or persons shall be assessed or rated or liable to be assessed or rated, or liable to pay to any county, borough, parochial or other local rates or cesses, in respect of any land houses, or buildings, or parts of houses or buildings, belonging to any society instituted for purposes of science, literature, or the fine arts exclusively, either as tenant or as owner, and occupied by it for the transaction of its business, and for carrying into effect its purposes, provided that such society shall be supported wholly or in part by annual voluntary contributions, and shall not, and by its laws may not make any dividend, gift, division or bonus in money unto or between any of its members, and provided also that such society shall obtain the certificate of the barrister-at-law or lord advocate as hereinafter mentioned

Scientific, etc societies, supported by voluntary contributions and dividing no profits exempted from rates upon obtaining the certificate hereinafter mentioned

2 Provided always, that before any society shall be entitled to the benefit of this Act such society shall cause three copies of all laws, rules, and regulations for the management thereof signed by the president or other chief officer and three members of the council or committee of management and countersigned by the clerk or secretary of such society, to be submitted in England, Wales and Berwick-upon-Tweed to the barrister at-law for the time being appointed to certify the rules of friendly societies there, and in Scotland to the lord advocate, or any deputy appointed by him to certify the rules of friendly societies there, and in Ireland to the barrister for the time being appointed to certify the rules of friendly societies there, for the purpose of ascertaining whether such society is entitled to the benefit of this Act, and such barrister or lord advocate, as the case may be, shall give a certificate on each of the said copies that the society so applying is entitled to the benefit of this Act, or shall state in writing the grounds on which such certificate is withheld, and one of such copies, when certified by such barrister or lord advocate, shall be returned to the society, another copy shall be retained by such barrister or lord advocate and the other of such copies shall be transmitted by such barrister or lord advocate to the clerk of the peace for the borough or county where the land or buildings of such society in respect of which such exemption is claimed shall be situated, and shall by him be laid before the recorder or justices for such borough or county at the general quarter sessions, or adjournment thereof, held next after the time when such copy shall have

Such societies to cause three copies of their rules of management to be submitted to the barrister or person appointed to certify the rules of friendly societies, who shall certify therein that society is entitled to exemption, or state his ground for withholding his certificate

One certified copy to be returned to the society, one to be retained by the barrister and the third transmitted to the clerk of the peace for confirmation at sessions and to be deposited

been so certified and transmitted to him as aforesaid and the recorder or justices then and there present are hereby authorised and required without motion, to allow and confirm the same and such copy shall be filed by such clerk of the peace with the rolls of the sessions of the peace in his custody, without fee or reward

Certain alterations made in the rules to be certified and deposited in like manner

3 If the laws, rules and regulations of any such society shall be altered, so as to affect or relate to the property or constitution of such society, such alteration shall within one calendar month after the same shall have been made, be submitted to such barrister or lord advocate and such barrister or lord advocate shall certify as aforesaid and such rules, when so certified shall be filed with the clerk of the peace as aforesaid, and in the meantime such society shall be entitled to the benefit of this Act, as if no such alterations had been made provided always that if the said barrister or lord advocate

In case of refusal to certify society to cease to be entitled to exemption

shall refuse to certify, that then, subject to such appeal as is hereinafter provided the said society shall cease to be entitled to the benefit of this Act from the time when such alterations shall come into operation

Fee to barrister etc to be paid with expense of transmission of rules by society

4 Provided always, that the fee payable to such barrister or lord advocate for perusing the laws, rules, and regulations of each society or the alterations made therein and giving such certificate or statement as aforesaid, shall not at any one time exceed the sum of one guinea which, together with the expence of transmitting the rules to and from the said barrister or lord advocate, shall be defrayed by each society respectively.

Reference to quarter sessions where certificate is refused

5 Provided always, that in case any such barrister or lord advocate shall refuse to certify that any such society is entitled to the benefit of this Act, it shall then be lawful for any such society to submit the laws, rules, and regulations thereof to the court of quarter sessions for the borough or county where the land or buildings of the society shall be situated together with the reasons so assigned by the said barrister or lord advocate as aforesaid, and the recorder or justices at such quarter sessions shall and may, if he or they think fit, order the same rules to be filed, notwithstanding such refusal as aforesaid, and such filing shall have the same effect as if the said barrister or lord advocate had certified as aforesaid

Appeal to quarter sessions by any person assessed to any rate from which any society is exempted against decision of barrister etc granting certificate

6 Provided also that any person or persons assessed to any rate from which any society shall be exempted by this Act may appeal from the decision of the said barrister or lord advocate in granting such certificate as aforesaid to the said court of quarter sessions within four calendar months next after the first assessment of such rate made after such certificate shall have been filed as aforesaid, or within four calendar months next after the first assessment of such rate made after such exemption shall have been claimed by such society, such appellant first giving to the clerk or secretary of the society in question, twenty-one days previously to the sitting of the

said court, notice in writing of his intention to bring such appeal, together with a statement in writing of the grounds thereof, and within four days after such notice entering into a recognizance before some justice, with two sufficient sureties, to try such appeal at and abide the order of and pay such costs as shall be awarded by the recorder or justices at such quarter sessions, and at such quarter sessions such recorder or justices shall on its being proved that such notice and statement have been given as aforesaid, proceed to hear such appeal according to the grounds set forth in such statement and not otherwise, and if the certificate of the said barrister or lord advocate shall appear to him or them to have been granted contrary to the provisions of this Act, shall and may annul the same, and shall and may according to their discretion award such costs to the party appealing or appealed against as he or they shall think proper, and his or their determination concerning the premises shall be conclusive and binding on all parties to all intents and purposes whatsoever

THE LANDS CLAUSES CONSOLIDATION ACT, 1845.

(8 & 9 Vict., cap 18)

AN ACT FOR CONSOLIDATING IN ONE ACT CERTAIN PROVISIONS USUALLY INSERTED IN ACTS AUTHORISING THE TAKING OF LANDS FOR UNDERTAKINGS OF A PUBLIC NATURE

[8th May, 1845]

133. And be it enacted, that if the promoters of the undertaking become possessed by virtue of this or the Special Act or any Act incorporated therewith of any lands charged with the land tax, or liable to be assessed to the poor's rate, they shall from time to time, until the works shall be completed and assessed to such land tax or poor's rate, be liable to make good the deficiency in the several assessments for land tax and poor's rate by reason of such lands having been taken or used for the purposes of the works, and such deficiency shall be computed according to the rental at which such lands, with any building thereon, were valued or rated at the time of the passing of the Special Act, and on demand of such deficiency the promoters of the undertaking or their treasurer shall pay all such deficiences to the collector of the said assessments respectively, nevertheless, if at any time the promoters of the undertaking think fit to redeem such land tax they may do so in accordance with the powers in that behalf given by the Acts for the redemption of the land tax

Until completion of works promoters shall make good any deficiency of land tax and poor's rate caused by lands being taken

Land tax may be redeemed

1 See the Housing, Town Planning, &c., Act, 1909 (9 Edw VII, c 44), s 34 of which provides that the above section shall not apply in the case of any lands of which a local authority becomes possessed by virtue of the Housing Acts

THE DISTRESS FOR RATES ACT, 1849
(12 & 13 Vict., cap. 14)

AN ACT TO ENABLE OVERSEERS OF THE POOR AND SURVEYORS OF THE HIGHWAYS TO RECOVER THE COSTS OF DISTRAINING FOR RATES

[*11th May, 1849*]

[PREAMBLE]

Costs of obtaining Warrant of Distress for Poor Rate

[1] It shall be lawful hereafter for all Justices of the Peace, if in their Discretion they shall so think fit, in any Warrant of Distress they shall make and issue for the levying of any Sum or Sums to which any Person or Persons is or are now or may hereafter be rated or assessed in or by any Rate or Assessment for the Relief of the Poor or for the Highways in *England* or *Wales*, or in or by any other Rate or Assessment which by Law now or hereafter is or shall be directed to be enforced or recovered in the same Manner as a Poor Rate, or in any Warrant for the levying of any Arrears of the same, to order that a Sum, such as they may deem reasonable, for the Costs and Expenses which such Overseers or Surveyors, or the Persons applying for such Warrant, shall have incurred in obtaining the same, shall also be levied of the Goods and Chattels of the Person or Persons against whom such Warrant shall be granted, together with the reasonable Charges of the taking, keeping, and selling of the said Distress.

In default of distress for non-payment of rates justices may issue warrant of commitment

2 [*Recital of 13 Eliz., c. 2, s. 2*]   When to any Warrant of Distress for the levying of any Sum or Sums to which any Person or Persons may hereafter be rated or assessed in or by any Rate or Assessment hereinbefore mentioned it shall be returned by the Constable or Person having the Execution of such Warrant that he could find no Goods or Chattels, or no sufficient Goods or Chattels, whereon to levy such Sum or Sums, together with the Costs of or occasioned by the levying of the same, it shall be lawful for any Two or more Justices of the Peace before whom the same shall be returned, or for any Two or more Justices of the Peace for the same County, Riding, Division, Liberty, City, Borough or Place, if in their Discretion they shall so think fit, to issue their Warrant of Commitment against the Person with relation to whom such Return shall be so made as aforesaid in the Form (D) in the Schedule to this Act annexed or in any form to the like Effect and thereby order such Person to be imprisoned in the Common Gaol or House of Correction for any time not exceeding Three Calendar Months, unless the Sum or Sums therein mentioned shall be sooner paid; and every such Warrant of Commitment made or issued in Default of Distress as aforesaid shall be made as well for the Nonpayment of the Costs and Expenses so as aforesaid incurred in obtaining such Warrant of Distress, if the same shall be so

ordered as aforesaid, and the Costs attending the said Distress and also the Costs and Charges of taking and conveying the Party to Prison (the Amount of such several Costs, Expenses, and Charges being stated in such Warrant of Commitment), as for the Nonpayment of the Sum or Sums alleged to be due for the said Rates respectively

3   For the saving of Expense in the levying of any Sum or Sums for Rate and Costs as aforesaid it shall be lawful to make and issue One Warrant of Distress against any Number of Persons neglecting or refusing to pay the same, in the Form in the Schedule to this Act annexed; but nothing herein shall be deemed or construed to authorise Justices in like manner to grant or issue One Warrant of Commitment against several Persons in default of Distress as aforesaid

One Warrant may be issued against any number of persons

4   The Warrant aforesaid may be directed to the Churchwardens and Overseers of the Poor, or the Overseers of the Poor, or the Surveyors of the Highways, respectively, and to the Constable of the Parish or Township, and to any other Person or Persons, or to any One or more of them, as by the Justices granting the same shall be deemed fit

To whom Warrants shall be directed

5   Every Summons to be issued against any Person for Non-payment of any Sum for which he or she is or shall be so rated or assessed as aforesaid shall be directed to such Person and may be in the Form (B) in the Schedule to this Act annexed or in any Form to the like Effect, and the same may be served by any Churchwarden or Overseer of the Poor, or Surveyor of the Highways, respectively, or Constable or other Person, to whom it shall be delivered for that Purpose, upon the Person to whom it is so directed, by delivering the same to the Party personally or by leaving the same with some Person for him or her at his or her last Place of Abode; and the Person who shall serve the same in manner aforesaid shall attend at the time and Place and before the Justices in the said Summons mentioned, to depose if necessary to the service of the said Summons; and if, upon the Day and at the Place appointed in and by the said Summons for the appearance of the Party so summoned, such Party shall fail to appear accordingly in obedience to such Summons, then and in every such Case, if it be proved upon Oath or Affirmation to the Justices then present that such Summons was duly served as aforesaid a reasonable time before the time so appointed for his or her Appearance as aforesaid, it shall be lawful for such Justices of the Peace in their Discretion, if they shall so think fit, to proceed *ex parte*, in the same Manner to all Intents and Purposes as if such Party had personally appeared before them in obedience to the said Summons

Summons for non-payment of rate

6   In all Cases where any Proceedings shall be taken to compel Payment of any Sum for which any such

On payment of Rate and Costs Proceedings to cease

Person shall be so rated or assessed as aforesaid, if at any Time before such Person shall be committed to and lodged in Prison for Nonpayment thereof, or for or by reason of its being returned to such Warrant of Distress as aforesaid that there are no Goods or Chattels or no sufficient Goods or Chattels of such Person whereon the same may be levied as aforesaid, such Person shall pay or tender to the Churchwardens or Overseers of the Poor, or any of them, or to the Surveyor of Highways respectively, or other Person authorised to collect or receive such Rate, the Sum so sought to be recovered, together with the Amount of all Costs and Expenses up to that Time incurred in the Proceedings so taken to compel Payment thereof as aforesaid, then and in every such Case the Person to whom such Sum and Costs shall be so paid or tendered shall receive the same, and thereupon no further Proceedings for the Recovery of the same shall be had or taken

Form in
Schedule valid

8   The Forms in the Schedule to this Act contained, or Forms to the same or the like Effect, shall be deemed good, valid, and sufficient in Law

SCHEDULE

(A. 1)

Complaint of the Overseers or Surveyors against One Rate payer

to wit } Be it remembered, That on the   Day of   in the Year of our Lord   the [Churchwardens and Overseers of the Poor, or the Surveyors of the Highways] of the Parish of   in the County of   aforesaid, by C.D. One of the said [Overseers or Surveyors], complain to the undersigned, [One] of Her Majesty's Justices of the Peace in and for the said [County], that A B of the said [Parish], being a Person duly rated and assessed to [the Relief of the Poor, or the Maintenance of the Highways] of the said Parish, in and by a Rate* made on the   Day of   in the Year   in the Sum of   hath not paid the same or any Part thereof, but hath refused so to do Wherefore the said [Churchwardens and Overseers or Surveyors], by C D. aforesaid, pray that the said A B may be summoned to appear before Two of Her Majesty's Justices of the Peace, to show Cause why he hath not paid and refuses to pay the said Sum.

C D

Made and exhibited before me
    at   in the County of
    on this   Day of   1849
                                L F

*Or, in and by several Rates made on   and
on   in the several Sums of   and of

(A 2)

Complaint against Several Rate-payers.

            } BE it remembered, That on the   Day of
to wit. }   in the Year of our Lord   the
[Churchwardens and Overseers of the Poor, *or* the Surveyors of the
Highways] of the Parish of   in the [*County*] of
      aforesaid, by *C D*, One of the said [Overseers *or*
Surveyors], complain to the undersigned [*One*] of Her Majesty's
Justices of the Peace in and for the said [*County*], that the several
Persons whose Names are mentioned and set out in the Schedule
hereunder written, being Persons duly rated and assessed to [the
Relief of the Poor, *or* the Maintenance of the Highways] of the said
Parish, in and by the Rates in the said Schedule mentioned, in certain
Sums set down opposite to their respective Names in the said
Schedule, have not respectively paid the said sums or any part
thereof, but have respectively refused so to do. Wherefore the said
[Churchwardens and Overseers, *or* Surveyors], by *C D* aforesaid, pray
that said several Persons may respectively be summoned to appear
before Two of her Majesty's Justices of the Peace, to show Cause
respectively why they have not paid and refuse to pay the said Sums
respectively.

SCHEDULE

Names of the Ratepayers	Residence	Under Rate dated the 1849			Arrears due under Rate dated the 1848			Total Sum due		
		£	s	d	£	s	d	£	s	d
A B	(here state it)	1	7	0	1	7	0	2	14	0
I K		0	13	0				0	13	0
L M					0	18	0	0	18	0
N P		0	14	4	0	14	4	1	8	0

C D

Made and exhibited before me
   at   in the County of   }
   on this   Day of   1849. }
                   E F }

(B)

Summons upon the Complaint.

To A B of

WHEREAS Complaint hath this Day been made before the undersigned, [*One*] of Her Majesty's Justices of the Peace in and for the
[*County*] of   by the [Churchwardens and Overseers of
the Poor, *or* Surveyors of the Highways] of the Parish of

in the said [*County*], that you, being a Person duly rated and assessed to [the Relief of the Poor, *or* the Maintenance of the Highways] of the said Parish, in and by a Rate made on the   Day of   1849, in the Sum of   , hath not paid the same or any Part thereof, but have refused so to do These are therefore to command you, in Her Majesty's Name, to be and appear on   at   o'clock in the Forenoon, at before such Two or more Justices of the Peace for the said [*County*] as may then be there, to Show Cause why you have not paid and refuse to pay the same, otherwise you shall be proceeded against by Default as if you had appeared, and be dealt with according to Law

Given under my Hand and Seal, this   Day of in the Year of our Lord   at   in the [*County*] aforesaid

E F

Take notice, that you have already incurred the under-mentioned Costs, viz

	s	d
Clerk to the Justices - - - - -		
Overseer [*or* Surveyor], for obtaining the Summons -		
Constable, for serving ditto - - - -	1	0
Ditto Travelling Expenses at Threepence per Mile,		
Total -		

If the Amount of these Charges, together with the rate claimed, be paid to the Overseer [*or* Surveyor] before the Day on which the Summons is returnable all further Proceedings will be stopped

(C 1.)

Warrant of Distress against One Rate-payer.

To the Overseers of the Poor [or to the Surveyors of the High ways] of the Parish of   in the [*County*] of and to the Constable of   and to all other Peace Officers in the said [*County*]

WHEREAS on   last past a Complaint was made before E F One of Her Majesty's Justices of the Peace in and for the [*County*] of   by the [Churchwardens and Overseers of the Poor, *or* Surveyors of the Highways] of the Parish of in the said [*County*], that A B, being a Person duly rated and assessed to the Relief of the Poor [*or* to the Maintenance of the Highways] of the said Parish in and by a Rate made on

in the Sum of   had not paid the same or any
Part thereof, but had refused so to do, and now at this Day, to wit,
on   at   the Parties aforesaid appear before us,
the undersigned **Two of Her Majesty's Justices of the Peace** in and
for the said County [*or* the said Churchwardens and Overseers, *or*
Surveyors, by *C D*, One of the said Overseers, *or* Surveyors, appear
before us, the undersigned, **Two of Her Majesty's Justices of the
Peace** in and for the said County, but the said *A B* although duly
called, doth not appear by himself, his Counsel or Attorney and it is
now satisfactorily proved to us on Oath that the said *A B* has been
duly served with the Summons in this Behalf, which required him to
be and appear here at this Day before such Two or more Justices of
the Peace as should now be here, to answer the said Complaint, and
to be further dealt with according to Law], and now having heard
the Matter of the said Complaint, and it being now duly proved to us
upon Oath [in the Presence and Hearing of the said *A B*], that an
Assessment for the [Relief of the Poor *or* the Maintenance of the
Highways] of the said Parish of   and for other Purposes
chargeable thereon according to Law, dated the   was
duly made, allowed, and published, and that the said *A B* is therein
and thereby assessed at the Sum of   aforesaid,° and that
the said sum hath been duly demanded of the said *A B*, but that he
hath not paid, and hath refused and still refuses to pay the same, and
the said *A B* now not showing to us any sufficient Cause for not
paying the same, These are therefore to command you, in Her
Majesty's Name forthwith to make Distress of the Goods and Chattels
of the said *A B* and if within the Space of [*Five*] Days after the
making of such Distress the said Sum, and the sum of
for the Costs incurred by the said [Churchwardens and Overseers *or*
Surveyors] in obtaining this Warrant, together with the reasonable
Charges of taking and keeping the said Distress, shall not be paid,
that then you do sell the said Goods and Chattels so by you distrained
and out of the Money arising by such Sales you retain the said Sums
of   and   rendering the Overplus on Demand,
to the said *A B*, the reasonable Charges of taking keeping, and selling
the said Distress being first deducted, and if no such Distress can be
found that then you certify the same unto us, to the end that such
further Proceedings may be had herein as to the Law doth appertain

  Given under our Hands and Seals, this   Day of
in the Year of our Lord   at   in the [*County*]
aforesaid

                                                        E F
                                                        G H

  ° And that a certain other Assessment for the Relief, *&c to the
Asterisk if there be Arrears*

(C 2)

Warrant of Distress against several Rate-payers

To the Overseers of the Poor [or the Surveyors of the Highways]
of the Parish of   in the [*County*] of   and
to the Constables of   and to all other Peace Officers
in the said [*County*]

WHEREAS on   last past a Complaint was made before
E F, One of Her Majesty's Justices of the Peace in and for the
[*County*] of   by the [Churchwardens and Overseers of the
Poor, or the Surveyors of the Highways] of the Parish of
in the said [*County*], that the several Persons whose Names are
mentioned and set forth in the Schedule hereunder written, being
Persons duly rated and assessed to [the Relief of the Poor, or Maintenance of the Highways] of the said Parish in and by the Rates in
the Schedule in that Complaint and in this Warrant underwritten, in
certain Sums set down opposite to their respective Names in the said
Schedule, had not respectively paid the said Sums or any part thereof
but had respectively refused so to do; and now at this Day, to wit,
on   at   the said [Churchwardens and Overseers,
or Surveyors] by *C D*, One of the said Overseers, or Surveyors, and
I B, *I K*, and *L M*, some of the said Parties in the said Schedule
mentioned, appear before us, the undersigned, Two of Her Majesty's
Justices of the Peace in and for the said [*County*], but the said *N P*,
although duly called, doth not appear by himself, his Counsel or
Attorney; and it is now satisfactorily proved to us on Oath that the
said *N P* has been duly served with the Summons in this Behalf,
which required him to be and appear here at this Day before such
Two or more Justices of the Peace as should now be here to answer
the said Complaint, and to be further dealt with according to Law;
and now having heard the Matter of the said Complaint against the
said several Parties and it being now duly proved to us upon Oath, in
the Presence of the Parties so appearing as aforesaid, that an Assessment for [the Relief of the Poor] of the said Parish of
and for other Purposes chargeable therein according to Law, dated
the   was duly made, allowed, and published, and that the
said several Persons whose Names are mentioned and set out in the
Schedule hereunder written are therein and thereby assessed at the
Sums set down opposite to their respective Names in the said Schedule, and that the said several Sums have been duly demanded of
them respectively, but they have not nor hath any of them paid the
said Sums or any of them, or any Part thereof respectively, but they
have refused and still do refuse to pay the same respectively, and
have not, nor hath any of them, showed to us sufficient Cause for
not paying the same: These are therefore to command you, in Her
Majesty's Name, forthwith to make Distress of the Goods and

Chattels of the several Persons whose Names are mentioned and set out in the Schedule hereunder written, and if within the Space of Five Days after the making of such Distresses respectively the said several Sums set opposite to their respective Names at which they were so rated and assessed as aforesaid, and the said several Sums for Costs incurred by the said [Churchwardens and Overseers, or Surveyors] also set opposite to their respective Names, together with the reasonable Charges of taking and keeping the said Distress in each Case, shall not be paid, that then you do sell the Goods and Chattels of the Party so making default so by you distrained, and out of the Money arising by such Sales respectively you retain the Sums so set opposite to the Name of each Party whose Goods you shall have so sold rendering to him the Overplus, the reasonable Charges of taking keeping and selling the said Distress being first deducted and if in any of the Cases mentioned in the Schedule hereunder written no such Distress can be found, that then you certify the same unto us, to the end that such further Proceedings may be had herein as to the Law doth appertain

SCHEDULE

Names of Ratepayers	Residence	Under Rate dated 1849			Arrears due under Rate dated 1848			Costs			Total		
		£	s	d	£	s	d	£	s	d	£	s	d
A B	(here state it)	1	7	0	1	7	0	0	6	0	4	0	0
I K		0	13	0				0	2	0	0	15	0
L M					0	18	0	0	3	0	1	1	0
N P		0	11	4	0	14	4	0	5	0	1	13	0

Given under our Hands and Seals, this   day of
in the Year of our Lord   at   in the [County]
aforesaid

E F
G H

(D)

Warrant of Commitment in Default of Distress

To the Overseers of the Poor [or the Surveyors of the Highways] of the Parish of   in the [County] of
and to the Constable of   and to all other Peace Officers in the said [County], and to the Keeper of the [House of Correction] at   in the said [County]

WHEREAS on   last past a Complaint was made before
E F. Esquire, One of Her Majesty's Justices of the Peace in and for

the said [*County*] of   by the [Churchwardens and Overseers of the Poor, *or* Surveyors of the Highways] of the Parish
of   in the said [*County*], that *A B*, being a Person duly
rated to the [Relief of the Poor, *or* Maintenance of the Highways] of
the said Parish, in and by a Rate made on   in the Sum
of   had not paid the same or any Part thereof, but had
refused so to do, and afterwards on   it   the
Parties aforesaid appeared before *E F* and *G H*, Esquires, Two of
Her Majesty's Justices of the Peace in and for the said County
[*or* the said Churchwardens and Overseers, *or* Surveyors by *C D*,
One of the said Overseers, *or* Surveyors appeared before *E F* and
G H, Esquires, Two of Her Majesty's Justices of the Peace in and
for the said County, but the said *A B*, although duly called, did not
appear by himself, his Counsel or Attorney, and it was then satisfactorily proved to the said Justices that the said *A B* had been duly
served with the Summons in that Behalf, which required him to be
and appear there at that Day before such Two or more Justices of the
Peace as should then be there, to answer the said Complaint, and to
be further dealt with according to Law], and then having heard the
Matter of the said Complaint, and it being then duly proved to the
said Justices upon Oath [in the Presence and Hearing of the said
A B] that an Assessment for the [Relief of the Poor, *or* the Maintenance of the Highways] of the said Parish of   dated
the   was duly made, allowed, and published, and that the
said *A B* was therein and thereby assessed at the Sum of
aforesaid and that the said Sum had been duly demanded of the said
A B, but that he had not paid, and had refused and still refused
to pay the same, and the said *A B* then not showing to the said
E F and *G H* any sufficient Cause for not paying the same, the said
Justices thereupon then issued a Warrant to   commanding
them to levy the said Sum of   and the Sum of
for the Costs incurred in obtaining that Warrant, by Distress and Sale
of the Goods and Chattels of the said *A B* And whereas it now
appears to me, the undersigned, One of Her Majesty's Justices of the
Peace in and for the said [*County*], as well by the Return of the
said   to the said Warrant of Distress as otherwise, that
the said   hath made diligent Search for the Goods and
Chattels of the said *A B*, but that no sufficient Distress whereon to
levy the said Sums above mentioned could be found These are therefore to command you the said [Churchwardens and Overseers, *or*
Surveyors] and Constable and Peace Officers, *or* some or one of you,
to take the said *A B*, and him safely to convey to the [*House of
Correction*] at   aforesaid, and there deliver him to the said
Keeper, together with this Precept And I do hereby command you
the said Keeper of the said [*House of Correction*], to receive the said
A B into your Custody in the said [*House of Correction*], there to

imprison him for the Space of   unless the said Sums of   and   together with the Sum of   for the Costs attending the said Distress, and the further Sum of   being the Costs and Charges of this Commitment, and of taking and conveying the said *A B.* to Prison, making in the whole the Sum of   shall be sooner paid unto you the said Keeper, and for your so doing this shall be your sufficient Warrant

Given under my Hand and Seal this   Day of   in the Year of Our Lord   at   in the [*County*] aforesaid

L S (L S)

THE QUARTER SESSIONS ACT 1849.

(12 & 13 Vict, cap 45)

AN ACT TO AMEND THE PROCEDURE IN COURTS OF QUARTER SESSIONS IN ENGLAND AND WALES, AND FOR THE BETTER ADVANCEMENT OF JUSTICE IN CASES WITHIN THE JURIS-DICTION OF THOSE COURTS   [*28th July, 1849*]

[PREAMBLE]

[1][1] In every case of appeal (except as hereinafter mentioned) to any Court of Quarter Sessions fourteen clear days notice of appeal at least shall be given, and such shall be sufficient notice, any Act or Acts, or any rule or practice of any Court or Courts, to the contrary notwithstanding, and such notice of appeal shall be in writing, signed by the person or persons giving the same, or by his, her, or their attorney on his, her, or their behalf, and the grounds of appeal shall be specified in every such notice 'Provided always, that it shall not be lawful for the appellant or appellants, on the trial of any such appeal, to go into or give evidence of any other ground of appeal besides those set forth in such notice

Notice of Appeal to Quarter Sessions

2 None of the provisions hereinbefore contained relating to notices of appeal shall be construed to affect or alter the law as to notice of appeal against a summary conviction, or against an order of removal, or against an order under any statute relating to pauper lunatics, or against an order in bastardy, or against any proceeding under or by virtue of any of the statutes relating to Her Majesty's revenue of excise or customs, stamps, taxes, or post-office, but the law with regard to notices of all such appeals shall be deemed and taken to be the same as if the provisions hereinbefore contained had not been enacted

This Act not to affect appeal in certain matters

3 [*Recital*] Upon the hearing of any appeal to any Court of Quarter Sessions no objection on account of any defect in the form of setting forth any ground of appeal shall be allowed, and

Certain objections not to prevail

---

[1] Section 1 is repealed so far as relates to appeal against order of Court of summary jurisdiction, 47 & 48 Vict, c 43 s 4.

no objection to the reception of legal evidence offered in support of any ground of appeal shall prevail, unless the Court shall be of opinion that such ground of appeal is so imperfectly or incorrectly set forth as to be insufficient to enable the party receiving the same to enquire into the subject of such statement and to prepare for trial;

Amendment

Provided always, that in all cases where the Court, shall be of opinion that any objection to any ground of appeal, or to the reception of evidence in support thereof, ought to prevail, it shall be lawful for such Court, if it shall so think fit, to cause any such ground of appeal to be forthwith amended by some officer of the Court, or otherwise, on such terms as to payment of costs to the other party or postponing the trial to another day in the same Session or to the next subsequent Sessions, or both payment of costs and postponement as to such Court shall appear just and reasonable

Costs in frivolous or vexatious appeals

4 If in any notice of appeal the appellant or appellants shall have included any ground or grounds of appeal which shall in the opinion of the Court determining the appeal be frivolous or vexatious, such appellant or appellants shall be liable, if the Court shall so think fit, to pay the whole or any part of the costs incurred by the respondent or respondents in disputing any such ground or grounds of appeal, such costs to be recoverable in the manner hereinafter directed as to the other costs incurred by reason of such appeal

General powers as to costs of appeals

5 Upon any appeal to any Court of Quarter Sessions, the Court before whom the same shall be brought may, if it think fit, order and direct the party or parties against whom the same shall be decided to pay to the other party or parties such costs and charges as may to such Court appear just and reasonable, such costs to be recoverable in the manner provided for the recovery of costs upon an appeal against an order or conviction by the Summary Jurisdiction Act, 1848

11 & 12 Vict., c 43

Costs where appeal is not prosecuted

6 And for the more effectual prevention of frivolous appeals, any Court of Quarter Sessions upon proof of notice of any appeal to the same Court having been given to the party or parties entitled to receive the same, though such appeal was not afterwards prosecuted or entered, may, if it so think fit, at the same Sessions for which such notice was given, order to the party or parties receiving the same such costs and charges as by the said Court shall be thought reasonable and just to be paid by the party or parties giving such notice, such costs to be recoverable in the manner last aforesaid

Powers of amendment on appeal or certiorari

7. [*Recital*] If upon the trial of any appeal to any Court of Quarter Sessions against any order or judgment made or given by any Justice or Justices of the Peace, or if upon the return to any writ of certiorari any objection shall be made on account of any omission or mistake in the drawing up of such order or judgment and it shall be shown to the satisfaction of the Court that sufficient grounds

were in proof before the Justice or Justices making such order or giving such judgment to have authorised the drawing up thereof free from the said omission or mistake, it shall be lawful for the Court, upon such terms as to payment of costs as it shall think fit, to amend such order or judgment, and to adjudicate thereupon as if no such omission or mistake has existed Provided always, that no objection on account of any omission or mistake in any such order or judgment brought up upon a return to a writ of certiorari shall be allowed unless such omission or mistake shall have been specified in the rule for issuing such certiorari

8 [*Recital*] Where any recognizance or recognizances which shall have been entered into within the time by law required before any Justice or Justices for the purpose of complying with any such condition of appeal shall appear to the Court before which such appeal is brought to have been insufficiently entered into, or to be otherwise defective or invalid, it shall be lawful for such Court, if it shall so think fit, to permit the substitution of a new and sufficient recognizance or new and sufficient recognizances to be entered into before such Court in the place of such insufficient, defective, or invalid recognizance or recognizances, and for that purpose to allow such time, and make such examinations, and impose such terms as to payment of costs to the respondent or respondents, as to such Court shall appear just and reasonable, and such substituted recognizance or recognizances shall be as valid and effectual to all intents and purposes as if the same had been duly entered into at any earlier time or times as required by any statute or statutes for that purpose.

Defective recognizances

9 The decisions of the Court of Quarter Sessions upon the hearing of any appeal, as to the sufficiency of the statement of any ground or grounds of appeal, and as to the amending or refusing to amend any order or judgment of a Justice or Justices appealed against, or the statement of any ground or grounds of appeal, and as to the substitution of any new recognizance or recognizances as aforesaid, shall be final, and shall not be liable to be reviewed in any Court, by means of a writ of certiorari or mandamus, or otherwise

Decisions of Sessions as to statement of grounds amendment or recognizances to be final

10 Every Court of Quarter Sessions on the trial of any offence within its jurisdiction, whenever any variance or variances shall appear between any matter in writing or in print produced in evidence, and the recital or setting forth thereof in the indictment shall have the same power in all respects to cause the indictment to be amended, which is given to courts of oyer and terminer and general gaol delivery with regard to offences tried before such last-mentioned courts by virtue of an Act of the twelfth year of Her Majesty's reign, intituled "An Act for the removal of defects in the administration of criminal justice", and after such amendment the trial shall proceed in the same manner in all respects, both with regard to the liability of witnesses to be indicted for perjury and otherwise, as if no such variance or variances had appeared

Amendment of indictments by Quarter Sessions

11 & 12 Vict, c 46

Special case, after notice given of appeal to Quarter Sessions

11 At any time after notice given of appeal to any Court of Quarter Sessions against any judgment, order, rate, or other matter (except an order in bastardy, or a proceeding under or by virtue of any of the statutes relating to Her Majesty's revenue of excise or customs, stamps, taxes, or post office), for which the remedy is by such appeal, it shall be lawful for the parties, by consent, and by order of any Judge of one of the Superior Courts of Common Law at Westminster, to state the facts of the case in the form of a special case for the opinion of such Superior Court, and to agree that a judgment in conformity with the decision of such Court and for such costs as such Court shall adjudge, may be entered on motion by either party at the Sessions next or next but one after such decision shall have been given, and such judgment shall and may be entered accordingly, and shall be of the same effect in all respects as if the same had been given by the Court of Quarter Sessions upon an appeal duly entered and continued

Arbitration after notice given of appeal to Quarter Sessions

12 [*Recital of 9 William III, c 15, as to arbitrations*] At any time after notice given of appeal to any Court of Quarter Sessions against any order, rate, or other matter (except a summary conviction, or an order in bastardy, or any proceeding under or by virtue of any of the statutes relating to Her Majesty's revenue of excise or customs, stamps, taxes, or post office), for which the remedy is by such appeal, it shall be lawful for the parties, by themselves or their attorneys, and by order of a Judge of Her Majesty's Court of Queen's Bench to submit the matter or matters of such appeal to the award or umpirage of any person or persons, . and every award or umpirage duly made under this Act shall be as binding and effectual to all intents as if the same had been a regular judgment of the said Court of Quarter Sessions, and shall and may, on the application of either party, be enrolled among the records of the said Court of Sessions.

Arbitration by order of Court of Quarter Sessions

13 It shall be lawful for any Court of Quarter Sessions before which any appeal (except against a summary conviction, or an order in bastardy, or any proceeding under or by virtue of any of the statutes relating to Her Majesty's revenue of excise or customs stamps, taxes, or post office), shall be brought, to order with consent of the parties or their attornies, that the matter or matters of such appeal be referred to arbitration to such person or persons and in such manner and on such terms as the said Court shall think reasonable and proper . . and the award of the arbitrator or arbitrators, or umpirage of the umpire, may, on motion by either party at the Sessions next or next but one after such award or umpirage shall have been finally made and published, or after the decision of the Court of Queen's Bench on any motion for setting aside the same, be entered as the judgment of the Court of Quarter Sessions in the appeal and shall be as binding and effectual to all intents as if given by the said Court

14. If upon any reference to arbitration under this Act it shall be made to appear to the Court of Queen's Bench that, either from the death of the arbitrator, or arbitrators, or umpire or from any other cause, it has become impossible that an award or umpirage can be made, it shall be lawful for the said Court to order the Court of Quarter Sessions to enter continuances and hear the appeal

Where reference becomes abortive, Court of Queen's Bench may order Sessions to hear the appeal

[S 15 *repealed 54 & 55 Vict. c 67 (S L R)*]

16 No recognizance entered into pursuant to any statute or statutes for the prosecution and trial of any appeal shall be deemed to be forfeited by such agreement as aforesaid for the statement of a special case without previously going to the Court of Quarter Sessions, or by any submission to arbitration under the provisions of this Act.

Recognizances not to be forfeited by statement of special case or submission to arbitration

17 And whereas by the Levy of Fines Act, 1822, provision is made for authorizing and levying and recovery of fines, issues, amerciaments, and forfeited recognizances set, imposed, lost, or forfeited by or before any Justice or Justices of the Peace in England, and whereas it is expedient that the subsequent proceedings in such cases should be uniform, be it enacted, that the proceedings subsequent to such authority given for so levying and recovering as aforesaid, shall and may be the same in all respects in the case of such fines, issues, and amerciaments as are by the said Act provided, permitted, and required in the case of such forfeited recognizances

3 Geo IV, c 46

Recovery of fines, etc., imposed by Justices

18 In all cases where any order shall be made by any Court of Quarter Sessions, it shall be lawful for the Court of Queen's Bench, or for any Judge of that Court at Chambers, upon the application of any person entitled to enforce such order, and upon the production of a copy of such order under the hand of the clerk of the peace or his deputy, and upon proof of refusal or neglect to obey such order, to order and direct such order of the Court of Quarter Sessions to be removed into the said Court of Queen's Bench, and thereupon such order shall be of the same force and effect, and may be enforced in the same manner as a rule made by the said Court of Queen's Bench, and all the reasonable costs and charges attendant upon such application and removal shall be recoverable in like manner, as if the same were part of such order

Enforcement of orders after removal by certiorari

19 Nothing in this Act contained shall extend to Scotland or Ireland

Extent of Act

[SS 20, 21 *repealed 38 & 39 Vict c 66 (S L R)*]

THE POOR RATES RECOVERY ACT 1862
(25 & 26 Vict, cap. 82)

AN ACT FOR THE MORE ECONOMICAL RECOVERY OF POOR RATES AND OTHER LOCAL RATES AND TAXES

[*7th August, 1862*]

[PREAMBLE]

1 Where any Number of Local Rates and Taxes, whether of the same or of different Kinds, are due from the same Person, the Rates

Consolidation of Proceedings for the Recovery of Rates

and Taxes so due may be included in the same Information, Complaint, Summons, Order, Warrant, or other Document required by Law to be laid before Justices or to be issued by Justices, and every such Document as aforesaid shall as respects each Rate or Tax comprised in it, be construed as a separate Document, and its Invalidity as respects any one Rate or Tax shall not affect its Validity as respects any other Rate or Tax comprised in it

No Costs shall be allowed in respect of several Informations, Complaints Summonses, Orders, Warrants, or other such Documents as aforesaid, in Cases where in the Opinion of the Justices or Court having Jurisdiction over the said Costs, One Information, Complaint, Summons, Order, Warrant, or other Document as aforesaid might have sufficed, regard being had to the Provisions of this Act

---

THE UNION ASSESSMENT COMMITTEE ACT, 1862

(25 & 26 Vict, cap 103)

AN ACT TO AMEND THE LAW RELATING TO PAROCHIAL ASSESSMENTS IN ENGLAND

[7th August, 1862]

WHEREAS it is expedient that more effectual Provision should be made for securing uniform and correct Valuations of Parishes in the Unions of *England*

Interpretation 4 & 5 Will IV, c 76 — 1 The words used in this Act shall be construed in like Manner as the words contained in the Poor Law Amendment Act, 1834, and the word "Committee" shall signify the Assessment Committee provided for by this Act, and this Act shall be termed "The Union Assessment Committee Act, 1862"

Short Title

Appointment of the Assessment Committee by Board of Guardians — 2 The Board of Guardians of every Union, formed under the Poor Law Amendment Act, 1834, shall in every year at their first meeting after the annual Election of Guardians, appoint from among themselves any Number not less than Six nor more than Twelve to be a Committee . . . . to be called the Assessment Committee of the Union, for the Investigation and Supervision of the Valuations to be made as herein-after mentioned within such Union, and for the Performance of such said Acts and Duties as herein-after mentioned

Repealed as far as regards Metropolis

Where Union has the same Bounds as a Borough Names of Assessment Committee to be transmitted to Town Council who — [3 Where any Union shall have the same Bounds as a Municipal Borough, the Clerk to the Guardians of such Union shall, upon the Appointment of the Assessment Committee, if directed by the said Guardians to do so, transmit in Writing the Names of the Persons so appointed to the Town Council of such Borough, and such Council may thereupon, if they think fit, appoint from themselves a certain Number, not exceeding the number appointed by the Board of Guardians, who shall, until they respectively cease to be Members of

the Town Council or decline to act, forthwith form Part of the *may appoint additional members*
Assessment Committee for such Union and the said Council may
from Time to Time supply any Vacancies in the Number of Persons
appointed by them]

4 If the Guardians shall neglect or be prevented from making such *Provision in case of neglect to appoint*
Appointment at the Meeting above specified, the Poor Law Board
shall by their Order appoint some other Day on which the Guardians
shall make such Appointment

5 If any   .   . Guardian being a Member of the *Supply of vacancies*
Committee cease to be Guardian, or resign his Seat at such Committee or die or become incapable of acting as such Member, the
Board of Guardians shall with all convenient Speed appoint an
[*ex-officio* or elected[1]] Guardian, to supply the Vacancy

6 During any Vacancy in any Assessment Committee the other or *Continuing members may act during vacancies*
continuing Members of such Committee may act, and shall have the
same Powers and Jurisdiction as if no such Vacancy had happened

7 The Authority of the Committee appointed for any Union under *Extent of committee's authority*
this Act shall extend over every Parish comprised in such Union

8 The Committee shall hold their First Meeting at the Board *Meetings when and where to be held etc*
Room of the Union on a Day to be fixed by the Board of Guardians
and the subsequent Meetings of the Committee shall be holden at
such Times and at such Place and upon such Notice and Requisition
as they shall from Time to Time appoint and any Guardian of the
Union may be present at any Meeting of the Committee, but shall not
be entitled to take part in the Proceedings thereof

9 All Acts, Orders, Matters, and things by this Act authorised or *Majority and quorum at meetings*
directed to be made or done by the Committee may be made or done
by the major Part of the Members of such Committee who shall be
present at a meeting, the whole Number present together at such
Meeting not being less than Three and not less in any Case than One
Third of the whole Number of which such Committee consists , and
when upon any Question there shall be an Equality of Votes the
presiding Chairman shall have a Second or Casting Vote

10 The Committee shall employ the Clerk or Assistant Clerk of *Committee may employ and pay clerk*
the Board of Guardians as their Clerk, with such Remuneration for
his services as the Poor Law Board shall sanction

11 The Committee shall cause a Minute of their Proceedings and *Proceedings to be entered in books and signed*
of the Names of the Members who attend each Meeting, to be duly
made from Time to Time in Books to be provided for that Purpose,
which shall be kept by their Clerk, under their Superintendence, and
every such Entry shall be signed by the presiding Chairman of the
Assessment Committee present at the Meeting at which the Proceed- *Such entries evidence*
ing took place , and such Entry, purporting to be so signed, shall be
received as Evidence in all Courts, and before all Judges, Justices,

---

[1] Words in brackets repealed 56 & 57 Vict, c 73, s 89.

and others, without Proof of such Meeting having been duly convened or held, or of the Persons attending such Meeting having been or being Members of the Committee, or of the Signatures of the Members, all of which Facts shall be presumed until the contrary be proved, and all such Books shall at all seasonable Times be open to the Inspection of every Person rated to the Relief of the Poor in any Parish or Place in the Union, without any Fee being demanded for such Inspection and all such Persons shall be entitled at all seasonable Times to take Copies or Extracts from the said Books, without paying any Fee for the same, and if, on Request made for that Purpose, the Clerk of the Committee refuse to permit any such Person to inspect any such Books, or to take Copies or Extracts therefrom, as aforesaid, such Clerk shall for every such Offence be liable to a Penalty not exceeding Five Pounds upon a summary Conviction for the same before Two Justices of the Peace

Books to be open to inspection

12 The Board of Guardians shall in the Month of April in every Year report the Proceedings of their Assessment Committee to the Poor Law Board

Proceedings of committees to be reported

13 The Committee by their Order may from Time to Time require the Overseers Assistant Overseers, Constables, Assessors Collectors and any other Persons having the Custody of any Books of Assessment of any Taxes or Rates, parliamentary or parochial or of the valuation of any parish or having the collection or management or any such taxes or rates to make Returns in Writing to the Committee, at such Times and Places as they may appoint, of all such Particulars as they may direct in relation to such Taxes, Rates or Valuations, or any Property included therein, so far as relates to the Union for which they act, and may require the Persons having the Custody of any such Books as aforesaid to make and transmit to the Committee Copies of or Extracts from such Books, or to permit such Copies or Extracts to be made by such Persons as the Committee may in that behalf direct, and may from Time to Time require any Persons having the Custody of any such Books or the Collection or Management of any such Taxes or Rates as aforesaid, to attend before them at a Time and Place to be mentioned in the Order in this Behalf, and to produce all Parochial and public Books of Assessment Rates, Rate Books, Valuations, Apportionments, Tithe and other Maps, Plans, Surveys, and other Public Documents in their Custody or Power, and may examine all Persons who shall attend before them Provided always that nothing herein contained shall authorise the Production of Valuations or Assessments which by any Provision of Law at present are not suffered to be made public.

Committee may require returns from Overseers, etc

and may require production of rates etc, and examine persons attending before them

[14 Subject to any Order as hereinafter referred to which may be made by the Committee, the Overseers of each Parish in the Union shall, within Three Calendar Months after the Appointment of such Committee, make a List of all the rateable Hereditaments in such

Repealed as regards Metropolis

Overseers to prepare valuation lists

Parish, with the annual Value thereof respectively in so much of the Form shown in the Schedule annexed to the Act Sixth and Seventh *William* the Fourth, Chapter Ninety-six, as is set out in the Schedule to this Act, and unless such Overseers think that the Valuation then last acted upon in assessing the Rate for the Relief of the Poor correctly shows the full annual rateable Value of all such Hereditaments, they shall revise such Valuation, and such Overseers shall sign every List so made by them as aforesaid, and such List shall be styled ' The Valuation List ")]

[15   The gross estimated Rental for the Purpose of the Schedule to this Act shall be the Rent at which the Hereditament might reasonably be expected to let from Year to Year, free of all usual Tenant's Rates and Taxes, and Tithe Commutation Rentcharge, if any   Provided that nothing herein contained shall repeal or interfere with the Provisions contained in the First Section of the said Act (Six and Seven *William* the Fourth, Chapter Ninety-six), defining the net annual Value of the Hereditaments to be rated.]

Repealed as regards Metropolis
Definition of gross estimated rental

16   The Committee by their Order may from Time to Time enlarge the Time within which the First Valuation Lists under this Act shall be made by the Overseers of all or any of the Parishes in the Union, and for ensuring a uniform and correct Valuation of every Parish in the Union may direct that any existing Valuation of the rateable Hereditaments in any Parish be revised, in whole or in part, or a new Valuation of such Hereditaments be made by the Overseers, or the Committee may, with the Consent of the Board of Guardians of the Union, after Notice shall have been sent to every Guardian thereof, in any Case appoint some Person for either of the Purposes aforesaid, and may direct such Person to make and sign the Valuation List instead of the Overseers, and every Valuation List so made and signed shall be delivered by such Person to the Overseers of the Parish to which the same relates.

Committee may enlarge the time for making first valuation lists, and may give directions concerning valuations and valuation lists and may appoint persons to make the same

17   The Valuation List for each Parish, made and signed by the Overseers, or delivered to them, as herein-before provided, shall be deposited by the Overseers in the Place in such Parish in which Rate Books are deposited or kept [and a copy of such Valuation List shall be forthwith delivered to the Board of Guardians], and the Overseers shall give public Notice of the Deposit of such List on the *Sunday* next following the Deposit of such List, and such Notice shall be given in the same Manner, and all Persons assessed or liable to be assessed to the Relief of the Poor of such Parish shall have the like Right of inspecting, and of demanding and taking Copies of and Extracts from such List as in the case of a Poor Rate allowed by the Justices and the Overseers shall, at the Expiration of Fourteen Days from the Time of the Notice given of the Deposit of such List, transmit the same to the Committee and any Overseer or other Ratepayer within the Union shall have the Right of inspecting and taking Copies of and Extracts from any of the Lists so transmitted

Valuation lists, to be deposited for inspection and afterwards transmitted to the committee
Part within brackets repealed as regards Metropolis

Objections to valuation list

18 Any Overseer or Overseers of any Parish in any Union who shall have Reason to think that such Parish is aggrieved by the Valuation List of any Parish within such Union, or any Person who may feel himself aggrieved by any Valuation List on the Ground of Unfairness or Incorrectness in the Valuation of any Hereditaments included therein, or on the Ground of the Omission of any rateable Hereditament from such List, may at any Time after the Deposit as aforesaid of such List, and before the Expiration of Twenty eight Days after the Notice of the Deposit as aforesaid, give to the Committee and to the Overseers a Notice in Writing of his Objection, specifying the Grounds thereof, and where the Ground of any Objection shall be Unfairness or Incorrectness in the Valuation of any Hereditament in respect of which any Person, other than the Person objecting, is liable to be rated, or the Omission of such Hereditament, also give Notice in Writing of such Objection and of the Ground thereof, to such other Person

Committee to hold meetings to hear objections

19 The Committee shall hold such Meetings as they may think necessary for hearing Objections to the Valuation Lists, and shall Twenty-eight Days at least before holding every Meeting for hearing Objections to Valuation Lists, other than Meetings by Adjournment, cause Notice of such Meeting to be given to the Overseers of the several Parishes to which such Lists relate, and such Overseers shall, on the *Sunday* next following the Receipt of such Notice, publish the same in the Manner in which Notice of a Rate allowed by Justices is by Law required to be given, and the Committee may at any such Meeting hear and determine such Objections, or may from Time to Time adjourn any such Meeting, and adjourn or postpone the Hearing or further hearing and Determination of any such Objections, and may, where they think fit, direct Notice of any such Objections to be given by the Overseers or by the Persons objecting to Third Parties before the further Hearing thereof but the Committee shall not be required to hold a Meeting for hearing Objections to the Valuation List of any Parish, unless such Notice in Writing as herein before mentioned of some Objection or Objections thereto have been given to the Committee and where a Meeting is holden for hearing Objections to the Valuation List of any Parish, the Committee shall not hear any Objection to such Valuation List unless such notice as aforesaid of such objection have been given to the Committee and to the Overseers , and where the Ground of such Objection is Unfairness or Incorrectness in the Valuation of any Hereditament of any other Person than the Person objecting, or the omission of such Hereditament, also to such other Person by the Person objecting, except where the Overseers, by themselves or any other Person on their Behalf, and in the Case aforesaid such other Person as aforesaid, by himself or any other Person on his Behalf, consent to the Hearing of such Objection, and in such Case the Committee may, if they see fit, hear the same ,

and where the Committee see fit to hear the same they shall act in relation thereto in like manner as if Notice of such Objection had been duly given

20 The Committee may whether any objection be or be not made to any such Valuation List, and either before or after any Meeting for hearing Objections, make such Alterations in the Valuation of any Hereditaments included in any Valuation List, and insert therein any rateable Hereditament omitted therefrom, and make such Corrections in Names, Descriptions, and Particulars in any Valuation List, and upon such Information, as to them may seem sufficient, and may, with the Consent of the Guardians as aforesaid, appoint or employ a Person to survey and value the rateable Hereditaments comprised in any such Valuation List or any of them, or omitted therefrom, or may take such other Means as they may think necessary for ascertaining the Correctness thereof, and when the Committee have heard and determined all such Objections as aforesaid, and have made such Alterations, Insertions, and Corrections in any Valuation List as to them may seem proper, they shall approve the same under the Hands of Three Members of the Committee present at the Meeting at which the same is approved, with the Date of such Approval.

Committee may correct valuation lists, and when corrected shall approve the same

21. Where the Committee make any alteration in the Valuation of any Hereditaments included in or insert therein any rateable Hereditament omitted from, any such Valuation List, they shall cause such Valuation List with such Alteration or Insertion, to be deposited for Inspection in manner herein-before provided concerning the Valuation List made by or delivered to the Overseers, and shall cause the like Notice to be given of such Deposit as is required in the Case of a Valuation List so made or delivered as aforesaid, and shall appoint a Day, not less than Seven Days nor more than Fourteen Days from the Re-deposit of such Valuation List, for the Hearing of any Objections to the Valuation List as so altered, and when the Committee have heard and determined any such Objections, or have made such further Alterations, Insertions and Corrections in such Valuation List, they shall approve the same in manner hereinbefore provided

Valuation list when altered to be deposited for inspection etc

[22 In case any Ratepayer shall under the existing Law appeal to the Special Sessions or Quarter Sessions against any Rate made for the Relief of the Poor in any Parish, and the Result of such Appeal shall be to amend the Rate appealed against, the Assessment Committee shall alter the Valuation List of the said Parish in conformity with the Decision so made]

Repealed as regards Metropolis

If on appeal a rate is amended the valuation list to be altered

[23 Every Valuation List, when approved by the Committee, shall be delivered to the Overseers of the Parish to which the same relates, and shall be preserved at the like Place and in the like Custody, and be subject to the like Resort thereto, and be delivered over from Time to Time in like Manner, as the Books are wherein Rates and Assessments for the Relief of the Poor for the same Parish are

Repealed as regards Metropolis

Custody, etc of valuation list after approval

entered, and shall be produced by the Overseers before the Justices, upon Application, for the Allowance of Rates, and at the Special or General or Quarter Sessions when any Appeal is to be heard, and also at such Times and Places as the Committee may from Time to Time direct]

Repealed as regards Metropolis
Lists to be deemed valuation lists in force

[24 Every Valuation List approved by the Committee, and delivered to the Overseers of the Parish to which the same relates shall with and subject to the Alterations and Additions for the Time being made therein or thereto by any supplemental Valuation Lists so approved and delivered, be the Valuation List in force in such Parish, except in the case of any Parish, as is herein-after referred to in which the Poor Rate, or Assessment for the Poor Rate, is made under the Authority of a Local Act until a new Valuation List in substitution for the same be approved and delivered in like Manner]

Repealed as regards Metropolis
Overseers to prepare supplemental valuation lists in case of additions to or alterations in the rateable property of the parish

[25 When and so often as any property not included in the Valuation List in force in any Parish becomes rateable, or where, by reason of any Alteration in the Occupation of any Property included in such List, such Property becomes liable to be rated in Parts not mentioned in such List as rateable Hereditaments and separately valued therein, and when and so often as it shall appear to the Overseers that any rateable Property included in such List has been increased or reduced in Value since the Valuation thereof, whether by Building, Destruction of Building, or other Alteration in the Condition thereof or otherwise, the Overseers of the Parish in each of the Cases aforesaid shall, as soon as conveniently may be, make a supplemental Valuation List showing the annual rateable Value according to the Judgment of the Overseers of the Property so become rateable, or of the Parts so become liable to be rated separately, or of the Property so increased or reduced in Value, as the Case may be]

Repealed as regards Metropolis
Committee may from time to time direct new valuation, and new or supplemental valuation lists

[26 The Committee by their Order may from Time to Time, where they see fit, upon the Application of any person aggrieved by the Valuation List in force in any Parish, or where they themselves think the same expedient, direct a new Valuation of all or any of the rateable Hereditaments in such Parish, and a new Valuation List in substitution for such Valuation List as aforesaid, or a Supplemental List in substitution for any Part thereof or in addition thereto, to be made by the Overseers or the Committee may, with such Consent as aforesaid, appoint a Person for such Purposes, and the Committee may, in directing such new Valuation and the making of such new or supplemental Valuation List, give and make all such or the like Directions and Provisions in relation thereto as they are authorised under this Act to give and make in relation to the Valuations and Valuation Lists first directed and authorised to be made under the Act]

Repealed as regards Metropolis

[27. All the Provisions of this Act in relation to signature, Deposit, Objections, Approval, and otherwise concerning the Valuation List first directed and authorised to be made under this Act of the rateable Hereditaments in any Parish shall be applicable to every new or supplemental Valuation List to be made under this Act]

28 [In every Parish where a Valuation List under this Act has been approved and delivered to the Overseers, no Rate for the Relief of the Poor, or other Rate which by Law is required to be based upon the Poor Rate, shall be of any Force, unless the Hereditaments, included in such Rate except as hereinafter provided, be rated according to the annual rateable Value thereof appearing in the Valuation List in force in such Parish , and instead of the declaration required by the Second Section of the said Statute of the Sixth and Seventh Years of *William* the Fourth, Chapter Ninety-six, the Overseers shall before the Rate shall be allowed by the Justices, sign a Declaration according to the Form set forth in the Schedule hereunto annexed] Provided always, that where by reason of any Alteration in the Occupation of any Property included in such List such Property has become liable to be rated in Parts not mentioned in such List as rateable Hereditaments, and separately rated therein, such Parts may, where a supplemental Valuation List showing the annual rateable Value of such Parts has not been approved and delivered as hereinbefore required and whether such List has or has not been made, be rated according to such Amounts as shall be fair apportioned Parts of the annual rateable Value appearing in such Valuation List in force as aforesaid of the Hereditaments out of which such Parts have been constituted

[29 The Provisions of Section Twenty-eight shall not apply to any Poor Rate made by any Vestry, Trustees. Guardians, Commissioners, Overseers, or other Persons authorised by any Local Act to make the Rate for the Relief of the Poor in any Parish, or the Assessment on which such Rate is made]

30 When the Assessment Committee for any Union shall have approved Valuation Lists for all the Parishes comprised within such Union, the Guardians of such Union, in computing the Amount of Contribution to the Common Fund for the several Parishes, shall thenceforward take the annual rateable Value of the Property in such Parishes respectively from the Valuation Lists for the Time being lastly approved of for such Parishes respectively, any Statute to the contrary notwithstanding Provided that in case any Parish comprised in any Union shall receive any Sum of Money as a Contribution in aid of the Poor Rate of such Parish, for or in respect of Government Property within such Parish and used for Public purposes, the annual value of such property according to the Estimate (if any) of such Value on which the Amount of the Sum of Money so received is computed, or if there be no such Estimate then the annual value of such property, estimated in the Mode provided by the Act Sixth and Seventh *William* the Fourth, Chapter

Provisions as to first valuation lists to apply to new and supplemental lists

Part within brackets repealed as regards Metropolis

After a valuation list is approved, no rate to be of force unless made according to such list

Repealed as regards Metropolis

Savings for places under Local Acts

In computing amount of contributions to common fund the annual new rateable value to be taken from approved valuation lists

Ninety-six, for making an Estimate of the annual rateable Value of Property liable to be rated to Rates for the Relief of the Poor, shall be included by the Overseer or Overseers in the Valuation List of such Parish, and shall be added to the annual rateable Value of the Property in such Parish in computing the Amount of Contribution to the Common Fund for the several Parishes in such Union

Repealed as regards Metropolis

Copy of valuation lists to be deposited in Board Room

[31 The Committee shall cause a Copy of the Valuation List for the Time in force for every Parish in the Union to be made and deposited at the Board Room or other convenient Place to be appointed by the Board of Guardians in the Custody of the Clerk, which Copy shall be open at seasonable Times to the Inspection of any of the Guardians of the Union, and of any Overseer of any Parish within the Union, without Charge, and of any Ratepayer within the Union on Payment of One Shilling, such Fee to be carried to the Account of the Common Fund]

Repealed as regards Metropolis

Appeal against valuation list

[32 If the Overseer or Overseers of any Parish in any Union shall have Reason to think that such Parish is aggrieved by the Valuation List of any Parish within such Union, whether it be on the Ground that the rateable Hereditaments comprised in the Valuation List of such Parish are valued at Sums beyond the annual rateable Value thereof, or on the Ground that the rateable Hereditaments comprised in the Valuation List of some other Parish in such Union are valued at Sums less than the annual rateable Value thereof, it shall be lawful for such Overseer or Overseers, with the Consent of a Vestry summoned for the Purpose of considering the Expediency of giving such consent, to appeal to the Quarter Sessions for the County or Borough in which the greatest Number of Parishes belonging to the Union is situate or, in case the Number of Parishes in any Two or more such Jurisdiction is equal to the Quarter Sessions for the County or Borough having Jurisdiction over the Parish in which the Workhouse of the Union is situate at the Sessions to be holden after the Expiration of a Month after the Allowance of and Deposit of such Valuation List as aforesaid against such Valuation List of the Parish which shall appear to be over-valued or under-valued, and if in any Case any such Overseer or Overseers appeal against the Valuation List of any other Parish on the Ground that the rateable Hereditaments in such List are valued at less than the annual rateable Value thereof, such Overseer or Overseers shall give Fourteen clear Days' Notice in writing previous to the First Day of the said Quarter Sessions at which the Appeal is to be made of the Intention to appeal, and the Grounds thereof, to the Overseers of the Poor of such Parish, and to the Guardians of the Union comprising such Parish, and if any Overseer or Overseers of any Parish appeal against the Valuation List of such Parish on the Ground that the rateable Hereditaments in such List are valued beyond the annual rateable Value thereof, such Overseer or

Overseers shall give Fourteen Days' Notice in Writing previous to the Quarter Sessions at which the Appeal is to be made of the Intention to Appeal, and the Grounds thereof, to the Guardians of the Union in which such Parish is situate, the said Court shall be empowered to hear and determine such Appeal, and either confirm such Valuation List, or correct such Irregularities or Inaccuracies as shall be proved to exist therein as to them may appear fair and just ; but no such Valuation List shall upon such Appeal be quashed or destroyed in regard to any other Parish unless the Court deem it necessary to proceed to the making of an entire new Valuation List as herein after provided]

[33 It shall be lawful for the Court of Quarter Sessions upon any such Appeal, instead of hearing the said Appeal, to adjourn the same, and to order upon the Application of the Appellant or Respondent in such Appeal, a Survey or Valuation of any of the Parishes in respect of which such Appeal shall be made, and to fix the next or some subsequent Sessions for receiving such Survey or Valuation, and for hearing and determining such Appeal ; and such Court shall also thereupon appoint a proper Person to make such Survey or Valuation, and the Person so appointed shall have Power, with or without assistants, to enter upon and survey measure and value all the Hereditaments liable to be assessed to the Rates for the Relief of the Poor within the Parish or Parishes mentioned in such Order, and such Survey and Valuation shall be reported to the Quarter Sessions on Adjournment fixed as aforesaid for receiving the same and the Court then and there assembled shall hear and determine the said Appeal in the Manner herein-before set forth]

[34 The Charges and Expenses of any such Survey and Valuation so ordered shall be deemed Costs in such Appeal and abide the Event thereof, and the Court before which any such Appeal is heard and determined may order the Costs in and about the Appeal to be paid by either the Appellant or Respondent Party, as they in their Discretion may think fit ; but where any Appeal is made on the Ground that the rateable Hereditaments of any Parish comprised in the Valuation List of such Parish are valued beyond the annual rateable Value thereof, if the Court on such Appeal determine in favour of the Appellants, such Court shall ascertain the Costs and charges incurred by such Appellants in and about such Appeal, and shall order the Board of Guardians of the Union in which such Parish is situate to pay the same to the Appellants out of the Money raised for the Common Fund for the several Parishes in such Union]

[35 Nothing herein contained shall be construed to prevent the Owners of Tenements from compounding for the Rates to be assessed on the same, in such Manner as they were by any Statute or Statutes enabled to do before the passing of this Act]

Repealed as regards Metropolis
Proceedings on appeal

Repealed as regards Metropolis
Costs of new valuation and appeal

Repealed as regards Metropolis
Act not to prevent composition for rates

Repealed as regards Metropolis

Saving of exemptions and special rules of rating

[36 Nothing herein contained shall extend or be taken to render liable to be rated any Property, or any Person in respect of any Occupation not now by Law rateable of any Property, or to deprive any Property, or the Occupier of any Property, of the Benefit of any Exemption, in whole or in part, to which such Property or Occupier is now by Law entitled, from any Poor Rate or other Rate which by Law is required to be based upon the Poor Rate, or to render liable to be rated, according to the annual rateable Value thereof, any Property which under any Local Act or otherwise is entitled to be rated upon a fixed Amount, or according to any special or exceptional Principle of Valuation, whether such Property shall or shall not be included in any Valuation List in force under this Act, or shall in anywise affect the Provisions of "The *Cambridge* Award Act, 1856" or the Act of the Seventeenth and Eighteenth *Victoria* relating to the Relief of the Poor in the City of *Oxford*]

19 & 20 Vict, c xvii
17 & 18 Vict c ccxix

Committee may allow compensation for returns, etc and expenses

37 The Committee may allow such Compensation for any Returns, Copies, or Extracts, or any Valuation, or Valuation List or other Act, Matter, or Thing to be made or done in pursuance of their Order and such Expenses connected therewith, as to the Committee in each Case seems just

Remuneration to clerk and expenses of Committee

38 The Remuneration allowed by the Committee to their Clerk and all expenses incurred by them for the common use and Benefit of the several Parishes within the Union for which they are appointed, shall be paid by the Guardians of the said Union, and be charged upon the Common Fund thereof

Repealed as regards Metropolis

Expenses of valuation, etc when to be paid out of poor rates, of parishes and when out of common fund

[39 The Expenses of making any Valuation and Valuation List of any Parish, or any of such expenses, whether such Valuation and Valuation List respectively be made by the Overseers or by any person appointed by the Committee, shall be charged upon the Poor Rates of such Parish if the Valuation made by direction of the Committee shall exceed by One Sixth the Amount of the Valuation delivered to them by the Overseers, and upon the Common Fund of the said Union if the Valuation so made as last mentioned shall not exceed by One Sixth the Valuation so delivered as aforesaid]

Penalty for non attendance, etc in obedience to order of the Committee

40 Every person who wilfully refuses to attend in obedience to any lawful Order of any such Committee, or to give evidence or refuses to produce any Rate Book, Assessment or Valuation which may be lawfully required to be produced before such Committee, shall for every such Offence be liable to a penalty not exceeding Twenty Pounds upon a summary Conviction for the same before Two Justices of the Peace, and every person who wilfully injures, defaces, conceals or destroys such Rate Book, or who upon any Examination before any such Committee wilfully gives false Evidence, shall be deemed guilty of a Misdemeanour

Injuring, etc rate books a misdemeanour

Repealed as regards Metropolis

[41 Every Order and Notice made or given by the Committee under this Act, may be in Writing or Print, or partly in Writing and partly in Print, and shall be sufficiently authenticated if signed by their Clerk, and may be served by the same or a Copy thereof being delivered personally or sent by the Post to the Party on or to whom such Order or Notice purports to be made or given, or by being delivered at his usual Place of Abode.] *Authentication and service of orders and notices of the Committee*

[42 Any Notice or Statement required to be served upon the Committee may be served by being left at the Office of the Clerk to the Board of Guardians, or sent through the Post Office, addressed to the Committee at such Clerk's Office, or by being delivered personally to their Clerk, or at his usual Place of Abode] *Repealed as regards Metropolis Service of notices, etc on the Committee*

[43 In every Parish until a Valuation List has been approved and delivered to the Overseers under this Act, every Rate made for the Relief of the Poor in such Parish, shall be made in the Form and contain the Particulars required by the said Act of the Sixth and Seventh Years of King *William* the Fourth , and after such Valuation List has been so approved and delivered, every such Rate, except in any Parish where the Poor Rate or the Assessment for the same is made under the Provisions of a Local Act as aforesaid, shall show the annual Rateable Value of each Hereditament comprised therein according to the Valuation List in force in such Parish] *Repealed as regards Metropolis Form of poor rate 6 & 7 Will 4, c 96*

44 All the Powers, Authorities, Provisions, Clauses, and Regulations now in force relating to the Assessment, Collection, and levying of Poor Rates (save so far as the same are hereby repealed or altered) shall be good, valid, and effectual for the Purposes of assessing, levying collecting, and enforcing the Payment of such Rate and for carrying this Act into execution. *Provisions concerning the assessment etc , of poor rates to be applicable to rates made according to this Act*

[45 And whereas there are divers Unions or Incorporations for the Relief of the Poor, formed under Local Acts and under the Act of the Twenty-second Year of King *George* the Third, Chapter Eighty-three, which may desire to adopt the Provisions of this Act Be it enacted, That any such Union or Incorporation, on Resolution to that effect of a Majority, at Two successive Meetings of the Body, having under the Constitution of such Union or Incorporation the Management of the Relief of the Poor within the same, may, by Writing under the Hand of the presiding Chairman of the Second of such Meetings, apply to the Poor Law Board to be included in this Act , and such Union or Incorporation, upon the Consent of the Poor Law Board being given to such Application under its Seal, shall be so included ; and such Consent so signified shall be Evidence that such Application was in all respects duly made according to the Provisions above mentioned , and such Regulations shall thereafter be made from time to time by the said Board, with the Consent of such Body, as may be necessary to render the Provisions of this Act conformable with the Provisions of the Act under which the said Union or Incorporation shall have been formed] *Repealed as regards Metropolis Powers for Unions under Local Acts or 22 Geo III c 83, to be included in this Act*

46 This Act shall extend only to *England* *Extent of Act*

SCHEDULE

(SECTION 14.)

VALUATION LIST for [*the Parish or Place for which the List is made*], *in the County of*

Name of Occupier	Name of Owner	Description of Property	Name or Situation of Property	Estimated Extent	Gross Estimated Rental	Rateable Value

Signed this   day of

A B } Overseers of the Poor of
C D }   the Parish aforesaid

DECLARATION TO BE ADDED TO THE RATE

WE, the undersigned, do hereby declare that One of us, or some Person on our Behalf, has examined and compared the several Particulars in the respective Columns of the above Rate with the Valuation List made under the Authority of the Union Assessment Committee Act 1862, in force in this Parish (or Township), and the several Hereditaments are, to the best of our Belief, rated according to the Value appearing in such Valuation List

} Churchwardens.

} Overseers

THE UNION ASSESSMENT COMMITTEE AMENDMENT ACT, 1864.

(27 & 28 Vict, cap. 39.)

AN ACT TO AMEND THE UNION ASSESSMENT COMMITTEE ACT, 1862

[*14th July, 1864*]

(PREAMBLE RECITES 25 & 26 VICT, c 103).

Repealed as regards Metropolis

[1. Before any Appeal shall be heard by any Special or Quarter Sessions against a Poor Rate made for any Parish contained in any

Union to which the Union Assessment Committee Act, 1862, applies, the Appellant shall give Twenty-one Days' Notice in Writing previous to the Special or Quarter Sessions to which such Appeal is to be made of the Intention to Appeal, and the Grounds thereof, to the Assessment Committee of such Union: Provided, that after the First Day of *August* next no Person shall be empowered to appeal to any Sessions against a Poor Rate made in conformity with the Valuation List approved of by such Committee, unless he shall have given to such Committee Notice of Objection against the said List, and shall have failed to obtain such Relief in the Matter as he deems just, and which Objection, after Notice given at any Time in Manner prescribed by the said Act with respect to Objections, the Committee shall hear, with full Power to call for and amend such List, although the same has been approved of, and no subsequent List has been transmitted to them, and if they amend the same shall give Notice of such Amendment to the Overseers, who shall thereupon Alter their then current Rate accordingly]

2 The Assessment Committee of such Union may, with the consent of the Guardians of such Union, after Notice shall have been sent to every Guardian, appear as Respondents to such Appeal, but in the Name of the Guardians of such Union, in like Manner, and with the same Incidents, and subject to the same Liabilities, and entitled to the same Remedies and Rights, as in the Case of Persons other than the Overseers to whom Notice of Appeal may be given

3 The Costs which the Committee may incur in consequence of becoming Respondents to such Appeal, or of having received Notice thereof, shall, if not recovered from the Appellants, as well as any Costs the Committee may be ordered to pay to the Appellants, be paid by the Guardians and charged to the Common Fund of the Union, unless the Court before whom such Appeal is heard shall direct that such Costs, or any Part thereof shall be charged to the Parish, the Rate of which is appealed against

4 Where a Valuer is appointed by the Assessment Committee he shall make his Valuation in Writing, showing the Particulars of the several Hereditaments comprised therein, and the Amounts at which he has valued the same respectively, and shall sign such Valuation, which shall be open to Inspection in like Manner and with the same Incidents with respect to the taking of Copies or Extracts as the Minute Books of the Committee

5. Within Fourteen Days after the Transmission to the Assessment Committee of any Valuation or Supplemental Valuation List the Committee shall give Notice to every Railway, Telegraph, Canal, Gas and Water Company named in such List as the Occupier of any Property included therein, and not having any Office or Place of Business in the Parish to which such List relates, of the Sum or Sums set down as the rateable Value of the Property purporting to be

---

Marginal notes:

Notice of appeal against poor rate to be given to the Assessment Committee of Union 25 & 26 Vict c 103

No appeal against rate made in conformity with valuation list unless objection has been made to list

Assessment Committee to hear such objections

Committee may with consent of guardians appear as respondents on appeal

Provision is to costs of committee on appeals

Valuation of valuer to be made in writing and signed and to be open to inspection

Notice of Valuation to be given to companies named as occupiers but not having places of business in the parish

occupied by such Company or Companies, and such Notice may be served by being transmitted through the Post to the Principal Office of the Company, or One of their principal Offices when there shall be more than One

Justices in certain cases not disqualified for hearing appeals

6 No Justice of the Peace shall be disqualified for acting in the Determination of any Appeal against a Poor Rate at any Quarter or Special Sessions by reason of such Justice being rated, or being liable to be rated, in some other Parish in the Union than that for which the Rate appealed against is made

Expenses of Overseers as to Valuation List, etc., incurred with consent of Vestry or allowed by Assessment Committee may be charged on poor rates

7 When the Overseers of any Parish incur any Expense in making out any Valuation List or Supplemental List, or in revising or valuing any of the rateable Hereditaments of such Parish, under the Provisions of the Union Assessment Committee Act, 1862, with the Consent of the Vestry given by express Resolution, after due Notice, they may charge such Expense, so far as the same may be authorised by the Vestry, upon the Poor Rate, and if no Vestry Meeting be held, or no Decision arrived at on the Subject, then to the Extent which the Assessment Committee shall allow   Provided that as regards the Valuation of the Property, no Expense shall be so charged upon the Poor Rate unless the Consent of such Committee to the procuring of such Valuation by the Overseers shall have been given previously to the same being made

Power to Guardians with the order of the Poor Law Board to borrow money for valuation expenses by charge on poor rates of union or on parish

8 If the Assessment Committee order a Valuation, with the Consent of the Board of Guardians, to be made of all the rateable Hereditaments of any Parish, the Guardians of the Union may, if they think fit, apply to the Poor Law Board for an Order to enable them to borrow the requisite Amount to pay the Cost of such Valuation, and if the said Board shall issue their Order, the said Guardians may borrow the same and charge the Poor Rates of the several Parishes in the Union with the Repayment of the same by not more than Five equal Annual Instalments, and where the Parish for which the Valuation is made shall, by reason of any Provision in the said Union Assessment Committee Act or this Act, be liable to pay the Cost of such Valuation, the said Guardians shall charge the annual Instalments, and the Interest payable therewith, to such Parish, and may recover the same as and with the usual Contributions

Repealed as regards Metropolis

Totals of rental and rateable value of property included in lists to be sent to Clerks of the Peace

[9 The Clerk of every Assessment Committee shall send annually in the month of *December* Copies of the Totals of the gross estimated Rental and rateable Value of the Property included in the Valuation Lists of the several Parishes within the Union and where such Totals have been altered by any Supplemental Valuation List or Lists then of such Totals as altered, to the Clerk or respective Clerks of the Peace of the County or Counties within which such Parishes respectively may be situate]

Power of Assessment Committee

10 If there be no Map or Plan of any Parish available for the Use or sufficient for the Purposes of the Assessment Committee, the

Committee may, with the Consent of the Guardians, after notice as aforesaid, and under the Authority of an Order of the Poor Law Board, appoint a competent Person to make a Map or Plan of such Parish, and the Cost thereof shall be charged either to the Common Fund, or to the Parish, as may be directed by the Poor Law Board

under order of Poor Law Board to order Map or Plan to be made

[11 Any Overseer who wilfully omits to make the Declaration required to be made by the Union Assessment Committee Act, 1862, or makes the same falsely, knowing the same to be untrue, shall be liable for every such Offence to a Penalty not exceeding Five Pounds, upon a summary Conviction for the same before Two Justices of the Peace]

Separate returns Metropolis Penalty on Overseers omitting to make declaration required by 25 & 26 Vict c 103, or making false declaration

12 The Provisions of the Union Assessment Committee Act, 1862, shall, so far as the same are not contrary hereto, be incorporated herewith, and the Terms used herein shall be construed in like Manner as in that Act

25 and 26 Vict., c 103 incorporated herewith

13 This Act may be cited as " The Union Assessment Committee Amendment Act, 1864 "

Short title

THE POOR LAW AMENDMENT ACT, 1868.

(31 & 32 Vict, cap 122)

AN ACT TO MAKE FURTHER AMENDMENTS IN THE LAWS FOR THE RELIEF OF THE POOR IN ENGLAND AND WALES

[*31st July, 1868*]

o   o   o   o   o

29 Where an appeal is brought against the poor rate of a parish in a union, and may appear to involve a principle in which some neighbouring parish has a common interest, it shall be lawful for the guardians of the unions comprising such parishes to enter into an agreement mutually to bear the costs which may be properly incurred in and about the trial of such appeals on the part of the several respondents as well as the costs of the appellants, if any which may be awarded against the respondents, in such proportions as shall be fixed and determined with reference to the amount of interest of the several unions in the question or otherwise as shall appear just, and the said agreement shall continue binding upon the several boards of guardians and their respective successors in succession until the several appeals shall have been finally determined

Power for guardians of unions mutually to bear the costs of several appeals involving the same common principle

30 When the assessment committee in any union shall have finally approved of any valuation list, whether original substitutional, or supplemental they shall cause the total of the entries in the columns for the gross estimated value and the rateable value to be ascertained and entered at the foot of the same, and shall retain such list for the use of the guardians, to be dealt with in the manner provided by the thirty first section of the Union Assessment Committee Act, 1862,

Repeal as regards Metropolis Fair copies of approved valuation lists to be given to overseers, instead of originals 25 & 26 Vict., c 103

and shall deliver a fair copy of the same to the overseers signed by the three members of the committee who approved of the same ; and such copy shall be countersigned by the clerk of the committee, and shall be preserved by the overseers and dealt with by them in all respects as the lists made out by them would have been dealt with accordingly to the law now in force, and it shall not be necessary for the said committee to cause any other copy to be made

31 Where any valuation list heretofore approved, or the copy hereafter to be made, shall be lost injured or destroyed the overseers of the parish to which it relates may apply to the clerk of the guardians for a copy of the same, and the clerk, upon payment of a reasonable compensation, not exceeding three shillings for one hundred separate rateable hereditaments, shall give such copy, and certify the same to be a true copy of the list deposited with the said guardians, and such certified copy shall be henceforth available as the original

32 The guardians may, upon the application of the assessment committee, after notice sent in the manner required by the Union Assessment Committee Act. 1862, appoint some competent person to assist the committee in the valuation of the rateable hereditaments of the union for such period as they shall see fit, at a salary or other settled remuneration to be paid out of the common fund

33 When any person shall occupy any new house or other building in the parish where the poor rate is not made under the provisions of a local Act, which house or building was incomplete, or not fit for occupation, or was not entered as such in the valuation list in force in the parish at the time when the current rate for the time being was made, the overseers may enter such house or building with the name of the occupier thereof, and the date of the entry in the rate book, and require the occupier to pay such amount as according to their judgment shall be the proper sum, having due regard to the rateable value of such house or building, and the time which shall have elapsed from the making of the current rate to the date of such entry, and the person so charged shall be considered as actually rated from such date, and shall be liable to pay the sum assessed in like manner, and subject to the like penalty of distress, and with the like power of appeal, as if he had been assessed for the same when the rate was made Provided, that when the said overseers shall so enter the said house or building in the rate book they shall forward to the assessment committee of the union comprising such parish, if any such there be, a supplemental list with reference to such house or building and the same shall be dealt with in all respects and with the like incidents and consequences, as a supplemental list made by the overseers under section twenty-five of the Union Assessment Committee Act, 1862

39 When a poor rate shall be made and assessed upon any land or premises and the occupier thereof is not living on such land or premises nor in the parish for which the rate shall be made, or the owner if assessed for such rate in the place of the occupier, is not living in such parish, a demand of the rate in writing delivered to the person having the custody of the land or premises, or if no such person can be found, then affixed upon some conspicuous part of the land or premises, shall be deemed a sufficient demand to justify proceedings for the non-payment of such rate, and where the residence or place of abode of the person assessed is not known to the overseers, and cannot be ascertained upon inquiry at the said land or premises the summons for the non-payment of the rate may be served in like manner

Demand of poor rate, or summons for non payment, may be made on the premises where occupier is not resident in parish

40 When a poor rate is assessed upon any corporation aggregate, joint stock or other company, or any conservators or other public trustees, a demand for payment, either made by letter sent through the post addressed to the clerk or secretary or other principal officer of the corporation, company, conservators, or trustees at the office of such corporation, company conservators, or trustees or made personally upon such clerk, secretary, or officer at such office shall be deemed a sufficient demand, and a summons for the non-payment of such rate may be served in like manner

Service of demand of rate from a corporation or a company, and of summons, for non payment

46. This Act may be cited and described for all purposes as "The Poor Law Amendment Act, 1868"

Short title

- -

THE SUNDAY AND RAGGED SCHOOLS (EXEMPTION FROM RATING) ACT, 1869

(32 & 33 Vict, cap 40)

AN ACT TO EXEMPT FROM RATING SUNDAY AND RAGGED SCHOOLS.

[*26th July, 1869*]

[PREAMBLE]

1   Every authority having power to impose or levy any rate upon the occupier of any building or part of a building used exclusively as a Sunday school or ragged school may exempt such building or part of a building from any rate for any purpose whatever which such authority has power to impose or levy   provided that nothing in this Act contained shall prejudice or affect the right of exemption from rating of Sunday or infant schools, or for the charitable education of the poor in any churches, district churches, chapels, meeting houses, or other premises, or any vestry rooms belonging thereto, or any part thereof, by virtue of the Poor Rate Exemption Act, 1833

Sunday and ragged schools may be exempted from rates for relief of poor etc

3 & 4 Will IV, c. 30

Interpretation of terms

2 A ' Sunday school" shall mean any school used for giving religious education gratuitously to children and young persons on Sunday, and on weekdays for the holding of classes and meetings in furtherance of the same object, and without pecuniary profit being derived therefrom.

A "Ragged school" shall mean any school used for the gratuitous education of children and young persons' of the poorest classes, and for the holding of classes and meetings in furtherance of the same object, and without any pecuniary benefit being derived therefrom except to the teacher or teachers employed

Extent of Act

3. This Act shall not extend to Ireland

Short title

4 This Act may be cited as "The Sunday and Ragged Schools (Exemption from Rating) Act, 1869 '

THE POOR RATE ASSESSMENT AND COLLECTION ACT, 1869

(32 & 33 Vict , cap 41.)

AN ACT FOR AMENDING THE LAW WITH RESPECT TO THE RATING OF OCCUPIERS FOR SHORT TERMS AND THE MAKING AND COLLECTING OF THE POOR'S RATE

[*26th July, 1869*]

[PREAMBLE]

Lessees for short terms may deduct poor rate from rent

1 The occupier of any rateable hereditament let to him for a term not exceeding three months shall be entitled to deduct the amount paid by him in respect of any poor rate assessed upon such hereditament from the rent due or accruing due to the owner, and every such payment shall be a valid discharge of the rent to the extent of the rate so paid

Amount of rate payable by occupier

2 No such occupier shall be compelled to pay to the overseers at one time or within four weeks a greater amount of the rate than would be due for one quarter of the year

Owners may agree to pay the rate, and be allowed a commission

3 In case the rateable value of any hereditament does not exceed twenty pounds, if the hereditament is situate in the metropolis or thirteen pounds if situate in any parish wholly or partly within the borough of Liverpool, or ten pounds if situate in any parish wholly or partly within the city of Manchester or the borough of Birmingham, or eight pounds if situate elsewhere, and the owner of such hereditament is willing to enter into an agreement in writing with the overseers to become liable to them for the poor rates assessed in respect of such hereditament, for any term not being less than one year from the date of such agreement, and to pay the poor rates whether the hereditament is occupied or not, the overseers may,

subject nevertheless to the control of the Vestry, agree with the owner to receive the rates from him, and to allow to him a commission not exceeding twenty-five per cent on the amount thereof

4 The Vestry of any parish may from time to time order that the owners of all rateable hereditaments to which section three of this Act extends, situate within such parish, shall be rated to the poor rate in respect of such rateable hereditaments, instead of the occupiers, on all rates made after the date of such order, and thereupon and so long as such order shall be in force the following enactments shall have effect

(margin: Vestries may order the owner to be rated instead of the occupier)

1 The overseers shall rate the owners instead of the occupiers, and shall allow to them an abatement or deduction of fifteen per centum from the amount of the rate

2 If the owner of one or more of such rateable hereditaments shall give notice to the overseers in writing that he is willing to be rated for any term not being less than one year in respect of all such rateable hereditaments of which he is the owner, whether the same be occupied or not, the overseers shall rate such owner accordingly, and allow to him a further abatement or deduction not exceeding fifteen per centum from the amount of the rate during the time he is so rated

3 The Vestry may by resolution rescind any such order after a day to be fixed by them, such day being not less than six months after the passing of such resolution, but the order shall continue in force with respect to all rates made before the date on which the resolution takes effect

Provided that this clause shall not be applicable to any rateable hereditament in which a dwelling-house shall not be included

5 When an owner who has become liable to pay the poor rate omits or neglects to pay, before the fifth day of June in any year, any rate or any instalment thereof which has become due previously to the preceding fifth day of January, and has been duly demanded by a demand-note delivered to him or left at his usual or last known place of abode, he shall not be entitled to deduct or receive any commission, abatement, or allowance to which he would, except for such omission or neglect, be entitled under this Act, but shall be liable to pay, and shall pay, such rate or instalment in full

(margin: Owners omitting to pay rates before the fifth day of June to forfeit commission)

6 [1] The statute thirteenth and fourteenth Victoria, chapter ninety-nine, with respect to the rating of small tenements, and so much of any local statute as relates to the rating of ...ers instead of occupiers, are hereby repealed, so far as the same apply to any poor rate made after this Act comes into operation

(margin: Repeal of 13 and 14 Vict, c 99, etc, so far as applies to the poor rate)

[1] 13 & 14 Vict c 99, is wholly repealed 38 & 39 Vict c 66, (S L R)]

Constructive payment of the rate

7. Every payment of a rate by the occupier, notwithstanding the amount thereof, may be deducted from his rent as herein provided, and every payment of a rate by the owner, whether he is himself rated instead of the occupier, or has agreed with the occupier or with the overseers to pay such rate, and notwithstanding any allowance or deduction which the overseers are impowered to make from the rate, shall be deemed a payment of the full rate by the occupier for the purpose of any qualification or franchise which as regards rating depends upon the payment of the poor rate.

Where owners omit to pay rates, the occupier paying the rate may deduct the amount from the rent

8. Where an owner who has undertaken, whether by agreement with the occupier or with the overseers, to pay the poor rates, or has otherwise become liable to pay the same, omits or neglects to pay any such rate, the occupier may pay the same and deduct the amount from the rent due or accruing due to the owner, and the receipt for such rate shall be a valid discharge of the rent to the extent of the rate so paid.

Owners to give lists of occupiers, and liable to penalty for wilful omission

9. Every owner who agrees with the overseers to pay the poor rate, or who is rated or liable to be rated for any hereditament instead of the occupier, shall deliver to the overseers, from time to time, when required by them, in writing, a list containing the names of the actual occupiers of the hereditaments comprised in such agreement, or for which he is so rated or liable to be rated, and if any such owner wilfully omits to deliver such list when required to do so, or wilfully omits therefrom or mistakes therein the name of any occupier, he shall for every such omission or mis-statement be liable, on summary conviction, to a penalty not exceeding two pounds.

Notice to occupiers of rates in arrear, 30 & 31 Vict. c. 102

10. Section twenty eight of the Representation of the People Act, 1867, with respect to notice to be given of rates in arrear shall apply to occupiers of premises capable of conferring the parliamentary franchise, although the owners of such premises have become liable for the rates assessed thereon under the provisions of this Act.

Liability of owner under agreement

11. Where the owner has become liable to the payment of the poor rates, the rates due from him, together with the costs and charges of levying and recovering the same, may be levied on the goods of the owner and be recovered from him in the same way as poor rates may be recovered from the occupier.

Recovery of rates unpaid by the owner

12. Notwithstanding the owner of any such rateable hereditament as aforesaid has become liable for payment of the poor rates assessed thereon, the goods and chattels of the occupier shall be liable to be distrained and sold for payment of such rates as may accrue during his occupation of the premises, at any time whilst such rates remain unpaid by the owner, subject to the following provisions:

1 That no such distress shall be levied unless the rate has been demanded in writing by the overseers from the occupier, and the occupier has failed to pay the same within fourteen days after the service of such demand

2 That no greater sum shall be raised by such distress than shall at the time of making the same be actually due from the occupier for rent of the premises on which the distress is made

3 That any such occupier shall be entitled to deduct the amount of rates for which such distraint is made, and the expense of distraint from the rent due or accruing due to the owner, and every such payment shall be a valid discharge of the rent to the extent of the rate and expenses paid

13 Every owner of any hereditament for the rates of which he has become liable shall have the same right of appeal (subject to the same conditions and consequences) against the Valuation Lists and the poor rates as if he were the occupier thereof *Owner may appeal against valuation list and rate*

14 The overseers of every parish when they make a poor rate shall set forth in the title of the rate the period for which the same is estimated, and if the same is payable by instalments, the amount of each instalment and the date at which each instalment is payable, provided that if the necessities of the parish shall require it another rate may be made before such period shall have elapsed *The overseer to state the period for which the rate is made* *Proviso*

15 The overseers who make the poor rate for a period exceeding three months may declare that the same shall be paid by instalments at such times as they shall specify, and thereupon each instalment only shall be enforceable as and when it falls due, and the payment of any such instalment shall, as respects any qualification or franchise depending upon the payment of the poor rate, be deemed a payment of such rate in respect of the period to which such instalment applies *Overseers may make poor rate payable by instalments*

16 [1] If the occupier assessed in the rate when made shall cease to occupy before the rate shall have been wholly discharged, or if the hereditament being unoccupied at the time of the making of the rate become occupied during the period for which the rate is made, the overseers shall enter into the rate book the name of the person who succeeds or comes into the occupation, as the case may be, and the date when such occupation commences, so far as the same shall be known to them, and such occupier shall thenceforth be deemed to have been actually rated from the date so entered by the overseer, and shall be liable to pay so much of the rate as shall be proportionate to the time between the commencement of his occupation and the expiration of the period for which the rate was made, in like manner and with the like remedy of appeal, as if he had been rated when the rate was made, and an outgoing occupier shall remain liable in like manner for so much and no more of the rate as is proportionate to the time of his occupation within the period for which the rate was made. *Provision for successive occupiers, and for occupiers coming into unoccupied hereditaments*

[1] See the Poor Rate Assessment and Collection Act, 1869, Amendment Act, 1882 (45 & 46 Vict., c 20), s 3

When the poor rate shall be deemed to be made

17. A poor rate shall be deemed to be made on the day when it is allowed by t'_ justices, and if the justices sever in their allowance, then on the day of the last allowance

Evidence of making and publication of rates

18. The production of the book purporting to contain a poor rate, with the allowance of the rate by the Justices, shall, if the rate is made in the form prescribed by law be *prima facie* evidence of the due making and publication of such rate

Overseers to insert names of all occupiers in the rate

Penalty for omission

19. The overseers in making out the poor rate shall in every case whether the rate is collected from the owner or occupier, or the owner is liable to the payment of the rate instead of the occupier, enter in the occupiers column of the rate book the name of the occupier of every rateable hereditament, and such occupier shall be deemed to be duly rated for any qualification or franchise as aforesaid, and if any overseer negligently or wilfully and without reasonable cause omits the name of the occupier of any rateable hereditament from the rate, or negligently or wilfully misstates any name therein, such overseer shall for every such omission or misstatement be liable on summary conviction to a penalty not exceeding two pounds, provided that any occupier whose name has been omitted shall notwithstanding such omission and that no claim to be rated has been made by him, be entitled to every qualification and franchise depending upon rating, in the same manner as if his name had not been so omitted

Interpretation

20. The word "overseer" shall include every authority that makes an assessment for the poor rate, the words "poor rate" shall mean the assessment for the relief of the poor and for the other purposes chargeable thereon according to law and in the Metropolis shall extend to every rate made by the overseers, and chargeable upon the same property as the poor rate, the word "owner" shall mean any person receiving or claiming the rent of the hereditament for his own use, or receiving the same for the use of any corporation aggregate, or of any public company or of any landlord or lessee who shall be a minor, a married woman, or insane or for the use of any person for whom he is acting as agent the word "parish" shall signify every place for which a separate overseer can be appointed, the word "vestry" shall include not only the vestry of a parish existing under the authority of some general or special Act of Parliament, or by special custom or otherwise, but also the meeting of the inhabitants of any township, vill, or place having a separate overseer, and for which a separate poor rate is made, held after notice given in like manner as is required by law in regard to the meetings of vestries, and the word "Metropolis" shall include only the Metropolis as defined by the Metropolis Management Act 1855

18 & 19 Vict., c. 120

Extent

21. This Act shall not extend to Scotland or to Ireland

Short title

22. This Act may be cited as "The Poor Rate Assessment and Collection Act 1869"

THE VALUATION (METROPOLIS) ACT, 1869 [1]

(32 & 33 Vict., cap 67)

AN ACT TO PROVIDE FOR UNIFORMITY IN THE ASSESSMENT OF RATEABLE PROPERTY IN THE METROPOLIS

[*9th August, 1869*]

[PREAMBLE]

Preliminary

1. The Union Assessment Committee Act 1862, is in this Act referred to as "the principal Act" and the principal Act, and the Union Assessment Committee Act, 1864 (amending the same), shall for the purposes of this Act, and so far as is consistent with the tenor thereof, be incorporated with this Act, and the expression 'this Act, in the principal Act, and any expression referring to the principal Act which occurs in the said Act amending the same, or in any other Act or document, shall as regards places to which this Act extends, be construed to mean the principal Act as incorporated with this Act — *Construction* 25 & 26 Vict c 103, 27 & 28 Vict., c 39

2. This Act (including the Acts incorporated herewith) may be cited as the Valuation (Metropolis) Act, 1869 — *Short title*

3. This Act shall extend only to unions and parishes not in union, which are for the time being either wholly or for the greater part in value thereof respectively situate within the jurisdiction of the Metropolitan Board of Works appointed under the Metropolis Management Act, 1855 — *Extent of Act* 18 & 19 Vict c 120

4. In this Act, unless the context otherwise requires — *Interpretation*

The term "metropolis" means the unions and parishes to which this Act extends ,

The term "parish" means any place for which a separate poor rate is or can be made, or for which a separate overseer is or can be appointed

The term "union" means any union of parishes and any parish for which there is a separate assessment committee under this Act and the Acts incorporated herewith

The term 'ratepayer' [2] means every person who is liable to any rate or tax in respect of property entered in any valuation list

The term "year" means the twelve months commencing with the sixth of April and ending with the succeeding fifth of April and words referring to a year refer to the same period

---

[1] All powers and duties of the Clerk to the Managers of the Metropolitan Asylums District under this Act are transferred to the Clerk of the London County Council, and this Act is to be construed as if the County Council were substituted for the Managers (51 & 52 Vict., c 41), s. 44

The Poor Law Board in this Act mentioned is now the Local Government Board (see 34 & 35 Vict., c 70)

[2] See also the Valuation (Metropolis) Amendment Act, 1884 (47 & 48 Vict., c 5 s 2)

The term ' surveyor of taxes ' means any surveyor of taxes, inspector of taxes, or other officer appointed or to be appointed by the Commissioners either of Inland Revenue or of Her Majesty's Treasury for the purposes of any tax in respect of which a valuation is by this Act made conclusive

The term "overseers" includes any person or body of persons performing the duties of overseers so far as regards the assessment, making, and collection of rates for the relief of the poor

The term "vestry clerk" means the vestry clerk, if any, elected under the Vestries Act, 1850, or under a local Act, or, if there is no such clerk, the vestry clerk appointed under "The Metropolis Management Act 1855"

The term "hereditament" means any lands, tenements, hereditaments, and property which are liable to any rate or tax in respect of which the valuation list is by this Act made conclusive

The term "gross value" means the annual rent which a tenant might reasonably be expected, taking one year with another, to pay for an hereditament, if the tenant undertook to pay all usual tenant's rates and taxes, and tithe commutation rent-charge if any, and if the landlord undertook to bear the cost of the repairs and insurance, and the other expenses, if any, necessary to maintain the hereditament in a state to command that rent

The term "rateable value" means the gross value after deducting therefrom the probable annual average cost of the repairs, insurance, and other expenses as aforesaid.

Assessment Committee [1]

5 Where in any parish which is not included in any union formed under the Poor Law Amendment Act, 1834, and the Acts amending the same, there is for the time being a vestry elected according to the provisions of the Metropolis Management Act, 1855, but no assessment committee under the principal Act, the following provisions shall have effect

(1) Where in any such parish there is a board of guardians having power under any local Act to assess or make the rates for the relief of the poor, that board of guardians shall appoint an assessment committee

(2) Where any two of such parishes are united under a local Act for the purpose of assessing or making the rates for the relief of the poor, the guardians for such united parishes elected in pursuance of the Poor Law Amendment Act, 1834, and the Acts amending the same, shall appoint an assessment committee

[1] Under the London Government Act, 1899 (62 & 63 Vict., c 14), ss 13, 31, the Assessment Committee in case of a Poor Law Union being wholly within a Metropolitan Borough, is to be appointed by the Borough Council, and under the City of London (Union of Parishes) Act, 1907 (7 Edward VII, c cxl.), s 14 in the case of the City of London by the City Corporation

(3) In cases other than those before mentioned the vestry of such parishes shall appoint an assessment committee

(4) In every year the body who appoint an assessment committee under this section shall on a day fixed by such body between the fifteenth and twenty-ninth of April in that year, or some other date fixed by the Poor Law Board,[1] hold a meeting and appoint from among themselves an assessment committee (consisting of not less than six nor more than twelve in number) in the same manner, as near as may be, as if the parish or united parishes were in union and the appointing body a board of guardians within the meaning of the principal Act

All the provisions of this Act and the Acts incorporated herewith shall—

(a) in cases where the assessment committee is appointed by guardians under this section be construed as if such guardians, and the monies applicable by such guardians for the relief of the poor, were the guardians mentioned in the principal Act and the common fund and

(b.) in cases where the assessment committee is appointed by the vestry be construed, so far as is consistent with the tenor thereof, as if the terms vestry, members of the vestry, vestry clerk, assistant vestry clerk, and monies applicable to the payment of the expenses of a vestry under the Metropolis Management Act, 1855, were respectively substituted for the terms board of guardians, guardians, clerk of the board of guardians, assistant clerk of the board of guardians, and common fund, but nothing in such Acts relating to ex-officio guardians shall have any application in the case of a vestry

18 & 19 Vict, c 120

Making of Valuation Lists

6 The overseers of every parish to which this Act extends, within the time in this Act mentioned, shall make and sign a valuation list of their parish in duplicate, in accordance with this Act

Making of valuation lists

7 After the valuation list is signed by the overseers the same proceedings shall be had as are directed by the seventeenth eighteenth, nineteenth twentieth, and twenty-first sections of the principal Act, subject to the alterations made by this Act

Valuation lists to be dealt with under 25 & 26 Vict., c 103, ss 17 to 21

8 The overseers shall send one duplicate of the valuation list to the surveyor of taxes of the district at the same time that the other duplicate is deposited by them   The surveyor of taxes shall insert in the duplicate so sent to him the amount in his opinion of the gross value of the hereditaments comprised in such list where such amount differs from the amount inserted by the overseers, and shall transmit the duplicate to the assessment committee within twenty-eight days after he has received the same.

Duplicate sent to surveyor of taxes

---

[1] Now the Local Government Board , see 34 & 35 Vict c 70

Notice to occu-
pier of altera-
tion of value,
etc

9 In each of the following cases, namely,

(1.) Where the overseers of the parish insert in the valuation list some hereditament not previously assessed, or raise the gross or rateable value of some hereditament above the value stated in the valuation list for the time being in force or (where there is no valuation list) in the then last assessment to the poor rate, or

(2.) Where the assessment committee (otherwise than in determining an objection) alter a valuation list by inserting therein some hereditament, or by raising the gross or rateable value of some hereditament comprised therein.

the overseers shall immediately after the deposit or re-deposit of the list (as the case may be) serve on the occupier of such hereditament a notice of the gross and rateable value thereof inserted in the valuation list

Notice to state
time and mode
of objection

10 The notice of the deposit and re-deposit of the valuation list published by the overseers shall state the times at which and the mode in which objections are to be made

Grounds on
which persons
may object
before assess-
ment com-
mittee

11 Objections may be made before the assessment committee by any person authorised by this Act and the Acts incorporated herewith to object who feels himself aggrieved by reason of the unfairness or incorrectness of the valuation of any hereditament, or by reason of the insertion or incorrectness of any matter in the valuation list, or by reason of the omission of any matter therefrom, or by reason of such a valuation list as is required by this Act not having been transmitted by the overseers to the assessment committee. The notice of objection shall specify the correction which the objector desires to be made

Surveyor of
taxes, et., may
inspect copy,
and object to
valuation list

12 A surveyor of taxes, and any ratepayer in the parish, shall have the same right of inspecting, copying, taking extracts from, and objecting to any valuation list which relates to his district or parish as is given to any person by this Act and the Acts incorporated herewith

If overseers do
not transmit
list committee
to appoint a
person to do so

13 If the overseers of any parish fail to transmit such a valuation list as is required by this Act, the assessment committee shall appoint some person to make a valuation list, and may allow such person such remuneration in addition to his expenses as they think fit, and all expenses incurred by the assessment committee in pursuance of this section shall be paid by the guardians and charged by them to such parish.

The person so appointed shall have for the purposes of this section the same powers and duties as overseers, and the valuation list so made shall be dealt with in like manner as if it had been duly made and transmitted by the overseers

Valuation list
to be revised
certified and
sent to over-
seers &c

14 The assessment committee, within the time in this Act mentioned, shall revise the valuation list in accordance with this Act and the Acts incorporated herewith When they have finally approved such valuation list, they shall cause the totals of the gross and rateable value in such list to be ascertained and inserted in the list, and three

members of the committee present at the meeting at which the list is finally approved shall sign at the foot thereof such declaration of approval and certificate of compliance with this Act as is contained in Part One of the Second Schedule to this Act   One duplicate, so certified, shall be sent to the clerk of the managers of the metropolitan asylum district, and the other duplicate to the overseers of the parish to which it relates

15 The overseers of the parish, on receiving the duplicate of the valuation list so sent to them by the assessment committee, shall immediately deposit it in the place in which the rate books of the parish are kept, and shall publish notice of such deposit, and of the time and mode of making appeals, and of the grounds on which an appeal is allowed by this Act to be made

Deposit of duplicate of list in each parish

16 The certified valuation list so sent to the clerk of the managers of the metropolitan asylum district by the assessment committee shall be deposited at the office of such managers, and within the time in this Act mentioned shall be returned by such clerk to the same assessment committee

Deposit of list at office of the managers of metropolitan asylum district

17 The clerk of the managers of the metropolitan asylum district shall, within the time in this Act mentioned, cause the totals of the gross and rateable values of all the valuation lists to be printed, and a printed copy of all such totals to be sent to every assessment committee, and the overseers of every parish in the metropolis and in every county in which any parish to which any of such totals relate is situate, to the clerks of the peace for every such county, to the Commissioner of the Metropolitan Police, the Corporation of the City of London, the Metropolitan Board of Works, every district board in the metropolis, and the Poor Law Board   Every assessment committee, overseer, and ratepayer within the metropolis and every such county shall respectively be entitled to have printed copies of such totals on payment of one penny for each copy of all the said totals

Printing and distribution of totals of gross and rateable value in valuation list

Appeals —Special Sessions

18 In every petty sessional division in the metropolis the justices of the peace acting in and for such division shall, in every year at the time mentioned in this Act, hold a special sessions for hearing appeals under this Act against the valuation lists of the several parishes within such division

Holding of special session to hear appeals

19 Any ratepayer and any overseers of a parish, so far as respects the valuation list of such parish, and any surveyor of taxes, so far as respects the valuation list of any parish in the petty sessional division, may, if he or they feel aggrieved by any decision of the assessment committee on an objection made with respect to the unfairness or incorrectness of the valuation of any hereditament included in such list

Persons entitled to appeal to special sessions

but not otherwise, appeal against such decision to the special sessions The right to appeal to special sessions shall not deprive a person of any other right of appeal conferred on him by this Act

Extent of jurisdiction of special sessions

20 The justices in special sessions under this Act shall not hear any appeal touching any matter with respect to which notice of appeal to the general assessment sessions has been served in manner prescribed by this Act, and shall not hear any appeal touching any part or alter any part of the valuation list except the part relating to the value of an hereditament, and a decision of such justices and an alteration by them of the value of an hereditament in the valuation list of any parish shall affect only the rights of the ratepayers of such parish among themselves, and shall not of itself in any way alter the totals of the gross or rateable value of such list as settled by the assessment committee, but may form a reason for appeal against such totals to the assessment sessions and superior court as hereinafter mentioned

Powers of special sessions

21 The justices in special sessions under this Act may adjourn their court from time to time, as may be necessary for the performance of their duties, under this Act They shall have, with respect to the attendance and examination of witnesses, the taking of evidence, the keeping order in court the enforcing their orders, and all matters necessary for the execution of their duties under this Act, the same powers and jurisdiction as if they were assembled in petty sessions

Notice by special sessions of time of sitting

22 The justices in special sessions shall send a written notice of the time and place at which they will hold a special sessions for the purpose of hearing appeals with respect to any parish to the overseers of such parish, who shall publish it as soon as it is received by them

Appeals —Assessment Sessions [1]

Court of general assessment sessions

23 For the purpose of hearing appeals under this Act against any valuation list in the metropolis the justices of the peace appointed as herein-after mentioned shall at the time mentioned in this Act assemble and hold a court of general assessment sessions (in this Act referred to as the assessment sessions)

Appointment of members of general assessment sessions

24 The justices who are to form the court of general assessment sessions shall be appointed annually as follows

1 Three justices of the peace of the county of Middlesex (of whom the assistant judge of the court of the sessions of the peace of the said county shall be one) shall be appointed by the court of general quarter sessions or general sessions of the peace for the county of Middlesex

---

[1] By the Local Government Act 1888 (51 & 52 Vict., c 41), s 42 (10), the Quarter Sessions for the County of London are substituted for the Assessment Sessions, and it is provided that upon the hearing of any appeals in relation to property in the City of London such two members of the court of Quarter Sessions of the City of London as may be appointed by that court for the purpose, shall be entitled to attend and sit as members of the Quarter Sessions for the County of London

2 Two justices of the peace of the county of Surrey shall be appointed by the court of general or quarter sessions of the peace for the county of Surrey

3 Two justices of the peace of the county of Kent shall be appointed by the court of general sessions for the county of Kent

4 Two justices of the peace of the city of London shall be appointed by the court of the mayor and aldermen of the city of London in the inner chamber

The said justices shall be appointed in the month of October in every year, or at such other time as may be from time to time fixed by the appointing body   They shall hold office for twelve months beginning on the first of November, and any casual vacancy may be filled up by the appointing body

25 The justices in assessment sessions may from time to time appoint with the consent of the Poor Law Board a clerk and other persons to assist them in the performance of their duties under this Act, and may assign him or them such remuneration and such duties as the Poor Law Board may approve

Officers of general assessment sessions

26 The justices in assessment sessions may from time to time appoint one of their own number to act as their chairman, who shall have a second or casting vote, and they may from time to time determine on their quorum so that it be not less than three

Chairman quorum and powers of general assessment sessions

The court of general assessment sessions may adjourn from time to time, as may be necessary for the performance of their duties under this Act, and (for the purpose of giving judgment only) from place to place in the metropolis   They shall with respect to the attendance and examination of witnesses, to the taking of evidence, to the keeping of order in court, to contempt of court, to the enforcement of their orders, and to all matters necessary for the execution of their duties under this Act have the same jurisdiction and powers and be in the same position as a court of quarter sessions , and subject to the express provisions of this Act, shall conduct their proceedings, be convened and be in the same position, as near as may be, as if they were a court of quarter sessions

27 The justices in assessment sessions may, with the approval of one of Her Majesty's Principal Secretaries of State, make orders from time to time for the purpose of regulating the proceedings on appeals to them under this Act, and for determining the recognisances (if any) to be entered into by appellants in the case of appeals either to special sessions or to the assessment sessions

Orders as to proceedings and recognisances on appeals

28 The justices in assessment sessions may make a table of the fees which in their opinion should be paid to the clerks of special sessions and to the clerk of assessment sessions in the case of appeals under this Act, and shall lay such table before one of Her Majesty's Principal Secretaries of State in the same manner as the justices at quarter

Fees on appeals under Act

11 & 12 Vict., c. 43.

sessions may make and lay before such Secretary of State a table of fees, and all the provisions of section thirty of the Summary Jurisdiction Act, 1848 (which section relates to a table of fees and to the prohibition of clerks taking other fees), shall apply in the case of a table of fees made and the business done by the said clerks under this Act

All fees paid in the case of appeals to the assessment sessions shall be paid to the account of the receiver of the Metropolitan Common Poor Fund and shall be so paid and taken and accounted for in such manner as the Poor Law Board may from time to time by order prescribe

Places for hearing appeals

29 The justices in assessment sessions shall from time to time appoint the place in the metropolis where the appeals relating to each parish in the metropolis are to be heard, and may, if they think fit, divide the metropolis into districts for the purpose of appeals and appoint one or more places for every such district

Public notice of times of holding courts to be given

30 The justices in assessment sessions shall cause public notice to be given of the several times at which they will sit at the several places appointed for the hearing of appeals such notice may be given under the hand of their clerk, and shall be given by advertisement in some newspaper circulating generally in the metropolis and by sending a copy of such notice to every surveyor of taxes in the metropolis to every assessment committee which would have a right to appeal at such court, and to the overseers of every parish to which any appeal relates and to all the parties to the appeal

The overseers shall publish the notice as soon as it is received by them

Summons of certain officers as witnesses

31 The justices in assessment sessions may order any clerk to the Commissioners of Taxes, any surveyor of taxes, clerk of assessment committee, overseer, assistant overseer, or like officer in the metropolis to produce any documents relating to rates or taxes which such justices may consider necessary for determining an appeal, and do not relate to profits of trade or of concerns in the nature of trade

Any person who refuses, after tender of a reasonable sum for his expenses, to obey any order under this section shall be liable (on summary conviction before the justices in assessment sessions or any other two justices) to a penalty not exceeding five pounds

Persons entitled to appeal to assessment sessions

32 Any rate payer[1] and any surveyor of taxes, and any overseer with the consent of the vestry of his parish, who may feel aggrieved by any decision of the assessment committee, on an objection made before them to which he was a party, or by any decision of special sessions, whether he was a party or not, may appeal against such decision to the assessment sessions

---

[1] See also The Valuation (Metropolis) Amendment Act, 1864 (47 & 48 Vict, c 5), s. 2

Any assessment committee in the metropolis, or in the county in which the parish to which the appeal relates is situate, any overseers in the metropolis or such county, with the consent of the vestry of their parish, any ratepayer in the metropolis or such county, and any body of persons authorised by law to levy rates or require contributions payable out of rates in the metropolis or such county, may appeal to the assessment sessions if they or he feel aggrieved by reason—

(1) of the total of the gross value of any parish being too high or too low,

(2) of the total of the rateable value of any parish being too high or too low, or

(3) of their being no approved valuation list for some parish

Proceedings on Appeals

33 Notice in writing of every appeal,[1] whether to special sessions or the assessment sessions, specifying the correction which the appellant desires to have made in the valuation list, must be served, within the time of this Act mentioned, on the following persons namely,

in all cases on the surveyor of taxes of the district to which the appeal relates, and on the clerk of the assessment committee which approved the list wholly or partly questioned by the appeal

when the appeal relates to the unfairness or incorrectness of the valuation of or to the omission of an hereditament occupied by any person other than the appellant or to the incorrectness of any matter stated in the list with respect to any such hereditament, then on such person

if an assessment committee or a surveyor of taxes is the appellant, then also on the overseers of the parish to which the appeal relates

Provided that it shall not be necessary to serve any notice of appeal on the surveyor of taxes in any case in which the appeal relates only to the rateable value of any hereditament

The clerk of the assessment committee, on receiving notice of an appeal shall forthwith serve notice thereof on the clerk of the special sessions or of the assessment sessions, as the case may require

34 The justices in special sessions and in assessment sessions respectively shall in open court, hear and determine all appeals brought before them in such order as they may respectively from time to time appoint   They may adjourn the hearing from time to time and to any day not later than the day before which all appeals to them are required by this Act to be heard and in the case of assessment sessions for the purpose of obtaining the decision of any superior

(margin note: Notice of appeal to special or assessment sessions)

(margin note: Sessions to hear and determine appeals and alter list accordingly)

[1] The Valuation (Metropolis) Amendment Act, 1854 (47 & 18 Vict, c 5), s 3 providing for the inclusion of several assessments under one notice of appeal.

court to any day necessary for that purpose, and if from accident or mistake due notice of appeal has not been given, or if an additional notice of appeal appears to be required, they may, if they think it just, order notice of appeal to be given. They may confirm or alter the valuation list, so far as it is questioned by the appeal, in such manner as they think just, but shall not make any alteration in contravention of this Act. The clerk of the assessment committee or some deputy allowed by the assessment committee shall attend the court with the valuation list to which the appeal relates, and any alteration shall be made by the justice acting as chairman of the sessions in that list, and the said justice shall place his initials against such alteration.

Making of valuation list where none approved 35. If it appears to the justices in assessment sessions on any appeal that there is no approved valuation list for some parish, they may appoint some proper person (with such remuneration as they may appoint) to make a valuation list. Such person shall have for that purpose the same powers and duties as overseers.

The valuation list so made shall be deposited and otherwise made known to the persons interested in such manner as the court may direct, but in manner as near as may be as is provided in this Act with respect to the list originally made.

The costs of making such valuation list shall be paid by the assessment committee who failed to approve the list, and shall be deemed part of their expenses under the principal Act.

Assessment sessions may on application of parts to appoint order valuation 36. If any of the parties to the appeal apply to the justices in assessment sessions to direct a valuation of any hereditament with respect to which any appeal may be made, and if such applicant or applicants give such security as the court think proper to pay the costs of the valuation, the court may, in their discretion, appoint some proper person to make such valuation.

Adjournment to receive valuation list or valuation 37. Where the court appoint a person to make a valuation list or a valuation, they may fix some subsequent day, either before or after the day before which all appeals are required by this Act to be heard, for receiving such valuation list or valuation and may adjourn the hearing to that day.

Valuation to be in writing 38. The person so appointed to make a valuation shall make his valuation in writing signed by him, showing the particulars of the hereditaments comprised therein, and the amounts at which he has valued the same respectively.

Person making it to have power to enter Such person may at all reasonable times with or without assistants enter upon any of the hereditaments directed to be valued and may do thereon all acts necessary for completing the valuation.

Costs of appeal 39. The costs of any appeal, including the cost of any such valuation as aforesaid shall be in the discretion of the justices in special or assessment sessions (as the case may be), and shall be awarded by them to be paid by such parties to the appeal, and in such proportion as they think just

Costs (including the costs of making a valuation) so ordered to be paid may be recovered as if they had been awarded by a court of quarter sessions, and when ordered to be paid by parties other than a ratepayer shall be paid as in this Act mentioned

46. The same proceedings may be had by special case and certiorari or otherwise, for questioning any decision of the justices in assessment sessions, as may be had for questioning any decision of the justices in general or quarter sessions provided that every such certiorari shall be sued out within three months after the decision is given

At any time after notice given of appeal under this Act to the assessment sessions, it shall be lawful for the parties, by consent and by order of any judge of one of the superior courts of common law at Westminster, to state the facts of the case in the form of a special case for the opinion of any of those courts, and to agree that a judgment in conformity with the decision of that court, and for such costs as that court may adjudge, may be entered on the application of either party at the meeting of the justices in assessment sessions next or next but one after such decision has been given, and such judgment may be entered accordingly, and shall be of the same effect in all respects as if the same had been given by the assessment sessions upon an appeal duly brought before them and adjourned, and the justices shall, if necessary, hold a sessions or an adjourned sessions for this purpose

Notice in writing of the decision of any superior court in pursuance of this section shall be served by the clerk of the assessment sessions on the assessment committee which approved the list questioned on the appeal to such court

Appeal from decision of assessment sessions on points of law

47. Notice of every alteration in the valuation list, which alteration is made in consequence of any decision on any appeal to the special sessions, assessment sessions or a superior court shall as soon as possible be sent in writing by the clerk of the assessment committee to the overseers and surveyor of taxes of the parish and district respectively to which the list which is so altered relates, and such alteration shall be entered by the clerk of the assessment committee and by the overseers on the duplicates respectively deposited with them.

Notice of every alteration in the total of the gross and rateable value of any valuation list, which alteration is made in consequence of any decision on any appeal to the assessment sessions or a superior court, shall as soon as possible be sent, in writing by the clerk of the assessment committee to the clerk of the managers of the Metropolitan Asylum District, and the clerk of such managers shall send in writing such altered total to every person and body of persons who has power to levy or make any rate or assessment or require any contribution based on such total.

Notice of alteration of list to be sent to overseers

Times for Proceedings

Times within
which pro
ceedings in
making
valuation list
are to be done

42 With respect to the times within which proceedings under this Act and the Acts incorporated herewith are to be done, the following provisions shall have effect, that is to say,

(1) The overseers shall make and deposit the valuation list before the first of June in the first year after the passing of this Act

(2) The overseers shall transmit the valuation list to the assessment committee not sooner than fourteen and not later than seventeen days after notice is given of the deposit of such list

(3) Notice of any objection by any person other than the surveyor of taxes and the overseers shall be given before the expiration of twenty-five days after the list is deposited

(4) The assessment committee shall revise the valuation list before the first of October in the same year, and before the same day, but not less than sixteen days after the transmission of the list to them by the overseers shall hold a meeting for hearing objections to such list

(5) The assessment committee shall give notice of a meeting for hearing objections to a list not less than sixteen days before such meeting

(6) Notice of objection with respect to any list by the surveyor of taxes and by the overseers shall be given not less than seven days before the meeting at which objections to such list will be heard by the assessment committee

(7) The assessment committee shall send the valuation list to be re deposited within three days after it is approved by them, and shall appoint a day not less than fourteen nor more than twenty-eight days after such re-deposit for hearing objections to the alterations, of which objections seven days' notice shall be given by the objector

(8) The assessment committee shall finally approve and send the valuation list to the overseers, and the clerk of the managers of the metropolitan asylum district, before the first of November in the same year

(9) Notices of appeal to special sessions shall be given on or before the twenty-first day of November in the same year

(10.) The justices may hold the special sessions at any time after the thirtieth of November in the same year which will enable them to determine all appeals before the ensuing first of January.

(11) The clerk of the said managers shall send out the printed totals before the first of December in the same year, and shall return the valuation list to the assessment committee not sooner than fourteen or later than twenty-one days after the totals are sent out

(12) Notices of appeals to assessment sessions shall be given on or before the fourteenth of January in the same year

(13) The justices may hold the assessment sessions at any time after the first of February in the same year, which will enable them to determine all appeals (except where a valuation list or valuation is ordered) before the ensuing thirty-first of March

(14) Notice of the times at which the assessment sessions will be held at each place shall be given by the clerk ten days at least before the first court is held

Effect of Valuation List

43 The valuation list as approved by the assessment committee, and, if altered on any appeal under this Act to any sessions or a superior court, as so altered shall come into force at the beginning of the year (commencing on the sixth of April) succeeding that in which it is made, and shall last for five years, subject to any alterations that may be made by any supplemental or provisional list as hereinafter mentioned

Duration of valuation list

44 Notwithstanding any appeal under this Act which may be pending at the commencement of the year, the valuation list shall come into force unaltered, and every assessment, contribution, rate and tax in respect of which the valuation list is conclusive shall be made, required, levied, and paid in accordance with such valuation list, and where in consequence of the decision on any appeal under this Act to assessment sessions or a superior court an alteration in such valuation list is made which alters the amount of the assessment, contribution rate, or tax levied thereunder, the difference, if too much has been paid, shall be repaid or allowed, and if too little, shall be deemed to be arrears of the assessment, contribution, rate or tax (except so far as any penalty is incurred on account of arrears) and shall be paid and recovered accordingly

Rate to be levied notwithstanding appeal

45 The valuation list for the time being in force shall be deemed to have been duly made in accordance with this Act and the Acts incorporated herewith, and shall for all or any of the purposes in this section mentioned be conclusive evidence of the gross value and of the rateable value of the several hereditaments included therein, and of the fact that all hereditaments required to be inserted therein have been so inserted; that is to say,

Valuation list to be conclusive for purposes of certain rates, taxes and qualification

(1) For the purpose of any of the following rates which are made during the year that the list is in force, namely, the county rate, the metropolitan police rate, the church rate, the highway rate, the poor rate, the police, sewers, consolidated and other rates in the City of London, the sewers, lighting, general, and other rates, levied by order of district board or vestries, the main drainage improvement and other rates, and sums

assessed on any part of the metropolis by the Metropolitan Board of Works assessments for contributions under the Metropolitan Poor Act, 1867, and every other rate, assessment, and contribution levied, made, and required in the metropolis on the basis of value.

(2) For the purpose of any of the following taxes which become chargeable during the year that the list is in force, namely,

(a) The tax on houses levied under the House Tax Act, 1851, and the Acts therein incorporated or referred to.

(b) Any tax assessed in pursuance of the Income Tax Act, 1842, and any Acts continuing or amending the same, on any lands, tenements, and hereditaments in all cases where the tax is charged on the gross value, and not on profits.

(3) For the purpose of determining, so far as it is applicable, the value of any hereditament included therein for the purposes of the Acts relating to the sale of exciseable liquors, to the qualification of a juror, to the qualification of a vestryman, and an auditor of accounts under the Metropolis Management Act, 1855, and to the qualification of a guardian and of a manager under the "Poor Law Amendment Act, 1834," or the "Metropolitan Poor Act, 1867," at any time at which such value is required to be ascertained.

And in construing the Metropolitan Police Act, 1829, and the Acts amending the same, the last valuation for the time being acted upon in assessing the county rate shall be deemed to mean the valuation list for the time being in force.

And in construing the County Rates Act, 1852, and Acts referring to the valuation, estimate, basis, or standard for the county rate the valuation, estimate, basis, or standard shall be deemed to be the rateable value stated in such list.

And in construing the House Tax Act 1851, and the Acts therein incorporated or referred to, the full and just yearly rent shall be deemed to be the gross value stated in such list.

And in construing the Income Tax Act, 1842, and any Acts continuing or amending that Act, with respect to Schedules A and B thereof, annual value shall be deemed to mean the gross value stated in such list.[1]

Revision of Valuation List

46. Every valuation list shall be revised in manner directed by this Act, and such revision in every period of five years (the first of such periods beginning with the sixth of April one thousand eight hundred and seventy-one) shall be conducted as follows:

Marginal notes:
30 & 31 Vict., c. 6
14 & 15 Vict., c. 36, etc.
5 & 6 Vict., c. 35, etc.
18 & 19 Vict., c. 120
4 & 5 Will IV, c. 76
30 & 31 Vict. c. 6
10 Geo IV, c. 44
15 & 16 Vict., c. 81, etc.
14 & 15 Vict., c. 36, etc.
5 & 6 Vict., c. 35, etc.
Mode of revising valuation list

---

[1] See also The Financial Act, 1894 (57 & 58 Vict., c. 30) s. 5.

(1) In each of the first four years of such period a supplemental list shall, if necessary, be made out in the same form as the valuation list, and shall show all the alterations which have taken place during the preceding twelve months in any of the matters stated in the valuation list, but shall contain only the hereditaments affected by such alterations. If no alteration has taken place which makes a supplemental list necessary, the overseers shall send a certificate to that effect to the assessment committee in place of such list, which certificate may be in the form contained in the second schedule to this Act

(2) In the fifth year of every such period the overseers shall make a new valuation list

(3.) The same regulations shall be observed and the same proceedings shall be had in the case of a supplemental list, and a new valuation list as are directed by this Act and the Acts incorporated herewith in the case of the valuation list made in the first year after the passing of this Act

(4) A supplemental list and a new valuation list shall come into force at the beginning of the year succeeding that in which they are respectively made, in the same manner and subject to the same conditions as the valuation list made in the first year after the passing of this Act

(5) In each of the last four years of such period the valuation list which was in force on the day before the commencement of each such year, together with and as altered by the supplemental list, if any, which comes into force at the commencement of such year shall be the valuation list which is in force during that year

(6) A new valuation list when it comes into force shall supersede the valuation list which was in force during the fifth year of such period

47 If in the course of any year the value of any hereditament is increased by the addition thereto or erection thereon of any building, or is from any cause increased or reduced in value, the following provisions shall have effect

Provision for valuing a house built between the times at which the valuation list is made

(1.) The overseers of the parish in which such hereditament is situate may, and on the written requisition of the assessment committee or of any ratepayer of the union or of the surveyor of taxes for the district shall send to the assessment committee a provisional list containing the gross and rateable value as so increased or reduced of such hereditament

(2) A copy of the requisition shall be sent by the person making it to the clerk of the assessment committee, and if within fourteen days after the requisition has been served on the overseers they make default in sending such provisional list he shall forthwith summon the assessment committee, and the

assessment committee shall appoint a person to make such provisional list, in the same manner as is in this Act provided in the case of the overseers failing to transmit a valuation list

(3) On the receipt of the list the clerk of the assessment committee shall serve on the surveyor of taxes for the district a copy of the list, and shall serve on the occupier of any hereditament to which the list relates a copy of so much thereof as relates to that hereditament Every copy shall be accompanied by a notice specifying a day, being not less than fourteen days after the date of the service of the notice, on or before which any objection to the provisional list may be made, and stating the mode in which an objection is to be made. Such copy and notice shall be served in the same way as notices by an assessment committee are served

(4) An objection may be made to any such provisional list by the said occupier, and by the surveyor of taxes, or by either of them, by notice thereof in writing being served on the clerk of the assessment committee, on the overseers, on the surveyor of taxes, and on the occupier, or on such of them as the case may require

(5) The clerk of the assessment committee, on the receipt of the notice of any objection, shall forthwith summon a meeting of the committee, and give notice of the time and place of such meeting to the overseers, to the surveyor of taxes, and the occupier

(6.) The committee shall hear and determine on the objection in the same manner as if it were an objection to a valuation list, and may make such order as they think just

(7) If no objection is made, then on the expiration of the time for making objections, or if an objection is made, then as soon as the assessment committee have determined on the objection the assessment committee shall cause a copy to be made of the provisional list, with any alteration made in it by the committee, and shall return the list and the copy thereof, after being dated and signed by their clerk, to the overseers

(8) A provisional list signed as aforesaid, shall have operation from the date of the service by the clerk of the assessment committee of a copy of the list and notice on the occupier, and shall continue in force until the first list (supplemental or other) which is subsequently made comes into force

(9) Upon a provisional list coming into operation the overseers shall make such entries in the rate book for the then current poor rate as will bring the same into conformity with such list, and shall also enter therein the date at which such list is to come into operation, and shall charge the occupier of such hereditament with a proper proportion of such current poor

rate, regard being had to the time which has elapsed between the making of such rate and the said date and to the rateable value stated in such provisional list, and such occupier shall be considered as actually rated for such sum from the said date and be liable to pay the same, and the same may be enforced accordingly

(10) A provisional list during the time that it is in force shall be deemed to form part of the valuation list for the time being in force, and shall (so far as is necessary) be substitute for so much of that valuation list as relates to the same hereditament, and every rate and tax in respect of which the valuation list is conclusive, which are respectively made or charged after the provisional list comes into force, and the proportion of the current rate charged is before provided in this section shall be levied accordingly but if when the next revision of the valuation list takes place the list as approved and altered on appeal contains a smaller value for the hereditament comprised in a provisional list than the value stated in such provisional list, the amount of rate or tax which has been overpaid in consequence of the larger value having been stated shall be returned or allowed

(11) Nothing in this section shall affect the value on which any rate is made or sum is assessed or contribution required which is made, assessed, or required on the totals of the gross or rateable value of parishes or unions

Expenses

48 The costs of an appeal awarded against or incurred by any assessment committee or overseers shall be deemed to be expenses incurred under this Act and the Acts incorporated herewith, and shall be raised and paid accordingly. *(Costs of appeal, etc)*

Any costs or expenses awarded against or incurred by any surveyor of taxes shall be defrayed in the same manner as expenses are directed to be defrayed by the Acts relating to the taxes in respect of which the Valuation List is made conclusive.

49. The Commissioners of Inland Revenue may make such allowances as they think fit for remunerating any person employed by them in the execution of this Act and for the discharge of any costs or expenses incurred by him *(Allowances by Inland Revenue for expenses)*

50 The expenses of the assessment sessions and such remuneration as the Poor Law Board may from time to time allow to the clerk of the managers of the metropolitan asylum district, the clerk of the assessment sessions, and persons appointed to assist the assessment sessions as provided by the Act, and such costs and expenses incurred by such clerks and persons under this Act as the Poor Law Board may allow, after such audit as the Poor Law Board may direct, shall *(Expenses)*

be paid by the receiver of the Metropolitan Common Poor Fund out of any monies for the time being in his hands, and shall be paid at such times and in such manner and upon such precept of the Poor Law Board as the Poor Law Board may from time to time prescribe, and the Poor Law Board may require contributions for the purpose of raising such remuneration, expenses, and costs

Rules for formation of Valuation List

Form and contents of valuation list

51 The valuation list shall be made out in the form given in the second schedule to this Act [1]

5 & 6 Vict. c. 35

The overseers shall not include in such valuation list any hereditaments (except tithes or payment in lieu of tithes) which are charged according to Rule two in section sixty of the Income Tax Act, 1842 but shall include tithes and payments in lieu of tithes and every hereditament in their parish, and shall enter every hereditament in the valuation list in accordance with the classes mentioned in the third schedule to this Act so that the deductions to be made in ascertaining the rateable value may be calculated in accordance with that schedule

Deductions for rateable value

52 The per-centage or rate of deductions to be made from the gross value in calculating the rateable value for the purposes of this Act shall not exceed the amounts in the third schedule to this Act so far as the same are applicable.

Amount of gross value specified by the surveyor of taxes to be inserted unless disproved

53 When a surveyor of taxes gives notice of objection or of appeal, the amount specified in the notice as being in his judgment the gross value of any hereditament referred to in the notice shall be inserted in the valuation list by the assessment committee, special sessions, or assessment sessions, unless it is proved to the satisfaction of the assessment committee, special sessions or assessment sessions, that such amount ought not to be so inserted

Saving of exemptions and exceptional principles of valuation

54 Nothing contained in this Act or the Acts incorporated herewith shall affect any exemption or deduction from or allowance out of any rate or tax whatever, or any privilege of or provision for being rated or taxed on any exceptional principle of valuation

Returns

Occupier to make returns

55 In every year in which a new valuation list is made or in the month of March preceding any such year, every person [2] who is liable to be charged with any rate or tax in respect of which the valuation list is made conclusive shall, when required, make to the overseers of

5 & 6 Vict. c. 35

his parish such statement or return as a person chargeable under the Income Tax Act, 1842 and the Acts amending the same is bound to make

---

[1] See now The Agricultural Rates Order 1896, Schedule W 2.

[2] See also The Valuation (Metropolis) Amendment Act, 1884 (47 & 48 Vict. c. 5) s. 2

56 For the purpose of securing the proper making of such returns, the surveyor of taxes shall in the month of February preceding send to the overseers of each parish in his district a sufficient number of printed forms and notices and the overseers, within a month after the receipt thereof, shall serve a notice and form on every person in their parish required by this Act to make a return, and every person required by this Act to make a return shall make it within twenty-one days after the service of a notice and form on him

The forms and notices shall be such as are prescribed by the Income Tax Act or the Acts amending the same, or as the Treasury may from time to time prescribe, and any such form duly filled up and signed shall be deemed to be a sufficient return

The return shall be delivered to the overseers of each parish, and together with the valuation list shall be sent by them to the surveyor of taxes, and by the surveyor of taxes to the assessment committee

57 An assessment committee may, by order, require any person who is the owner or occupier or reputed owner or occupier of any hereditament in their union to send them a return in writing of all or any of the following things, viz, of the rent receivable or payable by him (as the case may be) for such hereditament, and of the person entitled to any tithe rentcharge charged on such hereditament, and of the amount of the same, and of the several persons by whom any tithe rentcharge is paid to him, and of the amounts paid by each such person, and of any other particulars respecting such hereditament as are required for the due execution of this Act and the Acts incorporated herewith   And every such owner or occupier shall obey such order within fourteen days after the service thereof on him

58 If any person wilfully refuses or neglects to make any return lawfully required under this Act within the times respectively limited by this Act in that behalf, he shall be liable, on summary conviction, to a penalty not exceeding five pounds

If any person wilfully makes or causes to be made a false return, he shall be liable, on summary conviction to a penalty not exceeding ten pounds

Miscellaneous.

59 With respect to any parish which is not included in any union of parishes, and in which there is no board of guardians, the following provisions shall have effect

> (1) The assessment committee of the adjoining unions shall act as the assessment committee of that parish, and where there is more than one such adjoining union the Poor Law Board shall determine the assessment committee which is to act for such parish

> (2) Every such parish shall, for the purposes of this Act and the Acts incorporated herewith but not for any other purpose, be deemed to be within the union of the assessment committee which acts for it

Surveyors of taxes to supply notices and forms for returns to overseers, who are to serve them

5 & 6 Vict c 35

Assessment committee may require returns from owner and occupier

Penalty for no, or false returns

Provision for cases where no guardians and where no overseers

(3) The masters of the bench, treasurer, governors or other body of persons in such parish, may, at the time appointed for the election of an assessment committee, appoint a person to be a member of such assessment committee in addition to the number elected under this Act and the Acts incorporated herewith

(4) Where there are no overseers the assessment committee shall appoint some person to perform the duties of the overseers under this Act and the Acts incorporated herewith, and may award him such remuneration as they think fit, and the person so appointed shall perform those duties, and shall, for that purpose have all the powers of overseers

(5) A proportionate share of the expenses of the assessment committee under this Act and the Acts incorporated herewith, and any remuneration paid to or expenses incurred by the person appointed by them under this or any other section to make a valuation list shall be charged on such parish, and the sums so charged shall be paid by the masters of the bench, treasurer, governor, or other body of persons, and section sixty-six, sixty-seven, and sixty-eight of the Metropolitan Poor Act, 1867, shall apply to such sums in the same manner as if the assessment committee and their clerk were the Poor Law Board and the receiver mentioned in those sections

30 & 31 Vict., c 6

Provision where vestry or the overseers Guardians may appoint a paid valuer to assist the assessment committee

59 Where the vestry or the guardians of any parish perform the duties of overseers with respect to a valuation list under this Act the list shall be signed by the vestry clerk or the clerk of the guardians

61 The guardians may, upon the application of the assessment committee, after notice sent in the manner required by the principal Act, appoint some competent person to assist the committee in the valuation of the hereditaments in the union for such period as they see fit, at a salary or other settled remuneration, to be paid out of the common fund

Assessment committee and overseers may give security for costs of valuation

62 Every assessment committee, with the consent of the guardians and every overseer, with the consent of the vestry of his parish, may for the purposes of any application for a valuation on any appeal, give security for paying the costs of such valuation. An assessment committee may give such security and may appear on any appeal by their clerk, and shall indemnify the said clerk against all monies, losses, and costs paid or incurred by him in consequence of such security or appearance

Use of public room for appeals, etc

63 Any room maintained out of the proceeds of any rate levied wholly or partly in the metropolis may (with the consent of the person or body corporate having the control of it) be used for hearing appeals and for other purposes of this Act

Evidence of valuation list, etc

64 A valuation list may be proved by the production of a duplicate or copy of such list purporting to be certified to be a duplicate or a true copy by the clerk of the assessment committee that approved it,

and such certificate shall state that the alterations (if any) made in the list in consequence of the decision on any appeal under this Act have been correctly made in the duplicate or copy so produced, and the clerk on application shall furnish a copy to any overseers on payment of a sum not exceeding the rate of three shillings for every hundred entries numbered separately   A provisional list may be proved by the production of a duplicate or copy thereof purporting to be certified to be a true copy by the clerk of the committee who signed it

65 All orders and notices under this Act and the Acts incorporated herewith shall be in writing or print, or partly in writing and partly in print, and if made or given by an assessment committee shall be sufficiently authenticated if signed by their clerk, and all orders, notices, and documents required by the same Acts to be served on or sent to any person or body of persons corporate or unincorporate may be either delivered to such person or the clerk of such body, or left at the usual place of abode of such person or clerk, or at the office of such clerk or body, or (if such abode or office cannot on reasonable inquiry be discovered) at the premises to which the order, notice, or document relates Service of notices, etc , by post, etc

They may also be served and sent by post, by a prepaid letter addressed to such person, or to the office of such body or to their clerk, and, if sent by post, shall be deemed to have been served and received respectively at the time when the letter containing the same would be delivered in the ordinary course of post, and in proving such service or sending it shall be sufficient to prove that the letter containing the notice was properly addressed and prepaid and put into the post

66 Any notice required by this Act to be published by the overseers shall, on the Sunday next following the receipt of such notice, or the document to which the notice refers, and the two following Sundays be published by them in the manner in which notice of a rate allowed by justices is required to be published Publication of notices by overseers

67 Where any documents are required by this Act to be deposited in the same place in a parish in which rate books are kept, every rate payer shall be at liberty to inspect and take copies of or extracts from such documents at any reasonable time, without fee or charge Inspection, etc of documents deposited with rate books

68 The duplicate of the valuation list, approved by the assessment committee, and sent to the overseers, as directed by this Act, the notices of alterations made on any appeal under this Act, and any provisional list, shall for all purposes be deemed to be part of the rate books of the parish, and shall be produced by the overseers before the justices upon any application for allowance of rates, and in any appeal under this or any other Act, and on any other occasion if so required, on which they are bound to produce such rate books, and any overseer who fails to produce such list in accordance with the provisions of this section shall be liable on summary conviction to a penalty not exceeding five pounds Valuation lists to be equivalent to rate books of parish

The duplicate of the valuation list returned to the assessment committee by the clerk of the managers of the Metropolitan Asylum District, and other documents in the possession of the assessment committee in pursuance of this Act shall be kept at the board room or other convenient place from time to time appointed by the guardians of the same union, but shall be deemed to be in the possession of the assessment committee and shall be produced by their clerk to the district auditor whenever required by him

Ratepayer etc. may inspect documents etc., in hands of clerk of managers or assessment committee

69 Any ratepayer, overseer, clerk of an assessment committee, or surveyor of taxes in the metropolis may, at all reasonable times without payment, inspect and take copies of and extracts from all valuation lists and documents which in pursuance of this Act are under the control of the clerk of the managers of the Metropolitan Asylum District or of the clerk of the assessment sessions

Any surveyor of taxes and any guardian and any overseer in a union, without payment, and any ratepayer in a union on payment of a fee not exceeding one shilling (to be carried to the common fund), may at any reasonable time inspect and take copies of and extracts from any valuation list, notices of objection, returns, and other documents in the possession or under the control of the assessment committee of that union

Any clerk of an assessment committee in the metropolis may inspect and take extracts from any valuation lists in the possession or under the control of the assessment committee of any other union in the metropolis

Any person who hinders a ratepayer, overseer, clerk of an assessment committee, or surveyor of taxes from so inspecting or taking copies of or extracts from any valuation list or document, or demands where not authorised by this Act a fee for allowing him so to do, shall be liable on summary conviction to a penalty not exceeding five pounds for each offence

[S 70 (*owner where rated to be deemed occupier*) repealed 47 & 48 Vict, c 5, s 2, which substitutes other provisions]

Amendment of error in rate by two justices

71 Any person who feels aggrieved by reason of any clerical or arithmetical error in a rate in the metropolis may apply to two justices of the peace or a magistrate sitting at any police court in the metropolitan police district, who after the applicant has given such notice to the overseers who made the rate and such persons as such justices or magistrates think just, may hear the case in like manner as in the case of summary proceedings, and amend the rate so far as respects such error

Omissions from the rate

72 Whenever the name of any person liable to be rated at the time the rate is made is omitted from any rate in the metropolis, or if any person is described in any such rate by a wrong name, the overseers may, after giving to such person seven clear days' notice of their intention apply to any two justices or any police magistrate as afore-

said, who may hear the case in like manner as in the case of summary proceedings, and insert the name so omitted, or correct the name so wrongly entered, and every such insertion and correction shall operate as if it had been part of the original rate   Provided that any person whose name is so inserted or corrected in any such rate may appeal against the same at the general quarter session of the peace which is holden next after such insertion or correction, in like manner as he might have appealed against the rate

73 Every poor rate made in the metropolis after the fifth of April one thousand eight hundred and seventy-one shall contain the particulars specified in the fourth schedule to this Act,[1] together with such other particulars as the Poor Law Board may from time to time by order direct, and the overseer shall sign the form of declaration which is given in that schedule before the rate is allowed by the justices And the justices shall not allow any rate at the foot of which the said declaration has not been added and signed

Form of rate and declaration

Any overseer who wilfully omits to make the said declaration or makes the same falsely shall be liable on summary conviction to a penalty not exceeding five pounds

74 The entry of the proceedings of the assessment committee at any meeting, and of the names of the members who attend that meeting, may be signed by the chairman of the next meeting of the committee, and every entry and minute purporting to be so signed shall be received in evidence in the same manner as if such entry or minute had been signed by the chairman of the meeting at which the proceedings took place, and the members were present

Amendment of 25 & 26 Vict , c 103, s 11

75 Nothing in this Act shall in any way alter or affect the mode of valuing or taxing any hereditament which is not included in any valuation list, or which is chargeable according to the profits and not according to the gross value, or the mode of charging the occupiers of land subject to a tithe rentcharge in respect of such tithe rentcharge.

Saving of powers to value property not included in a valuation list

76 Where for the purposes of the Acts relating to the duty on inhabited houses, or to the duties charged under Schedule B of the Income Tax Act, 1842, or to the sale of exciseable liquors, it is necessary to make a separate valuation of any hereditament by reason of its not being separately valued in any valuation list, the value of such hereditament shall be ascertained in the same manner as if this Act had not passed

Separate assessment of houses for purposes of house duty, income tax, and Licensing Acts

REPEAL OF ACTS

77.   So much of any   Acts, *Repeal* whether public or local and personal, as authorizes any valuation of hereditaments to be made for the purposes of any rate or tax in respect of which the valuation list is by this Act made

---

[1] See now The Agricultural Rates Order 1896, Schedule Y 2

conclusive, are hereby repealed, where they relate only to the metropolis absolutely, and in other cases so far as they relate to the metropolis . . . .

[First Schedule omitted because the Acts to which short titles are therein given are referred to in this Act by the short titles given by 59 & 60 Vict., c 14]

SECOND SCHEDULE

[Sections 14, 51]

Part I

VALUATION LIST for [*the parish or place for which the list is made*] in the Metropolitan Union of   [*or not being in Union*] in the County of

Number	
Name of occupier.	
Name of owner	
Description of property	
No of class	
Name or situation of property	
Extent	
Gross value as estimated by overseers	
Gross value as estimated by surveyor of taxes.	
Rate of deduction per cent	
Rateable value	
Gross value as finally determined by Assessment Committee	
Rateable value as finally determined by Assessment Committee	

Signed this   day of

A B } Overseers of the Poor of the
C D } parish aforesaid

We do hereby approve the above valuation list, and certify that in determining the gross and rateable value of the above hereditaments, the provisions of the Valuation (Metropolis) Act 1869, have been duly complied with

Signed this   day of

$\left.\begin{array}{l} A\ B \\ C\ D \\ E\ F \end{array}\right\}$ Members of the Assessment Committee of the Union

Note —The two last of the above columns (for gross and rateable value as determined by Assessment Committee) must be filled up, and the totals of those columns must be added up after the objections to the alterations have (if any) been heard, and before the list is finally approved

---

Part II

Form of Certificate where no supplemental list is sent

We, the Overseers of the parish of   , do hereby certify that no alteration has taken place in the matters stated in the valuation list of this parish which renders a supplemental list necessary.

$\left.\begin{array}{l} A.B. \\ C\ D \end{array}\right\}$ Overseers of the parish of

THIRD SCHEDULE.

[SECTIONS 51 & 52]

Showing the several classes into which the hereditaments inserted in a valuation list under this Act are to be divided

	Maximum rate of deductions
	Per cent or proportion
Class 1 Houses and buildings, or either of them, without land other than gardens where the gross value is under 20*l*	25, or ¼th
„ 2 Houses and buildings without land other than gardens and pleasure grounds valued therewith for the purpose of inhabited house duty where the gross value is 20*l*. and under 40*l*	20, or ⅕th
„ 3 Houses and buildings without land other than gardens and pleasure grounds valued therewith for the purpose of inhabited house duty where the gross value is 40*l* or upwards. .	16⅔, or ⅙th
„ 4 Buildings without land which are not liable to inhabited house duty and are of a gross value of 20*l* and under 40*l*. .	20, or ⅕th.
„ 5 Buildings without land which are not liable to inhabited house duty and are of a gross value of 40*l* or upwards	16⅔, or ⅙th
„ 6 Land with buildings not houses	10, or 1/10th
7. Land without buildings	5, or 1/20th
„ 8. Mills and manufactories	33⅓, or ⅓rd
9. Tithes, tithe commutation rent-charge, and other payments in lieu of tithe	To be determined in each case according to the circumstances and the general principles of law
„ 10 Railways, canals, docks, tolls, waterworks, and gasworks	
„ 11 Rateable hereditaments not included in any of the foregoing classes	

The maximum rate of deductions prescribed in this schedule shall not apply to houses or buildings let out in separate tenements, but the rate of deductions in such cases shall be determined as in classes 9, 10 and 11

FOURTH SCHEDULE

[SECTION 73]

FORM OF RATE [1]

RATE for the RELIEF of the POOR of the Parish of
    in the   Union, and for other purposes charge-
able thereon, according to law made this   day of
in the year of our Lord 18 , after the rate of   in the
pound, which is estimated to meet all the expenses for the above
purposes which will be incurred before the   of   next

No.	Name of occupier	Name of owner	Description of property rated	Name or Situation of property	Rateable value	Rate at in the pound

DECLARATION TO BE ADDED TO THE RATE.

We, the undersigned, do hereby declare that one of us, or some
person on our behalf, has examined and compared the several
particulars in the respective columns of the above rate with the
valuation list made under the authority of the Valuation (Metropolis)
Act, 1869, and now in force in this parish (or township) and the
several hereditaments are, to the best of our belief, rated according
to the value appearing in such valuation list, and do declare that the
total of the above rate amounts to   pounds
shillings and   pence

    ———————————— } Churchwardens

    ———————————— } Overseers

[1] See now The Agricultural Rates Order, 1896, Schedule Y 2

FIFTH SCHEDULE [1]

[SECTION 77]

DATE OF ACT.	TITLE OF ACT.
25 & 26 Vict., c. 102 ..	The Metropolis Management } impart Amendment Act, 1862 .. } namely,
	So much of Sections six, seven and thirteen as authorized or relates to the ascertaining the value of any hereditament with respect to the value of which the valuation list is conclusive, and so much of any Act as applies the provisions hereby repealed

1 Repealed 46 & 47 Vict., c. 39 (S.L R) except as to the repeal of so much of any Act is applies the provisions hereby repealed of 25 & 26 Vict., c 102

THE RATING ACT, 1874

(37 & 38 Vict., cap 54)

AN ACT TO AMEND THE LAW RESPECTING THE LIABILITY AND VALUATION OF CERTAIN PROPERTY FOR THE PURPOSE OF RATES.

[7th August, 1874.]

1. This Act may be cited as " The Rating Act, 1874 "   *Short title*

2. This Act shall not apply to Scotland or Ireland.   *Extent of Act*

3. [*Recital of 43 Eliz , c 2, which Act and the Acts amending the same are in this Act referred to as the Poor Rate Acts*]

The Poor Rate Acts shall extend to the following hereditaments in like manner as if they were mentioned in the Poor Relief Act, 1601 , that is to say,   *Abolition of certain exemptions from rating 43 Eliz., c 2*

> (1.) To land used for a plantation or a wood or for the growth of saleable underwood, and not subject to any right of common
>
> (2.) To rights of fowling of shooting, of taking or killing game or rabbits, and of fishing when severed from the occupation of the land , and
>
> (3) To mines of every kind not mentioned in the recited Act

4. The gross and rateable value of any land used for a plantation or a wood, or for the growth of saleable underwood, shall be estimated as follows —   *Valuation of land used as plantation, etc*

> (*a*) If the land is used only for a plantation or a wood, the value shall be estimated as if the land instead of being a plantation or a wood were let and occupied in its natural and unimproved state
>
> (*b*) If the land is used for the growth of saleable underwood, the value shall be estimated as if the land were let for that purpose
>
> (*c*) If the land is used both for a plantation or a wood and for the growth of saleable underwood the value shall be estimated either as if the land were used only for a plantation or a wood, or as if the land were used only for the growth of the saleable underwood growing thereon, as the assessment committee may determine

5 Where the rateable value of any land used for a plantation or a wood, or both for a plantation or wood and for the growth of saleable underwood, is increased by reason of the same being estimated in accordance with this Act, the occupier of that land under any lease or agreement made before the commencement of this Act, may, during the continuance of the lease or agreement, deduct from his rent any poor or other local rate or any portion thereof, which is paid by him in respect of such increase of rateable value, and every assessment committee, on the application of such occupier, shall certify in the valuation list or otherwise the fact and amount of such increase   *Deduction of rate by tenant of plantation, etc*

Valuation and rating of rights of shooting etc

6 —(1.) Where any right of fowling, or of shooting, or of taking or killing game or rabbits, or of fishing (hereinafter referred to as a right of sporting) is severed from the occupation of the land and is not let, and the owner of such right receives rent for the land, the said right shall not be separately valued or rated, but the gross and rateable value of the land shall be estimated as if the said right were not severed and in such case if the rateable value is increased by reason of its being so estimated, but not otherwise, the occupier of the land may (unless he has specifically contracted to pay such rate in the event of an increase) deduct from his rent such portion of any poor or other local rate as is paid by him in respect of such increase and every assessment committee, on the application of the occupier, shall certify in the valuation list or otherwise the fact and amount of such increase

(2) Where any right of sporting, when severed from the occupation of the land, is let, either the owner or the lessee thereof, according as the persons making the rate determine, may be rated as the occupier thereof

(3) Subject to the foregoing provisions of this section the owner of any right of sporting, when severed from the occupation of the land, may be rated as the occupier thereof

(4) For the purposes of this section, the person who, if the right of sporting is not let, is entitled to exercise the right, or who, if the right is let, is entitled to receive the rent for the same shall be deemed to be the owner of the right

Gross and rateable value of tin, lead and copper mines

7 Where a tin, lead or copper mine is occupied under a lease or leases granted without fine on a reservation, wholly or partly of dues or rent, the gross value of the mine shall be taken to be the annual amount of the whole of the dues payable in respect thereof during the year ending on the thirty-first day of December preceding the date at which the valuation list is made in addition to the annual amount of any fixed rent reserved for the same which may not be paid or satisfied by such dues

The rateable annual value of such mine shall be the same as the gross value thereof, except that where the person receiving the dues or rent is liable for repairs, insurance or other expenses necessary to maintain the mine in a state to command the annual amount of dues or rent, the average annual cost of the repairs, insurance, and other expenses for which he is so liable shall be deducted from the gross value for the purpose of calculating the rateable value

In the following cases, namely —

1 Where any such mine is occupied under a lease granted wholly or partly on a fine , and

2. Where any such mine is occupied and worked by the owner; and

3. In the case of any other such mine which is not excepted from the provisions of this Act and to which the foregoing provisions of this section do not apply,

the gross and rateable annual value of the mine shall be taken to be the annual amount of the dues or dues and rent at which the mine might be reasonably expected to let without fine on a lease of the ordinary duration, according to the usage of the country, if the tenant undertook to pay all tenant's rates and taxes and tithe rentcharge, and also the repairs, insurance, and other expenses necessary to maintain the mine in a state to command such annual amount of dues or dues and rent

The purser, secretary, and chief managing agent for the time being of any tin, lead, or copper mine or any of them, may if the overseers or other rating authority think fit be rated as the occupier thereof.

In this section—

The term " mine," when a mine is occupied under a lease, includes the underground workings and the engines, machinery, workshops, tramways, and other plant, buildings (not being dwelling-houses), and works and service of land occupied in connexion with and for the purposes of the mine, and situate within the boundaries of the land comprised in the lease or leases under which the due or dues and rent are payable or reserved

The term " dues " means dues, royalty, or toll, either in money or partly in money and partly in kind, and the amount of dues which are reserved in kind means the value of such dues

The term " lease " means lease or sett, or license to work, or agreement for a lease or sett, or license to work

The term " fine " means fine premium or foregift, or other payment or consideration in the nature thereof

8 Where any poor or other local rate which at the commencement of this Act any lessee licensee, or grantee of a mine is exempt from being rated to in respect of such mine, becomes payable by him in respect of such mine during the continuance of his lease grant or license, or before the arrival of the period at which the amount of the rent, royalty, or dues is liable to revision or re adjustment, he may (unless he has specifically contracted to pay such rate in the event of the abolition of the said exemption) deduct from any rent, royalty, or dues payable by him one half of any such rate paid by him *(margin: Deduction of rate by tenant of mine)*

Provided that he shall not deduct any sum exceeding what one half of the rate in the pound of such poor or other local rate would amount to if calculated upon the rent, royalty, or dues so payable by him

9 Where any occupier lessee, licensee, grantee, or other person is authorised by this Act to deduct any rate or sum in respect of a rate from any rent, royalty, or dues payable by him, then— *(margin: General provision as to deduction of rates)*

(1) Any payment so authorised to be deducted shall be a good discharge for such amount of rent, royalty, or dues is is equal to the amount of such payment and shall be allowed accordingly.

(2) Any payment so authorised to be deducted may be recovered as an ordinary debt from the person to whom the rent, royalty, or dues may be payable

(3) The person receiving the rent, royalty, or dues shall have the same right of appeal and objection with reference to the rate and to the valuation of the hereditament in respect of which the rate is payable as he would have if he were the occupier of such hereditament

Liability of property to local rates as well as poor rates 10 The hereditaments to which the Poor Rate Acts are extended by this Act, and which are thus made rateable to the relief of the poor, shall be rateable to all local rates in like manner as if the Poor Rate Acts had always extended to such hereditaments

Commencement of Act 11 This Act shall come into operation on the sixth day of April, one thousand eight hundred and seventy-five, and the expression "commencement of this Act" shall in this Act be construed accordingly

As to provisions of Sanitary Acts as defined by 35 & 36 Vict c 79 12 The provision of the Sanitary Acts as defined by the ¹Public Health Act, 1872, with respect to any special assessment of wood lands for the purpose of any rate under those Acts shall be deemed to extend to and include land used for a plantation or a wood or for the growth of saleable underwood, or for both such purposes, and made rateable by this Act to the poor rate

Saving as to mine where dues payable in kind 13 Nothing in this Act shall apply to a mine of which the royalty or dues are for the time being wholly reserved in kind, or to the owner or occupier thereof

[S 14 repealed, 46 & 47 Vict c 39 (S L R)]

Definitions of terms 15 In this Act, unless the context otherwise requires —

The term "gross value" has the same meaning as gross estimated rental in the Union Assessment Committee Act, 1862

25 & 26 Vict c 103 s 15 The term "local rate" means any county rate, borough rate, highway rate, and other local rate leviable upon property rateable to the relief of the poor

The term "valuation list" means, as regards any parish or place for which there is no valuation list the poor rate

The term "assessment committee" means, in relation to any parish or place where there is no assessment committee, the persons having power to make and assess the poor rate in such parish or place

---

¹ This Act is repealed 38 & 39 Vict c 55, s 343 see s 343 54 & 55 Vict, c 76 s 142, see ss 7

THE UNION ASSESSMENT ACT, 1880
(43 & 44 Vict, cap 7)

AN ACT TO EXTEND THE UNION ASSESSMENT COMMITTEE ACTS TO
SINGLE PARISHES UNDER SEPARATE BOARDS OF GUARDIANS

[*19th July, 1880*]

[*Preamble recites 25 & 26 Vict, c 103, s 45; 25 & 26 Vict c 103;
4 & 5 Will IV, c 76*]

1. This Act may be cited as the Union Assessment Act, 1880, and
together with the Union Assessment Committee Act, 1862, and the
Union Assessment Committee Amendment Act, 1864, may be cited as
the Union Assessment Acts, 1862 to 1880. *Short title 25 & 26 Vict, c 103 27 & 28 Vict, c 39*

2 Section forty-five of the Union Assessment Committee Act, 1862,
shall apply to a parish which is not included in a union of parishes,
and in which the relief of the poor is administered by a board of
guardians elected under the Poor Law Amendment Act, 1834, or under
any local Act, in like manner as near as may be as it applies to any
union or incorporation for the relief of the poor formed under a local
Act, and the Union Assessment Committee Act, 1862, and the Acts
amending the same, shall be construed accordingly, and in relation to
any such single parish the expression "common fund" in the said
Acts shall be construed to mean the money applicable for the relief of
the poor *Application of 25 & 26 Vict, c 103, s 45, to single parishes under separate boards of guardians 4 & 5 Will IV c 76 25 & 26 Vict, c 103*

3 This Act shall not extend to the Metropolis as defined by the
Valuation (Metropolis) Act, 1869 *Extent 32 & 33 Vict, c 67*

THE POOR RATE ASSESSMENT AND COLLECTION
ACT, 1869, AMENDMENT ACT, 1882
(45 & 46 Vict cap 20)

AN ACT TO AMEND THE POOR RATE ASSESSMENT AND COLLECTION
ACT 1869

[*3rd July, 1882*]

1 This Act shall be called the Poor Rate Assessment and Collection Act 1869, Amendment Act, 1882. *Short title*

2 This Act and the Poor Rate Assessment and Collection Act,
1869, as amended, shall be read as one Act *Interpretation 32 & 33 Vict c 41*

3 The provisions of the sixteenth section of the Poor Rate Assessment and Collection Act, 1869, so far as regards the payment of rates
by an outgoing occupier, shall extend and apply to any outgoing
occupier assessed in the rate, and such outgoing occupier shall only be
liable to pay so much of the rate as shall be proportionate to the time
of his occupation within the period for which the rate was made, notwithstanding he may not be succeeded in his occupation by an in-
coming tenant *Payment of rates by outgoing occupier to be proportionate to time of occupation*

Publication of rate where no parish church

4 In a parish in which there is no church or chapel of the parish, a poor rate, whether made before or after the passing of this Act, shall be deemed to have been duly published if, within fourteen days after the making of the rate notice thereof has been given by affixing such notice in some public and conspicuous place or situation in the parish

THE VALUATION (METROPOLIS) AMENDMENT ACT, 1884

(47 & 48 Vict, cap 5)

AN ACT TO AMEND THE VALUATION (METROPOLIS) ACT, 1869, BY GIVING GREATER FACILITIES FOR APPEAL TO OWNERS AND LESSEES OF HOUSES PAYING RATES AND TAXES IN THE PLACE OF THE OCCUPIERS

[28th March 1884]

[PREAMBLE RECITES 32 & 33 Vict, c 67]

Short title and construction

1 This Act may be cited as the Valuation (Metropolis) Amendment Act, 1884, and shall be read and construed as one Act with the Valuation (Metropolis) Act, 1869 (hereinafter called the principal Act)

Enabling owners and lessees to appeal

2 Where the owner or lessee of any hereditament is liable to be assessed for any rate or tax in the place of the occupier or tenant, or does in fact pay any such rate or tax in his place under any contract or arrangement with him, such owner or lessee shall for the purposes of this Act and the Acts incorporated therewith be deemed to be the occupier of such hereditament, and the person referred to as the ratepayer in sections nineteen and thirty-two of the principal Act, and the person who is to make to the overseers of this parish the statement or return referred to in the fifty-fifth section of the principal Act   Provided that any form of return order, notice, or document required to be given to or served on the occupier under the principal Act shall, except where the owner or lessee is liable to be assessed to or to pay any rate or tax in the place of the occupier, be deemed to be sufficiently given or served, notwithstanding this Act, if addressed to such occupier and left on the premises to which the return, order, notice, or document relates

One notice of objection may include one or more separately assessed hereditaments

3 Where any occupier or ratepayer, or any owner or lessee deemed to be an occupier or ratepayer within the meaning of section two of this Act, shall object to the valuation list in respect of any hereditaments, whether consisting of a house or houses subdivided into tenements separately assessed as hereditaments, or of separate houses or tenements not so subdivided, it shall be lawful for him to include in any one notice made in pursuance of section thirty-three of the principal Act or otherwise or in any one objection appeal, or other

proceeding under the principal Act and the Acts incorporated therewith, the whole or any one or more of the hereditaments separately assessed and comprised in one valuation list of which he is or is deemed to be the occupier or ratepayer.

THE ADVERTISING STATIONS (RATING) ACT, 1889.

(52 & 53 Vict., cap. 27.)

AN ACT TO AMEND THE LAW WITH RESPECT TO RATING PLACES USED FOR ADVERTISEMENTS

[*12th August 1889*]

[PREAMBLE.]

1 This Act may be cited as the Advertising Stations (Rating) Act, 1889   *Short title*

2 In this Act the term "owner" means the person for the time *Definitions* being receiving or entitled to receive the rackrent of the lands or premises in connection with which the word is used, whether on his own account or as agent or trustee for any other person, or who would so receive or be entitled to receive the same if such lands or premises were let at a rackrent, and the word "person" shall be deemed to include any body of persons whether corporate or unincorporate

3 Where any land is used temporarily or permanently for the *Rating land used for advertisements and not otherwise occupied* exhibition of advertisements, or for the erection of any hoarding, frame, post, wall or structure used for the exhibition of advertisements, but not otherwise occupied, the person who shall permit the same to be so used, or (if he cannot be ascertained) the owner thereof, shall be deemed to be in beneficial occupation of such land or part thereof, and shall be rateable in respect thereof to the relief of the poor and to all local rates, according to the value of such use as aforesaid

4 Where any land or hereditament occupied for other purposes *Rating occupied hereditaments used for advertisements* and rateable in respect thereof to the relief of the poor and local rates, is used temporarily or permanently for the exhibition of advertisements, or for the erection thereon or attachment thereto of any hoarding, frame, post, wall or structure used for the exhibition of advertisements, the gross and rateable value of such land or hereditament shall be so estimated as to include the increased value from such use as aforesaid

5 Where, under any power vested in them by any local or general *Use of hoarding in roads for advertisements* Act, any corporation, board, vestry, urban, sanitary or other authority shall grant a license for the temporary erection of any hoard, gantry, scaffold or other structure upon or over any part of any public highway, or upon or over any lands or hereditaments the property of such corporation, board, vestry, sanitary or other authority, such corporation, board, vestry, sanitary or other authority may include in such license a condition or conditions prohibiting the affixing of

any advertisement to any such hoard gantry, scaffold or other structure, or sanctioning the affixing of advertisements thereto upon payment of such sum and on such conditions as the corporation, board, vestry, sanitary or other authority granting the license may determine And any person using any such hoard, gantry, scaffold or other structure otherwise than as permitted by such license shall for every offence be liable to a penalty not exceeding five pounds, and a further sum not exceeding forty shillings for every day during which such offence shall be continued after notice in writing to discontinue such use shall have been given to such person by such corporation board, vestry, sanitary or other authority, which penalties may be recovered in a summary way by such corporation, board, vestry, sanitary or other authority.

The amount of any payments received or penalties recovered under this section shall be applied by the corporation, board, vestry, sanitary or other authority receiving the same in aid of the rate levied for the repair of the highway

Application of Act to Ireland

6 In the application of this Act to Ireland—

(1) Any land used temporarily or permanently for the exhibition of advertisements, or for the erection of any hoarding, frame, post, wall or structure used for the exhibition of advertisements, shall be deemed to be a rateable hereditament within the meaning of the several Acts relating to the valuation of rateable property in Ireland, and shall be separately valued accordingly under the provisions of the said Acts.

(2) The expression "local rates" shall include grand jury cess [1];

(3) Section four shall be read and construed as if after the words "shall be so estimated" there were inserted the words "for the purposes of the several Acts relating to the valuation of rateable property in Ireland."

[S 7 repealed, 8 Edw 7, c 49 (S L R)]

THE TITHE ACT, 1891

(54 & 55 Vict, cap 8)

AN ACT TO MAKE BETTER PROVISION FOR THE RECOVERY OF TITHE RENT-CHARGE IN ENGLAND AND WALES

[26th March, 1891.]

o   o   o   o   o   o

Rating of owner of tithe rent charge

6—(1) Any rate to which tithe rent-charge is subject shall be assessed on and may be recovered from the owner of the tithe rent-charge in the like manner and by the like process as on and from any occupying ratepayer, and so much of any Act as authorises any rate or tithe rent-charge to be assessed on, or recovered from the occupier of any lands out of which the tithe rent-charge issues is hereby repealed.

---

[1] Now Poor Rate (see 61 & 62 Vict, c 37.)

(2) If the collector of the rate satisfies the County Court that he is unable to recover in manner aforesaid any rate assessed on the owner of any tithe rent-charge, the Court may, after such service on the owners of the tithe rent-charge, and of the lands out of which the tithe rent-charge issues, as may be prescribed, and after hearing such owners, if they appear and desire to be heard, order the owner of the lands to pay such tithe rent-charge to the collector until the amount of the rate, and any costs allowed by the Court, are fully paid and the order may be executed as if it were an order under this Act for the payment of a sum due on account of the tithe rent-charge.

(3) The Court may, if satisfied that the circumstances justify it, make such order as aforesaid in respect of any future rate, either generally or during the time limited by the order.

(4) The expression "rate" in this section means a poor rate, highway rate, general district rate, borough rate, and every other rate assessed on an owner of tithe rent-charge by a public authority for public purposes, and the expression "collector" means the overseer[1] surveyor of highways, rate-collector, or other person authorised for the time being to collect the rate

Power of appeal[1]

(7) If any party in any action or matter under this Act shall be dissatisfied with the determination or direction of the Judge of the County Court in point of law or equity, or upon the admission or rejection of any evidence, the party aggrieved by the judgment, direction, decision, or order of the Judge may appeal from the same to the High Court, in such manner and subject to such conditions as may be for the time being provided by the rules of the Supreme Court regulating the procedure on appeals from inferior Courts to the High Court

THE LOCAL GOVERNMENT ACT, 1894
(56 & 57 Vict, cap 73)

AN ACT TO MAKE FURTHER PROVISION FOR LOCAL GOVERNMENT IN ENGLAND AND WALES

[*5th March, 1894*]

Powers and Duties of Parish Councils and Parish Meetings

5 —(1) The power and duty of appointing overseers of the poor, and the power of appointing and revoking the appointment of an assistant overseer, for every rural parish having a parish council, shall be transferred to and vested in the parish council and that council shall in each year, at their annual meeting, appoint the overseers of

Parish council to appoint overseers

1 See now 56 & 57 Vict, c 73 s 25

the parish, and shall as soon as may be fill any casual vacancy occurring in the office of overseer of the parish, and shall in either case forthwith give written notice thereof in the prescribed form to the board of guardians

(2)

(a) The churchwardens of every rural parish shall cease to be overseers, and an additional number of overseers may be appointed to replace the churchwardens, and

(b) references in any Act to the churchwardens and overseers shall, as respects any rural parish, except so far as those references relate to the affairs of the church, be construed as references to the overseers and

(c) the legal interest in all property vested either in the overseers or in the churchwardens and overseers of a rural parish, other than property connected with the affairs of the church, or held for an ecclesiastical charity, shall, if there is a parish council, vest in that council, subject to all trusts and liabilities affecting the same, and all persons concerned shall make or concur in making such transfers, if any, as are requisite for giving effect to this enactment

Transfer of certain powers of vestry and other authorities to parish council

6—(1) Upon the parish council of a rural parish coming into office, there shall be transferred to that council—

(a) The powers, duties and liabilities of the vestry of the parish except—

(i) so far as relates to the affairs of the church or to ecclesiastical charities, and

(ii) any power, duty, or liability transferred by this Act from the vestry to any other authority

(b) The powers, duties, and liabilities of the churchwardens of the parish, except so far as they relate to the affairs of the church or to charities, or are powers and duties of overseers, but inclusive of the obligations of the churchwardens with respect to maintaining and repairing closed churchyards whereever the expenses of such maintenance and repair are repayable out of the poor rate under the Burial Act, 1855 Provided that such obligations shall not in the case of any particular parish be deemed to attach, unless or until the churchwardens shall give a certificate, as in the Burial Act, 1855, provided, in order to obtain the repayment of such expenses out of the poor rate

18 & 19 Vict, c 125

(c) The powers, duties, and liabilities of the overseers or of the churchwardens and overseers of the parish with respect to—

(i) appeals or objections by them in respect of the valuation list, or appeals in respect of the poor rate, or county rate, or the basis of the county rate

o o o o o o

19 In a rural parish not having a separate parish council the following provisions shall,   subject to provisions made by a grouping order, if the parish is grouped with some other parish or parishes, have effect —

o   o   o   o   o   o

(4) All powers, duties, and liabilities of the vestry shall, except so far as they relate to the affairs of the church or to ecclesiastical charities, or are transferred by this Act to any other authority, be transferred to the parish meeting

(5) The power and the duty of appointing the overseers, and of notifying the appointment, and the power of appointing and revoking the appointment of an assistant overseer, shall be transferred to and vest in the parish meeting and the power given by this Act to a parish council of appointing trustees of a charity in the place of overseers or churchwardens, shall vest in the parish meeting ,

(6.) The chairman of the parish meeting and the overseers of the parish shall be a body corporate by the name of the chairman and overseers of the parish, and shall have perpetual succession, and may hold land for the purposes of the parish without license in mortmain , but shall in all respects act in manner directed by the parish meeting, and any act of such body corporate shall be executed under the hands, or, if an instrument under seal is required, under the hands and seals, of the said chairman and overseers ,

o   o   o   o   o   o

(10) On the application of the parish meeting the county council may confer on that meeting any of the powers conferred on a parish council by this Act ,

(11) Any act of the parish meeting may be signified by an instrument executed at the meeting under the hands, or if an instrument under seal is required, under the hands and seals of the chairman presiding at the meeting and two other parochial electors present at the meeting

20 The following provisions shall apply to boards of guardians —

(1) There shall be no ex-officio or nominated guardians

(2) A person shall not be qualified to be elected or to be a guardian for a poor law union unless he is a parochial elector of some parish within the union, or has during the whole of the twelve months preceding the election resided in the union, or in the case of a guardian for a parish wholly or partly situate within the area of a borough, whether a county borough or not, is qualified to be elected a councillor for that borough, and no person shall be disqualified by sex or marriage for

being elected or being a guardian So much of any enactment, whether in a public general or local and personal Act, as relates to the qualification of a guardian shall be repealed

(3) The parochial electors of a parish shall be the electors of the guardians of the parish, and if the parish is divided into wards for the election of guardians, the electors of the guardians for each ward shall be such of the parochial electors as are registered in respect of qualifications within the ward

(4) Each elector may give one vote and no more for each of any number of persons not exceeding the number to be elected

(5) The election shall, subject to the provisions of this Act, be conducted according to rules framed under this Act by the Local Government Board

(6 [1]) The term of office of a guardian shall be three years and one third, as nearly as may be, of every board of guardians shall go out of office on the fifteenth day of April in each year, and their places shall be filled by the newly elected guardians Provided as follows —

(a) Where the county council, on the application of the board of guardians of any union in their county, consider that it would be expedient to provide for the simultaneous retirement of the whole of the board of guardians for the union, they may direct that the members of the board of guardians for that union shall retire together on the fifteenth day of April in every third year, and such order shall have full effect, and where a union is in more than one county, an order may be made by a joint committee of the councils of those counties

(b) Where at the passing of this Act the whole of the guardians of any union, in pursuance of an order of the Local Government Board, retire together at the end of every third year, they shall continue so to retire, unless the county council, or a joint committee of the county councils, on the application of the board of guardians or of any district council of a district wholly or partially within the union, otherwise direct

(7) A board of guardians may elect a chairman or vice-chairman, or both, and not more than two other persons, from outside their own body, but from persons qualified to be guardians of the union, and any person so elected shall be an additional guardian and member of the board Provided that on the first election, if a sufficient number of persons who have been ex-officio or nominated guardians of the union, and have actually served as such, are willing to serve, the additional members shall be elected from among those persons

o o o o o o

[1] Extended by 63 & 64 Vict., c 16

33—(1) The Local Government Board may, on the application of the council of any municipal borough, including a county borough, or of any other urban district, make an order conferring on that council or some other representative body within the borough or district all or any of the following matters, namely, the appointment of overseers and assistant overseers, the revocation of appointment of assistant overseers, any powers, duties, or liabilities of overseers and any powers, duties, or liabilities of a parish council, and applying with the necessary modifications the provisions of this Act with reference thereto

Power to apply certain provisions of Act to urban districts and London

o o o o o o

(3) Any order under this section may provide for its operation extending either to the whole or to specified parts of the area of the borough or urban district, and may make such provisions as seem necessary for carrying the order into effect

(4) The order shall not alter the incidence of any rate, and shall make such provisions as may seem necessary and just for the preservation of the existing interests of paid officers

o o o o o o

(6) The provisions of this section respecting councils of urban districts shall apply to the administrative county of London in like manner as if the district of each sanitary authority in that county were an urban district, and the sanitary authority were the council of that district

o o o o o o

34.—Where an order of the Local Government Board under this Act confers on the council of an urban district, or some other representative body within the district, either the appointment of overseers and assistant overseers, or the powers, duties and liabilities of overseers, that order or any subsequent order of the Board may confer on such council or body the powers of the vestry under the third and fourth sections of the Poor Rate Assessment and Collection Act, 1869.

Supplemental provisions as to control of overseers in urban districts

32 & 33 Vict., c 41

o o o o o o

52—(5) All enactments in any Act, whether general or local and personal, relating to any powers, duties, or liabilities transferred by this Act to a parish council or parish meeting from justices, or the vestry, or overseers, or churchwardens and overseers shall, subject to the provisions of this Act and so far as circumstances admit, be construed as if any reference therein to justices, or to the vestry, or to the overseers, or to the churchwardens and overseers, referred to the parish council or parish meeting as the case requires, and the said enactments shall be construed with such modifications as may be necessary for carrying this Act into effect

Supplemental provisions as to transfer of powers

o o o o o o

THE AGRICULTURAL RATES ACT, 1896

(59 & 60 Vict , cap 16)

AN ACT TO AMEND THE LAW WITH RESPECT TO THE RATING OF OCCUPIERS OF AGRICULTURAL LAND IN ENGLAND, AND FOR OTHER PURPOSES CONNECTED THEREWITH.

[20th July, 1896]

Exemption of agricultural land from half of rates to which this Act applies

1 —(1) During the continuance of this Act[1] .   .   . the occupier of agricultural land in England shall be liable in the case of every rate to which this Act applies, to pay one half only of the rate in the pound payable in respect of buildings and other hereditaments

(2) This Act shall apply to every rate as defined by this Act, except a rate—

(a) which the occupier of agricultural land is liable, as compared with the occupier of buildings or other hereditaments, to be assessed to or to pay in the proportion of one half or less than one half, or

(b) which is assessed under any commission of sewers or in respect of any drainage, wall, embankment, or other work for the benefit of the land

Payment ont of Local Taxation Account in respect of deficiency arising from exemption

2 —(1) In respect of the deficiency which will arise from the provisions of this Act in the produce of rates made by the spending authorities in England, as hereinafter defined, there shall during the continuance of this Act—

(a) be paid to the Local Taxation Account an annual sum (in this Act referred to as the annual grant) of such amount as is certified under the provisions hereinafter contained ; and

(b) be issued from the Local Taxation Account by half-yearly payments out of the annual grant to each such spending authority a share of that grant of such amount as is certified under the provisions hereinafter contained

(2) The Commissioners of Inland Revenue, in such manner, by such payments, and under such regulations, as the Treasury direct, shall pay to the Local Taxation Account, out of[2] the proceeds of the estate duty derived in England from personal property, the annual sum required by this section to be paid to that account

(3) The first of those payments shall be made during the six months ending on the thirty-first day of March next after the passing of this Act, so as to make up a half-yearly payment to meet the issues to spending authorities on account of the six ensuing months

---

[1] This Act was continued by 1 Edw. 7, c, 13 s. 1, and 5 Edw 7, c. 8, s. 1, to March 31st, 1910

[2] By 7 Edw 7, c 13, s 17 (1), the payment is to be made out of the Consolidated Fund, instead of being thus charged

3.—(1) Where any spending authority require in any half-year or other period to raise from two or more parishes a sum by a rate to which this Act applies, they shall, in determining the net amount to be so raised, deduct the sum issuable to them in respect of the said rate on account of their share of the annual grant for the said half-year or other period, and the net amount after that deduction shall, where it would otherwise be raised in proportion to the rateable value, be raised in proportion to the assessable value of those parishes.

Contributions from more than one parish

(2) For the purposes of this section the assessable value of a parish shall be the rateable value thereof reduced by an amount equal to one-half of the rateable value of the agricultural land in the parish.

4.—(1) The Local Government Board shall, as soon as may be after the passing of this Act, certify the amount—

Certifying of annual sums payable in respect of deficiency

(a.) of the annual grant to be paid to the Local Taxation Account ; and

(b.) of the share of such grant to be paid annually to each spending authority

under this Act, and for that purpose shall determine in the prescribed manner the amount which for the purposes of this Act is to be taken as having been raised during the last year before the passing of this Act by any rate to which this Act applies for the expenditure of each spending authority

(2) Such proportion of the whole amount so taken to be raised in respect of any hereditaments or parishes as the Local Government Board estimate to be the proportion of the total rateable value of those hereditaments or parishes which represents the value of agricultural land, shall be taken for the purposes of this Act as the amount raised during the said year, by the said authority, by the said rate, in respect of agricultural land, and one-half of that amount shall be taken as the deficiency which will arise from the provisions of this Act in the produce of the said rate

(3) A sum equal to the total amount of the deficiencies thus estimated for all the spending authorities in England shall be the amount of the annual grant, and a sum equal to the deficiency thus estimated in the case of each spending authority shall be the share of that spending authority in the annual grant, and the Local Government Board shall certify the same accordingly

(4) The Local Government Board, in acting under this section shall obtain such information and make such enquiries, and in such manner as they think fit

(5) The Local Government Board may in case of error amend, or for the purpose of meeting any alteration in an area or authority to which a certificate relates may vary, a certificate under this section, and any such amendment or variation shall have effect from the date of the original certificate, or any later date fixed by the Board, but, save as aforesaid, a certificate shall be final and binding on all persons

Separate statement in valuation lists etc, of value of agricultural land

(6) The Local Government Board may give provisional certificates if they think necessary for the purpose of enabling the first payments to and out of the Local Taxation Account under this Act to be made, before they have sufficient information to enable them to give final certificates

5 In every valuation list and in the basis or standard for any county rate, and in any valuation made by the council of a borough or any other council for the purpose of raising the borough or other rate—

(*a*) where separate hereditaments are specified therein the value of agricultural land shall be stated separately from that of any building or other hereditament, and

(*b*) in every case the total rateable value of the agricultural land in each parish shall be stated separately from the total rateable value of the buildings or other hereditaments in such parish, and whenever a copy of the total of the rateable value of any parish is required to be sent to any person, such copy shall state both the above-mentioned totals, and

(*c*) where any hereditament consists partly of agricultural land and partly of buildings, the gross estimated rental of the buildings, when valued separately, in pursuance of this Act, from the agricultural land shall, while the buildings are used only for the cultivation of the said land, be calculated not on structural cost, but on the rent at which they would be expected to let to a tenant from year to year if they could only be so used, and the total gross estimated rental of the hereditament shall not be increased by the said separate valuation

6 —(1) For the purposes of this Act returns shall be made to the Local Government Board in accordance with the prescribed regulations—

(*a*) by every spending authority in relation to the sums actually received by them or their predecessors during the year next before the passing of this Act from any rate to which this Act applies, and

(*b*.) by every assessment committee or council whose duty it is to revise or make a valuation list, basis, standard or other valuation for any parish, in relation to the gross estimated rental and rateable value of that parish, and the proportion thereof which represents agricultural land, and

(*c*) by any such authority, committee or council in relation to any other prescribed information

(2) For the purpose of the returns, statements showing the gross estimated rental and rateable value of the agricultural land in a parish and, in the case of any hereditament separately valued which consists in part of agricultural land and in part of buildings or other heredita-

ments, of each such part, shall be made by the overseers of every parish, and corrected by the assessment committee and sent to the surveyor of taxes, and be subject to objection or appeal by the said surveyor and overseers before the assessment committee and the justices in special sessions and the court of quarter sessions and subject to the right of any aggrieved ratepayer to be heard upon the said appeal in such form within such times, and generally in such manner, and subject to such provisions, as may be prescribed   These provisions shall conform as nearly as circumstances will permit to the existing statutory law respecting valuation lists, as regards notices, rights to inspect and take extracts, the hearing of objections, and otherwise

(3) The Local Government Board may by order make regulations for the purpose of this section, and also generally for carrying into effect this Act, and those regulations shall be laid before both Houses of Parliament and, if neither House of Parliament within ten days passes a resolution adverse to the said order, they shall be binding in law until varied in the same manner, shall have effect as if they were enacted in this Act, and shall amongst other matters provide—

(a.) for fixing, with the concurrence of the Treasury, for the purpose of the division in the statements of agricultural land from buildings or other hereditaments, the minimum gross estimated rental and rateable value of the buildings or other hereditaments ,

(b) for giving effect to a notice of objection or appeal by the surveyor of taxes unless it is proved that such notice is unfair or incorrect ,

(c) for the temporary adoption by the county council or any other council of the division in the return between the total rateable value of agricultural land and that of buildings and other hereditaments ,

(d) for the alteration of the valuation list in accordance with the statements as finally settled and sending copies of the returns to spending authorities and for applying and adapting any statutory form or procedure respecting the valuation list or poor rate , and

(e) for adapting this Act to cases where there is no valuation list, or where a sum is raised by rate from an area not a parish

(4) The regulations may also provide fines for the breach thereof not exceeding forty shillings, or in case of any continuing offence not exceeding forty shillings a day during the continuance of the offence, and any such fine may be recovered as a crown debt or to an amount not exceeding one hundred pounds before a court of summary jurisdiction

7—[S s (1) repealed, 8 Edw. 7, c. 49 (S L R.)]

ss 2

As to
spending
authorities

(2) Every sum paid under this Act out of the local taxation account to any spending authority in respect of any rate shall, for the purpose of its application, of account and of audit, be deemed to have been raised by the said rate

[S s (3) repealed, 2 Edw 7, c 42 s 25 (3) 3 Edw 7, c 24, s 1]

As to limit of
rate or
expenditure in
case of any
local authority

8 —A limit imposed by any enactment on a rate shall be construed as being only a limit on the amount to be raised by that rate, and where by that limit or otherwise the sum to be raised or expended by a local authority is limited by any enactment by reference to a rate, the limit shall be varied so as to enable the local authority to raise or expend the same sum as they might have done if this Act had not passed, and in the case of a spending authority receiving any sum paid under this Act out of the local taxation account in respect of such rate, that sum shall be deemed to be part of the sum raised thereby

Definitions

9 —In this Act, unless the context otherwise requires—

The expression "rate" means a rate made during the continuance of this Act, the proceeds of which are applicable to public local purposes, and which is leviable on the basis of an assessment in respect of the yearly value of property, and includes any sum which, though obtained in the first instance by a precept, certificate, or other instrument requiring payment from some authority or officer, is or can be ultimately raised out of a rate as before defined

The expression 'rateable value' in the case of the county rate, or any other rate, levied according to any annual value not being rateable value as stated in the valuation list, means that annual value

25 & 26 Vict
c 103

27 & 28 Vict,
c 39

32 & 33 Vict,
c 67

The expression 'valuation list" means a valuation list under the Union Assessment Committee Acts, 1862 and 1864, or, in the metropolis, under the Valuation (Metropolis) Act, 1869

The expression "spending authority" means any of the local authorities in England mentioned in the schedule to this Act

The expression "occupier" includes owner where the owner is rated in place of the occupier

51 & 52 Vict,
c 41

The expression "local taxation account" has the same meaning as in the Local Government Act, 1888

The expression "prescribed' means prescribed by order of the Local Government Board

The expression "agricultural land" means any land used as arable meadow, or pasture ground only, cottage gardens exceeding one quarter of an acre market gardens, nursery grounds, orchards, or allotments, but does not include land occupied together with a house as a park, gardens, other than as aforesaid, pleasure-grounds, or any land kept or preserved mainly or exclusively for purposes of sport or recreation, or land used as a racecourse

The expression "cottage" means a house occupied as a dwelling by a person of the labouring classes

The expression "year" means the local financial year, that is to say, the twelve months beginning on the first day of April, or where the spending authority do not make up their accounts to that day on the nearest day thereto to which they do make up their accounts, or on any other prescribed day.

10.—This Act may be cited as the Agricultural Rates Act, 1896   *Short title*

SCHEDULE.

SPENDING AUTHORITIES.

County councils, councils of county boroughs, councils of boroughs and other urban districts and of rural districts, boards of guardians, the receiver of the metropolitan police district.

THE LONDON GOVERNMENT ACT, 1899

(62 & 63 Vict., cap 14)

AN ACT TO MAKE BETTER PROVISION FOR LOCAL GOVERNMENT IN LONDON

[*13th July, 1899.*]

Establishment of Metropolitan Boroughs

1.—The whole of the administrative county of London, exclusive of the City of London, shall be divided into metropolitan boroughs (in this Act referred to as boroughs), and for that purpose it shall be lawful for Her Majesty by [1] Order in Council, subject to and in accordance with this Act to form each of the areas mentioned in the First Schedule to this Act into a separate borough, subject, nevertheless, to such alteration of area as may be required to give effect to the provisions of this Act, and subject also to such adjustment of boundaries as may appear to Her Majesty in Council expedient for simplification or convenience of administration, and to establish and incorporate a council for each of the boroughs so formed   *Establishment of metropolitan boroughs in London*

* * * * * *

Powers of Borough Councils

4.—(1) . . Every elective vestry and district board in the county of London shall cease to exist, and, subject to the provisions of this Act and of any scheme made thereunder, their powers and duties, including those under any local Act, shall . be transferred to the council for the borough comprising the area within which those powers are exercised, and their property and liabilities   *Transfer to borough councils of powers from vestries and district boards*

---

[1] See Orders in Council (Stat Rules and Orders 1900 Nos 380 to 407, local) establishing the twenty-eight metropolitan boroughs

shall be transferred to that council, and that council shall be their successors, and the clerk of the council shall be called the town clerk, and shall be the town clerk within the meaning of the Acts relating to the registration of electors

Provided that in the case of borrowing powers so transferred, if the London County Council refuse their sanction, or do not within six months after application made give their sanction, to a loan, or attach conditions to their sanction an appeal shall lie to the Local Government Board, whose decision shall be final

*   *   *   *   *   *

(3) The powers of a borough council shall save as in this Act mentioned, extend to the whole of their borough

Provided that any power or duty of the council under any Act, whether general or local, conferring powers in relation to some particular parish or district or part of a parish or district, shall be exercised and performed by the council either throughout the borough or in a limited part thereof, or shall cease to be exercised and performed, as may be provided by a scheme under this Act, having regard to the object of the Act under which the power or duty arise and to the nature of any change of area or alteration of boundary made by or under this Act

*   *   *   *   *   *

Rates, Overseers and Audit

Levy of rates   10—(1) A scheme under this Act shall provide for all the expenses of a borough council being paid out of the general rate and for the discontinuance of a separate sewers rate and separate lighting rate, but shall make provision for protecting the interests of owners and occupiers of any hereditament which is exempt from any rate or liable to be assessed thereto at a less amount than other hereditaments

(2)   The general rate and the poor rate shall be assessed, made and levied together by the borough council as one rate, which shall be termed the general rate, and shall be assessed, made, collected, and levied, as if it were the poor rate, and all enactments applying or referring to the poor rate shall, subject to the provisions of this Act as to audit, be construed as applying or referring also to the general rate

(3) Where a borough comprises more than one parish, the amount to be raised to meet the expenses of the borough council, or other sums payable as part of those expenses, shall, subject to any provision required for the adjustment of local burdens, be divided between the parishes in proportion to their rateable value

1 See the London (Rating) Scheme, 1901 Appendix II *post*

(4) Where any of the adoptive Acts, or any local or other Act, does not extend to the whole borough, any rate required to meet the expenses incurred under the Act shall, subject to the provisions of any scheme under this Act, be levied together with, and as an additional item of, the general rate over the area to which the Act extends.

11.—(1)   The council of each borough shall be the overseers of every parish within their borough, and shall appoint such officers as may be required to assist in the transaction of the business, and shall defray the expenses of and incidental to the performance of the duties of overseers. Provided that the town clerk of each borough shall have the powers and duties and be subject to the liabilities of overseers with respect to the preparation of lists of voters and of jury lists in the borough, and any document required to be signed by overseers may be signed by the town clerk.

Provisions as to overseers and collection of rates

(2)   .   Every precept issued by any authority in London for the purpose of obtaining money which is ultimately to be raised out of a rate within a borough, other than a precept sent to guardians by the Local Government Board or by a body containing representatives elected by the guardians, shall be sent to the council at their office, addressed to the council or to the town clerk. Any such precept, if so sent and addressed, shall be deemed to be personally served on the council, and shall be executed by them. 'Precept' in this section includes any order, certificate, warrant, or other document of a like character, and the Local Government Board may settle the form of any precept as so defined.

(3)   .   All the rates collected in a metropolitan borough from any person by the council shall, as far as is practicable, be levied on one demand note, and the demand note shall be in a form approved by the Local Government Board, and shall state in manner provided in that form—

    (a) the rateable value of the premises in respect of which the rate is levied; and

    (b) the rate in the pound; and

    (c) the period for which the rate is made; and

    (d) the several purposes for which the rate is levied; and

    (e) the approximate amount in the pound required for each purpose (including, as far as is practicable, the proportionate amount of the estimated costs of and loss in collection); and

    (f) any matter required by section two of the London (Equalisation of Rates) Act, 1894, or any other enactment, to be stated in the demand note. 57 & 58 Vict, c 3

12.—As between landlord and tenant every tenant who, if this Act had not been passed, would have been entitled to deduct against or to be repaid by his landlord any sum paid by the tenant on account of the sewers rate, shall in like manner be entitled to deduct against or to be repaid by his landlord such portion of the general rate as represents the sewers rate. *In lieu of sewers rate or its equivalent*

Assessment
committees

32 & 33 Vict.,
c 67

13 —Where the whole of the poor law union is within one borough, the assessment committee shall, notwithstanding anything in section five of the Valuation (Metropolis) Act, 1869, be appointed by the borough council instead of by the board of guardians, and where the borough comprises the whole of two or more unions, the council shall appoint only one assessment committee for those unions and where the council appoint the assessment committee the town clerk shall act as the clerk to that committee

·   ·   ·   ·   ·   ·

Orders and Schemes

Appointment
of Commis
sioners and
preparation of
Orders and
schemes

15 —(1.) It shall be lawful for Her Majesty in Council to refer to a Committee of the Privy Council the appointment of Commissioners to prepare such Orders and Schemes as are required for carrying this Act into effect and the Committee may settle the Orders and Schemes so prepared, and may employ such persons as they may deem necessary for the purposes of this Act

(2) Before any Order in Council forming an area into a borough is made under this Act, the draft thereof shall be laid before each House of Parliament for a period of not less than thirty days during the session of Parliament, and if either of those Houses before the expiration of those thirty days presents an address to Her Majesty against the draft or any part thereof, no further proceedings shall be taken thereon, without prejudice to the making of any new draft Order

(3) The Commissioners shall for the execution of their duties under this Act have the like powers as inspectors of the Local Government Board

(4) Any expenses incurred by the Committee under this Act shall, to the amount certified by the Treasury, be paid by the London County Council out of the county fund

Provisions to
be made by
scheme

15 & 46 Vict ,
c 50

1 & 52 Vict
c 41

56 & 57 Vict ,
c 73

16 —(1) A scheme under this Act may make provision—

(a) for any matters which under this Act are to be regulated by scheme , and

(b) for any of the purposes, except police, for which a scheme may be made under Part Eleven of the Municipal Corporations Act, 1882, so far as those purposes are consistent with this Act , and

(c) for anything which may be done with respect to a parish by an order under section fifty-seven of the Local Government Act, 1888, or may be done under section thirty three of the Local Government Act, 1894, so, however, that parishes in different unions shall not be united except with the approval of the Local Government Board , and (*d*) for such adjustments as may be required for carrying into effect any of the provisions of this Act or for preventing any injustice with respect to the incidence of any rate or the discharge of any liability or otherwise, and in particular for such adjustments as may be required for the efficient maintenance of any libraries, baths, or wash-houses, which have been maintained under the provisions of any of the adoptive Acts, and

(*e*) for preserving, so far as may appear necessary or expedient, any right, power, exemption, or immunity heretofore exercised or enjoyed in respect of property belonging to or occupied by the Crown or any Government department, and

(*f*) for making such alterations in the boundaries of the electoral divisions for the purpose of school board elections as may be rendered necessary by any alteration in the area of the county of London, and

(*g*) for repealing or modifying any local Act other than the London Building Act, 1894, and

57 & 58 Vict.
c. ccxiii

(*h*) for carrying into effect this Act or any Order in Council made thereunder

and may contain any incidental, consequential, or supplemental provisions, which may appear to be necessary or proper for the purposes of the scheme

(2) In making adjustments by a scheme under this section regard shall be had to any composition, contribution or exemption, whether statutory or otherwise, which has heretofore existed in regard to any portion of any area dealt with under the scheme

(3) The provisions of the Municipal Corporations Act, 1882, as amended by the School Boards Act, 1885, with respect to a scheme under Part Eleven of the first-mentioned Act, shall apply in the case of any scheme under this Act with the necessary modifications, and any governors or trustees of the poor or other similar body under a local Act shall be deemed, but the London County Council shall not be deemed, to be a local authority within the meaning of those provisions There shall also be deemed to be local authorities within the meaning of the said provisions—

45 & 46 Vict,
c. 50
48 & 49 Vict
c. 38

(*a*) the mayor, commonalty, and citizens, and the Court of Aldermen of the City of London, so far as relates to any powers exercisable by them or by officers appointed by them respectively within the ancient borough of Southwark and

(*b*) the Dean and Chapter of the Collegiate Church of St Peter Westminster, so far as relates to any powers of local government exercisable by them or their officers within the borough of Westminster, and the Court of Burgesses of the ancient city of Westminster

(4.) Provided that notification in the "London Gazette" and in such other manner as the Committee of Council may direct, of a draft

scheme having been prepared or of a scheme having been settled,
and of the place where copies of it can be inspected and obtained,
shall be substituted for publication of the draft scheme or scheme
in the "London Gazette" or in the manner required by the seventh
schedule to the Municipal Corporations Act, 1882

45 & 46 Vict.,
c. 50

17.—(1) Every part of the administrative county of London
outside the City shall be situate in some borough and some parish,
and a parish shall not be situate in more than one borough or partly
in a borough and partly in the City

Rules as to
boroughs and
parishes

(2) An Order in Council under this Act may divide a parish or
place into parts for the purpose of giving effect to this section or of
constituting a satisfactory area for a borough, and, unless otherwise
provided by the Order or by a scheme under this Act each part shall
be a separate parish.

Detached parts
of parishes

18.—(1) Every part of a parish in London which is wholly
detached from the principal part of the parish shall by an Order in
Council under this Act be annexed to or divided between any of the
boroughs which it adjoins, and be either constituted a separate parish
or be annexed to or divided between any of the parishes which it
adjoins, so however that the provisions of this Act with respect to a
parish not being situate in more than one borough shall be observed

Provided that if the Commissioners under this Act make a special
report to Parliament that by reason of anything done under any of
the adoptive Acts, or for any other exceptional reason, it is impracticable to deal with a detached part of a parish in manner required by the
foregoing provisions of this section those provisions shall not apply

And, further, provided that the foregoing provisions of this section
shall not apply to the hamlet of Knightsbridge

(2) Where the county of London surrounds a detached part of a
parish in another county the foregoing provisions shall apply, and
the detached part shall for all purposes become part of the county
of London and of the appropriate county electoral division

(3) Where a detached part so becomes part of the county of
London, and is part of any urban district the remainder of which
adjoins the county of London, the whole of the district may, by Order
in Council, if it seems expedient after considering all the circumstances of the case, be added to and form for all purposes part of the
county of London and of the appropriate borough

(4) Where a detached part of a parish in the county of London is
wholly surrounded by any other county, the detached part shall for
all purposes become part of that county, and where a detached part
as aforesaid is surrounded by more than one county, that detached
part shall become part of such county as shall be determined by Order
in Council under this Act, and every such detached part shall, by
Order in Council, be either constituted a separate parish or annexed
to or divided between any parish or parishes which it adjoins, and be
added to the appropriate county district and county electoral division

(5) Nothing in this section shall apply to the City of London

(6) The London County Council and the council of any adjoining county shall be entitled to be heard on any alteration or proposed alteration of the area of the county of London

19.—(1) A[1] scheme under this Act shall provide for placing Woolwich under the general law applying to metropolitan boroughs and for the repeal of the application thereto of the provisions of the Public Health Acts and other enactments not applying to London and for the application thereto of the Metropolis Management Acts 1855 to 1893, and other enactments applying to London

Application of Act to Woolwich

(2) Subject to the provisions of any such scheme, this Act shall apply to Woolwich in like manner as if the local board of health thereof were an administrative vestry

(3) Nothing in this Act shall prevent the council of any borough consisting of or comprising Woolwich from continuing to make any contribution for the purpose of technical education hitherto made by any local authority, or from exercising any existing powers of carrying on a market

20.—(1) An Order in Council under this Act may either annex Penge to the borough of Lewisham or to the borough of Camberwell. or separate it from the county of London and make it form part of the county of Surrey or[2] of the county of Kent, and if it is so separated shall provide for constituting it an urban district, or for adding it to an adjoining county borough or urban district, and if necessary shall determine the county electoral division to which it is to belong

Special provision as to Penge

(2) A scheme under this Act shall make such provision as may be necessary for the apportionment and transfer of property and liabilities, and for the repeal of the application to Penge of the Metropolis Management Acts, 1855 to 1893, and any other enactments applying to London, and for the application thereto of the Public Health Acts and other enactments not applying to London[3]

21.—An Order in Council under this Act may[4] detach Kensington Palace from the borough of Westminster and attach it to the borough of Kensington.

Provision as to Kensington Palace

22.—The places known as the Inner and Middle Temples shall for the purposes of this Act be deemed to be within the City of London.

Provision as to the Temples

* * * * * *

23.—(3).   The churchwardens of every parish within a metropolitan borough shall cease to be overseers, and references in

Church affairs and charities

---

[1] See Stat Rules and Orders 1900, No. 626 (local)

[2] Penge is now an urban district of the County of Kent. See Stat Rules and Orders 1900, No 434 (local)

[3] See Order in Council Stat Rules and Orders 1900 No. 780 (local)

[4] See Stat Rules and Orders 1900, No 394 (local)

any Act to the churchwardens and overseers of any such parish shall, except so far as those references relate to the affairs of the church, be construed as references to the council of the borough comprising the parish, and the legal interest in all property vested either in the overseers or churchwardens and overseers of any such parish (other than property connected with the affairs of the church or held for an ecclesiastical charity within the meaning of the Local Government Act, 1894) shall, subject to the provisions of any scheme under this Act, vest in the borough council

51 & 57 Vict., c. 73

(4) Provision shall be made by scheme under this Act for substituting nominees of the borough council for overseers as trustees of any charity, due regard being had to the area benefited by the charity

* * * * *

Proceedings in case of doubts as to transfer of powers

29—If any question arises or is about to arise, as to whether any power, duty or liability is or is not transferred by or under this Act to the council of any metropolitan borough, or any property is or is not vested in any such council, that question, without prejudice to any other mode of trying it, may, on the application of the council, be submitted for decision to the High Court in such summary manner as, subject to any rules of court, may be directed by the court; and the court, after hearing such parties and taking such evidence (if any) as it thinks just, shall decide the question

* * * * *

Construction of Acts and savings

31—(1) Where any Act passed before the passing of this Act contains expressions referring to a borough, those expressions shall not be construed as referring to a metropolitan borough created by this Act unless applied thereto by or under the provisions of this Act or of any subsequent enactment

(2) Any enactment in any Act, whether general or local, referring to an authority whose powers or duties are transferred by or under this Act to a borough council shall be construed with the necessary modifications, including the substitution of the borough council for that authority and of the borough for the area of that authority.

* * * * *

57 & 58 Vict., c. 53

(4) Except so far as the areas of parishes and sanitary districts are altered by or under this Act, nothing in this Act shall affect the London (Equalisation of Rates) Act, 1894

[S s (5) repealed, S Edw. 7, c 49 (S L R)]

* * * * *

33—[S s (1) repealed, S Edw 7, c 49 (S L R).]

(2) Subject to the provisions of any scheme under this Act, and to such adaptations as may be made by Order in Council, sections eighty-five to eighty-eight of the Local Government Act, 1894 (which contain transitory provisions), shall apply in the case of boroughs and borough councils under this Act

Transitory provisions

56 & 57 Vict c 73

34 —In this Act, unless the context otherwise requires —

Definitions

The expression "administrative vestry" means a vestry having the powers of a vestry elected for a parish specified in Schedule A to the Metropolis Management Act, 1855, and the expression "elective vestry" means any vestry elected under the Metropolis Management Act, 1855

18 & 19 Vict c 120

The expression "rateable value" shall include the value of Government property upon which a contribution in lieu of rates is paid

The expressions "powers" "duties," "property" "liabilities," and "powers, duties, and liabilities," have respectively the same meanings as in the Local Government Act, 1888

51 & 52 Vict., c 41

The expression "adoptive Acts" means the Baths and Wash-houses Acts, 1846 to 1896, the Burial Acts 1852 to 1885, and the Public Libraries Acts, 1892 and 1893

The expression "local Act" includes a provisional order confirmed by an Act, and the Act confirming the order; and the expression "enactment" includes a provision of any such order

35 —(1) This Act may be cited as the London Government Act, 1899

Short title

SCHEDULES

FIRST SCHEDULE

[SECTION 1]

AREAS WHICH ARE TO BE BOROUGHS

The[1] parishes of—

Battersea.	Islington
Bethnal Green	Kensington
Camberwell.	Lambeth
Chelsea	Paddington.
Fulham.	St Marylebone
Hackney	St Pancras
Hammersmith	Shoreditch
Hampstead	

---

[1] In the case of each of these fifteen parishes the borough bears the name of the parish, and in the remaining cases the names are Stepney, Poplar, Wandsworth Southwark, Bermondsey, Holborn, Finsbury, Deptford Greenwich, Lewisham, Woolwich, Westminster and Stoke Newington respectively The boundaries are adjusted by the Orders referred to in footnote (1) p 629 ante, and by Stat Rules and Orders 1900, Nos 423 to 436 (local)

The area consisting of the parishes of Mile End Old Town and St. George's-in-the-East and the districts of the Limehouse and Whitechapel Boards of Works including the Tower of London and the liberties thereof

The district of Poplar Board of Works

The district of Wandsworth Board of Works

The area consisting of the parishes of St George the Martyr, Christchurch, Southwark St Saviour, Southwark, and Newington

The area consisting of the parishes of Rotherhithe, Bermondsey, Horselydown, and St Olave and St Thomas, Southwark

The area of the parliamentary division of Holborn.

The area consisting of the parliamentary divisions of East and Central Finsbury

The area of the parliamentary borough of Deptford.

The area of the parliamentary borough of Greenwich

The area of the parliamentary borough of Lewisham

The area of the parliamentary borough of Woolwich

The area of the ancient parliamentary borough of Westminster, comprising the parishes of St Margaret and St John, Westminster, the parish of St George, Hanover Square, the parish of St James, Westminster, the parish of St Martin-in-the-Fields, and the district of the Strand Board of Works, and including the Close of the Collegiate Church of St Peter, Westminster, and the Liberty of the Rolls

The area consisting of the parish of Stoke Newington and of the urban district of South Hornsey, or[1] so much thereof as may be incorporated with the county of London under this Act.

THE TITHE RENTCHARGE (RATES) ACT, 1899

(62 & 63 Vict, cap 17)

AN ACT TO AMEND THE LAW WITH RESPECT TO THE PAYMENT OF RATES ON TITHE RENTCHARGE ATTACHED TO BENEFICE

[1st August, 1899]

Exemption of owner of tithe rentcharge attached to a benefice from one half of rates to which Act applies

1 The owner of tithe rentcharge attached to a benefice shall be liable to pay only one-half of the amount of any rate to which this Act applies, which is assessed on him as owner of that tithe rentcharge, and the remaining one-half shall, on demand being made by the collector of the rate on the surveyor of taxes for the district, be paid by the Commissioners of Inland Revenue out of the sums payable by them to the Local Taxation Account on account of the estate duty grant

---

[1] The whole of the urban district is now in London see Stat Rules and Orders, 1900, No 435 (local)

2.—(1) In this Act, unless the context otherwise requires,— *Interpretation*

(a) The expression "estate duty grant" means[1] the grant made under section nineteen of the Finance Act, 1894, in substitution for the probate duty grant *57 & 58 Vict., c 30*

(b) The expression "benefice" includes all rectories with cure of souls, vicarages, perpetual curacies, endowed public chapels and parochial chapelries, and chapelries or districts belonging or reputed to belong, or annexed, or reputed to be annexed to any church or chapel, and districts formed for ecclesiastical purposes by virtue of statutory authority, and includes benefices in the patronage of the Crown or of the Duchy of Cornwall

(c) The expressions 'owner of tithe rentcharge" and "tithe rentcharge" have the same meanings respectively as in the Tithe Act, 1891. *51 Vict., c 8*

(2) This Act shall apply in the case of any person liable to pay rates in respect of any payment in lieu of tithe as in the case of the owner of tithe rentcharge

3 This Act may be cited as the Tithe Rentcharge (Rates) Act, 1899 *Short title*

4 —This Act shall apply to[2] every rate as defined by section nine of the Agricultural Rates Act, 1896 (except any rate which the owner of tithe rentcharge is liable, as compared with the occupier of buildings, to be assessed to or to pay in the proportion of one-half or less than one-half), which is made   .   . during[3] the continuance of the said Agricultural Rates Act, 1896 *Application and duration 59 & 60 Vict, c 16*

---

[1] This grant is now charged on and payable out of the Consolidated Fund. see 7 Edw 7, c 14, s. 17 (1)

[2] As to application to the London General Rate, see Stat Rules and Orders, Rev 1904 VIII, "London County," p 84

[3] That Act was continued to March 31st, 1910, by 1 Edw 7, c 13, s 1 and 5 Edw 7, c 8.

APPENDIX II.

THE AGRICULTURAL RATES ORDER, 1896.

[*28th July, 1896*]

* * * * * *

As to adapting the Statutory Form of the Valuation List and of the Poor Rate

ARTICLE XVI.—In every Parish in which there is any agricultural land as defined by the Act, any new or Supplemental Valuation List made after the Thirty first day of March, One Thousand eight hundred and ninety seven, shall be made out in the Form shown in Schedule W hereto, instead of being made in the Form shown in the Schedule to the Union Assessment Committee Act, 1862, and every rate made after that date which is now required to be made in the Form shown in the Schedule to the Parochial Assessments Act, 1836, shall in every such Parish be made in the Form shown in Schedule Y, thereto

* * * * * *

Application of Regulations to Metropolis

ARTICLE XVIII.—These regulations and the Forms in the Schedule thereto in their application to Parishes within the Metropolis as defined by the Valuation (Metropolis) Act, 1869 (hereinafter in this Article called "the said Act") shall have the following and any other necessary modifications :—

* * * * * *

(3) The Form shown in Schedules * * * W 2, and Y 2, shall be substituted for those shown in Schedules * * W and Y, respectively. * * *

SCHEDULE W

Form of Valuation List

VALUATION List for [*the Parish or Place for which the List is made*] in the County of

Name of Occupier	Name of Owner	Description of Property	Name or Situation of Property	Estimated Extent			Gross Estimated Rental	Rateable Value of Agricultural Land	Rateable Value of Buildings and other Hereditaments not being Agricultural Land
1	2	3	4	5			6	7	8
				A	R	P	£ s d	£ s d	£ s d

Signed this   day of

A B } Overseers of the Poor of the
C D } Parish aforesaid.

SCHEDULE W 2

I orm of Valuation List, in Parishes in Metropolis in which there is any Agricultural Land as defined by the Agricultural Rates Act, 1896

VALUATION LIST for [*the Parish or Place for which the List is made*] in the Metropolitan Union of   [or not being in Union], in the County of London

Number	Name of Occupier	Name of Owner	Description of Property	No of Class	Name or Situation of Property	Extent	Gross Value as estimated by Overseers	Gross Value as estimated by Surveyor of Taxes	Rate of Deduction per Cent	Gross value as finally determined by Assessment Committee	Rateable value as finally determined by Assessment Committee	Rateable Value of Agricultural Land	Rateable value of Buildings and other Hereditaments not being Agricultural Land
1	2.	3.	4.	5.	6.	7	8	9	10.	11	12.	13	14
							£ s d	£ s d		£ s d	£ s d	£ s d	£ s d

[To be signed and approved as required by the Valuation (Metropolis) Act, 1869]

SCHEDULE Y

Form of Rate to be substituted for the Form in the Schedule to the Parochial Assessment Act, 1836

AN ASSESSMENT for the Relief of the Poor of the Parish of _____ in the County of _____ and for other purposes chargeable thereon according to law, made this _____ day of _____ in the year of our Lord_____, after the Rate of _____ in the £ on Buildings and other Hereditaments not being Agricultural Land, and at one-half of the said Rate on Agricultural Land which is estimated to meet all the expenses for the above purposes which will be incurred before the _____ day of _____ next.*

No	Name of Occupier	Name of Owner	Description of Property	Name or Situation of Property	Estimated Extent.	Gross Estimated Rental	Rateable Value of Agricultural Land.	Rateable Value of Buildings and other Hereditaments not being Agricultural Land	Rate at d in the £ on Agricultural Land and at d in the £ on other Hereditaments
1	2	3	4	5	6	7	8	9	10
					A R P	£ s d	£ s d	£ s d	£ s d

* If a Rate is made payable by instalments the amount of each instalment and the date at which each instalment is payable are also to be set forth in the heading

SCHEDULE Y 2

Form of Rate to be substituted for the Form in the Schedule to the Valuation (Metropolis) Act, 1869, in Parishes in the Metropolis where there is any Agricultural Land as defined by the Agricultural Rates Act, 1896

RATES FOR THE RELIEF OF THE POOR of the Parish of _____ in the _____ Union, and for other purposes chargeable thereon according to law made this_____ ___ _day of_____in the year of our Lord 18_ _____, after the rate of _____ in the Pound, on Buildings and other Hereditaments not being Agricultural Land, and at one half of the said Rate on Agricultural Land, which is estimated to meet all the expenses for the above purposes which will be incurred before the   ...   day of   _____ next

No.	Name of Occupier	Name of Owner	Description of Property Rated	Name or Situation of Property	Rateable Value of Agricultural Land.	Rateable Value of Buildings and other Hereditaments not being Agricultural Land.	Rate at d in the £ on Agricultural Land and at d. in the £ on other Hereditaments
1	2	3	4	5	6.	7	8
					£ s d	£ s d	£ s d

[Add Declaration as required by the Valuation (Metropolis) Act, 1869]

COUNTY OF LONDON QUARTER SESSIONS.

The Valuation (Metropolis) Act, 1869

ORDERS

REGULATING THE PROCEEDINGS ON

APPEALS

UNDER THE ABOVE ACT, AND DETERMINING THE RECOGNIZANCES TO BE ENTERED INTO BY APPELLANTS

1. On an Appeal to Special Session from the decision of an Assessment Committee, the appellant and one surety shall, within seven days after giving notice of Appeal, enter into recognizances in the sum of £20 each, before a Justice of the Peace for the County, conditioned for the due prosecution of the Appeal, and for the payment of any costs ordered by the Special Sessions to be paid by the Appellant *Appellants to Special Sessions to enter into recognizances*

2. In lieu of entering into the recognizances prescribed by Order 1, the Appellant may, within the same period, deposit with the Clerk of the Special Sessional Division the sum of £20, as security for the due prosecution of the appeal and for the payment of costs, and the order of Special Sessions, upon hearing and determining the Appeal, shall direct in what manner, to what persons, and in what amounts such sums shall be applied and paid *Deposit in lieu of recognizances at Special Sessions*

3. On an Appeal to Quarter Sessions from the decision either of an Assessment Committee or of Special Sessions, the Appellant and two sureties shall, within seven days after giving notice of Appeal, enter into recognizances before a Justice of the Peace for the County, conditioned for the due prosecution of the Appeal, and for the payment of any costs ordered by the Quarter Sessions to be paid by the Appellant, and the amount of such recognizances shall be determined by such Justice, having regard to the nature of the Appeal, so that the amount be not less than £50 *Appellants to Quarter Sessions to enter into recognizances*

4. In lieu of entering into the recognizances prescribed by Order 3, the Appellant may, within the same period, pay into the London and Westminster Bank (Head Office), to a joint account in the names of the Chairman of the Court and of the Clerk of the Court, the sum *Deposit in lieu of recognizances at Quarter Sessions*

£50, and the receipt given by the bank for such payment shall be deposited with the Clerk of the Court, and shall be filed by him in proof of such payment Before making such payment, a *precipe* shall be obtained from the Clerk of the Court

Recognizances not required of Assessment Committees etc

5 Orders 1 to 4, both inclusive, shall not apply to Assessment Committees, Overseers, or Surveyors of Taxes

Mode of entering Appeals at Quarter Sessions

6 Appeals to Quarter Sessions shall be entered by lodging with the Clerk of the Court, on or before the 14th January a copy of the Notice of Appeal

Respondents at Quarter Sessions to give notice of intention to appear

7 In an Appeal to Quarter Sessions, the person or persons claiming to appear as Respondents, shall give notice in writing of his or their intention to appear, and shall state in the notice whether he, or they, intend to appear separately, or a joint Respondents with any other person or persons, and such Notice shall be delivered to the Clerk of the Court, and served on the Appellant within fourteen days after the time limited by Order No 6 for the entry of the Appeal, and the person or persons omitting to give such Notice shall not be heard, unless by special leave of the Court, until he or they shall have given such Notice or complied with such terms as the Court may think fit to direct or impose

The expression "person or persons" in this Order shall extend to and include a ratepayer, an occupier, a Surveyor of Taxes, an Assessment Committee, Overseers and any body of persons authorized by law to levy rates or require contributions payable out of rates

Appellants and Respondents at Quarter Sessions to state Cases

8 On, or before, the 1st February next following the entry of an Appeal to Quarter Sessions the Appellant shall state his case and the facts to be proved, and the points of law (if any) to be argued in support of the case, and shall deliver to the Clerk of the Court ten copies thereof for the use of the Court, and shall serve one copy on each Respondent, and, in like manner, each Respondent shall, on or before the same day, state his case, and the facts to be proved, and the points of law (if any) to be argued in support of the case, and shall deliver, in like manner ten copies thereof for the use of the Court, and shall serve one copy on the Appellant

Provided that this Order shall not apply to an Appeal in which the total rateable value appealed against does not exceed £300

Paper and printing

9 The Appellants' and Respondents cases shall be lithographed or printed on judicature paper, bookwise, or on white paper of the same size, and shall be endorsed longways, and the Notice of Appeal and all other documents supplied for the use of the Court, or required to be delivered to the Clerk of the Court, shall be written, lithographed or printed and endorsed as aforesaid

Papers to bear reference number

10 Every document supplied for the use of Quarter Sessions, or filed with the Clerk of the Court, shall contain, at the top of the first page, and on the endorsement, the year and reference number of the Appeal

11 When the terms of an Order to be made in any Appeal to Quarter Sessions have been agreed upon by the parties, particulars of such terms, signed by the parties or their Solicitors, shall be filed with the Clerk of the Court, and, at the next or some subsequent sitting of the Court, an Order may be made in accordance with such terms, upon motion made by either party, with the consent of the other party *Consent Orders*

12 Notices of motion to Quarter Sessions shall be served two clear days before the Court is moved, unless by special leave of the Court, and a copy of the Notice shall be filed with the Clerk of the Court. *Notices of motion*

13 Applications required to be made, and consents required to be given, at Quarter Sessions. shall be made and given by Counsel in open Court *Audience by Counsel*

14 One Counsel only for each party to the Appeal shall be heard at Quarter Sessions, unless by special leave of the Court *One Counsel only to be heard*

15 On Appeals to Quarter Sessions, the Counsel for the Appellant shall begin, except when a Surveyor of Taxes is the Appellant, in which case the Counsel for the Respondents shall begin   In cases in which there shall be more than one Respondent claiming to appeal separately. then Counsel shall be heard in the order determined by the Court at the time *Counsel for Appellant to begin*

16 No Order shall be made at Quarter Sessions affecting the gross value of a hereditament until proof has been given, orally or by affidavit, that Notice of Appeal has been served upon the Surveyor of Taxes *Orders affecting gross value*

17 When an Order made by Quarter Sessions involves an alteration in the Valuation List, the alteration shall not be initialled by the Chairman until the Order has been completed and taken up *Initialling Valuation Lists*

18 The costs ordered by Quarter Sessions to be paid by any of the parties to the Appeal, shall be taxed, in the usual manner, by the Clerk of the Court before the Order is settled *Costs to be taxed*

19 If the party ordered to pay the costs of an Appeal is dissatisfied with the taxation of costs by the Clerk of the Court, such party may carry in objections to the taxation, and the procedure thereupon shall be the same as in the High Court, so far as is practicable *Review of taxation*

20 The Solicitors of the parties shall attend the Clerk of the Court on settling any Order of the Court, at a time to be fixed by him, and shall produce all necessary papers *Solicitors to attend on settling Order of Court*

21 The dates and times prescribed by these Orders (except where fixed by statute) may be extended or varied in Appeals to Quarter Sessions by the Court of Quarter Sessions, upon such terms and conditions as to costs or otherwise as the Court may think fit *Extension of time*

22 The provisions of Section 65 of the Act with respect to the service of Orders and Notices under the Act shall apply to all documents required to be served under these Orders *Service of documents*

Interpretations

23 Such of the expressions in these Orders as are the same as those used in the Act, shall respectively bear the interpretation given to them by the Act

W R McCONNELL,

Chairman of Quarter Sessions

18th April, 1898

Approved,   M W RIDLEY

One of Her Majesty's

Principal Secretaries of State

WHITEHALL,

13th June, 1898

FORM OF RECOGNIZANCE ON APPEAL TO QUARTER SESSIONS OR SPECIAL SESSIONS.

In the County of London,

Special Sessional Division.

WE, the undersigned, severally acknowledge ourselves to owe to our Sovereign Lord the King, the several sums following, namely

of

as Principal, the sum of £   and

of

and   of

as sureties, the sum of £   each

to be levied on our several goods, lands, and tenements, if the said Principal fail in the condition hereunder written

Signed

Taken at   in the

County of London, the

day of

1   before me

Justice of the Peace for the County aforesaid

CONDITION

The condition of the above Recognizance is such that, if the above-bounden Principal shall duly prosecute an Appeal to the Court of Quarter Sessions for the County of London, under the Valuation (Metropolis) Act, 1869, and the Local Government Act, 1888, in respect of certain hereditaments described in the Valuation List for the Parish of   in the County of

London, as   and shall duly pay
the Costs which may be ordered by the said Court to be paid by him,
then this Recognizance shall be void, but otherwise shall remain in
full force.

N.B —This form may be adopted to an Appeal to Special Sessions
Notice of the Recognizance must be given to the Principal and to each
surety

DEPOSIT IN LIEU OF RECOGNIZANCE ON APPEAL TO SPECIAL SESSIONS

In the County of London,
        Special Sessional Division
  I   of
                      acknowledge that I have this day
deposited with the Clerk of the above-mentioned Division, the sum
of £20 to be held by him as security in lieu of a recognizance
to duly prosecute an Appeal to the Justices of the Special
Sessional Division above-mentioned, under the Valuation (Metropolis)
Act, 1869, in respect of certain hereditaments described in the
Valuation List of the Parish of   ·   in the County
of London as   and I undertake duly to
prosecute such Appeal as aforesaid, and to pay the costs which may
be ordered by the said Justices to be paid by me And I consent
to the said Clerk holding the above-mentioned sum, until the above
conditions are performed And I authorise him to apply and pay the
said sum in such manner, to such persons, and in such amounts as the
said Justices shall direct

    Dated this   day of   . I
           Signed
        Witness to the signature
        of the said

APPEALS TO SPECIAL SESSIONS.
The Valuation (Metropolis) Act, 1869

Table of Fees to be Paid to Clerks of Special Sessions.

	s.	d
Drawing notice of Special Sessions or of any adjournment ..	5	0

Preparing and forwarding by post to each Justice residing
    and acting within the Division and to the Overseers of
    each Parish within the Division, a duplicate of such
    notice 2s 6d each, the total amount being divided pro-
    portionately among the Parishes comprised in the
    Division, and the proportion due from each Parish to be
    paid by the Overseers

	s	d.
Recognizances by Appellant and two Sureties	6	0
Notice to Sureties and Appellant (each)	1	0
Upon making a Deposit in lieu of Recognizances	2	6
Entering Appeal (including Hearing and Witnesses) ..	10	0
Drawing and recording Order	5	0
If exceeding 5 folios, at per folio . .	1	0
Certified Order for the parties	5	0
If exceeding 5 folios, at per folio	0	4
Minutes of Order for perusal	2	6
If exceeding 5 folios, at per folio .	0	4
Upon repayment of Deposit .	2	6
Taxation of Costs	10	0
Each subpœna	5	0

W. R. McCONNELL,
Chairman of Quarter Sessions.
18th April, 1898

Approved,   M. W. RIDLEY.
One of Her Majesty's Principal
Secretaries of State

WHITEHALL,
13th June 1898

APPEALS TO QUARTER SESSIONS

The Valuation (Metropolis) Act, 1869

Table of Fees to be Paid to the Clerk of the Court

	s	d
Entering Appeal	5	0
Hearing Fee	13	4
Upon Making a Deposit in lieu of Recognizances ..	5	0
Drawing and recording every Order of Court	5	0
If exceeding five folios, at per folio . ..	1	0
Certified Order of Court for the parties	2	6
If exceeding five folios, at per folio	0	4
Minutes of Order for perusal	2	6
If exceeding five folios, at per folio	0	4
Drawing Special Case, at per folio	1	0
Attending Chairman Settling Case, for every hour's attendance . .. . }	10	0
Copy of the Case as settled, at per folio . .	0	4
Attending Chairman for Signature	10	0
Taxation of Costs, one shilling for every £2 or fraction of £2 of the amount of the bill as taxed .. .. }		

	s	d
Upon repayment of deposit	5	0
Each Subpœna	5	0
Filing each document requiring to be filed .	2	6
Printed List of Appeals, each copy	1	0
Printed Orders and Tables of Fees, each copy	1	0

W R. McCONNELL,

Chairman of Quarter Sessions
18th April, 1898

Approved   M W RIDLEY,

One of Her Majesty's Principal
Secretaries of State.

WHITEHALL,
13th June, 1898

STATUTORY RULES AND ORDERS, 1901 (No 208)

THE LONDON (RATING) SCHEME, 1901

WHEREAS by section fifteen of the London Government Act, 1899 (in this scheme referred to as the Act), it is enacted that it shall be lawful for Her Majesty in Council to refer to a Committee of the Privy Council the appointment of Commissioners to prepare such schemes as are required for carrying the Act into effect and that the Committee may settle the scheme so prepared

[*Recital of Sections 16 and 10 (1) (2) (4) of the Act*]

And whereas the Agricultural Rates Act, 1896, and the Tithe Rentcharge (Rates) Act, 1899, apply to the several rates in those Acts respectively mentioned

And whereas by an Order issued under section thirty-three of the Act, the Lord President of the Council ordered that for the purpose of subsections (1) and (2) of section ten of the Act and of the repeal of such of the enactment specified in the Third Schedule of the Act as relate to rating, the appointed day shall be the first day of April, one thousand nine hundred and one

And whereas the Commissioners appointed by the said Committee of the Privy Council have prepared a scheme containing the provisions hereinafter set forth

Now, therefore, pursuant to the Act, and every other power enabling them in that behalf, the said Committee have settled a scheme containing the provisions herein, and do hereby direct, order, and declare as follows —

1 —(1) Subject to the provisions of this scheme, as from the first day of April, one thousand nine hundred and one, all money to be

Provisions as to rates

raised by rates to meet the expenses of the council of every metropolitan borough, including the sums of money required to be levied by any precept served on the borough council, shall be paid out of the general rate, and a separate sewers rate and a separate lighting rate shall not be levied

(2) The proceeds of any rate levied before the said date which are at that date in the hands or under the control of the council of a metropolitan borough, or which may be received by the council after that date, shall be carried to the same account as that to which the proceeds of the general rate levied after that date are to be carried

2.—(1) In levying the general rate after the first day of April, one thousand nine hundred and one, effect shall be given to any exemption from any existing rate (whether that exemption is given by way of reduced assessment or by levying a differential rate in the pound or in any other manner) by means of the deduction from the total amount of the general rate which would otherwise be payable in respect of any hereditament to which the exemption applies of a proportionate part (corresponding to the exemption) of the amount produced by the rate in the pound which is treated as levied for the purposes in respect of which the exemption exists, or, in the case of a total exemption, equal to the whole amount so produced

Provided that an allowance, commission or deduction under the Poor Rate Assessment and Collection Act, 1869, shall not be deemed to be an exemption within the meaning of this provision

(2) Where in any metropolitan borough the owners or occupiers of any hereditaments or any class of hereditaments are entitled to any exemption the council of that borough shall apportion the total rate in the pound amongst the various purposes for which the general rate is levied, so as to show approximately the rate in the pound required for any purpose or any number of purposes in respect of which there is such an exemption, and shall enter the rates in the pound so apportioned in the heading of the rate, and the rates in the pound so apportioned and entered shall be treated as levied for the purposes in respect of which the exemption exists

(3) The relief given by the Agricultural Rates Act, 1896, shall be treated as an exemption to be given by way of deduction in accordance with this scheme and as applying to the part of the general rate which is treated as levied for purposes for which any existing rates to which that Act applied were levied

(4) Nothing in this scheme shall be construed as extending the duration of an exemption beyond the period during which it would have continued had the Act not been passed

3.—(1) Where, under the Act or otherwise, a rate is to be levied together with, and as an additional item of, the general rate over the whole of any parish in a metropolitan borough the rate shall be included in the general rate for that parish

(2) Where any sum to be raised by the council of a metropolitan borough is to be raised over an area not being the whole of a parish in the borough, the sum to be raised shall be raised by a rate levied together with, and as an additional item of, the general rate over that area

(3) Where by the Act or this scheme or any other scheme under the Act a rate is to be levied together with, and as an additional item of, the general rate, effect shall be given to exemptions in the case of that rate in the same manner as in the case of the general rate

(4) Where an additional item of the general rate is to be levied over part of a parish in any metropolitan borough the council of that borough may, with the consent of the Local Government Board, keep a separate book for the purposes of that additional item but in any such case the net amount to be collected in respect of the item shall be shown in a column of the rate-book for the general rate

4 The Tithe Rentcharge (Rate) Act, 1899, shall be treated as applying to so much of the general rate as is treated as levied for purposes for which the existing rates to which that Act applied were levied

Adaptation of 62 & 63 Vict. c 17

5 The Local Government Board may from time to time by order make such adaptations as they may deem necessary in any statutory form or provisions respecting any rate, so as to give effect to the provisions of the Act and this scheme, and any such order shall have effect as if embodied in this scheme

Form of rate book, etc

6 For the purposes of this scheme the expression ' existing rate ' means any rate leviable in a metropolitan borough before the first day of April, one thousand nine hundred and one.

Definition of existing rate

7 —(1) This scheme may be cited as the London (Rating) Scheme, 1901 and shall have effect subject to the provisions of any future scheme and to the provisions of any scheme dealing with any particular exemption from rates or liability to be assessed

Short title effect and construction

(2) The Interpretation Act, 1889 applies for the purpose of the interpretation of this scheme as it applies to an Act of Parliament.

STATUTORY RULES AND ORDERS, 1902 (No 210)

THE LONDON (ASSESSMENT COMMITTEES) SCHEME, 1902

WHEREAS by various Orders in Council under the London Government Act, 1899 (in this scheme referred to as the Act), twenty-eight metropolitan boroughs have been established and a council for each such borough has been established and incorporated

[*Recital of Sections 15 16, 13 and 10 of this Act*]

And whereas it is necessary, for the purpose of carrying the Act into effect, that such adaptations in the Valuation (Metropolis) Act, 1869, and the enactments incorporated with or amending that Act, should be made as are herein-after contained

And whereas the Commissioners appointed by the said Committee of the Privy Council have prepared a scheme containing the provisions herein-after set forth

Now, therefore, pursuant to the Act and every other power enabling them in that behalf, the said Committee have settled a scheme containing the provisions herein, and do hereby direct, order and declare as follows —

Adaptation of Valuation Acts

1 —(1) Subject to the provisions of this scheme, in cases where before the passing of the Act an assessment committee was appointed by a board of guardians and by virtue of the Act the committee is appointed by the council of a metropolitan borough, all the provisions of the Valuation (Metropolis) Act, 1869, and the enactments incorporated therewith or amending the same, shall be construed, so far as is consistent with the tenor thereof, as if references to the borough, council, members of the council, town clerk, and general rate, were substituted for references to the union, board of guardians, guardians clerk and assistant clerk of the board of guardians, and common fund

(2) The assessment committee so appointed by the council of a metropolitan borough shall be entitled to have, and shall have, in their possession and under their control any valuation lists, notices of objection, returns and other documents which were in the possession or under the control of the assessment committee appointed by the board of guardians

Provided that any officer authorised by the board of guardians in that behalf shall have the same right of inspecting and taking copies of, and extracts from, any of those documents without payment as a Surveyor of Taxes has under section sixty-nine of the Valuation (Metropolis) Act, 1869, and that section shall apply accordingly

Expenses of assessment committee appointed by borough council for part of borough

2 —Where the council of a metropolitan borough, as successors either of a board of guardians or of a vestry appoint an assessment committee which acts for part only of the borough, and an assessment committee appointed by a board of guardians acts for other parts of the borough, the expenses of the committee appointed by the borough council shall be defrayed by the council out of a rate levied together with, and as part of, the general rate of the parishes for which that committee acts

Short title and construction

3 —This scheme may be cited as the London (Assessment Committees) Scheme, 1902, and the Interpretation Act, 1889, applies for the purpose of the interpretation of this scheme as it applies to an Act of Parliament

APPENDIX III.

TABLES AND FORMS

.*. In Tables 1, 2 and 3 the difference in the gross estimated rentals in calculations of ⅙, ⅕ and ¼ is so small that the intermediate calculation only is given

TABLE 1.

Rates at 1s. in the £.

Weekly Rent, inclusive of Rates.	Gross Estimated Rental, less Rates	Rateable Value after deducting—		
		One sixth	One fifth.	One fourth
s d	£ s d	£ s d	£ s d	£ s d
1	4 2	3 6	3 3	3 0
3	12 6	10 6	10 0	9 3
6	1 5 0	1 0 0	1 0 0	18 6
1 0	2 10 0	2 2 6	2 0 0	1 17 6
2 0	5 0 0	4 2 6	4 0 0	3 15 0
3 0	7 10 0	6 5 0	6 0 0	5 12 6
4 0	10 0 0	8 5 0	8 0 0	7 10 0
5 0	12 10 0	10 10 0	10 0 0	9 5 0
6 0	15 0 0	12 10 0	12 0 0	11 5 0
7 0	17 10 0	14 10 0	14 0 0	13 0 0
8 0	20 0 0	16 15 0	16 0 0	15 0 0
9 0	22 10 0	18 15 0	18 0 0	16 15 0
10 0	25 0 0	20 15 0	20 0 0	18 15 0
11 0	27 10 0	23 0 0	22 0 0	20 10 0
12 0	30 0 0	25 0 0	24 0 0	22 10 0

TABLE 2.

Rates at 1s. 6d. in the £.

Weekly Rent inclusive of Rates	Gross Estimated Rental, less Rates	Rateable Value after deducting—		
		One-sixth	One fifth.	One fourth
s. d.	£ s d	£ s. d	£ s. d	£ s. d
1	4 1	3 6	3 3	3 0
3	12 3	10 0	10 0	9 3
6	1 4 6	1 0 0	1 0 0	18 6
1 0	2 9 0	2 0 0	2 0 0	1 17 6
2 0	4 18 0	4 2 6	3 17 6	3 12 6
3 0	7 7 0	6 2 6	5 17 6	5 10 0
4 0	9 16 0	8 5 0	7 15 0	7 7 6
5 0	12 5 0	10 5 0	9 15 0	9 5 0
6 0	14 14 0	12 5 0	11 15 0	11 0 0
7 0	17 3 0	14 5 0	13 15 0	12 15 0
8 0	19 12 0	16 5 0	15 15 0	14 15 0
9 0	22 1 0	18 5 0	17 15 0	16 10 0
10 0	24 10 0	20 10 0	19 10 0	18 5 0
11 0	26 19 0	22 10 0	21 10 0	20 5 0
12 0	29 8 0	24 10 0	23 10 0	22 0 0

TABLE 3

Rates at 1s. 9d. in the £.

Weekly Rent, inclusive of Rates	Gross Estimated Rental less Rate	Rateable Value after deducting—		
		One-sixth	One fifth	One fourth
s d	£ s d	£ s d	£ s d	£ s d
1	4 0	3 4	3 3	3 0
3	12 3	10 0	10 0	9 0
6	1 4 6	1 0 0	1 0 0	18 6
1 0	2 9 0	2 0 0	2 0 0	1 17 6
2 0	4 17 0	4 0 0	3 17 6	3 12 6
3 0	7 6 0	6 2 6	5 15 0	5 10 0
4 0	9 14 0	8 0 0	7 15 0	7 5 0
5 0	12 3 0	10 0 0	9 15 0	9 0 0
6 0	14 12 0	12 5 0	11 15 0	11 0 0
7 0	17 0 0	14 0 0	13 10 0	12 15 0
8 0	19 9 0	16 5 0	15 10 0	14 10 0
9 0	21 17 0	18 5 0	17 10 0	16 10 0
10 0	24 6 0	20 5 0	19 10 0	18 5 0
11 0	26 15 0	22 5 0	21 10 0	20 0 0
12 0	29 3 0	24 5 0	23 5 0	21 15 0

TABLE 4

Rates at 2s. in the £

Weekly Rent inclusive of Rates	At ⅙, or 16⅔ % for Repairs, Insurance, &c		At ⅕, or 20 % for Repairs Insurance, &c		At ¼, or 25 % for Repairs, Insurance, &c	
	Gross Estimated Rental less Rates	Rateable Value after deducting ⅙th	Gross Estimated Rental, less Rates	Rateable Value after deducting ⅕th	Gross Estimated Rental less Rates	Rateable Value after deducting ¼th
s d	£ s d	£ s d	£ s d	£ s d	£ s d	£ s d
1	4 0	3 4	4 0	3 3	4 0	3 0
3	12 0	10 0	12 0	10 0	12 0	9 0
6	1 1 0	1 0 0	1 4 0	19 0	1 1 0	18 0
1 0	2 8 0	2 0 0	2 8 0	1 17 6	2 8 0	1 15 0
2 0	4 16 0	4 0 0	4 16 0	3 17 6	4 17 0	3 12 6
3 0	7 4 0	6 0 0	7 4 0	5 15 0	7 5 0	5 10 0
4 0	9 12 0	8 0 0	9 13 0	7 15 0	9 13 0	7 5 0
5 0	12 0 0	10 0 0	12 1 0	9 15 0	12 2 0	9 0 0
6 0	14 8 0	12 0 0	14 9 0	11 10 0	14 10 0	11 0 0
7 0	16 16 0	14 0 0	16 17 0	13 10 0	16 19 0	12 15 0
8 0	19 4 0	16 0 0	19 5 0	15 10 0	19 7 0	14 10 0
9 0	21 12 0	18 0 0	21 13 0	17 5 0	21 15 0	16 5 0
10 0	24 0 0	20 0 0	24 2 0	19 5 0	24 4 0	18 5 0
11 0	26 8 0	22 0 0	26 10 0	21 5 0	26 12 0	20 0 0
12 0	28 16 0	24 0 0	28 18 0	23 0 0	29 0 0	21 15 0

TABLE 5.

Rates at 2s. 3d. in the £.

Weekly Rent inclusive of Rates.		At ⅙ or 16⅔ % for Repairs, Insurance, &c.						At ⅕, or 20 % for Repairs, Insurance, &c						At ¼, or 25 per cent. for Repairs, Insurance &c.					
		Gross Estimated Rental less Rates.			Rateable Value after deducting ⅙th.			Gross Estimated Rental, less Rates.			Rateable Value after deducting ⅕th			Gross Estimated Rental less Rates			Rateable Value after deducting ¼th		
s	d	£	s	d	£	s	d	£	s	d	£	s	d	£	s	d	£	s	d
	1		3	11		3	4		4	0		3	3		4	0		3	0
	3		12	0		10	0		12	0		10	0		12	0		9	0
	6	1	4	0	1	0	0	1	4	0		19	0	1	4	0		18	0
1	0	2	8	0	2	0	0	2	8	0	1	17	6	2	8	0	1	15	0
2	0	4	15	0	4	0	0	4	15	0	3	15	0	4	16	0	3	12	6
3	0	7	3	0	6	0	0	7	3	0	5	12	6	7	4	0	5	7	6
4	0	9	10	0	8	0	0	9	11	0	7	15	0	9	12	0	7	5	0
5	0	11	18	0	10	0	0	11	19	0	9	10	0	12	0	0	9	0	0
6	0	14	5	0	12	0	0	14	6	0	11	10	0	14	8	0	10	15	0
7	0	16	13	0	14	0	0	16	14	0	13	5	0	16	16	0	12	10	0
8	0	19	0	0	15	15	0	19	2	0	15	5	0	19	4	0	14	10	0
9	0	21	8	0	17	15	0	21	9	0	17	5	0	21	11	0	16	5	0
10	0	23	15	0	19	15	0	23	17	0	19	0	0	23	19	0	18	0	0
11	0	26	3	0	21	15	0	26	5	0	21	0	0	26	7	0	19	15	0
12	0	28	11	0	23	15	0	28	12	0	23	0	0	28	15	0	21	10	0

TABLE 6

Rates at 2s. 6d. in the £.

Weekly Rent inclusive of Rates.		At ⅙, or 16⅔ % for Repairs, Insurance, &c						At ⅕, or 20 % for Repairs, Insurance, &c						At ¼, or 25 % for Repairs, Insurance &c					
		Gross Estimated Rental less Rates.			Rateable Value after deducting ⅙th			Gross Estimated Rental, less Rates			Rateable Value after deducting ⅕th			Gross Estimated Rental less Rates.			Rateable Value after deducting ¼th		
s.	d	£	s	d	£	s	d	£	s	d	£	s	d	£	s	d	£	s	d
	1		3	11		3	4		3	11		3	3		3	11		3	0
	3		11	9		10	0		11	9		9	0		11	9		9	0
	6	1	3	6	1	0	0	1	4	0		19	0	1	3	6		17	6
1	0	2	7	0	2	0	0	2	7	0	1	17	6	2	8	0	1	15	0
2	0	4	14	0	3	17	6	4	15	0	3	15	0	4	15	0	3	12	6
3	0	7	1	0	5	17	6	7	2	0	5	12	6	7	3	0	5	7	6
4	0	9	8	0	7	17	6	9	9	0	7	12	6	9	10	0	7	2	6
5	0	11	15	0	9	15	0	11	16	0	9	10	0	11	18	0	9	0	0
6	0	14	3	0	11	15	0	14	4	0	11	5	0	14	5	0	10	15	0
7	0	16	10	0	13	15	0	16	11	0	13	5	0	16	13	0	12	10	0
8	0	18	17	0	15	15	0	18	18	0	15	5	0	19	0	0	14	5	0
9	0	21	4	0	17	15	0	21	5	0	17	0	0	21	8	0	16	0	0
10	0	23	11	0	19	15	0	23	10	0	19	0	0	23	15	0	17	15	0
11	0	25	18	0	21	10	0	26	0	0	20	15	0	26	3	0	19	10	0
12	0	28	5	0	23	10	0	28	7	0	22	15	0	28	11	0	21	10	0

TABLE 7.

Rates at 3s. in the £.

Weekly Rent inclusive of Rates		At ⅙, or 16⅔ % for Repairs, Insurance, &c.						At ⅕, or 20 % for Repairs, Insurance, &c.						At ¼ or 25 % for Repairs, Insurance, &c.					
		Gross Estimated Rental less Rates			Rateable Value after deducting ⅙th			Gross Estimated Rental, less Rates.			Rateable Value after deducting ⅕th			Gross Estimated Rental, less Rates.			Rateable Value after deducting ¼th		
s	d	£	s	d	£	s	d	£	s	d	£	s	d	£	s	d	£	s	d
	1		3	10		3	3		3	10		3	0		3	10		2	9
	3		11	6		9	6		11	6		9	0		11	6		8	6
	6	1	3	0		19	0	1	3	0		18	0	1	3	0		17	6
1	0	2	6	0	1	17	6	2	6	0	1	17	6	2	7	0	1	15	0
2	0	4	12	0	3	17	6	4	13	0	3	15	0	4	13	0	3	10	0
3	0	6	19	0	5	15	0	6	19	0	5	10	0	7	0	0	5	5	0
4	0	9	5	0	7	15	0	9	6	0	7	10	0	9	7	0	7	0	0
5	0	11	11	0	9	10	0	11	12	0	9	5	0	11	14	0	8	15	0
6	0	13	17	0	11	10	0	13	19	0	11	5	0	14	0	0	10	10	0
7	0	16	3	0	13	10	0	16	5	0	13	0	0	16	7	0	12	5	0
8	0	18	10	0	15	10	0	18	12	0	15	0	0	18	14	0	14	0	0
9	0	20	16	0	17	5	0	20	18	0	16	15	0	21	0	0	15	15	0
10	0	23	2	0	19	5	0	23	5	0	18	10	0	23	7	0	17	10	0
11	0	25	8	0	21	5	0	25	11	0	20	10	0	25	14	0	19	5	0
12	0	27	14	0	23	0	0	27	17	0	22	5	0	28	1	0	21	0	0

TABLE 8.

Rates at 3s. 4d. in the £.

Weekly Rent inclusive of Rates.		At ⅙ or 16⅔ % for Repairs, Insurance, &c						At ⅕, or 20 % for Repairs, Insurance, &c						At ¼, or 25 per cent for Repairs, Insurance, &c					
		Gross Estimated Rental less Rates.			Rateable Value after deducting ⅙th			Gross Estimated Rental, less Rates			Rateable Value after deducting ⅕th			Gross Estimated Rental, less Rates			Rateable Value after deducting ¼th		
s	d	£	s	d	£	s	d.	£	s	d.	£	s	d	£	s	d	£	s	d.
	1		3	9		3	0		3	9		3	0		3	9		2	9
	3		11	6		9	6		11	6		9	0		11	6		8	6
	6	1	3	0		19	0	1	3	0		18	6	1	3	0		17	6
1	0	2	6	0	1	17	6	2	6	0	1	17	6	2	6	0	1	15	0
2	0	4	11	0	3	15	0	4	12	0	3	12	6	4	12	0	3	10	0
3	0	6	17	0	5	15	0	6	18	0	5	10	0	6	19	0	5	5	0
4	0	9	3	0	7	12	6	9	4	0	7	7	6	9	5	0	6	17	6
5	0	11	8	0	9	10	0	11	9	0	9	5	0	11	11	0	8	15	0
6	0	13	14	0	11	10	0	13	15	0	11	0	0	13	17	0	10	10	0
7	0	16	0	0	13	5	0	16	1	0	12	15	0	16	4	0	12	0	0
8	0	18	5	0	15	5	0	18	7	0	14	15	0	18	10	0	13	15	0
9	0	20	11	0	17	0	0	20	13	0	16	10	0	20	16	0	15	10	0
10	0	22	17	0	19	0	0	22	19	0	18	5	0	23	2	0	17	5	0
11	0	25	2	0	21	0	0	25	5	0	20	5	0	25	8	0	19	0	0
12	0	27	8	0	22	15	0	27	11	0	22	0	0	27	15	0	20	15	0

TABLE 9.

Rates at 3s. 8d. in the £.

Weekly Rent, inclusive of Rates	At ⅙, or 16⅔ % for Repairs, Insurance &c				At ⅕, or 20 % for Repairs, Insurance, &c				At ¼, or 25 % for Repairs, Insurance &c			
	Gross Estimated Rental, less Rates.			Rateable Value after deducting ⅙th			Gross Estimated Rental less Rates			Rateable Value after deducting ⅕th			Gross Estimated Rental less Rates.			Rateable Value after deducting ¼th
s d	£	s	d	£	s	d	£	s	d	£	s	d	£	s	d	£	s	d
1		3	9		3	0		3	9		3	0		3	9		2	9
3		11	3		9	0		11	3		9	0		11	6		9	0
6	1	2	6		19	0	1	3	0		18	6	1	3	0		17	6
1 0	2	5	0	1	17	6	2	5	0	1	17	6	2	6	0	1	15	0
2 0	4	10	0	3	15	0	4	11	0	3	12	6	4	11	0	3	7	6
3 0	6	15	0	5	12	6	6	16	0	5	7	6	6	17	0	5	2	6
4 0	9	0	0	7	10	0	9	1	0	7	5	0	9	3	0	6	15	0
5 0	11	6	0	9	10	0	11	7	0	9	0	0	11	9	0	8	10	0
6 0	13	11	0	11	5	0	13	12	0	11	0	0	13	14	0	10	5	0
7 0	15	16	0	13	5	0	15	17	0	12	15	0	16	0	0	12	0	0
8 0	18	1	0	15	0	0	18	3	0	14	10	0	18	6	0	13	15	0
9 0	20	6	0	17	0	0	20	8	0	16	5	0	20	11	0	15	10	0
10 0	22	11	0	18	15	0	22	13	0	18	0	0	22	17	0	17	5	0
11 0	24	16	0	20	15	0	24	19	0	20	0	0	25	3	0	18	15	0
12 0	27	1	0	22	10	0	27	4	0	21	15	0	27	8	0	20	10	0

TABLE 10

Rates at 4s. in the £.

Weekly Rent inclusive of Rates	At ⅙, or 16⅔ % for Repairs, Insurance, &c				At ⅕, or 20 % for Repairs, Insurance, &c				At ¼, or 25 % for Repairs, Insurance &c.			
	Gross Estimated Rental less Rates.			Rateable Value after deducting ⅙th			Gross Estimated Rental less Rates.			Rateable Value after deducting ⅕th			Gross Estimated Rental, less Rates			Rateable Value after deducting ¼th
s d	£	s.	d.	£	s	d.	£	s	d	£	s	d	£	s	d	£	s	d.
1		3	9		3	0		3	9		3	0		3	9		2	9
3		11	3		9	0		11	0		9	0		11	3		9	0
6	1	2	6		19	0	1	2	6		18	0	1	2	6		17	0
1 0	2	5	0	1	17	6	2	5	0	1	15	0	2	5	0	1	15	0
2 0	4	9	0	3	15	0	4	9	0	3	10	0	4	10	0	3	7	6
3 0	6	14	0	5	12	6	6	14	0	5	7	6	6	16	0	5	2	6
4 0	8	18	0	7	7	6	8	19	0	7	2	6	9	1	0	6	15	0
5 0	11	3	0	9	5	0	11	4	0	9	0	0	11	6	0	8	10	0
6 0	13	7	0	11	5	0	13	9	0	10	15	0	13	11	0	10	5	0
7 0	15	12	0	13	0	0	15	14	0	12	10	0	15	16	0	11	15	0
8 0	17	17	0	14	15	0	17	18	0	14	5	0	18	2	0	13	10	0
9 0	20	1	0	16	15	0	20	3	0	16	5	0	20	7	0	15	5	0
10 0	22	6	0	18	10	0	22	8	0	18	0	0	22	12	0	17	0	0
11 0	24	10	0	20	10	0	24	13	0	19	15	0	24	17	0	18	15	0
12 0	26	15	0	22	5	0	26	17	0	21	10	0	27	3	0	20	5	0

TABLE 11.

Rates at 4s 6d. in the £

Weekly Rent, inclusive of Rates	At ⅙, or 16⅔ % for Repairs, Insurance, &c.		At ⅕ or 20 % for Repairs, Insurance, &c		At ¼, or 25 % for Repairs, Insurance, &c	
	Gross Estimated Rental, less Rates.	Rateable Value after deducting ⅙th	Gross Estimated Rental, less Rates	Rateable Value after deducting ⅕th	Gross Estimated Rental, less Rates.	Rateable Value after deducting ¼th
s d	£ s d	£ s d	£ s d	£ s d	£ s d	£ s d
1	3 8	3 0	3 8	3 0	3 8	2 9
3	11 0	9 0	11 0	9 0	11 0	8 0
6	1 2 0	18 6	1 2 0	17 6	1 2 6	17 0
1 0	2 4 0	1 17 6	2 4 0	1 15 0	2 5 0	1 12 6
2 0	4 8 0	3 12 6	4 8 0	3 10 0	4 9 0	3 7 6
3 0	6 12 0	5 10 0	6 12 0	5 5 0	6 13 0	5 0 0
4 0	8 15 0	7 5 0	8 16 0	7 0 0	8 18 0	6 12 6
5 0	10 19 0	9 0 0	11 0 0	8 15 0	11 2 0	8 5 0
6 0	13 3 0	11 0 0	13 4 0	10 10 0	13 7 0	10 0 0
7 0	15 7 0	12 15 0	15 9 0	12 5 0	15 11 0	11 15 0
8 0	17 10 0	14 10 0	17 13 0	14 0 0	17 16 0	13 5 0
9 0	1C 14 0	16 10 0	19 17 0	16 0 0	20 0 0	15 0 0
10 0	21 18 0	18 5 0	22 1 0	17 15 0	22 5 0	16 15 0
11 0	24 2 0	20 0 0	24 5 0	19 10 0	24 9 0	18 5 0
12 0	26 6 0	22 0 0	26 9 0	21 5 0	26 14 0	20 0 0

TABLE 12

Rates at 5s. in the £.

Weekly Rent inclusive of Rates	At ⅙, or 16⅔ % for Repairs, Insurance, &c		At ⅕, or 20 % for Repairs, Insurance, &c		At ¼, or 25 % for Repairs, Insurance, &c	
	Gross Estimated Rental, less Rates.	Rateable Value after deducting ⅙th	Gross Estimated Rental less Rates.	Rateable Value after deducting ⅕th	Gross Estimated Rental, less Rates.	Rateable Value after deducting ¼th
s d	£ s d	£ s d	£ s d	£ s d	£ s d	£ s d
1	3 6	3 0	3 6	3 0	3 9	3 0
3	10 9	9 0	10 9	8 6	11 6	8 6
6	1 1 6	18 0	1 1 6	17 6	1 2 0	16 6
1 0	2 3 0	1 15 0	2 3 0	1 15 0	2 4 0	1 12 6
2 0	4 6 0	3 12 6	4 7 0	3 10 0	4 8 0	3 5 0
3 0	6 9 0	5 7 6	6 10 0	5 5 0	6 11 0	4 17 6
4 0	8 12 0	7 2 6	8 13 0	6 17 6	8 15 0	6 12 6
5 0	10 15 0	9 0 0	10 17 0	8 15 0	10 19 0	8 5 0
6 0	12 18 0	10 15 0	13 0 0	10 10 0	13 3 0	9 15 0
7 0	15 1 0	12 10 0	15 3 0	12 5 0	15 7 0	11 10 0
8 0	17 4 0	14 5 0	17 7 0	13 15 0	17 10 0	13 5 0
9 0	19 7 0	16 5 0	19 10 0	15 10 0	19 14 0	14 15 0
10 0	21 10 0	18 0 0	21 13 0	17 5 0	21 18 0	16 10 0
11 0	23 13 0	19 15 0	23 17 0	19 0 0	24 2 0	18 0 0
12 0	25 16 0	21 10 0	26 0 0	20 15 0	26 5 0	19 15 0

TABLE 13.

Rates at 5s. 6d. in the £.

Weekly Rent, inclusive of Rates.		At ⅙, or 16⅔ % for Repairs, Insurance &c.		At ⅕, or 20 % for Repairs, Insurance, &c.		At ¼, or 25 % for Repairs, Insurance. &c.	
		Gross Estimated Rental, less Rates.	Rateable Value after deducting ⅙th	Gross Estimated Rental, less Rates	Rateable Value after deducting ⅕th	Gross Estimated Rental, less Rates.	Rateable Value after deducting ¼th
s	d	£ s d	£ s d	£ s d	£ s d	£ s d.	£ s d.
	1	3 6	3 0	3 6	3 0	3 6	2 6
	3	10 6	8 6	11 0	9 0	11 0	8 0
	6	1 1 0	17 6	1 1 6	17 6	1 1 6	16 0
1	0	2 2 0	1 15 0	2 3 0	1 15 0	2 3 0	1 12 0
2	0	4 5 0	3 10 0	4 5 0	3 10 0	4 6 0	3 5 0
3	0	6 7 0	5 5 0	6 8 0	5 0 0	6 9 0	4 17 6
4	0	8 9 0	7 0 0	8 10 0	6 15 0	8 12 0	6 10 0
5	0	10 11 0	8 15 0	10 13 0	8 10 0	10 16 0	8 0 0
6	0	12 14 0	10 10 0	12 16 0	10 5 0	12 19 0	9 15 0
7	0	14 16 0	12 5 0	14 18 0	12 0 0	15 2 0	11 5 0
8	0	16 18 0	14 0 0	17 1 0	13 15 0	17 5 0	13 0 0
9	0	19 1 0	15 15 0	19 4 0	15 5 0	19 8 0	14 10 0
10	0	21 3 0	17 10 0	21 6 0	17 0 0	21 11 0	16 5 0
11	0	23 5 0	19 5 0	23 9 0	18 15 0	23 14 0	17 15 0
12	0	25 8 0	21 5 0	25 11 0	20 10 0	25 17 0	19 10 0

TABLE 14.

Rates at 6s. in the £.

Weekly Rent inclusive of Rates.		At ⅙, or 16⅔ % for Repairs Insurance &c		At ⅕, or 20 % for Repairs, Insurance, &c.		At ¼, or 25 % for Repairs, Insurance, &c	
		Gross Estimated Rental, less Rates.	Rateable Value after deducting ⅙th	Gross Estimated Rental, less Rates.	Rateable Value after deducting ⅕th	Gross Estimated Rental less Rates.	Rateable Value after deducting ¼th
s	d	£ s d	£ s. d	£ s. d	£ s d	£ s d	£ s d
	1	3 6	3 0	3 6	3 0	3 6	2 6
	3	10 6	8 6	10 6	8 6	10 6	8 0
	6	1 1 0	17 6	1 1 0	17 6	1 1 0	16 0
1	0	2 2 0	1 15 0	2 2 0	1 12 6	2 2 0	1 12 0
2	0	4 3 0	3 10 0	4 4 0	3 7 6	4 5 0	3 2 6
3	0	6 5 0	5 5 0	6 6 0	5 0 0	6 7 0	4 15 0
4	0	8 6 0	7 0 0	8 8 0	6 15 0	8 10 0	6 7 6
5	0	10 8 0	8 15 0	10 10 0	8 10 0	10 12 0	8 0 0
6	0	12 10 0	10 10 0	12 11 0	10 0 0	12 15 0	9 10 0
7	0	14 11 0	12 5 0	14 13 0	11 15 0	14 17 0	11 5 0
8	0	16 13 0	13 15 0	16 15 0	13 10 0	16 19 0	12 15 0
9	0	18 14 0	15 10 0	18 17 0	15 5 0	19 2 0	14 5 0
10	0	20 16 0	17 5 0	20 19 0	16 15 0	21 4 0	16 0 0
11	0	22 18 0	19 0 0	23 1 0	18 10 0	23 7 0	17 10 0
12	0	24 19 0	20 15 0	25 3 0	20 0 0	25 9 0	19 0 0

TABLE 15

Rates at 6s 6d. in the £.

Weekly Rent, inclusive of Rates		At ⅙, or 16⅔ % for Repairs, Insurance, &c.						At ⅕, or 20 % for Repairs, Insurance &c.						At ¼, or 25 % for Repairs, Insurance &c.					
		Gross Estimated Rental less Rates.			Rateable Value after deducting ⅙th			Gross Estimated Rental, less Rates.			Rateable Value after deducting ⅕th			Gross Estimated Rental less Rates			Rateable Value after deducting ¼th		
s	d	£	s	d	£	s	d.	£	s	d	£	s	d	£	s	d	£	s	d
	1		3	5		2	9		3	5		2	9		3	6		2	6
	3		10	0		8	6		10	0		8	0		10	6		8	0
	6	1	0	0		17	0	1	1	0		17	0	1	1	0		16	0
1	0	2	1	0	1	15	0	2	1	0	1	12	6	2	2	0	1	12	6
2	0	4	2	0	3	7	6	4	3	0	3	5	0	4	4	0	3	2	6
3	0	6	3	0	5	2	6	6	4	0	5	0	0	6	5	0	4	12	6
4	0	8	4	0	6	17	6	8	5	0	6	12	6	8	7	0	6	5	0
5	0	10	5	0	8	10	0	10	6	0	8	5	0	10	9	0	7	17	6
6	0	12	5	0	10	0	0	12	8	0	10	0	0	12	11	0	9	10	0
7	0	14	6	0	12	0	0	14	9	0	11	10	0	14	13	0	11	0	0
8	0	16	7	0	13	10	0	16	10	0	13	5	0	16	14	0	12	10	0
9	0	18	8	0	15	5	0	18	11	0	14	15	0	18	16	0	14	0	0
10	0	20	9	0	17	0	0	20	13	0	16	10	0	20	18	0	15	15	0
11	0	22	10	0	18	15	0	22	14	0	18	5	0	23	0	0	17	5	0
12	0	24	11	0	20	10	0	24	15	0	20	0	0	25	2	0	18	15	0

TABLE 16

Rates at 7s. in the £.

Weekly Rent inclusive of Rates		At ⅙, or 16⅔ % for Repairs, Insurance, &c.						At ⅕, or 20 % for Repairs, Insurance &c.						At ¼ or 25 % for Repairs Insurance &c.					
		Gross Estimated Rental, less Rates.			Rateable Value after deducting ⅙th			Gross Estimated Rental less Rates			Rateable Value after deducting ⅕th			Gross Estimated Rental less Rates			Rateable Value after deducting ¼th		
s	d	£	s	d	£	s	d.	£	s	d	£	s	d	£	s	d	£	s	d
	1		3	4		2	9		3	4		2	8		3	5		2	6
	3		10	0		8	6		10	0		8	0		10	0		7	6
	6	1	0	0		17	0	1	0	0		16	0	1	1	0		15	0
1	0	2	0	0	1	12	6	2	1	0	1	12	6	2	1	0	1	10	0
2	0	4	1	0	3	7	6	4	1	0	3	5	0	4	2	0	3	0	0
3	0	6	1	0	5	0	0	6	2	0	4	17	6	6	4	0	4	12	6
4	0	8	1	0	6	15	0	8	2	0	6	10	0	8	5	0	6	2	6
5	0	10	1	0	8	5	0	10	3	0	8	0	0	10	6	0	7	15	0
6	0	12	2	0	10	0	0	12	4	0	9	15	0	12	7	0	9	5	0
7	0	14	2	0	11	15	0	14	4	0	11	10	0	14	8	0	10	15	0
8	0	16	2	0	13	10	0	16	5	0	13	0	0	16	9	0	12	5	0
9	0	18	2	0	15	0	0	18	5	0	14	10	0	18	11	0	14	0	0
10	0	20	3	0	16	15	0	20	6	0	16	5	0	20	12	0	15	10	0
11	0	22	3	0	18	10	0	22	7	0	18	0	0	22	13	0	17	0	0
12	0	24	3	0	20	0	0	24	7	0	19	10	0	24	14	0	18	10	0

TABLE 17

Rates at 7s 6d in the £.

Weekly Rent inclusive of Rates	At ⅙ or 16⅔ % for Repairs, Insurance, &c.		At ⅕ or 20 % for Repairs, Insurance, &c.		At ¼ or 25 % for Repairs, Insurance, &c.	
	Gross Estimated Rental less Rates.	Rateable Value after deducting ⅙th	Gross Estimated Rental less Rates	Rateable Value after deducting ⅕th	Gross Estimated Rental less Rates	Rateable Value after deducting ¼th
s d	£ s d	£ s d	£ s d	£ s d	£ s. d	£ s d.
1	3 3	2 9	3 4	2 9	3 4	2 6
3	10 0	8 6	10 0	8 0	10 0	7 6
6	1 0 0	17 0	1 0 0	16 0	1 0 0	15 0
1 0	2 0 0	1 12 6	2 0 0	1 12 6	2 1 0	1 10 0
2 0	3 19 0	3 5 0	4 0 0	3 5 0	4 1 0	3 0 0
3 0	5 19 0	5 0 0	6 0 0	4 15 0	6 2 0	4 12 6
4 0	7 18 0	6 10 0	8 0 0	6 7 6	8 2 0	6 2 6
5 0	9 18 0	8 5 0	10 0 0	8 0 0	10 3 0	7 10 0
6 0	11 18 0	10 0 0	12 0 0	9 10 0	12 3 0	9 0 0
7 0	13 17 0	11 10 0	14 0 0	11 5 0	14 4 0	10 15 0
8 0	15 17 0	13 5 0	16 0 0	12 15 0	16 5 0	12 5 0
9 0	17 17 0	14 15 0	18 0 0	14 10 0	18 5 0	14 0 0
10 0	19 16 0	16 10 0	20 0 0	16 0 0	20 6 0	15 5 0
11 0	21 16 0	18 5 0	22 0 0	17 10 0	22 6 0	16 15 0
12 0	23 15 0	19 15 0	24 0 0	19 5 0	24 7 0	18 5 0

TABLE 18

Rates at 8s. in the £.

Weekly Rent inclusive of Rates	At ⅙ or 16⅔ % for Repairs Insurance &c		At ⅕ or 20 % for Repairs Insurance, &c		At ¼ or 25 % for Repairs Insurance &c	
	Gross Estimated Rental less Rates	Rateable Value after deducting ⅙th	Gross Estimated Rental less Rates	Rateable Value after deducting ⅕th	Gross Estimated Rental less Rates.	Rateable Value after deducting ¼th
s d	£ s d	£ s d	£ s d	£ s d	£ s d	£ s d
1	3 3	2 9	3 3	2 9	3 4	2 6
3	10 0	8 6	10 0	8 0	10 0	7 6
6	1 0 0	17 0	1 0 0	16 0	1 0 0	15 0
1 0	1 19 0	1 12 6	1 19 0	1 12 6	2 0 0	1 10 0
2 0	3 18 0	3 5 0	3 19 0	3 2 6	4 0 0	3 0 0
3 0	5 17 0	4 17 6	5 18 0	4 15 0	6 0 0	4 10 0
4 0	7 16 0	6 10 0	7 18 0	6 5 0	8 0 0	6 0 0
5 0	9 15 0	8 0 0	9 17 0	7 17 6	10 0 0	8 0 0
6 0	11 14 0	9 15 0	11 16 0	9 10 0	12 0 0	9 0 0
7 0	13 13 0	11 5 0	13 16 0	11 0 0	14 0 0	10 10 0
8 0	15 12 0	13 0 0	15 15 0	12 10 0	16 0 0	12 0 0
9 0	17 11 0	14 10 0	17 14 0	14 5 0	18 0 0	13 10 0
10 0	19 10 0	16 5 0	19 14 0	15 15 0	20 0 0	15 0 0
11 0	21 9 0	17 15 0	21 13 0	17 5 0	22 0 0	16 10 0
12 0	23 8 0	19 10 0	23 13 0	19 0 0	24 0 0	18 0 0

TABLE 19.

Rates at 8s. 6d. in the £

Weekly Rent inclusive of Rates		At ⅙, or 16⅔ % for Repairs, Insurance, &c.						At ⅕, or 20 % for Repairs, Insurance, &c.						At ¼, or 25 % for Repairs, Insurance, &c.					
		Gross Estimated Rental less Rates			Rateable Value after deducting ⅙th			Gross Estimated Rental, less Rates			Rateable Value after deducting ⅕th			Gross Estimated Rental, less Rates.			Rateable Value after deducting ¼th		
s	*d*	£	*s*	*d*	£	*s*	*d*	£	*s*	*d*	£	*s*	*d*	£	*s*	*d*	£	*s*	*d.*
	1		3	2		2	6		3	3		2	6		3	3		2	6
	3		10	0		8	6		10	0		8	0		10	0		7	6
	6	1	0	0		17	0	1	0	0		16	0	1	0	0		15	0
1	0	1	18	0	1	12	6	1	19	0	1	12	6	1	19	0	1	10	0
2	0	3	17	0	3	5	0	3	18	0	3	2	6	3	19	0	3	0	0
3	0	5	15	0	4	15	0	5	16	0	4	12	6	5	18	0	4	7	6
4	0	7	13	0	6	7	6	7	15	0	6	5	0	7	18	0	6	0	0
5	0	9	12	0	8	0	0	9	14	0	7	15	0	9	17	0	7	7	6
6	0	11	10	0	9	10	0	11	13	0	9	5	0	11	17	0	9	0	0
7	0	13	9	0	11	5	0	13	12	0	11	0	0	13	16	0	10	5	0
8	0	15	7	0	12	15	0	15	10	0	12	10	0	15	16	0	11	15	0
9	0	17	6	0	14	10	0	17	9	0	14	0	0	17	15	0	13	5	0
10	0	19	4	0	16	0	0	19	8	0	15	10	0	19	14	0	14	15	0
11	0	21	2	0	17	10	0	21	7	0	17	0	0	21	14	0	16	5	0
12	0	23	1	0	19	5	0	23	6	0	18	15	0	23	13	0	17	15	0

TABLE 20.

Rates at 9s in the £.

Weekly Rent inclusive of Rates		At ⅙, or 16⅔ % for Repairs, Insurance, &c.						At ⅕ or 20 % for Repairs, Insurance, &c.						At ¼ or 25 % for Repairs, Insurance &c.					
		Gross Estimated Rental less Rates.			Rateable Value after deducting ⅙th			Gross Estimated Rental less Rates			Rateable Value after deducting ⅕th			Gross Estimated Rental, less Rates			Rateable Value after deducting ¼th		
s	*d*	£	*s*	*d*	£	*s*	*d.*	£	*s.*	*d.*	£	*s.*	*d*	£	*s*	*d*	£	*s*	*d*
	1		3	2		2	6		3	2		2	6		3	3		2	6
	3		10	0		8	6		10	0		8	0		10	0		7	6
	6		19	0		16	0		19	0		15	0		19	0		15	0
1	0	1	18	0	1	12	6	1	18	0	1	10	0	1	19	0	1	10	0
2	0	3	16	0	3	5	0	3	16	0	3	0	0	3	18	0	2	17	6
3	0	5	13	0	4	15	0	5	15	0	4	10	0	5	17	0	4	7	6
4	0	7	11	0	6	5	0	7	13	0	6	2	6	7	15	0	5	15	0
5	0	9	9	0	7	17	6	9	11	0	7	12	6	9	14	0	7	5	0
6	0	11	7	0	9	10	0	11	9	0	9	5	0	11	13	0	8	15	0
7	0	13	5	0	11	0	0	13	8	0	10	15	0	13	12	0	10	5	0
8	0	15	3	0	12	10	0	15	6	0	12	5	0	15	11	0	11	15	0
9	0	17	0	0	14	5	0	17	4	0	13	15	0	17	10	0	13	0	0
10	0	18	18	0	15	15	0	19	2	0	15	5	0	19	9	0	14	10	0
11	0	20	16	0	17	5	0	21	1	0	16	15	0	21	8	0	16	0	0
12	0	22	14	0	19	0	0	22	19	0	18	0	0	23	6	0	17	10	0

TABLE 21.

Rates at 9s. 6d. in the £.

Weekly Rent inclusive of Rates		At ⅙, or 16⅔ % for Repairs, Insurance, &c.						At ⅕ or 20 % for Repairs, Insurance, &c.						At ¼, or 25 % for Repairs, Insurance, &c.					
		Gross Estimated Rental, less Rates.			Rateable Value after deducting ⅕th			Gross Estimated Rental, less Rates			Rateable Value after deducting ¼th			Gross Estimated Rental less Rates.			Rateable Value after deducting ¼th.		
s	d	£	s.	d	£	s	d	£	s	d	£	s	d	£	s	d	£	s	d.
	1		3	1		2	6		3	2		2	6		3	2		2	6
	3		9	0		7	6		9	0		7	0		9	6		7	6
	6		18	0		15	0		19	0		15	0		19	0		15	0
1	0	1	17	0	1	10	0	1	18	0	1	10	0	1	18	0	1	7	6
2	0	3	14	0	3	2	6	3	15	0	3	0	0	3	17	0	2	17	6
3	0	5	12	0	4	12	6	5	13	0	4	10	0	5	15	0	4	5	0
4	0	7	9	0	6	5	0	7	11	0	6	0	0	7	13	0	5	15	0
5	0	9	6	0	7	15	0	9	8	0	7	10	0	9	12	0	7	5	0
6	0	11	3	0	9	5	0	11	6	0	9	0	0	11	10	0	8	10	0
7	0	13	0	0	10	15	0	13	4	0	10	10	0	13	8	0	10	0	0
8	0	14	18	0	12	10	0	15	2	0	12	0	0	15	7	0	11	10	0
9	0	16	15	0	14	10	0	17	0	0	13	10	0	17	5	0	13	0	0
10	0	18	12	0	15	10	0	18	17	0	15	0	0	19	3	0	14	5	0
11	0	20	10	0	17	0	0	20	15	0	16	10	0	21	2	0	15	15	0
12	0	22	7	0	18	10	0	22	13	0	18	0	0	23	0	0	17	5	0

TABLE 22.

Rates at 10s. in the £.

Weekly Rent inclusive of Rates.		At ⅙, or 16⅔ % for Repairs, Insurance, &c.						At ⅕, or 20 % for Repairs, Insurance, &c.						At ¼, or 25 % for Repairs, Insurance, &c.					
		Gross Estimated Rental less Rates.			Rateable Value after deducting ⅕th			Gross Estimated Rental less Rates.			Rateable Value after deducting ¼th			Gross Estimated Rental less Rates			Rateable Value after deducting ¼th		
s	d.	£	s	d.	£	s	d	£	s.	d	£	s	d	£	s	d	£	s.	d
	1		3	0		2	6		3	1		2	6		3	2		2	6
	3		9	0		7	6		9	0		7	0		9	6		7	6
	6		18	0		15	0		19	0		15	0		19	0		15	0
1	0	1	17	0	1	10	0	1	17	0	1	10	0	1	18	0	1	7	6
2	0	3	13	0	3	0	0	3	14	0	3	0	0	3	16	0	2	15	0
3	0	5	10	0	4	12	6	5	11	0	4	10	0	5	13	0	4	5	0
4	0	7	7	0	6	2	6	7	8	0	6	0	0	7	11	0	5	12	6
5	0	9	3	0	7	12	6	9	6	0	7	10	0	9	9	0	7	0	0
6	0	11	0	0	9	5	0	11	3	0	9	0	0	11	7	0	8	10	0
7	0	12	17	0	10	5	0	13	0	0	10	10	0	13	5	0	10	0	0
8	0	14	14	0	12	5	0	14	17	0	12	0	0	15	3	0	11	5	0
9	0	16	10	0	13	15	0	16	14	0	13	5	0	17	0	0	12	15	0
10	0	18	7	0	15	5	0	18	11	0	14	15	0	18	18	0	14	5	0
11	0	20	4	0	16	15	0	20	9	0	16	5	0	20	16	0	15	10	0
12	0	22	0	0	18	5	0	22	6	0	17	15	0	22	14	0	17	0	0

TABLE 23

Rates at 11s in the £.

Weekly Rent, inclusive of Rates		At ⅙, or 16⅔ % for Repairs, Insurance &c.						At ⅕, or 20 % for Repairs, Insurance, &c						At ¼, or 25 % for Repairs, Insurance, &c.					
		Gross Estimated Rental less Rates			Rateable Value after deducting ⅙th			Gross Estimated Rental, less Rates			Rateable Value after deducting ⅕th			Gross Estimated Rental less Rates			Rateable Value after deducting ¼th		
s	*d*	£	*s*	*d*	£	*s*	*d*	£	*s*	*d*	£	*s*	*d*	£	*s*	*d*	£	*s*	*d*
	1		2	11		2	6		3	0		2	6		3	0		2	3
	3		9	0		7	6		9	0		7	0		9	0		6	6
	6		18	0		15	0		18	0		14	0		18	0		13	0
1	0	1	16	0	1	10	0	1	16	0	1	10	0	1	17	0	1	7	6
2	0	3	11	0	3	0	0	3	12	0	2	17	6	3	14	0	2	15	0
3	0	5	7	0	4	10	0	5	8	0	4	5	0	5	10	0	4	2	6
4	0	7	3	0	6	0	0	7	4	0	5	15	0	7	7	0	5	10	0
5	0	8	18	0	7	7	6	9	1	0	7	5	0	9	4	0	6	17	6
6	0	10	14	0	9	0	0	10	17	0	8	15	0	11	1	0	8	5	0
7	0	12	10	0	10	10	0	12	13	0	10	0	0	12	18	0	9	15	0
8	0	14	5	0	11	15	0	14	9	0	11	10	0	14	15	0	11	0	0
9	0	16	1	0	13	5	0	16	5	0	13	0	0	16	11	0	12	10	0
10	0	17	17	0	14	15	0	18	1	0	14	10	0	18	8	0	13	15	0
11	0	19	12	0	16	5	0	19	17	0	16	0	0	20	5	0	15	5	0
12	0	21	8	0	17	15	0	21	13	0	17	5	0	22	2	0	16	15	0

TABLE 24

Rates at 12s. in the £.

Weekly Rent inclusive of Rates.		At ⅙, or 16⅔ % for Repairs, Insurance, &c.						At ⅕ or 20 % for Repairs, Insurance, &c						At ¼, or 25 % for Repairs, Insurance, &c.					
		Gross Estimated Rental less Rates.			Rateable Value after deducting ⅙th			Gross Estimated Rental, less Rates.			Rateable Value after deducting ⅕th			Gross Estimated Rental, less Rates.			Rateable Value after deducting ¼th		
s.	*d*	£	*s*	*d*	£	*s*	*d*	£	*s*	*d.*	£	*s*	*d*	£	*s*	*d*	£	*s*	*d*
	1		2	10		2	3		2	11		2	3		3	0		2	3
	3		9	0		7	6		9	0		7	0		9	0		6	6
	6		17	0		14	0		18	0		14	0		18	0		13	0
1	0	1	15	0	1	10	0	1	15	0	1	7	6	1	16	0	1	7	6
2	0	3	9	0	2	17	6	3	10	0	2	15	0	3	12	0	2	15	0
3	0	5	4	0	4	7	6	5	5	0	4	5	0	5	8	0	4	1	0
4	0	6	19	0	5	15	0	7	1	0	5	12	6	7	3	0	5	7	6
5	0	8	13	0	7	5	0	8	16	0	7	0	0	8	19	0	6	15	0
6	0	10	8	0	8	15	0	10	11	0	8	15	0	10	15	0	8	0	0
7	0	12	3	0	10	0	0	12	6	0	9	15	0	12	11	0	9	10	0
8	0	13	17	0	11	10	0	14	1	0	11	5	0	14	7	0	10	15	0
9	0	15	12	0	13	0	0	15	16	0	12	15	0	16	3	0	12	0	0
10	0	17	7	0	14	10	0	17	11	0	14	0	0	17	19	0	13	10	0
11	0	19	1	0	15	15	0	19	6	0	15	10	0	19	14	0	14	15	0
12	0	20	16	0	17	5	0	21	2	0	17	0	0	21	10	0	16	0	0

FORM OF NOTICE OF OBJECTION

To the Assessment Committee of the Union in the County of

and

[To the Churchwardens and Overseers of the Poor of the Parish of
]

[To the Overseers of the Poor of the Parish of
and the Parish Council of the said Parish]²

[To the Overseers of the Poor of the Parish of   ]³

[To the Overseers of the Poor of the Parish of   and
the Parish Meeting of the said Parish   ]⁴

in the said Union

I   of

being aggrieved by the Valuation List in force for the Parish of
hereby give you and each of you
notice that I feel aggrieved by the said Valuation List for the parish
aforesaid in which I am described as occupier of hereditaments,
situate and described as

and that I object to the List on the following grounds —

1 —That the said Valuation List is generally unequal, unfair and
incorrect

2 —That the principle upon which the annual value of the
hereditaments is estimated is erroneous

3 —That other hereditaments, similar in character and description
to the said hereditaments and occupied for purposes similar to those
for which the said hereditaments are occupied by me the Appellant, and
situate in the parish aforesaid, have not been valued for the said
Valuation List in the same manner or by the same method as have
the said hereditaments occupied by me.

4.—That the aforesaid Valuation List includes works, factories,
shops, dwelling houses and other hereditaments not being now
assessed upon an estimate of their full annual value, but being
assessed upon a sum less than the amount of such full value

---

¹ Insert the words in these brackets if an urban parish in which no Order of
the Local Government Board affecting the powers of the Overseers has been made
under the powers of the Local Government Act, 1894   If such an Order has been
made the notice must be in accordance with the terms thereof

² Insert the words in these brackets if a rural parish in which there is a Parish
Council

³ Insert the words in these brackets if a rural parish and no Order of the County
Council under the said Act.

⁴ Insert the words in these brackets if a rural parish in which there is not a
Parish Council and an Order of the County Council under the said Act

1, 2, 3 4. As to the whole see the provisions of the Local Government Act, 1894, on
pp 461 2 ante

5—That the net annual value of the said hereditaments, as estimated in the said Valuation List, is greater than the rent at which the same might reasonably be expected to let from year to year, free of all usual tenant's rates and taxes and tithe commutation rent charge, if any, and deducting therefrom the probable average annual cost of repairs, insurance, and other expenses necessary to maintain them in a state to command such rent

6—That in the valuation of the said hereditaments, machinery, stock in-trade, utensils and other personal property, not subject to valuation for purposes of Poor Rates, have been included

7—That sufficient deductions have not been made from the gross estimated rental to arrive at a net annual value of the hereditaments

8—That the said Valuation List does not include certain works, factories, shops and hereditaments which ought to be included therein.

9—That the said Valuation List is in other respects illegal, unequal, partial, oppressive and unjust

Dated this   day of   , 19 .

ANALYTICAL INDEX.

A.

C

D.

E

Z Z

I.

J.

N

DDD

S.

T.

INDEX TO APPENDIX I.

NOTE—The provisions of these Acts, as hereinafter set out, are taken from "The Statutes Second Revised Edition," the dots indicating the omission of words which have been repealed.

Lightning Source UK Ltd.
Milton Keynes UK
UKHW031931080421
381649UK00015B/349